VBA
Professional Projects

VBA
Professional Projects

Rachna Chaudhary
Taruna Goel
WITH
NIIT

ISBN: 1-931841-55-1

Library of Congress Catalog Card Number: 2001099838

Printed in the United States of America

02 03 04 05 06 RI 10 9 8 7 6 5 4 3 2 1

Publisher:
Stacy L. Hiquet

Marketing Manager:
Heather Buzzingham

Managing Editor:
Sandy Doell

Editorial Assistant:
Margaret Bauer

Book Production Services:
Argosy

Cover Design:
Mike Tanamachi

About NIIT

NIIT is a global IT solutions corporation with a presence in 38 countries. With its unique business model and technology-creation capabilities, NIIT delivers software and learning solutions to more than 1,000 clients across the world.

The success of NIIT's training solutions lies in its unique approach to education. NIIT's Knowledge Solutions Business conceives, researches, and develops all of its course material. A rigorous instructional design methodology is followed to create engaging and compelling course content.

NIIT trains over 200,000 executives and learners each year in information technology areas using stand-up training, video-aided instruction, computer-based training (CBT), and Internet-based training (IBT). NIIT has been featured in the Guinness Book of World Records for the largest number of learners trained in one year!

NIIT has developed over 10,000 hours of instructor-led training (ILT) and over 3,000 hours of Internet-based training and computer-based training. IDC ranked NIIT among the Top 15 IT training providers globally for the year 2000. Through the innovative use of training methods and its commitment to research and development, NIIT has been in the forefront of computer education and training for the past 20 years.

Quality has been the prime focus at NIIT. Most of the processes are ISO-9001 certified. It was the 12th company in the world to be assessed at Level 5 of SEI-CMM. NIIT's Content (Learning Material) Development facility is the first in the world to be assessed at this highest maturity level. NIIT has strategic partnerships with companies such as Computer Associates, IBM, Microsoft, Oracle, and Sun Microsystems.

About the Authors

Rachna Chaudhary is a development executive in the Knowledge Solutions Business (KSB) division of NIIT. At KSB, Rachna has designed, developed, tested, and implemented the instructor-led training program. Her primary responsibilities include training development executives, project management, instructional review, technical review, and ensuring ISO compliance.

Taruna Goel is an instructional designer for NIIT Ltd. She has been working in the capacity of both a team member and a mentor in the Knowledge Solutions Business (KSB) division of NIIT for the past three years. She has been developing and delivering content on technical courses in areas, such as operating systems, networking, security, database management systems, and graphical tools, such as Macromedia Flash and Macromedia Director. Taruna has designed custom training products for corporate clients, such as Microsoft, Course Technology, Netvarsity, and ITT. She has experience in developing content using various delivery media, such as instructor-led training, multimedia-based training, and web-based training. At NIIT, she has had additional responsibilities including project management and training. She holds a post-graduate degree in business management.

Contents at a Glance

Contents

Introduction

Goal of the Book

This book provides a hands-on approach to learning the Visual Basic for Applications (VBA) programming language. The book is aimed at readers with a basic knowledge of programming.

The book starts with a few overview chapters that cover the key concepts of VBA. These chapters act as an information store for programmers who need to brush up on their VBA knowledge. A major part of the book revolves around professional projects. These projects enable programmers to learn about various tasks by following a simple-to-complex approach. Each project covers a specific subject area and guides you by using practical scenarios. The projects range from a simple project using the Visual Basic Editor to complex projects using Visual Studio. NET. These projects help programmers to accomplish their goals by understanding the practical and real-life application of VBA.

In addition to the overview chapters and the professional projects, this book includes two additional sections, "Beyond the Lab" and "Appendices." The "Beyond the Lab" section serves as both a summary of what you have learned throughout the projects and as a road map for where you can go to expand on this knowledge. This section also covers the future direction of the programming language. The "Appendices" section acts as a quick reference for the VBA programming language. It also covers some tips and tricks on using VBA.

How to use this Book

This book is organized to facilitate a better grasp of content covered in the book. The various elements in the book include the following:

- **Analysis.** The book incorporates an analysis of code, explaining what it did and why, line-by-line.
- **Tips.** Tips provide special advice or unusual shortcuts with the product.
- **Notes.** Notes give additional information that may be of interest to you, but is not essential to performing the task at hand.

- **Cautions.** Cautions warn of possible disastrous results if a task is performed incorrectly.
- **New term definitions.** All new terms are italicized and defined as a part of the text.

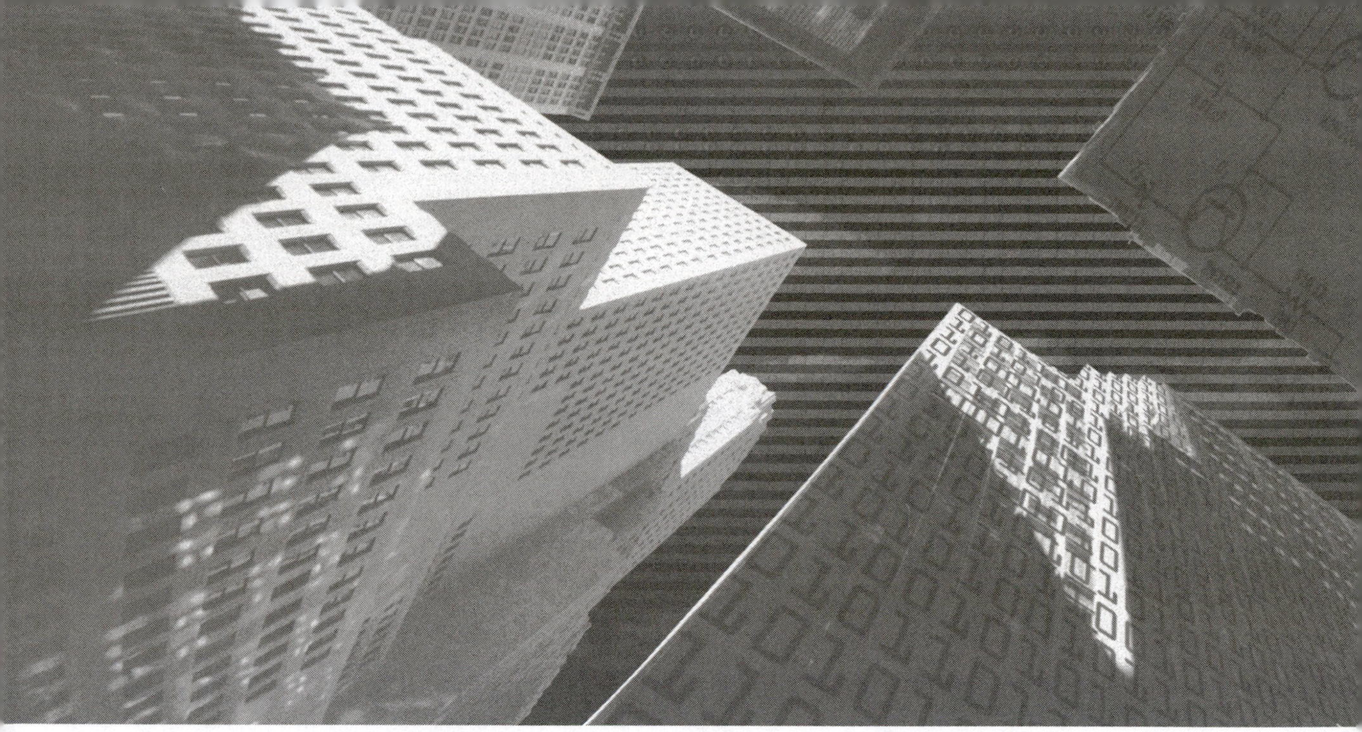

PART I

Introducing VBA

Chapter 1

VBA Overview

About a decade ago, Microsoft proposed VBA (*Visual Basic for Applications*) as a language for desktop applications. It came as a surprise to developers because they could now program Microsoft Office and other desktop applications. Visual Basic for Applications is the programming language used in several Microsoft and non-Microsoft products. It is fast becoming a standard as more and more third-party vendors authorize VBA to be included in their applications.

The universality of VBA as a programming language helps developers use a single programming language in various applications by learning only the object model of the application. As a result, instead of learning a separate language for each software application, the developers need to learn only one language.

You can use VBA to customize an application in a way in which complex actions can be performed at the click of a button.

In this chapter, you will learn about the concept of automating applications and how to automate tasks by using macros. You will also learn about the integrated programming environment associated with Visual Basic for Applications.

Automating Applications

The Microsoft Office suite consists of applications such as Word, Excel, PowerPoint, Access, Outlook, and FrontPage. Each application included in MS Office has a specific purpose. MS Word is a word processing application that is used to design documents. MS Excel is a spreadsheet application that is used to work with numbers, charts, and data maps. MS PowerPoint is used to create effective presentations. MS Access provides database management services. MS Outlook is a messaging application that is used to send and receive e-mail messages. MS FrontPage is used to create Web pages and Web sites. These Office applications are easy to use because they are Windows-based and use the graphical user interface.

These applications can be further customized either by automating a sequence of steps or by writing code to perform complex tasks. You can automate a sequence of steps by creating a macro, and you can write a code to perform complex tasks by using VBA.

The need to automate applications has given rise to the need for using macros and VBA. Increasingly, developers are realizing the need to create macros that combine the services of two or more applications. For example, a user may need a macro that can create an Excel chart from the data entered in an Access database and then include the chart in a document created in Word. You can use automation, which was earlier known as OLE automation, to accomplish this cross-application programming environment.

AUTOMATION

Automation is a process that allows an application to control objects in another application.

In a cross-application programming environment, the applications are controlled using VBA. For example, you can use VBA to perform automation between Microsoft Word and Microsoft Excel. This allows the Word application to control the objects contained in the Excel application, and the Excel application to control the objects contained in the Word application.

The following section looks at the key points of the object-based approach, which will help you to understand objects.

Object-Based Approach Toward Programming

The object model forms the basis of the object-based approach. Object-based methods are based on the conceptual framework provided by the object model. The *object model* refers to the logical arrangement of objects in an object-based application.

An object is a tangible entity that may exhibit some well-defined behavior. For example, a football is an object; it is a tangible, visible entity with a visible boundary. It is not necessary, however, for all objects to have a physical boundary. An organization does not have a physical boundary, but it has a conceptual boundary. Therefore, an organization is also an object.

An object has a state, it may display a behavior, and it has a unique identity.

The *state* of an object is indicated by a set of attributes and its values. For example, a bicycle can have states such as two wheels, number of gears, color, and so on.

Behavior refers to the change of these attributes over a period of time. Consider the example of the bicycle again. The bicycle can exhibit behavior such as braking, accelerating, changing gears, and so on.

Every object has a unique identity, which distinguishes it from another object. For example, an animal is identified by its species. Two objects may have the same behavior, may or may not have the same state, and will never have the same identity. The identity of an object never changes during its lifetime.

Following is a look at the benefits of the object-based approach toward programming.

Benefits of the Object-Based Approach

An object-based approach offers the following benefits:

- **Realistic modeling.** This refers to the objects surrounding us that model the real world. In other words, we live in a world of objects, and the object-based approach models the real world.
- **Reusability.** This refers to saving the procedures as external files, which can be used by other applications. The benefit of reusability translates to saving time and effort, which, in turn, results in cost benefits.
- **Resilience to change.** This refers to the flexibility of software to accommodate more objects over a period of time.

Visual Basic is another language that uses objects and models the real world. The following section looks at the similarities and differences between Visual Basic for Applications and Visual Basic.

VBA and VB

VBA is similar to VB in relation to the development environment. Both VBA and VB stem from the same programming language, BASIC. Both languages have the same level of object-orientation; that is, most of the properties and methods of objects, which are supported by VB, are also supported by VBA. However, you may find slight differences in the specific names of events or properties.

The difference between VBA and VB is that you can neither run VBA separately in an environment nor use it to create stand-alone applications. However, you can use VB to create tools for creating stand-alone components such as executable programs and COM components. VB is especially useful when building applications from scratch.

VBA is a complete programming language and can be used with any other application with which it has been integrated; that is, VBA requires a host application to support its functioning. A host application is an application, such as Word, Excel, or Access, which provides an integrated development environment for VBA programming. A host application has objects that are used by VBA to customize it. For example, Word has its set of VBA objects and Excel has its set of VBA objects. You will always have to open a host application to run VBA. Therefore, it is not possible to build stand-alone applications with VBA, but you can display the user forms created in any Office application by hiding the host application. This creates the illusion of a stand-alone application. Hence, VBA is best suited for customizing already existing applications.

Visual Basic for Applications

VBA is a programming language built into the Office suite of applications. When you open an application that is VBA-enabled, the Visual Basic for Applications environment is not displayed. Why? The VBA environment is loaded when a user performs an action that requires VBA to be activated. For example, if you want to create a macro, this will require VBA to load. The VBA environment is installed when you install the host application on your computer. It is loaded from the hard disk of your computer. The VBA environment is dependent on the host application. Therefore, quitting the host application closes the VBA environment associated with it.

NOTE

You should activate VBA only when the user action requires it. Loading VBA adds to the memory usage of the host application, and opening the VBA environment adds to the usage of memory.

In a VBA-enabled application, you can automate any operation supported by the application. VBA enables you to automate repetitive tasks. Consider a situation in which you have been assigned the task of collating sales data on a weekly basis. This task involves creating tables and entering data in them. The tables have to be in a specific style and size. You also need to fill in the same data in the first column and row of each table. One method to do this task is to create and format each table. Another method is to create a procedure for completing the task. You can thus write a procedure that can create a table with all the specifications.

There are various categories of tasks. A few tasks require repetitive actions to be performed, whereas some other tasks require decision-making activities to be performed. You can create macros to accomplish the tasks involving repetitive action, and you can use VBA to accomplish tasks involving decision making. VBA allows you to write procedures to automate tasks. You can save the procedures as external files and distribute these files to other people who perform the same tasks.

The following section shows you how to automate tasks using macros.

Introduction to Macros

A macro is a set of instructions put together as a single command in order to accomplish a task automatically. You can compare a macro with a batch file in DOS. A batch file is used to automate a group of tasks performed by the user.

You can create a macro either by recording the steps to perform a task or by programming in Visual Basic for Applications. Office applications, such as Word, Excel, PowerPoint, Outlook, and Access, support macros. The tools provided by Office applications to create macros are the Macro Recorder and the Visual Basic Editor. A macro recorder is used to automate repetitive tasks, whereas the Visual Basic Editor is used to automate tasks involving decision-making. You can assign a macro to a symbol (an icon on a toolbar), a key (on the keyboard), or a name that represents a list of commands, actions, or keystrokes.

You do not have to know any programming language to record a macro. The following section shows you how to record a macro.

Recording a Macro

A macro recorder is used to record the steps performed by a user to accomplish a task as a single command. You use the Record Macro dialog box to record a macro. The Record Macro dialog box is displayed in Figure 1-1.

The Record Macro dialog box enables you to customize the macro you are going to record. You can either attach a macro to a toolbar or assign a shortcut key(s) to execute it. The Record Macro dialog box helps specify the template or document where the macro will be stored.

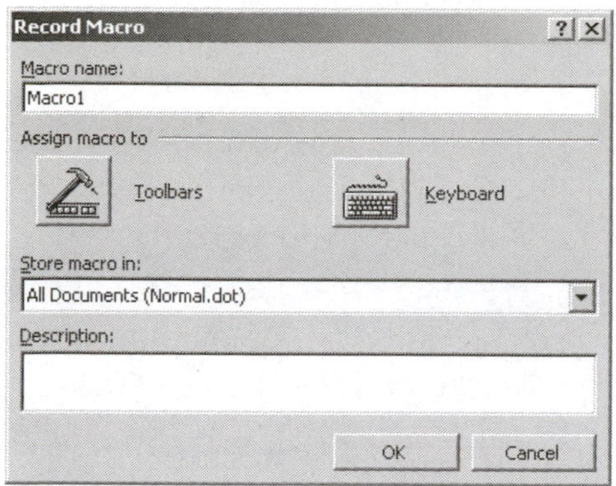

FIGURE 1-1 *The Record Macro dialog box*

The components of the Record Macro dialog box are as follows:

- **Macro name.** This is used to specify the name for the macro. The name of the macro must begin with alphabetical characters. You can specify a maximum of 80 letters and numbers and should not include spaces and symbols.
- **Assign macro to.** This is used to specify the location from where you would like to run a macro. You can run a macro from an icon on a toolbar, a shortcut key, or both.
- **Store macro in.** This is used to store the macro you are going to record in one of the instances of the host application.
- **Description.** This is used to enter the details associated with the macro. This can include any additional information that might help other users decide how to use the macro.

To record a macro, perform the following steps:

1. Select the Macro option from the Tools menu.
2. Click on the Record New Macro option.
3. Type the name to be assigned to the macro.
4. Click on OK.

Now, you have to click the required options to create a table and format it manually. When you start recording a macro, the Macro Recorder toolbar is displayed on the application window. The Macro Recorder toolbar consists of two buttons, Stop recorder and Pause recorder. See Figure 1-2.

FIGURE 1-2 *The Macro Recorder toolbar*

After you have finished recording a macro, click on the Stop recorder button.

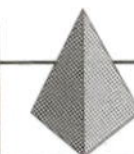

TIP

You should always plan the steps you want to record before starting the macro recorder.

If you record a step, you can edit it later. You will learn how to edit a recorded macro in the following section.

Editing a Macro

When you record a macro, the host application generates VBA code for that macro. You can view the VBA code for the macro by using the Macros dialog box. To view the VBA code for the macro, perform the following steps:

1. Select the Macro option from the Tools menu.
2. Click on the Macros option. The Macros dialog box appears, as shown in Figure 1-3.

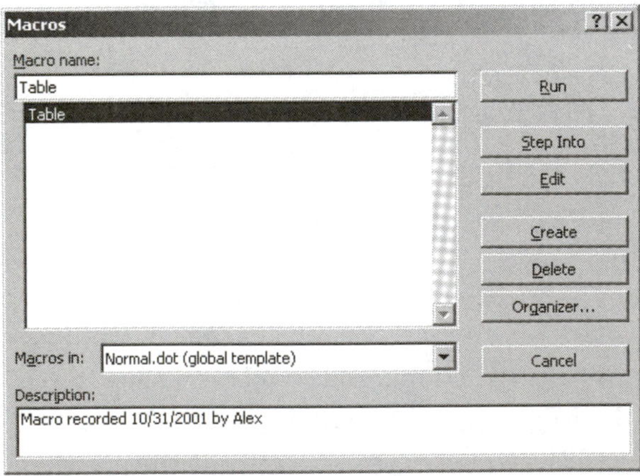

FIGURE 1-3 *The Macros dialog box*

3. Click on the Edit button to view the VBA code generated for the macro.

The code is displayed in the Visual Basic Editor window. See Figure 1-4.

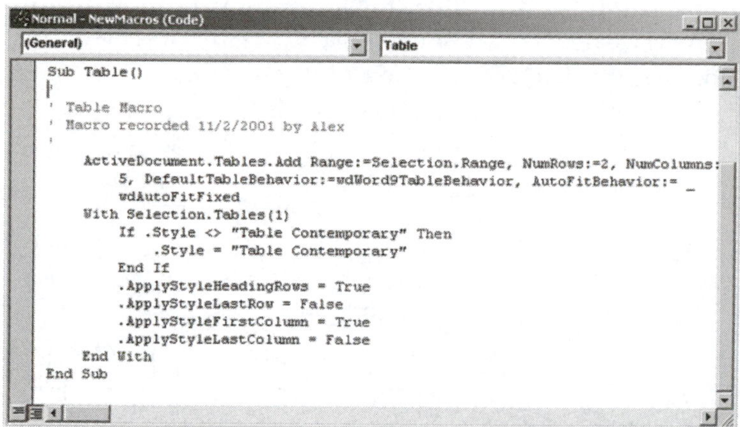
```
Sub Table()
'
' Table Macro
' Macro recorded 11/2/2001 by Alex
'
    ActiveDocument.Tables.Add Range:=Selection.Range, NumRows:=2, NumColumns:=
        5, DefaultTableBehavior:=wdWord9TableBehavior, AutoFitBehavior:= _
        wdAutoFitFixed
    With Selection.Tables(1)
        If .Style <> "Table Contemporary" Then
            .Style = "Table Contemporary"
        End If
        .ApplyStyleHeadingRows = True
        .ApplyStyleLastRow = False
        .ApplyStyleFirstColumn = True
        .ApplyStyleLastColumn = False
    End With
End Sub
```

FIGURE 1-4 *The VBA code generated for a macro*

Table 1-1 lists the options provided by the Macros dialog box and gives a description of each.

Table 1-1 Macros Dialog Box Options

Option	Description
Run	Executes the selected macro
Step in	Opens the VBA programming environment in debugging mode
Edit	Displays the VBA code for the selected macro
Create	Opens the blank Code window for the macro specified in the Macro name text box
Delete	Deletes the selected macro
Organize	Organizes the macros in the application

To summarize in the context of the Office application, we can say that there are two ways to create macros, one by using the macro recorder and other by using the Visual Basic Editor. The Macros dialog box is used to display the code in the Visual Basic Editor window. In other words, you can open the Editor window from the Macros dialog box. The next section takes a look at the Visual Basic Editor in detail.

Introduction to the Visual Basic Editor

The Visual Basic Editor is the tool provided by Microsoft to provide a programming environment for Microsoft Office applications. The Visual Basic Editor provides an integrated development environment based on the layout of the Visual Basic programming environment in Microsoft. All Office applications support the Visual Basic programming environment, and the programming interface is the same for all Office applications. You can use the Visual Basic Editor to create procedures and edit existing ones.

You can create a procedure that directs Microsoft Word to print labels automatically when the Company_labels document is opened. You can also create a procedure for building a Microsoft Excel graph from the data entered in a Microsoft Access database. You can store the related procedures as macros and, therefore, accomplish complex tasks involving decision making by executing the macros.

PROCEDURE

A *procedure* is a set of VBA instructions grouped together as a single unit to perform a specific task.

Opening the Visual Basic Editor

You have learned how to open the Editor window by using the Macros dialog box. This section looks at another way of opening the Editor window.

To open the Editor window, open a new instance of an Office application and perform the following steps:

1. Select the Macro option from the Tools menu.
2. Select the Visual Basic Editor from the Macro submenu. The Visual Basic Editor window appears, as shown in Figure 1-5.

Alternatively, you can use the shortcut key, Alt+F11, to open the Visual Basic Editor.

The following section looks at the components of the Visual Basic Editor interface.

Components of the Visual Basic Editor

The Visual Basic Editor consists of the following components:

- Menus
- Toolbars
- Project Explorer

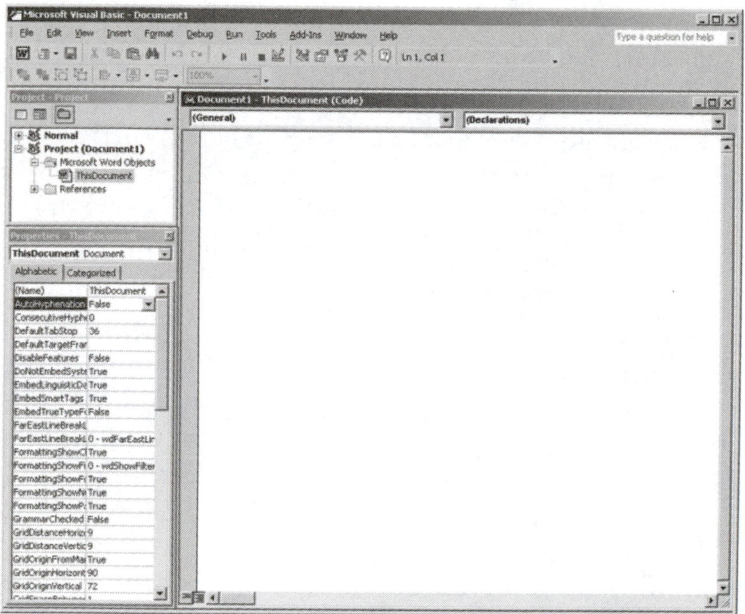

FIGURE 1-5 *The Visual Basic Editor window*

- Windows
- Object Browser
- Toolbox

Following is a look at each of these components in detail.

Menus

The Visual Basic Editor menus provide commands for handling files, viewing code and user forms, viewing various editor windows, debugging macros, running procedures and user forms, applying digital signatures, and so on.

Toolbars

A toolbar is a collection of commands that perform related actions. Toolbars represent shortcuts that are used to access menu items. The Visual Basic Editor provides the following toolbars:

- **Standard.** This toolbar contains commands in the form of buttons that perform a variety of functions. You can toggle between the Visual Basic Editor and the application. You can also insert objects into a project and perform edit operations, such as cut, copy, and paste. It also allows you to open the Project Explorer, the Properties window, and the Object Browser.

- **Edit.** This toolbar contains commands in the form of buttons that are used to edit the code written in the Code window. You can obtain information about the properties, methods, and constants in the Code window. It also enables you to add comments, delete comments, indent procedures, and bookmark procedures.
- **Debug.** This toolbar contains commands in the form of buttons that are used to debug the code.
- **UserForm.** This toolbar contains commands in the form of buttons that are used while working with forms.

Project Explorer

The Project Explorer window contains a list of all open instances of an application. These instances are displayed in the Project Explorer as projects.

Depending on the Office application, the contents of the Project Explorer window will vary. For example, if you have opened two Word documents, first.doc and second.doc, the Project Explorer will refer to them as `Project (first)` and `Project (second)`. In Excel and PowerPoint, the projects are displayed as `VBAProject (Book1)` and `VBAProject (presentation1)`, respectively. In Access, the projects are displayed as database names. For example, if a database, Sales, is open, the Project Explorer will display `Sales (Sales)` as the project name.

Figure 1-6 shows the Project Explorer of a Word application.

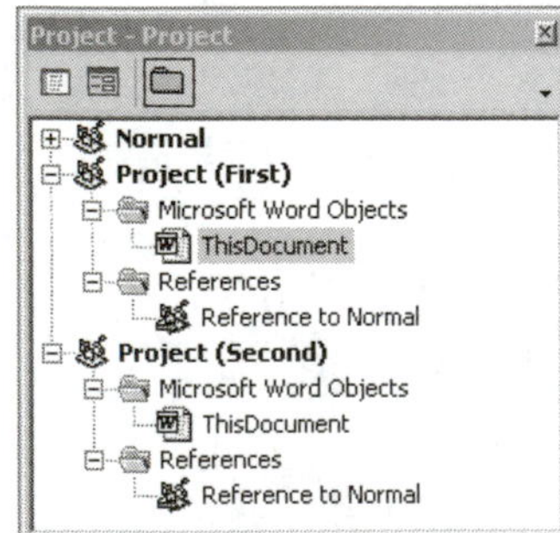

FIGURE 1-6 *The Project Explorer of a Word application*

Notice that each project in the Project Explorer, by default, contains a Microsoft Word Objects folder and a References folder. Each instance of an application is displayed as an object in the Project Explorer. The Microsoft Word Objects folder contains the `ThisDocument` object, which represents the current document. The Reference folder contains the reference to the template attached to the document.

The Project Explorer contains the following buttons:

- **View Code.** This is used to open the Code window for the object selected in the Project Explorer.
- **View Object.** This is used to view the object whose name is selected in the Project Explorer.
- **Toggle Folders.** This is used to display names of the folders in the Project Explorer.

Windows

The Visual Basic Editor window contains the following windows:

- Properties window
- Code window
- Immediate window
- Locals window
- Watches window

Properties Window

The Properties window allows you to control the behavior and appearance of an object. The object box displays the name of the selected object. There are two tabs in this window (see Figure 1-7). The Alphabetic tab arranges the property names alphabetically, and the Categorized tab groups the properties on the basis of the tasks they perform.

Each property is assigned a default value. You can use the Properties window to change the default value of a property.

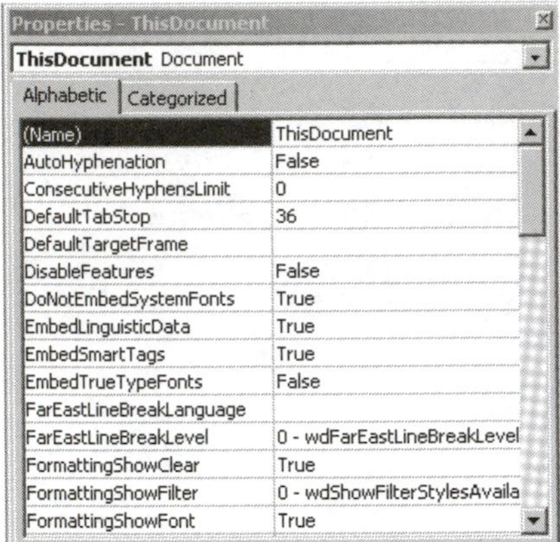

FIGURE 1-7 *The Properties window of a project*

Code Window

You use the Code window to write code for the application. The code is entered between the `Public Sub` and `End Sub` lines in the Code window. The `Public Sub` line denotes the beginning of the procedure whose name follows the word `Sub`, and the `End Sub` line marks the end of the procedure.

Each programming language has a set of keywords, which have a special meaning attached to them. The words `Public`, `Sub`, and `End` are keywords in VBA.

NOTE

You will learn about procedures in detail in Chapter 3, "Procedures, Functions, and Modules."

The Code window contains an Object list box and a Procedure list box. The Object list box either displays the word General or displays the type of object associated with the Code window, such as Workbook, Worksheet, or Document. You can click on the Object list box to display a list of other objects from which you can select. The Procedure list box displays the name of the current procedure. You can view the names of other procedures stored in the Module object by clicking on the Procedure list box. The Code window is displayed in Figure 1-8.

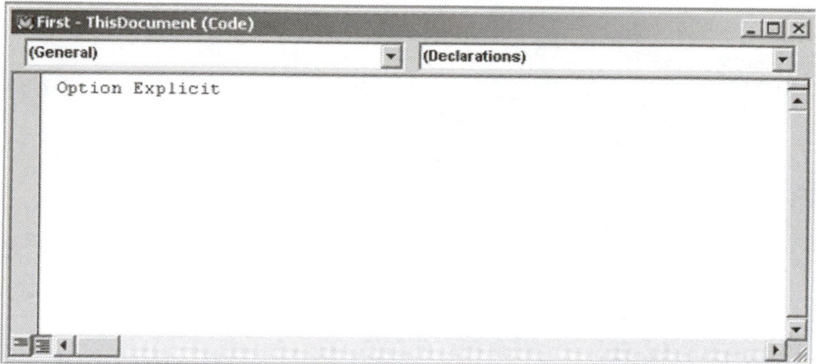

FIGURE 1-8 *The Code window*

Immediate Window

The Immediate window allows you to monitor the values assigned to variables and expressions. You can change the values of variables or expressions and test the result of expressions based on the new values. You can view the Immediate window from the View menu. See Figure 1-9.

FIGURE 1-9 *The Immediate window*

Locals Window

You can use the Locals window to monitor the values of variables within a procedure that is being executed. When the code runs, the values of variables are updated automatically in the Locals window. However, if a variable in the current procedure is not initialized, the value of the variable is displayed as `Empty` in the window.

You can open the Locals window from the View menu. See Figure 1-10.

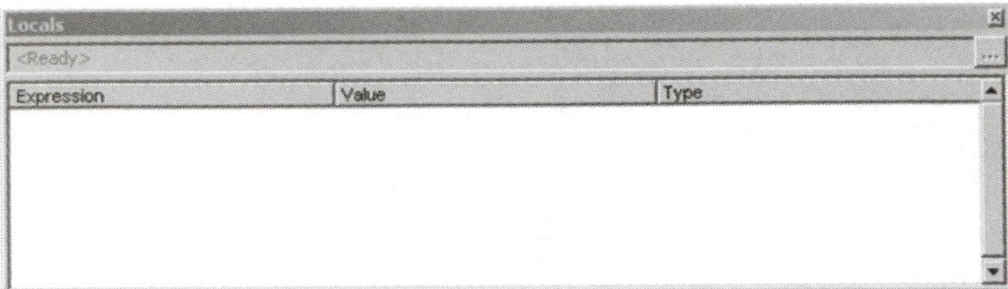

FIGURE 1-10 *The Locals window*

Watches Window

The Watches window is used to display watch expressions. You can view the value of the expression at the time of the transition to break mode. You can edit the value of the expression in the Watches window. The Edit field remains activated if the value entered is not valid. See Figure 1-11.

NOTE

You will learn more about this in Chapter 5, "Debugging and Error-Handling in VBA."

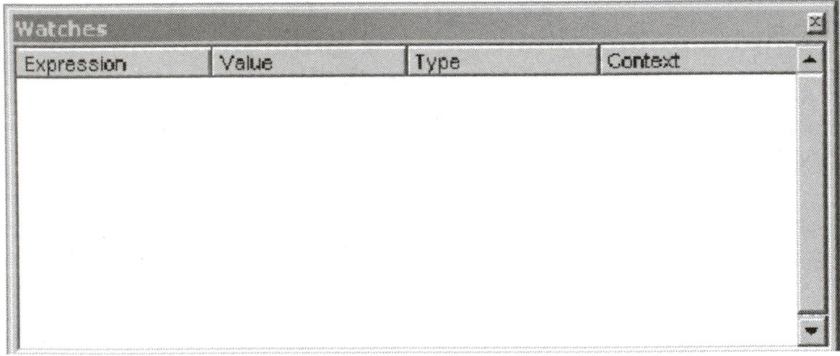

FIGURE 1-11 *The Watches window*

Object Browser

The Object Browser helps you browse through all the objects that are available in VBA in all the Office applications. It also lists all the available properties and methods of the objects. You can use the Object Browser to see what objects are available for the application.

To display Object Browser in the Visual Basic Editor, choose View, Object Browser or click on the Object Browser button on the Visual Basic toolbar.

The Object Browser is displayed as shown in Figure 1-12.

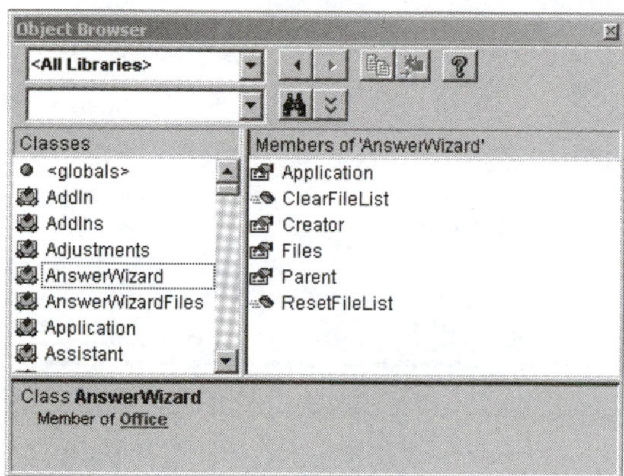

FIGURE 1-12 *The Object Browser*

The Object Browser dialog box displays the following:

- The Project/Library list displays the names of all the usable projects and libraries. These usable projects and libraries are used to select objects for the procedures.
- The Objects/Modules box displays the available objects and modules in relation to the object library or project that is selected in the Project/Library list.
- The Methods/Properties box displays the methods and properties that belong to an object.

> **LIBRARY**
>
> A *library* is a file that contains information about different classes, objects, procedures, and functions.

Toolbox

You can use controls such as text boxes, list boxes, and labels to display or accept data from users. You can accept data from users by using user forms. You can add a control by clicking on a button in the Toolbox and then drawing on the form. The form grid helps set and align the controls on the form. See Figure 1-13.

FIGURE 1-13 *The Toolbox*

Table 1-2 lists the controls in the Toolbox along with their description.

Table 1-2 Controls in the Toolbox

Option	Description
`Label`	Used to add text to a control or the form
`TextBox`	Used to accept data from the users
`CommandButton`	Used to carry out commands
`ListBox`	Used to display a list of values from which a user can select one
`CheckBox`	Used to indicate whether something is True or False
`OptionButton`	Used to display multiple options and turns on or off an option
`ComboBox`	Used to display a list of values from which the user can select or add a new value

Each control has a set of properties associated with it. VBA assigns a default name to each control that consists of the type of the control followed by a number. For example, when you insert the first list box control, the default name is ListBox1. Similarly, the second list box control is named ListBox2. You can change the Name property of the control to make it meaningful.

Summary

Visual Basic for Application is a programming language for desktop applications, and it is used to automate tasks. VBA differs from VB because VBA requires a host application to run and cannot be used to create a stand-alone application. On the other hand, VB is used to create stand-alone applications. VBA allows you to automate tasks either by using a macro recorder or by programming in VBA. You do not need to know any programming language to record a macro using a macro recorder, and you can edit a macro in the Visual Basic Editor.

Chapter 2

Variables, Constants, and Expressions

This chapter introduces you to the concept of variables, constants, and expressions in VBA programming. It also covers the various operators in VBA.

Variables in VBA

A *variable* is a temporary storage area in the memory used to store values. It is necessary to declare a variable before using it. *Declaring* a variable informs VBA of the name and data type of the variable you will be using. The data type of a variable specifies the type of values it can store. The type of value can be integer, string, long, and so on.

The `Dim` (`Dim` is short for dimension) keyword is used to declare a variable. The usage of the `Dim` keyword is as follows:

```
Dim variablename
```

Consider the following example:

```
Dim totalsales
totalsales=5
```

The first statement sets aside an area in memory with the name `totalsales`, which can store integer values. The variable is then assigned the value 5.

You can assign any name to a variable. However, you need to keep in mind the following points when declaring variables in VBA:

- Variable names must start with a letter and can be up to 255 characters long. However, most of the time, the length of a variable name is shorter.
- Variable names cannot contain characters such as +, -, /, *, !, <, >, ., <=, >=, <>, @, $, #, and &.
- Variable names cannot contain spaces. However, underscores are permissible.

The following are some of the valid variable names:

```
i
mary
total_score
howareyou
The_number_of_options_entered_by_the_user
```

Although all the variable names listed are valid examples, the last example is very long. You should preferably use short and logical variable names so that it is convenient to type the variable name repeatedly in the code.

The following are invalid examples of variable names:

`How r u`	Contains a space
`Hello!`	Contains an exclamation mark
`1user`	Does not start with a letter
`andrew+john`	Contains a + sign

You will now learn about the different data types of variables available in VBA.

Types of Variables

The data type of a variable specifies the kind of data the variable can store.

You specify the data type of a variable by including the `As` keyword in a `Dim` statement. The syntax is as follows:

```
Dim variablename As datatype
```

VBA supports the following data types for variables:

- `Boolean`
- `Byte`
- `Currency`
- `Date`
- `Decimal`
- `Double`
- `Integer`
- `Long`
- `Object`
- `Single`
- `String`
- `Variant`

The following sections discuss these data types in detail.

Boolean

You can use the Boolean data type to store Boolean values. Boolean variables can take only two values, True or False. A Boolean variable takes up two bytes of space. The declaration for a Boolean variable is as follows:

```
Dim product_availability As Boolean
```

The Boolean variable, when converted to another data type, returns –1 in case of a True, and a 0 in case of a False. In case of a numeric value being converted to a Boolean value, 0 returns False, and all the other numbers return True.

Byte

You can use the Byte data type to store integer values. It can store values from 0 to 255. The Byte data type is used for small values because it takes up the least memory (one byte) of all the data types.

Currency

The Currency data type is used for monetary or fixed-decimal calculations in which accuracy is an important issue. The value range for a Currency data type is up to 15 digits to the left of the decimal point and four digits to the right. Each Currency variable takes up eight bytes.

You can use type-declaration characters to implicitly declare variables. The type-declaration character for the Currency data type is @.

NOTE

A type-declaration character is a character that you append to the end of a variable name while declaring the variable implicitly. The type-declaration character informs VBA of the data type of the variable. On encountering the type-declaration character, VBA automatically declares the variable with the corresponding data type. The type-declaration character is used only while declaring a variable. Thereafter, you can use the variable name for its reference.

For example, the following statement declares a Currency data type by using the type-declaration character:

```
Dim mygrosssalary, mydepreciation as integer
mynetsalary@=mygrosssalary-mydepreciation
```

Date

You can use the Date data type for storing a date. Each Date variable takes up eight bytes each. The range of the Date data type is from January 1, 0100 to December 31, 9999 and the time from 0:00:00 to 23:59:59.

The date needs to be enclosed in hash signs when being assigned to the Date data type. For example:

```
Mydate = #6/5/01#
```

You can also specify the date in literals in the same way. For example:

```
Mydate = #June 6, 2001#
```

VBA converts the date specified in the preceding format to a number and displays it as 6/6/2001. You can also specify the time in a similar fashion.

Decimal

The Decimal data type is used to store signed integers scaled by powers of 10. Each Decimal variable takes up 12 bytes. The scaling factor specifies the number of digits to the right of the decimal point and can range from 0–28.

You cannot directly declare a variable of the Decimal data type in VBA. However, you can do so with the help of the Variant data type. You will look into the Variant data type later in the chapter.

Double

You can use the Double data type to store double-precision floating-point values ranging from –1.79769313486231E308 to –4.94065645841247E-324 for negative values and from 4.94065645841247E-324 to 1.79769313486232E308 for positive numbers. Double variables take up eight bytes each. The type-declaration character for the Double data type is #.

Integer

You can use the Integer data type to store integer values in the range of –32,768 to 32,767. Integer variables take up two bytes each. You can use the type-declaration character % to declare Integer variables. Integer variables can also be used to represent enumerated values. An *enumerated value* is a set of constants in which each has a special meaning in the context in which it is used.

Long

The `Long` data type is used for storing large signed integer values in the range of –2,147,483,648 to 2,147,483,647. `Long` variables take up four bytes each. You can use the type-declaration character & for declaring `Long` variables.

Object

The `Object` data type is used for storing addresses that reference objects. `Object` variables take up four bytes each. You can use the `Set` statement to assign object references to a variable declared as `Object`.

Single

The `Single` data type is used for storing single-precision floating-point numbers. A `Single` data type can store values in the range of –3.402823E38 to –1.401298E-45 for negative values and from 1.401298E-45 to 3.402823E38 for positive values. Single variables take up four bytes each. The type-declaration character used for the `Single` data type is !.

String

You can use the `String` data type for handling two types of strings in VBA:

- **Fixed-length strings.** A fixed-length string can store from 1 to 64,000 characters. As the name suggests, the number of locations in a fixed-length string is fixed and cannot be changed according to the string. If the string to be stored is shorter than the fixed length, VBA pads the string with trailing spaces; if the string to be stored is longer than the fixed length, VBA truncates the remaining data. For example, if "money" is stored in a fixed-length string of three characters, then only "mon" will be stored in the string. Hence, a variable-length string is preferable to a fixed-length string.
- **Variable-length strings.** A variable-length string can store strings of variable lengths. It can contain up to two billion characters.

Strings can contain letters, numbers, spaces, punctuation, and special characters. The type-declaration character for the `String` data type is $.

Variant

The `Variant` data type is the default data type and is assigned to all the variables whose data type is not declared. However, you can also declare a variable of the `Variant` data type explicitly in the following manner:

```
Dim myvariable as Variant
```

Variables declared of the `Variant` data type can contain string, date, Boolean, or numeric values and can automatically convert the data types of the values they contain. Each numeric `Variant` value requires 16 bytes of memory, and a string `Variant` value requires 22 bytes plus the storage required for the characters. Because of its capabilities, the `Variant` data type takes up a large amount of memory. Hence, it is a good practice to declare variables explicitly.

Another important point to note here is that the `Variant` data type cannot contain a fixed-length string value. To store strings of fixed length, you need to declare the variables explicitly as fixed-length strings.

Now that you know the different data types in VBA, the following section moves on to the declaration of variables.

Declaring Variables

As stated earlier, variables are declared using the `Dim` statement. The `Dim` statement declares a variable and allocates storage space to it. VBA allows you to declare variables implicitly or explicitly. Both methods have their advantages and disadvantages; however, it is always preferable to declare your variables explicitly at the start of the procedure. You will soon find out why.

Declaring Variables Implicitly

You cannot declare your variables explicitly before the start of a procedure and use them straightaway. Variables automatically get declared when their first use is encountered. This is known as *implicit declaration* of variables. When VBA encounters such variables, it checks whether a variable of the same name already exists. If no such variable is found, VBA creates the variable and assigns it the `Variant` data type. Remember that the `Variant` data type is the default data type and can contain any data type except for a fixed-length string.

The advantage of declaring variables implicitly is that you can declare variables as and when needed in the program. However, declaring variables implicitly also has certain disadvantages:

- We commit typing mistakes very often while coding. Consider a scenario in which you have declared a variable, `totalsales`, and the variable contains the value 50. While referencing the variable in the code, if you incorrectly type the variable name as `totlasales` instead of `totalsales`, VBA will not recognize this spelling mistake and will create another variable, `totlasales`, with the value 0. This may lead to unexpected results. To avoid such circumstances, you must explicitly declare variables before using them.
- The `Variant` data type takes up more memory than any other data type. Hence, declaring variables implicitly would mean that they would take up a lot of memory. If you are not using a large number of variables in a procedure, this may not be a big problem. However, if there are a number of variables to be used in a procedure and all of them are implicitly declared with the data type as `Variant`, they will take up a lot of memory, which would slow the procedure or may even cause it to run out of memory.

Because of the disadvantages of implicit declaration of variables, explicit declaration is preferable. The following section discusses explicit declaration of variables.

Declaring Variables Explicitly

Declaring a variable explicitly means declaring the variable before using it. VBA then allocates memory to the variable. Although you can declare variables at any place in the code, it is a good practice to declare all of them at the start of a program. You can always keep adding variables as and when you need them. Declaring variables explicitly has many advantages:

- Explicit declaration makes your code easier to read and debug.
- New variables are not created as a result of spelling mistakes, as is the case with implicit declaration.
- The code runs faster because VBA does not have to deal with the overhead of determining the data type of each variable while running it.

The only disadvantage of explicitly declaring variables is that you have to spend a little more time and effort in declaring variables at the start of the procedure. However, considering the advantages, it is worth the effort.

Choosing the Variable Scope

Whether you can use a variable in a particular procedure depends on where the variable was declared. That is, it depends on the scope of a variable. The *scope* of a variable refers to the accessibility of the variable. A variable that is created in a particular procedure can only be accessed within that procedure; it is *local* to the procedure in which it is created. To make a variable accessible to all the other procedures in the module, you need to declare the variable in the *General Declarations* section, in which case its scope becomes *public*. The scope of a variable can be *procedure*, *private*, or *public*.

The following sections look at each variable scope in detail.

Procedure Scope

A variable with procedure scope (also known as the procedure-level scope or the local scope) is accessible only in the procedure in which it is declared. The variable no longer exists when the procedure (in which it is declared) stops running. VBA kills the variable and releases the memory occupied by it.

Consider the following example, which declares a local variable, `sales_region`, in the procedure, `calculate_weekly_sales`:

```
Sub calculate_weekly_sales()
Dim sales_region as integer
...
End Sub
```

This example creates a procedure, `calculate_weekly_sales`. The variable, `sales_region`, is declared inside the procedure, `calculate_weekly_sales`, and is, therefore, local to the procedure. In other words, the variable can only be referenced inside the procedure, `calculate_weekly_sales`, and cannot be used outside this procedure. However, if you need to pass the value of `sales_region` to another procedure, you need to use the `Static` keyword or declare it using the public scope.

The procedure scope is the default scope of a variable. Any variable declared implicitly always has procedure scope.

Private Scope

It is often required to pass the values of variables from one procedure to another. This cannot be done if the variable has been declared with procedure scope. For this, you need to declare the variable with public or private scope.

A variable with private scope is available to all the procedures within the module in which it is created, but not to the procedures in other modules. Declaring a variable with private scope ensures that its value can be passed to all the procedures within that module. Unlike variables with procedure scope, variables declared with private scope retain their values as long as the project in which they have been created is running.

To declare a variable with public scope, you need to use the `Public` keyword or the `Dim` keyword.

Consider the following example:

```
Private pass_percentage as Boolean
Dim roll_no as integer
Sub disp_marks()
...
End Sub
```

This example creates a procedure, `disp_marks()`. The two variables, `roll_no` and `pass_percentage`, have been declared private by using the `Private` keyword and the `Dim` keyword, respectively. Note that the use of the `Dim` statement is similar to the earlier example; the difference is in the placement. In the earlier example, the `Dim` statement was placed inside the procedure, making the variable local in scope, whereas in this example, the `Dim` statement is placed before the start of the procedure, making the variable private in scope.

Public Scope

A variable declared with public scope is accessible to all the procedures and all the modules in the project that contains it.

A variable is declared public by using the `Public` keyword in the Declarations section at the beginning of a module. Variables with public scope retain their value as long as the project that contains them is running.

For example:

```
Public myvar as integer
```

This statement declares a public variable, `myvar`, of the `Integer` data type. The variable can be referenced from any procedure at any point in time during program execution.

Using the Static Keyword

Besides using the `Public`, `Private`, and `Dim` keywords, VBA also provides the `Static` keyword to help you preserve the values of variables between procedure calls. The variables declared using the `Static` keyword are known as *static variables*. Static variables are used in situations where you need to run a process multiple times and want to retain the value of the variable each time. Declaring the variable as static retains its value each time the process is run.

To declare a static variable, you need to use the `Static` keyword in place of the `Dim` keyword. The following statement declares the static string variable, `stritem`:

```
Static stritem as string
```

Constants

A *constant* is a named item that remains fixed throughout the execution of a program. Constants, unlike variables, do not change their values. A constant can be a number, a string, or any other value. Each application has its own set of constants, and new constants can be defined by a user. Once you have declared a constant, it can be used anywhere in the program instead of the actual value. VBA supports two types of constants: built-in constants and user-defined constants.

Built-in Constants

Every application has its own predefined built-in constants. These constants are assigned values. You can use these values to refer to the constants instead of their name. However, using names is preferable because it is difficult to remember the value for each constant. The names of the built-in constants (or intrinsic constants) begin with two letters indicating the application name. For example, the constants for Word objects begin with `wd`, the constants for PowerPoint begin with `pp`, and so on. Similarly, in VBA, the objects are referenced by prefixing the constants with `vb`. You can get a list of the constants provided for individual object libraries in VBA in the Object Browser.

User-defined Constants

In addition to built-in constants, VBA allows you to create your own constants. These constants are known as *user-defined constants*. Constants help in situations where you need to use a literal value many times. To declare constants, you need to use the `Const` statement. The syntax of the `Const` statement is as follows:

```
[Public¦Private] Const constantname [As type] = expression
```

where

`Public¦Private` specifies the scope of the constant. A constant declared inside a procedure is local to that procedure. However, it is optional.

`Const` is the keyword to declare user-defined constants.

`constantname` specifies the name of the constant. The name of the constant should adhere to the standard variable naming conventions.

`type` specifies the data type of the constant. A separate `As type` clause needs to be specified for each declaration of a constant. However, it is optional to specify the type.

`expression` specifies the value of the constant.

For example, the following statement declares a constant, `myconst`, and initializes it with a value, 50:

```
Private Const myconst as Integer = 50
```

You can specify more than one constant in a single statement. However, the data type for each constant should be included. Consider the following example:

```
Public Const roll_no as integer = 101, stud_name as string = Mary
```

Although the declaration of a constant looks similar to the declaration of a variable, there is a slight difference between the two. You initialize a constant at the time of declaration itself, unlike variables, which you may or may not initialize at the time of declaration. Once a constant is initialized, you cannot modify its value during program execution.

Variables and constants are used with operators to form expressions. The following section discusses operators.

Operators

Operators are symbols used in expressions to produce results. An expression is a combination of operators, operands, keywords, variables, and constants. Operators are used to work with the values in an expression. Operands are input values used by an expression on which the operation is performed. Operands can be variables, literals, or constant values. The combination of operands and operators in an expression produces results. However, an important point to remember while using expressions is that you should maintain data type consistency throughout an expression.

Data type consistency means that the operands in an expression should use compatible data types; otherwise a data type mismatch will occur. For example, you cannot combine a `Long` data type with a `String` data type. The operators used between the operands should also be compatible with the data types of the operands. For example, you cannot divide two strings. Last but not least, the output or the result of the expression should be stored in a variable whose data type is consistent with the data type of the result. For example, you cannot store a string expression in an Integer variable.

VBA supports four kinds of operators:

- **Arithmetic operators.** Used to perform mathematical calculations
- **Comparison operators.** Used to compare values
- **Concatenation operators.** Used to join two strings
- **Logical operators.** Used to develop logical structures

You will learn about each of these operators in detail in the following sections.

Arithmetic Operators

The Arithmetic operators supported by VBA are listed in Table 2-1:

Table 2-1 Arithmetic Operators in VBA

Operator	Name	Example	Result
+	Addition	5+5	10
–	Subtraction	5-2	3
–	Negation	-5	-5
*	Multiplication	5*5	25
/	Division	5/5	1
\	Integer division	6\5	1
^	Exponentiation	5^5	3125
Mod	Modulus	5 Mod 2	1

Comparison Operators

The Comparison operators are used in an expression to compare two or more numbers, strings, or variables. Comparison operators can take only two values, True (if the result of the expression is a true value) and False (if the result of the expression is a false value).

The various comparison operators supported by VBA are listed in Table 2-2.

Table 2-2 Comparison Operators in VBA

Operator	Name
=	Equal to
>	Greater than
<	Less than
>=	Greater than or equal to
<=	Less than or equal to
<>	Not equal to
Like	Like
Is	Is

Concatenation Operators

The Concatenation operator is used in an expression to combine text strings. You can use the ampersand (&) symbol to concatenate strings. For example, "hard" & "ware" would result in "hardware." You can use & to combine any kind of operands as long as its data type is `String`.

Logical Operators

The Logical operators in VBA are used to combine true/false expressions. The various logical operators supported by VBA are listed in Table 2-3.

In most cases, you will deal with one or two values with a single operator. But, what happens when several operators are being used in a single expression? In such a case, you can have multiple answers for the expression. For example, consider the expression 3+5*2. If you calculate the expression from the left, you get the answer 16. However, if you perform the multiplication first, followed by the addition, you get 13 as the answer. This problem is resolved with the help of *oper-*

Table 2-3 Logical Operators in VBA

Operator	Result
Eqv	Returns True if both the expressions are true or if both the expressions are false, and returns False otherwise.
And	Returns True if both the expressions are true, and returns False otherwise.
Imp	Returns False if the first expression is true and the second expression is false, and returns True otherwise.
Or	Returns True if at least one of the expressions are true, and returns False otherwise.
Xor	Returns False if both the expressions is true or if both the expressions are false, and returns False otherwise.
Not	Returns False if the expression is true, and returns True if the expression is false.

ator precedence. This order of precedence helps VBA follow a path for each part of the expression. But, what precedence does VBA follow?

Order of Precedence for the Operators

In case of multiple operators in an expression, VBA uses a predefined order of precedence for resolving ambiguity. Table 2-4 summarizes the order of precedence followed by VBA.

Table 2-4 Order of Precedence for the Operators in VBA

Order of Precedence	Operator
First	^
Second	-
Third	* and /
Fourth	\
Fifth	Mod
Sixth	+ and –
Seventh	&
Eighth	= < > <= >= <> Like Is
Ninth	And Eqv Imp Or Xor Not

You can see from Table 2-4 that multiplication precedes addition. Hence, the correct answer for the earlier example is 13, not 16. You will notice in the table that some operators (such as addition and subtraction, or multiplication and division) have the same order of precedence. This means that they can be evaluated in any order. For example, consider the expression 5+6–3. If you add first and then subtract, the answer would be 8. If you subtract first and then add, the answer remains the same. VBA evaluates operators with the same order of precedence from left to right.

Summary

This chapter introduced you to the concept of variables, constants, and expressions in VBA programming, and you were also introduced to operators and the operator precedence. This chapter is crucial because most of the programming that you will do in VBA will use variables, constants, and expressions.

Chapter 3

Procedures, Functions, and Modules

This chapter introduces the concept of *procedures*, *functions*, and *modules*. It begins with procedures, because they are the basic building blocks of programs.

Using Procedures

In VBA, you can use procedures to divide complex programs into smaller units. To execute one or more statements as a group, you can use procedures. Any code that you need to execute must be contained in a procedure.

When you use procedures, you can maintain and debug code easily. In addition, you can reuse existing procedures. In VBA, procedures are classified based on their functionality. The following sections look at the types of procedures.

Types of Procedures

In VBA, there are three types of procedures:

- `Sub` procedures
- `Function` procedures
- `Property` procedures

`Sub` procedures are the most common type of procedures and are also known as *Command macros*. `Sub` procedures can be called by using their names and do not return values to the process that calls them. `Function` procedures are also known as user-defined procedures and operate just like a program's built-in functions. Unlike `Sub` procedures, `Function` procedures cannot be called using their names but return values when executed. `Property` procedures are used to work with an object's properties. You can use `Property` procedures to create and modify an object's properties. The following sections discuss each of these procedures in detail.

Sub Procedures

A `Sub` procedure is a unit of code that is executed based on an event. A `Sub` procedure does not return any value when executed.

The syntax for `Sub` procedures is as follows:

```
[Public ¦ Private][Static] Sub <procedure name> [Arguments]
     [Statements]
End Sub
```

In the syntax, the keyword `Public` indicates that the procedure is available across different modules. To use a procedure within the current module, you specify the `Private` keyword. `Sub` and `End Sub` are VBA keywords that specify the beginning and end of `Sub` procedures, respectively.

When a `Sub` procedure is called, the statements contained between `Sub` and `End Sub` are executed.

The following is an example of a `Sub` procedure that prompts a user to specify his or her name and then displays the name in a message box:

```
Public Sub MyProcedure()
    Dim Myname As String
    MsgBox "This is the first Sub procedure that I have created."
    Myname = InputBox("Please specify your name")
    MsgBox ("Your name is: " & Myname)
End Sub
```

The output of this procedure is displayed in Figures 3-1 and 3-2.

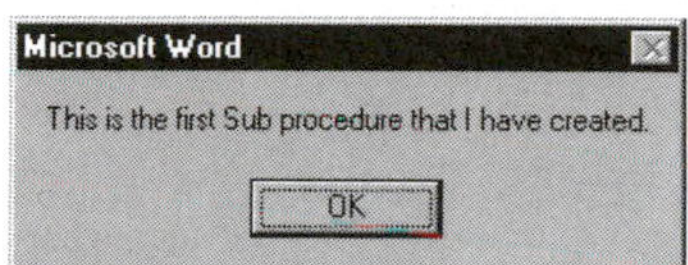

FIGURE 3-1 *A message box*

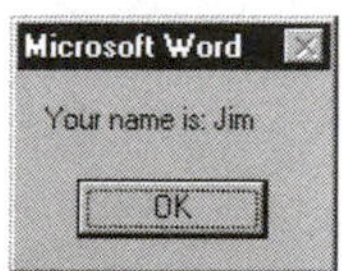

FIGURE 3-2 *A message box displaying the user name*

A `Sub` procedure can be further classified into `General` and `Event` procedures. The following sections discuss these procedures in detail.

General Procedures

You can use a `General` procedure to perform a single task. You can specify tasks that are common to various applications, such as connecting to a database, or tasks that are specific to an application, such as creating a formatted table in Microsoft Word. `General` procedures are `Public` and can be used across various modules. They are useful when tasks need to be performed repeatedly across various modules.

The syntax for `General` procedures is as follows:

```
[Public ¦ Private][Static] Sub <procedure name> [Arguments]
    [Statements]
End Sub
```

Event Procedures

You can use an `Event` procedure to perform a task that is based on an event. These procedures are executed when a specific event occurs, such as when a command button is clicked. `Event` procedures are always `Private` and can be used within the current module. To declare an `Event` procedure, you use the Code window in the Visual Basic Editor. After writing an `Event` procedure, you need to ensure that you do not rename the procedure or a control later. If you do so, the association between the objects and the event-handler is lost, and the procedure becomes a `General` procedure.

The syntax for `Event` procedures is as follows:

```
Private Sub < ObjectName_EventName > ([Arguments])
    [Statements]
End Sub
```

The following is an example of an `Event` procedure. In this procedure, when a command button is clicked, the message `"This is an example of an Event procedure."` is displayed.

```
Private Sub CommandButton1_Click()
     MsgBox "This is an example of an Event procedure."
End Sub
```

Function Procedures

A `Function` procedure is also used to execute a set of statements. However, a `Function` procedure returns values to the calling procedures. A `Function` procedure can accept and manipulate the values of arguments. You can use `Function` procedures to perform calculations.

The syntax for `Function` procedures is as follows:

```
[ Private ¦ Public ]  [ Static ]  Function < function name >  [ As < data type > ]
     [ Statements ]
End Function
```

In the syntax, the `As` keyword indicates the type of return value of a function.

The following is an example of a `Function` procedure. You can use this procedure to calculate the square root of two numbers.

```
Function fnSqrt (intNum As Integer) As Double
     fnSqrt = Sqr(intNum)
End Function
```

Property Procedures

You can use a `Property` procedure to access or assign a value to the property of an object. `Property` procedures are defined in objects. For example, to perform a task each time a specific property is set for an object, you can use a `Property` procedure. After you have defined a `Property` procedure, you do not need to call it implicitly.

The syntax for `Property` procedures is as follows:

```
[Public ¦ Private] [Static] Property {Get ¦ Let ¦ Set} propertyname_ [(Arguments)]
            [As type]
     [Statements]
End Property
```

In this syntax, the arguments `Get`, `Let`, and `Set` represent the three methods available with `Property` procedures. You use the `Property Get` procedure to declare the code that returns the value of a property, the `Property Let` procedure to set the value of a property, and the `Property Set` procedure to specify a reference to an object.

The following is an example of a `Property` procedure. It incorporates the use of the `Let` and `Get` methods to assign and retrieve the values of the variables, `intEmpCode` and `strEmpName`.

```
Public Property Let EmpCode(ByVal intletEmpCode As Integer)
     intEmpCode = intletECode
End Property
```

```
Public Property Get EmpCode() As Integer
     EmpCode = intEmpCode
End Property
Public Property Let EmpName(ByVal strletEmpName As String)
    strEmpName = strletEName
End Property
Public Property Get EmpName() As Integer
     EmpName = strEmpName
End Property
```

Now that you have learned about the various types of procedures, the following section explains how to pass arguments to procedures.

Passing Arguments to a Procedure

When you call a procedure, variables are passed to the calling procedure. These variables are known as *arguments*. By default, the arguments that you specify have the `Variant` data type. However, you can specify other data types for arguments, such as the `String` and `Integer` data types.

As you learned in Chapter 2, "Variables, Constants, and Expressions," you can pass an argument either by value or by reference. When you pass an argument by value, a copy of the variable is passed. Therefore, any changes that are made to the value by the procedure are made to the copy of the variable. You can use the `ByVal` keyword to specify that an argument is passed by value.

When you pass an argument by reference, the variable is passed to the procedure. Therefore, any changes made to the value are made permanently.

Now that you understand how to pass arguments to a procedure, you are ready to create procedures using the Visual Basic Editor.

Using the Visual Basic Editor to Create Procedures

In Chapter 1, "VBA Overview," you looked at the components of the Visual Basic Editor. You also learned how to record a macro by using the Record New Macro dialog box. The following section shows you how to create a simple procedure for Microsoft Word by using the Visual Basic Editor.

Creating a Procedure for Word

You will now create and execute a two-line procedure for Microsoft Word. To create this procedure, you need to use the Visual Basic Editor window. When you run this procedure, the Word application window is maximized and the last accessed document is opened in Word.

To create this procedure, you need to perform the following steps:

1. Start Microsoft Word.
2. Select the Tools > Macro > Visual Basic Editor command to display the Visual Basic Editor window.
3. Double-click on the `ThisDocument` item to open the Code window. The `ThisDocument` object specifies the current Word document.
4. From the `Objects` drop-down list, select the `Document` option. The Visual Basic Editor window automatically creates the stub of an `Open` event for the document object:

   ```
   Private Sub Document_New()
   End Sub
   ```

5. Both maximizing the application window and opening the recently accessed files are related to the `Application` object. You need to type `Application.W` and select the entry. In this case, you need to select the `WindowState` option. Figure 3-3 displays the Visual Basic Editor window.

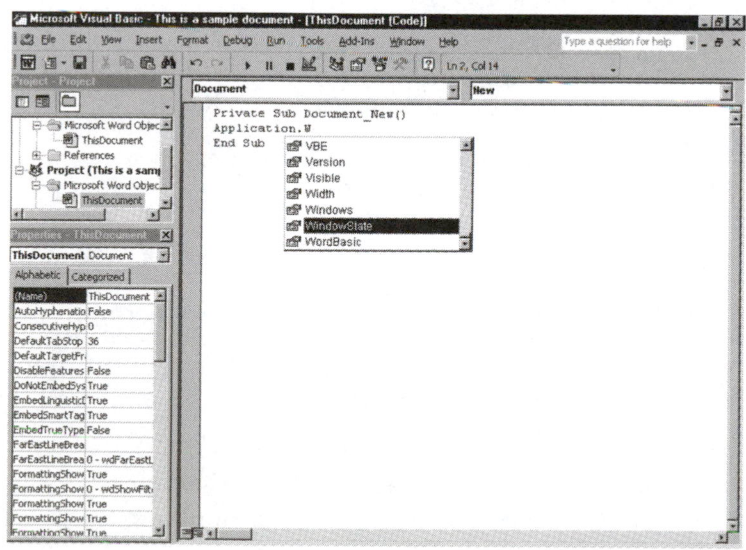

FIGURE 3-3 *The Visual Basic Editor window containing a code snippet*

6. After you select the `WindowState` option, you need to specify the List properties for this option. To do this, you need to type an = sign and select a constant. Here, you need to select the `wdWindowStateMaximize` item and press the Enter key to start a new statement.
7. You have specified that the application window should be maximized when the Word application is started. You now need to write a statement to open the most recently accessed file. To do this, type `Application.` and select `RecentFiles` from the `List Properties` drop-down list. Because you need to open the most recently accessed document, you need to specify `(1).` to indicate the first item in the list of recent files.
8. Next, select the `Open` constant from the `List Properties` drop-down list.
9. The procedure should now be displayed as follows:

```
Private Sub Document_New()
Application.WindowState = wdWindowStateMaximize
Application.RecentFiles(1).Open
End Sub
```

   Figure 3-4 displays the Visual Basic Editor window with the complete procedure.
10. To run this procedure, select the Close and Return to Microsoft Word option from the File menu.

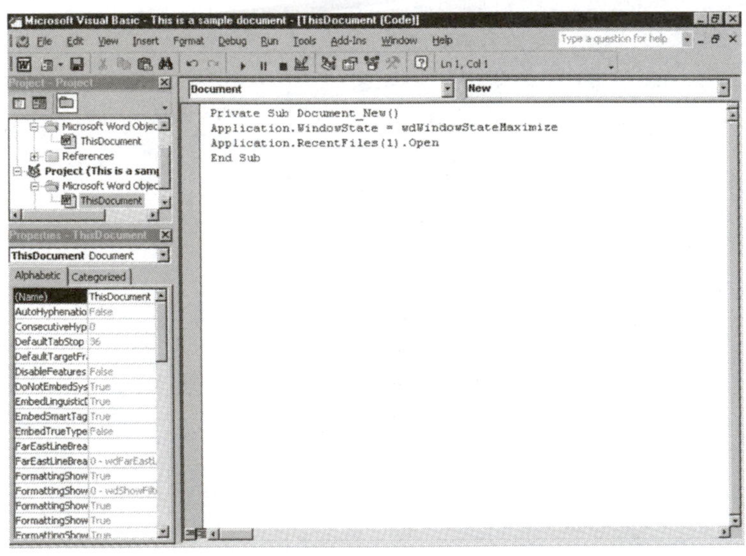

FIGURE 3-4 *The Visual Basic Editor window containing the complete procedure*

11. Now, open a sample document, make changes to it, and exit from Word.
12. Start the Word application again. The application window maximizes and the most recently accessed file is displayed.

You can declare procedures by writing the code in the Visual Basic Editor Code window or by using the Add Procedure dialog box. As shown in Figure 3-5, the Add Procedure dialog box allows you to create a procedure by specifying its name and type.

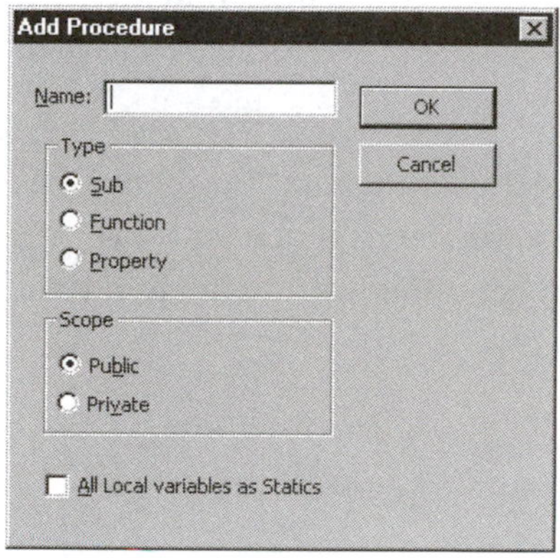

FIGURE 3-5 *The Add Procedure dialog box*

To declare a procedure by using the Add Procedure dialog box, you need to perform the following steps:

1. Open the module for which you need to declare a procedure.
2. Select the Procedure command from the Insert menu.
3. Specify the name of the procedure in the Name text box.
4. Specify the type of procedure that you need to create.
5. Specify the scope of the procedure as `Public` or `Private`.
6. Click on the OK button.

In the Add Procedure dialog box, you can also specify whether all the local variables declared will be *static*. If you select the All Local variables as Statics check box, the values of the variables within a procedure are preserved between procedure calls. Therefore, when a procedure is subsequently called, the values of the procedure-level variables are not started from scratch. To declare a static variable, you need to use the keyword `Static` instead of `Dim`.

Using Functions

A *function* is a type of procedure that returns a value and may or may not accept arguments. You typically use functions to perform a specialized task, such as calculating a student's grades.

VBA provides many built-in functions that you can use to perform multiple tasks, such as formatting an expression, converting the data type, or manipulating strings. You can also create user-defined functions to perform tasks that are specific to your application. For example, you might need to create a user-defined function to calculate the salary of an employee. You will learn more about such functions in later sections.

Although you can perform multiple tasks within a single function, you should create a user-defined function to perform a single specific task. When you specify a single task for a function, such as opening a file or accessing data to be displayed, you can reuse the function across various projects.

To use functions in VBA, you need to invoke them, as explained in the following section.

Calling Functions

To use functions, you need to call or invoke them from within a `Sub` procedure or another function. You can use the `Call` statement to invoke functions. You can either specify the `Call` keyword or simply specify the name of the function.

The syntax for `Call` statements is as follows:

```
[Call] name [, argumentlist]
```

In the syntax, `name` is the name of the function that you need to call. To call a function, you need to specify the `name` argument. The `argumentlist` argument is optional. You can use it to specify a comma-delimited list of variables or expressions that you need to pass to the function.

For example, to call the `MsgBox` function, you can specify the following:

```
MsgBox "Hello World!"
```

The `Call` keyword is optional. When you use the `Call` keyword, you need to enclose the `argumentlist` argument within parentheses as follows:

```
Call MsgBox ("Hello World!")
```

In VBA statements, you can use multiple sets of parentheses. The functions enclosed within the parentheses are evaluated first. However, instead of using multiple levels, you should limit the nesting to a few levels. This will not only help you read the code easily, but also troubleshoot it much faster.

Consider the following statement:

```
MsgBox Left(Right("This is a sample code.", 10),2)
```

Here, the statement uses three functions, `MsgBox`, `Left`, and `Right`. The `MsgBox` function is used to display a message box. The `Left` and the `Right` functions are used to display the specified number of characters from the left and the right of the string, respectively.

When this statement is evaluated, the `Right` function is evaluated before the `Left` function. The result is then passed to the `MsgBox` function and is displayed in a message box.

When you need to specify more than one argument for a function, you can pass the arguments to the function by using any of the three following methods:

1. You can specify the arguments without using their names, in the order in which a function expects them to be listed.

   Consider the time function `TimeSerial(hour, minute, second)`, which is used to display a date value for the specified hour, minute, and second.

   You can specify the arguments for this function without using their names as follows:

   ```
   MsgBox TimeSerial(12, 30, 2)
   ```

2. You can specify the arguments by using their names, in the order in which a function expects them.

   For example: `MsgBox TimeSerial(Hour:=12, Minute:=30, Second:=2)`

3. You can specify the arguments by using their names, in the order that you require.

   For example: `MsgBox TimeSerial(Minute:=30, Second:=2, Hour:=12)`

The fastest method to pass arguments is by specifying the arguments without their names in the order in which a function expects them. However, it is difficult to read the code without the argument names. Also, when you need to skip an argument, you need to specify a comma. Therefore, it is recommended that you use argument names to increase the readability of the code.

Now that you know how to invoke functions, the following sections discuss more about the various types of built-in functions provided by VBA.

Types of Built-in Functions

VBA has various types of built-in functions. The types of built-in functions are categorized based on their functionality. Here, you learn about the various types of built-in functions that you can use to perform tasks, such as convert data types, format expressions, and display the output.

Using Data Type Conversion Functions

At times, you might need to store data in a specific data type. In such cases, you can use VBA functions to convert data types.

The syntax for data type conversion functions is as follows:

```
function_name [expression/string/number]
```

In this syntax, `function_name` is the conversion function that you need to use, and `expression/string/number` is the expression, string, or number that you need to convert.

CAUTION

If you specify an expression that is outside the normal range for a data type, VBA generates an error.

Some of the common functions that you can use to convert one data type to another are listed in Table 3-1.

Table 3-1 Data Type Conversion Functions

Function(Arguments)	Data Type
CBool(*number*)	Boolean
CByte(*expression*)	Byte
CCur(*expression*)	Currency
CDate(*expression*)	Date
CDbl(*expression*)	Double
CDec(*expression*)	Decimal
CInt(*expression*)	Integer
CLng(*expression*)	Long
CSng(*expression*)	Single
CStr(*expression*)	String
CVar(*expression*)	Variant
CVErr(*errornumber*)	Variant of subtype Error
Asc(*string*)	Displays ANSI character code for the first character in the string
Chr(*number*)	Displays a number between 0 and 255 as a *String* for the specified character code
Hex(*number*)	Displays a string containing the hexadecimal value of a number
Oct(*number*)	Displays a string containing the octal value of a number
Str(*number*)	Displays a variant or a string representation of a number
Val(*string*)	Displays the number part of the string. If there is no numeric part, *Val* returns 0.

NOTE

When you use the `Str` function to return a string representation of a number, a leading space is reserved for the sign of the number. Consider the following example:

```
Dim ChangeString
ChangeString = Str(220)        'returns " 220"
ChangeString = Str(-220.01)    'returns "-220.01"
```

Using Format Functions

In addition to using functions to convert data types, you can also use them to format expressions. You can use the `Format` function to display the result of an expression in a logical and consistent format. For example, you can format expressions by adding commas in large numerals or specifying the percentage sign with figures.

The syntax for the `Format` function is as follows:

```
Format (expression[, format[, firstdayofweek[, firstweekofyear]]])
```

In this syntax, `expression` is a valid expression that you want to format. The `format` argument is optional, and you can use it to specify the named format expression or a user-defined format expression.

The `firstdayofweek` argument in the syntax is optional. You can use this argument to specify the day that starts the week. This option is required for date information. You can either use the default setting that is `vbSunday (1)` or specify `vbMonday (2)` and so on. To accept the system settings, you can use the `vbUse System (0)` argument.

The `firstweekofyear` argument is also optional, and you can use it to specify the first week of the year. This argument is also required for date information. You can either specify `vbFirstJan1` to specify the week in which January 1 falls, or you can use the system settings by specifying the `vbUseSystem (0)` argument. You can also specify `vbFirstFourDays (2)` to specify the first week with a minimum of four days in the year, or specify `vbFirstFullWeek (3)` to specify the first full week as consisting of seven days of the year.

VBA offers predefined numeric formats, date and time formats, and string formats. You will learn more about these later in this chapter. First, Table 3-2 lists some of the predefined numeric formats that you can use to format expressions.

Using String Manipulation Functions

You can use string variables to store, modify, and manipulate data. Some of the commonly used built-in string manipulation functions are listed in Table 3-3.

Table 3-2 Format Functions

Function(Arguments)	Description
General Number	Default numeric format with no thousand separator
Currency	Displays the number with two decimal places, a thousand separator, and the currency symbol. Negative numbers are displayed enclosed within parentheses.
Fixed	Displays the number with one integer place and two decimal places
Standard	Displays the number with the thousand separator, one integer place, and two decimal places
Percent	Displays the number multiplied by 100, with two decimal places and a percentage sign
Scientific	Displays the number in scientific notation where the most significant number is displayed to the left of the decimal, 2 to 30 decimal places are displayed to the right of the decimal, and E is followed by the exponent
Yes/No	Displays a non-zero number as *Yes* and a zero number as *No*
True/False	Displays a non-zero number as *True* and a zero number as *False*
On/Off	Displays a non-zero number as *On* and a zero number as *Off*

Table 3-3 String Manipulation Functions

Function(Arguments)	Description
InStr(*start, string1, string2, compare*)	Displays the character position of the first occurrence of *string2* in *string1* beginning at *start*
InStrRev(*stringcheck, stringmatch, start, compare*)	Displays the character position of the first occurrence of *stringmatch* in *stringcheck* beginning at *start*
LCase(*string*)	Displays a string in lowercase
Left(*string, number*)	Displays the specified number of character from the left of the string
Len(*string*)	Displays the number of characters in the string

(continues)

Table 3-3 String Manipulation Functions (continued)

Function(Arguments)	Description
LTrim(*string*)	Displays the string without the leading spaces
Mid(*string*, *start*, *length*)	Displays the specified number of characters beginning at *start* of the string
Right(*string*, *number*)	Displays the specified number of characters from the right of the string
RTrim(*string*)	Displays the string without the trailing spaces
Space(*number*)	Displays a string containing the number of spaces
StrComp(*string1*, *string2*, *compare*)	Displays the result of comparing *string1* and *string2*
String(*number*, *character*)	Displays the string containing the *number* of instances of *character*
StrReverse(*expression*)	Displays a string containing the characters in the *expression* in reverse order
Trim(*string*)	Displays the string without leading or trailing spaces
UCase(*string*)	Displays a string containing the string in uppercase

Using Mathematical Functions

You can use the built-in mathematical functions as operands for various expressions. Some of the commonly used mathematical functions are listed in Table 3-4.

In addition to the mathematical functions listed in Table 3-4, you can use certain derived functions. Some of these functions are listed in Table 3-5.

Table 3-4 Mathematical Functions

Function (Arguments)	Description
Abs(*number*)	Displays the absolute value of the number
Atn(*number*)	Displays the arctangent of the number
Cos(*number*)	Displays the cosine of the number

(continues)

Table 3-4 Mathematical Functions (continued)

Function (Arguments)	Description
Exp(*number*)	Displays the base of the natural logarithm raised to the power of the number
Fix(*number*)	Displays the integer portion of the number. If the number is negative, *Fix* returns the first negative integer greater than or equal to the number.
Hex(*number*)	Displays the hexadecimal value as a *Variant* of the number
Hex$(*number*)	Displays the hexadecimal value as a *String* of the number
Int(*number*)	Displays the integer portion of the number. If the number is negative, *Int* returns the first negative integer less than or equal to the number.
Log(*number*)	Displays the natural logarithm of the number
Oct(*number*)	Displays the octal value as a *Variant* of the number
Oct$(*number*)	Displays the octal value as a *String* of the number
Rnd(*number*)	Displays a random number between 0 and 1 as a *Single*
Sgn(*number*)	Displays the sign of the number
Sin(*number*)	Displays the sine of the number
Sqr(*number*)	Displays the square root of the number
Tan(*number*)	Displays the tangent of the number

Table 3-5 Derived Mathematical Functions

Function	Derived
Secant	Sec(X) = 1 / Cos(X)
Cosecant	Cosec(X) = 1 / Sin(X)
Cotangent	Cotan(X) = 1 / Tan(X)
Inverse Sine	Arcsin(X) = Atn(X / Sqr(-X * X + 1))
Inverse Cosine	Arccos(X) = Atn(-X / Sqr(-X * X + 1)) + 2 * Atn(1)
Hyperbolic Sine	HSin(X) = (Exp(X) – Exp(-X)) / 2
Hyperbolic Cosine	HCos(X) = (Exp(X) + Exp(-X)) / 2
Logarithm to base N	LogN(X) = Log(X) / Log(N)

Using Date and Time Functions

You use a date expression to return a `Date` value. You can either declare a variable as `Date` or use the date. To use the date, you need to enclose the date within hash signs as follows:

```
DateVar = #11/20/01#
```

VBA interprets dates as serial numbers. It uses December 31, 1899 as a starting point and represents the subsequent days as the number of days that have passed since then. Therefore, for January 1, 1900, the serial number is 1.

Similar to dates, the time is also represented by using serial numbers. Here, the starting point is midnight, which is given a value of 0, and the time is expressed as a fraction of a 24-hour day. When you use serial numbers to represent the date and time, it is easy to perform mathematical operations.

VBA offers certain built-in date and time functions. You can also define your own date and time functions. You will learn more about user-defined functions later in this chapter.

Table 3-6 lists some of the date and time functions provided by VBA.

You can use the Control Panel to specify the default formatting to be used by VBA to display the date and time. However, by default, if the date serial number does not contain a fractional component, the date is displayed in the `mm/dd/yy` format. Also, if the serial number does not contain an integer component, the time is displayed in the `hh:mm: AM/PM` format.

In addition to using functions to manipulate the data type or strings, you can use functions to display information or accept input from users. Next, you will learn how to use functions for user interaction.

Using User Interaction Functions

In VBA, you can use dialog boxes to accept input from and display output to users. You can use the `MsgBox` and `InputBox` functions to create dialog boxes with specific functionality. These dialog boxes are also known as *modal* dialog boxes.

You can use the user interaction functions to display dialog boxes. In the following sections, you will learn more about these functions and how to use them.

Table 3-6 Date and Time Functions

Function(Argument)	Description
CDate(*expression*)	Converts expression into a *Date* value
Date	Displays the current system date as a *Variant*
Dates$()	Displays the current system date as a *String*
DateAdd(*interval*, *number*, *date*)	Displays the resultant date after an interval of time is added to or subtracted from the date
DateDiff(*interval*, *date1*, *date2* [,*firstdayofweek*[,*firstweekofyear*]])	Displays the interval between *date1* and *date2*
DatePart(*interval*, *date* [,*firstdayofweek*[,*firstweekofyear*]])	Displays the date with its various components
DateSerial(*year*,*month*,*day*)	Displays a date value for the year, month, and day
DateValue(*date*)	Displays a date value for the date string
Day(*date*)	Displays the day of the month given by date
Hour(*time*)	Displays the hour component of time
Minute(*time*)	Displays the minute component of time
Month(*date*)	Displays the month component of date
Now	Displays the current system date and time
Second(*time*)	Displays the second component of time
Time	Displays the current system time as a *Variant*
Time$	Displays the current system time as a *String*
Timer	Displays the number of seconds since midnight
TimeSerial(*hour*,*minute*,*second*)	Displays a date value for the specified hour, minute, and second
TimeValue(*time*)	Displays a date value for the time string
Weekday(*date*)	Displays the day of the week as a number given by date
Year(*date*)	Displays the year component of date

Using the MsgBox Function

You can use the `MsgBox` function to display user-defined text within a dialog box.

The syntax for the `MsgBox` function is as follows:

```
MsgBox(prompt[, buttons][, title][, helpfile-context])
```

In the syntax, the `prompt` argument represents the string that you need to display as a message in the dialog box. You can specify a maximum of 1,024 characters in this argument. The `buttons` argument is a number that is a sum of values and specifies the number and type of buttons to be displayed, the icons of the default buttons, the identity of the default button, and the modality of the message box. The `title` argument specifies the string that will be displayed in the title bar of the dialog box.

Table 3-7 lists some of the frequently used argument settings for buttons.

Table 3-7 Argument Settings for Buttons

Constant	Value	Description
vbOKonly	0	Displays the OK button only
vbOKCancel	1	Displays the OK and Cancel buttons
vbOKAbortRetryIgnore	2	Displays the Abort, Retry, and Ignore buttons
vbYesNoCancel	3	Displays the Yes, No, and Cancel buttons
vbYesNo	4	Displays the Yes and No buttons
vbRetryCancel	5	Displays the Retry and Cancel buttons
vbCritical	16	Displays the Critical Message icon
vbQuestion	32	Displays the Warning Query icon
vbExclamation	48	Displays the Warning Message icon
vbInformation	64	Displays the Information Message icon
vbDefaultButton1	0	Specifies that the first button is the default
vbDefaultButton2	256	Specifies that the second button is the default
vbDefaultButton3	512	Specifies that the third button is the default
vbDefaultButton4	768	Specifies that the fourth button is the default
vbMsgBoxHelpButton	65536	Adds a Help button to the dialog box

Table 3-8 lists some of the `MsgBox` return values.

Table 3-8 MsgBox Return Values

Constant	Value	Button Selected
vbOK	1	OK
vbCancel	2	Cancel
vbAbort	3	Abort
vbRetry	4	Retry
vbIgnore	5	Ignore
vbYes	6	Yes
vbNo	7	No

The following is an example of how the `MsgBox` function can be used. In the example, a message box that contains the Yes, No, and Cancel buttons is displayed.

```
Private Sub Form_Load()
     Dim intResponse As Integer
     Dim strTitle As String
     strTitle = "Try MsgBox "
     intResponse = MsgBox("Application Stopped", 19, strTitle)
If intResponse = vbYes Then
     MsgBox "You clicked on Yes"
Else
     MsgBox "You did not click on Yes"
End If
End Sub
```

The output of the preceding example is displayed in Figure 3-6.

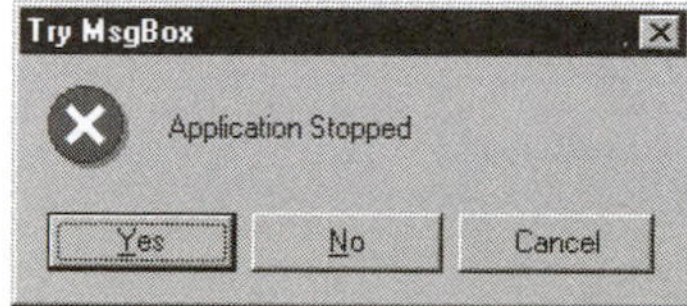

FIGURE 3-6 *A message box containing the Yes, No, and Cancel buttons*

Using the InputBox Function

You can use the `InputBox` function to accept user input in a dialog box. The function then returns the text entered by the user.

The syntax for the `InputBox` function is as follows:

```
InputBox(prompt[, title][, default][, xpos][, ypos])
```

In the syntax, the `default` argument refers to the string expression displayed in the text box as the default response. If you do not specify this argument, an empty text box is displayed. The `xpos` argument represents the horizontal distance between the left edge of the dialog box and the left of the screen. If you do not specify this argument, the dialog box is positioned horizontally. The `ypos` argument represents the vertical distance between the top edge of the dialog box and the top of the screen. If you do not specify this argument, the dialog box is positioned vertically, approximately one-third of the way down the screen.

The following is an example of the use of the `InputBox` function. In this example, a dialog box entitled `My InputBox`, which prompts users to specify their names, is displayed.

```
Private Sub Form_Load()
     Dim strMsg As String, strTitle As String, strName As String
     strMsg = "What is your name?"
     strTitle = "My InputBox"
     strName = InputBox(strMsg, strTitle, "Linda")
End Sub
```

The output of the this example is displayed in Figure 3-7.

FIGURE 3-7 *An input box prompting users to specify their names*

Using File Management Functions

In addition to data type conversion functions, format functions, string manipulations functions, mathematical functions, and date and time functions, VBA also offers specific file management functions that you can use to display information about files and folders. You can also use some of the functions to manipulate files and folders and access the contents of files.

Table 3-9 lists some of the file management functions.

Table 3-9 File Management Functions

Function(Argument)	Description
CurDir	Displays the path of the current drive
CurDir(*drive*)	Displays the path of the specified drive as a *Variant*
CurDir$(*drive*)	Displays the path of the specified drive as a *String*
Dir(*pathname, attributes*)	Displays the name of the file or folder. You can specify the wildcard characters, *?* and *, in the pathname argument. You can specify attributes such as Normal *{vbNormal (or 0)}*, Hidden *{vbHidden (or 2)}*, System *{vbSystem (or 4)}*, Volume Label *{vbVolume (or 8)}*, and Folder *{vbDirectory (or 16)}*.
FileDateTime(*pathname*)	Displays the date and time when the specified file was last modified
FileLen(*pathname*)	Displays a Long value representing the number of bytes in the specified file
GetAttr(*pathname*)	Displays an Integer value representing the sum of the attribute values for a file, directory, or folder. You can specify the directory, folder, or drive name in the pathname argument. You can specify the attribute values such as Normal {*vbNormal (or 0)*}, Read-only {*vbReadOnly (or 1)*}, Hidden {*vbHidden (or 2)*}, System File (not available on the Macintosh) {*vbSystem (or 4)*}, Directory or folder {*vbDirectory (or 16)*}, File has changes since the last backup (not available on Macintosh) {*vbArchive (or 32)*}, and Specified file name is an alias (available only on Macintosh) {*vbAlias (or 64)*}.

In addition to displaying information about files and folders, you can also use VBA file management statements to modify the current drive and folder, as well as create, delete, and rename files and folders.

Table 3-10 lists some of the file management statements that you can use to manipulate files and folders.

Table 3-10 File Management Statements

Statement(Argument)	Description
ChDir(*path*)	Changes the drive's default folder
ChDrive(*drive*)	Changes the default drive
FileCopy(*source*, *destination*)	Copies a disk file from one location to another

You have learned about the various built-in functions that you can use to perform specific tasks. In the following section you will learn more about how to create your own functions in VBA.

Creating User-Defined Functions

You can create user-defined functions in VBA just like you create procedures. A user-defined function cannot contain menu commands or mouse and keyboard actions. Therefore, you cannot record user-defined functions and need to write them manually. To write functions, you use the Code window for the module in which you need to create the functions. To create a user-defined function, you need to use the `Function` statement.

The syntax for the `Function` statement is as follows:

```
[Public ¦ Private] [Static] Function function_name [(argument_list)] [As type]
     [Statements]
     [function_name = expression]
      [Exit Function]
      [Statements]
      [function_name = expression]
End Function
```

In the syntax, `Public` is an optional keyword that you can use to make the function available to all the other procedures in other modules. If you need to make the function available to other procedures within the same module, you can use the `Private` keyword. The `function_name` is a required argument that specifies the name of the function. The naming convention for functions is similar to other VBA objects, such as procedures.

To specify a list of variables that represent the arguments that are passed to a function, you need to use the `argument_list` argument. The `type` argument is an optional argument that you can use to specify the data type of the argument, such as `Byte`, `Date`, or `Integer`. You can also specify the value that the function returns by using the `expression` argument.

NOTE

At times, you might specify a list of arguments, but the function may not require all the arguments. In such a case, you can specify an optional argument by including the `Optional` keyword before the argument.

To write a function in the Code window, follow these steps:

1. Open the module in which you need to create the function.
2. Type `Function` followed by the name of the function in the Code window and press the Enter key. You can also specify a list of arguments in a function enclosed within parentheses and separated by commas.
3. When you press Enter, VBA automatically inserts the `End Function` statement.
4. Then, you need to specify the statements within the `Function` and `End Function` lines. To ensure clarity, you need to indent each line of the statement.
5. In the statements, you also need to include a line that specifies the return value.

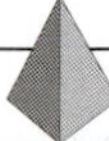

TIP

When you create a function, it is a good practice to describe what the function does by using comments. You can specify comments by using an apostrophe (') at the beginning of each comment line.

The following is a user-defined function that you can use to calculate the commission on the basis of the amount of sales. The user-defined function here is `CalculateCommission`, where `CalculateCommission = SalesQ` * (1.5 / 100). The user is prompted to specify the sales amount. The commission is then calculated and displayed in a message box.

```
Option Explicit
     Dim SalesQ As Currency 'specifies the quarterly sales
     Dim CalculateCommission As Currency
'specifies the function to calculate commission
Public Function CalComm() As Currency
     CalculateCommission = SalesQ * (1.5 / 100)
End Function
Public Sub Main()
     SalesQ = InputBox("Enter Sales Amount")
     Call CalComm
     MsgBox ("The commission amount  is: $" & CalculateCommission)
End Sub
```

The output of this example is displayed in Figure 3-8 and Figure 3-9.

FIGURE 3-8 *An input box prompting a user to specify the sales amount*

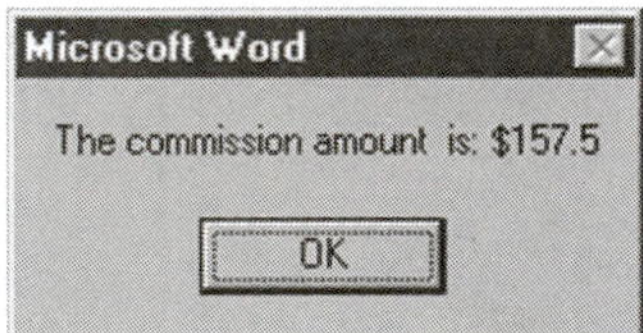

FIGURE 3-9 *A message box displaying the commission amount*

You can use the following function to extract the numeric component from a `Text` string in Excel:

```
Function GetNumber(rCell As Range)
     Dim IntCount As Integer, i As Integer
```

```
        Dim StrCount As String
        Dim lntNum As String
        StrCount = rCell
        For IntCount = Len(StrCount) To 1 Step -1
If IsNumeric(Mid(StrCount, IntCount, 1)) Then
            i = i + 1
        lntNum = Mid(StrCount, IntCount, 1) & lntNum
        End If
If i = 1 Then lntNum = CInt(Mid(lntNum, 1, 1))
        Next IntCount
        GetNumber = CLng(lntNum)
End Function
```

You can create different types of user-defined functions to perform specific tasks. You can also create user-defined functions for predefined numeric and date and time functions.

Table 3-11 lists some of the symbols that you can use to create user-defined functions for numeric formats.

Table 3-11 Creating User-Defined Functions for Numeric Formats

Symbol	Description
None	Displays the number without any formatting
(0)	Displays a digit or displays a zero if no number is specified
#	Displays a digit or does not display anything
%	Multiplies the expression by 100 and displays the percent character where it appears in the format string
(.)	Specifies the location of the decimal point
(,)	Specifies the location of the thousands separator
(:)	Specifies the hours, minutes, and seconds when time values are formatted
(/)	Specifies the day, month, and year when date values are formatted
(\)	Displays the next character in the format string
"ABC"	Displays the string enclosed in double quotation marks
(E- E+ e- e+)	Displays a number in scientific notation
- + $ ( )	Displays a literal character

Table 3-12 lists some of the symbols that you can use to create user-defined functions for date and time formats.

Table 3-12 Creating User-Defined Functions for Date and Time Formats

Symbol	Description
:	Separates different components of time value
/	Separates different components of date value
c	Displays the date as ddddd and time as ttttt in the system format
d	Displays the date (1 to 31) without a leading zero
dd	Displays the date (01 to 31) with a leading zero
w	Displays the day of the week as a number between 1 and 7
ww	Displays the week of the year as a number between 1 and 54
m	Displays the month without a leading zero as a number between 1 and 12
mm	Displays the month with a leading zero as a number between 01 and 12
q	Displays the quarter of the year as a number between 1 and 4
y	Displays the day of the year as an integer between 1 and 366
yy	Displays the year as a two-digit number between 00 and 99
h	Displays the hour as a number between 0 and 23
Hh	Displays the hour as a two-digit number between 00 and 23
N	Displays the minute as a number between 0 and 60
Nn	Displays the minute as a two-digit number between 00 and 60
S	Displays the seconds as a number between 0 and 60
Ss	Displays the seconds as a two-digit number between 0 and 60
ttttt	Displays the time in the system's default time format as hour, minute, and second
AM/PM	Displays AM or PM with the time value on the basis of the 12-hour clock
am/pm	Displays am or pm with the time value on the basis of the 12-hour clock

In VBA, a collection of procedures, functions, and event-handlers is called a *module*. Each application is a collection of modules. In the following section, you will learn more about modules and the types of modules.

Using Modules

Modules act as the basic building blocks of a project. They are containers that store code. When you organize code within modules, it is easier to maintain and debug the code and reuse the module across various projects.

In VBA, three types of modules are available:

- Form modules
- Standard modules
- Class modules

Form Modules

You can use Form modules to provide a user interface for an application. They are stored with the file extension `.frm`. Form modules contain all the controls on the form and the properties for these controls. You can also specify constant and variable declarations, procedures, and event procedures for the form and the controls.

By default, all the declarations in a Form module are `Private`. Therefore, the constant and variable declarations, procedures, and event procedures are not available to code outside the form.

Standard Modules

You can use Standard modules to store general procedures that can be invoked by procedures across other modules. Standard modules are stored with the file extension `.bas`. They contain declarations of constants, types, variables, procedures, and functions.

By default, all the constants, variables, and procedures that are declared in a Standard module are `Public`. Therefore they can be accessed by code in other modules, such as Form, Standard, and Class modules.

NOTE

Typically, all the procedures and functions that need to be globally accessed across a project are written in a Standard module.

Class Modules

You can use Class modules just like Form modules. The only difference between a Class module and a Form module is that the former does not have a visual component. You can use Class modules to create your own objects. To write the code for a class, you need to use the Class module.

An example of a Class module is a form. A form is an object that contains properties, such as the font, name, or caption; methods such as click; and predefined behavior. When you create a form, it becomes an independent module of code. Similarly, all the controls, such as command buttons and text boxes, are objects of their respective classes.

Summary

This chapter introduced you to the concept of procedures, functions, and modules in VBA programming. You learned about the types of procedures, how to pass arguments to procedures, and how to create simple procedures using the Visual Basic Editor. You then looked at functions and the various built-in functions. You also learned about the customized functions that you can create. Finally, you learned about modules and the types of modules. You are now well equipped to begin using procedures, functions, and modules to write code and develop applications using VBA.

Chapter 4

Arrays and Programming Constructs

In the previous chapters, you learned about the basics of programming in VBA. In this chapter, you will learn about arrays. You will also learn about the various types of programming constructs.

Arrays

As discussed in Chapter 2, "Variables, Constants, and Expressions," you can use variables to store values. However, the limitation of using variables is that each variable can store only one value at a time. Consider a situation in which you want to store 20 values in variables. It would be difficult and time-consuming to declare 20 variables and then assign values. Thus, variables are not a good option when the number of values to be stored is large. You can use arrays in such situations.

An *array* is a set of indexed data values stored sequentially. The values are stored in adjacent memory locations. Each set of data values stored as an array is treated as a separate variable. For the preceding example, you can declare an array which can store 20 values. The values in an array can be referenced individually at any point in the program. All the values in an array can be referenced by the same name (but with a different index number) and have the same data type.

Just like variables, you need to declare an array before using it. In the following section, you will learn how to declare an array.

Declaring Arrays

You can declare arrays the same way you declare variables by using the `Dim` statement. While declaring an array, you need to add a pair of parentheses to the array name. You can also specify the number of data values that the array can store, that is, the size of the array. For example, the following statement declares an array named `monthlysales` as the Integer data type containing 12 items:

```
Dim monthlysales(12) as Integer
```

You can declare either *fixed-size arrays* or *dynamic arrays*. I will talk about fixed-size arrays first.

An array whose size is specified at the time of declaration is a fixed-size array. For example, the `monthlysales` array you declared is an example of a fixed-size array. You can declare a fixed-size array that contains five strings as in the following statement:

```
Dim Names(5) As String
```

The `Names` array can store five strings. Each string is referred by its index number. The index number starts at 0. The first string in the array has the value `0`, and the last string has the value `4`.

```
Names(0)
Names(1)
Names(2)
Names(3)
Names(4)
```

The `Names` array is assigned the String data type. You can assign any data type to an array. The default data type of an array is Variant.

You will now learn about dynamic arrays.

In many situations you are not sure of the size of an array. You could take a guess and allocate memory. However, if your guess is too low and the array actually requires more memory than what is allocated, an error message is generated. On the other hand, if your guess is too high, VBA still allocates memory to the unused locations of the array, resulting in a waste of memory. To avoid these problems, you might need to allocate size to an array at runtime. For example, if you want to run a procedure that will store the name of each student in a list, and you do not know the number of students in the list, you can use a dynamic array.

You can declare a dynamic array by adding a pair of empty parentheses to the array name. For example, a dynamic array, `Names`, is declared as follows:

```
Dim Names() As String
```

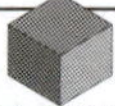

NOTE

You will learn about allocating size to a dynamic array with the help of the `ReDim` statement later in the chapter.

Apart from fixed-size and dynamic arrays, you can also specify the dimensions of an array by declaring it as *one-dimensional* or *multidimensional*. A one-dimensional array has only one dimension specified in the declaration. An example of a one-dimensional array is:

```
Dim Custname(10) As String
```

VBA supports a maximum of 60 dimensions.

You might want to declare an array as multidimensional. A two-dimensional array can be visualized as a table that consists of rows and columns. For example, you can declare a two-dimensional array named `StockRateArr` with three data values in each dimension as follows:

```
Dim StockRateArr(2,2) As Integer
```

Having declared an array, you want to store values in it. The next section deals with storing values in arrays.

Storing Values in an Array

To store values in an array, you need to refer to elements in an array. As discussed in the preceding section, each element in an array has an index number associated with it. The index number associated with a single data value in an array indicates its position in the array. The first element of an array has the index 0, and the last element has an index that is one less than the dimension of the array. You can either address the entire set of values in an array or refer to each value in the array separately. For example, you can reference the third data element in the array, `Names`, by using the following statement:

```
Names(2)
```

Similarly, you can use the index number and assignment operator to assign value to a particular data element in an array:

```
Names(2) = "John Smith"
```

The third element in the array, `Names`, is assigned the value `John Smith`.

By default, the indexing of items in an array starts at 0. You can use the `Option Base` statement to change the default index number. To do this, you need to declare the `Option Base` statement at the beginning of the code. For example, the following statement

```
Option Base 1
```

will change the default index number of the array from 0 to 1.

It is possible to increase or decrease the size of an array after you have declared it. You can do this with the help of the `ReDim` statement. In the next section, you will learn to change the size of an array after declaration by using the `ReDim` statement.

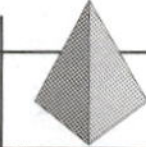

TIP

Working with arrays is much easier if you use `Option Base 1` statement because the index starts at 1, and referencing individual items of the array becomes easy.

Redimensioning an Array

Redimensioning an array refers to changing the size of the array. You might need to change the size of an array after you have declared it. Once an array is declared, it is allocated memory according to its size. If you want to increase or decrease the amount of memory allocated to the array, you can do so with the help of the `ReDim` statement. An example of modifying the size of an array is given below:

```
ReDim Names(7)
```

If the array, `Names`, has any values stored in it, the `ReDim` statement will erase the previously stored values. In case you want to change the size of an array without erasing the previously stored values, you use the `ReDim Preserve` statement as follows:

```
ReDim Preserve Names(10)
```

The preceding statement changes the size of the array, `Names`, to `10` and preserves the previously stored values.

Now, consider a situation in which you have an array with dimension `12`. You need to change the dimension of the array to `5` and preserve the first five data values. In this situation, you use the following `ReDim Preserve` statement:

```
ReDim Preserve Names(5)
```

This declaration preserves the values of the first five data elements and erases the rest.

Once arrays are declared and initialized, you can use them in functions and procedures just like variables. For example, you might need to perform some analysis based on the values stored in an array. You will learn about extracting information from an array in the next section.

Extracting Information from an Array

Arrays can be used in functions and procedures to store multiple values. The values from the array can be extracted to perform operations on those values. You need to specify the index number of the data element in an array to specify the position of the data value you want to extract. You can then use the `MsgBox` function to display the value stored in an array.

The following code declares an array, `InventoryListArr`, with dimension `9`:

```
Dim InventoryListArr(9) As String
```

The data elements in the array, `InventoryListArr`, store the following values:

```
InventoryListArr(0) = "Acrylic Sheets"
InventoryListArr(1) = "Brass Parker Adapter"
InventoryListArr(2) = "Bulk Head Connector"
InventoryListArr(3) = "Feed Thru Connector"
InventoryListArr(4) = "Wall Anchor"
InventoryListArr(5) = "Hilti Anchor"
InventoryListArr(6) = "Radiation Cable"
InventoryListArr(7) = "Coaxial Cable"
InventoryListArr(8) = "Bonded Shielding"
```

If you want to extract the sixth value of the `InventoryListArr` array and display it, you need to use the following statement:

```
MsgBox InventoryListArr(5)
```

The preceding statement gives the output as `Hilti Anchor`.

I will now discuss the various functions and statements that are used to manipulate arrays.

Manipulating Arrays

VBA provides the `IsArray`, `LBound`, and `UBound` functions to manipulate arrays. You can also use the `Erase` statement to manipulate the memory allocated to an array.

The following sections talk about each of these in detail.

The IsArray Function

At some point in the code you may need to find out whether a variable is an array or not. VBA provides the `IsArray` function to accomplish this.

The syntax of the `IsArray` function is as follows:

```
IsArray (varname)
```

In the syntax, `varname` denotes the name of the variable to be verified.

The `IsArray` function returns a True or a False value depending on the declaration of the variable. You can then take appropriate action based on the return value.

You might also need to find the upper bound value and the lower bound value of an array. You can do this with the help of the `LBound` and `UBound` functions.

The LBound and UBound Functions

The `LBound` and `UBound` functions are used to find the lower and upper bounds of an array. `LBound` is used to find the index number of the first item in an array, and `UBound` is used to find the index number of the last item in an array.

The syntax of the `LBound` and `UBound` functions is as follows:

```
LBound(array, [dimension])
UBound(array, [dimension])
```

In the preceding syntax, `array` refers to the name of the array. `Dimension` refers to the dimension of the array that should be returned. The default dimension is the first dimension. Consider the following example:

```
Dim CurProfitArr(300, 200, 33) As String
```

In the preceding statement, a multidimensional array, `CurProfitArr`, of `String` data type is declared.

To display the lower and upper bounds of all the dimensions of the `CurProfitArr` array, the following statement is given:

```
Dim CurProfitArr(300, 200, 33) As String
MsgBox UBound(CurProfitArr, 3)
MsgBox LBound(CurProfitArr, 1)
```

The result of the `UBound` function is displayed in Figure 4-1.

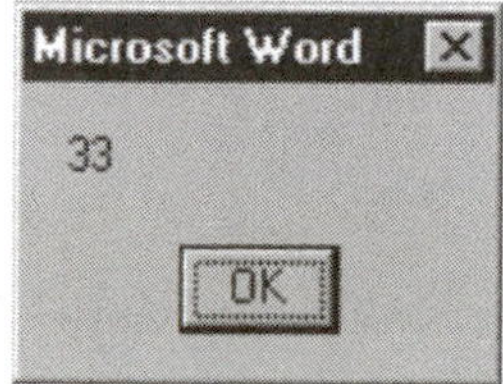

FIGURE 4-1 *Result of the UBound function*

The result of the `LBound` function is displayed in Figure 4-2.

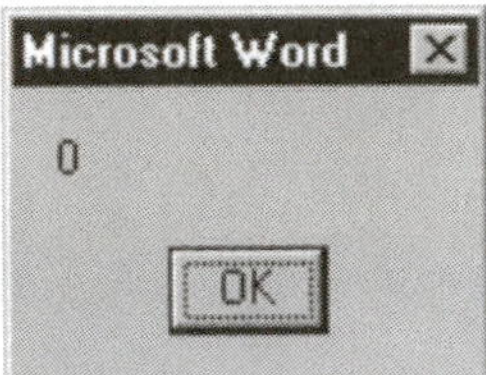

FIGURE 4-2 *Result of the LBound function*

The Erase Statement

When you declare an array, memory is automatically allocated to the array. Arrays can be deleted when you no longer require them. You can free the memory allocated to the array by erasing the contents of the array. The contents of an array can be erased by using the `Erase` statement. Consider the following example:

```
Erase CurProfitArr
```

The `Erase` statement removes the array `CurProfitArr` from memory.

In the preceding section, you learned about array variables—what they are and how are they used. The next section introduces you to the various programming constructs supported by VBA.

Programming Constructs

The statements written in a procedure or function are executed in the sequence they appear in the code. However, in a real-life situation, you need to make decisions in order to solve problems or perform an action repeatedly to achieve the desired result. You can use programming constructs for this purpose.

Programming constructs are of the following two types:

- Conditional constructs
- Looping constructs

You will learn about each type of programming construct in detail in the following sections.

Conditional Constructs

Conditional constructs are used to execute a group of statements repeatedly depending on the value of a condition. You can also control the flow of a program by using conditional constructs.

VBA supports the following types of conditional constructs:

- `If` construct
  - `If…Then…Else` construct
  - `If…Then…ElseIf…Else` construct
- `Select Case` construct

Each of these constructs is discussed in detail in the following sections.

The If Construct

The `If` construct is the most important conditional construct used in any programming language. Consider an example where you are responsible for checking the inventory of an organization. You need to order an item when the minimum reorder level is reached. You can use the `If` construct in such a situation. The `If` construct tests whether the item has reached the minimum reorder level and takes appropriate action based on the return value.

The `If` construct can take a lot of forms. The simplest `If` construct is the `If…Then` construct. The syntax of the `If…Then` construct is as follows:

```
If <condition> Then <Statement>
```

In this syntax, the `If` keyword is followed by a `condition` which will yield either the value True or the value False. If the value of the condition evaluates to True, the control of the program will move to the `Then` keyword, and the `statement` will be executed.

Here is an example of an `If…Then` construct:

```
If (Acrylic_Sheet.QOH.value = 50) Then MsgBox "The acrylic sheets need to be
ordered."
```

In the preceding example, if the quantity on hand of the acrylic sheets reaches 50, the message, "The acrylic sheets need to be ordered." is displayed.

You can also have a group of statements to be executed if the condition is met.

The syntax of the If statement with multiple statements is as follows:

```
If <condition> Then
    <Statements>
End If
```

The only difference between this syntax and the previous syntax is the keyword End If that denotes the end of the If construct. You need to use an End If clause if the Then keyword is followed by more than one statement.

Consider the following example that contains multiple executable statements:

```
If (Acrylic_Sheet.QOH.value = Acrylic_Sheet.ROL.value) Then
     MsgBox "The stocks for acrylic sheets need to be updated."
      Acrylic_Sheet.Font.Bold="True"
      Acrylic_Sheet.Font.Italic="True"
      Acrylic_Sheet.Forecolor="Red"
End If
```

NOTE

Properties used in the preceding example, such as Font.Bold and Font.Italic, are discussed in later chapters.

The preceding example compares the quantity on hand of the acrylic sheets with its minimum reorder level. If the values are equal, a message box is displayed, and the color and font properties of the acrylic sheet item are changed.

As stated earlier, the If construct can be used in a lot of different ways. The other If constructs are discussed in the following sections.

The If...Then...Else Construct

You can include an Else clause with an If construct to execute statements if the condition is not met. Consider a situation in which the user is prompted to enter the minimum reorder level for an item in the inventory. If the quantity on hand for that item is less than or equal to the minimum reorder level, then the font properties of the item are changed, otherwise they are changed in a different manner. You can use the If...Then...Else construct in this situation.

The syntax of the `If…Then…Else` construct is as follows:

```
If <condition> Then
        <Statements>
Else
        <Statements>
End If
```

In an `If…Then…Else` construct, the `condition` is evaluated first. Then, depending on the `condition`, the control is passed to the respective block of `statements`. If the `condition` is evaluated True, the `statements` in the immediate block are executed. If the `condition` is False, the statements in the `Else` block are executed.

The following code shows the use of the `If…Then…Else` construct:

```
If (item.QOH.value <= item.ROL.value) Then
      item.Font.Bold="True"
      item.Font.Italic="True"
      item.Forecolor="Red"
Else
      item.Font.Bold="False"
      item.Font.Italic="False"
      item.Forecolor="Blue"
End If
```

In the preceding example, if the quantity on hand is less than the reorder level, the font properties of the item in the list are changed to `Red`, `Bold`, and `Italic`, otherwise the color of the font is changed to `Blue`. Therefore, by looking at the inventory list, you can see which items need to be reordered.

The If...Then...ElseIf...Else Construct

You can use the `If…Then…ElseIf…Else` construct to evaluate multiple conditions. The statements associated with a specific condition are executed as soon as the condition is evaluated True. You use this construct in situations where you want to include a condition with the `ElseIf` statement so that the statements in the `ElseIf` block are executed if the condition is evaluated True.

The syntax of the `If…Then…ElseIf…Else` construct is as follows:

```
If <condition> Then                         first condition
        <Statements>
```

```
ElseIf condition                          second condition
        <Statements>
ElseIf condition                          third condition
        <Statements>
Else
        <Statements>
End If
```

In the preceding syntax, if the first condition is evaluated False, the second condition is evaluated. If the second condition is evaluated False, the control is passed to the statements in the `Else` block.

The following code uses the `If…Then…ElseIf…Else` construct:

```
If (item.QOH.value = item.ROL.value) Then
    MsgBox "You need to update the stock."
    Item.Font.Bold = "False"
    Item.Forecolor = "Black"
ElseIf (item.QOH.value < item.ROL.value) Then
    MsgBox "Quantity on hand is less than the reorder level. Please order the
       stock."
    Item.Font.Bold = "True"
    Item.Forecolor = "Red"
Else
    Item.Font.Bold = "False"
    Item.Forecolor = "Blue"
End If
```

The preceding example compares the quantity on hand for an item with its minimum reorder level. If both values are equal, the font color of the item is changed to `Black`. If the quantity on hand is less than minimum reorder level, the font color of the item changes to `Red`, and the font style changes to `Bold`. If neither condition is met, the font color is changed to `Blue`.

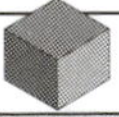

NOTE

An `If…Then…ElseIf…Else` construct can have several `ElseIf` blocks but only one `Else` statement.

The Nested If...Then...Else Construct

When an `If…Then…Else` construct is contained in another `If…Then…Else` construct, it is called a nested `If…Then…Else` construct. The syntax of the nested `If…Then…Else` construct is as follows:

```
If <condition> Then
    <Statements>
    If <condition> Then
        <Statements>
    Else
       <Statements>
    End If
Else
<Statements>
End If
```

In this syntax, each `If…Then…Else` construct is matched with an `End If` statement, which marks the end of that `If…Then…Else` construct. Nested `If…Then…Else` constructs are used in situations where you want multiple conditions to be evaluated one after the other.

Consider an example where the inventory data can be accessed only if the correct password is entered. The following example uses the nested `If…Then…Else` construct:

```
Dim strpass As String
strpass = InputBox("Enter Password")
  If Len(strpass) > 0 Then
    If Len(strpass) = 8 Then
      If (strpass) = "password" Then
        MsgBox "Password accepted"
      Else
        MsgBox "Incorrect Password"
      End If
    Else
        MsgBox "Please enter at least eight characters."
    End If
  Else
     MsgBox "Password cannot be blank"
  End If
```

In the preceding example, the user is asked to enter a password. The condition in the first `If` construct is evaluated. If the length of the password is less than zero, the control is passed to the `Else` block, and the `"Password cannot be blank"` message is displayed. If the length of the password is greater than zero, the control is passed to the next `If` construct. The length of the password is checked again. If the length is equal to `eight`, the control is passed to the next `If` construct. If the password entered by the user is `"password"`, the message, `"Password accepted"`, is displayed. If the condition in the second `If` construct is evaluated False, the control is passed to the `Else` block and the message, `"Please enter at least eight characters."` is displayed.

The Select...Case Construct

Multiple `If` constructs are difficult to handle when the number of conditions becomes large. It is a good practice to use the `Select...Case` construct in these situations.

The `Select...Case` construct is used to evaluate statements based on the value of a variable. An expression is provided at the beginning, and all the possible results are listed. When the value of the expression matches any of the listed results, the corresponding statements are executed. The syntax of the `Select...Case` construct is as follows:

```
Select Case <TestExpression>
    Case expression_1
      Statements
    Case expression_2
      Statements
    Case expression_n
      Statements
    Case Else
      Statements
End Select
```

In this syntax, `TestExpression` is evaluated and compared with each `Case` expression. The control is passed to the `Case` statement which equals the value of the expression. If none of the expressions match the value of the `TestExpression`, the control is passed to the `Case Else` statement. The `End Select` statement indicates the end of the `Select...Case` construct.

NOTE

You cannot have the same value in two case constants of a `Select…Case` construct.

The following example illustrates the use of the `Select…Case` construct:

```
Select Case (Item.QOH.value)
        Case Is = item.ROL.value
              Msgbox "The quantity on hand is equal to the reorder level."
              Item.Forecolor = "Black"
        Case Is < item.ROL.value
              Msgbox "The quantity on hand is less than the reorder level."
              Item.Forecolor = "Red"
              Item.Font.Bold = "True"
         Case Else
              Item.Forecolor = "Blue"
End Select
```

The preceding `Select…Case` construct compares the quantity on hand of an item and, depending on the result, displays the message and changes the font properties of the item in the inventory list.

You have learned about the conditional constructs that execute only once and stop when the condition is evaluated to true. In real life, there might be situations in which you have to repeat a set of statements a specific number of times. In such situations you can use looping constructs. The different looping constructs provided by VBA are discussed in the following section.

Looping Constructs

There might be situations in which you want to repeat a set of statements a specific number of times. Consider an example where the production manager of the organization has to generate a stock report for the inventory at the end of each week. You need to execute the same set of statements seven times to generate a report for each day of the week. You can incorporate this task by using looping constructs. The technique for executing the same lines of codes repeatedly is called *looping*. The repetition in a loop continues while the condition set for the loop remains True. The loop ends when the condition becomes False, and the control is passed to the statement following the loop.

VBA supports two types of looping constructs: the `For` construct and the `Do` construct.

The For Construct

The `For` construct is used to execute the code repeatedly for a fixed number of times. VBA supports the following types of `For` constructs:

- The `For...Next` construct
- The `For Each...Next` construct

These constructs are discussed next.

The For...Next Construct

The `For...Next` construct is used to perform an action repeatedly for a specified number of times. The number of times for which the action needs to be repeated is specified in the beginning.

The syntax for the `For...Next` construct is as follows:

```
For counter = start to end
                Statements
Exit For
                Statements
Next counter
```

The `counter` variable is used to determine the number of times that the statements within the construct are executed. The `counter` variable is increased by one each time the action is performed. The `counter` variable has a starting value and an ending value. The `Next` keyword passes the control to the `For` statement. You can use the `Exit For` statement to exit the `For...Next` construct.

The following code illustrates the use of `For...Next` construct:

```
Dim i As Integer
  For i = 1 To 10
     MsgBox "counter is" & i
  Next i
```

In this example, a message box is displayed `10` times. Each time the loop executes, the counter is increased by `1`. The message box displays the values stored in the counter one after another.

The For Each...Next Construct

The `For Each...Next` construct is used to perform an action repeatedly for each object in a collection.

NOTE

A *collection* is an object that contains a set of related objects. In a collection, the position of an object can change with each change in the collection.

The syntax for the `For Each...Next` construct is as follows:

```
For Each object In collection
            Statements
Next object
```

In this syntax, the statements are executed for each object in the specified collection. The `For Each` keyword is followed by the object name. The object name is followed by the `In` keyword specifying the collection name.

The following code illustrates the use of `For Each...Next` construct:

```
Dim dspform As Form
For Each dspform In Forms
Print dspform.name
Next dspform
```

In the preceding example, `dspform` is the `Object`, and `Forms` is the `Collection`. The loop displays the names of all the forms in the collection `Forms`. The `Next` keyword passes the control to the next object in the collection.

The Do Constructs

The `Do` constructs are more flexible than the `For` contructs. You can evaluate the condition in a `Do` construct and control the flow of the procedure accordingly. VBA provides the following `Do` constructs:

- `Do...While Loop`
- `Do...Loop While`
- `Do...Until Loop`
- `Do...Loop Until`

Each of these loops is discussed next.

The Do...While Loop Construct

The `Do...While Loop` construct is used to execute a set of statements repeatedly based on the value of the condition. The loop runs while the condition is evaluated True and exits when the condition becomes False.

The syntax of the `Do...While Loop` construct is as follows:

```
Do While (condition)
    Statements
Loop
```

In this syntax, the `condition` is evaluated first; afterwards, the `statements` in the loop are executed. The `Loop` keyword passes the control to the `Do While` statement until the `condition` is evaluated true.

The Do...Loop While Construct

The `Do...Loop While` construct is similar to the `Do...While Loop` construct. The only difference is that `Do...Loop While` runs at least once before evaluating the condition. The statements are executed repeatedly if the condition is evaluated True. Then, the loop continues to run until the condition becomes False.

The syntax of the `Do...Loop While` construct is as follows:

```
Do
    Statements
Loop While (condition)
```

In this syntax, the control passes from the `Do` keyword to the statements. The statements are executed, and the control is passed to the `Loop While` statement. The `condition` is evaluated. If the `condition` is evaluated True, the control is passed to the `Do` statement again. This process is repeated until the `condition` is evaluated False.

The following example illustrates the use of the `Do...Loop While` construct:

```
Dim strcode As Variant
Do
    strcode = InputBox("Enter the secret code")
    If strcode = " " Then End
Loop While (strcode <> "XDFGH01")
```

In the preceding example, the user is asked to enter the correct secret code. The loop is executed until the secret code entered by the user is correct.

The Do...Until Loop Construct

The `Do...Until Loop` construct is used to execute a set of statements while the condition is evaluated False. The construct stops running when the condition becomes True.

The syntax of the `Do...Until Loop` construct is as follows:

```
Do Until <condition>
    <Statements>
Exit Do
    <Statements>
Loop
```

In this syntax, the `condition` is evaluated first, and then the statements in the construct are executed. The statements are executed while the `condition` is False. The `Loop` keyword passes the control back to the `Do Until` statement. You can use the `Exit Do` statement to exit the loop.

The following example illustrates the use of the `Do...Until Loop`:

```
Dim tot_sales as integer
Do Until tot_sales > 2000
    tot_sales = amount.value*Price.value
Loop
```

In this example, the loop ends when the value of `tot_sales` is greater than `2000`.

The Do...Loop Until Construct

The `Do...Loop Until` construct is similar to the `Do...Until Loop` construct. However, in `Do...Loop Until`, the statement is executed at least once before evaluating the condition. The loop continues to run if the condition is evaluated False. The loop ends when the condition becomes True.

The syntax of the `Do...Loop Until` construct is as follows:

```
Do
    Statements
Loop Until (condition)
```

The following example illustrates the use of the Do…Loop Until construct:

```
Dim tot_sales as integer
Do
   tot_sales = amount.value*Price.value
Loop Until tot_sales > 2000
```

In this example, the control from the Do statement is passed to the tot_sales statement. The value of tot_sales is calculated, and then the condition is evaluated. If the value of tot_sales is greater than 2000, the loop ends. If the value of tot_sales is less than 2000, the control is passed again to the Do statement.

You can also use the Exit Do statement to exit an endless loop.

CAUTION

You should always use the Exit Do statement in the True block of a conditional construct.

Summary

In this chapter, you learned about arrays—their purpose, declaration, usage, and the various functions associated with them. Arrays are an important programming concept, and you will be using these concepts in later chapters. You also learned about the various programming constructs supported by VBA.

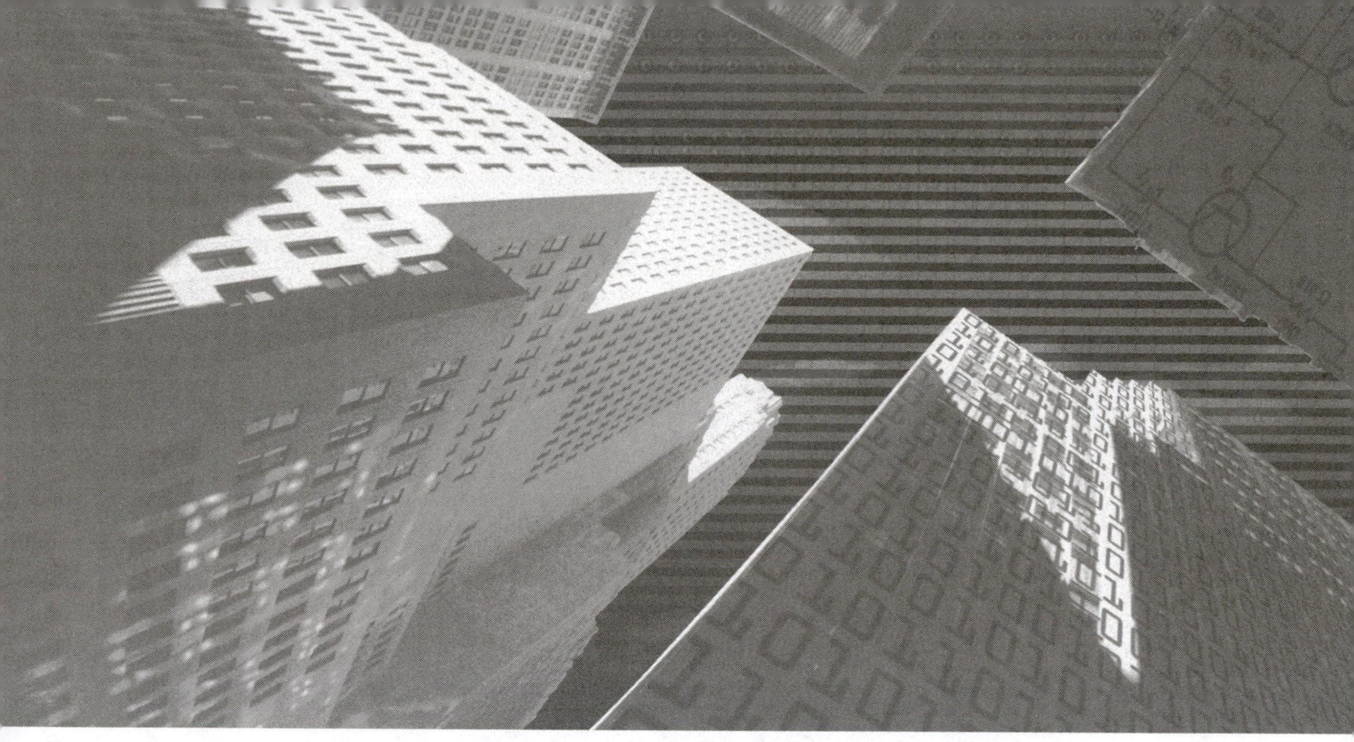

PART II

Advanced VBA Concepts

Chapter 5

Debugging and Error-handling in VBA

In this chapter, you will learn about the various debugging tools available in VBA. The chapter focuses on how to use these tools to recover from most programming errors.

What Is Debugging?

After you have written your code, you need to test it to check its accuracy. Two situations are possible while testing. The first is the ideal situation, in which your code behaves exactly as you want it to behave; that is, it produces the desired output. The second situation, however, is not as smooth. Your code does not produce the desired result, and you are unable to find the bug in the code. This is where debugging comes into the picture.

Debugging is the process of finding and removing errors (or bugs) from a program. A *bug* is a defect in the software that causes the program to malfunction. Simply put, debugging is nothing but taking a good, hard look at your code to identify errors.

If your code doesn't work as expected, you need to debug it to locate the bugs in it. Testing your application is the most important phase when developing applications and involves various stages. However, at a broad level, you need to perform the following steps while testing your code:

1. Test the code to check its accuracy. To ensure that the code works perfectly, you need to run it on different samples of data over a specific period of time.
2. If your code doesn't function the way it is meant to, you need to debug it. You can debug the code by using any of the debugging tools available. You will learn about the different debugging tools in this chapter.
3. Try to simulate different environments in which your code will be required to run, and check its accuracy. The focus is to check the portability of your code.
4. After you have successfully tested your code, you can document the observations, such as the circumstances under which the code would not function.

When an error occurs in the code, the first thing that you need to find out is the type of error. Detecting the type of error helps you decide the method you will use to rectify it.

You might think that an error is the same as a bug, but there is a slight difference between the two. An error can be a useful event that is generated through code. For example, if the user tries to enter a numeric value in the `name` field of a table, you can display your own error message to the user. This is a trappable error that can be handled by the programmer. A bug, on the other hand, is an unhandled error that causes a program to malfunction.

Errors can be classified into the following four categories: syntax errors, compile errors, run-time errors, and logic errors.

The following sections take a closer look at each type of error.

Syntax Errors

This is the most common type of error and is often caused by typing mistakes. Syntax errors arise as a result of misspelled keywords or punctuation. VBA catches almost all syntax errors. The VBA Editor displays a statement in red if it contains a syntax error. Although VBA displays an error message indicating the type of error that has occurred (which means that you just have to read that error message and make the appropriate changes), many times, you will find that the message displayed is of little help. See Figure 5-1.

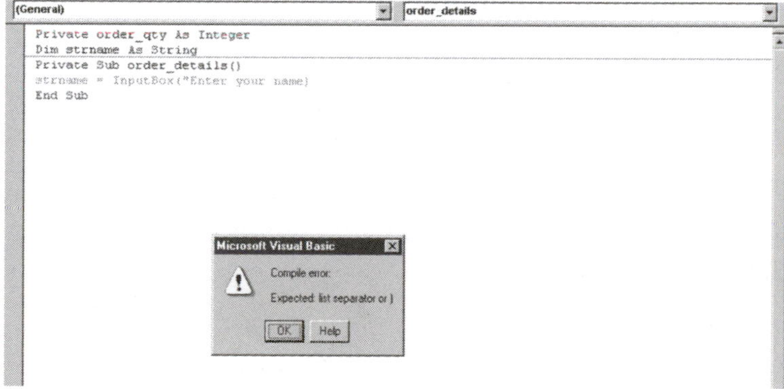

FIGURE 5-1 *The message box for the "Expected: line separator or)" message if you miss the ending quotes in the string*

Notice that the string, `"Enter your name`, does not have the concluding quotation mark. VBA displays the error message `Expected: list separator or )`. The error message doesn't tell the user that a quotation mark is missing but gives an arbitrary message instead.

Figure 5-2 shows another example of a syntax error.

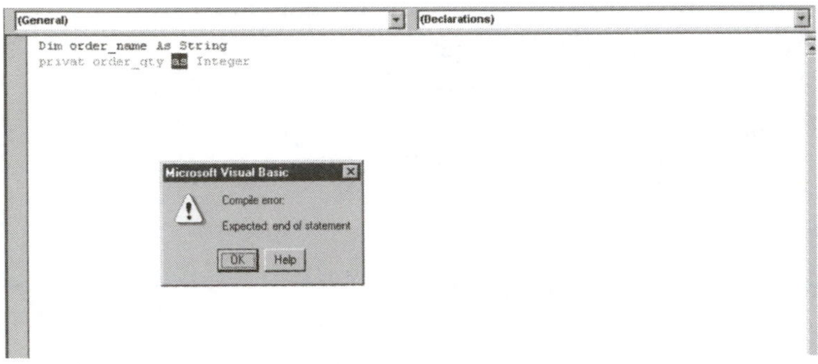

FIGURE 5-2 *The message box for the "Expected: end of statement" message if you do not include the "End Sub" statement*

Note that the VBA Editor displays an error message in the second statement. The syntax error occurs because the `private` keyword has been mistyped as `privat`. You will learn to debug such errors later in this chapter.

After you have written your code, you need to compile it before executing it. The errors that occur at compile time are known as compile errors.

Compile Errors

When VBA encounters a problem while compiling the code, a compile error occurs. A common example of a compile error is when you use a method for an object and the object doesn't support that method.

VBA traps some compile errors when you position the insertion point to the next line. See Figure 5-3.

VBA generates a compile error, `Expected: Then or GoTo`, because the `if` construct declared in the procedure, `result()`, does not have a corresponding `Then` or `GoTo` statement. VBA immediately traps this error and displays the statement in red when you move the insertion point to the next line. This vigilance in VBA prevents you from encountering this type of error deep into the execution of the code. However, certain compile errors are not as traceable as the example shown in Figure 5-3. Consider the example in Figure 5-4.

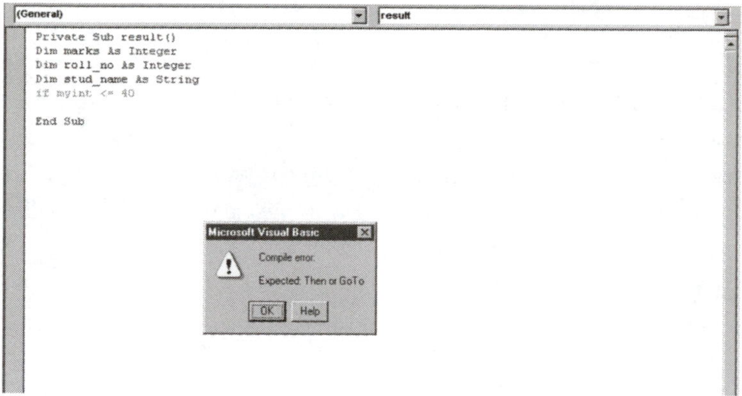

FIGURE 5-3 *The message box for the "Expected: Then or GoTo" message if you do not include the* `Then` *or* `GoTo` *statement with the* `if` *construct*

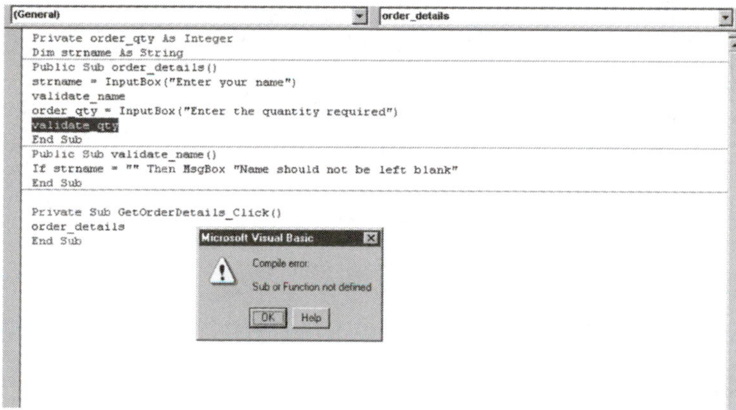

FIGURE 5-4 *This message box displays a compile error when you call a function that is not defined.*

Consider the example given in Figure 5-4. The procedure, `order_details`, accepts the user's name and the quantity required. It then calls the procedures, `validate_name` and `validate_qty`, to validate the data entered by the user. Although the code is syntactically correct, it gives a compile error when compiled. The compile error is generated because the code calls a procedure, `validate_qty`, which has not been declared in the code. VBA does not point out this error at the time of coding; it appears only when you compile the code.

You need to execute your code after you have successfully compiled it. The errors generated at the time of execution are called run-time errors.

Run-time Errors

The third category of errors, run-time errors, occurs when VBA encounters a statement that causes it to perform an impossible operation such as division by zero, opening or closing a document that does not exist, or closing a document when no document is open. When VBA encounters such statements, it displays a message box with the run-time error message. Run-time error numbers may also be displayed with messages. See Figure 5-5.

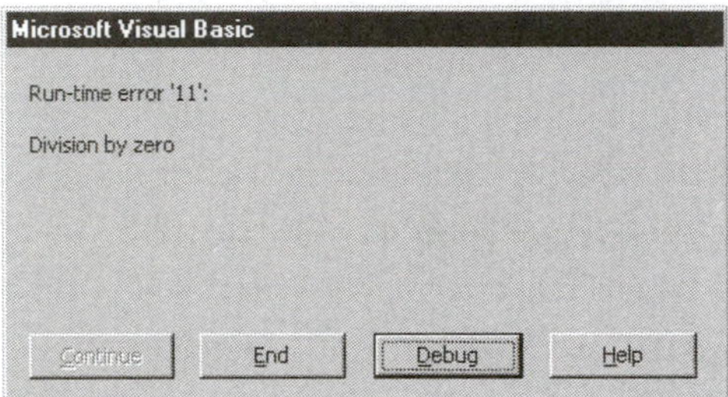

FIGURE 5-5 *This message box displays a run-time error when you divide a number by zero.*

You can click on the Debug button in the message box to see the statement in which the error has occurred. VBA highlights that statement and moves the insertion point there.

Another common example of a run-time error is the Type Mismatch error. This error is generated when you assign a value to a variable of a different data type. The error is displayed in Figure 5-6.

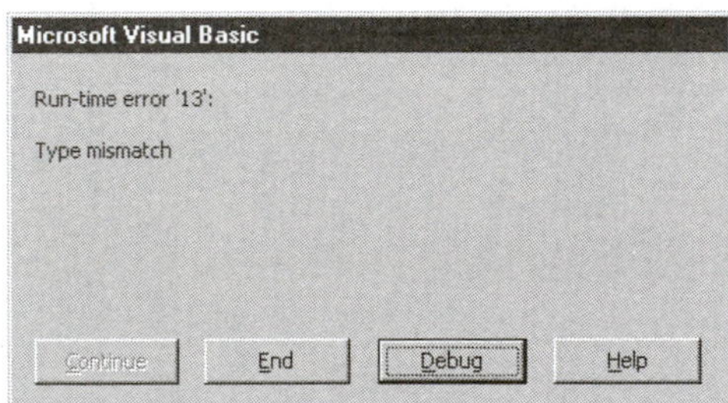

FIGURE 5-6 *This message box displays a Type Mismatch error.*

NOTE

To avoid run-time errors, you can track the values of your variables by using the Watches window which is discussed later in this chapter.

Apart from syntax, compile, and run-time errors, there is another category of errors that cannot be indicated by VBA. This category of error is known as logic errors.

Logic Errors

Logic errors are the most difficult type of error to find, since they arise because of the logic used in the program. They don't display any error messages to give you clues about what went wrong and where. However, sometimes they may generate run-time errors that enable you to identify the statement in which the error has occurred. This is the most difficult type of error because, if you have written modular code (modular code contains a number of functions, and one function calls another one, and so on), you will have to look into all the procedures to identify the location of the error. To ensure that the variables and expressions in your code are performing as expected, you can keep track of them with the help of the various debugging tools in VBA.

The following section looks at the various debugging tools available in VBA.

Debugging Tools in VBA

As stated earlier, the debugging tools help you debug your application. You can use these tools to keep track of the variables and expressions in your code. Some of the techniques you can use to debug codes include the break mode, stepping through procedures, and monitoring procedures.

The Break Mode

It is sometimes necessary to pause a procedure to see the current values of the variables and expressions. It also helps you monitor the flow of the procedure.

When you pause a procedure, VBA enters the *break* mode. When in break mode, the statement to be executed next is highlighted in yellow. You can enter the break mode in any of the following ways:

- By pressing the F8 key at the beginning of the procedure
- By using breakpoints (you will learn about breakpoints in the next section)
- By using the `Stop` statement
- By pressing Ctrl+Break while a procedure is running
- By using the run-time error dialog box (refer to Figure 5-5)

Breakpoints

You can set a breakpoint in a procedure if you know approximately where an error is occurring. Setting a breakpoint allows you to suspend the procedure in break mode at a specific statement. You can set breakpoints in procedures by using any of the following methods:

- Use the Debug menu option on the menu bar. Select the Toggle Breakpoint option from the drop-down menu.
- Press the F9 key.
- Click in the Margin Indicator Bar to the left of the Code window beside the statement at which you want to set the breakpoint.
- Right-click at the statement and select the Toggle, Breakpoint option.
- Click the Toggle Breakpoint button on the Debug toolbar.

The Debug toolbar is shown in Figure 5-7.

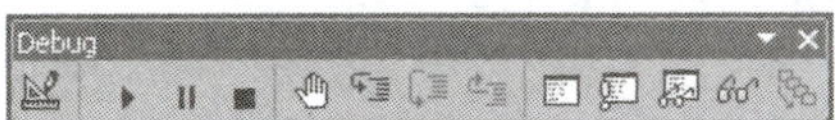

FIGURE 5-7 *The Debug toolbar*

The Debug toolbar contains buttons that are shortcuts to the menu items that are commonly used for debugging code. The various buttons on the Debug toolbar are listed in Table 5-1 along with their descriptions.

VBA allows you to set any number of breakpoints in a procedure. When you set a breakpoint, VBA highlights the statement in red and adds an indicator in the Margin Indicator Bar. Breakpoints are useful in situations where you want to track a bug in the program because they allow you to run the parts of a procedure that have no problem at all and break the execution where you think there may be a problem. Afterwards, you can examine the statements that might be problematic and watch their execution.

To remove a breakpoint, you need to place the insertion point at the statement containing the breakpoint and select the Toggle Breakpoint option. You can remove all the breakpoints in the module by selecting the Clear All Breakpoints option from the Debug menu, or you can press Ctrl+Shift+F9 to clear all the breakpoints.

Table 5-1 Buttons on the Debug Toolbar

Button	Name	Description
	Design Mode	Used to turn the design mode off and on
	Run Sub/User Form	Used to run the current procedure or the user form
	Break	Used to switch to the break mode
	Reset	Used to reset the project
	Toggle Breakpoint	Used to set or remove a breakpoint at the current statement
	Step Into	Used to execute one statement at a time
	Step Over	Used to execute one procedure or statement at a time in the Code window
	Step Out	Used to execute the remaining lines of the procedure that have the current execution point
	Locals Window	Used to display the Locals window
	Immediate Window	Used to display the Immediate window
	Watch Window	Used to display the Watches window
	Quick Watch	Used to display the Quick Watch dialog box
	Call Stack	Used to display the Calls dialog box

Using the Stop Statement

The `Stop` statement is used to suspend the execution of a procedure. It is similar to setting a breakpoint in the code. The syntax of the `Stop` statement is as follows:

```
Stop
```

On encountering the `Stop` statement, VBA automatically enters the break mode.

An important difference between the `Stop` statement and setting a breakpoint is that the `Stop` statement is a part of the code even when the project has been reloaded, whereas the breakpoints are cleared when the project is reloaded.

Exiting the Break Mode

You just saw that the break mode is a vital tool for debugging procedures in VBA because it allows you to examine your code in the Code window. To exit the break mode, you can use the following methods:

- Select Run Sub/Userform from the Run menu, or press the F5 key, or click on the Run Sub/Userform button on the Debug toolbar.
- Select the Reset option from the Run menu, or click the Reset button on the Debug toolbar.

The following section shows you how to debug code while stepping through procedures.

Stepping Through a Procedure

You may need to execute a procedure step-by-step to examine its flow, such as the way loops are executed and calls to other procedures are made. VBA provides four techniques to accomplish this:

- Stepping into a procedure
- Stepping over a procedure
- Stepping out of a procedure
- Stepping to a cursor position

Stepping Into a Procedure

Setting breakpoints in code is a good way of monitoring the code as and when it is executed. But setting breakpoints after every statement would be very tedious. This is where stepping comes into the picture. Stepping is done in conjunction with breakpoints. Stepping into a procedure allows you to execute one line at a time (in break mode) starting at the beginning of the procedure. You can select the Step Into option by the following methods:

- Select the Step Into option from the Debug menu.
- Click on the Step Into button on the Debug toolbar.
- Press the F8 key.

Keep stepping through the procedure by using any of these methods until you have reached the end of the procedure or you are ready to resume normal execution.

A procedure might call another procedure. If you want to step into each line of the called procedure as well, you can specify a breakpoint on the statement that makes the procedure call. You can then use any of the preceding methods to step into the called procedure. However, stepping into a procedure has a disadvantage. It is very time-consuming because it runs through each line of your code.

Stepping Over a Procedure

Stepping over a procedure allows you to run through a procedure without stepping into the called procedure. This means that if you are stepping into a procedure and you encounter a procedure call, Step Over would not go into the step-by-step execution of the called procedure. Then, on return from the called procedure, single-stepping resumes.

Once you are in the break mode, you can use any of the following methods to step over a procedure:

- Select the Step Over option from the Debug menu.
- Press Shift+F8.
- Click on the Step Over button on the Debug toolbar.

You should use the Step Over option when you are debugging a procedure that calls another procedure which you are sure is error-free. This is particularly useful when you are using procedures that have been tested and do not need to be debugged. You can step over such procedures and concentrate on the new ones in which errors are more likely to occur.

Stepping Out of a Procedure

The Step Out option is a combination of Step Into and Step Over. It allows you to execute the remainder of the procedure and breaks at the next line in the calling procedure. The Step Out option is helpful when you want to run through the rest of the procedure rapidly after you are finished with the part that you needed to watch step-by-step. You can invoke the Step Out option by using the following methods:

- Select the Step Out option from the Debug menu.
- Press Ctrl+Shift+F8.
- Click on the Step Out button on the Debug toolbar.

However, you might need to step over a couple of statements instead of stepping over an entire procedure. This is known as *stepping to the cursor position* and can be achieved by using the Run To Cursor option.

Stepping to a Cursor Position

The Run To Cursor option gives you the flexibility of placing the cursor on the line at which you want the execution to halt. You can invoke the Run To Cursor option by the following methods:

- Select the Run To Cursor option from the Debug menu.
- Press Ctrl+F8.

To step to a cursor position, enter the break mode, place the insertion point inside the line in which you want the execution to halt, and then use any of the preceding methods.

The Run To Cursor option is particularly useful when you have a number of loops in your code and you want to jump to the statement after the loop to save time.

In addition to using the stepping options, you can use the `Set Next Statement` and the `Show Next Statement` options to skip lines of code. To skip lines of code, place the insertion point at a statement that has not been executed. You can then use the `Set Next Statement` option from the Debug menu (or press Ctrl+F9) to tell VBA that this is the statement you want to be executed next. However, you need to be careful while using this option because VBA ignores all the lines in between, which means that the code may pose problems when those lines are executed.

The `Show Next Statement` option tells you which statement will be executed next. It is a useful feature, especially when you are monitoring many procedures and have lost track in the Code window.

Monitoring Procedures

A number of errors are generated due to expressions assuming unexpected values during execution. You can prevent this by monitoring the values of expressions while the procedure is in the break mode. VBA provides a number of tools to accomplish this. These tools will be dealt with in the following sections.

The Locals Window

VBA allows you to observe the values of variables and expressions at run-time. One of the tools for monitoring these values is the *Locals window*. The Locals window displays all the variables used in the current procedure along with their values and the properties of the currently loaded forms and controls when the procedure is in the break mode. The contents of the Locals window change when the execution switches from one procedure to another. The window is updated every time you switch between the run-time and the break modes. The Locals window can be displayed by using the following methods:

- Select the Locals Window option from the View menu.
- Click on the Locals Window button on the Debug toolbar.

The Locals window is displayed in Figure 5-8.

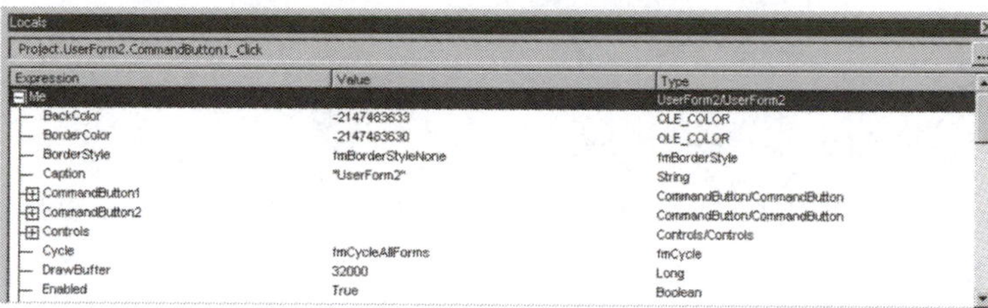

FIGURE 5-8 *The Locals window*

The Locals window displays the values of variables in a tree view, which you can expand or collapse to see as many details as you want.

The top line in the Locals window is the name of the module. The Expression column specifies the name of each expression in a procedure, listed under the name of the procedure in which it appears. The Value column displays the current value of an expression. The Value column can contain `Null`, `Empty`, or `Nothing` if the expression is empty. You can also change the values of variables in the Locals window by clicking the corresponding expression and typing the new value in the Values column. The Type column displays the data type of the expression. If the data type of a variable is `Variant`, the Value column specifies the data type, `Variant`, along with the data type that it is assigned.

To close the Locals window, click on the close button in the upper-right corner of the window.

The Locals window has a button marked with an ellipsis ([...]). You can click this button to display the Call Stack dialog box.

The Call Stack Dialog Box

When in the break mode, you can have a look at all the *active* procedure calls by using the Call Stack dialog box. Active procedure calls are the procedures currently loaded in memory.

When you execute a procedure, the procedure name is added to the list in the Call Stack dialog box. If the procedure calls another procedure, the name of the called procedure is also added to the list until the procedure is executed, at which time it is removed from the list. If procedure A calls another procedure, B, which in turn calls procedure C, the Call Stack dialog box will list all three procedures in the sequence: C,B,A. Thus, you can view a list of all the active procedures at any time. This information is useful when you need to check for errors but do not know which procedures are being called by other procedures. Thus, you can verify that the code has followed the right sequence of procedures.

To display the Call Stack dialog box, you can use one of the following methods:

- Select the Call Stack option from the View menu.
- Press Ctrl+L.
- Click on the Call Stack button on the Debug toolbar.

The Call Stack dialog box is displayed in Figure 5-9.

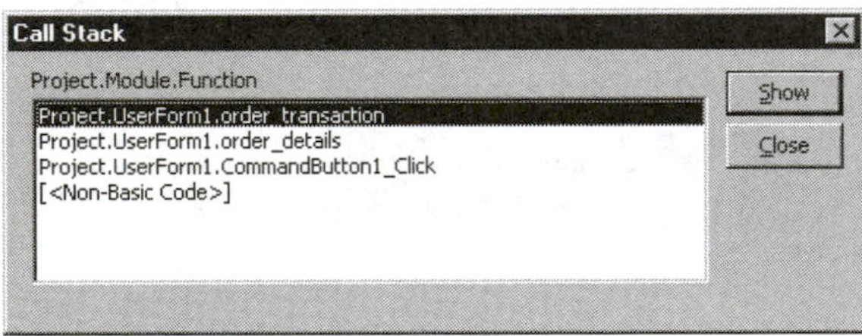

FIGURE 5-9 *The Call Stack dialog box*

In the dialog box, `order_transaction` is the currently active procedure and has been called from the procedure, `order_details`, which in turn has been called from the `CommandButton1_Click` procedure.

To close the Call Stack dialog box, click on the Close button.

The Immediate Window

The Locals window tells you about the current values of expressions. However, at times, you may require more information. This is possible with the *Immediate window*.

To display the Immediate window, you can use any of the following methods:

- Select the Immediate Window option from the View menu.
- Press Ctrl+G.
- Click on the Immediate Window button on the Debug toolbar.

The Immediate window is displayed in Figure 5-10.

FIGURE 5-10 *The Immediate window for a variable,* `myint`

The Immediate window can be used to query the local and global variables in the procedure and to execute commands. The commands typed in the Immediate window are executed as they would be executed if run from within the procedure. The Immediate window allows you to perform a number of tasks:

- Query the contents of a variable
- Set the value of a variable
- Create or destroy objects
- Execute single line commands

You can use the Immediate window to test portions of an application. You can execute the code in the Immediate window in both the break mode and the design mode.

When in the break mode, you can type a question mark in the Immediate window before the variable name or the expression that needs to be evaluated. When you have typed the command, press Enter, and the result will appear directly below the command.

There are a few restrictions on the code that you can type in the Immediate window:

- You cannot use declarative keywords such as `Dim`, `Private`, `Public`, `Static`, and so on inside the Immediate window.
- You cannot use multiline statements such as block `If` statements or block `For...Next` statements.
- You cannot set breakpoints in the Immediate window.

The reason behind these restrictions is that there is no logical connection between the statements in the Immediate window. Each line typed inside the Immediate window is treated in isolation.

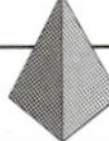

TIP

If you want to execute multiple statements in the Immediate window, you can type the statements in a single line with each statement separated by a colon.

When in the design mode, you can use the `Print` method of the `Debug` object in the Code window to print the values of variables and expressions in the Immediate window. The `Debug` object is used to send output to the Immediate window at run-time. It has two methods, the `Assert` method and the `Print` method. The `Assert` method is used to suspend execution conditionally at the statement in which the method is located, and the `Print` method is used to print text in the Immediate window. You will often use the `Print` statement to print text in the Immediate window in the design mode. The `Print` statement has the following syntax:

```
Debug.print [outputlist]
```

In the syntax, `outputlist` specifies the list of expressions to be printed in the Immediate window. If you do not specify anything in the output list, the `Print` method prints a blank line.

For example, suppose you have typed the following statement in your Code window in a procedure:

```
Debug.print "The quantity ordered is "; order_qty
```

The output of this statement is displayed in Figure 5-11.

FIGURE 5-11 *The output for the preceding line of code in the Immediate window*

The `Print` statement can also be used when in break mode. You can type the `Print` statement directly, followed by the expression.

For example:

```
Print myint
```

If you type this statement in the Immediate window and press the Enter key, it will print the value of the variable, `myint`. Note that you do not need to specify the `Debug` object while working with the `Print` method in the break mode.

Another tool used to monitor the values of expressions and variables while stepping through the code is the Watches window.

The Watches Window

The Watches window is a debugging tool with which you can change the values of variables and expressions in the break mode to see how the different values affect your code. To display the Watches window, use one of the following methods:

- Select the Watch Window option from the View menu.
- Click on the Watch Window button on the Debug toolbar.

The Watches window is displayed in Figure 5-12.

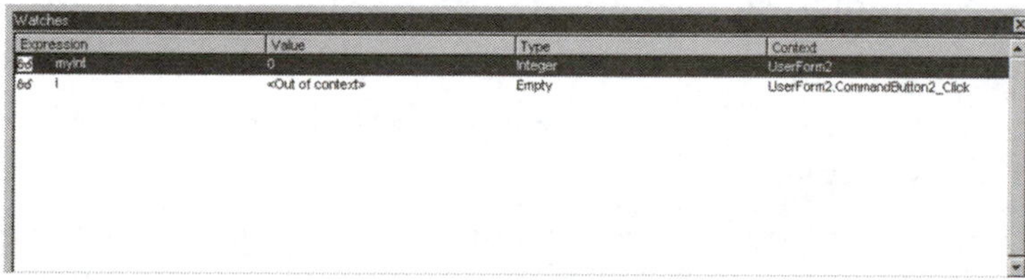

FIGURE 5-12 *The Watches window for a user form*

The Watches window displays four columns: Expression, Value, Type, and Context. The Expression column lists the names of the watched expressions and variables. The value of the expression is displayed in the Value column and the data type in the Type column. The Context column specifies the *context* of the expression. Context of an expression refers to the module and the procedure in which the expression is operating. The VBA Editor updates all the watch expressions whenever you enter the break mode and whenever you execute a statement in the Immediate window.

NOTE

If a variable or an expression specified in the Expression column has not been initialized, the Watches window will display `<out of context>` in the Value column.

In order to monitor expressions and variables, you need to specify watch expressions. These expressions are then displayed in the Expression column of the Watches window.

Setting Up Watch Expressions

Sometimes problems are difficult to trace, and you have to observe the behavior of a variable or expression throughout the procedure. Each variable or expression that you observe is known as a *watch expression*. You set up watch expressions by using the Add Watch dialog box. The steps to set up a watch expression by using the Add Watch dialog box are as follows:

1. Select the Add Watch option from the Debug menu. The Add Watch dialog box is displayed as shown in Figure 5-13. Another method of invoking the Add Watch dialog box is by right-clicking the Watch window and selecting the Add Watch option. You can also invoke the Add Watch dialog box by right-clicking in the Code window.
2. In the Expression dialog box, you need to specify the name of the variable, expression, user-defined function, or any other valid VBA expression that you want to evaluate.
3. Select the name of the procedure from the Procedure list box and the name of the module from the Module list box.
4. Next, select the watch type. The watch type specifies the way VBA will respond to the watch expression. There are three possible values for the watch type:

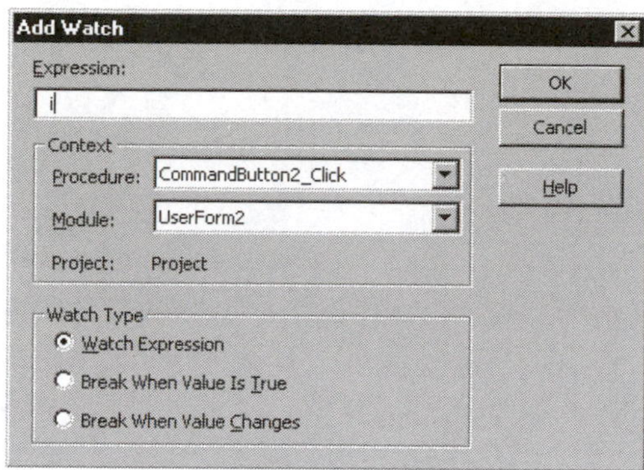

FIGURE 5-13 *The Add Watch dialog box for a user form*

- **Watch Expression.** The value of the expression is displayed in the watch pane whenever the program enters the break mode. This is the default option.
- **Break When Value Is True.** This triggers VBA to enter the break mode when the expression value becomes true (or non-zero).
- **Break When Value Changes.** This triggers VBA to enter the break mode whenever the value of the expression changes.

5. Click on the OK button.

After you have added a watch expression, you can monitor its value by entering the break mode and examining the expression in the Watches window. You can also modify the watch expressions at run-time, which means that you can add, edit, or delete them.

Editing Watch Expressions

You can edit a watch expression while in break mode. To do this, perform the following steps:

1. Click on the watch expression that you want to edit in the Watches window.
2. Select the Edit Watch option from the Debug menu to display the Edit Watch dialog box. The Edit Watch dialog box is displayed as shown in Figure 5-14.

   Alternatively, you can press Ctrl+W or double-click on the watch expression in the Watches window to edit it.

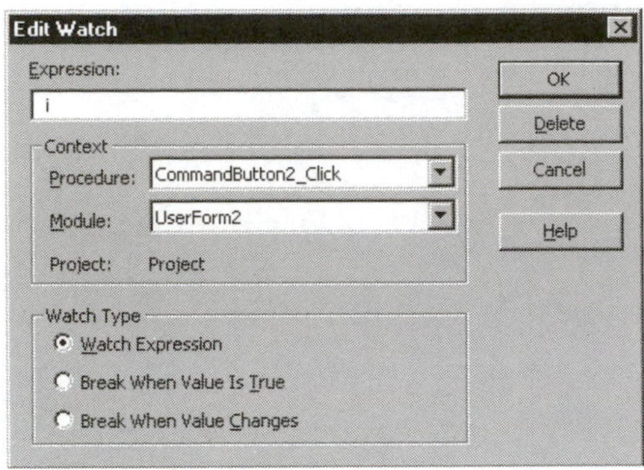

FIGURE 5-14 *The Edit Watch dialog box for a user form*

3. Make changes to the watch expression in the Edit Watch dialog box.
4. Click on the OK button to return to the Debug window.

You may want to delete the watch expressions that you no longer want to monitor. Expressions can be deleted by clicking on the Delete button in the Edit Watch dialog box.

There is another tool provided by VBA that helps you to determine the value of a variable or an expression quickly without having previously set a watch. This is the Quick Watch tool.

Quick Watch Tool

You may want to find the value of a variable or an expression without setting a watch expression. You can do this with the help of the *Quick Watch* feature. To use this feature, you invoke the Quick Watch dialog box which displays the context and value of the selected expression. To invoke the Quick Watch dialog box, use one of the following methods:

- Select the Quick Watch option from the Debug menu.
- Click on the Quick Watch button on the Debug toolbar.
- Press Shift+F9.

The Quick Watch dialog box is displayed in Figure 5-15.

The Add button in the dialog box can be used to add the expression to the Watches window.

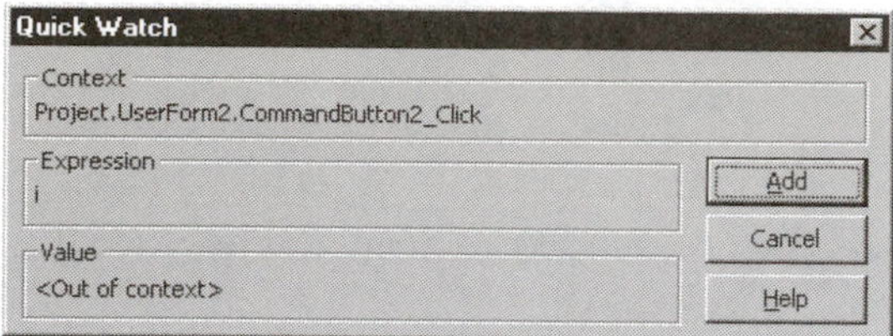

FIGURE 5-15 *The Quick Watch dialog box for a user form*

Another debugging tool is the Auto Data Tips tool. You can activate this tool by selecting the Options option from the Tools menu. The Options dialog box is displayed as shown in Figure 5-16.

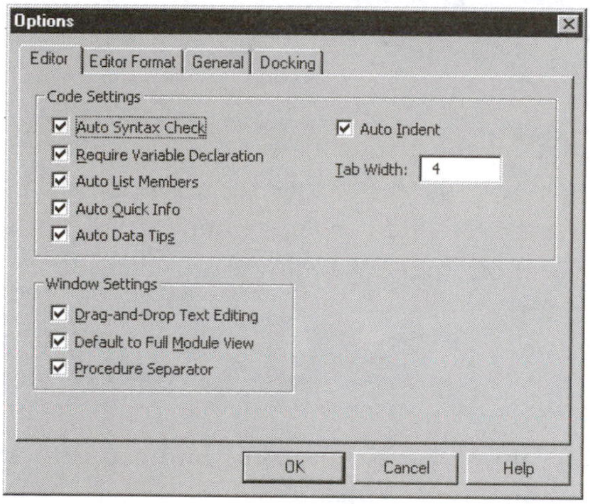

FIGURE 5-16 *The Options dialog box*

You need to check the Auto Data Tips option in the Editor tab. When you turn the Auto Data Tips feature on, you can determine the value of any variable just by resting the cursor over the variable in the Code window during break mode. The value of the variable will be displayed automatically as a tool tip.

You have looked at the debugging tools provided by VBA. However, you should always make a genuine effort to minimize errors in the code. Although the debugging tools discussed help trace your errors, they waste a lot of time and effort. In the next section, you will learn a few tips for avoiding errors in code.

Avoiding Errors

It's nearly impossible to write an application without any bugs in it. However, there are a few strategies that can be used to minimize them. You should develop a habit of using these strategies consistently while coding. The guidelines for minimizing errors are discussed in the following sections.

Use Comments in Code

There could be many procedures in your application. You may not remember what each procedure is doing if you look at your code after two weeks. Hence, it is always a good practice to insert comments in your code. However, commenting is an art. You should write only about the intention of your code, not about how it is being implemented.

Indent Code

To make your code readable, you need to indent it. Indenting makes the code easier to read and debug. You can indent your code by pressing Tab a specific number of times. Alternatively, you can enable the Auto Indent feature of VBA. To enable this feature, select the Options option from the Tools menu and check the Auto Indent check box in the Editor tab.

Modularize Code

Modularization refers to the breaking up of large procedures into a series of smaller procedures. Smaller procedures are easier to understand and debug.

Declare Variables Explicitly

You should declare all your variables explicitly before the start of a procedure. The advantages of declaring variables explicitly were discussed in Chapter 2, "Variables, Constants, and Expressions." You can add the statement

```
Option Explicit
```

at the top of the module to declare variables explicitly. Alternatively, you can check the Require Variable Declaration check box in the Editor tab of the Options option from the Tools menu.

Avoid Variants

The `Variant` data type is the default data type and can easily be used when you are not sure of the data type of a variable. However, as discussed in Chapter 2, the `Variant` data type is slower than any other data type and also takes up more space, hence, is difficult to move around in memory. For the two reasons stated, you should try to avoid the `Variant` data type in your code as much as possible.

CAUTION

If you have a variable that at some point may take a Null value, then you need to assign the `Variant` data type to it because `Variant` is the only data type that can contain a Null value. The same holds true for a function return value. If a function might need to return a Null value, the return value of the function must be `Variant`.

Turn on Syntax Checking

Syntax checking is another helpful feature provided by VBA. To turn this feature on, check the Auto Syntax Check check box of the Editor tab in the Options option of the Tools menu.

Be Careful with the Dim Statement

Consider the following `Dim` statement:

```
Dim mystr1, mystr2 as string
```

This statement seems to be a simple `Dim` statement, which declares two variables, `mysrt1` and `mysrt2`, of the type `String`. However, that is not the case. The `As` clause applies only to the variable immediately preceding it. Hence, the variable, `mystr2`, is assigned the data type `String`, and the variable, `mystr1`, is assigned the data type `Variant`. To declare both variables as `String`, you need to use separate `Dim` statements.

You have learned how to prevent errors and how to look for those that could not be prevented. However, run-time errors will still occur. VBA provides an efficient way of dealing with them. You can write error-handlers to trap these kinds of errors. *Error-handlers* are small pieces of code that analyze the errors encountered and take necessary action if they match the given error codes. The next section will introduce you to the concept of error-handling.

Error-handling

VBA responds to run-time errors by displaying error messages and stopping the execution of the code. However, run-time errors can be handled by including in your code error-handling features, which help you trap errors. Once an error is trapped, the program can prompt for action. The application becomes more robust when errors are handled in this manner.

When an error occurs in an application, VBA performs the following steps:

1. The application searches for an error-handling statement that transfers the control to the error-handler.
2. Once the error-handling code is executed, the control goes back to the statement in which the error occurred.

Therefore, it can be said that handling errors requires the following three steps:

1. Trapping the error
2. Writing the error-handler
3. Exiting the error-handler

You will learn about each of them in detail in the following sections.

Trapping an Error

The first thing that you need to do in error-handling is trap errors. Trapping an error means catching it to prevent it from stopping the execution of your code. Once the error is trapped, you can handle it accordingly. For trapping errors at run-time, you use the `On Error` statement.

The On Error Statement

The `On Error` statement is used to establish an error-handler so that, if a run-time error occurs, the execution jumps to the label specified in the `On Error` statement. The `On Error` statement helps you display your own error messages. The syntax for the `On Error` statement is as follows:

```
On Error GoTo line
```

In the syntax, `line` specifies the line to which the control would pass when a run-time error occurs.

For example, consider the following code snippet:

```
Private Sub calculate()
On Error GoTo validate_error
iresult = inum1/inum2
Print iresult
Exit Sub
Validate_error:
Msgbox "Runtime error - division by zero"
End Sub
```

This code specifies that the program will jump to the error-handler, `validate_error`, and will display the message, "Runtime error – division by zero" if there is an error in the third line.

The label used to identify the error-handler may be assigned any name according to the variable naming conventions. The label must have a colon at the end as shown in the preceding code snippet.

The `On Error` statement is usually placed at the start of a procedure so that it is *active* for the rest of the procedure. An error-handler is said to be active when an error occurs and the control moves to that error-handler. There are no restrictions on the number of error-handlers that can be placed in a procedure because different types of errors would require different types of action. However, only one error-handler can be enabled at a time.

An important point to note here is that since error-handlers are pieces of code, you need to ensure that an error-handler is not executed when there is no error. You can do this by inserting an additional `End Sub` statement, as is done in the preceding code snippet. The `End Sub` statement before the error-handler indicates the end of the procedure.

Another form of the `On Error` statement is the `On Error GoTo 0` statement. This statement is used to disable the error-handlers in the current procedure. VBA again starts trapping all subsequent errors.

Next, you will learn how to write an error-handler.

Writing an Error-handler

The `On Error` statement helps you trap errors. Once you have trapped an error, you want to take the appropriate action on it which will depend on your application. An error-handler should typically be coded for the following tasks:

- To display information to the user about the error generated
- To suggest a possible remedy to the user to resolve the error
- To enable the user to continue or cancel the operation

To decide upon the action that you would take, you first need to identify the type of error that has occurred. This can be done with the help of the `Err` object.

The Err Object

The `Err` object is a system object that stores information about run-time errors. When a run-time error occurs, the `Err` object is filled with information that can be used to identify the error and handle it. The `Err` object has properties that can be used to get specific numbers and descriptions, and methods that can be used to act on those errors programmatically.

The `Err` object has a number of properties, but the ones that are most commonly used are `Description`, `Number`, and `Source`.

Table 5-2 lists the properties of the `Err` object along with their descriptions.

Table 5-2 Properties of the Err Object

Property	Description
Number	Stores the Numerical ID of the last generated error. This is the default property.
Description	Stores information about the description of the error
Source	Contains the name of the object or the application in which the error has occurred
HelpFile	Contains the name of the help file
HelpContextID	Contains the help context ID corresponding to the error number
LastDLLError	Contains the system error code for the last call to a DLL

Using the properties of the `Err` object, you can easily determine which error has occurred. The `Err` object also comes equipped with two methods that you can use: `Raise` and `Clear`.

The Raise Method

At times, you may want display user-defined error messages rather than the system-defined error messages. You can use the `Raise` method of the `Err` object to generate user-defined errors. You may want to display user-defined messages when the program logic rules have been violated. The syntax of the `Raise` method is as follows:

```
Err.Raise Number, source, description, helpfile, helpcontext
```

In the syntax, all the parameters, except `Number`, are optional. The `Number` parameter specifies the number of the error that you want to generate.

If you have a chain of called procedures and if a procedure does not have an event-handler, the control moves up the chain until it finds the event-handler. The `Raise` method can, therefore, be used to pass an error condition back to a calling procedure. It can also be used to test your own error-handling codes.

If you are raising a user-defined error, the same procedure of error-handling applies. The execution jumps to the line defined in the `On Error` statement. The `Err` object's `Number` property is set to the argument given in the `Err.Raise` method. The other properties of the `Err` object are also set accordingly, if provided in the `Err.Raise` method. If no argument is specified, the default argument for the error number is used by VBA.

The Clear Method

You may want to clear the properties of the `Err` object once you have handled an error. This can be done with the help of the `Clear` method. The `Clear` method clears all the property settings of the `Err` object. The syntax of the `Clear` method is as follows:

```
Err.Clear
```

The `Clear` method sets the value of `Err.Number` back to zero.

Having handled errors, you need to come out of the error-handler. Next, you will learn about exiting error-handlers.

NOTE

The `Clear` method is automatically called whenever the `On Error`, `Exit Sub`, `Exit Function`, `Exit Property`, or `Resume` statement is called.

Exiting the Error-handler

First, you set an error trap in your application to trace an error. Then, you need to write an error-handler to display information about the error and suggest a possible remedy. Finally, you need to exit from the error-handler. To exit from an error-handler, the `Resume` statement is used.

The `Resume` statement can be used in the following three ways:

- `Resume`—This statement returns the control back to the statement that caused the error. If it is a procedure call, then the call is repeated and the procedure is run from the beginning. You should use the `Resume` statement when the error-handler has fixed the problem that caused the error and you want to continue from the same place where you left off. However, you need to be careful when using this form of the `Resume` statement because an endless loop occurs if the same statement fails again. A better way is to display a dialog box that provides a user with the option of either exiting from or resuming the procedure.
- `Resume Next`—This statement passes the control to the next statement following the statement that caused the error. You should use this statement when you want to ignore the statement that caused the error. This statement is usually used in conjunction with the `On Error` statement as follows:

  ```
  On Error Resume Next
  ```

  This statement returns the control to the next line in the program code, where the error occurred. This statement ignores the statement that caused the error.
- `Resume [linelabel]`—This statement takes the line label as a parameter. It passes the control to the line label specified. The execution then continues from that point onward. However, you need to place the label in the same procedure as the `Resume` statement.

NOTE

You can use the `Exit Sub` or `Exit Function` statement to exit a procedure in which an error has occurred. However, these statements should be placed ahead of the line where the error-handler begins so that the error-handler is not executed when there is no error.

Summary

In this chapter, you learned about the various debugging tools in VBA. You learned how you can use those tools to trace the type and cause of an error. You also looked at the strategies that you should use to minimize errors. Lastly, you learned about the various error-handling techniques in VBA with which you can handle run-time errors.

Chapter 6

Objects in VBA

In this chapter, you will learn about the object model of an application and how to use the properties, methods, and events associated with objects. You will also learn to find objects while working in the Visual Basic Editor and set references to object libraries.

The Object Model

An application in VBA is made up of a number of objects. Objects are elements that help structure an application. These objects or elements are organized in a specific manner to form the application.

An *object model* represents the hierarchy in which an application's objects are arranged. The objects at the top of the hierarchy are generic and those at the bottom are specific.

Each object model contains two types of objects: collection objects and individual objects. A collection object is a group of objects that are related to each other. You can refer to a collection as one unit. For example, you can have a collection called "books" that is made up of individual book objects.

Every element of an Office application can be referred to as an object. For example, in a Word application, a document, a bookmark, a paragraph, a character, a font, a comment, a range, and so on are objects. You can customize these objects by modifying the properties and methods associated with them. In the next two sections, I will discuss the properties and methods of an object.

Object Properties

Every object has a set of characteristics that controls its appearance and behavior. These characteristics are known as the *properties* of an object. For example, a Word `Document` object has a `Type` property, which stores the type of the document. You can use the properties of an object to return information about the object or change the attributes of the object. Each property of an object has a specific data type associated with it.

Table 6-1 lists the various objects and their properties.

You may want to modify the properties of an object at some point in the code. You can change the properties of an object either by using the Properties window or through code. The following syntax is used to modify the value of an object's property:

Table 6-1 Object Properties

Object	Properties	Description
Application object	DisplayScreenTips	Displays the comments, footnotes, endnotes, and hyperlinks as tips
	DisplayScrollBars	Displays horizontal and vertical scroll bars in all windows
	ActiveWindow	Represents the active window
	Name	Displays or sets the name of the application
Documents Collection object	Count	Returns the number of items in the Documents collection
	Creator	Returns a 32-bit integer that indicates the application in which the specified object was created
	Application	Returns the application object
ActiveWorkbook	Colors	Returns or sets colors in the palette for the workbook
	Readonly	Sets the workbook to Read-only
	Sheets	Returns a Sheets collection that represents all the sheets in the active workbook
	HasPassword	Checks whether the worksheet has a password

```
<object>.<property> = <value>
```

In the syntax, `object` refers to the name of the object, `property` refers to the name of the property, and `value` refers to the value to which you want to set the property. As you can see in the syntax, the object name and the property name are separated by a period (.).

The following example illustrates how to use an object's property:

```
CustFrm.Caption = CustomerForm
```

This example sets the value of the `Caption` property of the `CustFrm` object to `CustomerForm`.

NOTE

You cannot set values for all the properties of an object. You can set values only for the properties that are read-write-enabled. You cannot set values for read-only properties, such as `Line`, `Column`, and `AtEndOfFile`.

You have learned to modify the property of an object. You can also extract the current value of an object's property. The following syntax is used to find the value of a property and store it in a variable:

```
<Variable> = <object>.<property>
```

In the syntax, the value of the object's `property` will be stored in a `variable`.

Consider the following example:

```
Dim var As Variant
var = CustFrm.Caption
```

In the example, the value of the `Caption` property of the `CustFrm` object is stored in the variable, `var`.

Next, you will learn about object methods.

Object Methods

The properties of an object define the object, whereas methods tell what can be done with that object. Methods represent the actions associated with an object. Table 6-2 lists the various objects and their methods.

You can refer to a method in the same way you refer to a property:

```
<object>.<method>
```

In the syntax, `object` refers to the name of the object, and `method` refers to the name of the method.

The following example illustrates how to use an object method:

```
ActiveDocument.CheckGrammar
```

Table 6-2 Object Methods

Object	Methods	Description
Application object	Run	Runs a Visual Basic macro
	Resize	Sizes the Word application window or the specified task window
	ShowMe	Displays the Office Assistant or the Help window
	PrintOut	Prints part or all of the specified document
Document object	Add	Adds a new document to the Documents collection
	Open	Opens the specified document and adds it to the Documents collection
	Close	Closes the specified document(s)
	Save	Saves all the documents in the collection
ActiveWorkbook	Activate	Activates the first window associated with the Workbook
	Protect	Protects a Workbook so that it cannot be modified
	RemoveUser	Disconnects the specified user from the shared Workbook
	Unprotect	Removes protection from a sheet or Workbook

In this example, `CheckGrammar` is the method, and `ActiveDocument` is the currently active document. You can use this method to perform a grammar check on the currently active document.

You refer to a method depending on whether the method uses arguments. An argument is any constant, variable, or expression required by the method in order to perform the action properly.

```
<object>.<method> <argument list>
```

In the preceding statement, `argument list` refers to a list of the arguments required by the method, separated by commas.

The following example illustrates how to use an object method with an argument list:

```
Documents.Open FileName := "C:\Report.doc"
```

This example uses the `Open` method to open the file, `Report.doc`. `FileName` is the argument that specifies the name of the file to be opened.

Now that you have learned to use methods, I will discuss object events.

Object Events

VBA works on the *event-driven programming* model. The programs execute in response to *events*. An event is triggered by the system or occurs when you perform an action. For example, when you click on the Open command from the File menu in Word, an event is triggered. In response to this event, a Word document is opened.

Table 6-3 lists some common VBA events.

Table 6-3 Events

Event	Description
Open	Occurs when the specified object is opened
Activate	Occurs when the specified object becomes the active window
Deactivate	Occurs when the specified object is no longer the active window
Close	Occurs when the specified object is closed
Initialize	Occurs when the specified object is loaded into memory
QueryClose	Occurs before the UserForm object is closed
Resize	Occurs when the specified object is resized
Terminate	Occurs when all the references to an instance of an object are removed from memory

You can customize an application by using events. For example, you can display a message when a document is opened. To do this, you can write a procedure and associate it with the `Open` event. Such procedures are called *event-handlers*. Thus, event-handlers are special procedures that are executed every time a particular event occurs. You can write event-handlers by using the Code window. The Code window consists of two drop-down lists, the `Object` list and the `Procedure` list. The `Object` list displays the list of objects. The `Procedure` list displays all the events associated with the corresponding object.

Consider the following example in which you want to display a welcome message when the user opens a document. The steps are as follows:

1. Open the Code window.
2. Select the `Document` object in the `Object` list box.
3. Select the `Open` event in the `Procedure` list box. The event-handler for the `Open` event is displayed.
4. Enter the welcome message as shown in Figure 6-1.

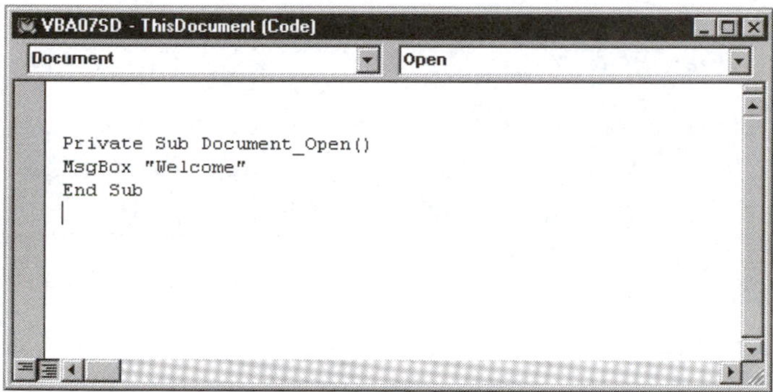

FIGURE 6-1 *The Code window*

Figure 6-1 displays the `Open` event-handler for the `Document` object. When you open a document, the message, `Welcome`, is displayed.

You can work with objects once you have assigned them to variables. In the next section, you will learn to access objects using variables.

Assigning Objects to Variables

As discussed in Chapter 2, "Variables, Constants, and Expressions," the `Object` data type is used for storing addresses that reference objects. You can declare a variable of the `Object` data type by using the `Dim` statement. After declaration, you can assign an object to the variable by using the `Set` statement. The `Set` statement is used to assign object references to a variable declared as `Object`.

The syntax of the `Set` statement is as follows:

```
Set <variable> = <object>
```

In the syntax, `variable` refers to the name of the variable, and `object` refers to the object to be assigned to the variable.

The following example declares a variable as `Object` and assigns an object to the variable, `DocAdd`.

```
Dim DocAdd As Object
Set DocAdd = Documents.Add
```

In the preceding statements, a variable, `DocAdd`, is declared as `Object`. The `Documents` collection has an `Add` method that adds a document to the collection. The address of the new document is assigned to the `DocAdd` variable. You can use the variable to access and modify the new document.

When you declare a variable as `Object`, some memory is allocated to it. The memory taken up by the variable can be released if you no longer require that variable. You can release the memory allocated to the variable by setting it to `Nothing`:

```
Dim DocAdd = Nothing
```

The preceding statement releases the memory allocated to the `DocAdd` variable.

While working with an application, you might want to search for a specific property of an object or find the various methods supported by the object. In the following section, you will learn about finding objects while working in the Visual Basic Editor.

Finding Objects

In order to customize an application, you need to be familiar with the objects of an application. VBA provides you with tools and options that help you find objects while working in the Visual Basic Editor.

The various tools and options used to find objects in VBE are the object browser, the online help, and the List Properties/Methods option.

I will discuss each of these in detail in the following sections.

The Object Browser

The Object Browser enables you to browse through all the available objects, object properties, object methods, and object events in a project. You can also view the procedures and constants available in a project. You can activate the Object Browser by using the Object Browser option from the View menu in the Visual Basic Editor. The Object Browser window is displayed in Figure 6-2.

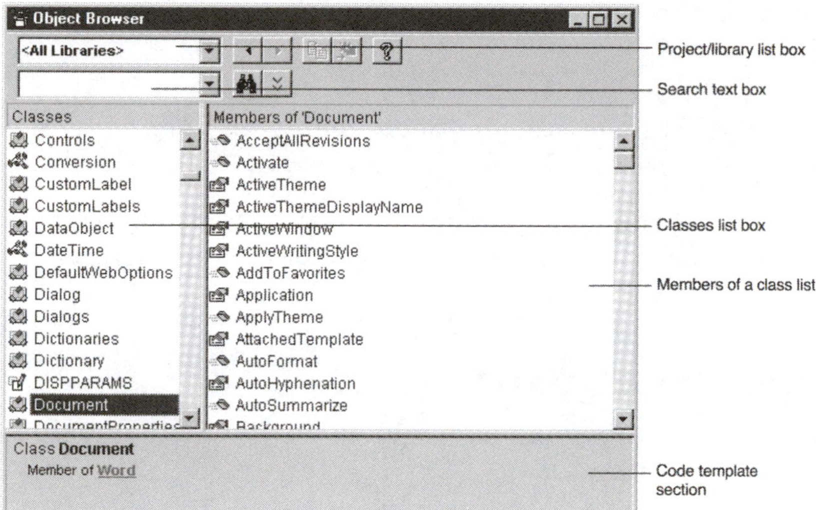

FIGURE 6-2 *The Object Browser window*

The components of the Object Browser are listed in Table 6-4.

Table 6-4 Components of the Object Browser

Components	Description
Help button	Invokes the Microsoft Visual Basic Help window
Project/Library list box	Contains the libraries and projects referenced in the project. A library refers to a file that contains information about the objects of the current application.
Search Text list box	Searches any property, method, event, or object in the Object Browser. To search for a specific object, you can enter the name of the search item in the text box and click on the Search button.
Classes list box	Contains the available classes of the selected library. A class defines the properties that control the object's appearance and the methods and events that control the object's behavior.
Members of <classname> list box	Lists the properties, methods, and events for the class selected in the Classes list
Code Template section	Displays the code templates for the selected property, method, or event

NOTE

The VBA library displays the available objects in the project in the Classes section.

Online Help

The Online Help provides a reference for all the objects in VBA. You can also access the properties, methods, and events associated with an object.

You can access the Online Help by selecting the Microsoft Visual Basic Help option from the Help menu or by pressing F1 in the Visual Basic Editor window. The Online Help window is displayed in Figure 6-3.

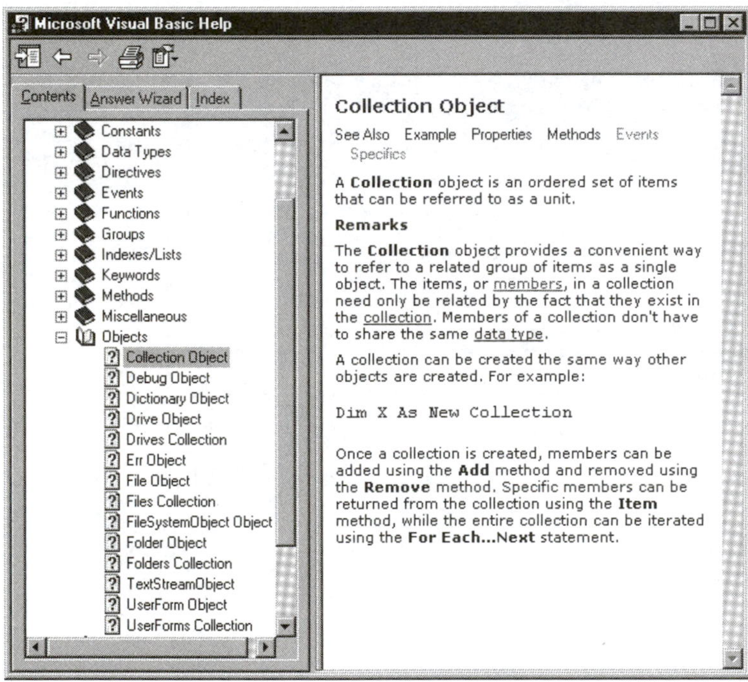

FIGURE 6-3 *The Online Help window*

The List Properties/Methods Option

The List Properties/Methods option provides an easy way to find the properties and methods of an object while working in the Code window. You can invoke the properties and methods list for the Code window by selecting the List Properties/Methods option from the Edit menu.

The properties and methods list for the Application method is displayed in Figure 6-4.

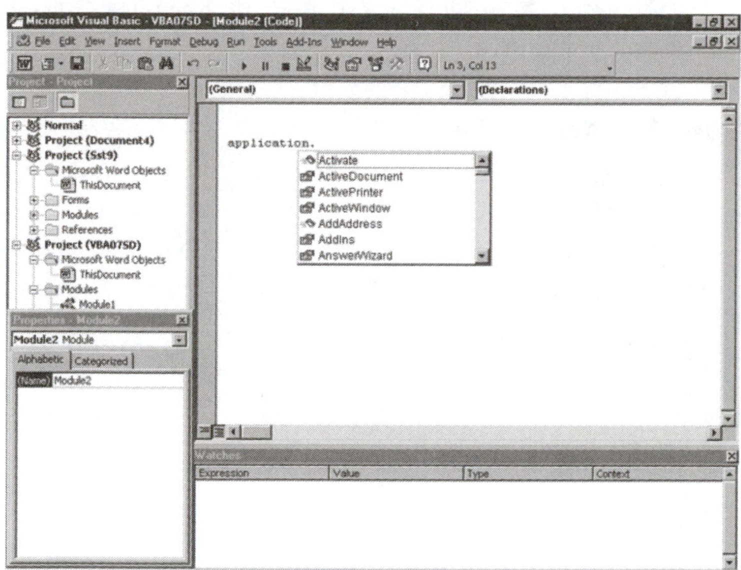

FIGURE 6-4 *The properties and methods list*

You have learned about object properties, methods, and events in the preceding sections. Every application has a set of objects. However, at times you might need to access objects from other applications. Objects from other applications can be referenced with the help of object libraries. The next section introduces you to object libraries and how to reference various object libraries.

Working with Object Libraries

An *object library* is a file that provides information about the available objects. When you start an application, VBA automatically loads the required object libraries for the application. If you want to access objects from other applications, you can add and remove object libraries. For example, if you want Excel's functionality in a Word application, you will need to add a reference to Excel within Word so that Excel objects are available in Word. Adding an object library to a project refers to making more objects available to the project, whereas deleting an object library from a project refers to removing the object libraries that you do not need to view or use, thus reducing the number of object references.

To add an object library, perform the following steps:

1. Select the Reference option from the Tools menu. The References dialog box displays as shown in Figure 6-5.

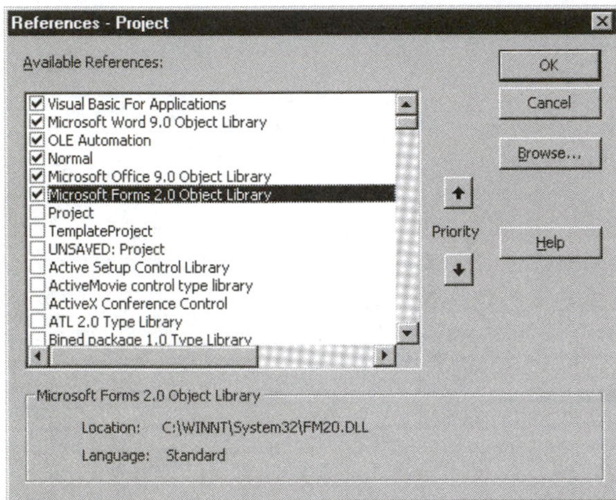

FIGURE 6-5 *The References dialog box*

2. Select the required object library.
3. Click on OK.

CAUTION

The object libraries required to use VBA are loaded when the Visual Basic Editor is opened. These libraries help you use VBA and the user forms of the host application. Do not try changing the set of libraries already loaded in the Visual Basic Editor.

The References dialog box also allows you to change the priority of the object libraries displayed in the Available Reference list box. You can use the Priority up arrow and down arrow to change the priority of an object library. You can also use the Browse button of the References dialog box to add more libraries to a project.

Summary

In this chapter, you learned about the object model of an application. You learned to use the properties, methods, and events of an object. You also learned how to use event-handlers. You were introduced to the object hierarchy and the tools used to find objects while working in the Visual Basic Editor. Finally, you learned to set a reference to an object library.

Chapter 7

Using Security Features in VBA

In a network-computing environment, you may need to work with shared applications and software. In addition, you may distribute your applications to other users. In situations such as these, you need to be aware of security features that you can use to ensure privacy and authentication. This chapter introduces you to the security features available in VBA. You can use these features to secure the applications that you create.

Security Features in VBA

When you share your applications with other users, the applications become susceptible to security risks. This is because applications are dynamic and interactive and involve complex code. Any user can access and tamper with the application code. Therefore, after you share your applications, you need to assure the users working with the software that the application code is unaltered. In addition, you need to prevent unauthorized code execution and tampering. Users of the application also need information about the publisher of the software. Users also need to specify particulars related to their identities so that they can access information for which they have exclusive access permission.

Therefore, to ensure a secure communication link, you need to implement security features that enable you to use and distribute macros and code in a public environment. The security features available in VBA are as follows:

- Digital Signatures
- Security Levels
- Password Protection of Code

A basic understanding of these features can enable you to protect your applications and code from data loss, attacks by malicious code and viruses, and unauthorized access. The first part of this chapter discusses digital signatures. However, to understand how to use digital signatures, you first need to understand the concept of digital certificates.

Digital Certificates

Just as each one of us has an identity card such as a passport or a driver's license, *digital certificates* are electronic identification cards. A digital certificate refers to the code that helps identify and authenticate an entity or an individual.

A digital certificate is issued to software developers by a *certification authority*. A certification authority is a trusted source or an organization that issues certificates either to an entity, such as a software company, or an individual. A digital certificate consists of information about the entity or individual to whom the certificate is issued. In addition, a digital certificate contains information about the certification authority. The certification authority is known as a certificate's *issuer*, and the individual or entity to whom the certificate is issued is known as the *subject* of the certificate. A digital certificate contains a subject's public key, the expiration date of the public key, the serial number of the certificate, and the digital signature of the issuer.

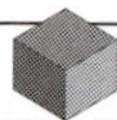

NOTE

A digital certificate may also contain information about the hierarchy of certifying authorities and is also known as a digital ID.

When you use digital certificates to sign applications, macros, or code, the information and the item are stored in a secure format. Digital certificates use the technology known as *public key cryptography*. This technology enables applications, macros, or code to be signed and certificates to be validated. In public key cryptography, a pair of *keys,* called *public key* and *private key,* is generated. The keys are used for decryption and encryption. Using this technology, data is encrypted with the *public key* and can be decrypted only by using the corresponding *private key*.

An individual or entity obtains a specific set of keys. The private key is made available only to the *subject* of the digital certificate, whereas the public key is made available to other users as a part of the digital certificate. Therefore, any user can encrypt a message and send it to you by using your public key. However, you can access the message only by decrypting it with your private key.

In addition to decrypting messages, you can use the private key to encrypt the digital certificate for authenticating your identity for other users. When users receive your certificate, they can validate the certificate by using the public key.

The process of public key cryptography is depicted in the following illustration.

PUBLIC KEY INFRASTRUCTURE

PKI (*Public Key Infrastructure*) enables users to exchange data over an unsecured network by using public and private keys. In PKI, users can work with digital certificates and digital signatures to authenticate or encrypt messages.

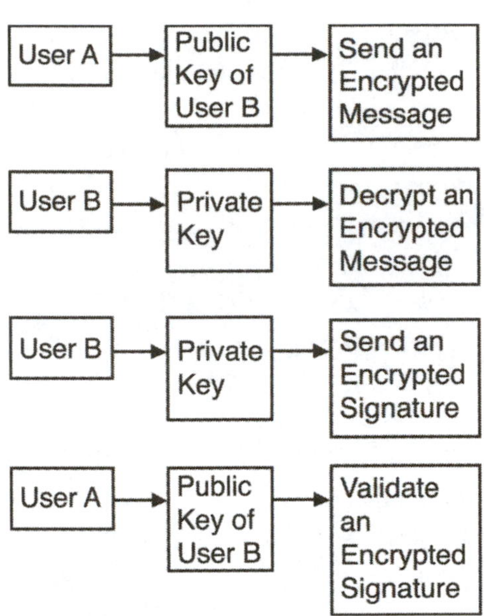

In the following sections, you will learn how to obtain a digital certificate and then how to install, export, remove, and view a digital certificate.

Obtaining a Digital Certificate

You can create your own digital certificates or obtain a digital certificate from various authorities. When you use digital certificates that you have created to sign projects, the projects are referred to as *self-signed* projects. Other users cannot use certificates that you create because they will be unable to establish your identity and run the self-signed projects due to security controls. Therefore, to make your applications, macros, or code available to multiple users, you should obtain a certificate from a commercial certification authority.

Various commercial certification authorities issue different types of certificates that you can use. Following are some of the commercial certification authorities:

- ViaCrypt
- Entrust Technologies
- VeriSign
- Thawte
- SecureNet

You need to select a suitable certificate based on your requirements. Two types of digital certificates are:

- Individual Software Publisher (Class 2) Digital ID
- Commercial Software Publisher (Class 3) Digital ID

An Individual Software Publisher (Class 2) Digital ID enables a developer to publish software independently and authenticates the developer. A Commercial Software Publisher (Class 3) Digital ID enables organizations to publish software. The Class 3 certificate provides higher levels of assurance.

After you have obtained a digital certificate, the next step is to install it. For the following example, assume that you are using the Microsoft technology known as *Microsoft Authenticode.* To make use of this technology and install a digital certificate, you need to use Internet Explorer version 4.0 or later.

NOTE

The Microsoft Authenticode technology enables users to download software to their computers after identifying the publisher of the software and ensuring that the software was not modified after it was signed.

Installing a Digital Certificate

When you want to work with digital certificates, you can either use existing certificates installed by various certifying authorities available with Internet Explorer or obtain new certificates. After you obtain a digital certificate from a certifying authority, you need to install the certificate by performing the following steps:

1. Start Internet Explorer version 4.0 or later.
2. Select the Internet Options command on the Tools menu to display the Internet Options dialog box.
3. Click on the Content tab to display the Certificates section.
4. Click on the Certificates button to display the Certificate Manager dialog box. The Certificate Manager dialog box consists of four tabbed pages: Personal, Other People, Intermediate Certification Authority, and Trusted Root Certification Authority. See Figure 7-1.

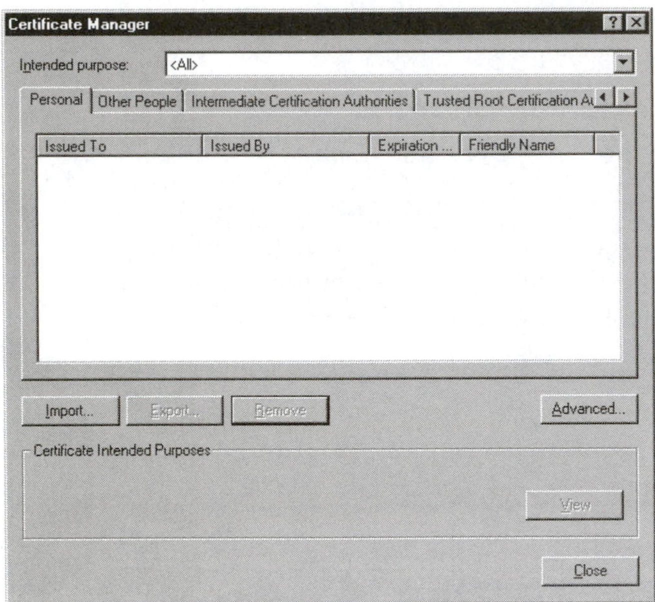

FIGURE 7-1 *The Certificate Manager dialog box*

The Personal tab consists of personal certificates that have an associated private key. By default, all certificates that identify a user by using the private key are listed in the Personal tab.

The Other People tab lists various certificates for which a user does not have a private key. These certificates help authenticate the identity of other users by means of public key cryptography.

The Intermediate Certification Authorities tab contains certificates for certifying authorities. These certificates are not root certificates.

The Trusted Root Certificates Authorities tab lists all certificates that are self-signed and enable you to rely on content that is authenticated by certification authorities.

5. Click on the Import button to display the Certificate Manager Import Wizard.
6. Click on the Next button to display the Select File To Import page of the wizard and specify the name of the file that you need to import.
7. Click on the Next button to display the Select A Certificate Store page. On this page, you need to specify the location where you need to store

the certificate. By default, Internet Explorer automatically stores certificates at a location based on the type of the certificate.

8. Click on the Next button to display the Completing The Certificate Manager page of the wizard. This page displays the certificate store, the type of content, and the file name. You need to click on the Finish button to complete the procedure for installing a digital certificate.
9. After you click on the Finish button, a message box is displayed confirming that the import was successful.

After you have installed a certificate, it is displayed in the appropriate certificate store in the Certificate Manager dialog box.

You have learned how to import a digital certificate. At times, you might need to export the certificate so that you can use it on other computers. You will now look at the steps to export a digital certificate.

Exporting a Digital Certificate

Exporting a digital certificate is similar to importing a digital certificate. To export a digital certificate, perform the following steps:

1. Open the Certification Manager dialog box and click on the certificate that you need to export.
2. Click on the Export button to display the Welcome to the Certification Manager Export Wizard page.
3. Click on the Next button. The Export Private Key with Certificate page is displayed. On this page, you can specify whether you want to export the private key with the certificate.
4. Click on the Next button to display the Certificate Export File page of the wizard. This is where you specify the format of the file that you need to create. The format of the file varies, depending on whether the private key is exported or not.

   If you do not export the private key, you can select from the following formats to export the certificate:

   - DER Encoded Binary x.509 (.CER)
   - Base64 Encoded x.509 (.CER)

◆ Cryptographic Message Syntax Standard – PKCS #7 Certificates (.p7b)

You use these formats to transfer a certificate and all the certificates listed in the certification path of the certificate from your computer to another computer or to a removable media device.

However, if you export the private key, you need to use the Personal Information Exchange – PKCS #12 (.PFX) format. This format transfers the certificate and the corresponding private keys from your computer to another computer or a removable media device. The Certificate Export File page of the wizard is displayed in Figure 7-2.

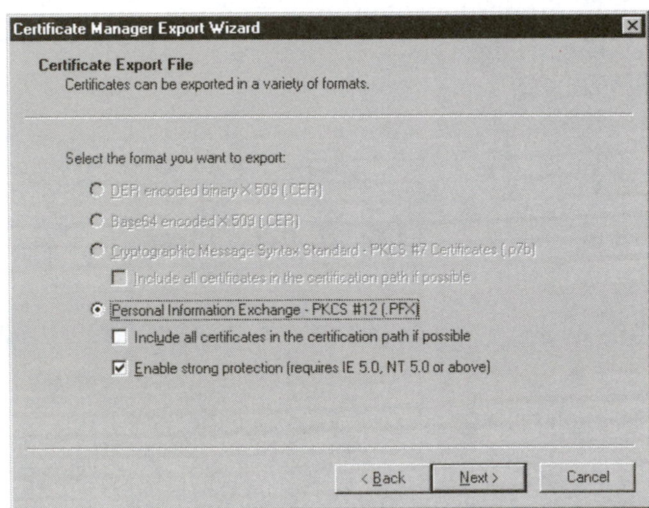

FIGURE 7-2 *The Certificate Export File page*

5. If you export a private key, you need to specify a password for it. The Password Protection For The Private Key page of the wizard is displayed. You need to specify the password required to encrypt the private key.
6. After you confirm the password and click on the Next button, the Export File Name page is displayed. Here, you need to specify the name of the file or browse for a location and enter the file name in the Save As dialog box.

7. Click on the Next button to display the Completing The Certificate Manager Export Wizard page.
8. To export the certificate to the specified file, click on the Finish button. A message box confirming that the certificate has been exported is displayed.

Removing a Digital Certificate

In certain situations, you may need to remove a digital certificate from the Certificate Manager dialog box. To remove a digital certificate, perform the following steps:

1. In the Certificate Manager dialog box, select the certificate that you need to remove.
2. Click on the Remove button. A message box is displayed to confirm the removal of the certificate. Click on the Yes button to complete the process.

NOTE

Different messages are displayed when you remove a personal certificate or a certificate from a commercial certification authority.

Viewing the Details of a Digital Certificate

In addition to adding or removing a digital certificate, you can also view the details of a digital certificate by performing the following steps:

1. Select the Internet Options command on the Tools menu in Internet Explorer.
2. Click on the Content tab to display the Certificates section.
3. Click on the Certificates button to display the Certificate Manager dialog box.
4. Select the certificate for which you need to view the details.
5. Click on the View button to display the Certificate dialog box.

   The Certificate dialog box is displayed in Figure 7-3. The dialog box consists of three tabbed pages. The General tab allows you to view the details about the entity to which the certificate is issued, the issuing authority, and the date of expiry of the certificate.

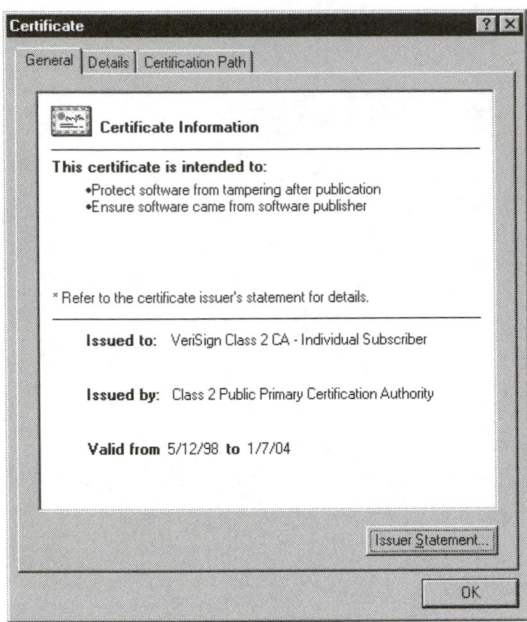

FIGURE 7-3 *The General page of the Certificate dialog box*

NOTE

You can view details of the certification authority by clicking on the Issuer Statement button in the General tab of the Certificate dialog box.

6. To view a list of the properties and extensions associated with the certificate, click on the Details tab. Figure 7-4 displays the Details tab of the Certificate dialog box.
7. To display the hierarchy of certificates associated with the specific certificate, click on the Certification Path tab. This page also provides you with the status of the certificate. Figure 7-5 displays the Certification Path tab of the Certificate dialog box.

TIP

You can also display the Certificate dialog box by double-clicking on the certificate name in the Certificate Manager dialog box.

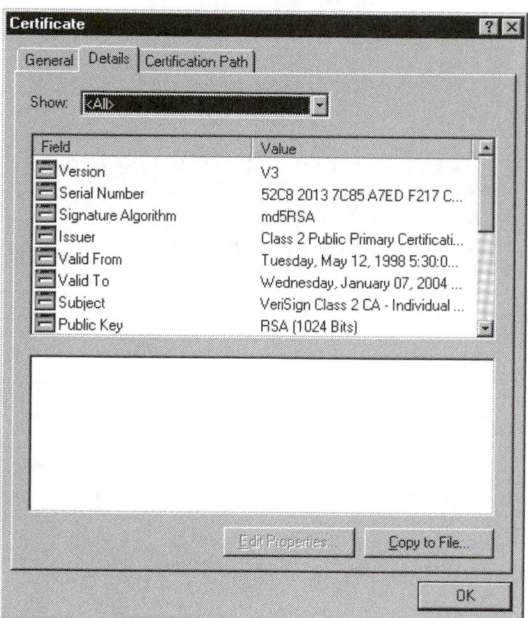

FIGURE 7-4 *The Details page of the Certificate dialog box*

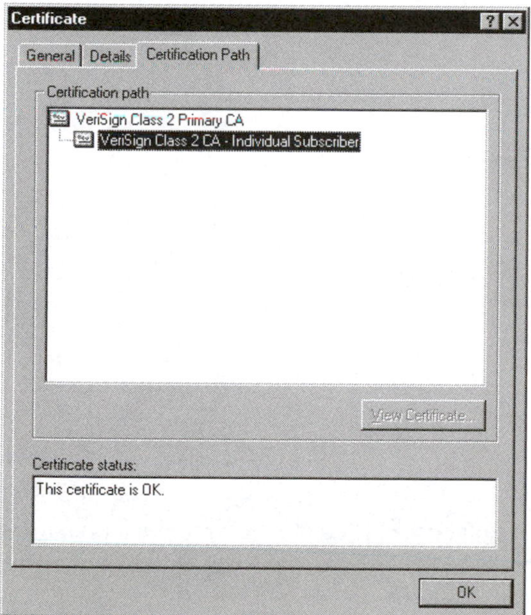

FIGURE 7-5 *The Certification Path page of the Certificate dialog box*

Editing the Properties of a Digital Certificate

In addition to viewing the details of a specific certificate, you can edit the properties of a certificate according to your requirements. To edit the properties of a certificate, click on the Edit Properties button on the Details tab of the Certificate dialog box.

After clicking on the Edit Properties button, the Certificate Properties dialog box is displayed (see Figure 7-6). You use this dialog box to specify a friendly name, a brief description of the certificate, and the purpose for the certificate. In the Certificate Properties dialog box, you can choose one of the option buttons to specify the purposes for the certificate.

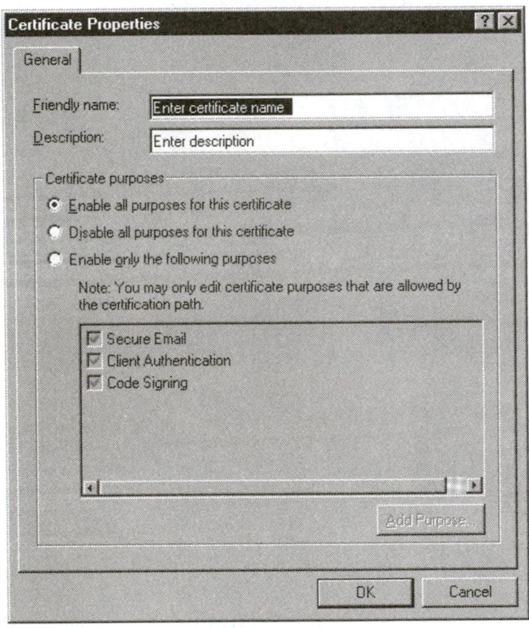

FIGURE 7-6 *The Certificate Properties dialog box*

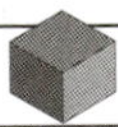

NOTE

You can only edit purposes in the list of purposes supplied by the certification authority and those that are listed in the certification path of the certificate.

Now that you have learned about digital certificates, the next section moves on to digital signatures and the procedures for using them to sign code and macros.

Using Digital Signatures

You can use a digital certificate to create a *digital signature*. A digital signature can be correlated with a block of code consisting of a string of zeros and ones. You typically use digital signatures to protect macros, procedures, forms, or code that you write in VBA. You can also use digital signatures for documents, templates, or add-ins.

You can create digital signatures by using DSA (*digital signature algorithm*). DSA is used to generate a pair of numbers that are computed within certain parameters. These are large, random numbers and are therefore unique. Digital signatures work in conjunction with the public key and the private key. An individual uses the private key to create a signature, and other users use the public key to verify the signature. Both the private and public keys are created using the same algorithm.

NOTE

The RSA algorithm developed by Ron **R**ivest, Adi **S**hamir, and Leonard **A**dleman is the most commonly used encryption and authentication algorithm and is included as part of Netscape Communicator and Internet Explorer.

When a user works with a digital signature, a summary of information of the original text is created using the *hash* function. This summary of information is known as the *message digest*. Although the original text is of variable length, the message digest is of a fixed length. The message digest is used with DSA and encrypted with the private key of the sender to create the digital signature. This digital signature is then sent with the message.

HASHING

Hashing transforms the strings contained in a message into a string of lesser value of a fixed length. This string represents the original string.

To assure users of your identity before they use the macros you created, you need to *sign* macro projects by using digital signatures. Other users can use the digital signature to check the integrity and determine whether any changes have been

NOTE

When you specify a digital signature, it applies to the entire project. Therefore, you cannot apply a digital signature to specific components of a project such as forms, classes, or modules.

made to the macro after its creation. When you use a digital signature to sign a file or a macro project, the digital certificate is added to the file or the macro project as an attachment and provides the user with a verifiable signature. You will now look at the steps to add a digital signature to a macro project.

Adding a Digital Signature to a Macro Project

To add a digital signature to a macro project, perform the following steps:

1. Open the file that contains the macro project that you need to sign.
2. Select the project in the Project Explorer window.
3. Select the Digital Signature command on the Tools menu to display the Digital Signature dialog box. See Figure 7-7.

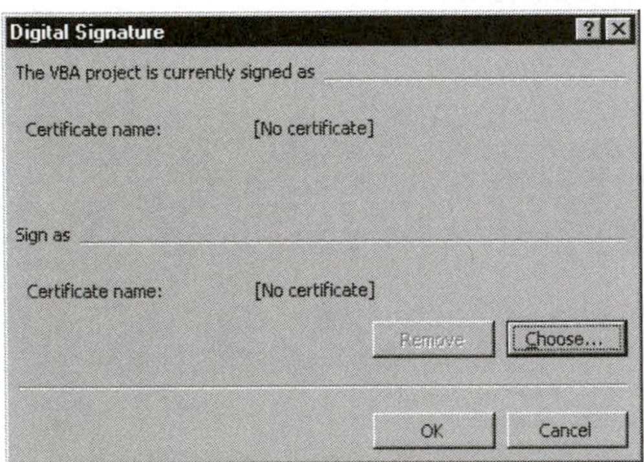

FIGURE 7-7 *The Digital Signature dialog box*

4. When you use this dialog box for the first time, it does not show any digital certificate. You can click on the Choose button to display the Select Certificates dialog box.
5. You need to specify a digital certificate in the dialog box and then click on the OK button to return to the Digital Signature dialog box.
6. Click on the OK button in the Digital Signature dialog box to add the digital signature to the macro project.

CAUTION

If you modify the code contained in a digitally signed project, the digital signature is removed from the project.

Removing a Digital Signature from a Macro Project

There are times when you may not require a specific digital signature in your macro project. You can remove digital signatures by using the Digital Signature dialog box. Click on the name of the digital signature in the dialog box, and then click on the Remove button. When you remove the digital signature, the dialog box displays [No Certificate] to indicate that the current project is not signed using any digital signature.

You can specify an appropriate level of security to ensure protection against macro viruses and malicious code. The following section discusses the various security levels and how to specify the security settings for macros.

Using Security Levels

To specify the appropriate level of security, you need specific security settings for macros. You can configure the security levels by using the Security dialog box. You can also use this dialog box to specify *trusted sources* so that executables or macros are checked for digital signatures before they are allowed to run.

Specifying Security Levels

To specify a level of security for macros, you need to display the Security dialog box by selecting the Security command on the Tools menu. See Figure 7-8.

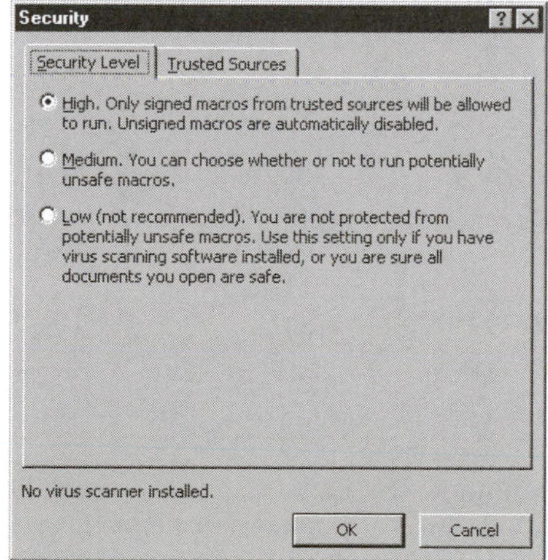

FIGURE 7-8 *The Security dialog box*

The Security dialog box contains two tabs, Security Level and Trusted Sources. You use the Security Level tab to specify the level of security as high, medium, or low.

When you specify the level of security as high, only signed macros from trusted sources are enabled. All unsigned macros are disabled. In this security setting, you can also run the macros you have created.

When you specify the level of security as medium, you can choose to enable or disable a macro individually before the macro is run.

When you specify the level of security as low, all macros are enabled; you do not have any protection against unsafe macros. This level of security is not recommended unless you are sure of all macros that you need to run.

In addition to the Security Levels tab, the Security dialog box contains the Trusted Sources tab.

Designating Trusted Sources

You use the Trusted Sources tab to specify trusted providers of macros or executable code. You can either specify a list of trusted sources as default or add trusted sources to the page. When you open a macro received from a trusted source, the macro is automatically enabled and no security warnings are displayed before running the macro.

Adding Sources

You can add sources either by using the sources identified in the templates and add-ins installed on your computer or by adding to the list of sources on the Trusted Sources tab. The Trusted Sources tab of the Security dialog box is displayed in Figure 7-9.

Before you add a source to the list of trusted sources, you need to specify the security settings as medium or high.

To add a trusted source, you need to run the component that contains the VBA code. After analyzing the code, a security warning is displayed. The Security Warning dialog box varies according to the type of document or executable code that is detected by the client application.

If you have specified the security settings as high and the application identifies an unsigned component, the client application will not enable the component to be

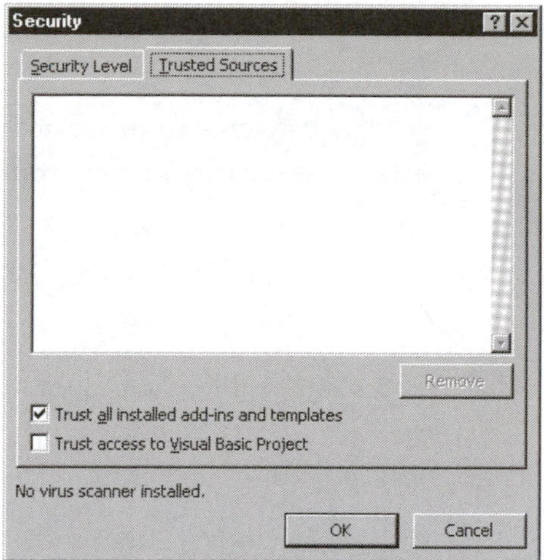

FIGURE 7-9 *The Trusted Sources page of the Security dialog box*

run. However, if you have specified the security settings as low, the Security Warning dialog box is displayed.

If an application detects a signed component, the client application displays a Security Warning dialog box that contains information about the publisher and the certification authority. In the Security Warning dialog box, you can click on the software name that is underlined to view details about the software. In addition, you can view details about the software publisher by clicking on the software publisher's name that is also underlined. You can also choose to rely on all subsequent content from the publisher and the specific certification authority.

The Security Warning dialog box is displayed in Figure 7-10.

Removing Sources

You can remove a previously trusted source by using the Trusted Sources tab in the Security dialog box. To remove a source, perform the following steps:

1. Open the Security dialog box.
2. Click on the Trusted Source tab to display the Trusted Source page.
3. Select the source that you need to remove.
4. Click on the Remove button to remove the source from the list.

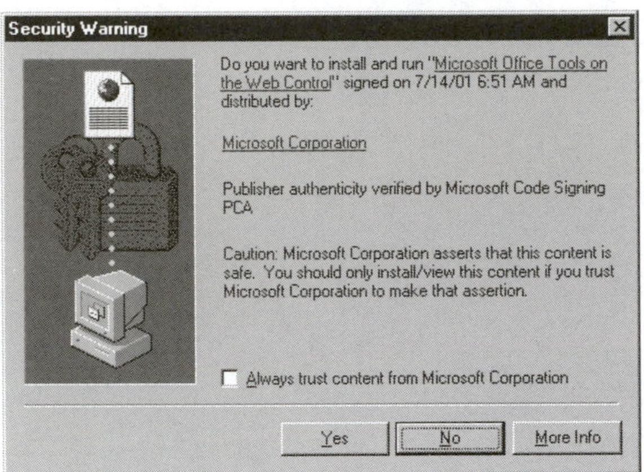

FIGURE 7-10 *The Security Warning dialog box*

You have learned about security measures such as digital signatures and macro security settings. VBA also allows you to use passwords to *lock* the project that you have created.

Using Password Protection

You can prevent unauthorized access to and modification of the code you have created. To do this, you can lock the project containing the code by using a password.

To lock a project, perform the following steps:

1. In the Visual Basic Editor, open the project that you need to lock.
2. Select the Project Properties command on the Tools menu to display the Project Properties dialog box.
3. Click on the Protection tab to display the Protection page.
4. To lock the project, select the Lock Project For Viewing check box and specify a password to view the project.
5. Click on the OK button to close the Project Properties dialog box.
6. You can work with the project and save the project. Subsequently, when you open the project in the Visual Basic Editor, the Project Password dialog box is displayed. You need to specify the password here and click on the OK button to open the project.

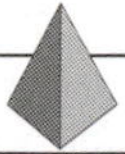

TIP

You can also right-click on the project name in the Project Explorer window to display the Project Properties dialog box.

CAUTION

You cannot lock a project without specifying a password.

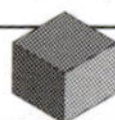

NOTE

If you specify an incorrect password for the project, the Project Locked dialog box displays the message, "Invalid Password."

Summary

In this chapter, you learned about the security features and tools available in VBA. You can use these features and tools to secure applications, secure code from unauthorized access and use, and enable code to be run across applications. You also learned about digital certificates and signatures to sign your code. In addition, you looked at the various levels of security that you can specify for macros. Finally, you learned about protecting your projects by using passwords.

PART III

Professional Project 1

Project 1

Creating a Contacts Book Application

Project 1 Overview

A contacts book application is a utility to store all the details from the Contacts folder in Outlook in a Word document. This utility acts like a mini Contact book in Word and helps display client contact details in a Word document. The tool has the following functionalities:

- The tool allows a user to add, modify, and delete contacts from within a Word document.
- The tool allows a user to print all contact details stored in the Contacts folder.

In this project, you will learn how to build this Outlook application. You will be working with forms and the properties, methods, and events of forms. You will also learn about various controls associated with forms and learn how to add code to the controls for the application given in this chapter. The concepts used to build the contacts book application are as follows:

- Outlook VBA programming
- Outlook Object Model
- Using OLE for Automation

Chapter 8

Project Case Study: Global Systems, Inc.

Global Systems, Inc. is a $100M company with headquarters in New York. The company manufactures network connectivity products such as adapters, routers, and switches. The company specializes in manufacturing high-quality products, which are produced as a result of high levels of quality management. It is a 17-year-old company with clients across the globe. The company has 10,000 experienced employees and operates from offices in 13 cities around the world.

Global Systems, Inc. offers products to a range of clients, large and small businesses and individual customers. The company sends proposals to the prospective clients and if the proposals are approved, a contract is signed between Global Systems, Inc. and the clients. A contract contains information such as the schedule, deliverables, cost, and delivery dates. Global Systems, Inc. caters to a number of clients across the globe; therefore, the company needs to send a large number of proposals on a daily basis. The details of all the clients of the company are stored in the Contacts folder in Microsoft Outlook and the proposal documents are created in Microsoft Word. It is required that each proposal document created in Word include the details of the clients such as the name, address, e-mail ID, and so on at the beginning of the document. However, the company is facing some problems, which are outlined in the following list:

- If a proposal needs to be sent to a number of clients, the Contacts folder in Outlook needs to be referred to repeatedly to look for the details of each client.
- Typing the details of each client consumes a lot of time and effort, especially when the number of clients is large.
- A list of all the clients cannot be printed from the Contacts folder in Outlook.

The company conducted a meeting to discuss these problems. One of the solutions suggested in the meeting was to create a tool that could store all the details from the Contacts folder in Outlook. The tool would act as a mini Contact book in Word and would display client details in a Word document. The functionality of the tool was also discussed in the meeting. All members approved of the proposal and a three-member team was formed to work on the project. The members of the team were:

- Tom Donaldson, Project Manager
- Mike Billing, developer
- Kate Turner, developer

The following sections discuss the main phases of the development life cycle (DLC) of the project, as identified by the development team.

Project Life Cycle

The development life cycle of the project involves the following phases:

- Requirements analysis
- Design
- Coding and construction
- Testing
- Application distribution

These phases are discussed in detail in the following sections.

Requirements Analysis

Requirements analysis is the first phase in a DLC. The development team analyzed the requirements of the project in this phase. To find about the requirements for the project, the team conducted interviews with the employees who send proposals to clients. The requirements of the project are as follows:

- All the contact details stored in the Contacts folder in Outlook should be made available in Word.
- The tool should allow a user to add, modify, and delete contacts and the same should be updated in Outlook.
- The tool should print all details stored in the Contacts folder as a single document.
- The modified list of contacts should be made available at any point of time.

Design

This is the second phase in the DLC. After analyzing the requirements of the project, the development team decided to create an interface for the tool. The team also decided on a broad-level functionality for the project. The team developed the following screens of the tool.

The Outlook Contacts Screen

This is the first screen to be displayed when a user runs the tool. The user selects a contact, and the related details of the selected contact are displayed. The details can then be inserted into a Word document. The user can also modify the details of the contacts in the Contacts folder by clicking on the Modify button. The tool also provides an option for printing a list of all contacts along with their details.

An illustration of this interface is depicted in Figure 8-1.

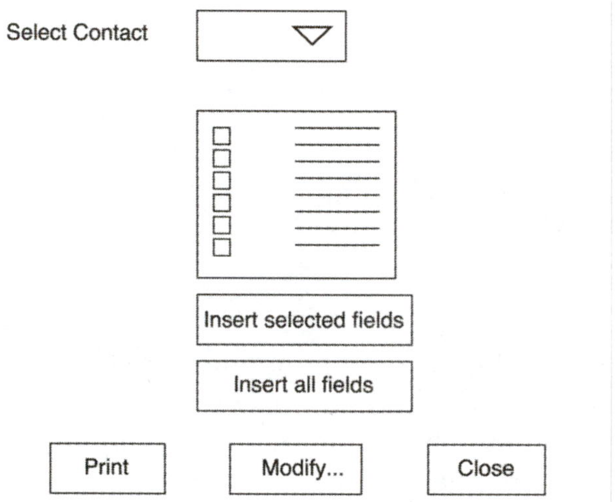

FIGURE 8-1 *The Outlook Contacts screen or the main screen is displayed.*

The Modify Contacts Screen

When the user clicks on the Modify button in the Outlook Contacts screen, the second screen, called the Modify Contacts screen, is displayed. This screen allows the user to modify the details of the selected contacts in the Contacts folder. The user can add, modify, or delete a contact, and the corresponding entry will be updated in Outlook's Contacts folder. An illustration of this interface is depicted in Figure 8-2.

The tool's functionality, as decided by the development team, is depicted in the flow chart in Figure 8-3.

Coding and Construction

In this phase, the application is coded. The input for this phase is the design document, and the design is then translated into code. The development team divided the

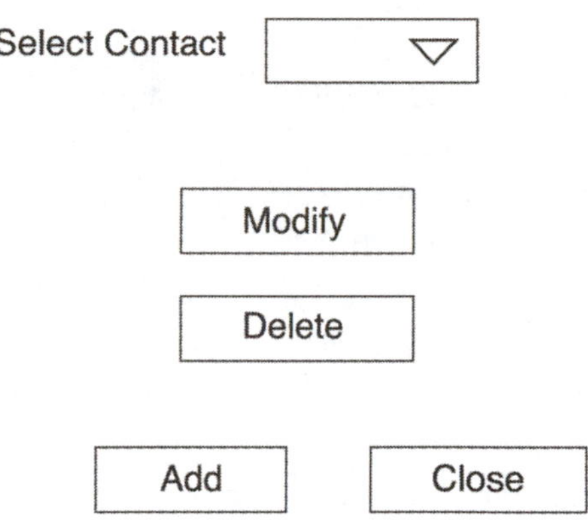

FIGURE 8-2 *The Modify Contacts screen or the second screen is displayed.*

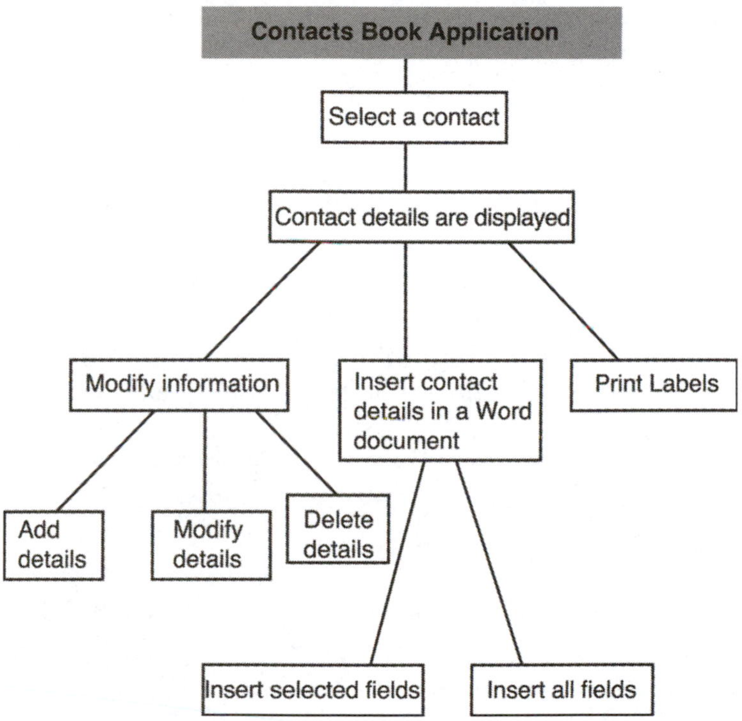

FIGURE 8-3 *The flow chart of the functionality of the Contacts Book application*

responsibilities of coding the tool among the team members. One team member was assigned the task of creating the interface, and the other was assigned the task of coding the application.

Testing

The application is tested during the testing phase. The modules in the application may be tested individually, or the entire application may be tested at once. For the Contacts Book application, the team decided to test the entire tool right away. The requirement for the tool to be tested is that the Microsoft Outlook folder should be open for the tool to run. In addition, the Contacts folder should include contact items. The development team created a *test plan outline* that consisted of details such as the requirements for the project, items to be tested, test deliverables, environmental needs, and so on. A *test specification document* was then prepared to help the testers check the application. The test specification document lists the procedures for testing the application. The testing team prepared a *test analysis report* after they tested the application. The report was submitted to the development team, who then made changes to the code based on the feedback in the report. A separate QA team was formed to ensure that the final product conformed to the defined levels of quality.

Distributing the Application

After the tool has been successfully tested, it needs to be distributed to all employees in the organization. However, it is important to obtain the approval of the QA team before the project is distributed. The Contacts Book application is an internal project for Global Systems, Inc.; therefore, the tool needs to be distributed over its network so that all employees have access to it. The development team has the responsibility of providing ongoing support in terms of installation and correcting any reported errors.

Summary

In this chapter, you looked at the development life cycle. The phases of the DLC of the Contacts Book application were also discussed. In the next few chapters, you will look at the creation and development of the tool.

Chapter 9

Creating the User Interface of the Application

In this chapter, you will learn to create the user interface for the Contacts Book application. You will learn about forms, their properties, methods, and events. This chapter also discusses various controls associated with forms.

Forms

A form is one of the main building blocks of a VBA application. Ideally, every application in VBA consists of one or more forms. Users interact with the controls placed on forms to obtain the required results. Therefore, forms function as data entry screens.

Forms are distinct objects that you need to add to your VBA project. To add forms to the Contacts Book application, open the Visual Basic Editor and choose the UserForm option from the Insert menu. Alternatively, you can select the Insert, UserForm option by right-clicking in the Project window. The Visual Basic Editor displays a user form as shown in Figure 9-1.

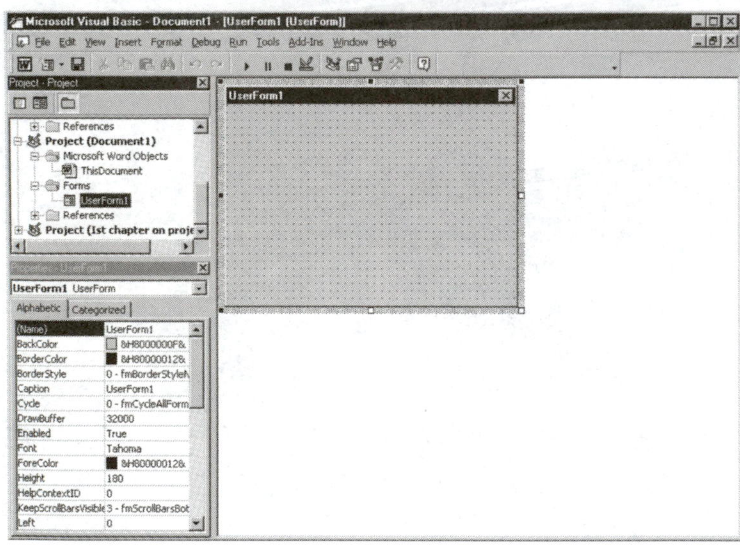

FIGURE 9-1 *A default user form is displayed in the Visual Basic Editor window.*

By default, the Visual Basic Editor creates a form with the name, `UserForm1`, unless the project already contains a user form by that name. The form is inserted into the `Forms` node of the project as shown in Figure 9-1.

You will see small dots displayed on the form in Figure 9-1. These dots constitute a grid. *Grids* help you place controls relative to each other on the form. You can switch off the display of this grid by performing the following steps:

1. Select the Options option from the Tools menu. The Options dialog box is displayed.
2. Select the General tab from the Options dialog box.
3. Clear the Show Grid check box in the Form Grid Settings group box.

The form is displayed without the grid. However, the grid saves time when aligning controls, therefore, the feature is turned on in the Contacts Book application.

The Contacts Book application has two screens according to the Design phase of the DLC. A sketch of the Outlook Contacts screen is displayed in Figure 9-2.

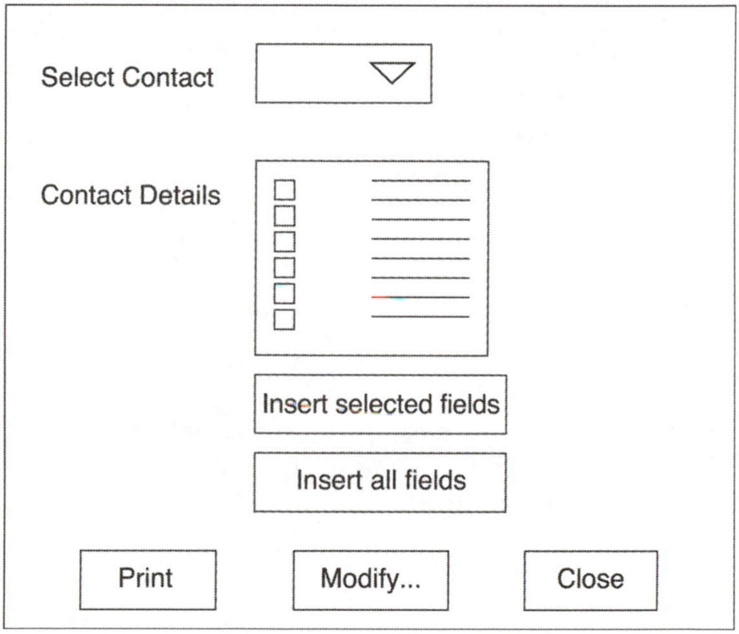

FIGURE 9-2 *The Outlook Contacts screen as designed by the development team*

The sketch of the Modify Contacts screen is displayed in Figure 9-3.

As you can see, both forms will have controls. A form can contain controls such as command buttons, labels, text boxes, and so on. Controls are discussed later in the chapter.

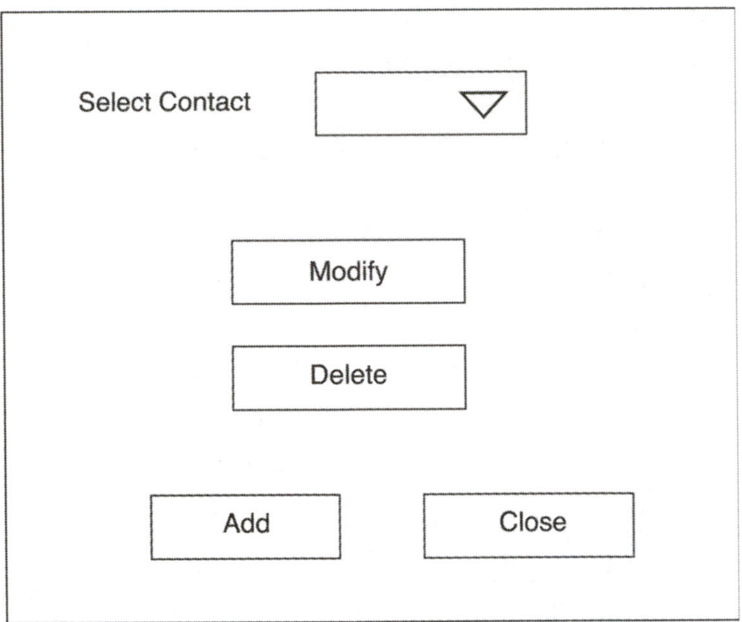

FIGURE 9-3 *The Modify Contacts screen as designed by the development team*

After you have added forms in the Contacts Book application, the next step is to change its design-time properties. The next section deals with the properties of forms.

Form Properties

Every object in VBA has properties and methods associated with it. Recall that properties are attributes or characteristics of an object, and methods define the actions associated with objects. The properties of an object are displayed in the Properties window. If the Properties window is not displayed, press F4 to display it. Alternatively, you can select the Properties Window option from the View menu or right-click on the form and select the Properties option from the shortcut menu.

Forms have properties such as `Name`, `Caption`, `BorderColor`, and `BorderStyle`. These properties can be set at design-time or run-time. For example, by default, when you create a user form, VBA assigns the name, `UserForm1`, to the user form. As a result, the `Name` property is set to `UserForm1`. You can change the `Name` property of the form at design time. It is recommended that you assign meaningful names to forms to avoid confusion when working with different forms.

You will now take a look at the properties of the `Outlook Contacts` form and the `Modify Contacts` form of the Contacts Book application. The Properties windows of the two forms are displayed in Figures 9-4 and 9-5.

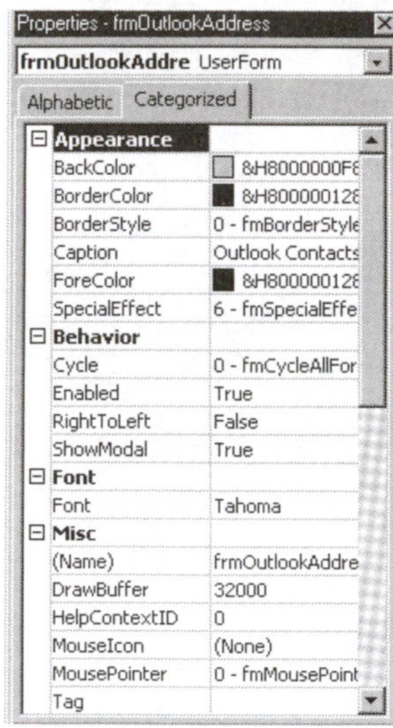

FIGURE 9-4 *The Properties window of the Outlook Contacts form*

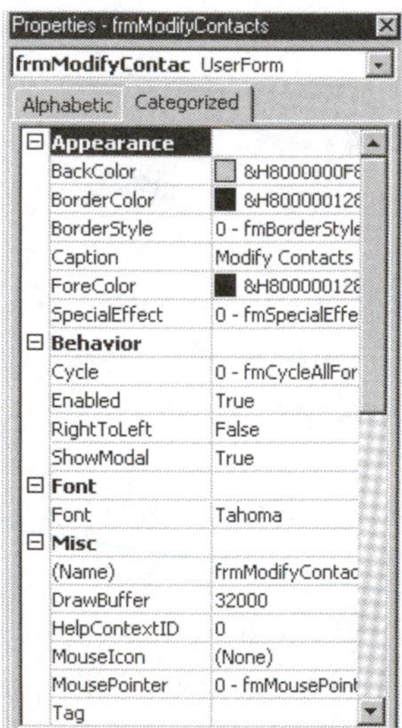

FIGURE 9-5 *The Properties window of the Modify Contacts form*

The Properties window provides two options, Alphabetic and Categorized, to list the properties of an object. If the Alphabetic tab is clicked, the properties of the selected object are displayed alphabetically. If the Categorized tab is clicked, the properties are displayed by classifying them into categories, such as `Appearance`, `Behavior`, and `Font`. You can expand a category by clicking on the plus sign (+) appearing alongside it. The default option is Alphabetic. In Figures 9-4 and 9-5, the properties are displayed according to categories.

NOTE

Any changes in the property settings that you make under the Alphabetic tab are also updated in the properties under the Categorized tab and vice versa.

The following sections discuss some of the categories of the properties of a form.

The Appearance Category

The `Appearance` category deals with properties related to the appearance or the look of a form. The various properties within the `Appearance` category are as follows:

- `BackColor`. This property is used to set the background color of a form. To select a background color, you can choose from the colors available in the drop-down list. The value of the `BackColor` property of the `Outlook Contacts` form and the `Modify Contacts` form of the Contacts Book application is `&H8000000F&`.
- `BorderColor`. This property is used to set the border color of a form. The border color can be selected in the same way as the background color. However, an important point to note here is that you need to assign a border to the form by using the `BorderStyle` property to implement the `BorderColor` property. The value of the `BorderColor` property for the forms of the Contacts Book application is `&H80000012&`.
- `BorderStyle`. This property is used to set a form's border style. This property can have two values, `fmBorderStyleSingle` to apply a border to the form and `fmBorderStyleNone` for no border. `fmBorderStyleNone` is the default value. The values can be selected from the drop-down list of the `BorderStyle` property. The value of this property for the forms of the Contacts Book application is `fmBorderStyleNone`.

- `Caption`. This property is used to specify the text that will be displayed in a form's title bar. The default caption specified for the first form is `UserForm1`. However, you should assign descriptive caption names to forms. The caption for the `Outlook Contacts` form is assigned as `Outlook Contacts`, and the caption for the `Modify Contacts` form is assigned as `Modify Contacts`.
- `ForeColor`. This property is used to set a form's foreground color for text. The foreground color can be selected in the same way as the background and border colors. The value of this property for the forms of the Contacts Book application is `&H80000012&`.
- `SpecialEffect`. This property is used to control the appearance of a form with respect to the form window (for example, sunken, raised, and so on). The default value of this property is `fmSpecialEffectFlat`, for no special effects. The forms of the Contacts Book application have default values for this property.

In this category, you have set the layout for the form. The next category deals with the behavior of the form.

The Behavior Category

The properties in this category specify how a user will interact with a form. The properties included in this category are as follows:

- `Cycle`. This property is used to determine the behavior of the form when the user presses the Tab key. The forms of the Contacts Book application have the value, `fmCycleAllForms`. If the value of this property is set to `fmCycleAllForms` and if the focus is on the last control, the focus passes to the first control on the next page.
- `Enabled`. This property is used to enable or disable a form. A `True` value enables a form, while a `False` value disables a form. The default value of the property is `True`. The forms of the Contacts Book application are enabled.
- `RightToLeft`. This property is used to change the tab order of the form. When set to `True`, on pressing the Tab key, the controls of the form are highlighted in the right-to-left direction instead of the usual left-to-right direction. The default value is `False`. The forms of the Contacts Book application have the default value for this property.

- `ShowModal`. This property is used to set the *modality* of a form. A `True` value is used to make a form modal. A modal form means that a user will not be able to interact with any other underlying application until the user closes the form. The default value for this property is `True`, and the forms of the Contacts Book application are assigned the default value for this property.

The next category deals with the default font used for a form.

The Font Category

This category consists of only one property, called `Font`. This property is used to set the font for the form. Fonts can be selected by clicking on the three-dot (...) button displayed when you click on the `Font` property. You need to set the value of the `Font` property to `Tahoma` for the forms of the Contacts Book application.

You have learned about the different properties of forms related to their appearance, behavior, and font. Other properties of a form that do not fit in any category are included in the `Misc` category, which is discussed in the next section.

The Misc Category

The properties that form the `Misc` category are as follows:

- `Name`. This property is used to set the name of a form. A form is referred to by this name in the code. When a new form is added, VBA automatically assigns a caption and a name to the form `UserForm1`. Although you can use the default names, user-defined, meaningful, and descriptive names are preferred because they make the code easier to read and debug.

TIP

You should use meaningful, user-defined names not only for form objects, but also for other objects.

The `Name` property is assigned the value `frmOutlookAddress` for the `Outlook Contacts` form and `frmModifyContacts` for the `Modify Contacts` form.

NOTE

You might get confused between the `Name` property and the `Caption` property of an object. The `Caption` property specifies the title of an object, which is displayed to the user. The `Name` property is never displayed on the object and is used to refer to the object in the VBA code. Although both the `Name` and `Caption` properties can be assigned the same value, they are assigned different values to avoid confusion.

- `DrawBuffer`. This property is used to specify the number of pixels that VBA needs to set aside in memory for a frame. You can specify any value in the range of 16,000 to 1,048,576. The default value of this property is `32,000`. The forms of the Contacts Book application are assigned the default value for this property.
- `HelpContextID`. This property specifies the topic number for the form in a Help file. The default value is `0`. The forms of the Contacts Book application are assigned the default values.
- `MouseIcon`. This property is used to create mouse icons. You can assign a picture by using this property, which will be displayed as a mouse icon when the cursor is on the form. The default value, `None`, is assigned to this property for the forms of the Contacts Book application. If you need to define custom mouse icons, you need to set the value of the `MousePointer` property to `fmMousePointerCustom`.
- `MousePointer`. This property is used to determine the appearance of the mouse pointer when the pointer is within the form. The default value `fmMousePointerDefault` is assigned to this property for the forms of the Contacts Book application.
- `Tag`. This property is used to provide additional information about a form. The property assigns a hidden string to the form, which is used to store extra information.
- `WhatsThisButton`. When set to `True`, this property displays the What's This? help button in the corner of the window.
- `WhatsThisHelp`. When set to `True`, this property displays a pop-up help window when the user clicks on a control after clicking on the What's This? help button.
- `Zoom`. This property is used to specify a percentage value by which a form can be viewed in an enlarged or reduced magnification.

The Picture Category

This category consists of properties related to inserting and aligning pictures in a form. The various properties in this category are as follows:

- `Picture`. This property is used to set a background picture for the form. The picture can be selected by clicking on the three-dot (...) button.
- `PictureAlignment`. This property is used to align a picture on the form. The picture can be aligned at the top-left, top-right, center, bottom-left, or bottom-right corner of the form.
- `PictureSizeMode`. This property is used to specify the location of the picture relative to the form.
- `PictureTiling`. This property is used to fill the background with multiple copies of an image if the image is small in size.

The Position Category

This category specifies the dimensions and position of a form inside an application window. The `StartUpPosition` property is an important property in this category and is used to specify the position of the form with respect to the application window or the screen. You can also specify your own values to position the form by using the `Left`, `Right`, `Height`, and `Width` properties.

In addition to positioning a form in an application window, you can also specify whether the form will display scroll bars. This is discussed in the next category of properties.

The Scrolling Category

The properties in this category determine whether a form displays scroll bars. It also contains properties that deal with the position of scroll bars such as `ScrollHeight`, `ScrollLeft`, `ScrollTop`, and `ScrollBottom`.

You have learned about the various form properties. As stated earlier, properties of an object can be set at design-time or run-time. You will now look at an example of setting properties at run-time.

Consider an example of a form which contains a frame. The frame consists of employee details. The frame should be displayed only when the employee code and password of the employee is validated. Therefore, the `Enabled` property of the `Frame` control should be set to `True` only after the employee has been successfully validated, otherwise it should be set to `False`. The following line of code accomplishes this.

```
Frame1.Enabled = False
```

In this code statement, `Frame1` is the name of the frame.

Therefore, properties can be set at run-time when values are assigned to properties after a user event has occurred.

CAUTION

You need to be careful while setting properties at run-time. When assigning values to properties, ensure that the values are valid, otherwise the application will generate a run-time error.

Properties help you set the attributes of an object. Objects are created for user interaction. These objects respond to user interactions through events. In the next section, you will learn about form events.

Form Events

An object has a set of properties and events associated with it. *Events* are actions recognized by a program. An event can be a user-generated event, such as the click of a mouse button, or a system-generated event, such as running out of memory. For each event associated with a control, you can write event-handlers. An *event-handler* is a procedure that you can write to process events. When an event occurs, VBA looks for the corresponding event-handler code in the program and transfers the control to the event-handler. To write an event-handler, double-click on the object and write the code in the code module for the object. You can also use the procedure drop-down list to select the event with which you want to work.

Some of the most commonly used form events are:

- `Initialize`. This event is generated when a form is created at run-time.
- `Load`. This event is generated when a form is loaded in memory.
- `Activate`. This event is generated if a form window is the currently active window.
- `Click`. This event is generated when a user clicks on the empty part of a form.

- `DblClick`. This event is generated when a user double-clicks on an empty part of a form.
- `Resize`. This event is generated when a user resizes a form.
- `Deactivate`. This event is generated when a form is not currently active.
- `Terminate`. This event is generated when a form is set to `Nothing`.

Some keyboard- and mouse-related events are used quite often. These are discussed in the following list:

- `KeyDown`. This event is generated when a user presses or holds down a key or key combination.
- `KeyPress`. This event is generated when a user presses and then releases a key.
- `KeyUp`. This event is generated when a user releases the key or the key combination that was held down by using the `KeyDown` event.
- `MouseDown`. This event is similar to the `KeyDown` event. It is generated when a user presses or holds down a mouse button.
- `MouseMove`. This event is generated when a user moves the mouse pointer inside the form window.
- `MouseUp`. This event is generated when a user releases the mouse button that was held down by using the `MouseDown` event.

In order to interact with a form, every form has controls associated with it. The next section discusses controls.

Form Controls

Recall the two forms of our application, `Outlook Contacts` and `Modify Contacts`. (Refer to Figures 9-2 and 9-3.) Now that you have set up the design-time properties of the two forms, you need to design the forms. Designing a form refers to placing controls on the form. Controls are objects with their own sets of properties and methods. A form is also an object. There are a number of controls in VBA including `command button`, `combo box`, `list box`, and `frame`. You will now place controls on the forms of the Contacts Book application, align them to get the required layout, and set the design-time properties for each control.

Inserting Controls

When you insert a user form, it is an empty form, which is of little use to anyone. You need to add controls to the form for it to be of any use to the application. The Toolbox is a warehouse of all the controls that you need on a form. To display the Toolbox, select the Toolbox option from the View menu. The Toolbox is displayed as shown in Figure 9-6.

FIGURE 9-6 *The standard Toolbox in the Visual Basic Editor window*

To add a control to the form, click on the control that you want to include, and drag the control to the required location on the form. The commonly used controls in VBA are discussed in the following section.

The Label Control

This is the simplest control and is used to display text on the screen. The `Label` control is used to display descriptive text on the form such as the title of any field, captions, or precise instructions. Although labels are mostly used to display text, they can also be used to assign captions to controls that do not have their own captions, such as text boxes and list boxes. Labels are unbound controls. Unbound controls cannot be bound to any other control, and the value of an unbound control does not change as you move from one record to another. Just as all objects, the `Label` control also has a set of properties, methods, and events associated with it. The default property for a `Label` control is `Caption`, and the default event is the `Click` event.

To add a `Label` control, click on the `Label` control in the Toolbox and move the control by dragging it onto the form.

Now, for the Contacts Book application, refer to Figure 9-2. In order to create the `Outlook Contacts` form, you need to give the caption, `Select a Contact:`, to inform the user that one of the contacts has to be selected from the available list of contacts. Next, you need to give the caption, `Contact Details`, and display the details of the selected contact to the user.

The important properties of the `Select a Contact:` label along with their values for the `Outlook Contacts` form are as follows:

- Name—`Label1`
- Caption—`Select a Contact:`

The rest of the properties of the label are the same as that of the form object, which was discussed in the earlier section.

You can add the `Contact Details` label to the `Outlook Contacts` form in a similar manner. You can also add labels for the `Modify Contacts` form in the same manner.

The ComboBox Control

After adding the `Label` control to the `Outlook Contacts` form, you need to add the `ComboBox` control in front of the label, `Select a Contact`. A `ComboBox` control is used to provide the user with a range of choices. To add a combo box to the `Outlook Contacts` form, click on the `ComboBox` control in the Toolbox and drag the control over the form. Some of the properties of the `ComboBox` control along with their values for the `Outlook Contacts` form are discussed in the following list:

- `Name—cboContactList`
- `ColumnWidth—90 pt; 1 pt; 1 pt; 1 pt; 1 pt; 1 pt`. This property specifies the width of each column in the list box.
- `Value`. This property is the default property for a `ListBox` control and specifies the state of a given control.
- `ColumnCount—6`. This property sets the number of elements to be displayed in the list.
- `ColumnHeads`. When set to `True`, this property displays the list columns with headings.
- `MultiSelect`. This property specifies whether the user can make multiple selections in the list.
- `Text`. This property returns the selected item.

The default property of the `ComboBox` control is the `Value` property, and the default event is the `Change` event. The `Change` event occurs when the user changes the selection in the `ComboBox` control.

The ListBox Control

Now you need to add a ListBox control in front of the label, Contact Details. This control is similar to the ComboBox control. The ListBox control is also used to list a range of values to the user. The ComboBox control combines a text box with a list box. The difference between a ListBox control and a ComboBox control is that you cannot enter your own values in a list box; however, this is possible in the case of a combo box. The properties of the ListBox control for the Outlook Contacts form are as follows:

- Name—LstFieldList
- Height—83.3
- Left—84
- ListStyle—fmListStyleOption. This property allows you to change the visual presentation of your list box.
- MultiSelect—fmMultiSelectMulti. This property indicates whether a list box allows multiple selections.
- TabIndex—2. This property is used to set the tab order of controls.
- Top—48
- Width—126

The default property of the ListBox control is the Value property, and the default event is the Click event.

The TextBox Control

The TextBox control is used to enter text, numbers, cell references, and so on. It is the most common control used for data input. Some of the key properties of a TextBox control are as follows:

- EnterFieldBehavior. This property is used to define the behavior of the TextBox control when the user accesses the text box by using the Tab key. The value, fmEnterFieldBehaviorSelectAll, specifies that only the text within the field should be selected, and the value, fmEnterFieldBehaviorRecallSelect, specifies that only the text that the user last selected should be displayed.
- AutoTab. This property specifies whether a tab should be entered automatically when the user has entered the maximum number of characters in the text box.

- AutoWordSelect. When set to True, this property selects a whole word when the user drags the cursor through the text in the text box.
- DragBehavior. This property makes the drag-and-drop feature for a text box available or unavailable.
- EnterKeyBehavior. This property specifies the behavior of a text box when the user presses the Enter key when the focus is on the text box. VBA creates a new line or shifts the focus to the next control depending upon the value of the property.
- HideSelection. This property determines whether VBA displays any selected text in a text box.
- MultiLine. This property determines whether a text box can contain multiple lines of text.

The default property for a TextBox control is the Value property, and the default event for the TextBox control is the Change event.

The CommandButton Control

The CommandButton control is a push button that is used to start, interrupt, or end an action. Some of the key properties of the CommandButton control are discussed in the following list:

- Cancel. When set to True, the button is highlighted when the user presses the Esc key.
- Caption. This property returns the text that appears on the CommandButton control.
- Default. When this property is set to True, the button is selected when the user presses the Enter key.
- TakeFocusOnClick. This property defines whether the command button takes focus when the user clicks on it.

The default property of a CommandButton control is the Value property, and the default event for the CommandButton control is the Click event.

Going back to the Contacts Book application, you need to add five command buttons to the Outlook Contacts form. (Refer to Figure 9-2.) The CommandButton control can be added by moving the control to the form. After adding the command buttons, set the design-time properties of the command button as follows:

- `Caption`. The five command buttons should be assigned the names `Insert Selected Fields >`, `Insert All Fields >>`, `Print Labels…`, `Modify Contacts…`, and `Close`.
- `Name`. The names of the command buttons are `cmdInsertSelected`, `cmdInsertAll`, `cmdPrint`, `cmdModify`, and `cmdClose`.
- `Top`. The values of the command buttons are `138`, `168`, `204`, `204`, and `204`.
- `Width`. The values of the command buttons for the `Width` property are `95`, `95`, `70`, `95`, and `70`.
- `Height`. The height for all the controls is `24`.
- `Left`. The left position of the command buttons is `84`, `84`, `6`, `84`, and `186`.
- `TabIndex`. The values for this property are `3`, `4`, `8`, `7`, and `5`. The `TabIndex` property specifies the position of the objects.

TIP

Instead of sizing controls manually, you can select the Make Same Size option from the Format menu. This option uses one of the selected controls as a "base" upon which all the other controls are sized.

You have added controls to the `Outlook Contacts` form. You have also set the properties of the controls. Similarly, you can add controls to the `Modify Contacts` form.

The following sections discuss the remaining controls.

The Frame Control

The `Frame` control acts as a container for controls and is used to create groups of two or more controls. The `Frame` control is used when you need to logically group controls. The `Frame` control is also used in situations when you need to move a set of controls as one unit. To add a `Frame` control to the form, click on the `Frame` control on the Toolbox and move the control to the form. Some of the properties of the `Frame` control are discussed in the following list:

- `Cycle`. This property is used to shift the focus to another control when the user is on the last control in the frame.
- `InsideHeight`. This property returns the height of the area inside the form.

- `InsideWidth`. This property returns the width of the area inside the form.
- `KeepScrollBarsVisible`. This property determines whether a frame will display scroll bars.
- `PictureSizeMode`. This property determines how a background picture will be displayed.

The default event of the `Frame` control is the `Click` event.

The CheckBox Control

If you want to give the user a choice between two values, you can use the `CheckBox` control. When the user selects the check box, a special mark is displayed on the check box, and the current setting of the check box becomes `True`, `On`, or `Yes`. If the user clicks on the check box again, the mark disappears, and the setting changes to `False`, `Off`, or `No`. The distinct properties of a `CheckBox` control are as follows:

- `TripleState`. This property determines whether a check box can have the `Null` state along with the `True` and `False` states.
- `SpecialEffect`. This property is used to control the visual appearance of a check box.
- `Value`. This property indicates whether a check box is selected or cleared.
- `Accelerator`. This property is used to provide quick access to a check box.

The default property for a `CheckBox` control is `Value`, and the default event for a `CheckBox` control is the `Click` event.

You have added controls to the two forms of the Contacts Book application. You have also set the design-time properties of the controls. Figures 9-7 and 9-8 display the two forms of the application.

All the controls discussed so far were a part of the Toolbox. However, you can also use user-defined controls that are not a part of the standard Toolbox. User-defined controls are discussed in the following section.

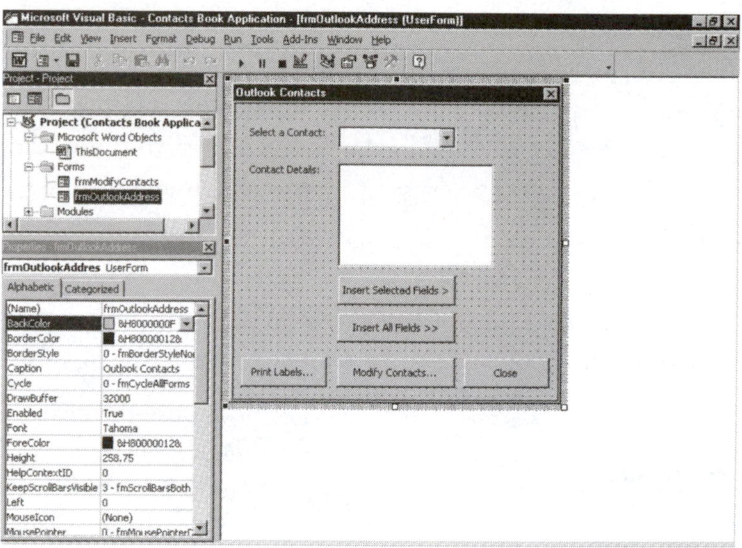

FIGURE 9-7 *The* `Outlook Contacts` *form of the Contacts Book application*

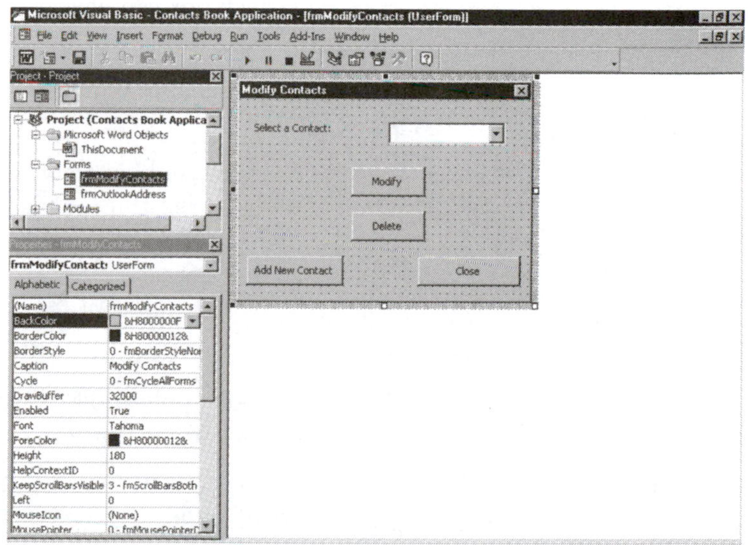

FIGURE 9-8 *The* `Modify Contacts` *form of the Contacts Book application*

Using User-Defined Controls

By default, the Toolbox displays only the standard controls available in an application. However, you may be required to work with additional custom controls. You can add controls to the existing controls in the Toolbox by performing the following steps:

1. Click on the Toolbox to activate it.
2. Select the Additional Controls option from the Tools menu. Alternatively, you may select the Additional Controls option by right-clicking on the control page in the Toolbox. The Additional Controls dialog box is displayed as shown in Figure 9-9.

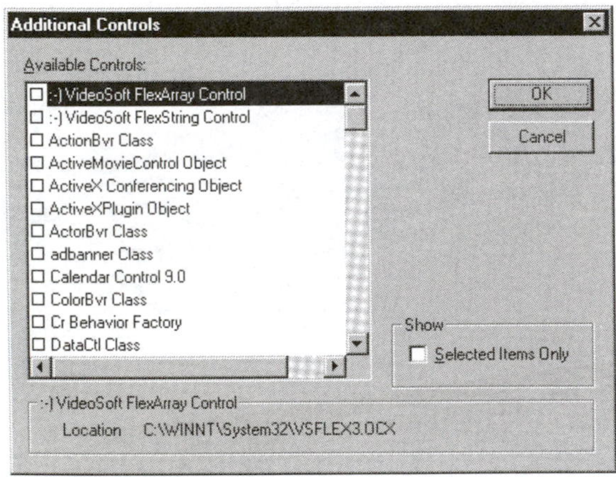

FIGURE 9-9 *The Additional Controls dialog box*

3. Select the check boxes of the controls that you want to add to your form. The controls will now appear as icons in the Toolbox and you can use them just as you use the default controls.

To add user-defined controls to the Toolbox, create a separate page in the Toolbox. Then, add the new controls to that page to avoid confusion between the default and user-defined controls. To add a new page to the Toolbox, right-click on the Toolbox tab and select the New Page option from the shortcut menu. The Toolbox appears as shown in Figure 9-10.

Right-click on the New Page tab and click the Rename option to rename the page. You can now add user-defined controls to this page.

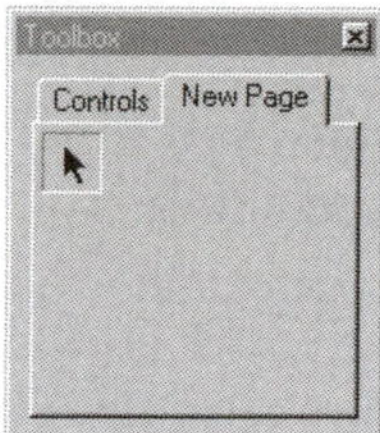

FIGURE 9-10 *The Toolbox with a new page*

The user-defined controls that you use in a project can also be used in other projects. This also holds true for the standard controls that you have used with a particular set of properties. You can also create a group of controls placed on a form and use it as one unit in another project.

NOTE

A group is a collection of controls that you want to treat as a single unit. As a result, you can format, size, or move the controls just like a single control. To group two or more controls, select the controls and select the Group option from the Format menu. Alternatively, you can use the UserForm toolbar's Group button after selecting the controls. To ungroup controls, select the Ungroup option from the Format menu or click on the UserForm toolbar's Ungroup button.

You have created two forms for the Contacts Book application. These forms are required to perform a few actions. For example, when a user clicks on the Modify button of the `Outlook Contacts` form, the `Modify Contacts` form is displayed. The actions that an object can perform are known as methods. The next section deals with the different form methods available in VBA.

Form Methods

A method is an action performed by an object. Some of the most commonly used form methods are `Show`, `Hide`, and `Unhide`. These methods are discussed in detail in the following sections.

The Unload Method

You can unload a form from memory when it is no longer required. It is good practice to unload forms to make memory space available. To unload a form, you need to specify the following statement:

```
Unload <form name>
```

If you want to unload the form currently running, you can give the following statement:

```
Unload me
```

The Show Method

The `Show` method is used to display a form on the screen. The form can be displayed on the screen without explicitly loading the form. The syntax of the `Show` method is

```
<form name>.Show
```

In the Contacts Book application, the `Modify Contacts` form should be displayed when a user clicks on the Modify button of the `Outlook Contacts` form. To accomplish this, you need to write the following code in the `Click` event of the Modify button:

```
Private Sub cmdModify_Click()
Unload Me
frmModifyContacts.Show
End Sub
```

This code snippet is executed when a user clicks on the Modify button of the `Outlook Contacts` form. The code unloads the current form, `Outlook Contacts`, from the memory and displays the `Modify Contacts` form to the user.

The Hide and Unhide Methods

Another commonly used form method is the `Hide` method. This method is used to hide a form. If you run the `Hide` method without explicitly loading the form in the memory, VBA will load it automatically. The syntax of the `Hide` method is

```
Hide <form name>
```

When an object is hidden, it becomes invisible, and its `Visible` property is set to `False`. Although the controls of a hidden object are not accessible to a user, they are available in memory. The `Hide` method always hides the form with its current settings. This implies that if the form is displayed again, the existing settings are restored.

To make the form visible again, use the `Unhide` method. The syntax of the `Unhide` method is

```
Unhide <form name>
```

You can use the methods discussed to perform actions on objects.

After you have created forms in an application, you can share them across applications, as discussed in the next section.

Sharing Forms Across Applications

Forms created in a VBA application can be shared across all VBE-enabled applications, which means you can reuse such forms. Therefore, you do not need to create forms from scratch and can use the available forms of other projects. VBA offers two ways of sharing forms:

- Importing and exporting forms
- Dragging the form object from one application to another

Each method is discussed in detail in the following sections.

Importing and Exporting Forms

You can share forms across applications by importing and exporting forms as files. A form can be exported to a separate file, and this file can be imported into other VBE-enabled projects. You need to carry out the following steps to import and export forms:

1. Click on the form that needs to be exported in the Project Explorer window.
2. Select the Export File option from the File menu. Alternatively, you can press Ctrl+E. The Export File dialog box is displayed, as shown in Figure 9-11.

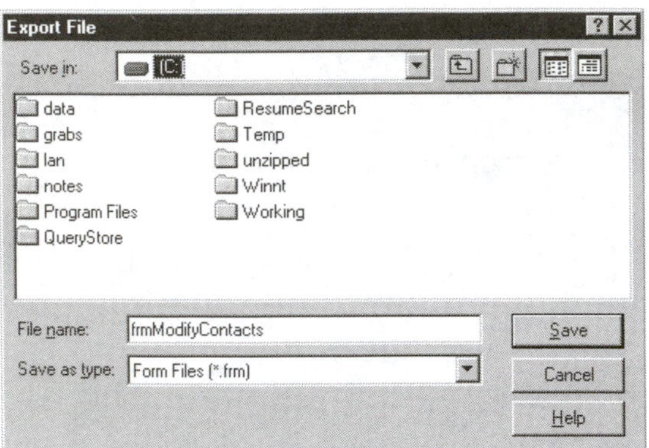

FIGURE 9-11 *The Export File dialog box*

3. Specify the file name and location of the file to be stored in the Export File dialog box and click on the Save button.
4. To import the exported file into another project, click on the project into which you want to import the file.
5. Select the Import File option from the File menu. Alternatively, you can press Ctrl+M. The Import File dialog box is displayed, as shown in Figure 9-12.

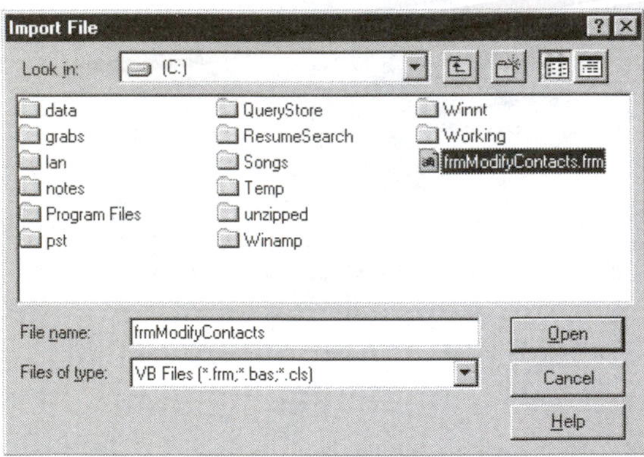

FIGURE 9-12 *The Import File dialog box*

6. Select the form file, which you need to import, from the Import File dialog box, and click on the Open button. The selected form will be added to the project.

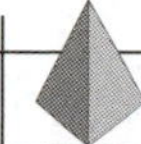

TIP

You can also use the Export File option to create a form file that can be used as a backup in case of failures.

Importing and exporting forms as files allow you to share forms across applications, however there is an easier method available. The next section deals with sharing forms by dragging form objects.

Dragging Form Objects

If you import and export many forms, you may end up cluttering your hard disk. A solution to this problem is to drag form objects. You can drag the form object from the Project Explorer window of a project to the Project Explorer window of the other project. You can move the form to the name of the Project in the Project Explorer window. If, however, the project is in a different application, you need to open and arrange the application in advance to be able to move the form to that application.

Summary

In this chapter, you learned about forms, their properties, events, and methods. You also learned about controls and how to set their design-time properties. You created the two forms of the Contacts Book application. You also added controls to the forms and set their design-time properties. In the next chapter, you will learn to work with the forms created in this chapter.

Chapter 10

Working with User Forms

In this chapter, you will learn to work with user forms. You created the forms for the Contacts Book application in the previous chapter. This chapter also shows you how to add code to the controls for the application and discusses user-defined status bar messages.

Working with Controls

Designing the user interface of an application is the first step in developing a project. The next step is to add code to the application, that is, link controls with procedures. The functionality of the Contacts Book application was discussed in Chapter 8, "Project Case Study: Global Systems, Inc." In order to work with controls, you need to retrieve the values of the controls and attach events and procedures to them.

You created the two forms for this application in the previous chapter. However, to be able to attach code to the form, you need to retrieve the responses of a user. You have used the `Label`, `ComboBox`, `ListBox`, and `CommandButton` controls in the application. The next section deals with displaying and retrieving values from these controls.

Displaying and Retrieving Values in a ListBox Control

To retrieve values from a list box in the Contacts Book application, you first need to display the items to a user. To display items in a `ListBox` control in the Contacts Book application, you need to initialize a user form and then add the items to be listed. To do this, you need to create a procedure in the Code window for the `ListBox` control. You can select the Code window by selecting the Code option from the View menu. Alternatively, you can right-click on the form and select the View Code option from the shortcut menu.

TIP

The simplest way of reaching the Code window is by double-clicking on the control for which you want to write the code.

If you want to display the list box to a user when the form is first displayed in the Contacts Book application, you need to add items to the list box in the `Initialize` event of the form. This is because the `Initialize` event is the first method to be called when an application is executed.

The contact details for the selected contact need to be displayed to the user in the list box (refer to Figure 9-7). The contact details are retrieved from the Contacts folder of Outlook. Therefore, the combo box items need to be added at the `User-Form`'s `Initialize` event. To add items to a list box, the `AddItem` method of the `ComboBox` control is used. The `AddItem` method is used as shown in the following code snippet:

```
lstEmpCode.AddItem "E001"
lstEmpCode.AddItem "E002"
lstEmpCode.AddItem "E003"
lstEmpCode.AddItem "E004"
```

In this code snippet, `lstEmpCode` is the name of the list box, and the string included in double quotation marks is the item to be inserted into the list box.

The `AddItem` method is specified as follows in the Contacts Book application for `cboContactList` in the `UserForm_Intilialize` event:

```
For Each oItm In oNspc.GetDefaultFolder(olFolderContacts).Items
       With Me.cboContactList
       .AddItem (oItm.FullName)
       .Column(1, x) = oItm.JobTitle
       .Column(2, x) = oItm.CompanyName
       .Column(3, x) = oItm.BusinessAddress
       .Column(4, x) = oItm.BusinessTelephoneNumber
       .Column(5, x) = oItm.Email1address


End For
```

The preceding code snippet retrieves the job title, company name, business address, business telephone number, and e-mail address of each of the contacts of the Contacts folder and displays them in the list box. Recall that the `MultiSelect` property of the `ListBox` control was set to `fmMultiSelectMulti` in Chapter 9, "Creating the User Interface of the Application," which allowed multiple selections. Therefore, the preceding code will display the job title, company name, business address, business telephone number, and e-mail address for each contact in the list box, and the user can select the details that need to be included in the Word document.

The `Value` property of the `ListBox` control is used to retrieve values from a single-select list box. The use of the `Value` property is as follows:

```
Msgbox "Your employee code is: " & lstEmpCode.Value
```

However, to retrieve values from a multiselect list box, as in the Contacts Book application, the `Value` property cannot be used. This is because the `Value` property returns a `Null` value when it is used in a multiselect list box. The `Selected` property is used to retrieve values from a multiselect list box. The `Selected` property is used to determine the selected rows in the list box, and the `List` array is used to return the contents of the selected rows.

In the Contacts Book application, the following code snippet is used to insert the contact details into a Word document:

```
Public Sub AddtoDoc(All As Boolean)
      Dim itm As Variant
            With lstFieldList
                  For x = 0 To .ListCount - 1
                       If All Then .Selected(x) = All
                           If .Selected(x) = True Then
                               With Selection
                                    .InsertAfter (lstFieldList.List(x))
                                    .Collapse (wdCollapseEnd)
                                    .Paragraphs.Add
                               End With
                           End If
                  Next x
            End With
End Sub
```

You need to display the names of the contacts in a combo box to allow a user to select a contact. The next section deals with displaying and retrieving values from a `ComboBox` control.

Displaying and Retrieving Values in a ComboBox Control

Displaying values in a `ComboBox` control is similar to displaying values in a `ListBox` control. The `ComboBox` control also has an `AddItem` method to add items to the combo box. The following code snippet adds items to the combo box at the `UserForm_Initialize` event:

```
Private Sub UserForm_Initialize
        CmbEmpName.AddItem "Mary"
        CmbEmpName.AddItem "Joseph"
        CmbEmpName.AddItem "Steve"
        CmbEmpName.AddItem "Rita"
End Sub
```

The `ComboBox` control does not allow multiple selections. Therefore, the `Value` property of the `ComboBox` control can be used to retrieve the selected value. Consider the following statement:

```
MyName = cmbEmpName.Value
```

This statement retrieves the value selected by the user.

In the Contacts Book application, the combo box should display the name of the contact retrieved from the Contacts folder in Outlook. To do this, write the following code:

```
Private Sub cboContactList_Change()
        Dim x As Integer
                With lstFieldList
                        If .ListCount > 0 Then
                                For x = 0 To .ListCount - 1
                                        .RemoveItem (0)
                                        Next x
                        End If
                    For x = 0 To cboContactList.ColumnCount - 1
                        .AddItem (Me.cboContactList.Column(x))
                         Next x
                End With
End Sub
```

The following sections discuss other important controls of the Contacts Book application.

Returning a Value from a CheckBox Control

A check box can have only two values: `True` or `False`. Therefore, the easiest way to retrieve a value from a check box is to use the `Value` property of the control with the `If…Then` construction. Consider the following example:

```
If chkReorderLevel.Value = True Then
…' Take appropriate action'
End If
```

The preceding code snippet checks the value of the check box, `chkReorderLevel`.

If the value retrieved is `True`, the appropriate action is taken. You can also add an `ElseIf` clause with the `If` construction in the code snippet that will be executed if you clear the check box.

Returning a Value from a TextBox Control

A text box is the most commonly used control for user input. To retrieve a value from a `TextBox` control, you need to check its `Value` or `Text` property after the control loses focus.

NOTE

The `Value` and `Text` properties return the same information for a `TextBox` control.

For example, to display the information entered by a user in the text box `txtName`, you need to write the following statement:

```
Msgbox txtName.text
```

At times, you may need to allow multiple lines of text in a text box. VBA supports single-line and multi-line text boxes. To create a multiline text box, set the `MultiLine` property of the text box to `True`. You can now enter multiple lines of text in the text box.

Table 10-1 summarizes the `Value` properties of controls.

Table 10-1 Value Properties of Controls

Control	Return Value
`CheckBox`	`True` if selected, `False` if cleared, and `Null` otherwise
`ComboBox`	Position of the selected item in the list, where 1 is the first item
`ListBox`	Position of the selected item in the list, where 1 is the first item
`TextBox`	Value entered in the text box

You have probably noticed system-defined status bar messages in other applications. Status bar messages are used to keep a user informed about the progress of the procedure that is being executed. However, you can also display your own status bar messages in an application. In the next section, you will learn to display messages for a user-defined status bar in the Contacts Book application.

Displaying Status Bar Messages

Status bar messages inform a user about the current state of a procedure. The `StatusBar` property is used to display text messages at the bottom of the screen. For example, the following line of code displays a message on the status bar:

```
StatusBar = "Processing..."
```

In the Contacts Book application, the `StatusBar` property is used to specify status bar messages to a user.

To retrieve a value from a `StatusBar` property, the `DisplayStatusBar` property is used. The `DisplayStatusBar` property returns `True` if the status bar is displayed and `False` otherwise.

Summary

In this chapter, you learned to work with user forms. You also learned to display and retrieve values from controls such as a text box, list box, combo box, and check box, and learned to display user-defined status bar messages to a user.

Chapter 11

Using Automation

This chapter will introduce you to the concepts of object linking and embedding and automation. It also discusses various methods that you can use to automate an application.

Using OLE for Automation

OLE, or object linking and embedding, is used to integrate and automate various applications and enable data exchange within these applications. Using OLE, you can work with application objects, properties, and methods. The OLE framework is comprised of three components: *objects*, *servers*, and *clients*.

An object can be defined as an instance of a class within a server that exposes properties and methods. A server application makes its objects available to other applications and development tools that support automation, such as VBA. For example, MS Word as a server exposes objects such as `Application`, `Document`, or `Paragraph`. Similarly, MS Outlook as a server exposes objects such as `Application`, `ContactItem`, `TaskItem`, and `AppointmentItem`. On the other hand, a client application uses VBA to access and control these objects exposed by the server application by invoking methods of the objects or changing the object's properties.

The Component Object Model (COM) is the backbone of OLE. COM defines how the server and client applications interact with each other. The server and client applications communicate with each other using *interfaces*, which are simply a set of related functions. These interfaces help manage the data exchange between server and client applications.

Automation is a feature of COM. You can use automation to work with application objects by applying various methods to the objects or modifying the object properties. Automation enables you to access the objects, methods, properties, and events of one application from another application. Microsoft Office applications, such as Word, Outlook, and Excel, support automation.

In the Contacts Book application, the Outlook application is controlled from the Word application. To work with automation, a reference has to be set to the other application's object library. In addition, you must create an instance of the application. The following section describes the procedure for referencing object libraries and the concepts of early and late binding.

Referencing Object Libraries

You can access information about the various objects available in an application by using the application's *object library*. This object library consists of information about objects, methods, and properties available for automation. Although you can write a program without manually specifying a reference to the other application's object library, it is a good practice to add a reference. By doing this, the code runs faster, and all the applications objects, methods, and properties are available using the IntelliSense feature of VBA.

Consider a situation in which you might need to access the objects available in Outlook from within Word. To do this, you can either declare a variable as `Outlook.Application` or declare the variable as an `Object` in your code. Because the `Object` data type specifies any `Object` reference, the code containing the variable as an `Object` will run more slowly than the code containing the variable as `Outlook.Application`.

Early Binding versus Late Binding

Applications that support automation are known as *automation controllers* and *automation servers*. Automation controllers are applications that work with the automation server's objects. All Microsoft Office applications can act as both automation servers and automation controllers. *Binding* is the method by which COM links automation servers and automation controllers. During binding, an object variable is connected to the `Automation` object on the automation server.

To start an automation session, you can use either *early* binding or *late* binding. The following section discusses each type of binding and the associated methods.

Early Binding

In early binding, the binding between objects and variables occurs at the time of compilation. To ensure early binding, you need to specify a reference to the automation server's object library in the current VBA project. Here, the object variable is connected to the `Automation` object on the automation server.

You can specify the reference to the automation server's object library by using the Tools menu in the Visual Basic Editor window. To specify a reference for an object library, you need to select the References option from the Tools menu. The References dialog box is displayed as shown in Figure 11-1.

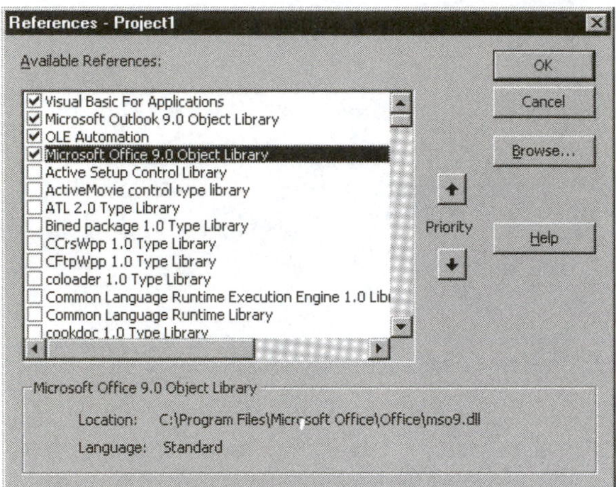

FIGURE 11-1 *The References dialog box displaying the available references*

In the References dialog box, you can select the application's object library that you need in your current VBA project. However, you must ensure that you do not add references to object libraries that are not used by the program. This is to minimize the time required to compile the project.

After you add a reference to an object library, you can initialize the application. In this example, early binding has been used to initialize the Outlook application.

```
Set myApp = New Outlook.Application
```

NOTE

A reference to an application's object library is available in a program even after you distribute the program.

To implement early binding, you use the `New` keyword.

The New Keyword

To access automation objects by using early binding, you need to use the `New` keyword within the `Dim` statement. You can use the `New` keyword with the `Dim` statement to declare an object variable of a specific type. When you use the `New` keyword, VBA creates the object implicitly. Therefore, an instance of the object is created, and you do not need to use the `Set` statement to create an instance of the object.

The syntax for the `Dim` statement with the `New` keyword is as follows:

```
Dim varName As New Application.ObjectType
```

In this syntax, `varName` is the name of the object variable, and `Application.ObjectType` specifies the `Automation` object. Here, `Application` is the name of the application, such as Word, Outlook, or Excel, and `ObjectType` is the object class type.

Following is an example of the `New` keyword with the `Dim` statement:

```
Dim myOLApp As New Outlook.Application
```

Although the `New` keyword results in early binding, when you use the `New` keyword, an object is created before it is actually used. Therefore, many programmers prefer to use late binding.

Late Binding

In late binding, the binding between objects and variables occurs when the application is executed. Therefore, object variables are not connected to the `Automation` object on the automation server until the application is executed. This causes the program to run slowly, because VBA has to resolve all object references. In the following example, the variable `myobj` is declared as an `Object` and is used to create an instance of the Outlook application:

```
Dim myobj as Object
        Set myobj = CreateObject("Outlook.Application")
```

To implement late binding, you can use the `CreateObject` method or the `GetObject` method. The following section describes these automation objects in detail.

The CreateObject Method

At times, you may need to create an instance of an application if it is not already opened. You may also need to use a new instance of the application. To do this, you can use the `CreateObject` method. The `CreateObject` method creates an object explicitly. The syntax for the `CreateObject` method is as follows:

```
objApplication.CreateObject(ObjectName)
```

In this syntax, `objApplication` represents the `Application` object. The `ObjectName` argument specifies the class name of the object that you need to create such as `Application`, `Document`, or `Workbook`.

When you use the `CreateObject` method, you need to use the `Set` keyword to create a new instance of the specified `Automation` object.

Consider an example in which `OutApp` is an object variable. To create a new instance of Outlook's `Application` object, you need to specify the following code:

```
Set OutApp = CreateObject("Outlook.Application")
```

If a variable is declared as an `Object`, late binding is used. For example, consider the following statements:

```
Dim OutApp as Object
Ser OutApp = CreateObject("Outlook.Application")
```

However, if the variable is declared as a specific type of class, then early binding is used. For example, consider the following statements:

```
Dim OutApp as Outlook.Application
Set OutApp = CreateObject("Outlook.Application")
```

In the Contacts Book application, you will use the `CreateObject` method to create an instance of Outlook from Word.

The GetObject Method

Sometimes, an application might already be open, and you may not need to create a new instance of the application. In such situations, it is better to use the `GetObject` method and work with the current instance of the application. The syntax for the `GetObject` method is as follows:

```
GetObject(PathName, Class)
```

In this syntax, `PathName` refers to the name of the file that you need to work with, such as a drive, folder, or file name. The `Class` argument is used to specify the class of the object that you need to access. The syntax for the `Class` argument is as follows:

```
AppName.ObjectType
```

In this syntax, `AppName` specifies the name of the application whose object you need to access, and `ObjectType` specifies the type of object that you need to create.

The following code illustrates the use of the `GetObject` method. The `GetObject` method has been used to work with an instance of Word and open an existing document.

```
Sub OpenDoc()
Dim mydoc As Word.Document
Set mydoc = GetObject("C:\test.doc", "Word.Document")
mydoc.Application.Visible = True
With mydoc
.Paragraphs(1).Range.InsertBefore "This is an example of the GetObject method."
End With
Set mydoc = Nothing
End Sub
```

If you refer to an application object that is not currently running, an automation error is generated by VBA. Therefore, your code should incorporate error-handling procedures. These procedures check whether the application is already running. If this is the case, the `GetObject` method is used to work with its instance. In contrast, if the application is not running, the `CreateObject` method is used to create a new instance of the application.

The following code illustrates the use of such error-handling procedures. Here, the procedure checks whether the Word application is already running. If the application is running, the `GetObject` method is used to create a reference to Word's `Application` object. If the application is not running, the `CreateObject` method is used to create an instance of Word's `Application` object.

```
Sub OpenDocument()
    On Error GoTo OpenWord
    Dim WdApp As Word.Application
    ' Create a reference to the existing Word Application object
    Set WdApp = GetObject(, "Word.Application")
    With WdApp
        ' Display Word
        .Visible = True
    End With
    Set WdApp = Nothing
```

```
'If Word is not already running then a new instance is created
OpenWord:
    ' Create a new instance of Word's Application object
     Set WdApp = CreateObject("Word.Application")
    Resume Next
End Sub
```

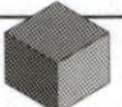

NOTE

When you use the `GetObject` method, the `Visible` property, by default, is set to True. However, when you use the `CreateObject` method, the `Visible` property is set to False.

Summary

This chapter introduced you to the concepts of OLE and automation. You also learned about early and late binding and the procedure for adding references to object libraries. With this information, you can now automate the Contacts Book application and add functionality to the application.

Chapter 12

Adding Functionality to the Contacts Book Application

In this chapter, you will add functionality to the Contacts Book application by using Outlook VBA programming. The discussion starts by describing the logic of the Contacts Book application, and then the Outlook object model. Finally, you will learn how to implement the Outlook object model in the Contacts Book application to automate the application.

Understanding the Logic of the Contacts Book Application

As discussed in Chapter 8, "Project Case Study: Global Systems, Inc.," the Contacts Book application consists of two screens. The Outlook Contacts screen is the main screen. Using this screen, a user can view contact details, add the details to a Word document, and print mailing labels. In addition, the user can click on the Modify button and view the Modify Contacts screen. In the Modify Contacts screen, the user can add contacts, modify the details of existing contacts, and delete contacts. An event is attached to every control on the two screens. Each event further calls specific procedures. These procedures are related to the functionality of the Outlook application. Figure 12-1 illustrates the procedures associated with the different functions on the screens of the Contacts Book application.

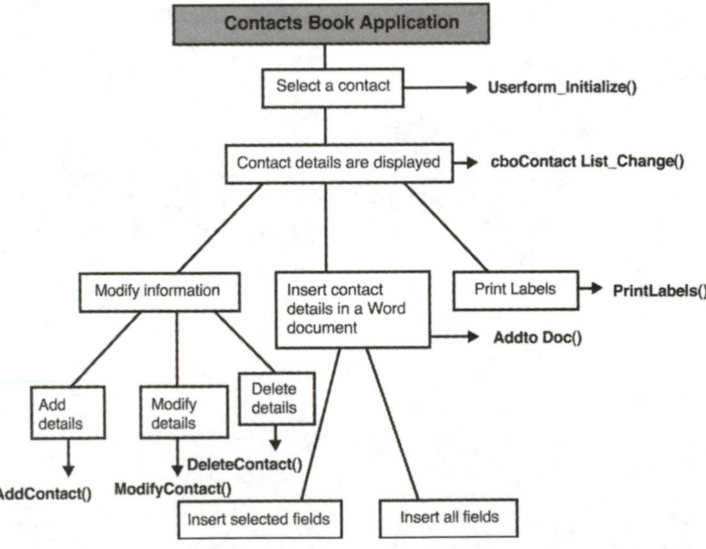

FIGURE 12-1 *Different procedures associated with the Contacts Book application*

To write these procedures and automate the Contacts Book application, you first need to understand the Outlook object model. The following section briefly describes the model and some important methods and properties.

Introduction to the Outlook Object Model

As you learned in Chapter 6, "Objects in VBA," an object model represents the hierarchy in which an application's objects are arranged. The following sections discuss the Outlook object model and the procedure to automate the model.

You can use the Outlook object model to manipulate the data stored in Outlook folders. You can programmatically control the Outlook bar and work with selected items in folders. By using the model, you can control item-level and application-level windows. Although the Outlook object model is huge and consists of approximately 60 objects and multiple methods, properties, and events, it offers less functionality than the Word or Excel object models. The Outlook object model emphasizes items and the folders in which items are stored.

You can use the Outlook object model to customize Outlook as per your requirements. The main components of the model are as follows:

- `Application`
- `NameSpace`
- `Folder`
- `Items`
- `Explorer`
- `Inspector`

In the Outlook object model, the `Application` object consists of the `NameSpace` object. The `NameSpace` object contains the `Folder` object, which in turn contains `MAPIFolder` objects. These `MAPIFolder` objects represent all the available folders in a given data source, such as a MAPI (*Messaging Application Programming Interface*) message store. A MAPI message store represents the data stored in a personal folder (.pst) in Outlook. MAPI message stores are the only data sources currently supported by Outlook.

The `MAPIFolder` objects contain objects that represent all the Outlook items in the data source. Each Outlook item consists of programmable objects that enable you to control that item. In addition, there is an `Explorer` object associated with each folder and an `Inspector` object associated with each item, as illustrated in Figure 12-2.

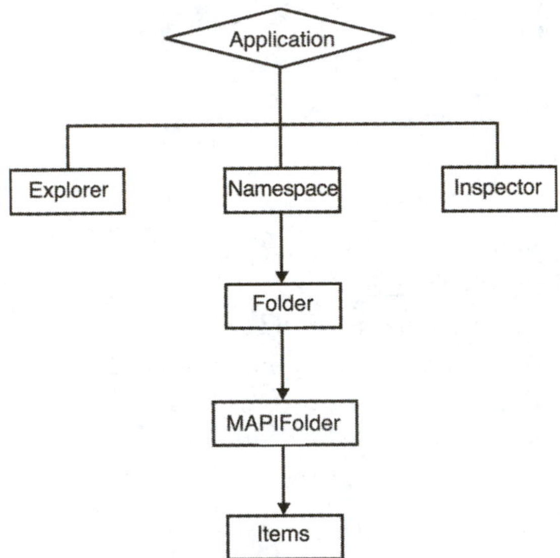

FIGURE 12-2 *The main components of the Outlook object model*

The following sections describe the various components of the Outlook object model in detail.

The Application Object

The `Application` object represents the Outlook application. It is the root object of the Outlook object model. You can use the `Application` object to gain access to all other objects in the object model. You can also create new items and objects by using the `Application` object. You can directly create new items without going through the entire object hierarchy. For example, the following code creates an Outlook mail item in VBA:

```
Application.CreateItem(olMailItem).Display
```

You can also use the `Application` object to refer to other objects that represent the Outlook interface, such as the `Explorer` and `Inspector` objects. You will learn about the Explorer and Inspector objects later in this chapter. As you learned in Chapter 11, "Using Automation," you can return an Application object in any other application by using the CreateObject method or the GetObject method.

The NameSpace Object

The NameSpace object is the root object for a data source. It represents any recognized data source, such as a MAPI message store. You can use the NameSpace object to log on and log off the data source, return default folders such as Inbox and Contacts, and access the data sources owned by other users. You can return MAPI message stores by using the GetNameSpace("MAPI") expression.

The following example depicts the use of the NameSpace object and the GetNameSpace("MAPI") expression to gain access to the Contacts folder in Outlook:

```
Set myOlApp = CreateObject("Outlook.Application")
Set myNameSpace = myOlApp.GetNameSpace("MAPI")
Set myFolder = myNameSpace.GetDefaultFolder(olFolderContacts)
```

The Folder Objects

The Outlook object model contains two types of Folder objects: Folders Collection and MAPIFolder. You can use the Folders Collection object to work with a collection of folders. The Folders Collection object contains all the MAPIFolder objects in the specified message store. You can use the MAPIFolder object to work with a specific folder, such as a personal folder.

The Folders Collection Object

As the name suggests, the Folders Collection object is a collection of folders. The Folders Collection object represents folders in a specified hierarchy. You can specify multiple levels of folders. Each folder contains various Outlook items and other MAPI folders. You can use various events, properties, and methods to manipulate and navigate the various items and folders. You can refer to the Folders Collection object by using any one of the following:

- GetDefaultFolder method
- PickFolder method
- Folder property of the NameSpace object

The following sections take a closer look at each of these.

The GetDefaultFolder Method

The `GetDefaultFolder` method returns the default folder for the specified type. The syntax for the `GetDefaultFolder` method is

```
NameSpace.GetDefaultFolder (FolderTypeEnum)
```

where `NameSpace` is the `NameSpace` object. `FolderType` specifies the type of folder. For the `FolderType` argument, you can specify values, such as `olFolderCalendar`, `olFolderContacts`, and `olFolderInbox`.

Consider the following example. Here, the `GetDefaultFolder` method is used to return the Calendar folder in Outlook:

```
Set myOlApp = CreateObject("Outlook.Application")
Set myNameSpace = myOlApp.GetNameSpace("MAPI") Set myOlApp.ActiveExplorer.CurrentFolder
  = myNameSpace.GetDefaultFolder(olFolderCalendar)
```

The PickFolder Method

In addition to using the `GetDefaultFolder` method, you can use the `PickFolder` method of the `NameSpace` object. The syntax for the `PickFolder` method is

```
NameSpace.PickFolder
```

where `NameSpace` is the `NameSpace` object.

When you use the `PickFolder` method, the Select Folder dialog box is displayed. A user can specify a folder in this dialog box and proceed. If the user clicks on the OK button in the Select Folder dialog box, the `MAPIFolder` object corresponding to the selected folder is returned. If the user does not select a folder, the return value is `Nothing`.

The Folder Property

In addition to using the `GetDefaultFolder` or `PickFolder` methods, you can use the `Folder` property of the `NameSpace` object to refer to the `Folders Collection` object. You can use the `Folder` property to return the `Folders Collection` object from a `NameSpace` object or another `MAPIFolder` object. If you need to return a single `MAPIFolder` object, you can use `Folders(`*`index`*`)`, where *`index`* is the index number of the folder or the folder name.

Consider an example. The following code returns a folder named `Client Contacts` from a folder called `ClientFolder`:

```
Set OlApp = CreateObject("Outlook.Application")
Set NameSpace = OlApp.GetNameSpace("MAPI")
Set ClientFolder = NameSpace.GetDefaultFolder(olFolderContacts)
Set NewFolder = ClientFolder.Folders("Client Contacts")
```

The MAPIFolder Object

The `MAPIFolder` object represents an Outlook folder. The `MAPIFolder` object can include folders and other `MAPIFolder` objects.

You can refer to a MAPI folder by using any one of the following methods:

- `GetDefaultFolder` method
- `GetFolderFromID` method
- `GetSharedDefaultFolder` method of the `NameSpace` object

You learned about the `GetDefaultFolder` method in the `Application` object. The next section describes the `GetFolderFromID` method and the `GetSharedDefaultFolder` method.

The GetFolderFromID Method

Each Outlook item, such as a message or a contact, has a unique ID field. This field is known as `EntryID`. The `EntryID` field is generated by the messaging storage system such that the item can be used with the MAPI folder that stores the item. Similar to `EntryID`, the MAPI folder has a unique ID field known as `StoreID`.

When you use the `GetFolderFromID` method, you need to specify the `EntryID` of the item and the `StoreID` of the MAPI folder to retrieve the specific MAPI folder.

The syntax for the `GetFolderFromID` method is

```
NameSpace .GetFolderFromID(EntryIDFolder, [StoreID])
```

where `NameSpace` refers to the `NameSpace` object. The `EntryIDFolder` and `StoreID` arguments are used to specify the `EntryID` of the item and the `StoreID` of the MAPI folder, respectively.

The `GetFolderFromID` method is typically used in complex situations in which both `EntryID` and `StoreID` need to be referenced quickly.

The GetSharedDefaultFolder Method

The `GetSharedDefaultFolder` method is used to retrieve the specified default folder of a particular user. The syntax for the `GetSharedDefaultFolder` method is

```
NameSpace.GetSharedDefaultFolder(RecipientObject, FolderTypeEnum)
```

where `NameSpace` refers to the `NameSpace` object. The `RecipientObject` argument is used to specify the owner of the folder. The `FolderTypeEnum` argument is used to specify the type of folder, such as `olFolderCalendar`, `olFolderContacts`, or `olFolderJournal`.

The MAPIFolder Object Properties

Some of the important `MAPIFolder` object properties and their descriptions are listed in the Table 12-1.

Table 12-1 The MAPIFolder Object Properties

Properties	Descriptions
`Application`	Returns an application object that represents Outlook for an object.
`Class`	Returns the constant that represents the object's class, such as `olContact`, `olApplication`, or `olFolder`.
`DefaultItemType`	Returns the default type of item stored in a folder. The different types of items are `OlItemType` constants, such as `olAppointmentItem(1)`, `olContactItem(2)`, `olJournalItem(4)`, `olMailItem(0)`, `olNoteItem(5)`, `olPostItem(6)`, and `olTaskItem(3)`.
`Folders`	Returns the collection of folders that represents all folders stored in a specific folder or namespace.
`Items`	Returns the collection of items in a specific folder.
`Name`	Returns the name of a specific item.

The MAPIFolder Object Methods

You can use various methods of the `MAPIFolder` object to manipulate folders and items.

The `MAPIFolder` object methods and their description are listed in Table 12-2.

Table 12-2 The MAPIFolder Object Methods

Methods	Description
`CopyTo`	Copies a specific folder to the destination folder. Returns a `MAPIFolder` object that represents the copy of the folder.
`Delete`	Deletes a specific folder.
`Display`	Displays a window representing the contents of a specific folder or a specific item.
`GetExplorer`	Returns a window initialized with a specific folder as the current folder.
`MoveTo`	Moves a specific folder to the destination folder.

Outlook Items

In addition to the `Application`, `NameSpace`, and `Folders` objects, the Outlook object model also consists of Outlook items. Just like folder objects, there are two item objects, the `Items Collection` and `Item`. You can use the `Items Collection` object to work with items present within a folder. You can use the `Item` object to manipulate objects that represent standard item types in Outlook, such as `AppointmentItem`, which represents an appointment, or `MailItem`, which represents a mail message.

Types of Items

The `Items Collection` object consists of different objects depending on the type of folder that you have specified. You can work with Outlook items, such as `AppointmentItem`, `ContactItem`, `JournalItem`, `MailItem`, `MeetingRequestItem`, `NoteItem`, and `PostItem`.

Some of the important Outlook items, their default properties, and a brief description are listed in Table 12-3.

Table 12-3 Outlook Items

Item	Default Property	Description
`AppointmentItem`	Subject	Represents an appointment in a Calendar folder.
`ContactItem`	FullName	Represents a contact in a Contacts folder.
`JournalItem`	Subject	Represents a journal entry in a Journals folder.
`MailItem`	Subject	Represents a mail message in an Inbox folder, which can be any mail folder.
`NoteItem`	Subject	Represents a note in a Notes folder.
`TaskItem`	Subject	Represents a task in a Tasks folder.

To return an item, you can use `Items (index)`, where `index` is either an integer with the first item in a folder specified as `1` or a property of the Outlook item.

Outlook items are objects that you can create. To create these objects, you need to use the `Application` object's `CreateItem` method. The next section discusses the `CreateItem` method.

The CreateItem Method

You can use the `CreateItem` method to create a new default Outlook item. The syntax for the `CreateItem` method is

```
Application.CreateItem(ItemType)
```

where `Application` is the `Application` object and `ItemType` is a constant that specifies the type of Outlook item that you need to create, such as `olAppointmentItem(1)`, `olContactItem(2)`, `olJournalItem(4)`, `olMailItem(0)`, `olNoteItem(5)`, `olPostItem(6)`, or `olTaskItem(3)`.

In the following example, a new appointment item is created and displayed using the `CreateItem` method:

```
Set myOlApp = CreateObject("Outlook.Application")
Set myNameSpace = myOlApp.GetNameSpace("MAPI")
Set myFolder = myNameSpace.GetDefaultFolder(olAppointmentItem)
Set myItem = myOlApp.CreateItem(olAppointmentItem)
myItem.Display
```

The Explorer Object

The Outlook object model also includes the `Explorer` object. The `Explorer` object represents an Outlook window used to display the contents of a folder. To return an `Explorer` object, you can use the `ActiveExplorer` method of the `Application` object or the `GetExplorer` method of the `MAPIFolder` object.

The ActiveExplorer Method

The `ActiveExplorer` method returns the topmost `Explorer` object. This method returns the active `Explorer` object with which a user is currently working. If the user is not working with any `Explorer` object, the `ActiveExplorer` method returns `Nothing`.

The syntax for the `ActiveExplorer` method is

```
Application.ActiveExplorer
```

where `Application` is the `Application` object.

The GetExplorer Method

The `GetExplorer` method of the `MAPIFolder` object returns an `Explorer` object that represents a new inactive window for the specified `MAPIFolder` object. You can use the `GetExplorer` method to return a new `Explorer` object and display the contents of a folder.

The syntax for the `GetExplorer` method is

```
MAPIFolder.GetExplorer([DisplayMode])
```

where `MAPIFolder` is the `MAPIFolder` object and `DisplayMode` is an optional argument to specify a constant representing the format for displaying the folder. You can specify values representing the format for displaying the folder, such as `olFolderDisplayNormal(0)`, `olFolderDisplayFolderOnly(1)`, or `olFolderDisplayNoNavigation(2)`.

When you specify the `olFolderDisplayNormal` display mode, the new `Explorer` object is displayed with all the components of the Outlook interface, such as the Outlook bar, the folder list, and navigation commands to move to other folders in that `Explorer` object. In the `olFolderDisplayFolderOnly` display mode, the `Explorer` object is displayed with no Outlook bar or folder list. However, the navigation to other folders is available. In the `olFolderDisplayNoNavigation` display mode, the Explorer object is displayed with no Outlook bar or folder list, and the navigation to other folders in that Explorer object is not available. By default, the Explorer object's display mode is the olFolderDisplayNormal type.

After you create a new Explorer object by using the GetExplorer method, you need to use the object's Display method to make the Explorer object visible.

The Inspector Object

Just as the Explorer object is used to display the contents of a folder, you can use the Inspector object in the Outlook object model to display the contents of an Outlook item. The Inspector object represents the window in which the contents of an Outlook item are displayed. For example, when you open an Outlook item, such as a contact or a task, the window in which the item is displayed is the Inspector object.

Similar to the Explorer object, you can return an Inspector object by using either the ActiveInspector method of the Application object or the GetInspector method of the Item object.

The ActiveInspector Method

The ActiveInspector method returns the topmost Inspector object. This method returns the active Inspector object with which a user is currently working. If the user is not working with any Inspector object, the ActiveInspector method returns Nothing.

The syntax for the ActiveInspector method is

```
Application. ActiveInspector
```

where Application is the Application object.

The GetInspector Method

The GetInspector method of the Item object returns an Inspector object that represents a new inactive window for the specified Outlook item. You can use the GetInspector method to return a new Inspector object to display the contents of an item.

The syntax for the `GetInspector` method is

```
Item.GetInspector
```

where `Item` is the Outlook `Item` object.

NOTE

After you create a new `Inspector` object, you need to make the new item visible by using the `Display` method.

Now that you have learned about the Outlook object model, you will take a look at how to implement the Outlook object model in the Contacts Book application.

Automating the Contacts Book Application

Listing 12-1 contains the complete code for the Contacts Book application. The code for the Contacts Book application is available at `www.Premierpressbooks.com/downloads.asp`. The following sections briefly describe various procedures used in the Contacts Book application.

Listing 12-1 The Contacts Book Application Code

```
'The code for the frmOutlookAddress user form
Private Sub cmdClose_Click()
Unload Me
End Sub

Private Sub cmdInsertAll_Click()
Call AddtoDoc(True)
End Sub

Private Sub cmdInsertSelected_Click()
Call AddtoDoc(False)
End Sub
```

```
Private Sub cmdModify_Click()
Unload Me
frmModifyContacts.Show
End Sub

'This procedure is used to initialize the Outlook Application
Private Sub UserForm_Initialize()
        Dim oApp As Outlook.Application
        Dim oNspc As NameSpace
        Dim oItm As ContactItem
        Dim x As Integer
        If Not DisplayStatusBar Then
        DisplayStatusBar = True
        End If
        StatusBar = "Please Wait..."
        x = 0

        'Create an instance of outlook
        'Reference its MAPI Interface
        'Reference MAPI's Contact Folder

        Set oApp = CreateObject("Outlook.Application")
        Set oNspc = oApp.GetNamespace("MAPI")

        'For each item in the Contacts folder
        'display specific information.
        'You can specify one or more fields of information
        'to be displayed.

        For Each oItm In oNspc.GetDefaultFolder(olFolderContacts).Items
        With Me.cboContactList
        .AddItem (oItm.FullName)
        .Column(1, x) = oItm.JobTitle
        .Column(2, x) = oItm.CompanyName
        .Column(3, x) = oItm.BusinessAddress
        .Column(4, x) = oItm.BusinessTelephoneNumber
        .Column(5, x) = oItm.Email1address
```

```
        End With
        x = x + 1
        Next oItm
        StatusBar = "Adding Contact Details..."
        Set oItm = Nothing
        Set oNspc = Nothing
        Set oApp = Nothing
End Sub
'This procedure is used to display specific information of
'the selected contact item in the combo box.

Private Sub cboContactList_Change()
        Dim x As Integer
        With lstFieldList
        If .ListCount > 0 Then
        For x = 0 To .ListCount - 1
        .RemoveItem (0)
        Next x
        End If
        For x = 0 To cboContactList.ColumnCount - 1
        .AddItem (Me.cboContactList.Column(x))
        Next x
        End With
End Sub

'This procedure is used to insert the selected
'fields into a word document at the current cursor position.

Public Sub AddtoDoc(All As Boolean)
        Dim itm As Variant
        With lstFieldList
        For x = 0 To .ListCount - 1
        If All Then .Selected(x) = All
        If .Selected(x) = True Then
        With Selection
        .InsertAfter (lstFieldList.List(x))
        .Collapse (wdCollapseEnd)
        .Paragraphs.Add
```

```
        End With
        End If
        Next x
        End With
End Sub

Private Sub cmdPrintLabels_Click()
Dim Msg, Style, Title, Help, Ctxt, Response, MyString
Msg = "The labels will be printed in a new Word document. Do you need to print mailing
   labels for the contacts?" ' The message displayed in the message box
Style = vbYesNo + vbDefaultButton1 + vbQuestion 'The buttons displayed in the message
   box
Title = "Print Labels"     ' The title of the message box.
         ' Display message.
Response = MsgBox(Msg, Style, Title, Help, Ctxt)
If Response = vbYes Then     ' If the user selects yes, then print labels
    Call PrintLabels
End If
End Sub

'This procedure is used to print the contact information
'in a new word document as labels.

Sub PrintLabels()

    On Error GoTo ErrorHandler

   Dim oApp As New Outlook.Application
   Dim oNspc As Outlook.NameSpace
   Dim fld As Outlook.MAPIFolder
   Dim itms As Outlook.Items
   Dim oItm As Outlook.ContactItem

   Set oNspc = oApp.GetNamespace("MAPI")

SelectContactFolder:
   Set fld = oNspc.PickFolder
   Debug.Print "Default item type: " & fld.DefaultItemType
```

```
    If fld.DefaultItemType <> olContactItem Then
      MsgBox "Please select a Contacts folder.", vbExclamation, "Select Contacts"
      GoTo SelectContactFolder
   End If

     Dim appWord As New Word.Application
     Dim docWord As New Word.Document
     docWord.Activate


     Set itms = fld.Items
     For Each oItm In itms
         With Selection
         'the labels are printed in blue color in the bold format
            Selection.Font.Color = wdColorBlue
            Selection.Font.Bold = True
            .TypeParagraph
            .TypeText Text:="----------------------------------"
            .TypeParagraph
            .TypeText Text:=oItm.FullName
            .TypeParagraph
            .TypeText Text:=oItm.JobTitle
            .TypeParagraph
            .TypeText Text:=oItm.CompanyName
            .TypeParagraph
            .TypeText Text:=oItm.BusinessAddress
            .TypeParagraph
            .TypeText Text:=oItm.BusinessTelephoneNumber
            .TypeParagraph
            .TypeText Text:="----------------------------------"
             End With
      Next

ErrorHandlerExit:
   Exit Sub

ErrorHandler:
   MsgBox "Error No: " & Err.Number & "; Description: " & Err.Description,
```

```
vbExclamation, "Print Labels"
   Resume ErrorHandlerExit

   frmOutlookAddress.Show

End Sub

'The code for the frmModifyContacts user form.

Private Sub cmdClose_Click()
Unload Me
frmOutlookAddress.Show
End Sub

Private Sub UserForm_Initialize()
      Dim oApp As Outlook.Application
      Dim oNspc As NameSpace
      Dim oItm As ContactItem
      Dim x As Integer
      If Not DisplayStatusBar Then
      DisplayStatusBar = True
      End If
      StatusBar = "Please Wait..."
      x = 0

      'Create an instance of outlook
      'Reference its MAPI Interface
      'Reference MAPI's Contact Folder

      Set oApp = CreateObject("Outlook.Application")
      Set oNspc = oApp.GetNamespace("MAPI")

      'For each item in the Contacts folder
      'display specific information.

      For Each oItm In oNspc.GetDefaultFolder(olFolderContacts).Items
      With Me.cboContactList
      .AddItem (oItm.FullName)
```

```
        .Column(1, x) = oItm.JobTitle
        .Column(2, x) = oItm.CompanyName
        .Column(3, x) = oItm.BusinessAddress
        .Column(4, x) = oItm.BusinessTelephoneNumber
        .Column(5, x) = oItm.Email1address

        End With
        x = x + 1
        Next oItm
        StatusBar = "Adding Contact Details..."
        Set oItm = Nothing
        Set oNspc = Nothing
        Set oApp = Nothing
End Sub

Private Sub cmdModify_Click()
Call ModifyContact
Call Refresh
End Sub

'This procedure is used to open the Outlook Contact form of an
'existing contact such that it can be modified.

Sub ModifyContact()
strFullName = cboContactList.Text

Dim oApp As Outlook.Application
Dim oNspc As NameSpace
Dim itms As Items
Dim oItm As ContactItem

'Create an instance of outlook
'Reference its MAPI Interface
'Reference MAPI's Contact Folder

    Set oApp = CreateObject("Outlook.Application")
    Set oNspc = oApp.GetNamespace("MAPI")
    Set itms = _
```

```
        oNspc.GetDefaultFolder(olFolderContacts).Items

        'Search for the items that need to be modified.

        For Each oItm In itms
            If oItm.FullName = strFullName Then
                oItm.Display
             MsgBox "The contact item has been modified.", vbInformation, "Modify
                Contacts"
             Exit Sub
             End If
          Next
           'If no entry found for the specific contact
          MsgBox "Please select a contact.", vbExclamation, "Modify Contacts"
End Sub

Private Sub cmdDelete_Click()
Call DeleteContact
Call Refresh
End Sub

'This procedure is used to refresh the combo box contents
'after a contact has been deleted/modified/added.

Sub Refresh()
      cboContactList.Clear
      x = 0
      Set oApp = CreateObject("Outlook.Application")
      Set oNspc = oApp.GetNamespace("MAPI")
   For Each oItm In oNspc.GetDefaultFolder(olFolderContacts).Items
      With Me.cboContactList
      .AddItem (oItm.FullName)
      End With
      x = x + 1
      Next oItm
      Set oItm = Nothing
      Set oNspc = Nothing
      Set oApp = Nothing
```

```
End Sub

'This procedure is used to delete a specific Outlook Contact item.

Sub DeleteContact()
strFullName = cboContactList.Text

Dim oApp As Outlook.Application
Dim oNspc As NameSpace
Dim itms As Items
Dim oItm As ContactItem

'Create an instance of outlook
'Reference its MAPI Interface
'Reference MAPI's Contact Folder

    Set oApp = CreateObject("Outlook.Application")
    Set oNspc = oApp.GetNamespace("MAPI")
    Set itms = _
    oNspc.GetDefaultFolder(olFolderContacts).Items

  'Search for the items that need to be deleted.

    For Each oItm In itms
        If oItm.FullName = strFullName Then
            oItm.Delete
         MsgBox "The contact item has been deleted!", vbInformation, "Modify Contacts"
            Exit Sub
         End If
      Next
      'If no entry found for the specific contact
      MsgBox "Please select a contact.", vbExclamation, "Modify Contacts"

End Sub

Private Sub cmdAdd_Click()
Call AddContact
```

```
Call Refresh
End Sub

'This procedure is used to start a new Outlook Contact item form
'after a user clicks the Add New Contact button to add contacts.

Public Sub AddContact()
        On Error GoTo AddContact_Error
        Dim spObj As Object, oItm As Object

        ' Create an instance of OutLook object
        Set spObj = CreateObject("Outlook.Application")

        ' Create and display a new contact form
        Set oItm = spObj.CreateItem(olContactItem)
         oItm.Display

        ' Quit Outlook.
         Set spObj = Nothing
         MsgBox "The contact item has been added.", vbInformation, "Modify Contacts"
         Exit Sub

AddContact_Error:
        MsgBox "Error: " & Err & " " & Error, vbExclamation, "Add Contact"
        Exit Sub
End Sub

'The code for Module1

Sub ShowContacts()
frmOutlookAddress.Show
End Sub
```

The UserForm_Initialize Procedure

Listing 12-2 contains the code for the `UserForm_Initialize` procedure. This section discusses the code for the procedure and analyzes the code step-by-step.

Listing 12-2 The UserForm_Initialize Procedure

```
'This procedure is used to initialize the Outlook Application

Private Sub UserForm_Initialize()
    Dim oApp As Outlook.Application
    Dim oNspc As NameSpace
    Dim oItm As ContactItem
    Dim x As Integer
    If Not DisplayStatusBar Then
    DisplayStatusBar = True
    End If
    StatusBar = "Please Wait..."
    x = 0

    'Create an instance of outlook
    'Reference its MAPI Interface
    'Reference MAPI's Contact Folder

    Set oApp = CreateObject("Outlook.Application")
    Set oNspc = oApp.GetNamespace("MAPI")

    'For each item in the Contacts folder
    'display specific information.
    'You can specify one or more fields of information
    'to be displayed.

    For Each oItm In oNspc.GetDefaultFolder(olFolderContacts).Items
    With Me.cboContactList
    .AddItem (oItm.FullName)
    .Column(1, x) = oItm.JobTitle
    .Column(2, x) = oItm.CompanyName
    .Column(3, x) = oItm.BusinessAddress
```

```
            .Column(4, x) = oItm.BusinessTelephoneNumber
            .Column(5, x) = oItm.Email1address

        End With
        x = x + 1
        Next oItm
        StatusBar = "Adding Contact Details..."
        Set oItm = Nothing
        Set oNspc = Nothing
        Set oApp = Nothing
End Sub
```

The `UserForm_Initialize` procedure allows a user to work with the Contacts folder in Outlook. In this procedure, three variables are declared: `oApp`, `oNspc`, and `oItm`. The `oApp` variable represents the Outlook `Application` object, and the `oNspc` variable represents the `NameSpace` object. To list the collection of items in the Contacts folder, the `oItm` variable is used.

First, you need to establish a reference to an instance of Outlook in Word. Then, you need to create a new instance of Outlook. Here, the `CreateObject` function is used to create a new instance of Outlook. Then, the `GetNameSpace` method is applied to the `Application` object such that a reference can be made to a particular folder in Outlook. By using the `GetNameSpace` method, you can refer to the MAPI interface of the Outlook application. After a reference to the MAPI interface is established, the procedure refers to each item in the Contacts folder in Outlook by using the `GetDefaultFolder` method. The `GetDefaultFolder` method is applied to the `NameSpace` object with `olFolderContacts` as the argument such that the Contacts folder is returned.

After the Contacts folder is returned, specific information about the contact items is added to a combo box in the user form of the Contacts Book application. To do this, the `Items` property is used. In the case of the Contacts Book application, you need to display information including full name, job title, company name, business address, business telephone number, and the e-mail address of each contact item. However, you can specify other types of information for a Contact item object, such as birthday, gender, hobby, home address, mailing address, and mobile telephone number.

To list the details of each contact item, the code uses the `For...Each` loop. To display specific information about each contact item in the Contacts folder, the `AddItem` method of the combo box is used to add the details of each contact in separate columns. This creates a new Outlook item for each contact in the items collection for the folder.

When the `UserForm_Initialize` procedure is run, the `cboContactList` combo box in the `frmOutlookAddress` form is filled with items from the Contacts folder. Figure 12-3 displays the Contacts Book application with the `cboContactList` combo box filled with details of contacts.

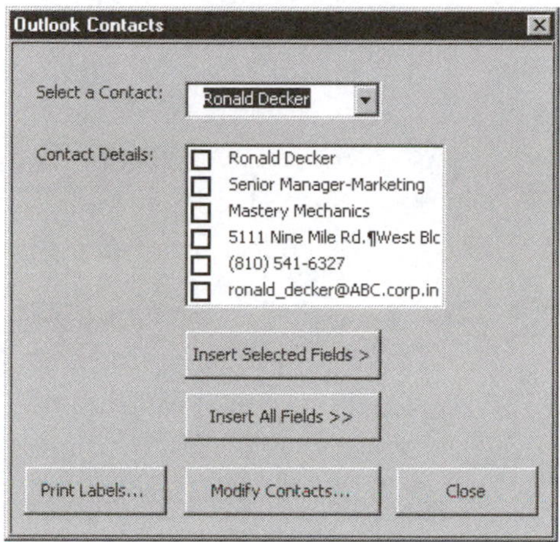

FIGURE 12-3 *The Contacts Book application displays contact details after the* `UserForm_Initialize` *procedure is executed.*

To display specific information about the selected contact item in the `cboContactList` combo box, you need to apply the `Change` event to the `cboContactList` object. The following section explains the code for the `cboContactList_Change` procedure.

The cboContactList_Change Procedure

Listing 12-3 contains the code for the cboContactList_Change procedure.

Listing 12-3 The cboContactList_Change Procedure

```
'This procedure is used to display specific information of
'the selected contact item in the combo box.

Private Sub cboContactList_Change()
       Dim x As Integer
       With lstFieldList
       If .ListCount > 0 Then
       For x = 0 To .ListCount - 1
       .RemoveItem (0)
       Next x
       End If
       For x = 0 To cboContactList.ColumnCount - 1
       .AddItem (Me.cboContactList.Column(x))
       Next x
       End With
End Sub
```

The cboContactList_Change procedure displays specific information about a selected contact item in the cboContactList combo box. In the procedure, a variable x is declared as Integer. The procedure uses the List property to return a set of list entries in the cboContactList combo box.

The procedure uses the AddItem and RemoveItem methods and the ListCount property. In the code, the AddItem method adds an item to the list. In the Contacts Book application, the AddItem method adds a row to the list of items. The syntax for the AddItem method is

```
Variant = object.AddItem( [item [,varindex]])
```

where object is a valid object. The item argument is optional and can be used to specify the item or row that you need to add. The number of the first item or the first row is 0. The varindex argument is also optional and can be used to specify the position where the new item or row needs to be placed in the object.

In the code, the `RemoveItem` method removes the specified row from a list in the combo box. The number of the first row is `0`.

The `cboContactList_Change` procedure also uses the `ListCount` property to return the number of items in the `lstFieldList` list box control. When the procedure is run, the specific columns of information about the selected contact are displayed as separate rows in the `lstFieldList` list box control.

In addition to listing the items in the Contacts folder and displaying specific information about each item, the Contacts Book application also enables a user to enter specific details of a contact in a Word document at the current cursor position. The procedure for obtaining this functionality in the main screen of the Contacts Book application is the `AddtoDoc` procedure. The next section describes the `AddtoDoc` procedure.

The AddtoDoc Procedure

Listing 12-4 contains the code for the `AddtoDoc` procedure.

Listing 12-4 The AddtoDoc Procedure

```
'This procedure is used to insert the selected
'fields into a word document at the current cursor position.

Public Sub AddtoDoc(All As Boolean)
       Dim itm As Variant
       With lstFieldList
       For x = 0 To .ListCount - 1
       If All Then .Selected(x) = All
       If .Selected(x) = True Then
       With Selection
       .InsertAfter (lstFieldList.List(x))
       .Collapse (wdCollapseEnd)
       .Paragraphs.Add
       End With
       End If
       Next x
       End With
End Sub
```

When the AddtoDoc procedure is executed, the selected fields or all fields of information about the selected contact are inserted into the current Word document. In this procedure, the InsertAfter method is used to insert the specified information. After the InsertAfter method is applied, the selection expands to include the new text. In addition to the InsertAfter method, the Collapse method is applied to the selection. After the Collapse method is applied, the selection is collapsed to the start or end position. Here, the Collapse method is applied to specify the selection as an insertion point at the end of the previous selection.

Finally, the Add method is applied to the Paragraphs collection to add a new blank paragraph after the selection.

Figure 12-4 displays selected fields of a contact inserted into a Word document.

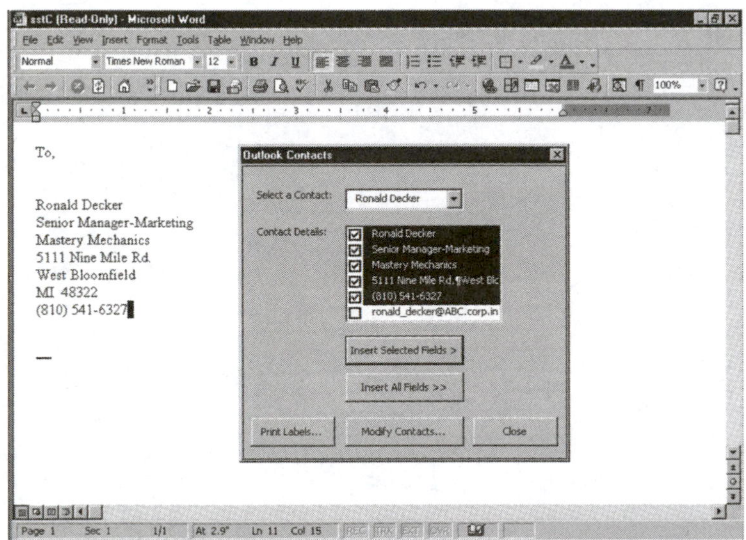

FIGURE 12-4 *Specific details of a contact added to a Word document using the Contacts Book application*

The Contacts Book application also enables a user to print mailing labels for each contact item in the Contacts folder. To do this, the PrintLabels procedure is used. The following section describes the code for the PrintLabels procedure.

The PrintLabels Procedure

Listing 12-5 contains the code for the `PrintLabels` procedure.

Listing 12-5 The PrintLabels Procedure

```
'This procedure is used to print the contact information
'in a new word document as labels.

Sub PrintLabels()

     On Error GoTo ErrorHandler

    Dim oApp As New Outlook.Application
    Dim oNspc As Outlook.NameSpace
    Dim fld As Outlook.MAPIFolder
    Dim itms As Outlook.Items
    Dim oItm As Outlook.ContactItem

    Set oNspc = oApp.GetNamespace("MAPI")

SelectContactFolder:
    Set fld = oNspc.PickFolder
    Debug.Print "Default item type: " & fld.DefaultItemType
     If fld.DefaultItemType <> olContactItem Then
       MsgBox "Please select a Contacts folder.", vbExclamation, "Select Contacts"
       GoTo SelectContactFolder
    End If

      Dim appWord As New Word.Application
      Dim docWord As New Word.Document
      docWord.Activate


      Set itms = fld.Items
      For Each oItm In itms
          With Selection
          'the labels are printed in blue color in the bold format
             Selection.Font.Color = wdColorBlue
```

```
                Selection.Font.Bold = True
                .TypeParagraph
                .TypeText Text:="-----------------------------------"
                .TypeParagraph
                .TypeText Text:=oItm.FullName
                .TypeParagraph
                .TypeText Text:=oItm.JobTitle
                .TypeParagraph
                .TypeText Text:=oItm.CompanyName
                .TypeParagraph
                .TypeText Text:=oItm.BusinessAddress
                .TypeParagraph
                .TypeText Text:=oItm.BusinessTelephoneNumber
                .TypeParagraph
                .TypeText Text:="-----------------------------------"
                 End With
        Next

ErrorHandlerExit:
   Exit Sub

ErrorHandler:
   MsgBox "Error No: " & Err.Number & "; Description: " & Err.Description,
      vbExclamation, "Print Labels"
   Resume ErrorHandlerExit

   frmOutlookAddress.Show

End Sub
```

The `PrintLabels` procedure starts with establishing a reference to the `MAPIFolder` object of Outlook. In the `PrintLabels` procedure, the `PickFolder` method is used to display the Select Folder dialog box of Outlook. If a user does not select a valid Contacts folder, a message box specifying the same is displayed.

```
Dim appWord As New Word.Application
Dim docWord As New Word.Document
docWord.Activate
```

To print mailing labels for all contact items in the Contacts folder, the procedure functions in conjunction with a new Word document. First, an instance of the Word application is created, and then a new Word document is created and activated.

```
Set itms = fld.Items
     For Each oItm In itms
          With Selection
          'the labels are printed in blue color in the bold format
             Selection.Font.Color = wdColorBlue
             Selection.Font.Bold = True
             .TypeParagraph
             .TypeText Text:="---------------------------------"
             .TypeParagraph
             .TypeText Text:=oItm.FullName
             .TypeParagraph
             .TypeText Text:=oItm.JobTitle
             .TypeParagraph
             .TypeText Text:=oItm.CompanyName
             .TypeParagraph
             .TypeText Text:=oItm.BusinessAddress
             .TypeParagraph
             .TypeText Text:=oItm.BusinessTelephoneNumber
             .TypeParagraph
             .TypeText Text:="---------------------------------"
              End With
     Next
```

The procedure then specifies each item as a contact item. For each item in the selection, specific fields of information need to be added to mailing labels. Although you can choose from any of the contact item properties, in the Contacts Book application, the full name of the contact and the contact's job title, company name, and business address are inserted in the given order. In addition, a line is inserted at the beginning of contact information to mark the end of the label. Figure 12-5 shows how mailing labels for all contacts are added and displayed in a new Word document.

The Contacts Book application also enables a user to modify information about contacts, add new contacts, and delete contacts. The following sections describe various procedures that help perform these tasks.

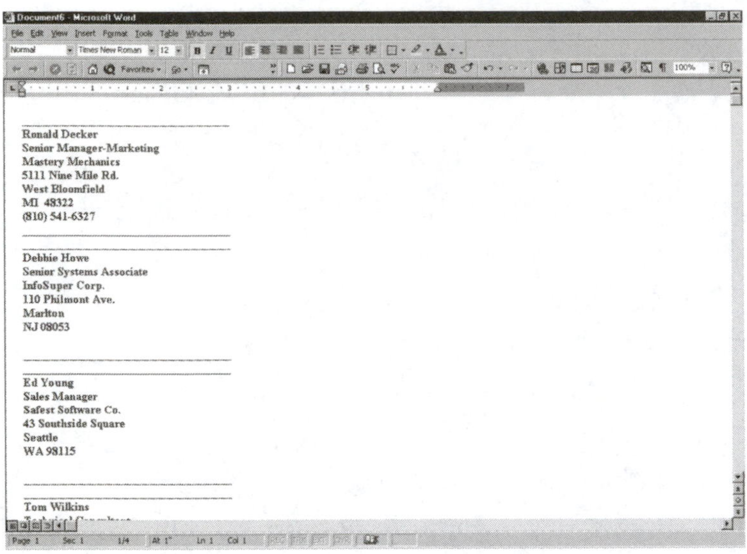

FIGURE 12-5 *Mailing labels added to a new Word document for all the contact items in the Contacts folder*

The AddContact Procedure

Listing 12-6 contains the code for the `AddContact` procedure.

Listing 12-6 The AddContact Procedure

```
'This procedure is used to start a new Outlook Contact item form
'after a user clicks the Add New Contact button to add contacts.

Public Sub AddContact()
         On Error GoTo AddContact_Error
         Dim spObj As Object, oItm As Object

         ' Create an instance of OutLook object
         Set spObj = CreateObject("Outlook.Application")

         ' Create and display a new contact form
         Set oItm = spObj.CreateItem(olContactItem)
          oItm.Display

         ' Quit Outlook.
```

```
        Set spObj = Nothing
        MsgBox "The contact item has been added.", vbInformation, "Modify Contacts"
        Exit Sub

AddContact_Error:
        MsgBox "Error: " & Err & " " & Error, vbExclamation, "Add Contact"
        Exit Sub
End Sub
```

The `AddContact` procedure starts with referencing the Outlook application. When the `AddContact` procedure is executed, a new Outlook Contact Item form is displayed. A user can enter details in the new form and then close the form.

When the new contact item is added, the Outlook application is closed by specifying its reference as `Nothing`. This is required to make available the memory resources being utilized by the Outlook `Application` object. The procedure then displays a message box specifying that the new contact is added.

Similar to the `AddContact` procedure, the Contacts Book application also includes the `ModifyContact` and `DeleteContact` procedures.

The ModifyContact Procedure

Listing 12-7 contains the code for the `ModifyContact` procedure.

Listing 12-7 The ModifyContact Procedure

```
'This procedure is used to open the Outlook Contact form of an
'existing contact such that it can be modified.

Sub ModifyContact()
strFullName = cboContactList.Text

Dim oApp As Outlook.Application
Dim oNspc As NameSpace
Dim itms As Items
Dim oItm As ContactItem
```

```
'Create an instance of outlook
'Reference its MAPI Interface
'Reference MAPI's Contact Folder

    Set oApp = CreateObject("Outlook.Application")
    Set oNspc = oApp.GetNamespace("MAPI")
    Set itms = _
    oNspc.GetDefaultFolder(olFolderContacts).Items

    'Search for the items that need to be modified.

    For Each oItm In itms
        If oItm.FullName = strFullName Then
            oItm.Display
         MsgBox "The contact item has been modified.", vbInformation, "Modify
            Contacts"
         Exit Sub
         End If
      Next
       'If no entry found for the specific contact
      MsgBox "Please select a contact.", vbExclamation, "Modify Contacts"
End Sub
```

In the `ModifyContact` procedure, the contents of the `cboContactList` combo box are matched with the full name of a contact item stored in the Contacts folder of Outlook. When a user selects a particular contact item's name from the `cboContactList` combo box control and clicks on the Modify button on the user form, the `ModifyContact` procedure is executed. The `Display` method is used to display the specific item such that changes can be made to the contact's details. Figure 12-6 displays a contacts form that appears after a user selects a contact and clicks on the Modify button on the Modify Contacts screen of the application.

After the contact item is modified, the `MsgBox` function is used to display a message box specifying that the contact item is modified.

The DeleteContact Procedure

Listing 12-8 contains the code for the `DeleteContact` procedure.

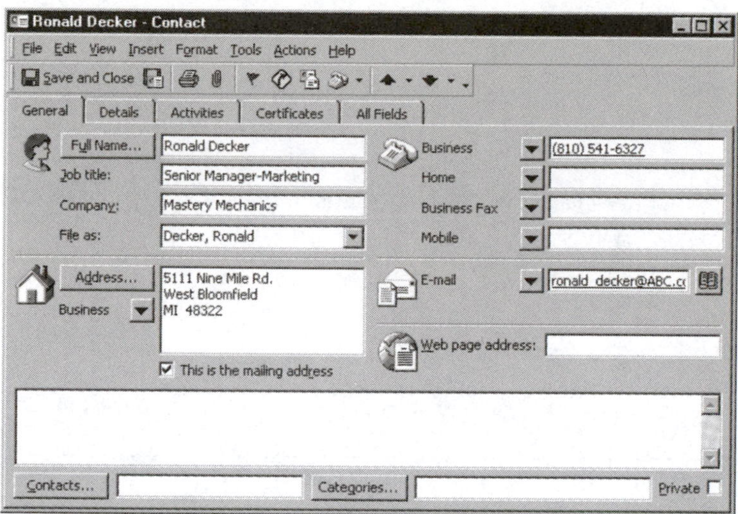

FIGURE 12-6 *The contacts form of a contact available for modification after the* `ModifyContact` *procedure is executed*

Listing 12-8 The DeleteContact Procedure

```
'This procedure is used to delete a specific Outlook Contact item.

Sub DeleteContact()
strFullName = cboContactList.Text

Dim oApp As Outlook.Application
Dim oNspc As NameSpace
Dim itms As Items
Dim oItm As ContactItem

'Create an instance of outlook
'Reference its MAPI Interface
'Reference MAPI's Contact Folder

    Set oApp = CreateObject("Outlook.Application")
    Set oNspc = oApp.GetNamespace("MAPI")
    Set itms = _
    oNspc.GetDefaultFolder(olFolderContacts).Items
```

```
    'Search for the items that need to be deleted.

      For Each oItm In itms
          If oItm.FullName = strFullName Then
              oItm.Delete
           MsgBox "The contact item has been deleted!", vbInformation, "Modify Contacts"
              Exit Sub
           End If
        Next
        'If no entry found for the specific contact
        MsgBox "Please select a contact.", vbExclamation, "Modify Contacts"
End Sub
```

In the `DeleteContact` procedure, the contents of the `cboContactList` combo box are matched with the full name of a contact item stored in the Contacts folder of Outlook. When a user selects a particular contact item's name from the `cboContactList` combo box control and clicks on the Delete button on the user form, the `DeleteContact` procedure is executed. The `Delete` method is used to delete the specific item from the Contacts folder in Outlook.

After the contact item is deleted, the `MsgBox` function is used to display a message box specifying the same.

In addition to the `AddContact`, `ModifyContact`, and `DeleteContact` procedures, the Contacts Book application includes a `Refresh` procedure. The following section discusses the `Refresh` procedure.

The Refresh Procedure

Listing 12-9 contains the code for the `Refresh` procedure.

Listing 12-9 The Refresh Procedure

```
'This procedure is used to refresh the combo box contents
'after a contact has been deleted/modified/added.

Sub Refresh()
        cboContactList.Clear
        x = 0
```

```
        Set oApp = CreateObject("Outlook.Application")
        Set oNspc = oApp.GetNamespace("MAPI")
    For Each oItm In oNspc.GetDefaultFolder(olFolderContacts).Items
        With Me.cboContactList
        .AddItem (oItm.FullName)
        End With
        x = x + 1
        Next oItm
        Set oItm = Nothing
        Set oNspc = Nothing
        Set oApp = Nothing
End Sub
```

The `Refresh` procedure is used to update the contents of the `cboContactList` combo box after a contact item has been added, modified, or deleted from the Contacts folder. This procedure is similar to the `UserForm_Initialize` procedure. Just as with the `UserForm_Initialize` procedure, the `Refresh` procedure fills the `cboContactList` combo box with the full names of all contact items stored in the Contacts folder in Outlook.

Summary

In this chapter, you learned about the Outlook object model and the various components of the Outlook object model, and you looked at how to add code and implement various procedures in the Contacts Book application. In the next chapter, you will learn to execute the Contacts Book application.

Chapter 13

Using the Contacts Book Application

In this chapter, you will learn how to compile and run the Contacts Book application that you have developed. You will also learn how to distribute the application as a Word template file.

Compiling the Application

To compile the Contacts Book application, you need to add a simple, one-line code in a new Standard module for the current project. To do this, you need to first insert a new module in the current project. To insert a new Standard module in the current project, you need to select the Module command from the Insert menu in the Visual Basic Editor window.

To add the code, double-click on the module and open the Code window. Then, add the following lines of code in the module:

```
Sub ShowContacts()
frmOutlookAddress.Show
End Sub
```

In this code, the `Show` method is used to display the `frmOutlookAddress` form of the Contacts Book application. After you add this code and run the application, the VBA project is saved as a Word macro named `ShowContacts` and is available in the current Word document.

The following section explains the procedure to run the application using the Macros dialog box in the current Word document.

Running the Application

To run the Contacts Book application, you need to select the Macros command from the Tools menu in the current Word document in which you have created the VBA project.

After you select the Macros command, the Macros dialog box is displayed. Here, you need to select the `ShowContacts` macro and click on the Run button. The Macros dialog box is displayed with the `ShowContacts` macro as shown in Figure 13-1.

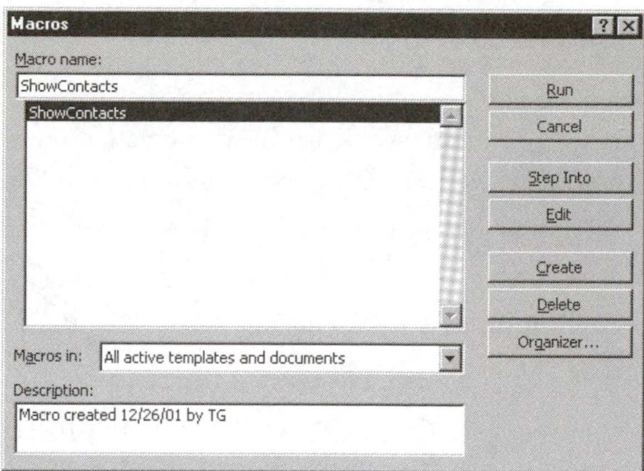

FIGURE 13-1 *The Macros dialog box containing the* `ShowContacts` *macro*

After you click on the Run button in the Macros dialog box, the main screen of the Contacts Book application is displayed as shown in Figure 13-2. You can then work with the Contacts Book application to perform the required tasks.

At times, you may need to distribute and share an application with other users. This is discussed in the next section.

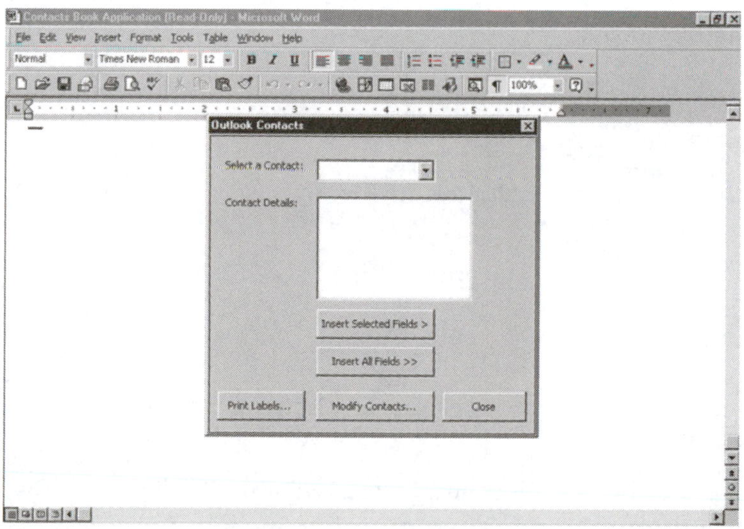

FIGURE 13-2 *Contacts Book application displayed in the current Word document*

Distributing the Application

You can either distribute the Word document in which the VBA project is saved or create a template file for the application. Here, you learn how to create a template file for the Contacts Book application. When you create a template file for the `ShowContacts` macro, the Contacts Book application is executed automatically each time a new Word document is created from a Word template file.

To distribute the Contacts Book application as a template file, perform the following steps:

1. Create a new Word template file. To do this, select New from the File menu and select the Template option button in the New dialog box as displayed in Figure 13-3.

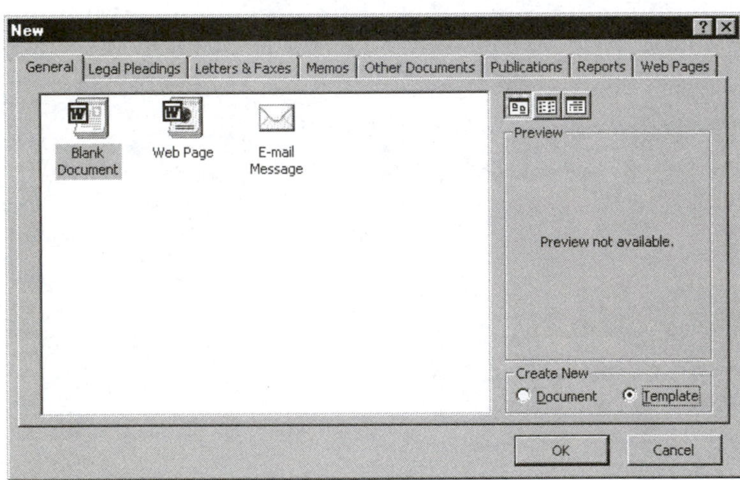

FIGURE 13-3 *The New dialog box*

2. Save the template file as the `Contacts Book Application.dot` file.
3. In the `Contacts Book Application.dot` file, select the Macros command from the Tools menu and click on the Organizer button in the Macros dialog box.
4. After you click on the Organizer button, the Organizer dialog box is displayed with the current page as Macro Project Items. The Organizer dialog box is displayed in Figure 13-4.

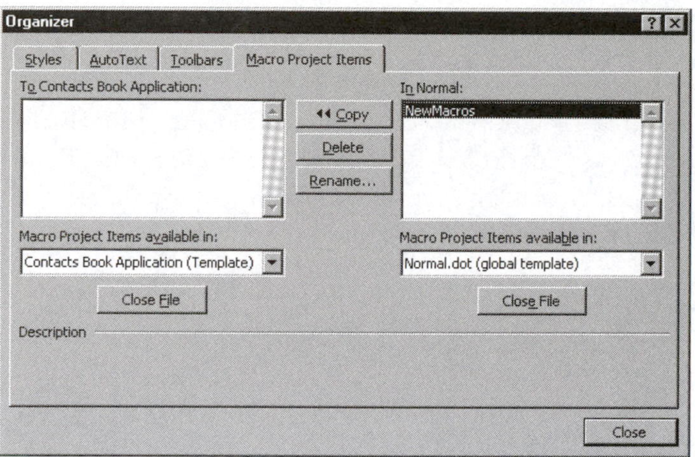

FIGURE 13-4 *The Organizer dialog box*

5. In the Macro Project Items page of the Organizer dialog box, click on the Close File button in the left pane of the dialog box. The Close File button is a toggle button. After you click on the button, the button name changes to Open File.
6. Click on the Open File button in the left pane to browse for the Contacts Book application VBA project document.
7. Similarly, browse for the `Contacts Book Application.dot` file in the right pane of the Organizer dialog box.
8. Next, click on each of the forms and modules present in the document containing the Contacts Book application VBA project in the left pane and then click on the Copy button to copy all the items to the `Contacts Book Application.dot` file in the Organizer dialog box. The Organizer dialog box is displayed in Figure 13-5, depicting that all forms and modules are copied from the Word document to the template file.
9. After copying all forms and modules from the VBA project Word document into the `Contacts Book Application.dot` file, click on the Close button in the Organizer dialog box.
10. Save the `Contacts Book Application.dot` file.
11. Open the Visual Basic Editor window in the `Contacts Book Application.dot` file and open the Code window for the `ThisDocument` object.

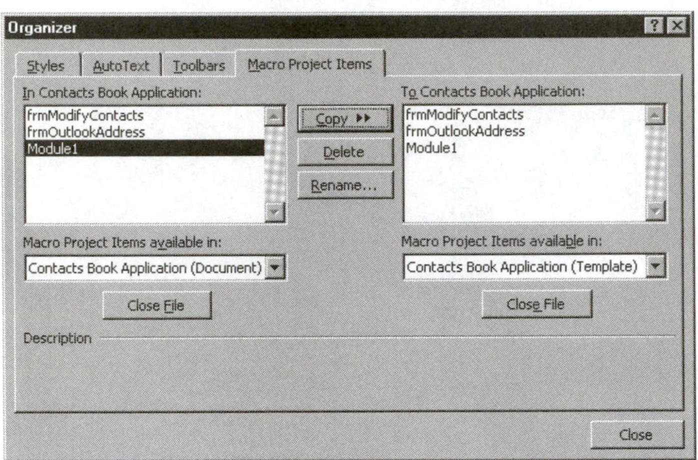

FIGURE 13-5 *The Organizer dialog box depicting the macro project saved in a template file*

12. Add the following lines of code to the `New` event for the `Document` object:

```
Private Sub Document_New()
frmOutlookAddress.Show
End Sub
```

    This piece of code ensures that each time a new document is opened using the `Contacts Book Application.dot` file, the Contacts Book application executes automatically. The Code window is displayed in Figure 13-6.

13. Add the reference to the Outlook object model in the `Contacts Book Application.dot` file by using the References dialog box available in the Visual Basic Editor window.
14. After you double-click on the `Contacts Book Application.dot` file to open a new Word document, the main screen of the Contacts Book application is displayed.

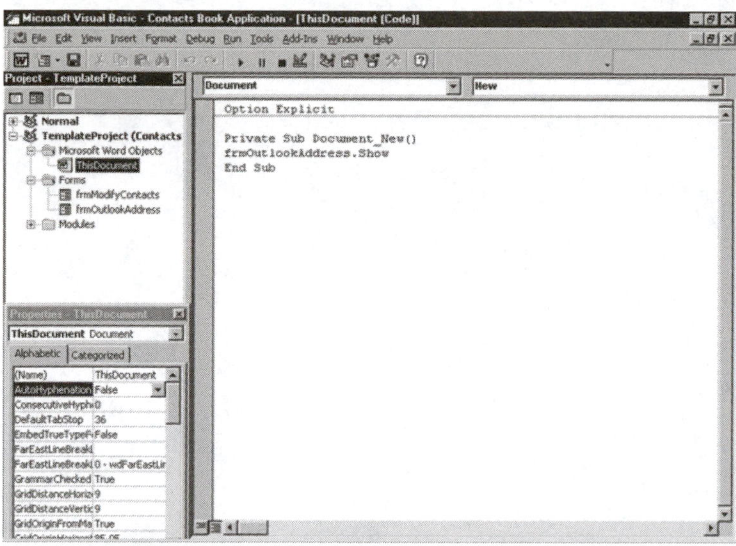

FIGURE 13-6 *The Code window for the ThisDocument object*

Summary

In this chapter, you learned to compile and run the Contacts Book application by using the Macros dialog box within the current Word document. You also learned how to distribute the Contacts Book application as a Word template file and execute the Contacts Book application automatically when a new Word document is created from a Word template file.

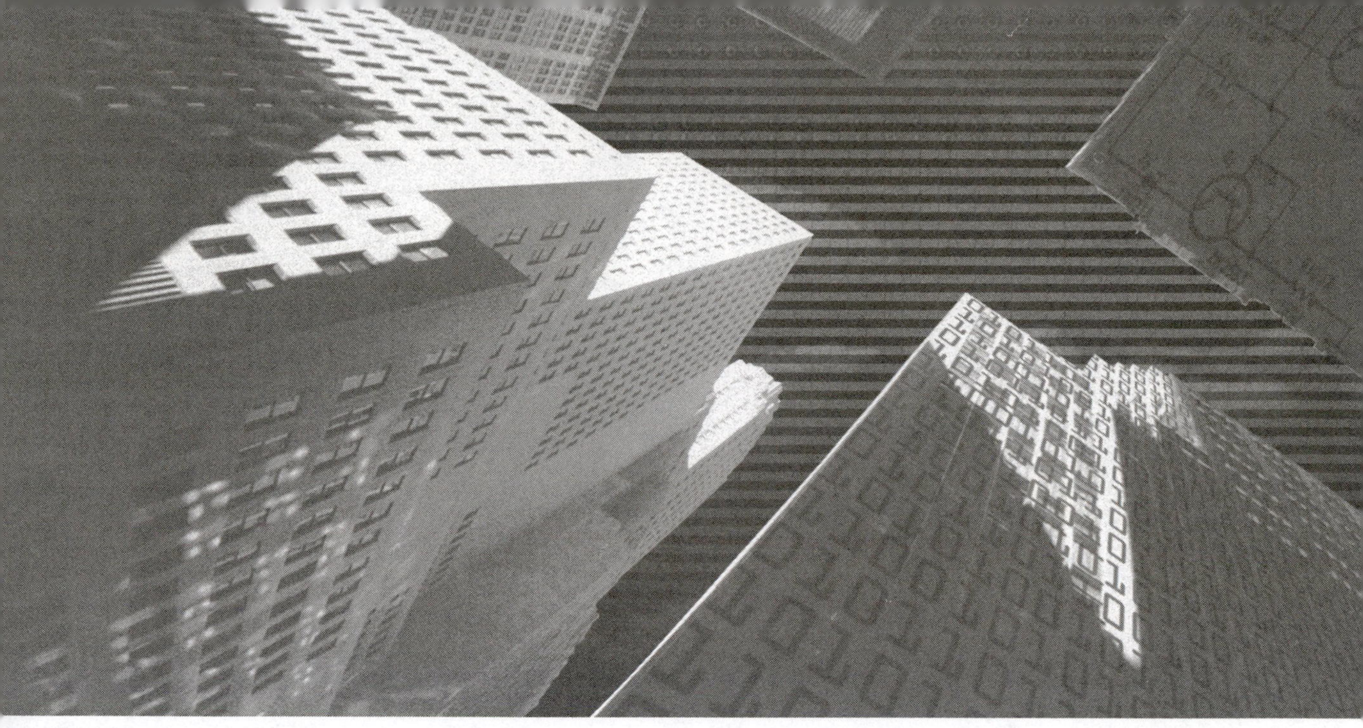

PART IV

Professional Project 2

Project 2

Creating a Skill Search Application

Project 2 Overview

A skill search application can be used by big organizations to search for details of employee skills pertaining to specific technologies. The tool has the following functionalities:

- The application allows a user to search for the skill details document of various employees based on either the skills and years of experience or the name of the employee.
- All documents that meet the search criterion are displayed as a list along with a link to the skill details document of the employee, experience in the particular technology, and the total experience.
- Users can open and view the skill details document of the selected employee within the application.

The Skill Search application has been built using Visual Basic .NET. In this project, you will learn how to build this Skill Search application and how to deploy this application on the Web. You are also introduced to the .NET Framework.

The concepts used to build the Skill Search application are as follows:

- .NET Framework
- Visual Studio.NET
- VB .NET
- Enhanced Components of Visual Studio.NET IDE
- Working With Databases by using VB .NET and ADO.NET
- Introduction to ASP.NET
- Working with Web Forms

Chapter 14

Project Case Study: Red Sky IT Systems

Red Sky IT Systems is one of the largest software and services company in the United States. The company offers Internet-based software solutions to banking, accounting, insurance, manufacturing, and healthcare industries across the globe. The company is based in New York and has seven branches across the U.S. The company has approximately 500 employees in its various offices.

At Red Sky IT Systems, each project manager leads a team of 3 to 5 developers. The responsibility of the project managers is to coordinate the activity of the team members so that development work is completed on time as per client requirements. At the start of a project, developers are allocated to various projects on the basis of their current skill sets. To perform this task, project managers need to scan through the skill details document of each employee. However, since Red Sky IT Systems is a large company and the number of projects and employees has grown, it is becoming increasingly difficult for project managers to view the skill details document of each employee. To solve this problem, a meeting of all project managers and senior managers was held. The team decided to build an application that could be used to search for details of employee skills pertaining to specific technologies. This would help in effective resource allocation. In addition, because most project managers will need to use the application, the team has decided to deploy the application on the Internet for easy accessibility.

A four-member team was created to build and deploy the application. Ed Young, a project manager, was leading the team of three developers, Larry Williams, Corrine Wallace, and Lee Mitchell. The team decided to call the application Skill Search.

The next sections discuss the development life cycle (DLC) of the project as identified by the team.

Project Life Cycle

The development life cycle of the project involves the following major phases:

- Requirements analysis
- Design
- Coding and construction
- Testing
- Application distribution

These phases are discussed in detail in the following sections.

Requirements Analysis

The development team at Red Sky IT Systems analyzed the requirements of the project based on the feedback received from project managers. In addition, the team tried to understand the requirements for the Skill Search application by interviewing the recruitment team of the company. The project requirements, as analyzed by the development team, are as follows:

- The application should allow a user to search the skill details document of various employees either by skills and years of experience or employee name.
- All documents meeting the search criteria should be displayed as a list along with a link to the skill details document of the employees, experience in the particular technology, and the total experience.
- Users should be able to open and view the skill details document of the selected employee within the application.
- The back-end database for the application should be developed in Microsoft Access and should contain information such as employee name, employee code, location, home address, work phone, mobile phone, e-mail address, name of the document containing the skill details, skills, the total experience in a skill, and so on.
- The Skill Search application needs to be built using Visual Basic .NET. In addition, the application needs to be deployed on the Web.

Design

Based on the requirements analysis, the development team decides to design a user interface and the back-end database for the application.

While designing the user interface, the development team decides to incorporate three main screens for the Skill Search application. The team also considers and analyzes the functionality of each screen. Following are the screens of the application that need to be developed.

The Splash Screen

The `Splash` screen is the first screen to be displayed when a user starts the Skill Search application. This screen is visible for a few seconds, at which time the next screen appears automatically. The user can also click anywhere on the `Splash` screen to display the next screen.

A sketch of this screen as designed by the development team is displayed in Figure 14-1.

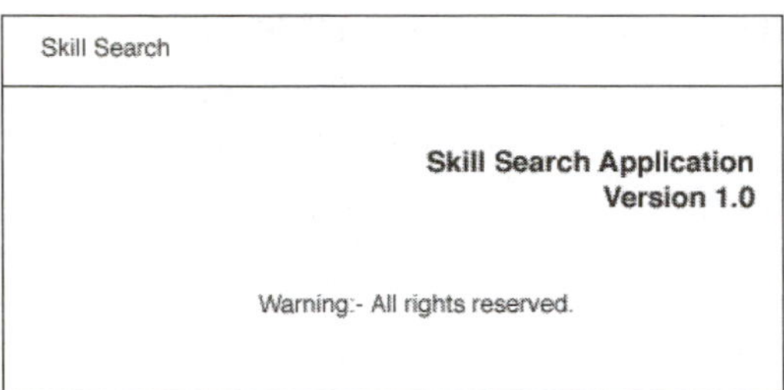

FIGURE 14-1 *The* `Splash` *screen of the Skill Search application*

The Search Screen

After the `Splash` screen is closed, a user can view the main screen of the Skill Search application. This screen is the `Search` screen. Using this screen, a user can search the skill details document of the employees by the required skills or the name of the employees. The screen also includes an `Exit` button that will allow users to close the application.

A sketch of this screen is depicted in Figure 14-2.

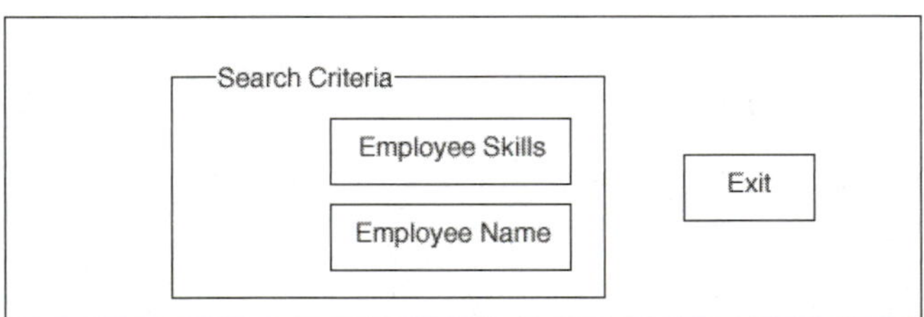

FIGURE 14-2 *The* `Search` *screen displaying options for the search*

The Search by Technology Screen

After a user clicks on the `Employee Skills` button in the `Search` screen, the second screen, called the `Search by Technology` screen, is displayed. This screen allows a user to enter the name and years of experience of the required skill area as the search criteria. Using this screen, the user can also select from a drop-down list of various technologies and search for all employees with work experience in a particular technology. The user can click on the `Search` button to list the skill details documents or click on the `Back` button to view the main screen.

After the user clicks on the `Search` button, the search results are displayed. The search results include a list of employees with knowledge of the selected technology. The list contains the name of the skill details file of the employee, the experience in the specific technology (expressed as the number of months), and the overall experience of the employee (also expressed as the number of months).

A sketch of this screen is depicted in Figure 14-3.

FIGURE 14-3 *The* `Search by Technology` *screen of the Skill Search application*

To access the skill details document of a specific employee, a user can double-click on the list entry for that employee.

The Search by Employee Name Screen

After a user clicks on the `Employee Name` button in the `Search` screen, a new screen called `Search by Employee Name` is displayed. This screen allows the user to select the name of the employee from an available drop-down list box or type the name of the employee. A sketch of this screen is depicted in Figure 14-4.

The user can click on the `Back` button to view the main screen. To perform the search, the user needs to click on the `Search` button. The results of the search display information, such as employee name, employee code, location, e-mail address of the employee, and a link to the skill details document. If the name of the employee does not exist in the database, a message box stating the same is displayed. However, if the name of the employee specified by the user exists in the database, then the relevant information is displayed.

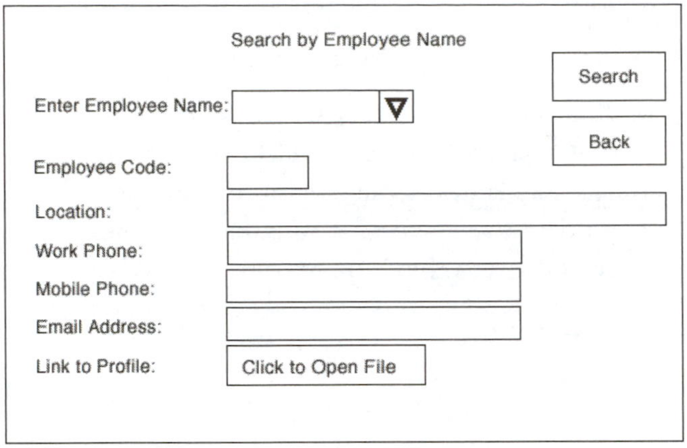

Search by Employee Name

Search

Enter Employee Name:

Back

Employee Code:

Location:

Work Phone:

Mobile Phone:

Email Address:

Link to Profile: Click to Open File

FIGURE 14-4 *The* `Search by Employee Name` *screen of the Skill Search application*

Designing the Database

After discussing the interface of the tool, the team finalized the design of the database that will serve as the back end for the application. As per the requirements, the database needs to be developed in Access. The development team designed an Access table and named it `Skill_Info`. This table contained the following fields of information about the employees:

- `Name`
- `Location`
- `Home_Address`
- `Work_Phone`
- `Res_Phone`
- `EmpCode`
- `Mobile_Phone`
- `Email_Id`
- `File_Name`
- `Total_Exp`
- `Qualification`
- `Certification`
- `Skill1_Name`
- `Skill1_Exp`

- `Skill2_Name`
- `Skill2_Exp`

The database design is displayed in Figure 14-5.

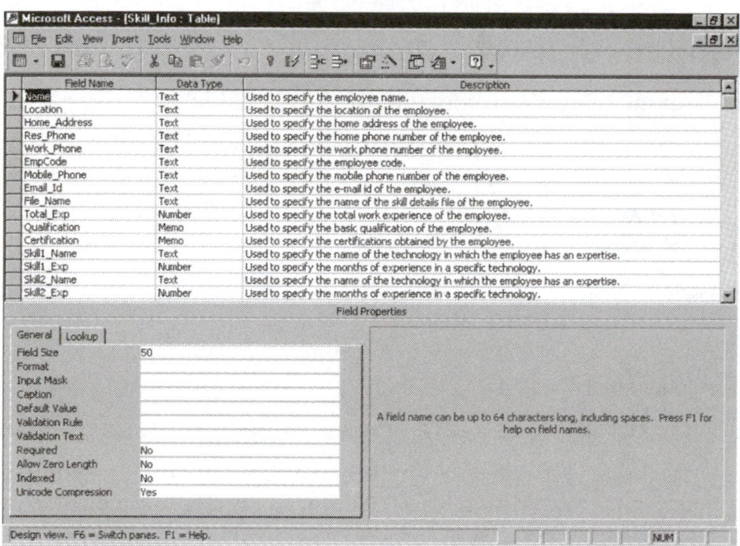

FIGURE 14-5 *The database design for the* `Skill_Info` *table in Access*

After completing the design phase, the development team moves to the next phase of the development life cycle, which is coding and construction.

Coding and Construction

After the requirements for the application are analyzed and the design for the interface is decided, the next phase of DLC is coding and construction. In this phase, the development team will code the Skill Search application by using VB .NET. The project manager, Ed Young, has assigned the task of coding the tool to different team members.

Testing

In the testing phase, the Skill Search application needs to be tested as per the requirements identified at the beginning of the project. In the case of the Skill Search application, the development team decided to implement a comprehensive test plan that will be used by testers in addition to the testing guidelines. The test report for the application will then be submitted to the development team, who will make the appropriate changes and debug the application. After the testing phase, the application will be ready for distribution.

Distributing the Application

After the Skill Search application is developed and tested, the development team needs to distribute the application to various project managers in the company. In addition, the team needs to deploy the application on the Web for easy access. The development team has the responsibility of providing constant support in terms of installation and debugging any errors.

Summary

In this chapter, you looked at the phases of the DLC of the Skill Search application. In the next few chapters, you will look at the creation and development of the application by using VB .NET. The Skill Search application needs to be developed using VB .NET. Therefore, the next chapter introduces you to the concept of the .NET Framework and the components and features of the .NET Framework.

Chapter 15

Overview of the .NET Framework

One of the requirements of the Skill Search application is that it be created in VB .NET by using the .NET Framework. This chapter discusses the .NET Framework, its components, and features, and introduces you to the Visual Studio .NET suite of programs.

Introduction to the .NET Framework

Imagine a situation in which you need to develop applications that are accessible using a variety of clients, such as palmtop computers and cellular phones, and are able to run across different operating systems. In such a situation, the .NET Framework provides you with the necessary solution. The .NET Framework is the latest product launched by Microsoft. The .NET Framework helps integrate various programming languages and services. It provides multi-language support that enables you to develop, execute, and deploy Web-based applications by using various languages. With the help of the related .NET compilers, the framework currently supports more than 20 languages, such as C, C++, Visual Basic, C#, Pascal, JScript, Perl, and Python. The framework consists of classes and services and acts as a layer between the applications you develop and the operating system. The .NET Framework comprises two main components: CLR (*common language run-time*) and the .NET Framework class library.

CLR (Common Language Run-Time)

In earlier versions of Visual Basic, each programming language in the Visual Studio suite had a separate run-time environment. Therefore, each language executed in a different domain, making it difficult to achieve interoperability among the applications. The .NET Framework has solved this problem and enables you to implement cross-language interoperability by using CLR.

CLR, an important component of the .NET Framework, forms the base of the .NET Framework. This run-time environment controls code execution and provides services such as memory management, thread management, and security management. CLR manages the interaction between the code and the operating system. The code executed by CLR is known as *managed* code. The code that does not operate with CLR is known as *unmanaged* code. Managed code provides *metadata* to CLR. This metadata is the minimum level of information provided by the code so that services of CLR, such as memory management, are utilized by the code. The metadata is stored with the compiled code and contains information about the types, methods, and references in the code. CLR uses metadata to locate and load classes, generate native code, and provide security.

Some of the features of CLR are listed as follows:

- Cross-language integration
- Cross-language exception handling
- Enhanced security

CLR helps eliminate memory leaks and invalid memory references. Objects are managed and removed from memory after all the references are deleted. This feature is known as *garbage collection*. In addition, CLR implements a code verification infrastructure known as CTS (*common type system*). This system is a standard used by all languages that support CLR. CTS defines the framework and rules by which objects interact, therefore allowing cross-language integration. For example, you can define a class in C# from a base class defined in VB .NET. CTS ensures that data types, such as `String` and `Integer`, are implemented in the same manner in all languages that support CLR.

CLR also provides JIT (*just-in-time*) compilation. This feature helps enhance the performance of an application because code is run in the native language of the computer on which the code is being executed. When managed code is run, the compiler converts the source code into MSIL (*Microsoft intermediate language*). MSIL is a set of CPU-independent instructions for loading, storing, initializing, and calling methods. MSIL also performs operations such as arithmetic and logical operations, direct access to memory, and exception handling.

Before the code is executed, MSIL has to be converted to the native computer language which is CPU-specific. A JIT compiler converts MSIL to the native computer language. CLR provides a JIT compiler for each type of CPU architecture that is supported by CLR. Therefore, you can write a set of MSIL which is JIT-compiled and then executed on CPUs with different architectures.

An important feature of JIT compilation is that the code is compiled only when required. Therefore, whenever the code is required, the JIT compiler converts the code to native code and ensures that memory is optimally allocated to the application. The entire process of how a JIT compiler works is depicted in Figure 15-1.

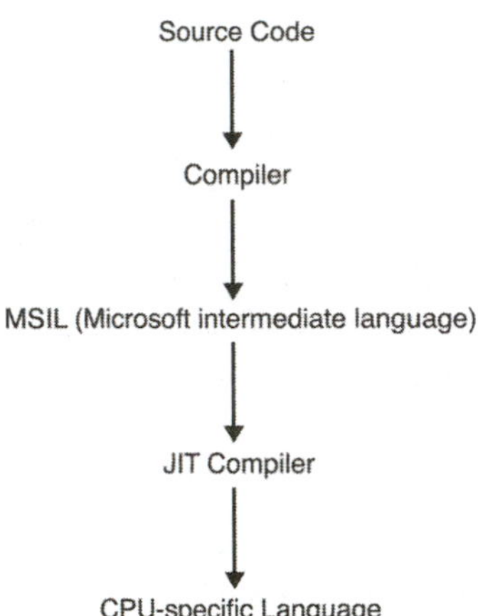

FIGURE 15-1 *The process of JIT compilation depicted using a flow chart*

The following section discusses the next important component of the .NET Framework, the .NET Framework class library.

The .NET Framework Class Library

The .NET Framework class library comprises object-oriented reusable and extensible classes that are integrated with CLR. This library is common to various programming languages. Therefore, you can use the same library to develop applications in Visual C++ and Visual Basic. These classes act as a foundation for developing applications and implementing cross-language inheritance. You can also develop third-party components that can be integrated with the class library. Although earlier versions of VB .NET offered the feature of inheritance, it was only *interface* inheritance. The .NET Framework offers *implementation* inheritance, which allows you to develop applications by creating new classes from existing ones.

Using the .NET Framework class library, you can perform various programming tasks such as connecting to a database, manipulating data, and accessing files. You can also develop specific applications and services.

The .NET Framework class library uses a syntax-naming scheme to group related types, such as classes and structures. This syntax-naming scheme is known as a *namespace*. The `System` namespace is at the top of the hierarchy and contains all other classes. You need to include the `System` namespace in most of the applications that you develop. The .NET Framework uses a dot (.) as a delimiter between namespaces and classes. For example, `System.Console` is used to represent the `Console` class of the `System` namespace. Because classes are grouped into namespaces, you can have two classes with the same name but belonging to different namespaces or hierarchies.

When you build applications, you need to import one or more namespaces for the types that you need to use in your application. Table 15-1 lists some of the namespaces available in the .NET Framework class library with a brief description of each.

Table 15-1 Namespaces in the .NET Framework Class Library

Namespace	Description
`Microsoft.CSharp`	Used to compile and generate code in Visual C# .NET
`Microsoft.Jscript`	Used to compile and generate code in JScript
`Microsoft.VisualBasic`	Used to compile and generate code in Visual Basic .NET
`Microsoft.Win32`	Used to manipulate the system registry and manage operating system events
`System`	Used to manage exceptions and define data types, events, event-handlers, interfaces, and attributes

Now that you have learned about the components of the .NET Framework, the following section briefly describes the features of the .NET Framework.

Features of the .NET Framework

The .NET Framework provides features that enable you to design and develop complete solutions. Some of the important features of the .NET Framework are:

- Consistent and simplified programming
- Management of resources
- Support for debugging
- Use of assemblies
- Management of security

The following sections briefly discuss each of these features.

Consistent and Simplified Programming

The .NET Framework enables you to use a consistent object-oriented programming model that involves more than 20 programming languages currently supported by the .NET Framework. This simplifies programming because you can use a preferred programming language and reuse existing code. In addition, in the .NET Framework, all classes are logically grouped into namespaces. Therefore, the hierarchy of classes is available to you at any time. You can also extend the functionality of these classes by using inheritance. Further, the .NET Framework supports the use of Internet technologies, such as HTML and XML, and other Web standards, which enable you to build and deploy Web-based applications easily.

Management of Resources

At times, it may become difficult for you to program the management of system resources, such as memory, network connections, and files manually. However, if these resources are not managed optimally, the program might function unpredictably. To solve this problem, the .NET Framework offers the feature of garbage collection. During garbage collection, CLR automatically tracks the use of system resources, destroys the objects after they are used, and reallocates the memory.

Support for Debugging

Consider a situation in which you have an ASP application that contains VB COM components. If you had to debug this application, you would have to make use of Visual InterDev to debug the ASP code and VB to debug the COM components. To solve this problem, the .NET Framework now enables you to debug applications by using a common, integrated debugger. This debugger can be used in various languages while the program is running. Therefore, even if your application is written in different languages, you can make use of the integrated debugger to debug the application. You can also use the debugger to debug remote programs.

Use of Assemblies

The .NET Framework allows you to create assemblies. An *assembly* is a collection of one or more classes which are used in multiple applications. You can use assemblies to build applications. Although an assembly usually consists of classes, it can also contain other files associated with your application such as graphics or resource files. You can create such assemblies and store them on the hard disk of your computer. Such assemblies are known as *static* assemblies. You can also work with *dynamic* assemblies that are created at run-time.

Management of Security

In the .NET Framework, security is achieved using the CAS (*code access security*) model and role-based security. You can use CAS to control access permissions for the code. In the CAS model, CLR imposes restrictions on managed code by using objects knows as *permissions*. The code can, therefore, be used to perform only the permitted tasks, which also prevents unauthorized users from misusing the code. This also ensures that by using the .NET Framework, you can download trusted code from the Internet and prevent that code from gaining access to system resources.

Role-based security is another security mechanism implemented in the .NET Framework. This mechanism allows you to implement security based on the designation of a user known as the *principal*. Using role-based security, you can specify permissions for the principal. Using the .NET Framework, the individual and group permissions are validated for the principal.

The features of the .NET Framework not only help increase developer productivity, but also enable organizations to address changing market requirements by developing, deploying, and maintaining reliable enterprise solutions.

Now that you have learned about the .NET Framework, you should learn more about the Visual Studio .NET suite of languages. The following sections introduce you to Visual Studio .NET and the important programming tools included in its suite.

Introduction to Visual Studio .NET

Visual Studio .NET is based on the .NET Framework. You can use a single shared IDE (*integrated development environment*) of Visual Studio .NET to create solutions for the .NET Framework. The Visual Studio .NET IDE is applicable to various programming languages supported by Visual Studio .NET.

You can use Visual Studio .NET to build Web-based, desktop, and mobile applications. Visual Studio .NET is a development environment that enables you to work with the .NET Framework and build reliable XML Web services. Some of the important programming tools included in the Visual Studio .NET suite are:

- Visual Basic .NET
- Visual C++ .NET
- Visual C# .NET

The next sections briefly discuss each of these.

Visual Basic .NET

Unlike the earlier versions of Visual Basic, Visual Basic .NET is an object-oriented programming language and supports implementation inheritance. Visual Basic .NET has many new features, such as multithreading, overloading, and exception handling, which enable you to build and maintain programs easily and handle different types of data by using the same programming logic. In addition, Visual Basic .NET is compliant with CLS (*Common Language Specification*). CLS is a set of features that define the basic language features required by various applications. Using CLS, objects expose only those features that are common to all the languages with which they interact. This ensures that you can use the objects, classes, or components that you create in Visual Basic .NET in other languages that are CLS-compliant and allows interoperability between applications, irrespective of the language used to create the application.

All managed types in Visual Basic .NET are derived from the `System.Object` class. In addition, you can use the Visual Studio IDE to develop server-side components and Web applications easily by using Server Explorer.

Visual C++ .NET

Visual C++ is the new version of the C++ programming language and includes features such as support for managed extensions and attributes. Managed extensions enable you to convert existing components so that they are compatible with the .NET Framework. Therefore, you can continue to write C++ code in existing programs and reuse the code.

You can use Visual C++ to work with managed and unmanaged code in an application simultaneously. When working with managed code, you can use the .NET

Framework class library to interoperate with all other languages that support CLR.

In addition to managed extensions, Visual C++ also supports attributes. You can use attributes to simplify COM programming in Visual C++. Attributes are Visual C++ keywords that are interpreted by the compiler and extend the functionality of the existing code by modifying the functionality of the code or including additional code.

Visual C# .NET

Visual C# is a new language developed with C and C++ as its base and incorporates the best features of C and C++. You can use Visual C# to build high-end applications that can be run on the .NET Framework.

Using Visual C#, you can work with both managed and unmanaged code. Using managed code, you can derive the benefits of CLR and work with the .NET Framework class library to create applications. In contrast, you can use unmanaged code to bypass the .NET Framework and interact directly with the underlying operating system.

You can also use Visual C# to convert existing Windows applications to Web applications by using Internet standards, such as HTML and XML, which are supported by Visual C#.

Visual Studio .NET also offers other features, such as Web Forms, Windows Forms, Web services, and XML support.

Web Forms

Visual Studio .NET provides Web Forms to enable you to create Web pages for Web-based applications. Web Forms use the technology offered by ASP.NET. Here, the code runs on the server side and produces dynamic Web pages on the client side. You can use Web Forms to display information to users in any browser or on a mobile device. You can also use the functionality and features of a specific Web browser and target the output accordingly.

You can use Web Form controls to design an extensive user interface for your Web-based applications.

Windows Forms

Visual Studio .NET supports Windows Forms that you can use to create Windows applications based on the .NET Framework. Windows Forms are object-oriented and consist of an extensible set of classes. You can use these classes to implement *visual inheritance,* which can be used to inherit a form from an existing form and, therefore, reuse code.

Using Windows Forms, you can manipulate and access system resources such as the Windows registry and local files. You can also use Windows Forms to create a user interface by using various graphic classes and Windows GDI (*graphic device interface*).

Web Services

Web services are the most significant contribution of the .NET Framework. You can use Web services to exchange data between applications by using XML. To create Web services, you can use the ASP.NET Web Service template. Web services do not have interfaces. For example, the Microsoft Passport Authentication service is a Web service that uses Passport authentication to validate users visiting the Microsoft Web sites.

You can use Web services to access specific functionality at the server side remotely. Web services are applications, and their functionality is available to users on the Internet. Web services provide methods that are accessible to other applications by using XML for data interchange.

By using Web services, organizations can share data and provide real-time solutions to meet client requirements.

XML Support

Visual Studio .NET offers support for XML. The .NET Framework includes two classes in the `System.Xml` namespace: `XmlReader` and `XmlWriter`. To implement these classes, you can use two objects, namely `XmlTextReader` and `XmlTextWriter`. Visual Studio .NET provides an XML Designer that you can use to create and edit XML documents and create XML schemas.

Summary

In this chapter, you learned about the major components and important features of the .NET Framework. This chapter also introduced you to the Visual Studio .NET suite of programs. In the next chapter, you will learn about Visual Basic .NET in detail and the differences between Visual Basic 6.0 and Visual Basic .NET. This will enable you build the Skill Search application in Visual Basic .NET and deploy it on the Web.

Chapter 16

Introduction to VB.NET

As stated in the case study of the Skill Search application, one of the requirements of the application is that it should be built using VB.NET. In Chapter 15, "Overview of the .NET Framework," you learned about the .NET Framework and the various components of Visual Studio.NET. In this chapter, you will learn about VB.NET. This chapter discusses the differences between VB 6.0 and VB.NET, as well as the object-oriented features of VB.NET and also introduces the methods for upgrading your existing VB 6.0 applications to VB.NET.

Overview of VB.NET

VB.NET is one of the most powerful programming tools available in the Visual Studio.NET programming suite. It provides a fast and efficient way of developing applications based on the .NET Framework. One of the main differences between VB.NET and the earlier versions of VB is that VB.NET is an object-oriented language and it supports features such as multithreading, inheritance, and overloading. The next section discusses the new features in VB.NET.

Features of VB.NET

In addition to the basic features of programming, such as variables, data types, arrays, constants, operators, expressions, statements, procedures, and functions, VB.NET supports a host of other features. This section takes you through a journey of some of the new features in VB.NET.

The new features in VB.NET are as follows:

- **Assemblies.** An *assembly* can be defined as a collection of one or more classes. Assemblies can be used to build applications.
- **Namespaces.** A *namespace* is used to organize the objects present in the assembly. A namespace consists of classes, structures, and interfaces that can be used in your application. An assembly can have more than one namespace. You will learn about namespaces in detail later in the chapter.
- **Object-oriented features.** VB.NET supports all the features of an object-oriented programming language, such as abstraction, encapsulation, inheritance, and polymorphism. You will learn about the features of an object-oriented programming language in detail in the next section.
- **Adding references.** You can add references to objects that are external to an application. References can be added to objects by using the Add

Reference option from the Project menu. Once a reference is added to a namespace, you can use the `Imports` statement to refer to that namespace in the assembly. The syntax of the `Imports` statement is as follows:

```
Imports [Alias = ] NameSpace
```

In the preceding statement, `Alias` is the alternate name of the namespace and is optional. `NameSpace` is the name of the namespace being referred to.

- **Visual Inheritance.** VB.NET allows developers to inherit forms from an existing form. This feature offers code reusability and enhanced productivity.
- **Exception handling.** VB.NET supports structured exception handling, which catches errors at run-time.
- **Multithreading.** VB.NET supports multithreading, which enables an application to perform multiple tasks simultaneously.

The next section focuses on the language differences between the earlier versions of VB and VB.NET.

Language Differences in VB.NET

Although VB.NET is quite similar to the earlier versions of VB, there are a few differences. VB.NET uses the same syntax as the earlier versions except for a few changes. The various language changes in VB.NET are discussed in the following sections.

Changes in Array Declaration and Size Declaration

In VB 6.0, an array declared using the `Dim` statement with its dimensions mentioned in the declaration is a fixed-size array, which cannot be modified using the `ReDim` statement. For example:

```
Dim MyArray ( 0 to 5) As String
```

The preceding statement creates a fixed-size array named `MyArray`.

However, you cannot create fixed-size arrays in VB.NET. Therefore, you can always use the `ReDim` statement to modify arrays created in VB.NET. Another point to note here is that the `ReDim` statement in VB.NET is always used to resize an array and it cannot be used to declare an array for the first time, which was the case with VB 6.0.

VB 6.0 also allows you to change the lower bound of an array by using the `Option Base` statement. VB.NET does not provide this feature. Therefore, an array declared in VB.NET always has a base 0.

Changes in Data Type

The various changes in the data type are as follows:

- VB.NET does not support the `Currency` data type. You can use the `Decimal` data type to store currency values.
- VB.NET provides a `DateTime` data type to store date values.
- The default data type in VB 6.0 is the `Variant` data type. The default data type in VB.NET is the `Object` data type.
- In VB 6.0, you can specify the length of the `String` data type. For example, the following line of code declares a `String` data type of length 5:

  ```
  Dim MyString As String * 5
  ```

  However, in VB.NET, you cannot specify a fixed-length string.

Statement Changes

In addition to the data type and array declaration changes, there are a few changes in statements such as `While…Wend` and `GoSub` and the usage of the `Dim` statement in VB.NET. These are discussed in the following list:

- The `While…Wend` statement in VB 6.0 is used to execute a set of statements based on a condition. In VB.NET, the `While…Wend` statement is replaced by the `While…End While` statement.
- You can use the `GoSub` statement in VB 6.0 to call a subprocedure. VB.NET does not support the `GoSub` statement. You can use the `Call` statement to call a procedure in VB.NET.
- You learned about the `Dim` statement in Chapter 2. Recall that when you declare more than one variable in a single `Dim` statement, all variables except the last are assigned the `Variant` data type, which is the default data type.

  For example, consider the following statement:

  ```
  Dim MyVar1, MyVar2, MyVar3 As Integer
  ```

  In this statement, the variables `MyVar1` and `MyVar2` are assigned the `Variant` data type, and the variable `MyVar3` is assigned the `Integer` data type. However, this is not true for variables declared in VB.NET. All variables that are declared using the `Dim` keyword are assigned the same data type in VB.NET. Therefore, the preceding line of code when written in VB.NET assigns all the three variables to the `Integer` data type.

As mentioned earlier, one of the main features of VB.NET is its object-oriented nature. The next section discusses the features of an object-oriented programming language.

What Is Object-Oriented Programming?

An *object* is the main building block of an object-oriented programming language. In an object-oriented programming language, each application is made up of objects. Simply put, an object could be anything around you such as a pen, a newspaper, a watch, or this book that you are reading right now. An object is an entity that has certain attributes or properties and exhibits some type of behavior. Related objects can be grouped together to form a *class*. For example, Porsche, Cadillac, and Rolls Royce are all cars. They share the same basic properties such as color, number of wheels, model, and all of them are used to drive. Therefore, they can be put together in a class named cars.

In a programming language, an object is an instance of a class and consists of properties and methods. Objects and classes together form the basis of an object-oriented programming language. How does an object-oriented programming language help you as a programmer? You will see the answer to this question after becoming familiar with the features of an object-oriented programming language.

An object-oriented programming language supports the following features:

- Abstraction
- Encapsulation
- Inheritance
- Polymorphism

Each of these features is discussed in detail in the following sections.

Abstraction

Suppose you want to buy a car. Consider the features that you look for in a car before buying it, such as the color, model, price, and so on. As a consumer, you might not be too interested in the internal working of the car, therefore you only look at the essential details and ignore the nonessential details. This phenomenon is known as *abstraction*. In a programming language, abstraction allows you to focus on the essential details of an object and ignore the nonessential details; it helps you ignore the complexity of an object. Similar to all other object-oriented programming languages, VB.NET enables abstraction with the help of classes and objects. An object is an instance of a class, and a class is a group of related objects. A class has common properties and displays similar behavior. Object-oriented programming languages allow users to specify the properties and methods of objects while building classes. Therefore, as a programmer, abstraction helps you expose only the essential details of an object and hide the nonessential ones.

How do you ignore the nonessential details of an object? This is done with the help of encapsulation, which is discussed in the next section.

Encapsulation

To ignore the nonessential details of an object, you can hide them. While driving a car, you cannot see the internal processing within the car. All the internal processing of the car is hidden because it is encapsulated. Encapsulation refers to hiding the nonessential components of an object. It is a method of implementing abstraction.

In any programming language, encapsulation hides the internal implementation of a class from the user. Encapsulation displays only the properties and methods of an object to the user and hides the other nonessential details. Therefore, as a programmer, you can hide the complexity of an object from the user. Encapsulation is also known as data hiding.

In addition to hiding the nonessential details of an object in a class, you can also derive an object or a class from another class. This phenomenon is known as *inheritance*. The next section discusses inheritance.

Inheritance

Inheritance is another important feature of object-oriented programming languages and is used to reuse objects and classes. Inheritance means deriving an object or a class from an existing object or class. For example, children may inherit the characteristics of parents. When a class is derived from another class, the derived class is known as the *subclass* or the *derived* class, and the class from which it is derived is known as the *base* class or the *deriving* class. The derived class can access the properties and methods of the base class. You can also add methods and properties to the derived class to enhance its functionality. In addition, the derived class can also override the properties and methods of the base class.

You can create hierarchies of objects by using inheritance. For example, consider a class `space`. The `solar system` class is derived from the `space` class, and the `earth` class is derived from the `solar system` class. The `earth` class inherits all the properties and methods of the `solar system` class, and the `solar system` class inherits all the properties and methods of the `space` class. All classes in VB.NET can be inherited.

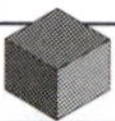

NOTE

All classes in VB.NET are derived from the `Object` class. The `Object` class is a part of the `System` namespace.

Inheritance allows developers to reuse code and create specific user-defined classes from generic classes.

Polymorphism

When created, an object can exist in more than one form. For example, to buy a car, you can either contact a dealer or the car manufacturing company directly. In object-oriented terminology, this phenomenon is known as *polymorphism*. Here, the company and the dealer are two separate classes that behave differently to the same order. Polymorphism means that classes or objects can exist in different forms. From the programming point of view, this means that you can declare a method of the same name in a derived class as in a base class. However, the method in each class performs different tasks.

When a call to this method is made, how does the compiler decide which method to execute? The answer to this question lies in *binding*.

When two classes have a method with the same name, the compiler associates each method with the class by identifying the type of object that was used to invoke the object. This process of associating a method with an object is known as binding. Binding can be of two types: *early binding* and *late binding*. When the method is associated with its object at the time of compilation, it is known as early binding or static binding. However, you will notice that the type of an object is often not known at the time of compilation, and the objects are created dynamically. In such cases, the method is linked with its object at run time, and this is known as late binding or dynamic binding.

You have learned about the advantages of an object-oriented programming language. One of the key advantages of an object-oriented programming language is that you can reuse code by creating classes and using them in several applications. The next section discusses the implementation of the object-oriented features in VB.NET.

Object-Oriented Features in VB.NET

As discussed in the previous section, objects and classes form the basis of an object-oriented language. The same is applicable in VB.NET. The controls used for designing a form are classes. When you drag a control on the form, you create a class of that particular control.

Recall that an object is an instance of a class. An object is a combination of code and data. Each object is associated with properties, methods, and events that are used to manipulate the data of the object. The properties, methods, and events of an object are defined by the class from which it was created. Therefore, an object is nothing but an instance of a class.

Objects in VB.NET are created using the `Dim` statement. The syntax is given in the following statement:

```
Dim ObjName as ClassName
```

In this statement, `ObjName` refers to the name of the object, and `ClassName` refers to the name of the class from where the object will be created. The syntax for accessing a property of an object is as follows:

```
ObjName.Property
```

In the preceding statement, `ObjName` is the name of the object, and `Property` specifies the property of the object.

To perform certain tasks, an object uses the methods defined in a class. A method is accessed in the same way as a property. The syntax of a method is as follows:

```
ObjName.Method()
```

You can also attach events to objects. To attach an event to an object, you need to declare an event by using the `Event` keyword. Events are always declared within classes. Consider the following example:

```
Event MyEvent()
```

This statement declares an event named `MyEvent`.

You need to create classes in VB.NET to implement the object-oriented features. To create a class, choose the Add Class option from the Project menu and give a name to the class. The `Class` keyword is used to declare a class. The syntax to declare a class is as follows:

```
[AccessModifier][Keyword] Class ClassName
----
----
End Class
```

In the preceding code snippet, `AccessModifier` specifies the accessibility of a class such as `Private`, `Public`, `Protected`, or `Friend`.

`Keyword` specifies whether other classes can inherit the class. `Keyword` can take one of two values: `NotInheritable` or `MustInherit`.

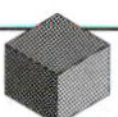

NOTE

Access modifiers are used to implement abstraction or encapsulation. For example, to enable other classes to access the properties and methods of a class, you need to specify the `Public` access modifier. Similarly, to prevent other classes from accessing the properties and methods of a class, you can use the `Private` access modifier.

Each class has a set of properties and methods. To create a property for a class, you can use the `Property` keyword. The `Property` keyword can also be used to declare procedures that can be used to assign and retrieve property values. These procedures are known as *property* procedures. The syntax for a property procedure is as follows:

```
Property MyProperty() As DataType
----
----
End Property
```

Once you have declared a property procedure, you need to assign values to a property by using the `Set` keyword. The property procedure is then executed as soon as that property changes. The `Set` statement takes the property value as a parameter. The syntax of the `Set` statement is as follows:

```
Set (Value as Type)
    ClassVariable=Value
End Set
```

To retrieve a value from a property procedure, you can use the `Get` keyword. The syntax of the `Get` statement is as follows:

```
Get PropertyName = ClassVariable
End Get
```

You have learned how to create classes, assign properties, and attach methods and events to a class in this section. You will now learn to implement inheritance.

As discussed earlier, inheritance enables you to create multiple derived classes from a base class. To derive a class from a base class, you use the `Inherits` keyword. The syntax for using the `Inherits` statement is as follows:

```
[AccessModifier] Class ClassName
    Inherits OtherClass
End Class
```

In the preceding code snippet, `ClassName` refers to the name of the derived class, and `OtherClass` is the name of the deriving class.

VB.NET provides various keywords in addition to the `Inherits` statement that enable you to implement inheritance. Following is a list of these keywords:

- `Inherits`. This keyword is used with classes and inherits all nonprivate members of the specified class.
- `MustInherit`. This keyword is used with classes and specifies the class as a base class.
- `NotInheritable`. This keyword is used with classes and specifies that the class cannot be used as a base class.
- `Overridable`. This keyword is used with procedures and specifies that the procedure can be overridden in the derived class.
- `MustOverride`. This keyword is used with procedures and specifies that the procedure must be overridden in the derived class.

- `NotOverridable`. This keyword is used with procedures and specifies that the procedure cannot be overridden in the derived class.
- `Overrides`. This keyword is used with procedures and specifies that the procedure overrides the procedure of the base class.

In addition to using these keywords while declaring classes, you can also use them while declaring *procedures* and *fields*. As you leaned in Chapter 2, a procedure is a set of statements that performs a specific task. A field is a variable that is declared inside a class and is accessible from other classes. You will learn more about fields in the next section.

Declaring Class Members in VB.NET

As with all object-oriented programming languages, you can declare class members within a class in VB.NET. Class members consist of properties, methods, variables, and fields. You will learn about each of the following in detail in the next sections:

- Constructors
- Destructors
- Methods
- Fields
- Properties

Constructors

Constructors are used to initialize objects. The `Sub New` procedure acts as a constructor in VB.NET. The `Sub New` procedure is the first procedure to be executed when an object of the class is created. You can use this procedure to initialize variables or perform other tasks before using an object of the class.

Every class in VB.NET is derived from the `Object` class. While creating a class, you first need to call the constructor of the `Object` class. You can call constructors from within the constructor of a base class or a derived class.

Destructors

Destructors are used to release memory and resources that were used by an object. The function of a destructor is contrary to that of a constructor. The `Sub Finalize` statement acts as a destructor in VB.NET. The `Sub Finalize` method is a protected method of the `Object` class and can be overridden in the classes that you create.

Methods

In addition to using constructors and destructors in a class, you can also define other methods in a class. The method of a class refers to the `Public Sub` or `Function` procedures declared inside a class. As you already know, a procedure is a set of statements that is executed to perform a specific task. Once you have written a procedure, it can be called from anywhere in the application. VB.NET allows you to define three types of procedures:

- `Sub`. This type of a procedure cannot return a value. You use the `Sub` and `End Sub` statements to define a `Sub` procedure. Typically, these procedures are used to define event handlers.
- `Function`. This type of a procedure returns values to the calling procedures. You use the `Function` and `End Function` statements to define a `Function` procedure.

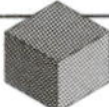

NOTE

Both `Sub` procedures and `Function` procedures can take arguments.

- `Property`. As discussed earlier in the chapter, the property procedure helps you assign and retrieve values of properties. The property procedure of an object is executed whenever the property of the object changes.

VB.NET enables developers to overload methods and allow code reuse. You can declare a method with the same name in the base class as well as in the derived class.

A class in VB.NET also consists of fields and properties in addition to constructors, destructors, and methods. Fields and properties of a class are discussed next.

Fields

As stated earlier, fields are variables of a class that can be accessed from anywhere within the application. You declare fields by using a single declaration statement as shown in the following code snippet:

```
Public Class SampleClass
    Public MyField As String


End Class
```

The `MyField` variable can be manipulated using the object of the `SampleClass` class.

Properties

Properties are used to define the attributes of a class. You use the property procedures to declare properties.

You have learned about the features of VB.NET and the differences between VB.NET and the earlier versions of VB. However, you might be wondering what to do with existing VB applications. VB.NET provides a solution to upgrade your existing VB applications to VB.NET, as discussed in the following section.

Upgrading Applications

There are two options for creating applications in VB.NET. You can create a new VB.NET application, or you can upgrade your existing application to VB.NET. The second option is a timesaver, and it also gives you the advantage of code reusability. VB.NET provides the Visual Basic Upgrade Wizard, which helps you upgrade existing applications. Before using the wizard, you need to consider a few key points. Some features of VB 6.0 are not supported by VB.NET. Therefore, before using the wizard, you need to change the following features to their corresponding features in VB.NET:

- OLE Container Control
- Data Control and Remote Data Control
- Dynamic Data Exchange (DDE)
- DHTML applications
- ActiveX documents
- Web Classes
- Visual Basic 5.0 Windows Common Controls

If your application uses any of these features, you first need to modify your application before upgrading it. Modifying the application could mean adding the functionality of the feature not supported by VB.NET again in VB.NET or looking for alternative features in VB.NET. However, you need to keep in mind the size of the application and the rework involved in adding the functionality in VB.NET before deciding upon the choice.

Having looked at the considerations before actually upgrading your application to VB.NET, you will now learn to use the Visual Basic Upgrade Wizard.

The Visual Basic Upgrade Wizard is an easy way of converting your existing applications to VB.NET. One of the main advantages of using this wizard is that it does not change the original application but creates a new VB.NET application instead. An important point to note here is that the wizard might not change the entire application to VB.NET. Therefore, you might be required to make some changes in the final application.

The steps to upgrade an existing application are as follows:

1. Open the required VB 6.0 project in VB.NET. When you open the project in VB.NET, the Visual Basic Upgrade Wizard is displayed as shown in Figure 16-1.

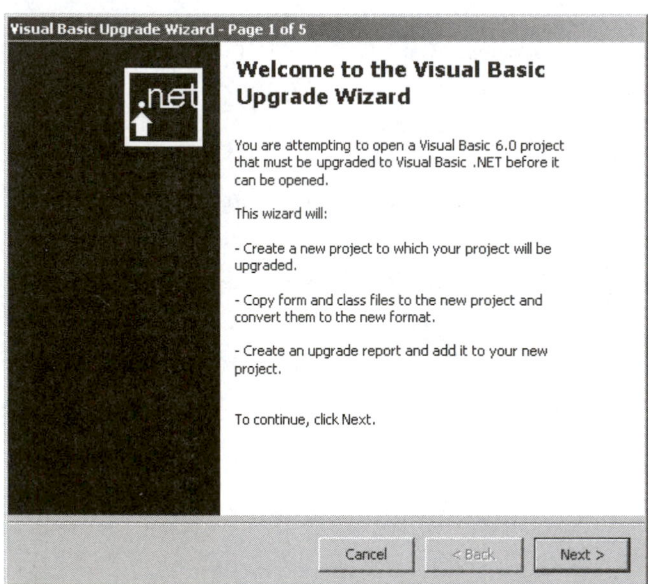

FIGURE 16-1 *The startup screen of the Visual Basic Upgrade Wizard*

2. Click on the `Next` button on the first screen on the wizard. The second screen of the wizard is displayed as shown in Figure 16-2.

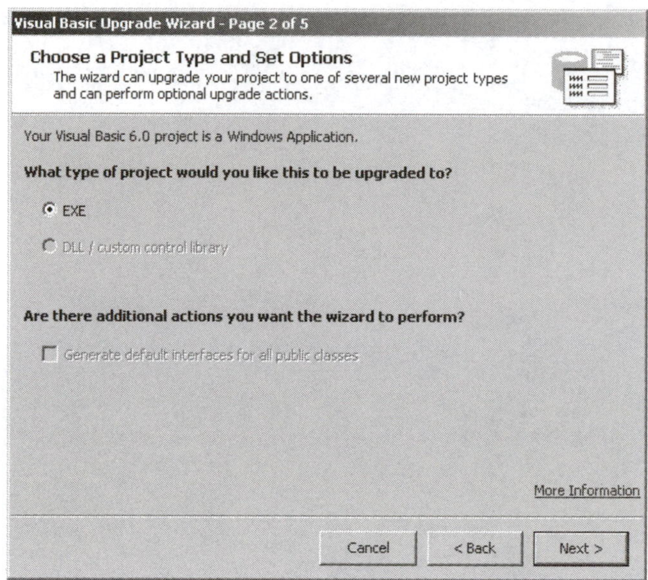

FIGURE 16-2 *This screen is used to select the project type as an .exe or a .dll.*

The second screen of the wizard enables you to specify the project type. You can specify whether you want to upgrade the project as an .exe project or a .dll project. In Figure 16-2, the .exe option is selected.

3. Click on the `Next` button to display the third screen of the wizard as shown in Figure 16-3.
4. Click on the `Next` button on the third screen of the wizard. The fourth screen is displayed as shown in Figure 16-4.
5. Click on the `Next` button to begin the upgrade process. Figure 16-5 displays the next screen of the wizard.
6. When the upgrade process is complete, you can view the new project in the Solution Explorer window as shown in Figure 16-6.
7. The Solution Explorer window also displays an .htm file, which is the upgrade report for the project. After the upgrade is complete, the Upgrade Wizard displays an upgrade report, which is in the HTML format. The upgrade report contains a list of issues that were not covered by

the wizard. You need to fix these issues before executing the application. The upgrade report is displayed as shown in Figure 16-7.

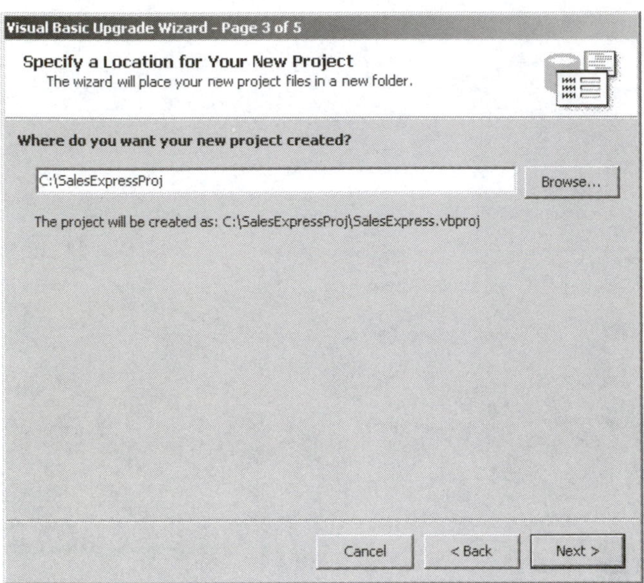

FIGURE 16-3 *This screen is used to select the location where the new project will be created.*

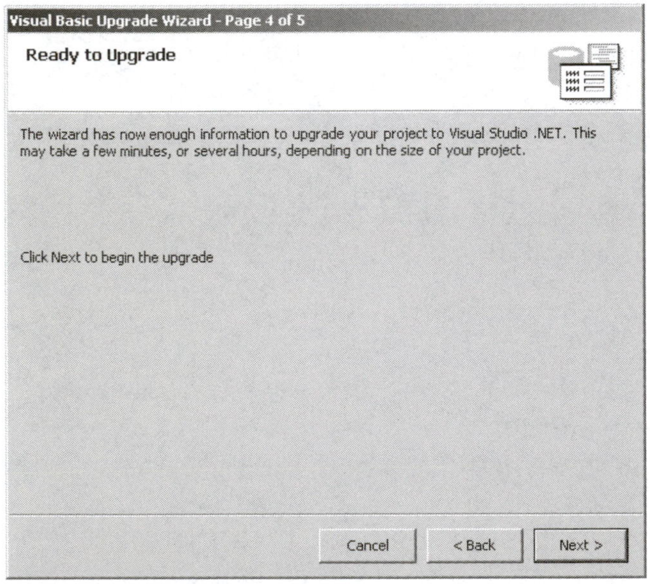

FIGURE 16-4 *The* `Ready to Upgrade` *screen of the wizard prompts the user to begin the upgrade process.*

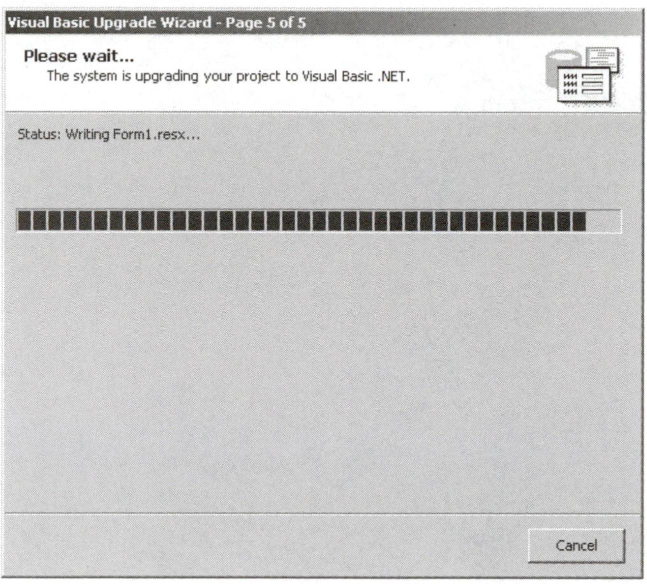

FIGURE 16-5 *This screen is displayed when the upgrade process is in progress.*

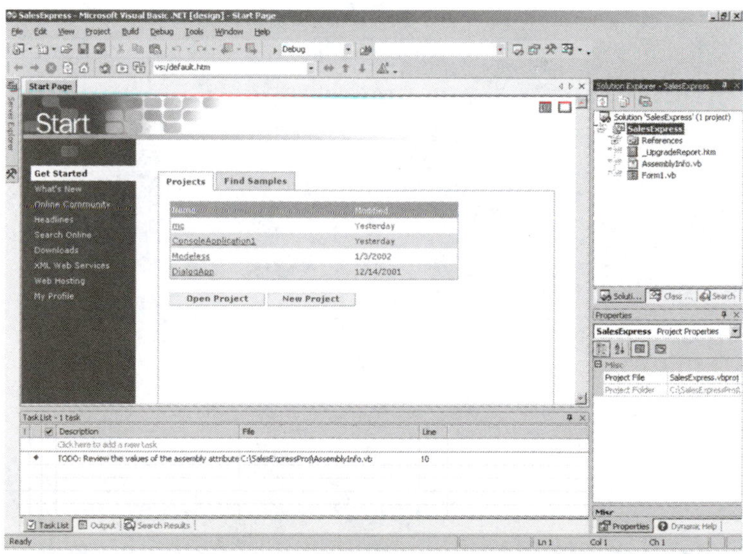

FIGURE 16-6 *The* `SalesExpress` *project in the Solution Explorer window after the project has been upgraded using the wizard*

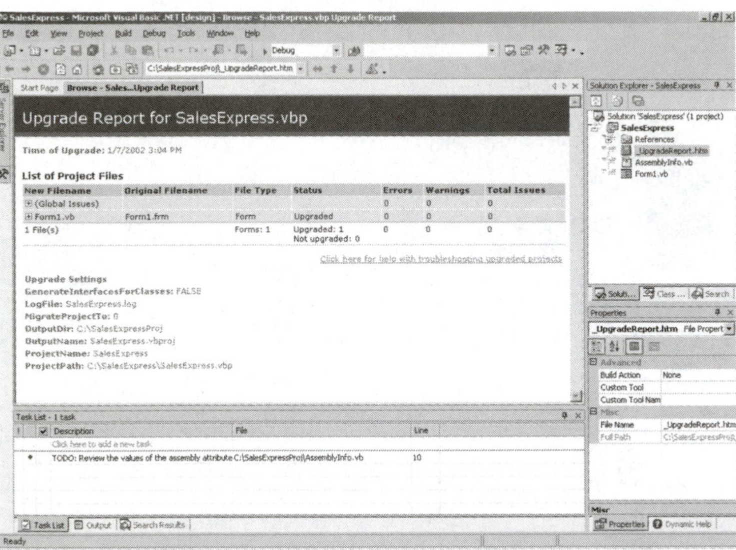

FIGURE 16-7 *The upgrade report for the* `SalesExpress` *project*

Summary

In this chapter, you were introduced to VB.NET. You learned about the differences between VB 6.0 and VB.NET. You also learned about the new features of VB.NET and how to upgrade other VB applications to VB.NET by using the Visual Basic Upgrade Wizard. In the next few chapters, you will develop the Skill Search application in VB.NET.

Chapter 17

The Integrated Development Environment

To create the Skill Search application using VB .NET, you need to understand the look and feel and the functionality of the development environment. In this chapter, you will learn about the integrated development environment (IDE) offered by Visual Studio .NET. The chapter starts with a discussion of the main features of the development environment and then discusses how to use the environment to create Windows- and Web-based applications.

Overview of the Integrated Development Environment

As you learned in Chapter 15, "Overview of the .NET Framework," Visual Studio .NET offers a single shared integrated development environment for all the languages within it, such as Visual Basic .NET, Visual C++ .NET, and Visual C# .NET. The Visual Studio .NET integrated development environment enables you to develop and build your applications easily using a wide range of tools accessible across various languages.

Enhanced Components of Visual Studio .NET IDE

The development environment of Visual Studio has been modified substantially from previous versions. Unlike the development environment available earlier with each programming language, Visual Studio .NET IDE is oriented toward developing Web-based and distributed applications. The following sections discuss some of the enhanced components of Visual Studio .NET IDE.

Start Page

Each time you start Visual Studio .NET, the Start page is displayed. The Start page is the default home page of the Visual Studio .NET IDE Web browser. The Start page acts as a central location from where you can access various options and obtain information regarding how to use the .NET Framework. The Start page is displayed in Figure 17-1.

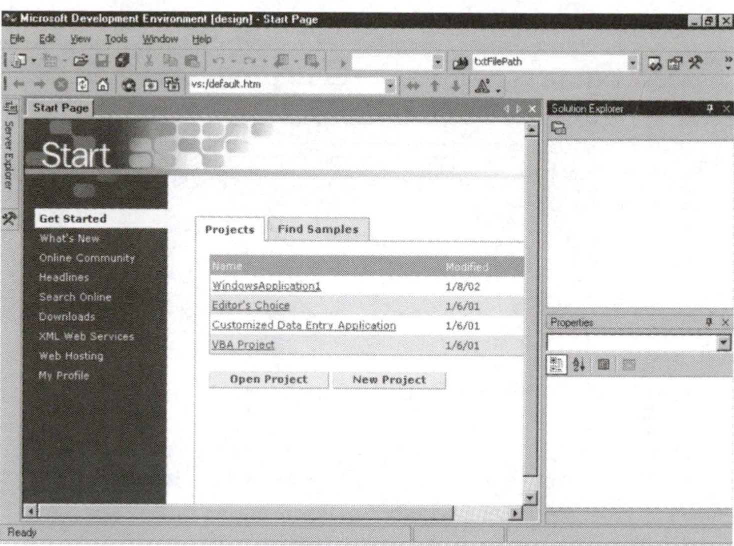

FIGURE 17-1 *The Start page of Visual Studio .NET IDE*

Using the Start page, you can access MSDN Online and view online help about the .NET Framework. You can view discussions and read product news using the Start page. In addition, you can access existing projects and create new projects.

In addition to accessing information, you can use the Start page to customize IDE as per your individual requirements and preferences. For example, you can specify the keyboard scheme as Visual Basic 6, Default, or Visual C++ 2 and specify window layout as Visual Studio Default, Visual Basic 6, or Student Window Layout.

TIP

If the Start page is not displayed automatically, you can display the page using the Show Start Page option from the Help menu.

Table 17-1 lists the various links available on the Start page and a brief description of each link.

Table 17-1 Links Available on the Start Page

Links	Description
Get Started	Used to access existing projects and create new projects
What's New	Used to access information about Visual Studio .NET products, resources, and updates
Online Community	Used to access links to various Web sites and newsgroups
Headlines	Used to access links to the latest news and technical articles available on MSDN Online Web site
Search Online	Used to search for information about a specific topic using the MSDN Web site
Downloads	Used to download development tools, code samples, service packs, and updated products of Visual Studio .NET available on the Web
Web Hosting	Used to access Visual Studio .NET Web Hosting Portal to host and view Web applications and services developed using Visual Studio .NET
My Profile	Used to specify the user preferences for Visual Studio .NET IDE

NOTE

To start Visual Studio .NET, select Start, Programs, Microsoft Visual Studio .NET 7.0, Microsoft Visual Studio .NET 7.0.

Solution Explorer

Imagine a situation in which the application that you are creating in Visual Studio .NET is complex and contains various projects. You may need to continuously access these projects when developing your application. To do this, you can use the Solution Explorer window.

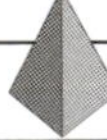

TIP

A *solution* is a collection of all projects and files required for an application.

Solution Explorer is the counterpart of Projects Explorer in earlier versions of Visual Studio. You can use Solution Explorer to display an organized view of projects and files associated with a solution. You can also view other *miscellaneous* files that are not directly associated with the project. However, these files enable you to build your applications, such as the files that reside on your computer's hard disk and are opened during the development of the project.

You can display the Solution Explorer window by selecting the Solution Explorer option from the View menu. Solution Explorer is displayed in Figure 17-2.

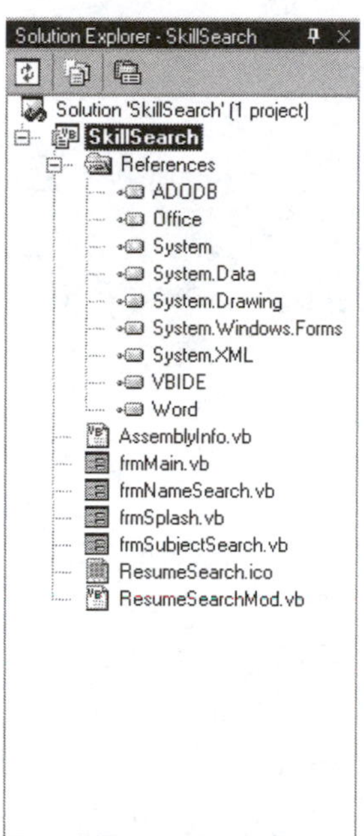

FIGURE 17-2 *The Solution Explorer window displaying a view of projects and associated files*

You can use the Solution Explorer window to simplify file management tasks. For example, you can open, copy, edit, or rename files and add or remove items from a solution. You can also disassociate an item from a project. To do this, you can right-click on the item in Solution Explorer and select the Exclude from Project option.

When you double-click on an item in Solution Explorer, the item opens in the editor or the tool associated with the item. Therefore, you can use Solution Explorer to work with multiple files simultaneously. When you right-click on an item in the window, a context menu is displayed. The options available in this menu vary with the type of item that you select in the Solution Explorer window.

The Solution Explorer window also displays a list of references added to the solution, such as references made to various libraries, namespaces, or data connections.

In addition to various files and projects, the Solution Explorer window displays a toolbar. The buttons on the toolbar are dynamic and change with respect to what you select in the Solution Explorer window. For example, if you select a form in the window, the View Code, View Designer, Refresh, Show All Files, and Properties buttons are available on the toolbar. However, when you select a reference, only the Refresh, Show All Files, and Properties buttons are displayed.

NOTE

When you select multiple files in the Solution Explorer window, only the buttons common to the files are displayed in the toolbar.

Server Explorer

At times while building your applications, you might need to access resources available on other computers on the network, such as a database existing on a server. To manage servers, Visual Studio .NET IDE offers the Server Explorer window. The Server Explorer window is a new server development window offered by Visual Studio .NET IDE. To display the Server Explorer window, select the Server Explorer option from the View menu. The Server Explorer window is displayed in Figure 17-3.

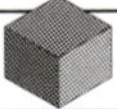

NOTE

A database connection is a link to a database.

You can use Server Explorer to make database connections to SQL servers and other databases and access available XML services within your existing projects. However, to gain access to resources on other computers, such as services, processes, event logs, and database objects, you need to have the required permissions to the computer.

FIGURE 17-3 *The Server Explorer window displaying available data connections and servers*

The Server Explorer window displays two different nodes to access servers and database objects on the network. These are the Data Connections and the Servers nodes.

You can use the Data Connections node to display the different connections that you have added to the current solution. The Data Connections node also lists various database objects, such as stored procedures, functions, tables, and views.

You can use the Servers node to display a list of the servers that are connected to your computer. You can use the Server Explorer window to connect to any listed server to which you have the required access permissions. The Server node also displays system resources, such as messaging queues and event logs available on the servers.

To program the database connections and data components, you need to add them to your current project. To add a component or a service, you can simply drag the required component or service from the Server Explorer window to your current project. This creates a reference to the component or the service. For instance, if you select and drag an event log component from an existing server to your current project, Visual Studio .NET IDE automatically creates an `EventLog` component that interacts with the specific event log component on the server.

You can use the Server Explorer window toolbar to refresh the connection and connect to a database or a server.

Dynamic Help

Imagine a situation in which you are developing your application and need immediate help related to the current task that you are performing. The Visual Studio .NET IDE provides you with Dynamic Help that you can use to access information related to the current selection or task. You can display the Dynamic Help window by selecting the Dynamic Help option from the Help menu.

All information displayed in the Dynamic Explorer window is categorized into three sections: Help, Samples, and Getting Started. When you point the cursor to a specific item or select an item in IDE, the Dynamic Help window filters the topics available in MSDN and displays the information that is relevant to the current development task. For example, if you select the Server Explorer window and view the Dynamic Help, the Dynamic Help window displays all information related to the Server Explorer window and connecting to databases. The Dynamic Help window is displayed in Figure 17-4.

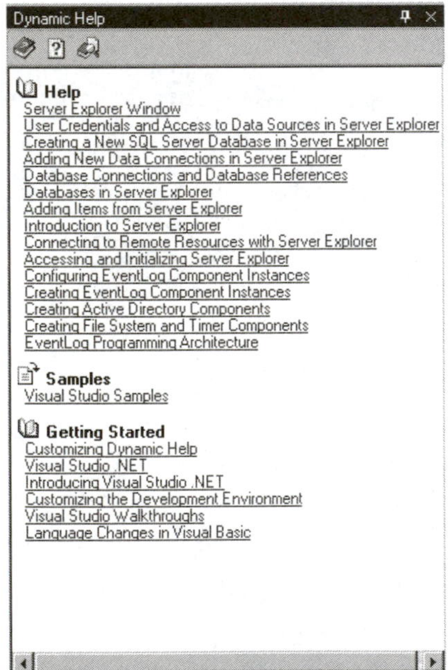

FIGURE 17-4 *The Dynamic Help window displaying information specific to the Server Explorer window*

Toolbox

To design applications in Visual Studio .NET IDE, you can use the various controls available in the Toolbox. You can view the Toolbox by selecting the Toolbox option from the View menu. The Toolbox is displayed in Figure 17-5.

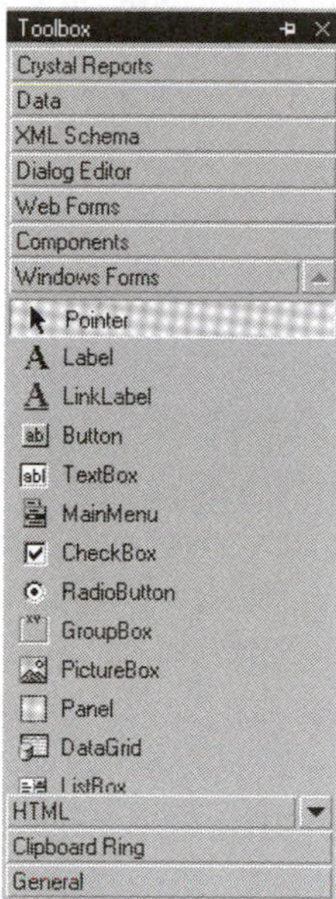

FIGURE 17-5 *The Toolbox displaying different controls categorized in tabbed pages*

The various controls available in the Toolbox are categorized into different tabs on the basis of the functionality of the controls. The different tabs of the Toolbox change depending on the current editor or designer that a user is working in. The Toolbox contains a few controls by default. However, you can also add custom controls to the Toolbox. Table 17-2 lists some of the main tabs available in the Toolbox and a brief description of each tab.

Table 17-2 Some Tabs Displayed in the Toolbox

Tab Name	Description
General	Displays the Pointer control, default controls for a project, and custom controls
Data	Displays data objects related to Visual Basic or C# Forms, such as DataSet and DataView
Components	Displays controls related to Visual Basic or C# designers

continues

Table 17-2 (continued)

Tab Name	Description
XML Schema	Displays controls related to ADO.NET Datasets and XML Schemas
Web Forms	Displays controls related to Web Forms and other validation controls
HTML	Displays controls related to Web pages and Web Forms
Clipboard Ring	Displays the Pointer control and the last 12 items added to Clipboard
Windows Forms	Displays controls related to Windows Forms and Windows applications

Class View Window

You can use the Class View window to display a hierarchical view of different solutions and projects. To display the Class View window, select the Class View option from the View menu. The Class View window is displayed in Figure 17-6.

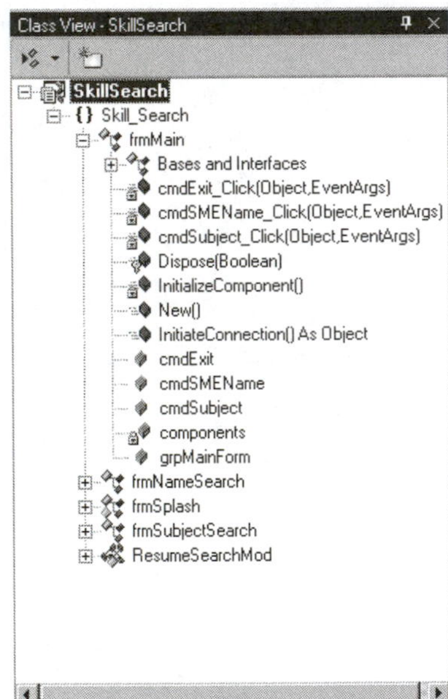

FIGURE 17-6 *The Class View window displaying various components of a project*

As you already know, each project is made of components, such as namespaces, classes, interfaces, forms, functions, and variables. You can view an organized listing of these components in the Class View window. The window also displays the organization of the components within a project such that you can comprehend the relationship between various components of a project.

In addition to viewing the components of a project, you can use the Class View window to view the code associated with a method. To do this, you need to right-click on the name of the method and select the Browse Definition option from the context menu.

You can use the toolbar available on the Class View window to sort components alphabetically, by type, or by access properties. You can also group the components of each project on the basis of their types. The toolbar also displays the New folder button. You can use this button to create virtual folders to group frequently used components. Therefore, you can access these components easily.

Properties Window

Unlike the other windows in Visual Studio .NET IDE, the Properties window resembles its counterpart in the previous versions of Visual Studio. You can use the Properties window to view the properties for a selected component. You can display the Properties window by selecting the Properties option from the View menu.

You can use the Properties window to view and modify the properties of files, folders, the current project, and solution. In addition, you can use the Properties window to modify the properties of various controls that you add to your forms. The Properties window displays properties specific to the item or component selected in IDE. For example, when you select a label component in a Windows Form, the properties for the label component are displayed in the Properties window. The Properties window is displayed in Figure 17-7.

Task List

Another enhanced feature of Visual Studio .NET IDE is the Task List window. You can use the Task List window to view error messages and display warnings during code compilation. The Task List window also displays a list of tasks. You can add new tasks and delete existing tasks. In addition, you can mark tasks as you complete them. You can also specify the priority of tasks as low, normal, and high. To display the Task List window, select the Task List option from the Other Windows submenu from the View menu.

When you double-click on an error item in the Task List window, the item opens in the appropriate Visual Studio editor at the specific location where an error is encountered in the code. The Task List window is displayed in Figure 17-8.

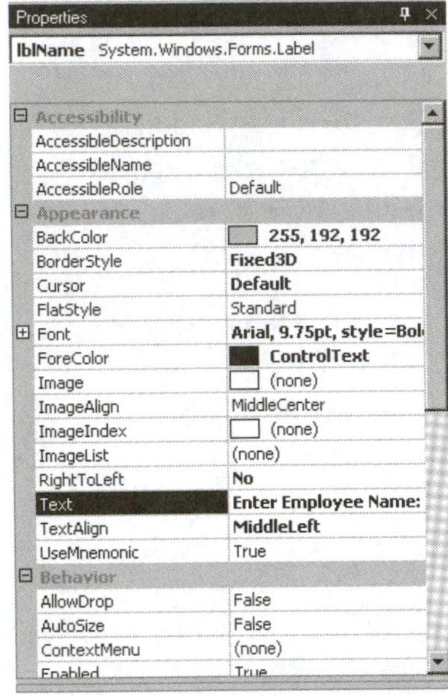

FIGURE 17-7 *The Properties window of the selected label component*

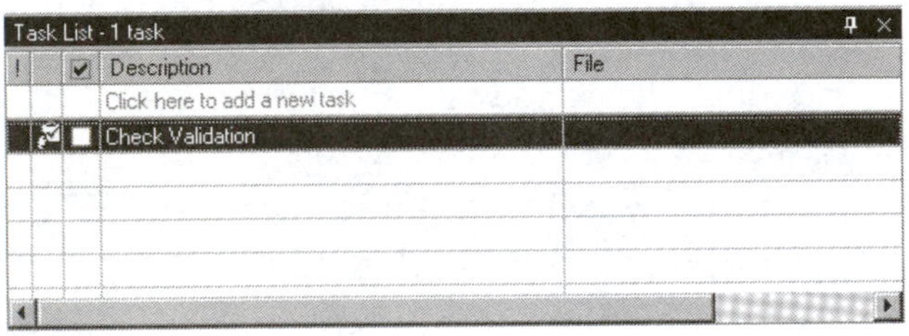

FIGURE 17-8 *The Task List window in Visual Studio .NET IDE*

You can also use the Task List window to add comments to the application code for future reference. For instance, if other developers need to work with the application that you have created, you can add appropriate comments in the code.

When you compile an application, by default all errors listed in the Task List window are marked as high priority, whereas all warnings are assigned normal priority.

Command Window

In addition to the Task List window, Visual Studio .NET IDE contains the Command window. You can use the Command window to execute various commands, such as open and save or debug and evaluate expressions. To display the Command window, select the Command Window option in the Other Windows submenu from the View menu. The Command window is displayed in Figure 17-9.

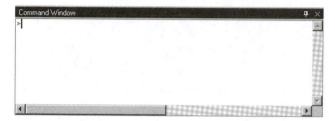

FIGURE 17-9 *The Command Window used to execute commands in Visual Studio .NET IDE*

You can use the Command window in two modes: the Command mode and the Immediate mode. The Command mode is useful for executing Visual Studio commands, such as add project, open file, find, replace, and navigate. You can execute commands that do not exit in the menu or you want to specify the commands directly instead of using the menu. On the other hand, you can use the Immediate mode for executing statements or evaluating and debugging expressions. You can also use the Immediate mode for viewing or modifying the values of variables during debugging.

IntelliSense

Visual Studio .NET IDE incorporates the use of IntelliSense. This feature enables developers write better code, which is less prone to errors. You can make use of the IntelliSense feature to handle compiled languages as well as HTML and XML. You can obtain specific and immediate information about items within code, such as tags, properties, and values. This feature enables you to implement automatic statement completion and syntax notification while you are writing the code.

You looked at the enhanced features of Visual Studio .NET IDE. The next section discusses how you can work with and manage various windows available in IDE.

Working with Windows

While working in IDE, you might need to work with multiple windows simultaneously. For example, during your project development, you might need to work with the Solution Explorer window, Properties window, and the Toolbox at the same time. To avoid cluttering the space and work efficiently within IDE, you can use the window management features of Visual Studio .NET IDE.

Hiding Windows

You can automatically hide various windows in IDE using the Auto Hide feature. When you enable the Auto Hide feature, the hidden window is displayed as a tabbed page in IDE. To display the window again, you can simply click on the tab.

To enable the Auto Hide feature, you click on the pushpin icon available on each window in IDE, such as Solution Explorer, Task List, and Properties. The push-pin icon is a toggle button, and you use it to either enable or disable the Auto Hide feature.

Figure 17-10 displays hidden windows displayed as tabbed pages in IDE.

FIGURE 17-10 *Hidden windows are displayed as tabbed pages in Visual Studio .NET IDE*

Docking Windows

In addition to hiding windows, you can also attach windows to other windows by dragging the window. When you attach a window to other windows, the window is available in the *tab-linked* mode. Therefore, all the attached windows are displayed as tabs within a single window.

Figure 17-11 displays windows in the tab-linked mode.

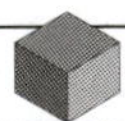

NOTE

In addition to hiding and attaching windows, you can navigate through the various open windows by using the Back and Forward buttons available in Visual Studio .NET IDE.

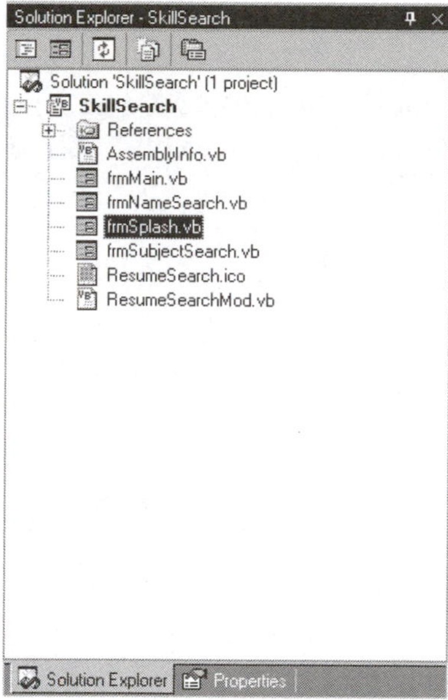

FIGURE 17-11 *The Properties window and Solution Explorer displayed in the tab-linked mode.*

In the previous sections, you learned about Visual Studio .NET IDE and the enhanced features of IDE. In the next section, you will learn how the Skill Search application has been designed using Visual Studio .NET IDE.

Designing the Skill Search Application Using Visual Studio .NET IDE

As per the requirements analysis for the Skill Search application, the application has to be designed as both a Windows application and Web application. Therefore, for the application and both Windows Forms and Web Forms need to be designed. This section details the process of designing Windows Forms and Web Forms for the Skill Search application.

Using Windows Forms

As you already know, a *form* is a window that is displayed when you are working with any application. A form acts as a user interface to the application. You can create forms to accept information from and display information to a user.

Windows Forms is a new feature offered by the .NET Framework. When working with Windows Forms, you can make use of other .NET features, such as a common application framework, managed code, object-oriented design, and enhanced security. You can also use Windows Forms to build ADO.NET-based applications by using XML.

All applications that you create using Windows Forms are based on the `System.Windows.Forms` namespace. Windows Forms are instances of classes. Therefore, when you create a form, a class is derived from `System.Windows.Forms.Form`. In addition, when you display a form at run-time, an instance of the class is created.

To use Windows Forms in your application, you need to first create a new Windows application using the File menu. When you create a new Windows application, a Windows Form is added to the application by default. You can then add various controls to forms and specify properties and events for forms. Figure 17-12 displays a new Windows application with a default Windows Form.

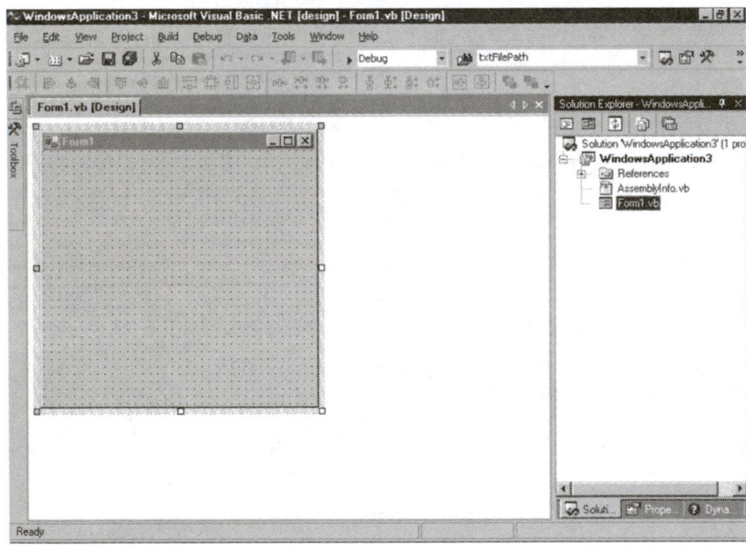

FIGURE 17-12 *Default Windows Form added to a new Windows application*

To work with Windows Forms, you need to use *Windows Forms Designer* available in Visual Studio .NET IDE. Windows Forms Designer enables you to add components and controls to your forms. Using Windows Forms Designer, you can also add default events or other events, such as the `Load` event for the form. In addition to adding controls, you can edit the `Text` property for controls and specify the placement of controls on the form. Windows Forms Designer acts as *Rapid Development Tool* and enables you to create Windows applications easily.

The Toolbox tabs available for Windows Forms include the Windows Forms tab, the Data tab, and the Components tab. Some of the Windows Forms controls are `Label`, `TextBox`, `ListBox`, `CheckBox`, and `RadioButton`. The Data tab and the Components tab include controls such as `DataSet`, `DataView`, `MessageQueue`, `EventLog`, and `Timer`.

The following sections briefly describe the various forms and related properties used in the Skill Search application.

Splash Screen

The Splash screen for the Skill Search application has been designed using Windows Forms. A `Timer` control has been added to the Splash screen so that the screen is displayed for only for a few seconds when the Skill Search application is executed. The design view of the Splash screen is displayed in Figure 17-13 with the Windows Form and the Properties window for the Splash screen.

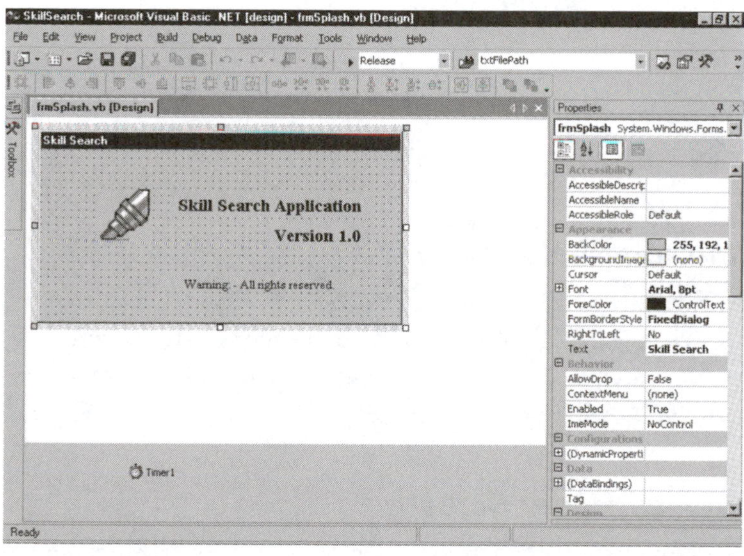

FIGURE 17-13 *The Splash screen designed in Visual Studio .NET IDE*

Search Screen

The Search screen is the main screen of the Skill Search application. The screen contains a few `Button` controls and `Label` controls. A user can click on either the Employee Name or the Employee Skills button to access other forms in the Skill Search application. The design view and the Properties window for the Search screen are displayed in Figure 17-14.

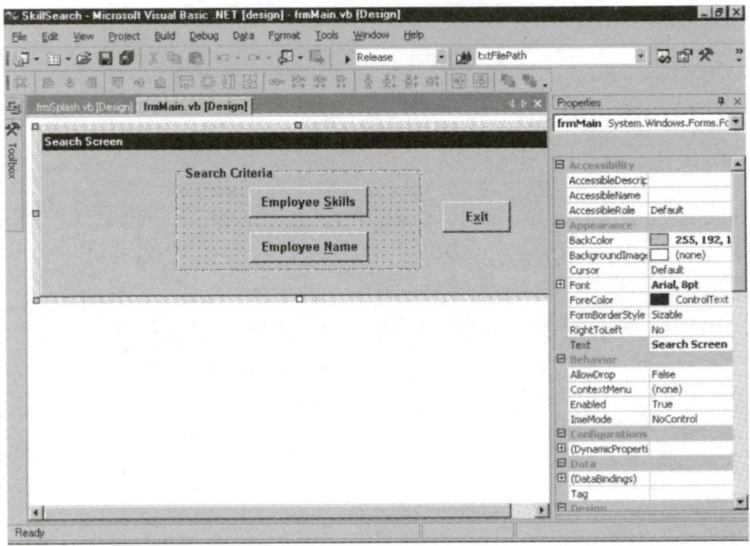

FIGURE 17-14 *The Search screen for the Skill Search application*

Search by Technology Screen

If a user clicks on the Employee Skills button on the Search screen, the Search by Technology screen is displayed. This Windows Form includes various controls, such as `Label`, `Button`, `TextBox`, and `ListBox`. The design view and the Properties window for the Search by Technology screen are displayed in Figure 17-15.

Search by Employee Name Screen

If a user clicks on the Employee Name button on the Search screen, the Search by Employee Name screen is displayed. This screen includes a `ComboBox` control that acts as both a `TextBox` and a `ListBox` control. The design view and the Properties window for the Search by Employee Name screen are displayed in Figure 17-16.

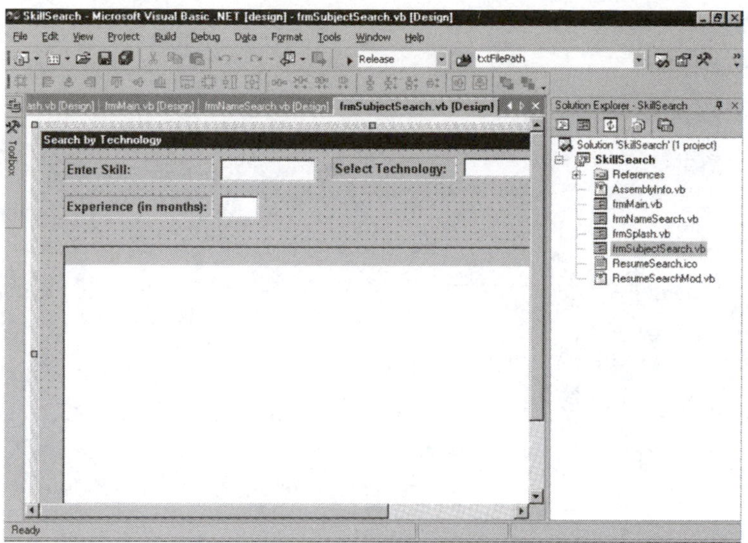

FIGURE 17-15 *The Search by Technology screen as designed in Visual Studio .NET IDE*

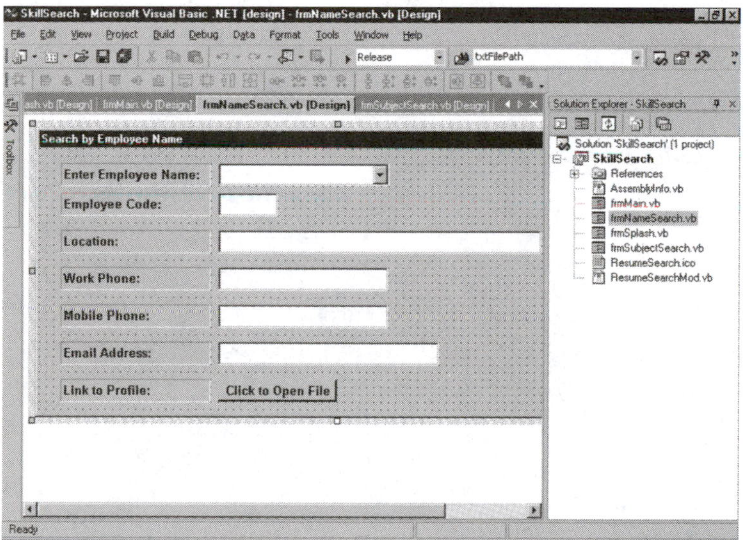

FIGURE 17-16 *The Search by Employee Name screen for the Skill Search application*

Using Web Forms

In addition to building Windows applications, you can also build Web-based applications using Web Forms. The choice between using Windows Forms and

Web Forms is dependent on the application that you are trying to build. For example, if you are creating an application that needs fast processing speed and requires using the system resources of the client application, such as a Word processor, you will need to build a Windows application. If you are creating a virtual shopping mall that has to be accessible to users over the Internet, the choice is obvious, and you would use Web Forms.

WAP

WAP (*Wireless Application Protocol*) is a worldwide standard for accessing and delivering information to wireless devices. WAP specification is a global wireless protocol specification for all wireless networks. You can use the WAP architecture as a combination of an application framework and a network framework to implement wireless Web services.

The Skill Search application has to be deployed on the Web. Therefore, you would need to build a Web application using Web Forms.

Web Forms use the technology offered by ASP .NET. ASP .NET is based on the .NET Framework and supports various programming languages, such as Visual Basic .NET, Visual C++, and Visual C# for server-side programming. You can use ASP .NET to create Web applications and Web services.

You will learn more about ASP.NET in Chapter 20, "Working with ASP.NET."

A Web Forms page incorporates a *markup* file that contains the visual, XML-based representation of the page, such as HTML, XML, and WML file. In addition, a Web Form includes a source file that contains the event-handling code. Both the markup file and the source file are stored on the server and generate a Web page for the client application.

XML

XML is a language used to create Web applications. It is a W3C standard that provides format to present structured data. The data is stored in XML documents. XML documents act like databases; however, they store data in plain text to enable multiple platforms to support that data.

As you learned in Chapter 15, "Overview of the .NET Framework," using Web Forms you create Web pages that are targeted either at any browser or a specific browser. You can also target Web pages to mobile devices that use technologies such as WAP and XML.

You can create Web Forms using the Web Forms Designer available in Visual Studio .NET IDE. You can add various controls to a Web Form using different tabs of the Toolbox, such as Web Forms, Data, HTML, and Components. To add code behind controls, you can simply double-click on the controls and add the event code. In addition, you can choose the language you are most comfortable with to add the relevant code.

Summary

In this chapter, you learned about Integrated Development Environment of Visual Studio .NET. You looked at the various enhanced features of IDE. In addition, you learned how to use Windows Forms and Web Forms in the Skill Search application. With this information, you can create a rich user interface for your Windows and Web applications.

Chapter 18

Working with Databases by Using VB.NET and ADO.NET

You created the user interface for the Skill Search application in the previous chapter. Next, you need to create a database in Microsoft Access 2000 to store the resumes of employees. The database will act as the back end for the application. In this chapter, you will learn to work with databases by using VB.NET and ADO.NET. You will also learn about database connectivity and manipulating information in a database.

Database Architecture

Typically, all applications have to perform some kind of database access. Database access refers to connecting to the database, retrieving information from the database, and manipulating information. The database architecture consists of the following components:

- **User Interface.** The user interacts with the user interface of the application. The user interface may contain forms that display information and accept user inputs.
- **Database Engine.** The database engine is responsible for reading, writing, and updating the database. It acts as an interface between the user interface and the data store. The database engine used for Microsoft Access is the *Jet Database Engine.*
- **Data Store.** The data store is a set of files that contain database tables. However, a database is considered to be passive, because it cannot work on the data on its own.

A database application can be categorized into the following three types:

- **Single user DBMS.** A single-user database allows only one user to view or manipulate data.
- **Multi-user DBMS.** A multi-user database allows more than one user to view or manipulate data.
- **Client/Server DBMS.** In a client/server DBMS system, both the database engine and the data store are located on one server. Multiple client applications can then send requests for the services of the engine.

For the Skill Search application, you need to create a `Skills` database in Microsoft Access 2000. The `Skill_Info` table present in the `Skills` database is used to store the details of employees of Red Sky IT Systems. The fields of the `Skill_Info` table are as follows:

- `Name`. Stores the name of an employee.
- `Location`. Stores the work address of an employee.
- `Home_Address`. Stores the home address of an employee.
- `Res_Phone`. Stores the home phone number of an employee.
- `Work_Phone`. Stores the work phone number of an employee.
- `EmpCode`. Stores the employee code of the employee.
- `Mobile_Phone`. Stores the mobile phone number of an employee.
- `Email_Id`. Stores the e-mail address of the employee.
- `File_Name`. Stores the name of the Word file that contains the skill information of an employee.
- `Total_Exp`. Stores the total work experience of an employee.
- `Qualification`. Stores the qualification details of the employee.
- `Certification`. Stores the certification details of an employee, if any.
- `Skill1_Name`. Stores the main skill of an employee. The skills of employees are categorized into main skill and secondary skill.
- `Skill1_Exp`. Stores the total work experience of an employee in the main skill area.
- `Skill2_Name`. Stores the name of the secondary skill of an employee.
- `Skill2_Exp`. Stores the total work experience of an employee in the secondary skill area.

After the structure of the `Skill_Info` table is created, the fields of the table are then populated with records.

An application can access data by using different methods. These methods are used for database connectivity in an application. These methods are as follows:

- Data Access Objects (DAO)
- Open Database Connectivity (ODBC)
- Remote Data Objects (RDO)
- ActiveX Data Objects (ADO)

The following sections discuss each one of them in detail.

Data Access Objects (DAO)

DAO is a library of objects that represent the structure of the database and the data that it contains. These objects can be used to manipulate the data in the database from the code. You can also use the DAO objects to create tables and queries and access remote data sources. The various DAO objects are listed in Table 18-1.

Table 18-1 Objects of the DAO Model

Object	Description
`DBEngine`	This object represents the Microsoft Jet Database engine. This object has methods such as the `CompactDatabase` method and the `RepairDatabase` method.
`Workspace`	This object is an instance of the `DBEngine` object.
`Error`	This object represents an error that might occur when using any of the DAO objects.
`Database`	This object represents an open database in the `Workspace`. You can refer to all the open `Database` objects in the `Workspace` object by using the `Databases` collection.
`User`	This object defines a user account for a workgroup database.
`Group`	This object is used to represent a group in the workgroup database.
`TableDef`	This object represents the table in a `Database` object. You can also refer to all the table definitions in the `Database` object by using the `TableDefs` collection.
`QueryDef`	This object represents a query in a `Database` object. You can also refer to all the query definitions in the `Database` object by using the `QueryDefs` collection.
`RecordSet`	This object represents the records in a base table or from a query. You can also use the `RecordSets` collection to refer to all the open `RecordSet` objects in the `Database` object.
`Container`	This object stores the built-in objects contained in the database. Each built-in object is a `Document` object. For example, table, query, and so on.
`Field`	This object represents a column of information. It contains the value of a particular field for the current record for a `RecordSet` object.
`Index`	This object specifies the order in which the records are placed in a `TableDef` object.

NOTE

A workgroup is a group of users in a multi-user environment. All users of a workgroup share data. Every workgroup maintains a workgroup information file that contains user account and group account. The user account stores the user's name and personal ID (PID). The group account, on the other hand, is a collection of user accounts and is identified by a group name and PID.

The object hierarchy in DAO supports two types of environments:

- **Microsoft Jet.** This environment is used for working with Microsoft Jet Databases (.MDB files), Jet-connected Open Database Connectivity (ODBC) databases, and installable Indexed Sequential Access Method (ISAM) databases.
- **ODBCDirect.** This environment is used to connect to the remote ODBC database directly. You do not need to load the entire Jet engine if you are using ODBCDirect.

You can use the properties and methods of the previously listed objects to manipulate the data stored in the database. You will learn about the various operations that can be performed by these objects, such as creating a database, connecting to a Jet database, and so on, in the next section.

Operations Using DAO Objects

The basic steps that you perform to access data from a database are as follows:

1. Declare variables for the objects.
2. Establish a workspace session.
3. Open the database.
4. Open the recordset for the table.

One of the basic operations that you need to perform while working with the DAO objects is to connect to a database. However, you need to invoke a workspace instance before creating the database. A new workspace session can be created using the `CreateWorkspace` method of the `DBEngine` object. The syntax of the `CreateWokspace` method is as follows:

```
DBEngine.CreateWorkspace (Name, User, Password, UseType)
```

In the this syntax:

- `Name` refers to the name given to the workspace.
- `User` refers to the username of the person connected to this database session.
- `Password` refers to the password of the person connected to this database session.
- `UseType` refers to the type of workspace created. The `dbUseJet` keyword is used to create a Microsoft Jet workspace, and the `dbUseODBC` keyword is used to create an ODBCDirect workspace.

Consider the following example, which creates a Microsoft Jet workspace:

```
Dim myws as Workspace
Set myws = DBEngine.CreateWorkspace (Name:="Myspace", User:="John"
   Password:="XXXX" UseType:=dbUseJet)
```

An important point to note here is that the Jet engine creates a default workspace every time you open a database.

Once a workspace is created, you can use the `CreateDatabase` method of the `Workspace` object to create a Jet database from scratch. The syntax of the `CreateDatabase` method is as follows:

```
Workspace.CreateDatabase (Name, Locale, Option)
```

In this syntax:

- `Workspace` refers to the `Workspace` object where you want the database to be created.
- `Name` refers to the name or the path of the new database.
- `Locale` refers to a constant that specifies the collating order for the database. The collating order of a database is used when performing comparisons or sorting.
- `Option` refers to a constant value that specifies whether the database is encrypted. It also specifies the version of the Jet database. The possible values for this option are listed in Table 18-2.

Table 18-2 Constant Values for Option in the CreateDatabase Method

Constant	Description
dbEncrypt	This value indicates that the database will be encrypted. It has a default value of 2.
dbVersion10	This value indicates that the database created will use the Jet 1.0 version.
dbVersion11	This value indicates that the database created will use the Jet 1.1 version.
dbVersion20	This value indicates that the database created will use the Jet 2.0 version.
dbVersion30	This value indicates that the database created will use the Jet 3.0 version.

Once created, you can open a database by using the `OpenDatabase` method of the `Database` object. The syntax of the `OpenDatabase` method is as follows:

```
Workspace.OpenDatabase (Name, Options, ReadOnly, Connect)
```

In this syntax:

- `Workspace` refers to the `Workspace` object in which the database will be opened.
- `Name` refers to the path of the database file.
- `Options` is used to open a database with exclusive access. The default value is `False`.
- `ReadOnly` is used to open the database with read-only access. The default value is `False`.
- `Connect` refers to a string that specifies extra parameters for opening the database.

After you have opened the database, you can open the `RecordSet` object by using the `Open RecordSet` method of the `Database` object. The syntax of the `OpenRecordSet` method is as follows:

```
Database.OpenRecordset (Name, Type, Options, LockEdit)
```

In this syntax:

- `Database` refers to the `Database` object that contains the data for the recordset.
- `Name` refers to a string specifying the source for the recordset. It can be a table name, query name, or a SQL statement.
- `Type` refers to the type of recordset that you want to create. The various recordset types available are listed in Table 18-3.

Table 18-3 Recordset Types

Type Constant	Description
`dbOpenTable`	This type refers to a base table or an attached table in the `Open Database` object. An attached table is a table in another database. Some operations, such as indexing and sorting, are allowed only on table-type recordsets.
`dbOpenDynaset`	This type refers to a set of records from a table or an attached table, or the results of queries containing fields from one or more tables. It enables you to extract data from more than one table. It is dynamic because it allows you to update records by adding, editing, and deleting.
`dbOpenSnapshot`	This type is similar to a dynaset-type recordset, except that you cannot update records in a snapshot-type recordset. Therefore, the records in a snapshot are static.
`dbOpenForwardOnly`	This is similar to a snapshot-type recordset, except that you can only scroll forward through its records.

- `Options` refers to one or more constants that are used to specify the characteristics of the new recordset. These constant values are listed in Table 18-4.

Table 18-4 Constant Values for the Characteristics of a Recordset

Constant	Description
`dbAppendOnly`	This value specifies that you can append only new records. This constant is used only with dynaset-type recordset.
`dbSeeChanges`	This value generates an error if more than one user tries to edit a record at the same time.
`dbDenyWrite`	This value prevents users from editing and adding records.
`dbInconsistent`	This value allows you to update all fields in a multiple-table query recordset. This value is used only with the dynaset recordset.
`dbConsistent`	This value allows you to update a single field in a multiple-table query recordset. This value is used only with the dynaset recordset.

- `LockEdit` refers to a constant value that specifies the locking attributes of the recordset. The various constant values that can be assigned to the recordset are `dbReadOnly`, `dbPessimistic`, `dbOptimistic`, `dboptimisticValue`, and `dbOptimisationBatch`.

The `OpenDatabase` method and the `OpenRecordset` method are used for the Jet database engine. If you want to connect to a non-Jet database, you need to attach the data source to an existing Jet database as a new `TableDef` object.

NOTE

Although you can directly use the `OpenDatabase` method for a non-Jet database, the recordset operations perform faster if you link the database to a Jet database.

To connect to a Jet database, a Jet database is opened, and the `TableDef` object is created using the `CreateTableDef` method of the `Database` object. You can set the properties of the `TableDef` object to set up the `TableDef`. However, the most commonly used properties are the `Connect` property and the `SourceTableName` property. The general usage of these properties is as follows:

```
TableDef.Connect = databasetype;DATABASE = path
```

In this syntax, `TableDef` is the `TableDef` object, and `databasetype` specifies the type of the database that you are attaching. The various types are dBASE III, dBASE IV, dBASE 5.0, Paradox 3.x, Paradox 4.x, Paradox 5.x, Lotus WK 1, Lotus WK 2, Lotus WK 3, HTML Import, HTML Export, ODBC, Excel 3.0, Excel 4.0, Excel 5.0, Excel 8.0, Text, and Exchange 4.0. `Path` specifies the drive and directory that contain the table that you want to use.

The `SourceTableName` property is used to specify the table that you want to use. You need to assign the name of the table to this property.

You need to create a `TableDef` object variable to hold the `TableDef`. After the `TableDef` object is created, you can use the `TableDef` object as a Jet table.

TIP

Once created, you can add the object to the `TableDefs` collection by using the `Append` method.

This section discussed the DAO method for accessing data in a database. As stated earlier, you can also use OBDC to interact with a database. This is discussed in the next section.

Open Database Connectivity (ODBC)

In the preceding section, you learned that DAO allows you direct access to the Jet databases through the Jet database engine. You also learned that to attach to non-Jet databases you can attach the table to an existing Jet database. However, both options result in many disadvantages. Both methods require the Jet engine to access data, and the direct method of accessing data from the Jet engine is very slow. Therefore, to overcome these problems, the ODBCDirect method is used.

To work with the ODBCDirect method, you need to create the ODBCDirect workspace. You can create an ODBCDirect workspace by specifying a constant value `dbUseODBC` in the `CreateWorkspace` method of the `DBEngine`. Recall the syntax of the `CreateWorkspace` method:

```
DBEngine.CreateWorkspace (Name, User, Password, UseType)
```

You need to assign the value of `UseType` as `dbUseODBC` to specify an ODBCDirect workspace.

Consider the following example, which creates an ODBCDirect workspace:

```
Dim myODBCws As Workspace
Set myODBCws = DBEngine.CreateWorkspace (Name:= "ODBCWorkspace", User:= "John",
   Password:= "xxxx" , UseType:= "dbUseODBC)
```

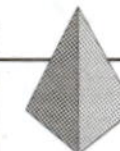

TIP

You can also define the cursor type that you want to use inside the workspace in ODBCDirect. You can specify the cursor type by using the `DefaultCursorDriver` property. The possible values for this property are `dbUseDefaultCursor`, `dbUseODBCCursor`, `dbUseServerCursor`, `dbUseClientBatchCursor`, and `dbUseNoCursor`.

To connect to a database in ODBCDirect, you first need to define the data source. You can define a data source by using the Administrative Tool's Data Sources Icon from the Control Panel. The steps to define a data source are listed below.

1. Click on the Administrative Tools option in the Control Panel.
2. Click on the Data Sources (ODBC) option from the Administrative Tools option to display the ODBC Data Source Administrator dialog box as shown in Figure 18-1.

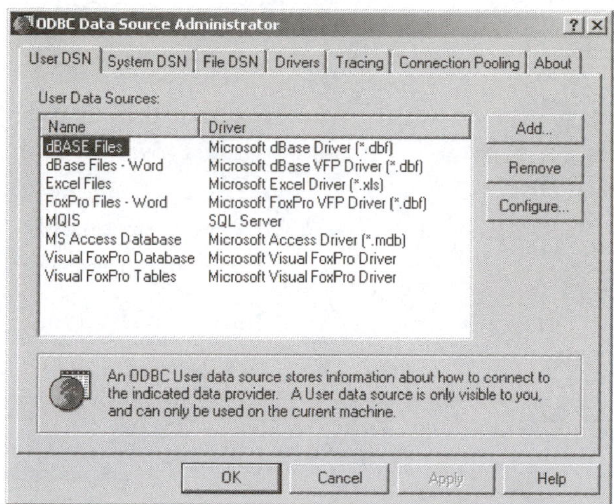

FIGURE 18-1 *The default ODBC Data Source Administrator dialog box*

3. Click on Add in the User DSN tab to display the Create New Data Source dialog box as shown in Figure 18-2.

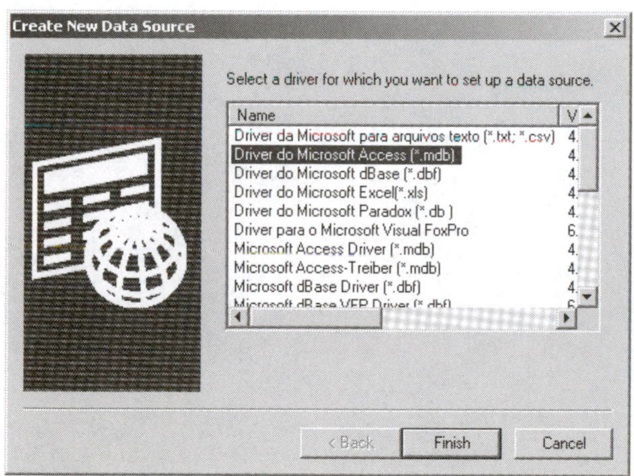

FIGURE 18-2 *The Create New Data Source dialog box allows you to select the type of driver to be used for the data source.*

4. Click on Driver do Microsoft Access (*.mdb) and click on Finish. The ODBC Microsoft Access Setup dialog box is displayed as shown in Figure 18-3.

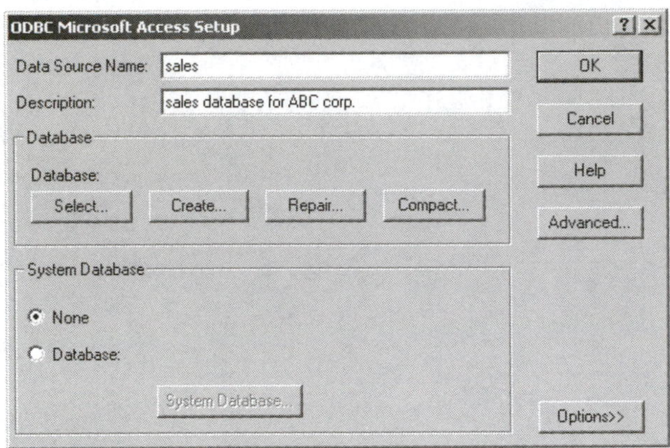

FIGURE 18-3 *This dialog box is used to specify the name and description of the data source.*

5. Enter the name of the data source in the Data Source Name text box. You can also enter a description for the data source in the Description text box.
6. Click on the Select button to display the Select Database dialog box as shown in Figure 18-4.

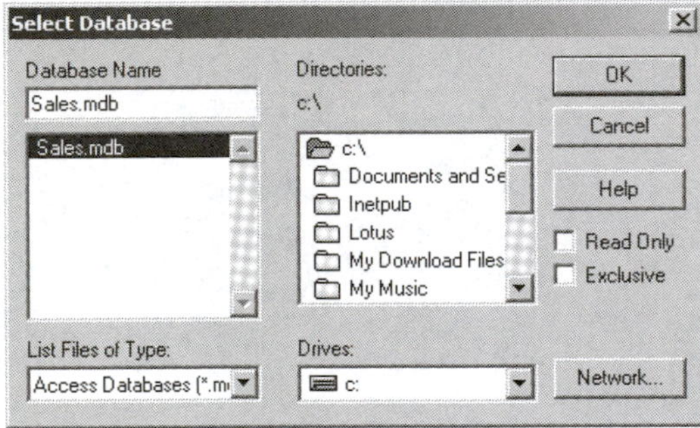

FIGURE 18-4 *This dialog box is used to specify the location of the data source.*

7. Select the database from its location. The ODBC Microsoft Access Setup dialog box will now also display the location of the database as shown in Figure 18-5.

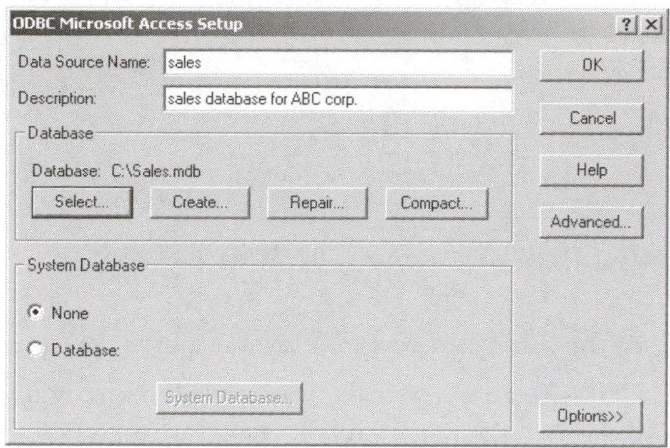

FIGURE 18-5 *The ODBC Microsoft Access Setup dialog box after the user has specified the name, description, and location of the data source*

8. The data source name will now appear in the ODBC Data Source Administrator dialog box as shown in Figure 18-6. Click on the OK button in the OBDC Data Source Administrator dialog box.

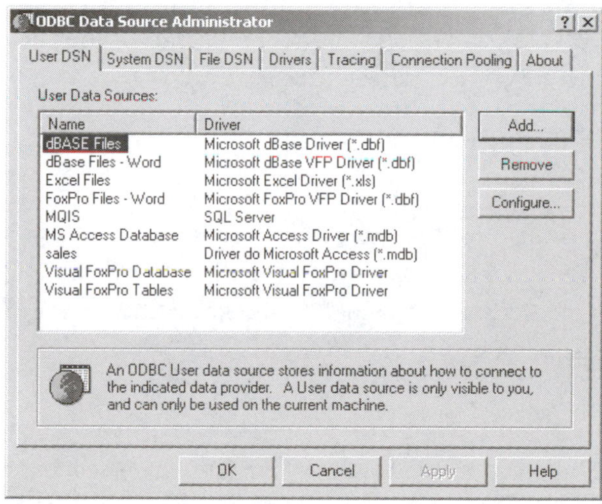

FIGURE 18-6 *The newly added data source name* `sales.mdb` *in the ODBC Data Source Administrator dialog box*

After you have defined the data source to be used, you can then establish a connection with the database. You learned that the `OpenDatabase` method of the `Database` object is used to connect to the data source. The same can be used in an ODBCDirect workspace. However, you can also establish a `Connection` object.

The syntax of the `OpenDatabase` method when applied to the ODBCDirect workspace is as follows:

```
ODBCWorkspace.OpenDatabase (Name, Options, ReadOnly, Connect)
```

In this syntax:

- `ODBCWorkspace` refers to the ODBCWorkspace in which the database will be opened.
- `Name` specifies the name of the data source to which you want to connect.
- `Options` refers to a constant value that determines whether the user will be prompted while establishing the connection. The possible values for this option are `dbDriverNoPrompt`, `dbDriverPrompt`, `dbDriverComplete`, and `dbDriverCompleteRequired`.
- `ReadOnly` specifies the read-only access for the database.
- `Connect` refers to a string that can be used to specify the extra parameters to open a database.

You can use the `Connect` property when connecting to an ODBC data source in a client/server model. However, you need to specify a few more parameters such as the user ID (UID), password (PWD), and so on. The general syntax of the `Connect` property when connecting to an ODBC data source is as follows:

```
Object.Connect = "ODBC; DATABASE = dbname; UID = user ID; PWD = password;
  DSN = datasource
```

Using the `OpenDatabase` method is the most preferred way of connecting to a data source in an ODBCDirect workspace. However, another method for data connectivity is the `OpenConnection` method of the `Connection` object. The syntax of the `OpenConnection` method is as follows:

```
ODBCWorkspace.OpenConnection (Name, Options, ReadOnly, Connect)
```

After you have established the connection, you can invoke the `OpenRecordset` method to work with the ODBCDirect recordsets. The syntax of the `OpenRecordset` method used with ODBCDirect is the same as discussed in the previous section. However, there are a few changes as listed here:

- ODBCDirect workspace does not support the table-type recordset. Therefore, you cannot use the `dbOpenTable` constant for the `Type` argument in the syntax of the `OpenRecordset` method.

- The default value of the `Type` argument in `OpenRecordset` method is `dbOpenForwardOnly`.
- The default value for the `LockEdit` argument in `OpenRecordset` is `dbReadOnly`.
- You can return multiple `Recordset` objects from a single `OpenRecordset` method.

CAUTION

It is important to note here that ODBCDirect does not support indexing and methods such as `Seek`, `FindLast`, `FindFirst`, `FindNext`, and `FindPrevious`.

Returning more than one recordset object is a distinct feature of ODBCDirect. It can return multiple recordset objects in a single call to the `OpenRecordset` method. This can be done by specifying multiple SQL Select statements in the `Name` argument of the `OpenRecordset` method as follows:

```
Set myrs = con.OpenRecordset ("SELECT * FROM publishers;
   " & "SELECT * FROM authors")
```

However, you need to keep a few points in mind before using this technique of returning multiple recordset objects:

- This technique cannot be used on Jet databases.
- Updating the returned recordsets is not possible because they have read-only access.
- The returned object will act like a forward-only snapshot recordset.

In this section, you learned about ODBC, ODBCDirect, and the various operations performed for database connectivity by using ODBCDirect. In the next section, you will learn about RDO, which is used for remote connectivity.

Remote Data Access (RDO)

DAO allows you to access data from a database only when there is a connection with the database. To provide a more efficient way of accessing data, Microsoft developed the Remote Access Data Objects (RDO). RDO can be considered as an advancement over DAO. However, an interesting point to note is that RDO was designed for accessing data from connected databases.

RDO enables you ODBC-based data access from databases on servers such as SQL Server databases. Both RDO and ADO were designed for relational databases.

In the following section, you learn the basics of working with a database by using the Active Data Objects.

ActiveX Data Objects (ADO)

The various operations of database connectivity such as establishing a connection, connecting to the data source, and data manipulation are possible with the help of ADO.

To use ADO in your project, you first need to create a reference to the ADO library, which acts as a COM component. To add a reference to your project, click on the Add Reference option from the Project menu to display the Add Reference dialog box as shown in Figure 18-7.

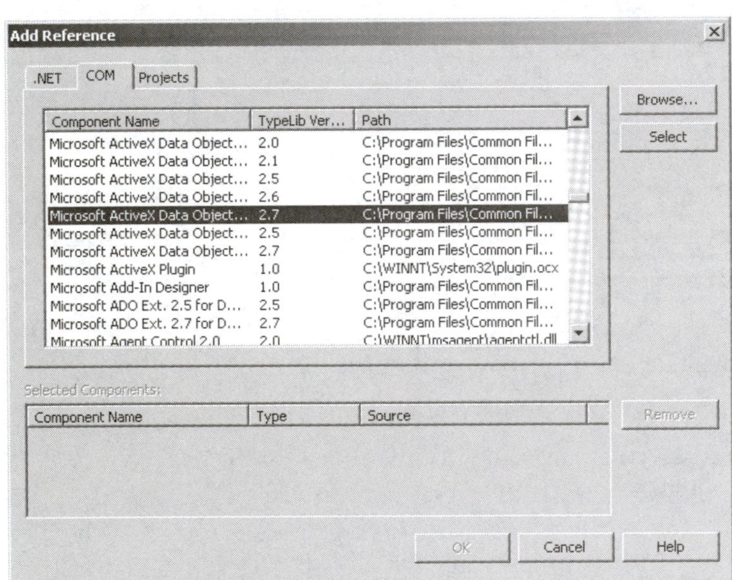

FIGURE 18-7 *The Add Reference dialog box*

Click on the COM tab to display the COM components and select the Microsoft ActiveX Data Objects 2.7 Library. Click on Select to add the item to the list of selected components, and then click on OK to add the component to the project.

Establishing Connection

Recall that to access data in a database, you first need to establish a connection with the database. You can establish a connection with the database by using the `Connection` object of ADO. To establish a connection, you need to create a new `Connection` object. The ADO library is referenced as ADODB in code. Therefore, to create a new `Connection` object, you need to write the following code:

```
Dim myADOConnection As New ADODB.Connection()
```

You connect to a data source by using the `Open` method of the `Connection` object. The syntax of the `Open` method is as follows:

```
Objectvariable.Open ([ConnectionString] As String, [User ID] As String,
   [Password] As String, [Options] As Long)
```

In this syntax:

- `ConnectionString` refers to a string that specifies connection information such as the data source name, the name of the data provider, username, password, name of the database driver, and the data source server name.
- `User ID` refers to the name of the user when connecting to the data source. `User ID` is an optional argument.
- `Password` refers to the password specified by the user when connecting to the data source. This is an optional argument.
- `Options` refers to a value that specifies whether the `Connection` object should return synchronously or asynchronously.

It is a good practice to close a data source explicitly when you no longer need it. You can close a connection to the database by using the `Close` method of the `Connection` object. The syntax of the `Close` method is as follows:

```
myADOConnection.Close()
```

Once you have established a connection with the data source, you can create a `Recordset` object to manipulate data by using ADO. The `Recordset` object can contain the result of a table, query, or a stored procedure. You can then use the recordset to add, edit, delete, find, and navigate records.

Consider a situation in which two users are manipulating the same data at the same time. This may result in a collision and considerable loss of data. You can prevent such situations by locking. The next section discusses the various locking schemes in ADO.

Locking Schemes

All recordsets make use of one or more locking schemes. A locking scheme determines when the data is locked and cannot be used by others. The locking scheme that you choose depends upon the situation in which you want to use it. You might need a stronger locking scheme in situations where you want to prevent multiple users from accessing data. However, you might not need this type of locking scheme in situations where there is no such conflict. The various locking schemes are as listed in Table 18-5. The default is `adLockReadOnly`.

Table 18-5 Locking Scheme for Recordsets in ADO

Lock Type	Description
`adLockReadOnly`	This value specifies read-only access to records. This is the default option and is used with static cursors and forward-only cursors.
`adLockPessimistic`	This value specifies the locking by the provider itself. The provider usually locks records at the data source immediately upon editing.
`adLockOptimistic`	This value specifies that the provider locks the records only when you call the Update method and not at the time of editing.
`adLockBatchOptimistic`	This value specifies that the records are locked in Batch Update Mode.

Creating ADO Recordsets

To create a recordset, you need to use the `Open` method of the `Recordset` object. The syntax of the `Open` method is as follows:

```
Object.Open ([Source], [ActiveConnection], [CursorType], [LockType], [Options])
```

In this syntax:

- `Source` refers to a SQL statement or a table name. This is an optional argument.

- `ActiveConnection` refers to a data source and is used to accept a `Connection` object.
- `CursorType` refers to the type of cursor o be used. The possible values are `adOpenStatic`, `adOpenForwardOnly`, `adOpenDynamic`, and `adOpenKeyset`.
- `LockType` refers to the type of locking scheme to be used.
- `Options` is used to provide additional options to the recordset.

Consider the following example, which creates a recordset:

```
my_rsSales.Open ("Sales" , my_ADOConnection)
```

This line of code creates a recordset with the default cursor and lock settings.

To work with databases, you also need to work with the *fields*. Fields are the data elements in a table. To access fields, you use the `Fields` collection as follows:

```
My_rsSales . Fields (" ProductName") . Value = " Chair"
```

Note that an exception will occur at run time if you misspell a field.

To access data from fields in a recordset, it is important that the recordset is pointed at the desired record. A recordset might also point to the beginning-of-file or end-of-file. This can be tested by determining the value of the BOF and EOF property of the recordset.

NOTE

The beginning-of-file is encountered when the recordset is positioned immediately after the first record of the recordset. The end-of-file is encountered when the recordset is positioned immediately after the last record of the recordet.

If BOF returns a true value, you are at the beginning of the file, and if EOF returns a true value, you are at the end of the file.

TIP

If there are no records in the recordset, both BOF and EOF will return `True`.

Navigating Records in a Recordset

Once you have created a recordset, you will need to navigate through the different records that it contains. ADO provides a number of methods to navigate through records, as listed here:

- `MoveFirst`. This method is used to move to the first record in the recordset.
- `MoveNext`. This method is used to move to the next record in the recordset.
- `MovePrevious`. This method is used to move to the previous record in the recordset.
- `MoveLast`. This method is used to move to the last record in the recordset.

For example, consider the following code snippet that moves from one record to another and displays each using the `ShowRecord()` method until the end-of-file is encountered:

```
If Not (my_rsSales.EOF)
    My_rsSales.MoveNext
    Call ShowRecord()
End If
```

To add records in a recordset, you need to call the `AddNew()` method of the `Recordset` object. On encountering the `AddNew()` method, the cursor is positioned to a new record. You can then enter the field values and save the record by calling the `Update()` method of the `Recordset` object. You can also call the `CancelUpdate()` method if you do not want to add the record.

You might need to edit the information stored in records. ADO provides a simple way of editing records. Make changes to the specific fields of the record and call the `Update()` method of the `Recordset` object. The changes will be made. If, however, you want to cancel the changes you made, call the `CancelUpdate()` method of the `Recordset` object to cancel the changes.

You can delete records when you no longer need them. To delete a record, you first need to position the record pointer to the record that you want to delete and call the `Delete()` method of the `Recordset` object. The specified record will be deleted.

ADO.NET is the new database technology that is built on ADO. ADO is still considered a good data-access solution especially for desktops, however if you are writing a large-scale application for an e-commerce site, ADO.NET proves to be more than useful. Therefore, ADO.NET is used for database connectivity in the Skill Search application. The following section discusses the concepts of ADO.NET.

Introducing ADO.NET

ADO.NET is the latest offering by Microsoft for database connectivity. One of the biggest advantages of using ADO.NET is its disconnected architecture. All traditional applications maintained an open database connection, which did not prove to be useful because of the database resources it consumed. If a component established a connection with a database and held it open for a long time, it consumed a lot of expensive database resources; however, it was needed for only a small percentage of that time. This overhead of database connections was even more when the number of users grew. This disadvantage ceases to exist in ADO.NET.

As stated, ADO.NET uses a disconnected architecture, therefore it solves the problem of scalability by reducing the number of active connections and also makes data transfer from one component to another easier.

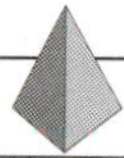

TIP

If, however, you need to use a connected architecture to the underlying database, you should use ADO instead of ADO.NET.

ADO.NET stores the disconnected data in a `DataSet`. A `DataSet` is similar to a recordset in ADO, but with a little difference. A recordset in ADO always resembles a single table even if the data that it contains is from different tables. The resultant recordset is made up of rows and columns. However, a `DataSet` in ADO.NET can store multiple tables in its cache. You can then retrieve data from these tables, set relationships between tables, or join tables. Therefore, a `DataSet` acts like a mini database but with a subset of the data or tables from the database.

The tables in a `DataSet` can be from multiple databases, for example, a SQL database and an ORACLE database. The `DataSet` adapter object is used to hold the information about the connection to the underlying database. You can use the methods of the `DataSet` adapter object to retrieve and update data. However, you need to provide the appropriate SQL statements or stored procedure names for retrieving and updating data.

When passing data from one `DataSet` to another, XML is used. Therefore, if you want to write a `DataSet` to disk, you can do that in an XML format. An ADO recordset, on the other hand, uses a binary format that cannot be used on any other platform. XML uses a text-based standard that can be used by any platform.

Objects of ADO.NET

You will find a number of objects in ADO.NET that sound similar to the ones in ADO. However, you need to be careful while using them because you may assume certain capabilities of these objects based on your knowledge of ADO, which might not exist in their ADO.NET counterpart.

As you already know by now, the first step is to make the database connection. ADO.NET provides the `oleDbConnection` object and the `SQLConnection` object to connect to a data source. The `oleDbConnection` object uses OLE DB for connection. The `SQLConnection` object uses a local driver to connect to a SQL Server and results in better performance than the OLE DB. Because the Skill Search application does not uses SQL Server, this section discusses how to use `oleDbConnection`.

To connect to a data source, you need to define the connection string, create the connection object, and open the connection.

Consider the following code snippet, which defines the variable, and creates and opens the connection:

```
Dim myString As String = "Provider = SQLOLEDB.1; Data Source = Sales;" "UID = sa;
   PWD = ; Initial Catalog = northwind;"
Dim myConn As New oleDbConnection()
    myconn.ConnectionString = connString
    myconn.Open()
```

The `Open()` method is used to open a connection with the database. Next, you need to create a command to run against the database. You can do this by using the `OleDbCommand` object or the `SqlCommand` object if you are using a `SqlConnection`.

You learned to establish a connection to the database and create commands to retrieve the records. However, as with ADO, you cannot store these records in a connection or a command; you need an object that can hold these records.

There is another method of retrieving records in ADO.NET in addition to the `DataSet` method. It is known as the `DataReader`.

You can use `DataSet` to access records that result from a query. Consider a situation in which you want to retrieve a large amount of data and do not want to consume a lot of memory. You can use a `DataReader` in such cases. A `DataReader` is an object that reads data. It is used to read the data one record at a time in a forward-only mode. It allows you to examine one record at a time and then moves on to the next one. Because only one record is read at a time, only one record is in memory, and, therefore, the memory requirement is cut down significantly. However, if you want to scroll through the data or make changes to it, you should store the data in a `DataSet`.

The `DataSet` object that you learned about is a combination of one or more `DataTable` objects. A `DataSet` object is used to retrieve data from the database and stores it in a `DataTable` object inside a `DataSet`. Therefore, in ADO.NET the `DataSet` acts as a collection of tables where each table may contain data from multiple tables in the underlying database.

To create and fill the `DataSet`, you need to first create a `DataSetAdapter` object. You then need to set a reference to the `OleDbCommand` or the `SqlCommand` that will be used to provide the records. This is displayed in the following lines of code:

```
Dim myCommand As New OleDbDataAdapter()
myCommand.SelectCommand = myCom
```

The `Fill()` method of the `DataSetAdapter` object is used to execute the statement in the command object.

Next, you need to create a `DataSet` object and call the `Fill()` method on the `DataSetAdapter` object. The new `DataSet` created is passed as an argument to the `Fill()` method. The second parameter to the `Fill()` method is the name of the `DataTable` inside the `DataSet`.

Consider the following lines of code, which create a `DataTable` inside the `DataSet`:

```
Dim dsSales As New DataSet()
myCommand.Fill (dsSales, "Products")
```

A table named `Products` is created inside the `DataSet` when you execute this code. When a `Fill()` method is encountered, a table with the table name that you specify is automatically created if a table with the specified name does not already exist in the database. The schema of the table matches that of the result that you get back from the query. However, you can also define the table schema explicitly, in which case the `Fill()` method simply inserts the data into the table.

An important point to note here is that in ADO.NET, objects are independent of each other. This can be seen in the previous example where there is no property in the `DataSetAdapter` that binds it to a particular `DataSet` and vice versa.

You can also define relationships between tables if you have multiple tables in a `DataSet`. Therefore, you can insert, update, or delete records in the tables in the `DataSet` or in the underlying database.

ADO.NET with VB.NET

VB.NET consists of a number of controls for accessing data from an application. You can view the various controls in VB.NET by creating a new Windows application project in VB.NET and clicking on the Toolbox. Click on the Data tab at the top and a series of controls appear in the drop-down list, as shown in Figure 18-8.

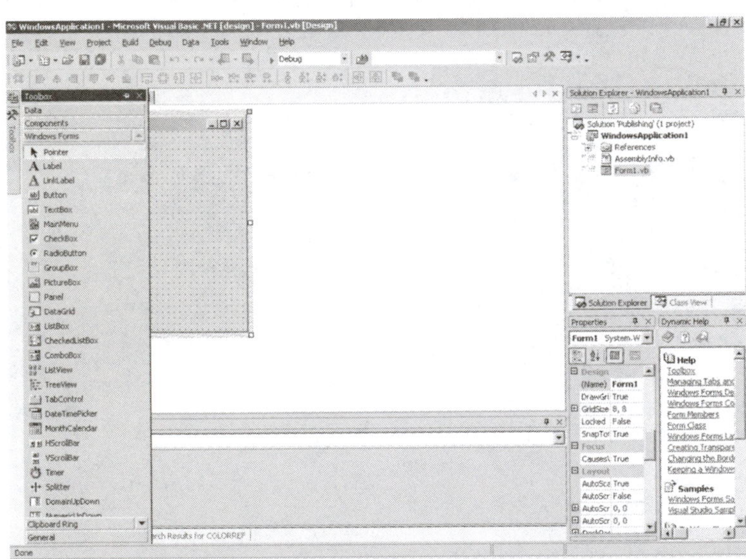

FIGURE 18-8 *A list of the controls of the Toolbox in the Data tab*

In VB.NET, controls that do not have a visual interface appear in a window below the form.

In addition to using the controls on the Toolbox, you can also use components. Components can be considered forms without the visual part. All forms can share components. You can thus have a single component, and all forms can connect to it. To add a component to your project, select the Add New Item option from the Project menu and double-click on the Component Class icon. A new component, `Component1`, will be added to your project.

VB.NET provides an option for creating a data-driven form easily by using the Data Adapter Configuration Wizard.

To invoke the wizard, open the Toolbox and click on the Data tab. Now, drag an `OleDbDataAdapter` control to the component. The Data Adapter Configuration Wizard will be invoked automatically when you drop the control on the component. The steps to follow for the wizard are as follows:

1. The first screen of the wizard provides general information about the wizard. Figure 18-9 displays the first screen of the wizard.

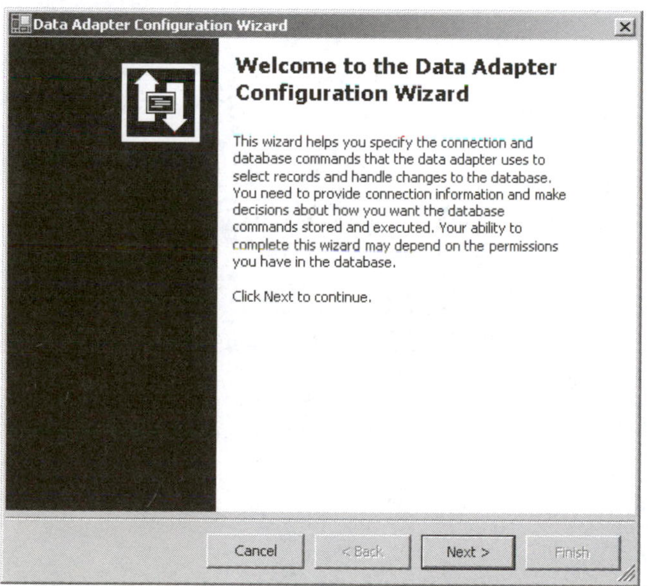

FIGURE 18-9 *The welcome screen of the Data Adapter Configuration Wizard*

2. Click on the Next button to advance into the wizard. The screen appears as shown in Figure 18-10.

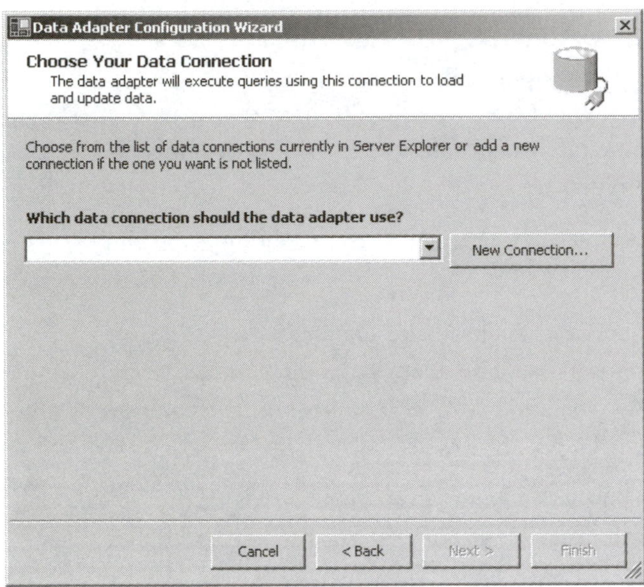

FIGURE 18-10 *This screen is used to specify the data connection for the data adapter.*

3. The screen displayed in Figure 18-10 prompts the user to choose the Data Connection to be used with the Data Adapter. If you do not have any prior data connection, you need to click on the New Connection button, which displays the Data Link Properties dialog box as shown in Figure 18-11.
4. Click on the Provider tab on the Data Link Properties dialog box and select the Microsoft OLE DB Provider for SQL Server option to establish connection with an SQL database.
5. Click on the Connection tab on the Data Link Properties dialog box and specify the server name, user name, and the database name on the server. The Data Link Properties dialog box now appears as shown in Figure 18-12.
6. You can test your connection by clicking on the Test Connection button. Click on the OK button to go back to the Data Adapter Configuration Wizard as shown in Figure 18-13.

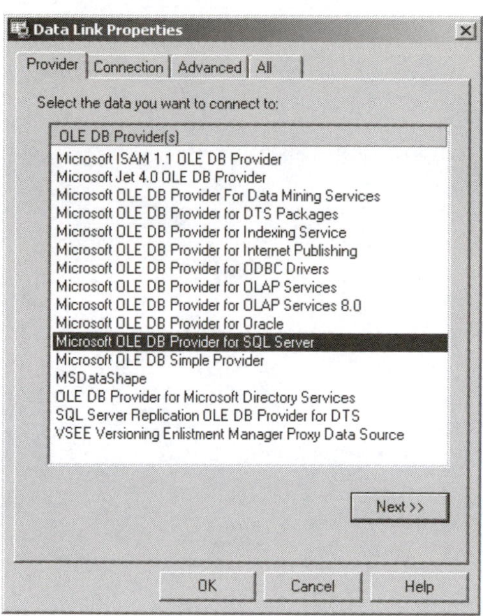

FIGURE 18-11 *The Data Link Properties dialog box*

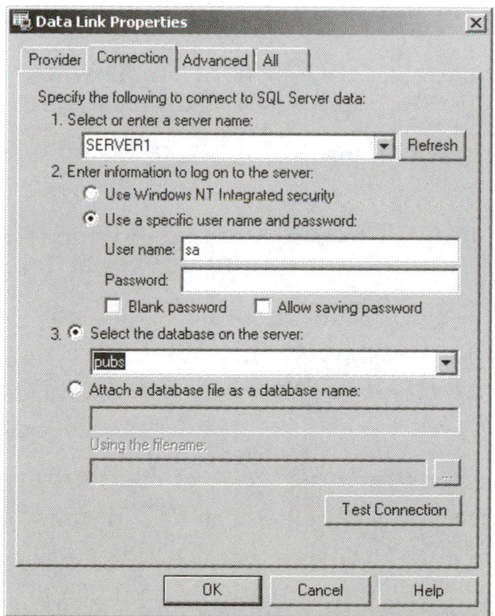

FIGURE 18-12 *The Data Link Properties dialog box with specific values for the server name, user name, and the database name*

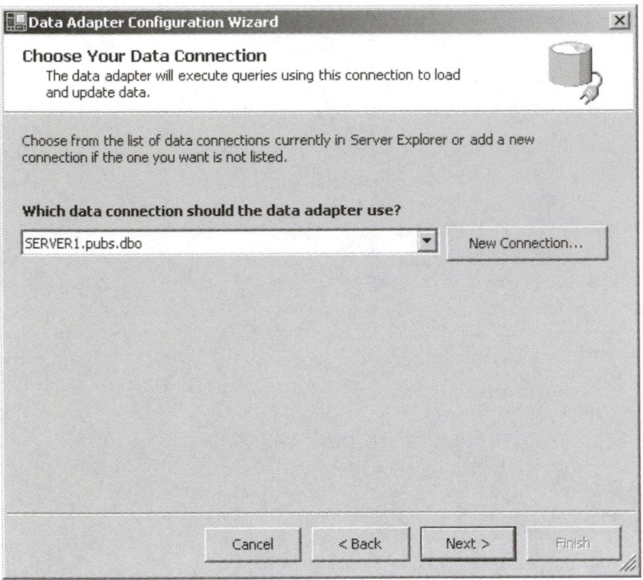

FIGURE 18-13 *This screen displays the name of the data connection that you just set up.*

7. The Data Configuration Wizard displays the connection that you just set up. Click on the Next button. The wizard now appears as shown in Figure 18-14.
8. The wizard now prompts you to choose a query type to determine how Data Adapter will access the database. Choose the appropriate option and click on the Next button. The wizard appears as shown in Figure 18-15.
9. You can see two buttons in Figure 18-15. The first one is the Advanced Options button that is used for operations such as insertions, updating, and deletions. The second one is the Query Builder button that is used for launching the SQL Builder. Write the query in the text box as shown in Figure 18-15, and click on the Next button. The wizard displays the last screen as shown in Figure 18-16.
10. Clicking on the Next button brings you to the last screen of the wizard. This screen also provides some general information. Click on Finish and the wizard exits.

When you click on the Finish button of the wizard, you come back to the Component1.vb [Design] tab. You will see in Figure 18-17 that two controls have been added on the design surface: `oleDbDataAdapter1` and `oleDbConnection1`.

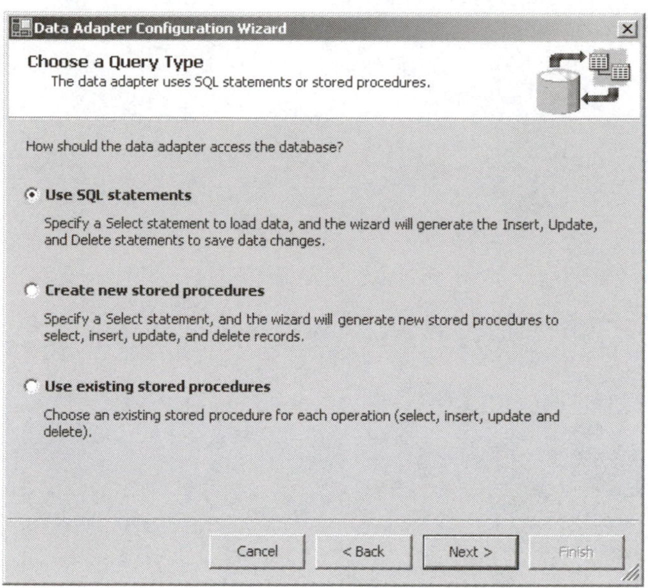

FIGURE 18-14 *This screen is used to specify the type of database access, that is, using SQL statements or stored procedures.*

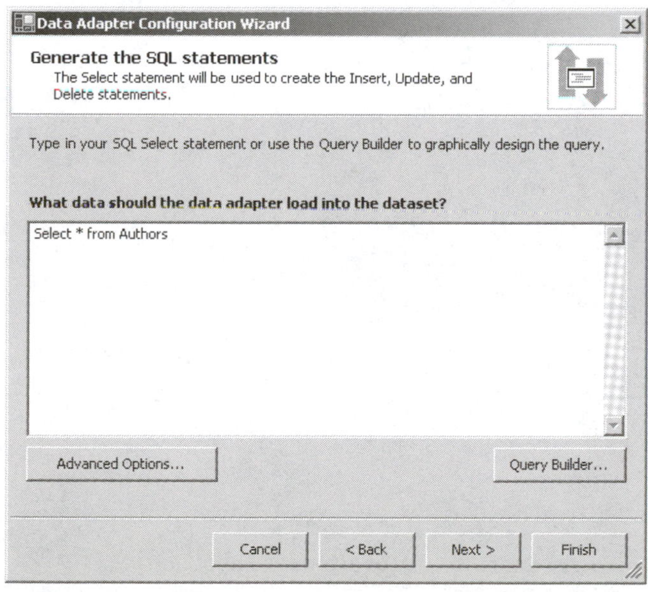

FIGURE 18-15 *This screen is used to specify the SQL statement that is used for retrieving records from the database.*

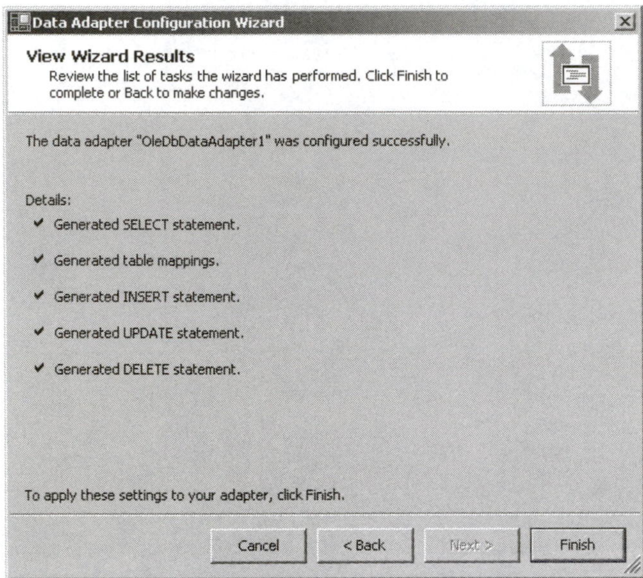

FIGURE 18-16 *This screen is the last screen of the wizard and displays information related to the query that was processed.*

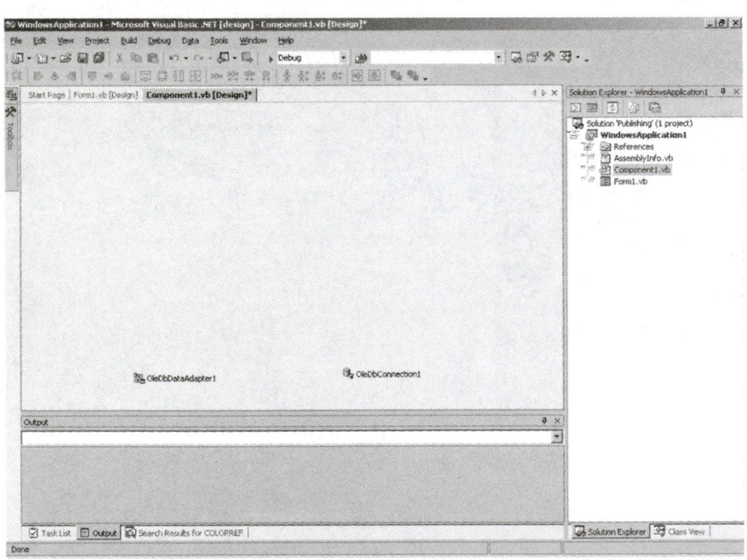

FIGURE 18-17 *The Component screen with two controls:* `oleDbDataAdapter1` *and* `oleDbConnection1`

When you click on `oleDbConnection1` and view the Properties window, you will see the connection string, database, server, provider, and other information related to the connection. The `oleDbDataAdapter1` control describes your actual query.

The Data Adapter Configuration Wizard helps you to connect to a database. Next, you need to move the records from the database to a `DataSet`.

Click on the form and choose the Generate Dataset option from the Data menu. The Generate Dataset option creates a `DataSet` object that will store the object in memory just as the ADO `Recordset` object did.

The Generate Dataset dialog box opens when you choose the Generate Dataset option. The dialog box is displayed in Figure 18-18.

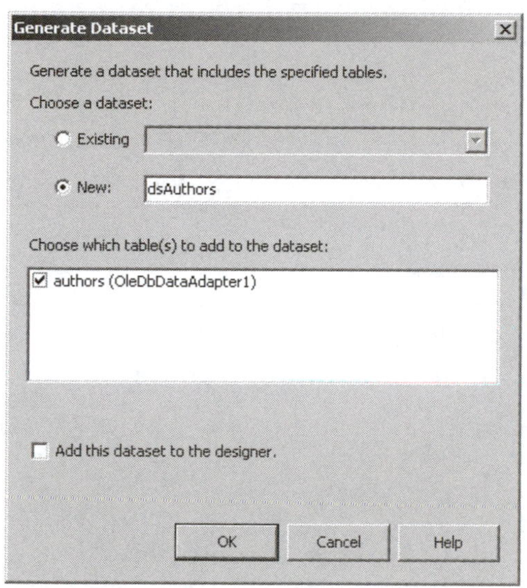

FIGURE 18-18 *The Generate Dataset dialog box*

In Figure 18-18, you need to enter a name for the DataSet. You can also choose the tables to be added to the DataSet.

Click on the OK button after specifying the information in Figure 18-18. You will see that a new file `dsSales.xsd` is added in the Solution Explorer window. XSD is an XML Schema Definition file.

You have learned to connect to a data source by using the Data Adapter Configuration Wizard. There is an alternative method available. It is known as the Data Form Wizard. The steps to perform in the Data Form Wizard are as follows:

1. Right-click on the project node and select the Add option from the shortcut menu that appears.
2. Select the Add New Item option from the Add menu and click on the Data Form Wizard. The wizard will be invoked. The first screen of the wizard when it is invoked is displayed in Figure 18-19.

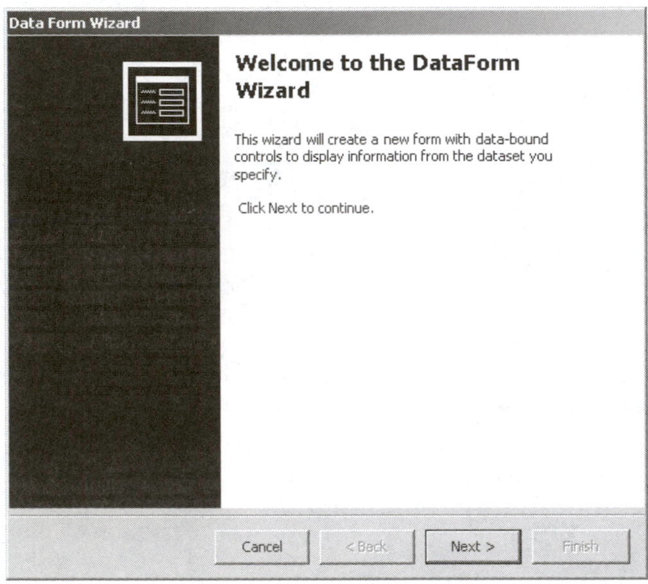

FIGURE 18-19 *The welcome screen of the Data Form Wizard*

3. Click on the Next button to advance into the wizard. Figure 18-20 displays the next screen of the wizard.
4. This screen is used to specify the name of the DataSet. The drop-down list displays a list of available DataSets for your project. Click on the Next button after selecting the desired DataSet. The wizard now displays the screen shown in Figure 18-21.

Data Form Wizard

Choose the dataset you want to use

The dataset contains the tables and columns to work with in your form.

The wizard helps you create a new dataset. Alternatively, you can use a dataset already defined in your project or one provided by a Web service.

Which dataset do you want to use?

Create a new dataset named:

Use the following dataset:

WindowsApplication1.dsAuthors

Available tables:

authors

Cancel < Back Next > Finish

FIGURE 18-20 *This screen is used to create or specify the name of a DataSet.*

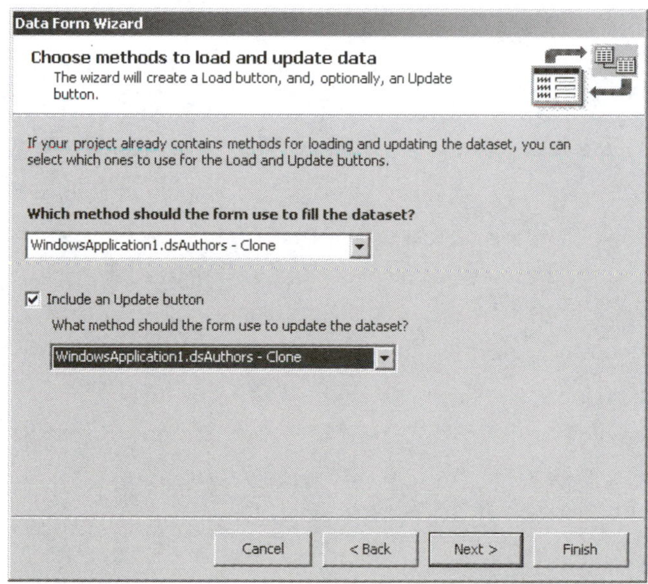

FIGURE 18-21 *This screen is used to specify the method to be used for filling the DataSet.*

5. This screen is used to specify the method that you want to use to load the data source. The figure also displays a checkbox for Include an Update button. You can check this checkbox to enable you to manipulate data as you work with it. Click on the Next button to display the screen in Figure 18-22.

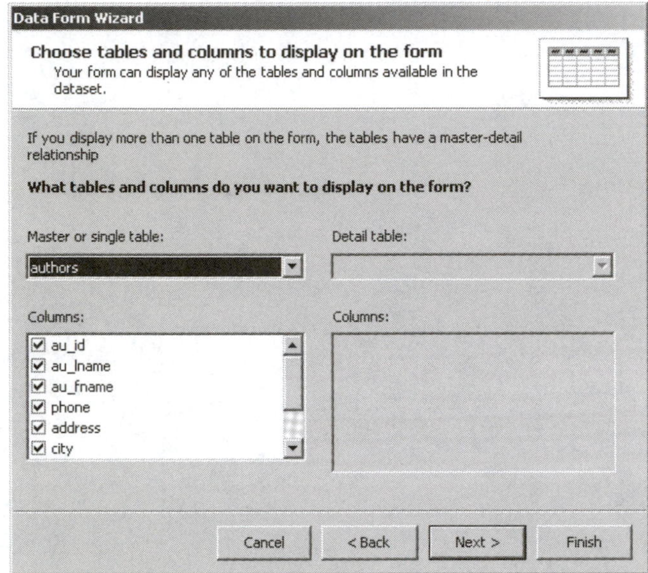

FIGURE 18-22 *This screen is used to specify the tables and columns that you want to display on the form.*

6. You use this screen to specify the table and the fields from the table that you want to display on the form. You can choose from the available list of tables and columns. Choose the required columns and click on the Next button. The screen in Figure 18-23 is displayed.
7. This screen is used to choose the display style for the records. If you choose the grid style, all records are displayed in a row-column format. If you choose the single record style, records are displayed in text boxes. Click on the Finish button to exit the wizard.

After you exit from the wizard and the form is loaded, click on the Load button. The DataSet will be automatically filled with the records, and the first record is displayed on the form.

The next section discusses XML integration with VB.NET and ADO.NET

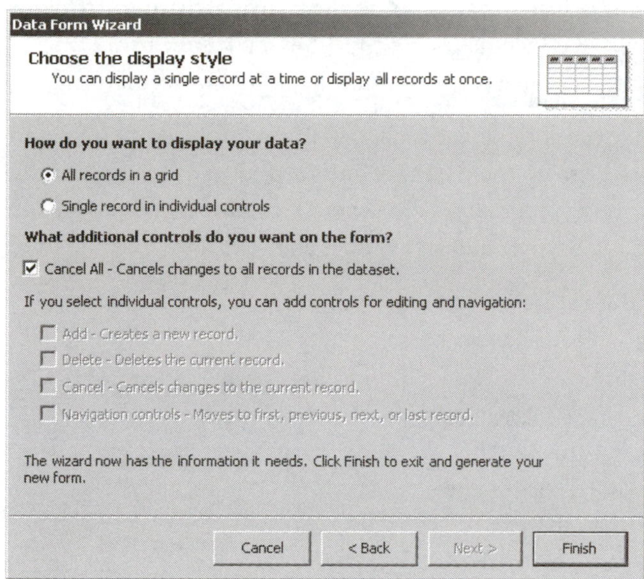

FIGURE 18-23 *This screen is the last screen of the wizard and is used to specify the display style for the records on the form.*

XML Integration with .NET

As already stated in the previous section, ADO.NET uses XML to transfer data from one `DataSet` to another. XML is used to provide a mechanism to transfer structured or relational information in a text-only format that can support multiple platforms. Today, XML is seen as the ideal choice for businesses to pass data.

Most of Microsoft's .NET is XML-based. This is made possible by the inclusion of two classes: `XmlReader` and `XmlWriter`. The two objects that are used to implement these classes are `XmlTextReader` and `XmlTextWriter`. The namespace `System.Xml` contains these classes. XML and .NET can be used together to read or write data whether it is XML or relational data.

To bind relational data from a `DataSet` with the XML Document Object Model (DOM), Microsoft provides the `XmlDataDocument`. It is used to load and manipulate relational or XML data.

.NET also allows you to validate your XML against an XML schema. An XML schema defines the structure of your XML document. You can also share your schema with others. If everyone uses the same schema, it will be a big advantage for businesses that need to share data across disparate systems.

Having learned about the concepts of database connectivity by using different methods, you can implement the concepts in the Skill Search application.

The `frmNameSearch.frm` form displays the employee name and the related employee fields, such as employee code, location, work phone, mobile phone, and e-mail address, which are picked from the database and displayed according to the selection made from the list box. The database connectivity is maintained in the `Load` event of the form. The code for `frmNameSearch_Load()` is as follows:

```
Private Sub frmNameSearch_Load(ByVal sender As System.Object,
   ByVal e As System.EventArgs) Handles MyBase.Load
         Call PopulateNamesCombo()       'This function populates the Employee
            Names Combo Box with the names retrieved from the database
         '  Dim firstvalue As String
         '  firstvalue = cmbNames.Items.Item(0)
           cmbNames.Text = ""
           Call DoTasks(False)
           cmdNameSearch.Focus()
         '  Call cmdNameSearch_Click(Me, New System.EventArgs())
     End Sub
```

The preceding code snippet calls a function, `PopulateNamesCombo()`, that is used to populate the combo box with values of employee names retrieved from the database. The user can then select the employee name from this combo box. The code for this function is as follows:

```
Function PopulateNamesCombo() As Object
         Dim Conn_Object As New ADODB.Connection()
'Function to add Employee Name entries in the 'Name of the Employee' ComboBox
         Dim recset_Object As New ADODB.Recordset()
         If Len(Trim(Application.StartupPath)) > 3 Then
             Conn_Object.Open(("Provider=Microsoft.Jet.OLEDB.4.0;" &
                "Data Source=" & Application.StartupPath & "\Skills.mdb"))
         Else
             Conn_Object.Open(("Provider=Microsoft.Jet.OLEDB.4.0;" &
                "Data Source=" & Application.StartupPath & "Skills.mdb"))
         End If
         recset_Object.CursorType = ADODB.CursorTypeEnum.adOpenKeyset
         recset_Object.LockType = ADODB.LockTypeEnum.adLockOptimistic
         recset_Object.let_ActiveConnection(Conn_Object)
```

```
        recset_Object.Open("Select Name from Skill_Info")
        If (recset_Object.RecordCount = 0) Then
            recset_Object.Close()
            Conn_Object.Close()
            Call frmNameSearch_Load(Me, New System.EventArgs())
            MsgBox("Sorry, no Employee names were found in the Skills database !!",
               MsgBoxStyle.Information + MsgBoxStyle.OKOnly, "SkillSearch Tool")
            cmbNames.Focus()
            GoTo MoveOut
        Else
            recset_Object.MoveFirst()
            While Not recset_Object.EOF()
                cmbNames.Items.Add((recset_Object.Fields("Name").Value))
                recset_Object.MoveNext()
            End While
            recset_Object.Close()
            Conn_Object.Close()
        End If
MoveOut:
    End Function
```

When the user selects an employee name and the value in the combo box changes, the `cmbNames_SelectedIndexChanged()` subroutine is called. The code for this procedure is as follows:

```
Private Sub cmbNames_SelectedIndexChanged(ByVal sender As Object, ByVal e As
System.EventArgs) Handles cmbNames.SelectedIndexChanged
        On Error GoTo ErrHandler
' This function is invoked when the entries in the Employee Names ComboBox get changed
        Dim checkreturnvalue As Boolean
        checkreturnvalue = ValidateEmpName()
        If (checkreturnvalue = False) Then
            GoTo MoveOut
        End If

        Dim temprecset As New ADODB.Recordset()

        temprecset.CursorType = ADODB.CursorTypeEnum.adOpenKeyset
        temprecset.LockType = ADODB.LockTypeEnum.adLockOptimistic
```

```
            temprecset.ActiveConnection = MastDBConn_Obj
            temprecset.Open("Select Name, EmpCode, Location, Work_Phone, Mobile_Phone,
               Email_Id, File_Name from Skill_Info where Name like '%" &
               Trim(cmbNames.Text) & "%'")

            If (temprecset.RecordCount = 0) Then
                temprecset.Close()
                Dim Pattern As String
                Pattern = "FALSE"
                Call DoTasks(Pattern)
                MsgBox("Sorry, your query did not generate any results !!",
                   MsgBoxStyle.Information + MsgBoxStyle.OKOnly, "SkillSearch Tool")
                cmbNames.Focus()
                cmbNames.SelectionStart = 0
                cmbNames.SelectionLength = Len(Trim(cmbNames.Text))
                GoTo MoveOut
            Else
                Dim Pattern As String
                Pattern = "TRUE"
                Call DoTasks(Pattern)

                cmbNames.Text = temprecset.Fields("Name").Value
                txtAddress.Text = temprecset("Location").Value
                txtPhoneNo.Text = temprecset("Work_Phone").Value
                txtEmailId.Text = temprecset("Email_Id").Value
                txtEmpCode.Text = temprecset("EmpCode").Value
                txtMobile.Text = temprecset("Mobile_Phone").Value
                ProfileName = temprecset("File_Name").Value
                temprecset.Close()
            End If
            Exit Sub
ErrHandler:
            MsgBox("The following error(" & CStr(Err.Number) & ") was encountered:" &
               Chr(13) & Err.Description, MsgBoxStyle.Information + MsgBoxStyle.OKOnly,
               "SkillSearch Tool")
MoveOut:
    End Sub
```

One of the requirements of the application is that it should be deployed on Web. The Web version also has the same interface. The user enters the name of the employee or the skill and clicks on the Search button. The skill-related file of the employee is then displayed to the user based upon the filename in the database for the related employee. The code for the `frmSubjectSearch_load()` subroutine is as follows:

```
Private Sub frmSubjectSearch_Load(ByVal sender As System.Object, ByVal e As
   System.EventArgs) Handles MyBase.Load
         Call PopulateSkillListBox()
         Call StepsToPerform("FALSE")
    End Sub
```

This subroutine calls the `PopulateSkillListBox()` function that is used to fill the list box with the skills of all employees. The user can then select a skill from the list box and the corresponding skill-related file resume will be displayed to the user. The code of the `PopulateSkillsListBox()` is as follows:

```
Function PopulateSkillListBox()
         Dim Conn_Object As New ADODB.Connection()
'Function to add Primary Skills in the Skills ListBox
         Dim recset_Object As New ADODB.Recordset()

         If Len(Trim(Application.StartupPath)) > 3 Then
              Conn_Object.Open(("Provider=Microsoft.Jet.OLEDB.4.0;" &
                 "Data Source=" & Application.StartupPath & "\Skills.mdb"))
         Else
              Conn_Object.Open(("Provider=Microsoft.Jet.OLEDB.4.0;" &
                 "Data Source=" & Application.StartupPath & "Skills.mdb"))
         End If

         recset_Object.CursorType = ADODB.CursorTypeEnum.adOpenKeyset
         recset_Object.LockType = ADODB.LockTypeEnum.adLockOptimistic

         recset_Object.let_ActiveConnection(Conn_Object)
         recset_Object.Open("Select Distinct Skill1_Name from Skill_Info")

         If (recset_Object.RecordCount = 0) Then
              recset_Object.Close()
```

```
            Conn_Object.Close()
            MsgBox("Sorry, no Skill entries were found in the Skills database !!",
               MsgBoxStyle.Information + MsgBoxStyle.OKOnly, "SkillSearch Tool")
            lstSkills.Focus()
            GoTo MoveOut
        Else
            recset_Object.MoveFirst()
            While Not recset_Object.EOF()
                lstSkills.Items.Add((recset_Object.Fields("Skill1_Name").Value))
                recset_Object.MoveNext()
            End While
            recset_Object.Close()
            Conn_Object.Close()
        End If
MoveOut:
    End Function
```

Summary

In this chapter you learned about database connectivity by using DAO, ODBC, RDO, ADO, and ADO.NET. You also learned about the database connectivity wizards such as the Data Adapter Configuration Wizard and the Data Form Wizard. You created the table to be used in the Skill Search application and also learned about the database connectivity to be used in the application. In the next chapter, you will code the application.

Chapter 19

Coding the Skill Search Application

In this chapter, you will add functionality to the Skill Search application. You will code the application in VB.NET. This chapter discusses the logic of the Skill Search application and the various functions to be used in the application.

Working with the Skill Search Application

As discussed in Chapter 14, "Project Case Study: Red Sky IT Systems," the Skill Search application consists of four screens:

- `Splash` screen
- `Search` screen
- `Search by Technology` screen
- `Search by Employee Name` screen

The `Splash` screen is the first screen to be displayed, as shown in Figure 19-1.

FIGURE 19-1 *The* `Splash` *screen of the Skill Search application*

The `Splash` screen disappears after some time. Listing 19-1 contains the code for the `Splash` screen.

Listing 19-1 Code for the Splash Screen

```
Dim FirstEntry As Boolean
    Private Sub Timer1_Tick(ByVal eventSender As System.Object, ByVal eventArgs As
       System.EventArgs) Handles Timer1.Tick
         Call DoTask()
```

```
End Sub
Private Sub DoTask()
    If (FirstEntry = False) Then
        Me.Hide()
        Dim FirstScreen As New frmMain()
        FirstScreen.Show()
        FirstScreen.Visible = True
        FirstEntry = True
    End If
End Sub
```

The `Splash` screen is displayed for a few seconds, after which the next screen, the `Search` screen, is displayed. The main function used in the `Splash` screen code is the `DoTask()` function, which displays the `Search` screen to the user after the specified time interval has expired.

The `Search` screen is displayed in Figure 19-2.

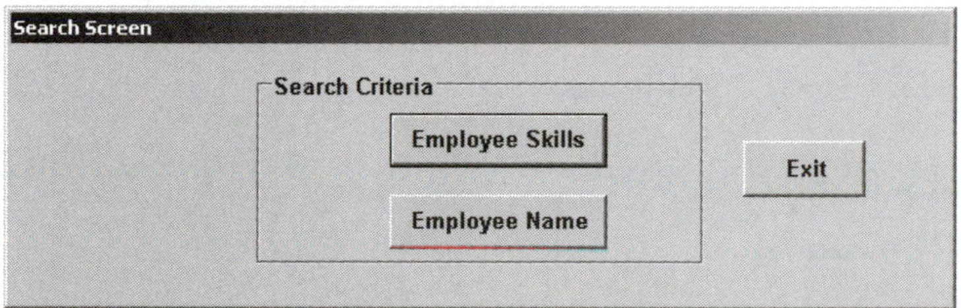

FIGURE 19-2 *The* `Search` *screen of the Skill Search application*

The `Search` screen displays the two options for the search criteria, searching by employee skills or by employee name. The screen also displays an `Exit` button that is used to exit out of the application. The user can click on either of the two search options available, and based on the selection the next screen is displayed to the user. The code for the `Search` screen of the application is given in Listing 19-2.

Listing 19-2 Code for the Search Screen

```
    Private Sub cmdSubject_Click(ByVal sender As System.Object, ByVal e As
      System.EventArgs) Handles
    cmdSubject.Click ' This function is invoked when the 'Subject' button is clicked
        Dim ValidateMDBExistence As String
        If Len(Trim(Application.StartupPath)) > 3 Then
            ValidateMDBExistence = Dir(Application.StartupPath & "\" & "Skills.mdb")
        Else
            ValidateMDBExistence = Dir(Application.StartupPath & "Skills.mdb")
        End If
        If UCase(ValidateMDBExistence) <> UCase("Skills.mdb") Then
            MsgBox("Unable to locate 'Skills.mdb' database in application folder,
              please check.",
            MsgBoxStyle.Information + MsgBoxStyle.OKOnly, "SkillSearch Tool")
            Exit Sub
        End If
        Call InitiateConnection()
        Me.Hide()
        Dim SubjSearchForm As New frmSubjectSearch()
 Create an instance of the form 'frmSubjectSearch'
        SubjSearchForm.Show()
    End Sub
    Private Sub cmdSMEName_Click(ByVal sender As System.Object, ByVal e As
      System.EventArgs)
     Handles cmdSMEName.Click
 ' This function is invoked when the 'SME Name' button is clicked
        Dim ValidateMDBExistence As String
        If Len(Trim(Application.StartupPath)) > 3 Then
            ValidateMDBExistence = Dir(Application.StartupPath & "\" & "Skills.mdb")
        Else
            ValidateMDBExistence = Dir(Application.StartupPath & "Skills.mdb")
        End If
        If UCase(ValidateMDBExistence) <> UCase("Skills.mdb") Then
            MsgBox("Unable to locate 'Skills.mdb' database in application folder,
              please check.",
```

```
                MsgBoxStyle.Information + MsgBoxStyle.OKOnly, "SkillSearch Tool")
                Exit Sub
            End If
            Call InitiateConnection()
            Me.Hide()
            Dim NameSearchForm As New frmNameSearch()
' Create an instance of the form 'frmNameSearch'
            NameSearchForm.Show()
        End Sub
        Private Sub cmdExit_Click(ByVal sender As System.Object, ByVal e As
           System.EventArgs)
         Handles cmdExit.Click
' This function is invoked when the 'Exit' button is clicked
            If Len(LTrim(RTrim(StoreVal))) <> 0 Then
                MastDBConn_Obj.Close()
' Close the Database Connection
            End If
            End
        End Sub
        Function InitiateConnection()
            If Len(LTrim(RTrim(StoreVal))) = 0 Then
 'Open the Database connection on Form Load by providing connection string parameters
                If Len(Trim(Application.StartupPath)) > 3 Then
                    MastDBConn_Obj.Open(("Provider=Microsoft.Jet.OLEDB.4.0;" &
                       "Data Source="
                     & Application.StartupPath & "\Skills.mdb"))
                    StoreVal = "ConnectionOpened"
                Else
                    MastDBConn_Obj.Open(("Provider=Microsoft.Jet.OLEDB.4.0;" &
                       "Data Source="
                     & Application.StartupPath & "Skills.mdb"))
                    StoreVal = "ConnectionOpened"
                End If
            End If
        End Function
End Class
```

The flow of the functions of the `frmMain` form is depicted in Figure 19-3.

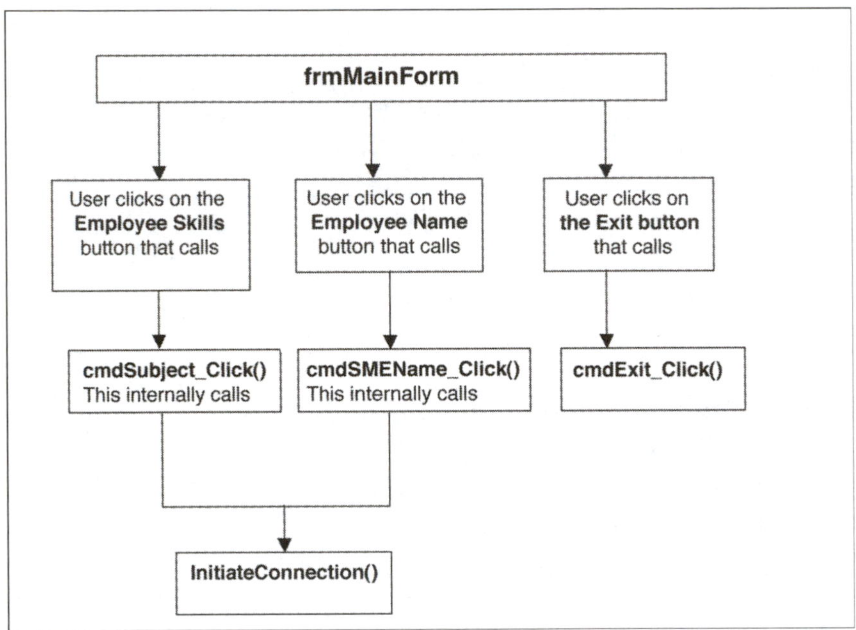

FIGURE 19-3 *Flow chart of the* `frmMain` *form*

The main functions for the search screen in the `frmMain` form along with their descriptions are listed in Table 19-1.

Table 19-1 Main Functions of the *frmMain* Form

Function Name	Description
`cmdSubject_Click()`	This function is executed when the user clicks on the `Employee Skills` button on the `Search` screen. The function validates the existence of the `Skills.mdb` database and displays a message box to the user if the database is not found. The execution then transfers to the `InitiateConnection()` function. The `cmdSubject_Click()` function then displays the `Search by Technology` screen depending upon the successful return value of the `InitiateConnection()` function.
`cmdSMEName_Click()`	This function is executed when the user clicks on the `Employee Name` button on the `Search` screen. The function validates the existence of the `Skills.mdb` database and displays a message box to the user if the database is not found. The execution then

	transfers to the `InitiateConnection()` function. The `cmdSMEName_Click()` function then displays the `Search by Technology` screen depending upon the successful return value of the `InitiateConnection()` function.
`cmdExit_Click()`	This function is executed when the user clicks on the `Exit` button on the `Search` screen. This function closes the database connection and exits out of the application.
`InitiateConnection()`	This function opens the ADO database connection with the MS Access 2000 database when the form is loaded.

If the user clicks on the `Employee Skills` button, the `Search by Technology` screen is shown to the user, as displayed in Figure 19-4.

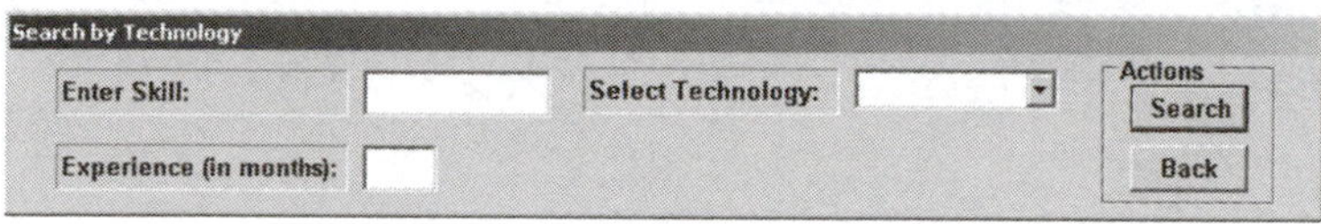

FIGURE 19-4 *The* `Search by Technology` *screen*

The user can enter the skill in the `Enter Skill` text box and the experience of an employee in the `Experience (in months)` text box and click on the `Search` button. The user can also select the skill from the `Select Technology` combo box. The corresponding skill details document of the employee will then be picked up from the database and displayed to the user, if a matching entry exists in the database. The `Back` button takes the user back to the `Search` screen. If the user leaves all the text boxes blank and clicks on the `Search` button, an error message box is displayed, as shown in Figure 19-5.

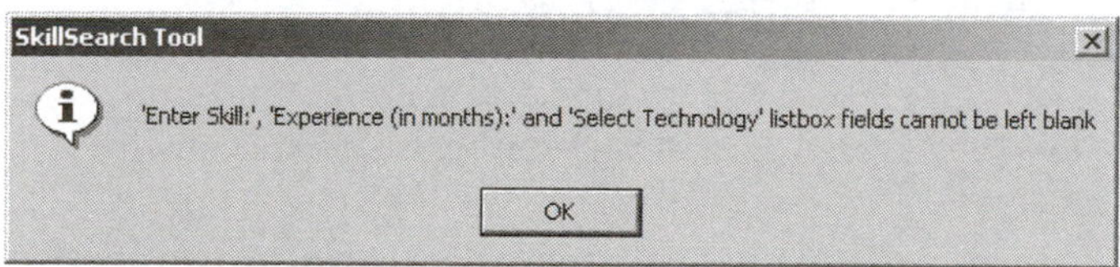

FIGURE 19-5 *This message box is displayed when the user leaves all the text boxes blank.*

If the text that the user entered in the text boxes does not match any of the records in the database, a message box as shown in Figure 19-6 is displayed.

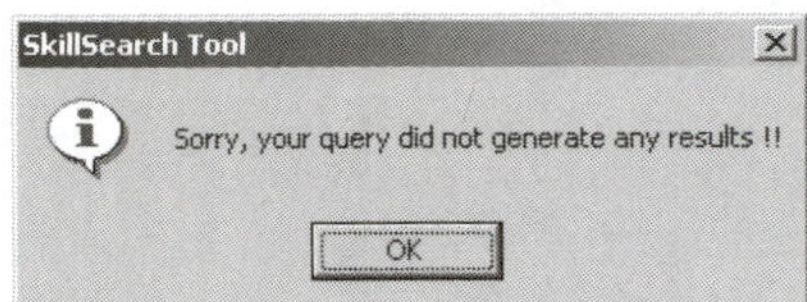

FIGURE 19-6 *This message box is displayed when the details entered do not match any record in the database.*

If, however, the details entered by the user match a record in the database, the `Search by Technology` screen is displayed with additional fields as shown in Figure 19-7.

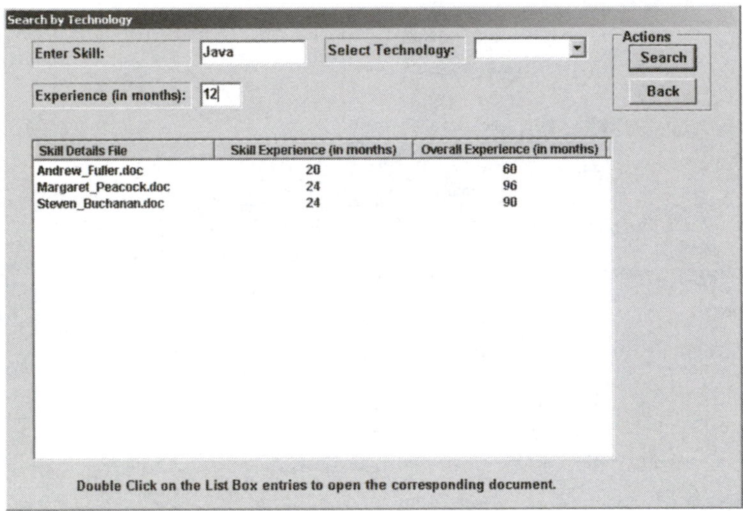

FIGURE 19-7 *The* `Search by Technology` *screen with additional fields*

The user can then double-click on an entry in the list box to open the corresponding skill details document in Word. The skill details document will be opened in Word as shown in Figure 19-8.

The code for the `Search by Technology` screen is given in Listing 19-3.

Listing 19-3 Code for the Search by Technology Screen

```
Dim ResumeArray(500, 3) As String
Private Sub cmdBack_Click(ByVal sender As System.Object, ByVal e As
   System.EventArgs) Handles
cmdBack.Click
    Me.Hide()
```

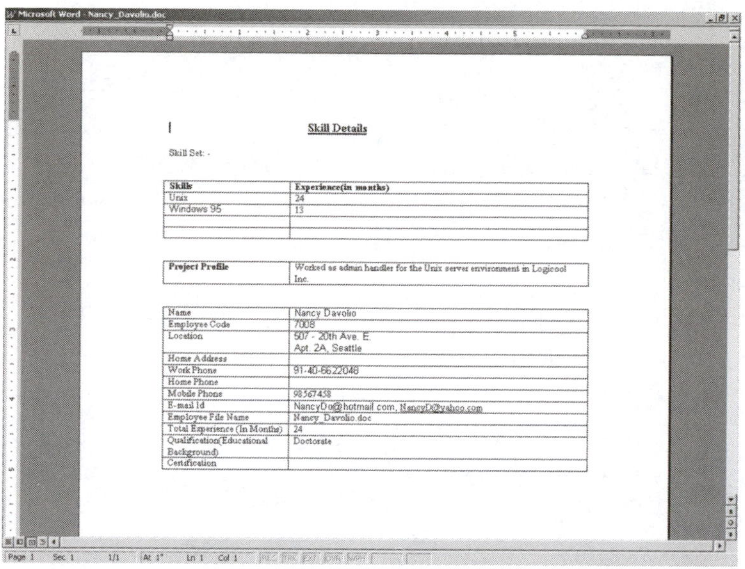

Skill Details

Skill Set: -

Skills	Experience(in months)
Unix	24
Windows 95	13

Project Profile	Worked as admin handler for the Unix server environment in Logicool Inc.

Name	Nancy Davolio
Employee Code	7008
Location	507 - 20th Ave. E. Apt. 2A, Seattle
Home Address	
Work Phone	91-40-6622048
Home Phone	
Mobile Phone	98567458
E-mail Id	NancyDo@hotmail.com, NancyD@yahoo.com
Employee File Name	Nancy_Davolio.doc
Total Experience (In Months)	24
Qualification(Educational Background)	Doctorate
Certification	

FIGURE 19-8 *The skill details document when opened in Word*

```
        Dim MainForm As New frmMain()       'Create an instance of the form 'frmMain'
        MainForm.Show()
    End Sub
    Private Sub cmdSearch_Click(ByVal sender As System.Object, ByVal e As
       System.EventArgs) Handles
    cmdSearch.Click
        On Error GoTo ErrHandler
        Dim checkreturnvalue As Boolean
        If (lstSkills.SelectedIndex() = -1) And Len(Trim(txtSkillName.Text)) = 0
           And Len(Trim(txtYears.Text)) =
        0 Then
'Check if the 'Skill Name' and 'Years of Experience' field entries have been
'entered by the user
            Call StepsToPerform("FALSE")
'This function is called with the parameter as 'FALSE' if entries have not been entered
            MsgBox("'Enter Skill:', 'Experience (in months):' and 'Select
               Technology' listbox fields cannot be left
```

```
        blank", MsgBoxStyle.Information + MsgBoxStyle.OKOnly, "SkillSearch
           Tool")
        txtSkillName.Focus()
        txtSkillName.SelectionStart = 0
        txtSkillName.SelectionLength = Len(Trim(txtSkillName.Text))
    End If
    If Len(Trim(txtSkillName.Text)) <> 0 Or (lstSkills.SelectedIndex() <> -1)
       Then
        If Len(Trim(txtYears.Text)) <> 0 Then
            If Len(Trim(txtSkillName.Text)) <> 0 Then
                checkreturnvalue = ValidateSkill()
' This function validates the 'Skill Name' field
                If (checkreturnvalue = False) Then
                    GoTo MoveOut
                End If
            End If
            checkreturnvalue = ValidateYrsofExp()
' This function validates the 'Years of Experience' field
            If (checkreturnvalue = False) Then
                GoTo MoveOut
            End If
            If Len(Trim(txtSkillName.Text)) <> 0 Then
                QueryPattern = "BOTHFROMTEXT"
                Call ProcessonBasisOfQuery(QueryPattern)
'This function is called with the parameter
                as "BOTHFROMTEXT" if valid entries are entered for both
                   'Skill Name' & 'Years of Experience'
                fields
                GoTo MoveOut
            End If
            If (lstSkills.SelectedIndex() <> -1) Then
                QueryPattern = "BOTHFROMLIST"
                Call ProcessonBasisOfQuery(QueryPattern)
'This function is called with the parameter
                 as "BOTHFROMLIST" if valid entries are entered for both
                    'Skill Name' List box & 'Years of
                  'Experience' fields
                GoTo MoveOut
```

```
                End If
            End If
        End If
        If Len(Trim(txtYears.Text)) = 0 Then
            If Len(Trim(txtSkillName.Text)) <> 0 Then
                checkreturnvalue = ValidateSkill()
' This function validates the 'Skill Name' field
                If (checkreturnvalue = False) Then
                    GoTo MoveOut
                Else
                    QueryPattern = "SUBJECT_TEXT"
                    Call ProcessonBasisOfQuery(QueryPattern)
'This function is called with the parameter as
                    'SUBJECT_TEXT' if valid entry is entered for 'Skill Name'
                       textbox only
                    GoTo MoveOut
                End If
            End If
            If (lstSkills.SelectedIndex() <> -1) Then
                QueryPattern = "SUBJECT_LIST"
                Call ProcessonBasisOfQuery(QueryPattern)
'This function is called with the parameter as
                "SUBJECT_LIST" if valid entry is selected for 'Skill Name' list box
                GoTo MoveOut
            End If
        End If
        If Len(Trim(txtSkillName.Text)) = 0 And (lstSkills.SelectedIndex() = -1) Then
            If Len(Trim(txtYears.Text)) <> 0 Then
                checkreturnvalue = ValidateYrsofExp()
' This function validates the 'Years of Experience' field
                If (checkreturnvalue = False) Then
                    GoTo MoveOut
                End If
                QueryPattern = "YEARS"
                Call ProcessonBasisOfQuery(QueryPattern)
'This function is called with the parameter as
```

```
            "YEARS" if valid entry is entered for 'Years of Experience' field only
          End If
        End If
        Exit Sub
ErrHandler:
        MsgBox("The following error(" & CStr(Err.Number) & ") was encountered:" &
           Chr(13) & Err.Description,
        MsgBoxStyle.Information + MsgBoxStyle.OKOnly, "SkillSearch Tool")
MoveOut:
    End Sub
    Function ValidateSkill() As Boolean
'Function to validate the 'Skill Name' field
        Dim testSubjectContents As String
        testSubjectContents = Trim(txtSkillName.Text)
        If (Len(Trim(testSubjectContents)) = 0) Then     'Validate for blank entry
            Call StepsToPerform("FALSE")
            MsgBox("Blank entry found in the 'Enter Skill:' field !!",
               MsgBoxStyle.Information +
             MsgBoxStyle.OKOnly, "SkillSearch Tool")
            txtSkillName.Focus()
            txtSkillName.SelectionStart = 0
            txtSkillName.SelectionLength = Len(Trim(txtSkillName.Text))
            ValidateSkill = False
            Exit Function
        End If
        ValidateSkill = True
    End Function
    Function ValidateYrsofExp() As Boolean
'Function to validate the 'Years of Experience' field
        Dim testYrsofExpContents As String
        testYrsofExpContents = Trim(txtYears.Text)
        If (Len(Trim(testYrsofExpContents)) = 0) Then
'Validate for blank entry
            Call StepsToPerform("FALSE")
            MsgBox("Blank entry found in the 'Experience (in months):' field !!",
               MsgBoxStyle.Information +
            MsgBoxStyle.OKOnly, "SkillSearch Tool")
```

```
                txtYears.Focus()
                txtYears.SelectionStart = 0
                txtYears.SelectionLength = Len(Trim(txtYears.Text))
                ValidateYrsofExp = False
                Exit Function
            End If
            If (IsNumeric(testYrsofExpContents) = False) Then
'Validate for non-numeric entry
                Call StepsToPerform("FALSE")
                MsgBox("Non-numeric entry found in the 'Experience (in months):' field
                   !!", MsgBoxStyle.Information
               + MsgBoxStyle.OKOnly, "SkillSearch Tool")
                txtYears.Focus()
                txtYears.SelectionStart = 0
                txtYears.SelectionLength = Len(Trim(txtYears.Text))
                ValidateYrsofExp = False
                Exit Function
            End If
            ValidateYrsofExp = True
        End Function
        Function ProcessonBasisOfQuery(ByVal Pattern As String)
'This function generates the SQL query on
        the basis of the selection made by the user
            On Error GoTo ErrHandler
            Dim temprecset As New ADODB.Recordset()
            Dim jctr As Short
            Dim ictr As Short
            For ictr = 0 To 499
                For jctr = 0 To 3
                    ResumeArray(ictr, jctr) = ""
                Next jctr
            Next ictr
            temprecset.CursorType = ADODB.CursorTypeEnum.adOpenKeyset
            temprecset.LockType = ADODB.LockTypeEnum.adLockOptimistic
            temprecset.let_ActiveConnection(MastDBConn_Obj)
            If Pattern = "BOTHFROMTEXT" Then
' If both 'Skill Name' & 'Years of Experience' fields are entered by the user
                temprecset.Open("Select File_Name, Total_Exp, Skill1_Exp from
```

```
                Skill_Info where Skill1_Name like
              '%" & Trim(txtSkillName.Text) & "%'")
          ElseIf Pattern = "BOTHFROMLIST" Then
' If both 'Skill Name' List box entry & 'Years of Experience' fields
' are entered by the user
              temprecset.Open("Select File_Name, Total_Exp, Skill1_Exp from
                Skill_Info where Skill1_Name like
              '%" & lstSkills.Items.Item(lstSkills.SelectedIndex()) & "%'")
          ElseIf Pattern = "SUBJECT_TEXT" Then
' If only 'Skill Name' text box entry is entered by the user
             temprecset.Open("Select File_Name, Total_Exp, Skill1_Exp from Skill_Info
               where Skill1_Name like
               '%" & Trim(txtSkillName.Text) & "%'")
          ElseIf Pattern = "SUBJECT_LIST" Then
' If only 'Skill Name' list box entry is entered by the user
              temprecset.Open("Select File_Name, Total_Exp, Skill1_Exp from
                Skill_Info where Skill1_Name like
              '%" & lstSkills.Items.Item(lstSkills.SelectedIndex()) & "%'")
          ElseIf Pattern = "YEARS" Then
' If only 'Years of Experience' field is entered by the user
              temprecset.Open("Select File_Name, Total_Exp, Skill1_Exp from
                Skill_Info where Total_Exp = " &
              CShort(Trim(txtYears.Text)) * 12)
          Else
          End If
          If (temprecset.RecordCount = 0) Then
'Validate the condition if any records are returned by the SQL
          query
              Call StepsToPerform("FALSE")
              MsgBox("Sorry, your query did not generate any results !!",
                 MsgBoxStyle.Information +
              MsgBoxStyle.OKOnly, "SkillSearch Tool")
              txtSkillName.Focus()
              txtSkillName.SelectionStart = 0
              txtSkillName.SelectionLength = Len(Trim(txtSkillName.Text))
              GoTo MoveOut
          Else
              Call StepsToPerform("TRUE")
```

```
' Else store the returned field values in the array named as 'ResumeArray'
        Dim ValueEntered As Boolean
        Dim Counter As Short
        temprecset.MoveFirst()
        Counter = 0
        While Not (temprecset.EOF)
            ValueEntered = False
            For ictr = 0 To 499
                For jctr = 0 To 2
                    If (ResumeArray(ictr, 0) = "") Then
                        ResumeArray(ictr, 0) =
                          temprecset.Fields("File_Name").Value
                        ResumeArray(ictr, 1) =
                          temprecset.Fields("Total_Exp").Value
                        ResumeArray(ictr, 2) =
                          temprecset.Fields("Skill1_Exp").Value
                        ValueEntered = True
                        Counter = Counter + 1
                    End If
                    If (ValueEntered = True) Then
                        Exit For
                    End If
                Next jctr
                If (ValueEntered = True) Then
                    Exit For
                End If
            Next ictr
            temprecset.MoveNext()
        End While
        temprecset.Close()
        Dim CheckForBoth As Boolean
        CheckForBoth = False
        lstResumes.Items.Clear()
        For ictr = 0 To Counter
            For jctr = 0 To 2
                If ResumeArray(ictr, 0) <> "" Then
                    If (Pattern <> "YEARS") Then
                        If Pattern = "BOTHFROMTEXT" Or Pattern =
                          "BOTHFROMLIST" Then
```

```
                    If CInt(ResumeArray(ictr, 2)) >=
                       CInt(txtYears.Text) Then
                        CheckForBoth = True
                        Dim objListItem As ListViewItem
                        objListItem =
                        lstResumes.Items.Add(ResumeArray(ictr, 0))
                        objListItem.SubItems.Add(CStr(ResumeArray(ictr, 2)))
                        objListItem.SubItems.Add(CStr(ResumeArray(ictr, 1)))
                        Exit For
                    Else
                    End If
                Else
                    Dim objListItem As ListViewItem
                    objListItem =
                       lstResumes.Items.Add(ResumeArray(ictr, 0))
                    objListItem.SubItems.Add(CStr(ResumeArray(ictr, 2)))
                    objListItem.SubItems.Add(CStr(ResumeArray(ictr, 1)))
                    Exit For
                End If
            End If
            If (Pattern = "YEARS") Then
                Dim objListItem As ListViewItem
                objListItem = lstResumes.Items.Add(ResumeArray(ictr, 0))
                objListItem.SubItems.Add("")
                objListItem.SubItems.Add(CStr(ResumeArray(ictr, 1)))
                Exit For
            End If
        End If
    Next jctr
Next ictr
If (Pattern = "BOTHFROMTEXT" Or Pattern = "BOTHFROMLIST") And
   (CheckForBoth = False)
Then
```

```
                Call StepsToPerform("FALSE")
                MsgBox("Sorry, your query did not generate any results !!",
                   MsgBoxStyle.Information +
                MsgBoxStyle.OKOnly, "SkillSearch Tool")
                txtSkillName.Focus()
                txtSkillName.SelectionStart = 0
                txtSkillName.SelectionLength = Len(Trim(txtSkillName.Text))
            End If
        End If
        Exit Function
ErrHandler:
        MsgBox("The following error(" & CStr(Err.Number) & ") was encountered:" &
           Chr(13) & Err.Description,
        MsgBoxStyle.Information + MsgBoxStyle.OKOnly, "SkillSearch Tool")
     MoveOut:
    End Function
    Private Sub frmSubjectSearch_Load(ByVal sender As System.Object, ByVal e As
       System.EventArgs)
    Handles MyBase.Load
        Call PopulateSkillListBox()
        Call StepsToPerform("FALSE")
    End Sub
    Function StepsToPerform(ByVal CheckValue As String)
        If CheckValue = "FALSE" Then
           'Adjust the form display height & other controls display on the
        basis of current condition
            Me.Height = 112
        Else
            Me.Height = 488
        End If
        lstResumes.Visible = CheckValue
        lblInfo.Visible = CheckValue
    End Function

    Private Sub lstResumes_DoubleClick(ByVal sender As Object, ByVal e As
       System.EventArgs) Handles
    lstResumes.DoubleClick
        On Error GoTo HandleErr
```

```
'This function is invoked when a user double-clicks in the
     Resumes List box
    Dim CheckFileExistence1 As String
    Dim CheckFileExistence2 As String
    Dim tempStoreStr As String
    Dim FilePos As Short
    If lstResumes.SelectedItems.Count > 0 Then
        tempStoreStr = lstResumes.SelectedItems(0).Text
        FilePos = InStr(1, tempStoreStr, ".doc", CompareMethod.Text)
    End If
    Dim myWord1 As New Word.Application()
    Dim Word1 As New Word.Application()
    If (FilePos <> 0) Then
        tempStoreStr = Mid(tempStoreStr, 1, FilePos + 3)
        If Len(Trim(Application.StartupPath)) > 3 Then
            CheckFileExistence2 = Dir(Application.StartupPath & "\files\" &
               tempStoreStr)
        Else
            CheckFileExistence2 = Dir(Application.StartupPath & "files\" &
               tempStoreStr)
        End If
        If UCase(CheckFileExistence2) <> UCase(tempStoreStr) Then
            MsgBox("Unable to locate '" & tempStoreStr & "' document.",
               MsgBoxStyle.Information +
            MsgBoxStyle.OKOnly, "SkillSearch Tool")
            Exit Sub
        End If
        On Error Resume Next
       If Err.Number <> 0 Then
            Word1.Application.Visible = True
            Word1.Application.WindowState =
               Word.WdWindowState.wdWindowStateMaximize
            If Len(Trim(Application.StartupPath)) > 3 Then
                Word1.Documents.Open(FileName:=Application.StartupPath &
                   "\files\" & tempStoreStr)
            Else
                Word1.Documents.Open(FileName:=Application.StartupPath &
                   "files\" & tempStoreStr)
```

```
            End If
        Else
            myWord1.Parent.Windows(1).Visible = True
            myWord1.Application.WindowState =
              Word.WdWindowState.wdWindowStateMaximize
            If Len(Trim(Application.StartupPath)) > 3 Then
                myWord1.Documents.Open(FileName:=Application.StartupPath &
                  "\files\" & tempStoreStr)
            Else
                myWord1.Documents.Open(FileName:=Application.StartupPath &
                  "files\" & tempStoreStr)
            End If
        End If
        Err.Clear()
    End If
    Dim myWord2 As New Word.Application()
    Dim Word2 As New Word.Application()
    If (FilePos = 0) Then
        FilePos = InStr(1, tempStoreStr, ".DOC", CompareMethod.Text)
        tempStoreStr = Mid(tempStoreStr, 1, FilePos + 3)
        If Len(Trim(Application.StartupPath)) > 3 Then
            CheckFileExistence1 = Dir(Application.StartupPath & "\files\" &
              tempStoreStr)
        Else
            CheckFileExistence1 = Dir(Application.StartupPath & "files\" &
              tempStoreStr)
        End If
        If UCase(CheckFileExistence1) <> UCase(tempStoreStr) Then
            MsgBox("Unable to locate '" & tempStoreStr & "' document.",
              MsgBoxStyle.Information +
          MsgBoxStyle.OKOnly, "SkillSearch Tool")
            Exit Sub
        End If
        On Error Resume Next
        If Err.Number <> 0 Then
            Word2.Application.Visible = True
            Word2.Application.WindowState =
              Word.WdWindowState.wdWindowStateMaximize
```

```
                If Len(Trim(Application.StartupPath)) > 3 Then
                    Word2.Documents.Open(FileName:=Application.StartupPath &
                       "\files\" & tempStoreStr)
                Else
                    Word2.Documents.Open(FileName:=Application.StartupPath &
                       "files\" & tempStoreStr)
                End If
            Else
                myWord2.Parent.Windows(1).Visible = True
                myWord2.Application.WindowState =
                   Word.WdWindowState.wdWindowStateMaximize
                If Len(Trim(Application.StartupPath)) > 3 Then
                    myWord2.Documents.Open(FileName:=Application.StartupPath &
                       "\files\" & tempStoreStr)
                Else
                    myWord2.Documents.Open(FileName:=Application.StartupPath &
                       "files\" & tempStoreStr)
                End If
            End If
            Err.Clear()
        End If
HandleErr:
        If Err.Number = 52 Then
            MsgBox("Please see if the directory containing the Skills-related
               files is shared.",
            MsgBoxStyle.Information + MsgBoxStyle.OKOnly, "SkillSearch Tool")
        End If
    End Sub
    Function PopulateSkillListBox()
        Dim Conn_Object As New ADODB.Connection()
           'Function to add Primary Skills in the Skills
         ListBox
        Dim recset_Object As New ADODB.Recordset()
        If Len(Trim(Application.StartupPath)) > 3 Then
            Conn_Object.Open(("Provider=Microsoft.Jet.OLEDB.4.0;" & "Data Source=" &
            Application.StartupPath & "\Skills.mdb"))
        Else
            Conn_Object.Open(("Provider=Microsoft.Jet.OLEDB.4.0;" & "Data Source=" &
```

```
            Application.StartupPath & "Skills.mdb"))
        End If
        recset_Object.CursorType = ADODB.CursorTypeEnum.adOpenKeyset
        recset_Object.LockType = ADODB.LockTypeEnum.adLockOptimistic
        recset_Object.let_ActiveConnection(Conn_Object)
        recset_Object.Open("Select Distinct Skill1_Name from Skill_Info")
        If (recset_Object.RecordCount = 0) Then
            recset_Object.Close()
            Conn_Object.Close()
            MsgBox("Sorry, no Skill entries were found in the Skills database !!",
               MsgBoxStyle.Information +
            MsgBoxStyle.OKOnly, "SkillSearch Tool")
            lstSkills.Focus()
            GoTo MoveOut
        Else
            recset_Object.MoveFirst()
            While Not recset_Object.EOF()
                lstSkills.Items.Add((recset_Object.Fields("Skill1_Name").Value))
                recset_Object.MoveNext()
            End While
            recset_Object.Close()
            Conn_Object.Close()
        End If
MoveOut:
    End Function
    Private Sub lstSkills_SelectedValueChanged(ByVal sender As Object, ByVal e As
       System.EventArgs)
    Handles lstSkills.SelectedValueChanged
        txtSkillName.Text = CStr("")
    End Sub
    Private Sub lstSkills_SelectedIndexChanged(ByVal sender As Object, ByVal e As
       System.EventArgs)
     Handles lstSkills.SelectedIndexChanged
        txtSkillName.Text = CStr("")
    End Sub
End Class
```

The flow of the functions of the `frmSubjectSearch` form is depicted in Figure 19-9.

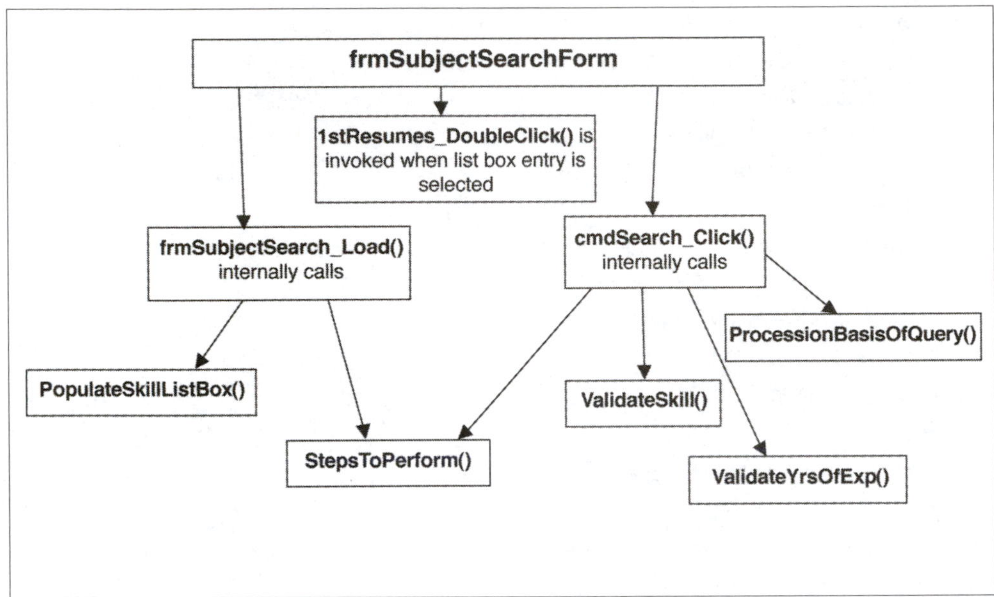

FIGURE 19-9 *Flow chart of the* `frmSubjectSearch` *form*

The main functions of the `frmSubjectSearch` form along with their description are given in Table 19-2.

Table 19-2 Main Functions of the frmSubjectSearch Form

Function Name	Description
`cmdBack_Click()`	This function is executed when the user clicks on the `Back` button on the `Search by Technology` screen. The function displays the previous screen (the `Search` screen) to the user.
`cmdSearch_Click()`	This function is executed when the user clicks on the `Search` button on the `Search by Technology` screen. The function calls the `ValidateSubject()` and the `ValidateName()` functions. A call to the `StepsToPerform()` function and the `ProcessonBasisOfQuery()` function is then made.
`ValidateSkill()`	This function is used to validate the user entry for the `Enter Skill` text box.

`ValidateYrsOfExp()`	This function is used to validate the user entry for the `Experience` text box.
`ProcessonBasisOfQuery()`	This function is used to generate the SQL query for search criteria that is based on the selection made by the user.
`StepsToPerform`	This function is used to adjust the form display area if an error is encountered. This is done so that only the relevant fields are shown to the user.
`lstSkills_Selected-ValueChanged()`	This function is used to assign the default value in the `Enter Skill` text box as blank.
`lstSkills_Selected-IndexChanged()`	This function is used to assign the default value in the `Enter Skill` text box as blank.
`PopulateSkillListBox()`	This function is used to populate the skill list box with values from the database.
`lstResumes_DoubleClick()`	This function is called when the user double-clicks on the list box containing the entries for the skill details documents. This function opens the corresponding document in Word.
`frmSubjectSearch_Load()`	This function is called when the form is first loaded. The function calls the `PopulateSkillListBox()` and the `StepsToPerform()` functions.

If the user clicks on the `Employee Name` button, the `Search by Employee Name` screen is displayed, as shown in Figure 19-10.

FIGURE 19-10 *The* `Search by Employee Name` *screen*

The user can enter or select the name of an employee and click on the `Search` button to display the corresponding skill details document file from the database. The `Back` button is used to go back to the `Search` screen. If the user leaves the employee name text box blank and clicks on the `Search` button, a message box as shown in Figure 19-11 is displayed.

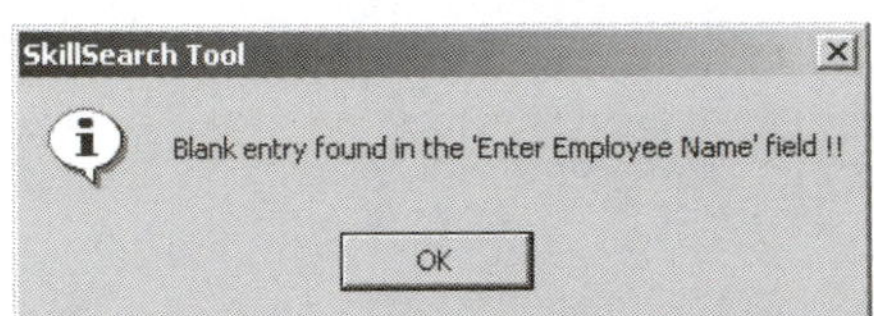

FIGURE 19-11 *The dialog box displayed when the user leaves the employee name field text box empty*

If the information entered by the user in the employee name text box does not match any of the records in the database, a dialog box as shown in Figure 19-12 is displayed.

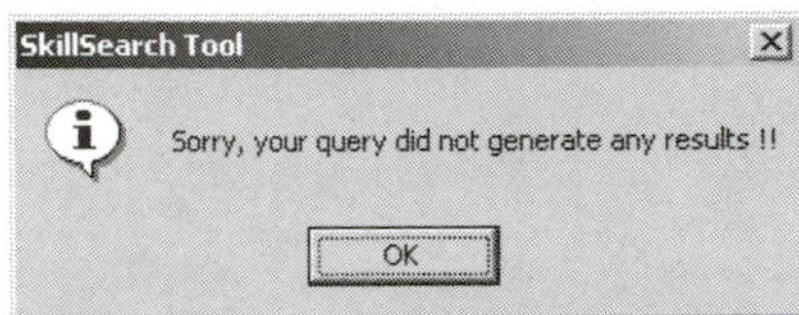

FIGURE 19-12 *This message box is displayed when the user input does not match any records in the database.*

If, however, the user input matches a record in the database, the `Search by Employee Name` screen is displayed with additional fields as shown in Figure 19-13.

FIGURE 19-13 *The* `Search by Employee Name` *screen with additional fields*

All the other fields are automatically displayed when the user selects an employee name, and a record for it is found in the database. The user can then click on the `Click to Open File` button to open the skill details document file in Word. The code listing for the `Search by Employee Name` screen is given in Listing 19-4.

Listing 19-4 Code for the Search by Employee Name Screen

```
    Dim ProfileName As String
    Private Sub cmbNames_SelectedIndexChanged(ByVal sender As Object, ByVal e As
       System.EventArgs)
    Handles cmbNames.SelectedIndexChanged
        On Error GoTo ErrHandler
' This function is invoked when the entries in the Employee Names ComboBox get
' changed
        Dim checkreturnvalue As Boolean
        checkreturnvalue = ValidateEmpName()
        If (checkreturnvalue = False) Then
            GoTo MoveOut
        End If
        Dim temprecset As New ADODB.Recordset()
        temprecset.CursorType = ADODB.CursorTypeEnum.adOpenKeyset
        temprecset.LockType = ADODB.LockTypeEnum.adLockOptimistic
        temprecset.ActiveConnection = MastDBConn_Obj
        temprecset.Open("Select Name, EmpCode, Location, Work_Phone,
           Mobile_Phone, Email_Id,
        File_Name from Skill_Info where Name like '%" & Trim(cmbNames.Text) & "%'")
        If (temprecset.RecordCount = 0) Then
            temprecset.Close()
            Dim Pattern As String
            Pattern = "FALSE"
            Call DoTasks(Pattern)
            MsgBox("Sorry, your query did not generate any results !!",
               MsgBoxStyle.Information +
            MsgBoxStyle.OKOnly, "SkillSearch Tool")
            cmbNames.Focus()
            cmbNames.SelectionStart = 0
            cmbNames.SelectionLength = Len(Trim(cmbNames.Text))
            GoTo MoveOut
        Else
            Dim Pattern As String
            Pattern = "TRUE"
            Call DoTasks(Pattern)
```

```
                cmbNames.Text = temprecset.Fields("Name").Value
                txtAddress.Text = temprecset("Location").Value
                txtPhoneNo.Text = temprecset("Work_Phone").Value
                txtEmailId.Text = temprecset("Email_Id").Value
                txtEmpCode.Text = temprecset("EmpCode").Value
                txtMobile.Text = temprecset("Mobile_Phone").Value
                ProfileName = temprecset("File_Name").Value
                temprecset.Close()
            End If
            Exit Sub
ErrHandler:
            MsgBox("The following error(" & CStr(Err.Number) & ") was encountered:" &
               Chr(13) & Err.Description,
            MsgBoxStyle.Information + MsgBoxStyle.OKOnly, "SkillSearch Tool")
MoveOut:
        End Sub
        Private Sub cmdBack_Click(ByVal sender As System.Object, ByVal e As
           System.EventArgs) Handles
        cmdBack.Click
            Me.Hide()
            Dim MainForm As New frmMain()
'Create an instance of the form 'frmMain'
            MainForm.Show()
        End Sub
        Private Sub cmdNameSearch_Click(ByVal sender As System.Object, ByVal e As
           System.EventArgs)
        Handles cmdNameSearch.Click
            On Error GoTo ErrHandler
This function is invoked when the 'Search' button is clicked by the user
            Dim checkreturnvalue As Boolean
            checkreturnvalue = ValidateEmpName()
'Validate the Employee Name entered by the user
            If (checkreturnvalue = False) Then
                GoTo MoveOut
            End If
            Dim temprecset As New ADODB.Recordset()
            temprecset.CursorType = ADODB.CursorTypeEnum.adOpenKeyset
            temprecset.LockType = ADODB.LockTypeEnum.adLockOptimistic
```

```
        temprecset.let_ActiveConnection(MastDBConn_Obj)
        temprecset.Open("Select Name, Location, Work_Phone, EmpCode,
           Mobile_Phone, File_Name,
       Email_Id from Skill_Info where Name like '%" & Trim(cmbNames.Text) & "%'")
        If (temprecset.RecordCount = 0) Then
            temprecset.Close()
            Dim Pattern As String
            Pattern = "FALSE"
            Call DoTasks(Pattern)
            MsgBox("Sorry, your query did not generate any results !!",
               MsgBoxStyle.Information +
            MsgBoxStyle.OKOnly, "SkillSearch Tool")
            cmbNames.Focus()
            cmbNames.SelectionStart = 0
            cmbNames.SelectionLength = Len(Trim(cmbNames.Text))
            GoTo MoveOut
        Else
            Dim Pattern As String
            Pattern = "TRUE"
            Call DoTasks(Pattern)
            cmbNames.Text = temprecset("Name").Value
            txtAddress.Text = temprecset("Location").Value
            txtPhoneNo.Text = temprecset("Work_Phone").Value
            txtEmailId.Text = temprecset("Email_Id").Value
            txtEmpCode.Text = temprecset("EmpCode").Value
            txtMobile.Text = temprecset("Mobile_Phone").Value
            ProfileName = temprecset("File_Name").Value
            temprecset.Close()
        End If
        Exit Sub
ErrHandler:
        MsgBox("The following error(" & CStr(Err.Number) & ") was encountered:" &
           Chr(13) & Err.Description,
        MsgBoxStyle.Information + MsgBoxStyle.OKOnly, "SkillSearch Tool")
MoveOut:
    End Sub
    Private Sub frmNameSearch_Load(ByVal sender As System.Object, ByVal e As
       System.EventArgs)
```

```
    Handles MyBase.Load
        Call PopulateNamesCombo()
'This function populates the Employee Names Combo Box with the
        names retrieved from the database
        '  Dim firstvalue As String
        '  firstvalue = cmbNames.Items.Item(0)
        cmbNames.Text = ""
        Call DoTasks(False)
        cmdNameSearch.Focus()
        '  Call cmdNameSearch_Click(Me, New System.EventArgs())
    End Sub
    Function ValidateEmpName() As Boolean
        Dim testSMENameContents As String
        testSMENameContents = Trim(cmbNames.Text)
        If (Len(Trim(testSMENameContents)) = 0) Then
 'Validate for blank entry
            MsgBox("Blank entry found in the 'Enter Employee Name' field !!",
               MsgBoxStyle.Information +
            MsgBoxStyle.OKOnly, "SkillSearch Tool")
            cmbNames.Focus()
            cmbNames.SelectionStart = 0
            cmbNames.SelectionLength = Len(Trim(cmbNames.Text))
            ValidateEmpName = False
            Exit Function
        End If
        ValidateEmpName = True
    End Function
    Function PopulateNamesCombo() As Object
        Dim Conn_Object As New ADODB.Connection()
 'Function to add Employee Name entries in the 'Name of the Employee' ComboBox
        Dim recset_Object As New ADODB.Recordset()
        If Len(Trim(Application.StartupPath)) > 3 Then
            Conn_Object.Open(("Provider=Microsoft.Jet.OLEDB.4.0;" & "Data Source=" &
            Application.StartupPath & "\Skills.mdb"))
        Else
            Conn_Object.Open(("Provider=Microsoft.Jet.OLEDB.4.0;" & "Data Source=" &
```

```
            Application.StartupPath & "Skills.mdb"))
        End If
        recset_Object.CursorType = ADODB.CursorTypeEnum.adOpenKeyset
        recset_Object.LockType = ADODB.LockTypeEnum.adLockOptimistic
        recset_Object.let_ActiveConnection(Conn_Object)
        recset_Object.Open("Select Name from Skill_Info")
        If (recset_Object.RecordCount = 0) Then
            recset_Object.Close()
            Conn_Object.Close()
            Call frmNameSearch_Load(Me, New System.EventArgs())
            MsgBox("Sorry, no Employee names were found in the Skills database
               !!", MsgBoxStyle.Information
            + MsgBoxStyle.OKOnly, "SkillSearch Tool")
            cmbNames.Focus()
            GoTo MoveOut
        Else
            recset_Object.MoveFirst()
            While Not recset_Object.EOF()
                cmbNames.Items.Add((recset_Object.Fields("Name").Value))
                recset_Object.MoveNext()
            End While
            recset_Object.Close()
            Conn_Object.Close()
        End If
MoveOut:
    End Function
    Function DoTasks(ByVal PatternEntered As String)
        If PatternEntered = "TRUE" Then
'Function to adjust the form display height and controls display on
       the basis of current condition
            Me.Height = 312
        Else
            Me.Height = 120
        End If
        lblEmpCode.Visible = PatternEntered
        txtEmpCode.Visible = PatternEntered
        lblMobile.Visible = PatternEntered
        txtMobile.Visible = PatternEntered
```

```
        lblLink.Visible = PatternEntered
        cmdLink.Visible = PatternEntered
        lblAddress.Visible = PatternEntered
        txtAddress.Visible = PatternEntered
        lblPhone.Visible = PatternEntered
        txtPhoneNo.Visible = PatternEntered
        lblEmail.Visible = PatternEntered
        txtEmailId.Visible = PatternEntered
    End Function
    Private Sub cmdLink_Click(ByVal sender As System.Object, ByVal e As
       System.EventArgs) Handles
    cmdLink.Click
        On Error GoTo HandleErr
'This function is invoked when a user double-clicks in the Resumes List box
        Dim CheckFileExistence As String
        Dim Word1 As New Word.Application()
        If Len(Trim(Application.StartupPath)) > 3 Then
            CheckFileExistence = Dir(Application.StartupPath & "\files\" &
               ProfileName)
        Else
            CheckFileExistence = Dir(Application.StartupPath & "files\" &
               ProfileName)
        End If
        If UCase(CheckFileExistence) <> UCase(ProfileName) Then
            MsgBox("Unable to locate '" & ProfileName & "' document.",
               MsgBoxStyle.Information +
            MsgBoxStyle.OKOnly, "SkillSearch Tool")
            Exit Sub
        End If
        On Error Resume Next
        If Err.Number = 0 Then
            Word1.Parent.Windows(1).Visible = True
            Word1.Application.WindowState =
               Word.WdWindowState.wdWindowStateMaximize
            If Len(Trim(Application.StartupPath)) > 3 Then
                Word1.Documents.Open(FileName:=Application.StartupPath & "\files\"
                   & ProfileName)
            Else
```

```
                Word1.Documents.Open(FileName:=Application.StartupPath & "files\"
                   & ProfileName)
            End If
        End If
        Err.Clear()
HandleErr:
        If Err.Number = 52 Then
            MsgBox("Please see if the directory containing the Skills-related
               files is shared.",
            MsgBoxStyle.Information + MsgBoxStyle.OKOnly, "SkillSearch Tool")
        End If
    End Sub
End Class
```

The flow of the functions of the `frmNameSearch` form is depicted in Figure 19-14.

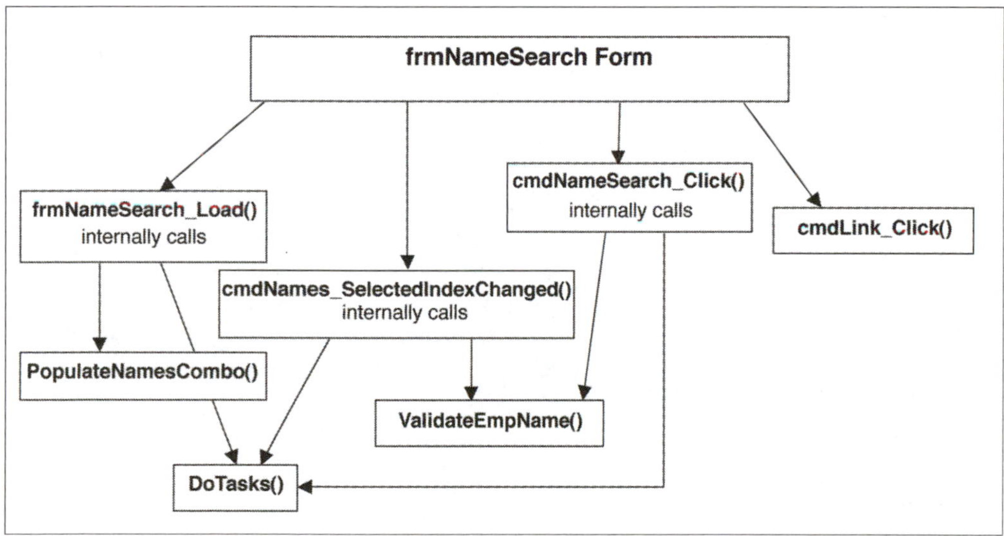

FIGURE 19-14 *Flow chart of the* `frmNameSearch` *form*

The main functions of the `frmNameSearch` are listed along with their description in Table 19-3.

Table 19-3 Main Functions of the frmNameSearch Form

Function Name	Description
`frmNameSearch_Load()`	This function is the first function to be called. The function calls the `PopulateNamesCombo()` function, which fills the `Enter Employee Name` combo box with the employee names. This function also calls the `DoTasks()` function.
`PopulateNamesCombo()`	This function fills the `Enter Employee Name` combo box with values from the `Skills` database.
`DoTasks()`	This function displays the employee-related fields based on the selected value of employee name.
`cmdLink_Click()`	This function is used to open the employee skill details file in Word.
`ValidateEmpName()`	This function validates the employee name entry as entered by the user against the values for employee names stored in the database.
`cmdBack_Click()`	This function displays the previous screen (the `Search` screen) to the user.
`cmdNames_SelectedIndexChanged()`	This function populates the employee-related fields when the user selects a different employee name from the drop-down combo box.
`cmdNameSearch_Click()`	This function is executed when the user enters the employee name in the text box and clicks on the `Search` button.

Summary

In this chapter, you coded the desktop version of the Skill Search application. You also learned all the main functions for the forms. Recall that you also need to deploy the application on Web. In the next chapter, you will learn to code the Web version of the application by using ASP.NET.

Chapter 20

Working with ASP.NET

This chapter introduces you to the basic concepts of ASP.NET. It answers some of the commonly asked questions, such as "What are the benefits of using ASP.NET?" and "How can it improve productivity in a development environment?" This chapter also describes the two different programming models in ASP.NET: Web Forms and Web Services. In addition, the chapter describes how to create interactive Web pages using ASP.NET.

Introducing ASP.NET

ASP.NET is a powerful server-based technology designed to build dynamic and structured Web applications. This technology is built in the .NET Framework, which is designed to build applications in the .NET environment. A common question that users ask is whether ASP.NET is the next version of ASP. Well, calling ASP.NET the next version of ASP may not be completely appropriate. Considering the fact that it has an entirely different programming model, perhaps it is more appropriate to call it a revolutionized technology. Does this mean that if you have applications running in ASP, you cannot use these applications in the .NET Framework? The good news is that ASP.NET is syntax-compatible with ASP. If you have existing applications in ASP, you can incrementally add ASP.NET functionality to them.

ASP.NET provides two programming models, Web Forms and Web Services, for Web developers to build enterprise-class Web applications. A Web form is the ASP.NET technology that helps you build form-based pages. Web Forms use the ASP.NET technology to create UI elements on the Web page. These elements are programmed at the server side.

A Web service is a Web application that provides functionality such as application logic, allowing application access by disparate devices. For example, your laptop device, mobile device, or your desktop machine can access Web Services by using Internet protocols, such as HTTP and XML. Note that Web Services are not tied to any particular component technology. This allows programs written in any language, using any component model, and running on any operating system to access Web Services.

Both these programming models use the different features of the ASP.NET technology. Some of the major features of ASP.NET are as follows:

- **Cross-language support.** ASP.NET provides support to multiple languages, such as Visual Basic, C#, and JScript. This feature allows you to author your application in any .NET-compatible language.
- **Multiple-tools support.** ASP.NET is compatible with WYSIWYG HTML editors and other programming tools, including Microsoft Visual Studio .NET. This allows you to build ASP.NET files using any text editor.
- **Compiling code.** Unlike its earlier versions, the code in ASP.NET is compiled and not interpreted. This improves the performance of request processing significantly. Compiling allows early binding and strong typing of the program code.
- **Caching service.** Another method by which ASP.NET optimizes the performance of request processing is providing extensive caching service. ASP.NET provides caching at three levels: page-level caching, fragment caching, and cache API. As their respective names suggest, page-level caching enables you to cache a complete page, and fragment caching enables the caching of only a portion of a page. The cache API exposes the ASP.NET cache engine to the programmers to cache their own objects. This allows programmers to have greater control over caching of their content. Note that both page-level caching and fragment caching use cache API.
- **Security.** ASP.NET uses Windows, Forms, MS Passport Authentication, or client certificates to authenticate user credentials. These authentication methods allow Web applications to customize content per the requesting identity or based on a set of roles that a requesting identity may belong to.
- **Migrating.** As mentioned earlier, ASP.NET allows easy migration from ASP. If your applications are in ASP and you want to migrate to ASP.NET, then all you need to do is change the file extensions from .asp to .aspx and add few lines of code. The .aspx file extension is used in the .NET Framework.
- **Debugging and tracing.** An important element of application development is debugging and tracing. This feature allows developers to debug and trace any errors in an application. In ASP.NET, you can use the built-in Visual Studio .NET debugging tools and trace method for tracing your Web pages.

- **State management.** State management is the process by which you maintain state and page information over multiple requests for the same or different pages. ASP.NET provides easy-to-use application and session-state facilities that are familiar to ASP developers and are readily compatible with all other .NET Framework APIs.
- **ASP.NET runtime.** The runtime feature in ASP.NET provides both reliability and improved deployment. Runtime manages system memory, which helps eliminate memory leaks and other traditional programming problems. In addition, it uses the Xcopy feature to ease the deployment of applications.
- **Accessing data.** ASP.NET provides functionalities that allow easy access of data from databases and also help manage this data.

The following sections provide a more detailed explanation of Web Forms and how this programming model leverages the benefits of ASP.NET in building Web applications. Note that this book will not be delving into the Web Services model.

NOTE

ASP.NET is supported on Windows 2000 and Windows NT 4 with Service Pack 6a, except Web Services. Web Services is supported on all platforms supported by the Microsoft .NET Framework SDK, except Windows 95.

Web Forms

Web Forms are an ASP.NET technology, which allow you to create powerful forms-based Web pages. These forms can be run on any browser. They leverage the benefits of the ASP.NET technology to automatically render the correct, browser-compliant HTML for features such as styles, layout, and so on. In addition, these forms provide a rich set of controls to create interactive and dynamic Web pages. You can program these controls in any Common Language Runtime (CLR) supported language, including Visual Basic, C#, and JScript. Using the CLR technology allows Web Forms to leverage the benefits of this technology, which allows managed execution environment, type safety, inheritance, and dynamic compilation for improved performance.

A Web form contains two major components: the visual component and the application logic.

- **Visual component.** The visual component of a Web form consists of a file that contains markup and elements specific to a Web form, such as static HTML or XML. This file is referred to as a page, and it carries the .aspx extension. It works as a container for the text and the controls you want to display in your Web page.
- **Application/programming logic.** The application logic contains the code you create to interact with the Web form. This code can be created in a code-inline model in which the code is written in the .aspx file. The other option is to use the code-behind model to create the code. In this model, the code is written in a separate file. However, please note that the choice between using the code-inline and the code-behind models is a matter of the Web developers' preference.

Before creating a Web form, it will be useful for you to know the processing cycle of a Web form.

Web Form Processing

The way in which Web Forms are processed may differ depending upon the client request. There are two methods to process a form: server processing and client processing.

In the server-side processing method, the request from the client is passed to the server for validation. Consider the example of a store that sells its products through the Internet. A customer looking to buy products from this store must fill out the order processing form. This form asks customers to enter the item they want to purchase and the desired quantity. When the customer submits this information, the form is sent to the server for validation. Depending upon the availability of the product, the form returns the relevant result to the customer and allows the customer to continue using the page.

The client-side processing method is commonly used for input validation where the client side processes the form. I will use the order processing form example to help you understand client-side processing. If the customers decide to buy the product, they are asked to fill in billing information. After this information is entered, the customers click on the Submit button to post the form. In this case, the form need not be submitted to the server for validation. To handle such interactions, you can create client-side scripting that validates the form for any missing information.

Now that you know about the two methods of Web form processing, the following sections discuss the different processing stages in the life cycle of a Web form. Note that there are several stages involved in Web form processing. However, in this chapter discusses the three primary stages: Page Load event, Event Handling, and Page Unload. These stages recur each time the Web form is requested or posted.

Page Load Event

Each time a Web page requires processing on the server side, the page must be posted back to the server and returned to the client for the user to continue using the page. For example, if the user uses the order processing form to inquiry about a product, the Web page (containing all products-related information) is sent to the server for processing. Before the server returns the page, it must be re-created. Therefore, each time a page is served from the server to the client, the page follows a sequence of events.

Event-Handling

The next step is to handle these events. You can accomplish this task by writing event-handling procedures. If you were to handle events such as the initialization of a page or the loading of a page, you must write the code in the `Page_Init` event or the `Page_Load` event. Note that all server controls are guaranteed to be loaded only in the `Page_Load` event. After the Init and Load events, the page is posted to the client. Now each time the user interacts with the page and the page is submitted to the server for processing, the page is re-created before it is submitted to the client, and the same sequence of events, `Page_Load` and `Page_Init`, are generated. For example, if the user clicks on the Submit button in the order processing form to place an order, the page is posted back to the server, and the code in the control's event-handler (`Submit_Click`) is executed. After processing, the page is re-created and the page follows the same Init and Load events. This slows down the performance of the Web form processing. ASP.NET has a solution to this problem. It uses the `IsPostBack` property of the Web form to check if the form is requested for the first time. If the page displays `False`, it means that the page has been requested for the first time. A `True` value indicates that the page is run as a result of a round trip. Therefore, using the `IsPostBack` property, you can make the page run the initialization code only once when it is requested for the first time.

Page Unload

Finally, when a user closes the page or exits from the browser, the page is unloaded from the memory and the Unload event is generated. Any de-initialization code can go in the `Page_Unload` event-handler.

Now that you know about the basic concepts of Web Forms, you are ready to create your first ASP.NET application using Visual Studio .NET.

Creating a Web Form

In this section, you create a Web form, main.aspx. This form allows a company to search for relevant data about an employee based on their skill sets. You must first create a project in Visual Studio .NET before you create the form. Name the project SkillsSearchWeb.proj. Follow these steps:

1. Open Microsoft Visual Studio .NET.
2. On the File menu, point to New, and then click on Project.
3. In the New Project dialog box (see Figure 20-1), perform the following tasks:
   - In the Project Types pane, select Visual Basic Projects.
   - In the Templates pane, select ASP.NET Web Application.
   - In the Location box, you can accept the default setting, which is **http://localhost** to define the location Web server where you want to create the project. If you want to specify any other location, enter the specific URL (including http://). Also, specify the name of the application in the Location box as main.aspx.
4. Click on OK.

   Notice that a new Web Form, WebForm1.aspx, opens in the Design view as displayed in Figure 20-2.

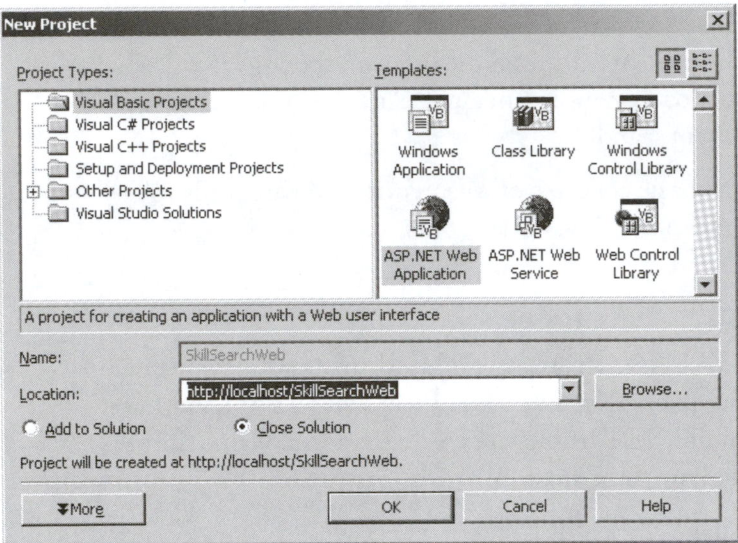

FIGURE 20-1 *The New Project dialog box*

5. In the File Name field of the Properties dialog box, change the name of the file to main.aspx.
6. Next, click on the HTML tab and add a reference to the .css file. This will enable you to use cascading style sheets. Drag the Styles.css file from Solution Explorer to the HTML page and drop it above the <head> tag. Notice that the following code is added.

```
<LINK rel="stylesheet" type="text/css"
href="http://localhost/WebForms/Styles.css">
```

Now that your base form is ready, you can add server controls to this form. Web Forms use the ASP.NET server controls to create the common UI elements in these pages. The following section provides a detailed description of the different types of server controls. You will then add these server controls to the form created in this section.

ASP.NET Server Controls

Creating a user interface that meets the requirements of broad range of Internet users is a challenging task. It is important to ensure that your Web site is well structured and organized. To design such a Web site, ASP.NET provides a rich

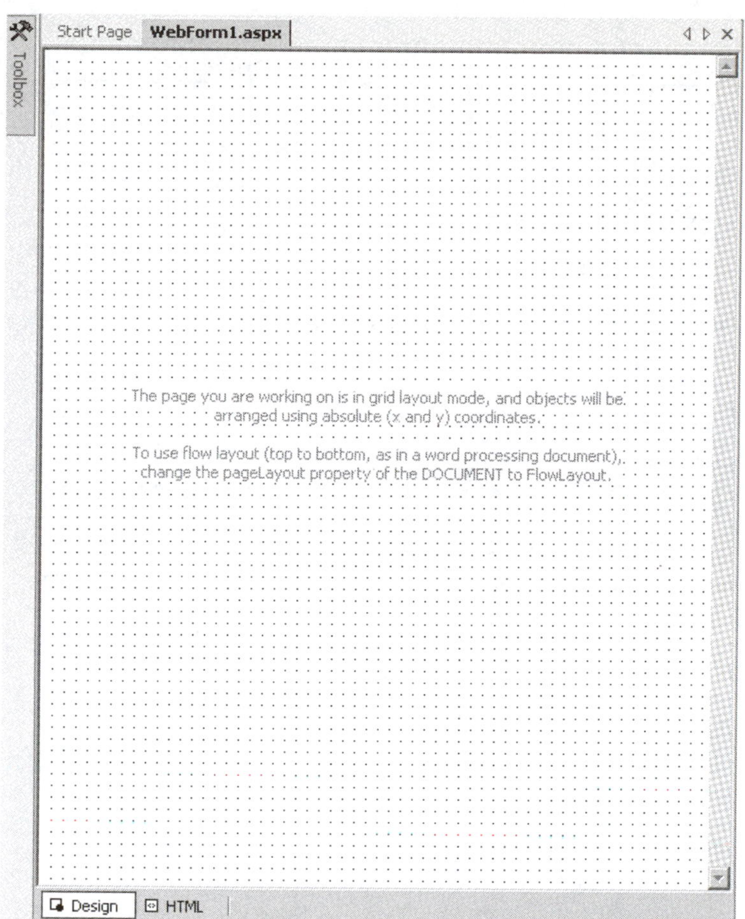

FIGURE 20-2 *The Design view of the Web form*

set of server controls that enables you to create interactive and dynamic Web pages. These are known as server controls because the events raised by the client are handled at the server end. Server controls are declared within an `.aspx` file using custom tags that contain a `runat="server"` attribute value. This attribute enables server-side events. If you do not set the `runat` attribute to `"server"`, the control works as a plain HTML control. The server tags must be enclosed within the form tags `<form runat="server"></form>`.

Table 20-1 describes some of the commonly accessed properties of a server control.

Table 20-1 Server Control Properties

Properties	Description
`ID`	Identifier for a control.
`Controls`	Collection of child controls.
`Page`	Element that contains the control.
`Parent`	Control to which a collection of controls belongs.
`ViewState`	Automatically saves the values of a Web form and the controls in the form during page processing.
`UniqueID`	Uniquely identifies a control.
`Visible`	Determines the visibility of a control.

There are four types of Server controls in ASP.NET: HTML, Web Server, Validation, and User. The following sections explain each of these controls in detail.

HTML Controls

HTML controls are similar to HTML elements. HTML controls contain some attributes that make them visible to the server. These controls can be programmed on the server. Any HTML element can be made into a control by adding the attribute `runat="server"`. Note that all HTML controls can be bound to a data source.

The names and descriptions of some of the HTML controls are given in Table 20-2.

Table 20-2 HTML Controls

Control	Description
`HtmlForm`	Defines an HTML form. The values of controls within the form are posted to the server when the form is submitted.
`HtmlInputText`	Displays text entered at design time that can be edited by users at run time, or changed programmatically.
`HtmlButton`	Defines a button control on the Web form. When clicked, it generates an event that was assigned to it.
`HtmlAnchor`	Creates Web navigation.
`HtmlTextArea`	Displays a large amount of text.

Web Server Controls

Web server controls are similar to HTML controls. However, they have more built-in features than the HTML controls. Apart from the traditional user-entry controls, such as text box and button controls, it contains special-purpose controls, such as Calendar. The names and descriptions of some of the Web server controls are given in Table 20-3.

Table 20-3 Web Server Controls

Control	Description
`TextBox`	Displays a text box where user can input text.
`Label`	Displays text that cannot be edited by the user.
`DropDownList`	Allows users to select one option from a list or enter text.
`ListBox`	Displays a list of choices. This type of list allows multiple selections.
`Image`	Displays an image.
`AdRotator`	Displays a sequence of images.
`CheckBoxList`	Creates a grouping of check boxes.
`RadioButton`	Displays a single button that users click to enable or disable the control.
`Calendar`	Displays a graphic calendar and gives the users the option to select a date.
`LinkButton`	Performs the task of a `Button` control, but is displayed like a hyperlink.
`ImageButton`	Renders images on a form.
`HyperLink`	Creates Web navigation links.
`Table`	Creates a table.
`Panel`	Creates a borderless division on the form that serves as a container for other controls.
`Repeater`	Displays information from a data set using a set of HTML elements and controls you specify, repeating the elements once for each record in the data set.
`DataList`	Like the `Repeater` control, but with more formatting and layout options, including displaying information in a table. The `DataList` control also allows you to specify editing behavior.
`DataGrid`	Displays information, usually data-bound, in tabular form with columns. Provides mechanisms to allow editing and sorting.

Validation Controls

Validation controls offer a way to check user input on a page. For example, they can be used to check if a value entered by a user in a date field matches a specified format. Table 20-4 lists the types of validation controls you can use in Web Forms.

Table 20-4 Validation Controls

Control	Description
`RequiredFieldValidator`	Ensures that the user does not skip a required entry.
`CompareValidator`	Uses the comparison operators, such as >, =, <, to validate user input with a predefined value of another control or a database field.
`RangeValidator`	Validates if the user input is within a predefined range for numbers, characters, or dates.
`RegularExpressionValidator`	Performs pattern matching of user input with a regular expression. For example, it checks for predictable sequences of characters, such as social security numbers, telephone numbers, zip codes, and so on.
`CustomValidator`	Checks the user's entry using validation logic that you code yourself. This type of validation allows you to check for values derived at run time.

Custom User Controls

Custom user controls make it easy for developers to code for user controls that can be reused in other applications. For example, developers can program for a header control file that can be used by other applications. This saves the effort to create and maintain separate header controls files for each application. Custom user controls can contain controls, images, or any valid HTML code. For instance, in a header control you can place a property that allows you to set the header for the application.

Adding Controls in a Web Form

In this section, you will enhance the Web form `SkillSearchWeb` created earlier. This is a search form that should enable a company to look for employee details based on the employee name or their skills. Create a main page, `main.aspx`, which contains two search options, `Employee Skills` and `Employee Name`. When the user clicks the `Employee Skills` button, the application should load a Search page called `EmpNameSearch.aspx`. The `Search` page should contain a `TextBox` control where the user can input the employee name for searching. Next, add a drop-down list box control that displays a list of skills that can be selected by the user to look for employees with matching details. Finally, add two buttons, `Search` and `Back`. If the employee name exists in the server database, the form should display the relevant details of the employee. If the employee name does not exist, the page should return an error message. Note that in this activity, you create the relevant event code for each control you add to a Web page.

To add the `Label`, `TextBox`, and `Drop-down list box` controls, follow these steps:

1. In the `main.aspx` form, click the Toolbox tab.
2. Click the Web `Forms` tab.
3. Add two button controls, `Employee Skills` and `Employee Name`, to the form. To add a button, drag the `Button` control from the Toolbox to the Design page. Figure 20-3 displays the controls in the Toolbox.
4. In the Properties page, define the name of this button as `Employee Skills`.
5. Next, add another button control, `Employee Name`, to the Web page.
6. The next step is to write the relevant event code for each button control. When the user clicks the `Employee Skills` button, the page should load a search page, `skills.aspx`, which contains the relevant employee skills search options. Add the following event code for the `Employee Skills` button:

   ```
   function SkillsClicked()
   {location.href = "Skills.aspx"
   return; }
   ```

7. For the `Employee Name` button control, add the following code. This code will load the `EmpNameSearch.aspx` page.

   ```
   function NameClicked()
   { location.href = "EmpNameSearch.aspx"
   return; }
   ```

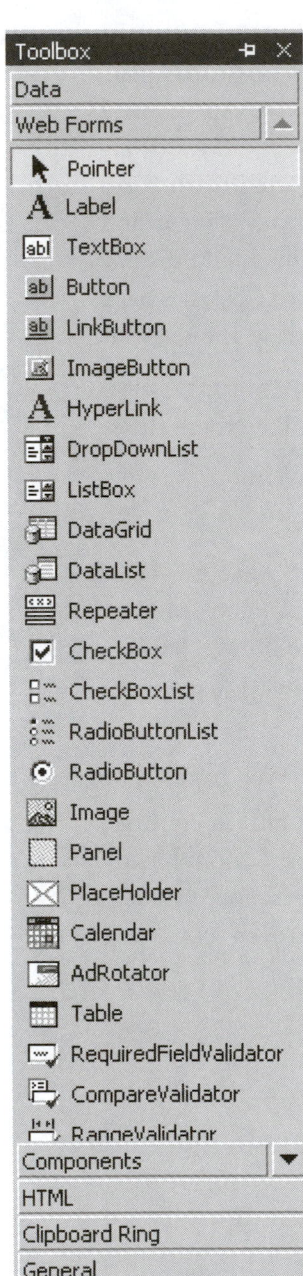

FIGURE 20-3 *The Toolbox controls*

8. The next step is to create a form, `skills.aspx`, which contains the query for the employee skills details. This page should contain the following labels and their corresponding controls:

Label	Name of the Control	Description
`Enter Skill`	*TextBox* control	User text
`Select Technology`	*Drop-down list box* control	Contains a list of skills
`Experience (in months)`	*TextBox* control	User text

9. Add a `CustomValidator` button control under the `Select Technology` drop-down list box. This control contains the following event code:

```
<td><asp:customvalidator id="CustomValidator_Skills_List"
style="Z-INDEX: 101; LEFT: 590px; POSITION: absolute; TOP:
323px" runat="server" ClientValidationFunction="listChange()"
ControlToValidate="lstSkills"></asp:customvalidator></td>
```

10. Note that the `CustomValidator` button control calls a function called `listChange()`. The code for this function follows. The function validates the following conditions based on the skill technology selected by the user:
    - Validate empty text fields.
    - Check if the user has entered the value 0 or less than 0 in the text fields.
    - Check for spaces entered by the user in the text fields.

    If the user has selected the correct entry from the drop-down list box, the Web form will load the page, `SkillSearch.aspx`, which contains the search result.

```
function listChange()
{
var skillname=document.frmSkills.lstSkills.options[document.frmSkills.lstSkills.
   selectedIndex].text
var noOfMonths=document.frmSkills.txtnoOfMonths.value;
      if (skillname != "<Select an entry from the list>") {
      var noOfMonthsLength=(document.frmSkills.txtnoOfMonths.value.length);

      if (noOfMonths=="") {
```

```
        noOfMonths=0;
        location.href = "Skillsearch.aspx" + "?skill=" + skillname + "&months="
          + noOfMonths;
    }

    if (noOfMonths!="") {
        checkyear =0;
        for( j=0; j<noOfMonthsLength ; j++) {
                    if (noOfMonths.charAt(j)==" ") {
        continue;
        }
    else {
        checkyear =1;
    break;
    }
    }

    if (checkyear == 0 ) {
        alert("Please enter some value in 'Experience (in months):' field.");
        document.frmSkills.txtnoOfMonths.value= "";
        document.frmSkills.txtnoOfMonths.focus();
    return;
    }

    if(isNaN(noOfMonths)) {
        alert("Non-numeric entry found in 'Experience (in months):' field.");
        document.frmSkills.txtnoOfMonths.value= "";
        document.frmSkills.txtnoOfMonths.focus();
    return;
    }
    location.href = "Skillsearch.aspx" + "?skill=" + skillname + "&months=" +
      noOfMonths;
    }
    } else {
        alert("Please select a valid skill from the technology listbox.");
        document.frmSkills.lstSkills.focus();
        return;
    }
}
```

11. Next, add a button control called `Search`. This button control contains the following event code:

```
<td align="middle"><input type="button" value="Search"
id="Search" name="cmdSearch" onclick="validateskill()"></td>
```

12. Note that the `Search` button calls a function called `validateskill()`. The code for this function follows. This function performs the following validations on the text fields:

    - Check if the text fields, `Enter Skill` and `Experience`, are empty.
    - Check for non-numeric values in the `Experience` field.
    - Check if the user has entered the value 0 or less than 0 in the text fields.
    - Check for spaces entered by the user in the text fields.

    For every incorrect format entered in the text fields, display the relevant error message. If all the relevant fields contain text in the correct format, the Web Form loads another page called `Skillsearch.aspx` that displays the search results.

```
function validateskill()
{
var skillname=document.frmSkills.txtSkill.value;
var noOfMonths=document.frmSkills.txtnoOfMonths.value;

var skillnameLength=document.frmSkills.txtSkill.value.length;
var noOfMonthsLength=document.frmSkills.txtnoOfMonths.value.length;

	if (noOfMonths=="")
	{
		if (skillname == "")
		{
				alert("Please enter some value in 'Enter Skill' field.");
				document.frmSkills.txtSkill.value= "";
				document.frmSkills.txtSkill.focus();
			return;
		}
	checkskill = 0;
	for( j=0; j<skillnameLength ; j++) {
		if (skillname.charAt(j)==" ") {
```

```
        continue;
    }
    else {
        checkskill=1;
        break;
    }
    }

    if (checkskill == 0 ) {
        alert("Please enter some value in 'Enter Skill' field.");
        document.frmSkills.txtSkill.value= "";
        document.frmSkills.txtSkill.focus();
    return;
        noOfMonths=0;
        location.href = "Skillsearch.aspx" + "?skill=" + skillname + "&months="
           + noOfMonths;
    return;
    }

    if ((noOfMonths!="") && (skillname == ""))
    {
        alert("Please enter some value in 'Enter Skill' field.");
        document.frmSkills.txtSkill.value= "";
        document.frmSkills.txtSkill.focus();
    return;
    }

    if (noOfMonths!="")
    {
        checkyear =0;
        for( j=0; j<noOfMonthsLength ; j++) {
                if (noOfMonths.charAt(j)==" ") {
                continue;
                }
                else {
                checkyear =1;
                break;
                }
```

```
            }

    if (checkyear == 0 ) {
            alert("Please enter some value in 'Experience (in months):'
               field.");
            document.frmSkills.txtnoOfMonths.value= "";
            document.frmSkills.txtnoOfMonths.focus();
    return;
}

    if(isNaN(noOfMonths)) {
            alert("Non-numeric entry found in 'Experience (in months):'
               field.");
            document.frmSkills.txtnoOfMonths.value= "";
            document.frmSkills.txtnoOfMonths.focus();
    return;
    }

    if (skillname == "")
    {
            alert("Please enter some value in 'Enter Skill' field.");
            document.frmSkills.txtSkill.value= "";
            document.frmSkills.txtSkill.focus();
    return;
    }
    checkskill = 0;
    for( j=0; j<skillnameLength ; j++) {
            if (skillname.charAt(j)==" ") {
            continue;
            }
            else {
                    checkskill=1;
            break;
            }
    }

    if (checkskill == 0 ) {
            alert("Please enter some value in 'Enter Skill' field.");
```

```
                    document.frmSkills.txtSkill.value= "";
                    document.frmSkills.txtSkill.focus();
          return;
          }
                    location.href = "Skillsearch.aspx" + "?skill=" + skillname +
                       "&months=" + noOfMonths;
                    return;
          }
}
```

13. Save the file.
14. The next step is to build and run the project. On the Build menu, click on Build Solution. The output is displayed in Figure 20-4.

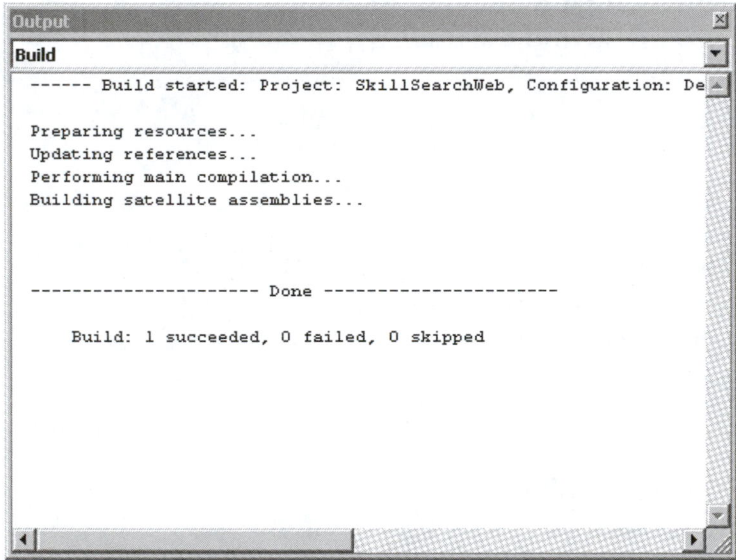

FIGURE 20-4 *The output of the Build*

15. To verify that your Web application will run in a browser, click on the Debug menu item and click on Start With Debugging to open the Web page in the Debug mode as displayed in Figure 20-5.

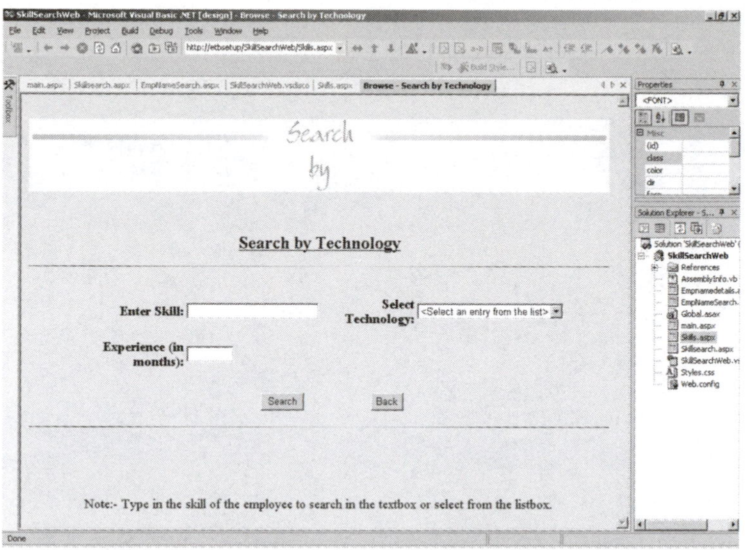

FIGURE 20-5 *The Skills form in the Web browser*

Summary

ASP.NET provides a scalable way to build and deploy powerful Web applications that can target any browser. It has been designed with scalability in mind, with features such as caching and session state. In addition, it is specifically tailored to improve performance in clustered and multiprocessor environments.

Chapter 21

Executing the Skill Search Application

You have coded the Skill Search application in the previous chapters. In this chapter, you will learn to execute the desktop version of the Skill Search application and learn the steps to distribute the application as an executable file.

Running the Skill Search Application

You need to install the Skill Search application on your computer to run the application. To install the application, you need to run the setup.exe file. The setup.exe file will automatically install the application in the default C drive on your machine.

The steps to run the setup.exe file are as follows:

1. Double-click on the setup.exe file to run the application setup wizard.
2. The first screen of the setup is a Welcome screen as shown in Figure 21-1. Click on the Next button on the screen to advance into the setup.

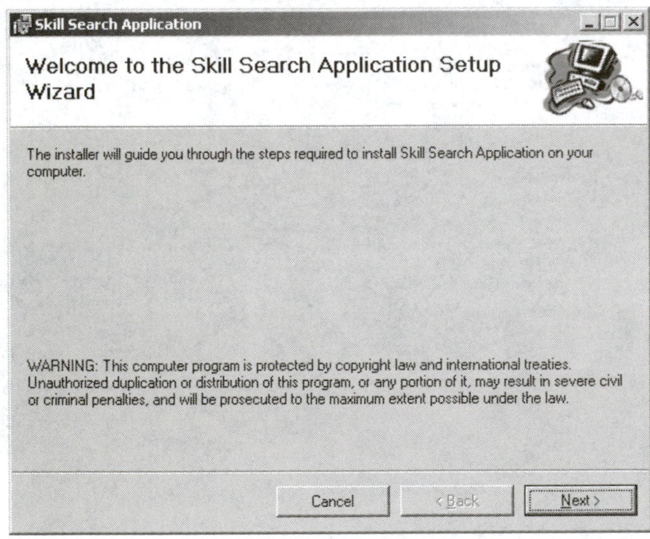

FIGURE 21-1 *The Welcome screen of the Skill Search application Setup Wizard*

3. The next screen appears as displayed in Figure 21-2. You can select the folder where you want the application to be stored by clicking on the Browse button.

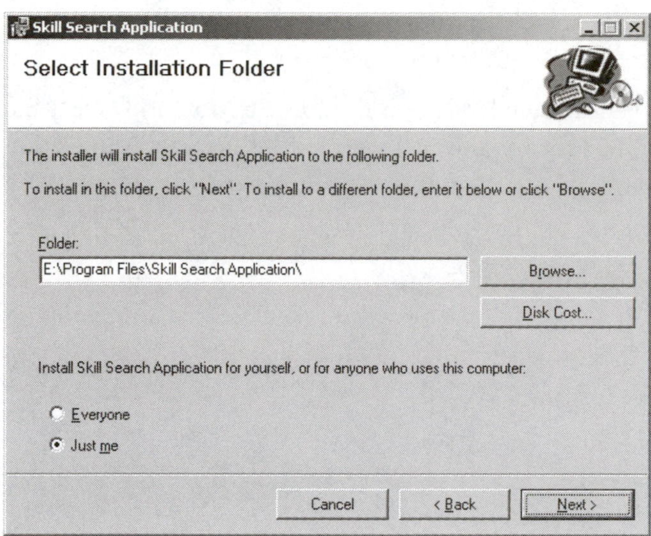

FIGURE 21-2 *This screen of the setup is used to specify the location where the Skill Search application will be stored.*

4. Click on the Next button to display the next screen of the wizard, as shown in Figure 21-3.

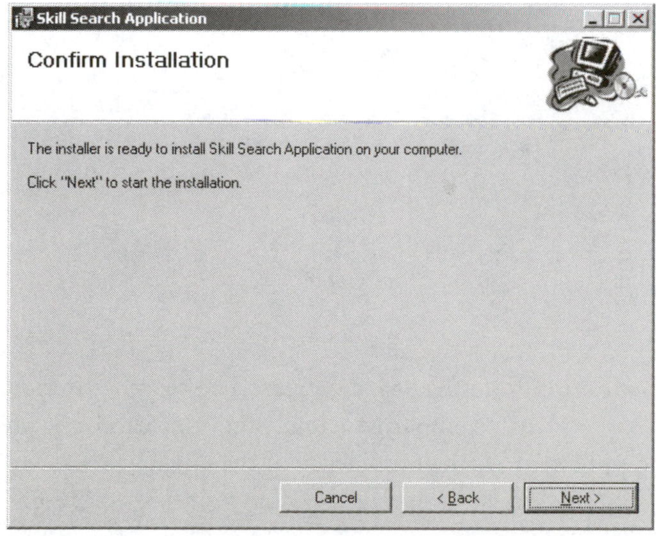

FIGURE 21-3 *This screen is used to start the setup process.*

5. Click on the Next button, and the setup will install the application at the specified location.

After the application has been installed, click on the Start button and select the Programs option from the Start menu. You will see the Skill Search Application option in the Programs suboption. Click on this option to run the application.

The `Splash` screen is the first screen to be displayed when the application is run. The `Splash` screen is displayed in Figure 21-4.

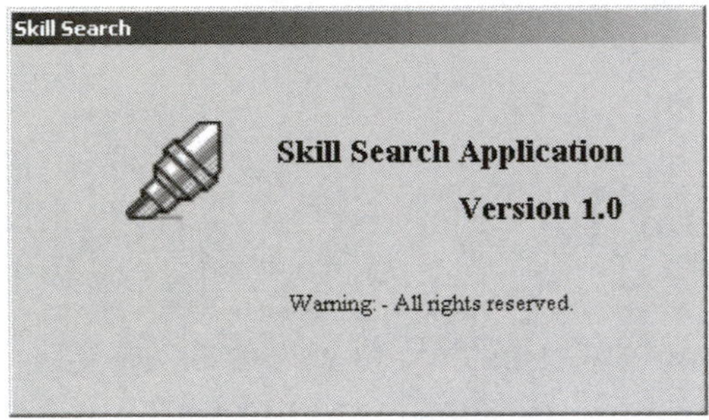

FIGURE 21-4 *The* `Splash` *Screen of the Skill Search application*

The `Splash` screen is displayed for only a few seconds after which the `Search` screen, as shown in Figure 21-5, is displayed to the user.

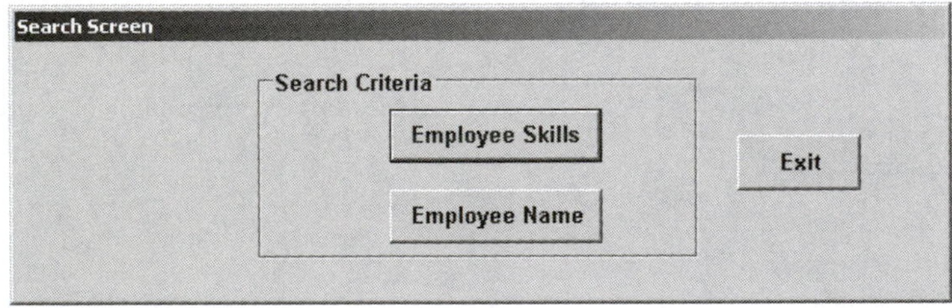

FIGURE 21-5 *The* `Search` *screen is used to specify the search criteria for the Skill Search application.*

The user can select a search criterion from the `Search` screen. The search criterion can be on the basis of employee skills or employee name. The user can click on the `Exit` button to quit the application. If the user clicks on the `Employee Skills` button, the `Search by Technology` screen is displayed as shown in Figure 21-6.

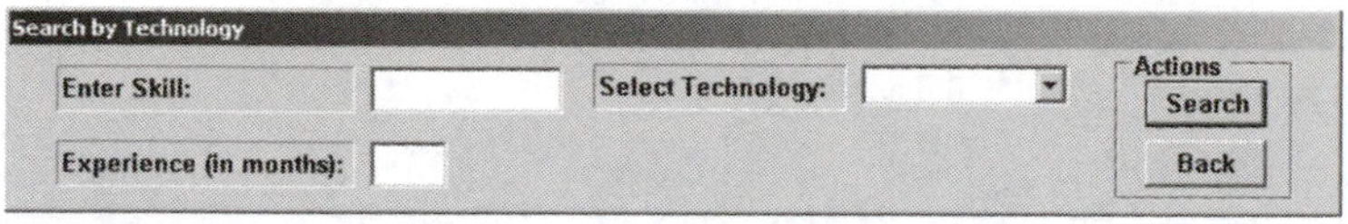

FIGURE 21-6 *This screen is used to search for the skills details document of an employee based on employee skills.*

The user can enter the employee skill in the `Enter Skill` text box or select the skill from the `Select Technology` combo box. The number of years of experience in the subject needs to be entered in the `Experience (in months)` text box. If the user input matches records in the database, the `Search by Technology` screen is displayed as shown in Figure 21-7.

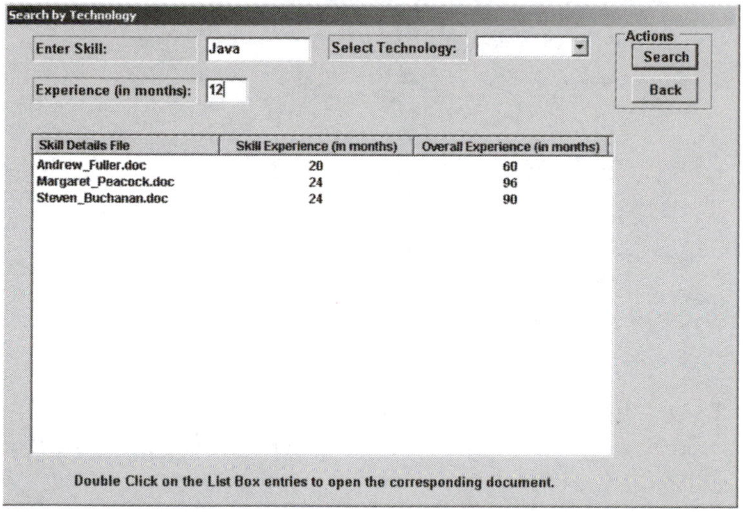

FIGURE 21-7 *This screen is displayed when matching records for the user inputs in the* `Search by Technology` *screen are found in the database.*

The user can then double-click on a list box entry to open the corresponding employee's skills details document in Word. The screen also has a `Back` button, which takes the user to the previous `Search` screen.

However, if the user clicks on the `Employee Name` button on the `Search` screen, the `Search by Employee Name` screen, as shown in Figure 21-8, is displayed.

The user can select the name of an employee from the `Enter Employee Name` combo box. The `Search` button is then used to search for the specific record in the

FIGURE 21-8 *This screen is used to search for the skills details document of an employee based on the employee name.*

database. If matching records are found in the database, the `Search by Employee Name` screen is displayed with additional fields, as shown in Figure 21-9.

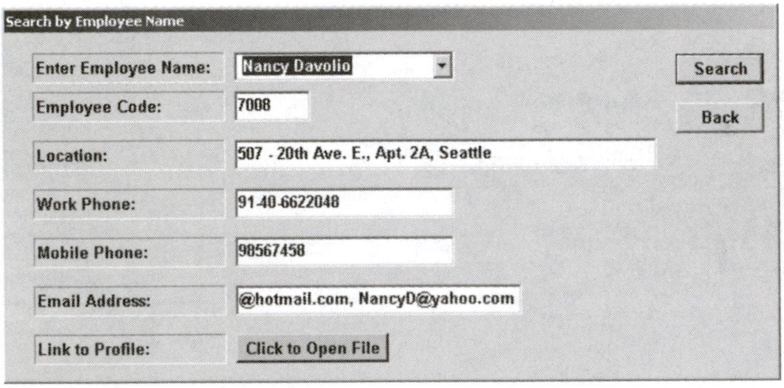

FIGURE 21-9 *The* `Search by Employee Name` *screen with additional fields is displayed.*

When the user selects an employee name, the rest of the fields of the `Search by Employee Name` screen, as displayed in Figure 21-9, are picked up directly from the database and displayed to the user.

The user can click on the `Click to Open File` button to open the corresponding skills details document in Word.

In this section, you learned about the execution and the screen displays of the Skill Search application. The next section discusses the steps to distribute the application as an .exe file.

Distributing the Application

You can distribute the Skill Search application as an .exe file to run the application. The steps to create a setup for the Skill Search application are as follows:

1. Open a new project in Visual Studio .Net and select the project type as Setup and Deployment Projects. Select the Setup Project option from the Templates list. The New Project dialog box is displayed as shown in Figure 21-10.

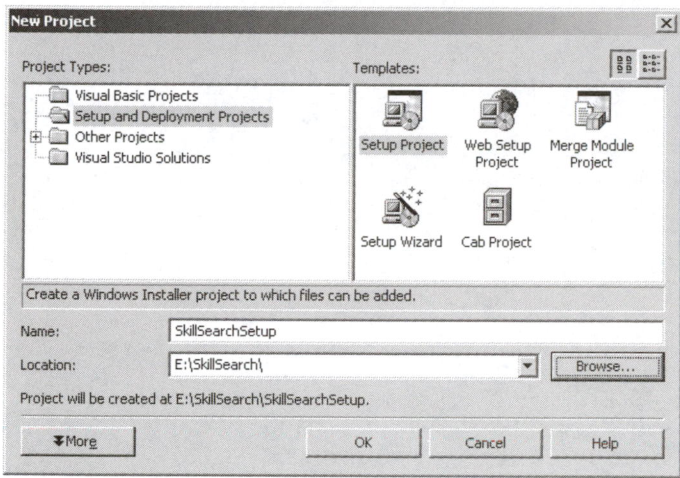

FIGURE 21-10 *This dialog box is used to specify the project type and template to be used.*

You also need to specify a name for the setup and the location where you want the setup to be created.

2. Next, you need to specify the files to be included in the setup. The files to be included in the setup are displayed in Figure 21-11.
3. After you have specified the files to be included in the setup, you need to build the application. To build the application, select the Build Solution option from the Build menu, as displayed in Figure 21-12.

   The setup will be created at the specified location.

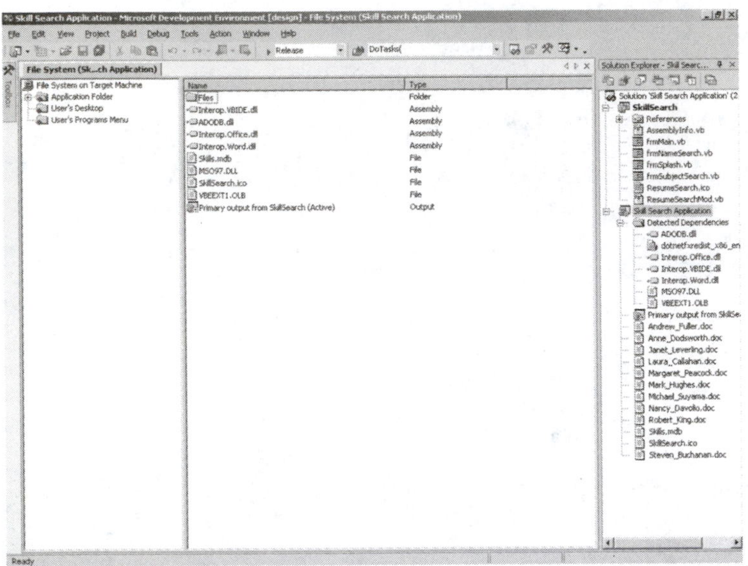

FIGURE 21-11 *This screen displays the setup files.*

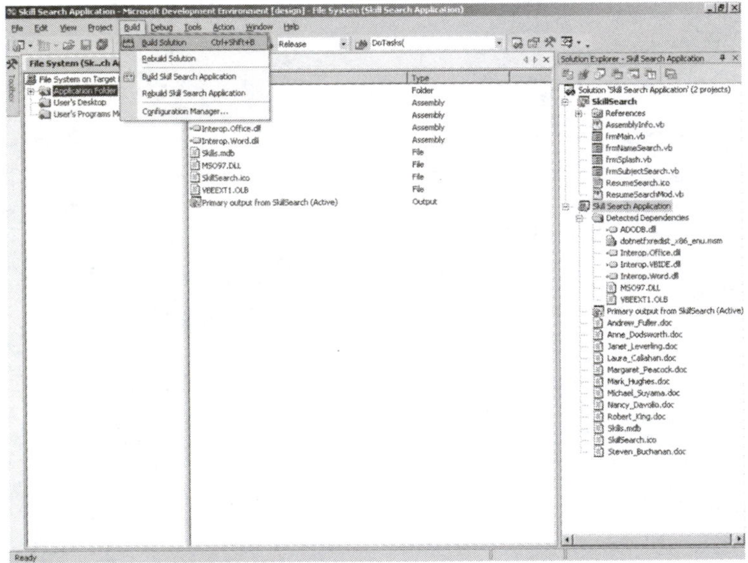

FIGURE 21-12 *The Build Solution option from the Build menu is displayed.*

Summary

In this chapter, you learned how to run the Skill Search application. You also learned about the steps to distribute the application as an .exe file.

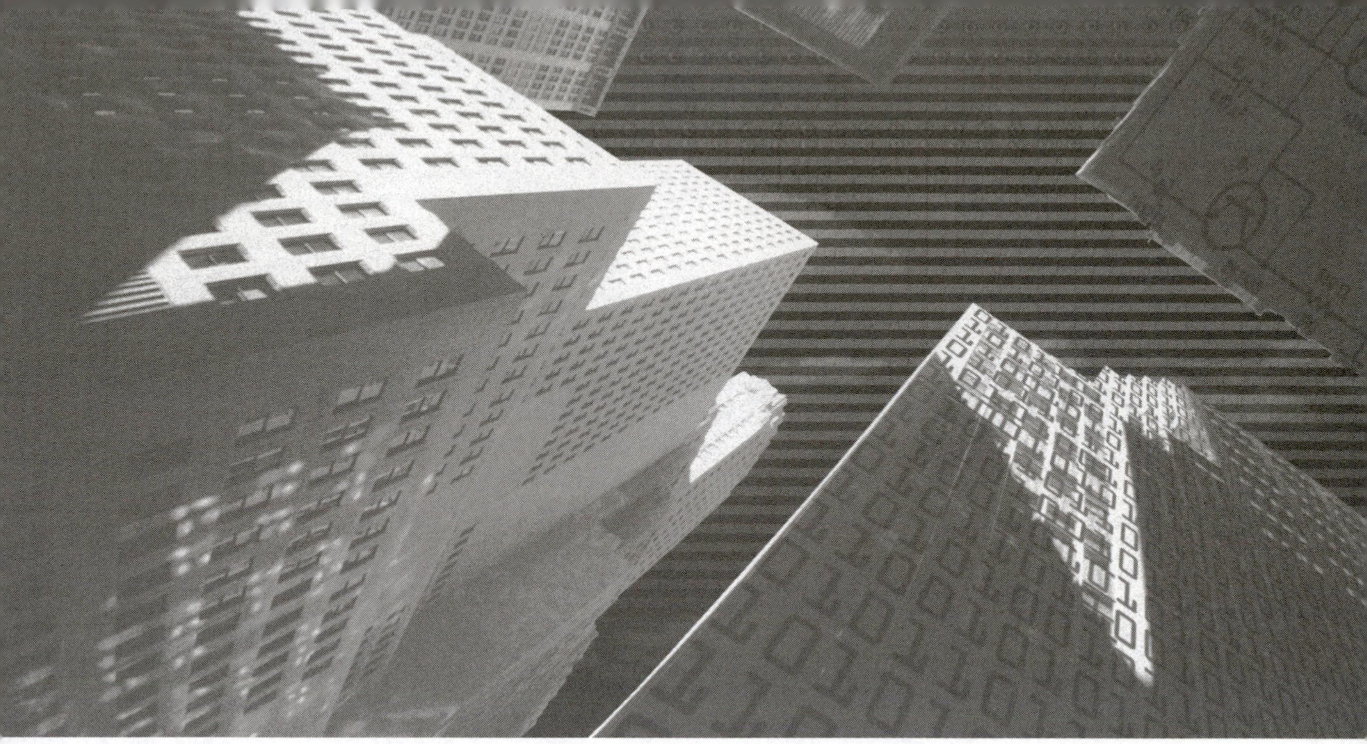

PART V

Professional Project 3

Project 3

Creating a Word Checker Tool

Project 3 Overview

A Word Checker tool can be used to automate the procedure for proofreading a document for any deviations from a specified style sheet. It can be used by organizations that specialize in editing and proofreading documents for corporate clients.

The tool has the following functionalities:

- The tool points out any deviations from the style specifications as mentioned in the standard style sheet document.
- The tool reports all deviations from the standard style sheet in a separate document.
- The tool highlights incorrect words in the document in a different color.
- The tool has a simple and user-friendly interface.

The Word Checker tool has been built using Visual Basic .NET. You will learn to work with Word Objects in this application.

Chapter 22

Project Case Study: Writers and Editors Inc.

Writers and Editors Inc. is a company based in New Jersey. The company specializes in editing and proofreading documents for individual customers and corporate clients. The company has an experienced staff of 150 professional editors, of which some are writers themselves. Therefore, the employees have experience with the kinds of errors that writers make.

The company provides both services and consultation to various types of clients, such as Fortune 500 companies, nonprofit organizations, and individual customers. As a result, editors and proofreaders are familiar with various types of documents, such as newsletters, featured articles, press releases, brochures, manuscripts, sales letters, manuals, reports, academic material, surveys, letters, and e-mails. The editors are also skilled at working with various subject areas, such as business writing, creative writing, technical writing, computing and the Internet, engineering, environment, marketing, finance, and medicine.

While editing, editors check for grammar, spelling, punctuation, capitalization, word usage, structural problems, stylistic problems, sentence structure, sentence clarity, and conciseness. While proofreading, editors and proofreaders perform a careful check on edited documents for any typographical, punctuation, or formatting errors or deviations from the style sheet.

At Writers and Editors Inc., the customers can specify the kind of final feedback that they require based on the type of document and services that the company provides. The feedback can comprise corrections in grammar and sentence structure or reviewing the overall look and feel of the document.

The company aims to provide the highest quality and fastest turnaround time at an affordable cost. In addition, the company has decided to automate some of the editing tasks. One such task is proofreading a document for any deviations from the specified style.

To accomplish this task, the company has outsourced the project to a software development company called Develop Minds Inc. At Develop Minds Inc., a team of programmers and developers has been allocated to develop the proofreading tool. The team consists of the project manager and three developers. You, as a part of this team, need to help automate the procedure of proofreading a document for any deviations from the specified style sheet by using a development tool called Visual Basic Application (VBA). Before you start creating the application, you must know the development life cycle (DLC) that you must follow. The life cycle of this project is discussed in the following sections.

Project Life Cycle

The DLC of the project involves the following phases:

- Requirements analysis
- Design
- Coding and construction
- Testing
- Application distribution

Requirements Analysis

Requirements analysis is the first phase in a DLC. The team at Develop Minds Inc. met with the editors at Writers and Editors Inc. to discuss the requirements of the proofreading tool in detail.

The proofreaders stated the following requirements for the tool:

- The tool must point out any deviations from the style specifications as mentioned in the standard style sheet document.
- The tool should report the deviations in a separate document.
- The standard file consists of two columns of text. The first column specifies the word, and the second column specifies a suggestion regarding the usage of the word.
- The tool must highlight incorrect spelling of words in the document.
- The tool should have a simple and user-friendly interface.

Design

In the Design phase of the DLC, the development team decides to create an interface for the tool. The team also decides on broad-level functionality for the tool.

The output format of the report is generated in a separate document, as shown in the following table. The first column specifies the incorrect words that the tool encounters and displays the exact text, the second column gives the page and line number where the erroneous text is located, and the third and last column suggests the change.

Incorrect Words	Pg# Ln#	Suggestion
2D	Pg 1 Ln 6	Use 2-D instead of 2D. Use 3D (without a hyphen) only if specified by product names.
2D	Pg 1 Ln 33	Use 2-D instead of 2D. Use 3D (without a hyphen) only if specified by product names.
2D	Pg 1 Ln 40	Use 2-D instead of 2D. Use 3D (without a hyphen) only if specified by product names.
2D	Pg 1 Ln 45	Use 2-D instead of 2D. Use 3D (without a hyphen) only if specified by product names.

The team decided to develop the following screens for the proofreading tool as per the requirements gathered in the requirements analysis phase of the project.

The Splash Screen

This is the first screen that is displayed when the user runs the Word Checker tool. This screen appears for some time and disappears after displaying the version number and the tool name.

An illustration of this interface is depicted in Figure 22-1.

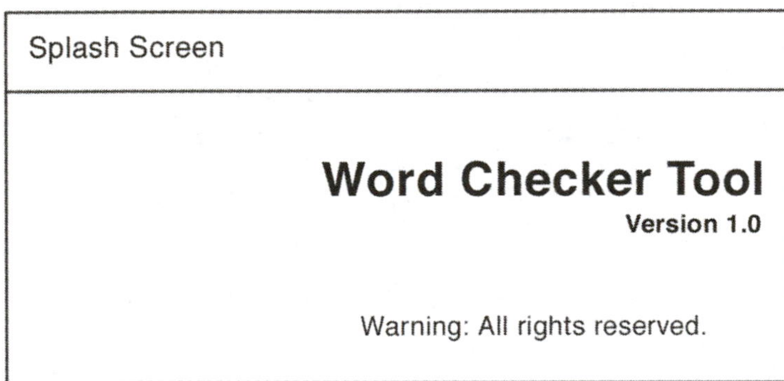

FIGURE 22-1 *The* `Splash` *screen of the Word Checker tool*

The Main Screen

After the `Splash` screen, the `Main` screen appears. On this screen, you need to mention the path of the script on which the tool is to be run, the path of the *stan-*

dard control file, and the path at which the final output report is to be stored. The user can either type the path or browse through the path.

An illustration of this interface is depicted in Figure 22-2.

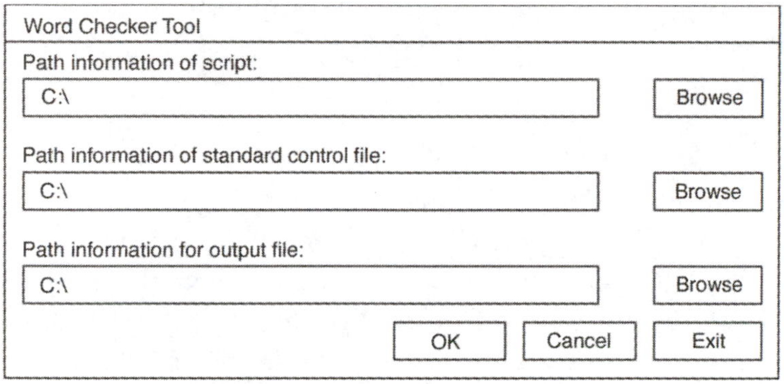

Word Checker Tool

Path information of script:

C:\ [Browse]

Path information of standard control file:

C:\ [Browse]

Path information for output file:

C:\ [Browse]

[OK] [Cancel] [Exit]

FIGURE 22-2 *The* `Main` *screen*

Coding and Construction

This is the third phase of the DLC. In this phase, the developer writes the code for the application. The input for this phase is the design document that is translated into code. In this phase, the development team divides the responsibilities of writing code and creating an interface for the tool among the team members. The output of this phase is a tool to proofread documents for checking the script against the standard control file that has been provided.

Testing

In the fourth phase of the DLC, the application is tested. The modules in the application can be tested individually or the entire application can be tested at once. In the case of the Word Checker tool, the team decides to test the complete application together. The tool is being tested for its ability to accurately proofread an edited document for any deviations from a standard style sheet document and typographical errors. To be able to test the tool accurately, the team must first create a test plan that states the guidelines for testing the tool. The development team decided upon a *test plan outline* that consists of details such as the requirements for the project, items to be tested, and test deliverables. A *test specification document*, which consists of the procedures to help testers test the application in the correct way was also prepared separately. The testing team then prepared a *test analysis report* specifying the errors along with the suggestions after the application is tested. The report was then submitted to the development team for incorporating the changes, if required, and correcting the errors reported in the test analysis report. A separate *Quality Assurance* (QA) team was formed to ensure that the final product conforms to the defined levels of quality.

Distributing the Application

This is the final phase in the DLC of the Word Checker tool. After the tool has been successfully tested, it needs to be distributed to various development teams, the testing team, and also to the subordinate teams. However, before the tool can be distributed, the QA team must sign off after checking that all the quality requirements of the tool are fulfilled. The Word Checker tool is an internal application of Develop Minds Inc. Therefore, the tool needs to be distributed over the network so that all the concerned teams can have access to the tool. The development team is responsible for providing constant support for installing and debugging any errors.

Summary

In this chapter, you looked at the DLC of the Word Checker tool. The various phases of the DLC were also discussed. In the next chapter, you look at the creation and development of the tool.

Chapter 23

Working with Word Objects in VBA

In this chapter, you will learn about working with the key objects of the Word object model and learn to work with the Word program options. You will also learn to work with properties, application objects, document objects, and objects used to represent text.

Introduction to Word Program Options

A Word document contains a lot of customization options. These options are available in the Options dialog box. Almost all these options are available to VBA procedures as property controls. The most commonly used controls belong to three key tabs in the Options dialog box. They are as follows:

- View tab
- General tab
- Edit tab

The controls for the options in each tab are used to either read the current status of an option or to change the value of the option.

The following sections discuss each option in these tabs.

View Tab

The options in the View tab are used to modify the display settings for Word screens, documents, objects, and windows. Most of these options are check boxes. Therefore, you can assign the `Boolean` values `True` or `False` to them. The `Boolean` value `True` selects a check box, whereas the `Boolean` value `False` clears the check box. The View tab of the Options dialog box is displayed in Figure 23-1.

Table 23-1 lists the components in the View tab along with their property control and description.

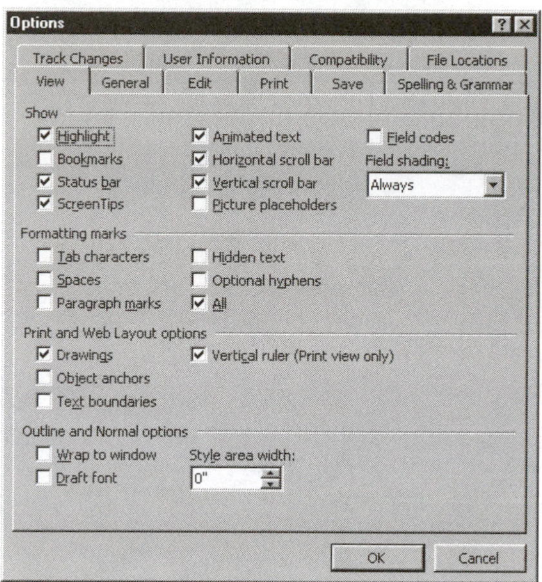

FIGURE 23-1 *The View tab of the Options dialog box*

Table 23-1 View Tab Controls

Option	Property	Description
Highlight	`Window.View.Highlight`	Turns highlight formatting on and off for the specified window
Bookmarks	`Window.View.ShowBookmarks`	Turns the display of bookmarks on and off for a specified window
Status bar	`Application.DisplayStatusBar`	Turns the status bar on and off for a specified window
Screen tips	`Window.DisplayScreenTips`	Turns the display of screen tips on and off for a specified window
Animated text	`Window.View.ShowAnimation`	Turns the display of animated text on and off for a specified window
Horizontal Scroll bar	`Window.Display-HorizontalScrollBar`	Turns the display of the horizontal scroll bar on and off for a specified window
Vertical Scroll bar	`Window.DisplayVerticalScrollBar`	Turns the display of the vertical scroll bar on and off for a specified window

continues

Table 23-1 continued

Option	Property	Description
Picture placeholders	`Window.View.ShowPicture-PlaceHolders`	Turns the display of picture placeholders on and off for a specified window
Field codes	`Window.View.ShowFieldCodes`	Turns the display of field codes on and off for a specified window
Field shading	`Window.View.ShowFieldCodes`	Turns the display of field codes on and off for a specified window
Tab characters	`Window.View.ShowTabs`	Turns the display of tab characters on and off for a specified window
Spaces	`Window.View.ShowSpaces`	Turns the display of dots to represent spaces between words on and off for a specified window
Paragraph marks	`Window.View.ShowParagraphs`	Turns the display of paragraph marks (¶) on and off for a specified window
Hidden text	`Window.View.ShowHiddenText`	Turns the display of hidden text with a dotted underline on and off for a specified window
Drawings	`Window.View.ShowDrawings`	Turns the display of drawings in Web layout or Print view on and off for a specified window
Object anchors	`Window.View.ShowObjectAnchors`	Turns the display of object anchors in Web layout or Print view on and off for a specified window
Text boundaries	`Window.View.Show-TextBoundaries`	Turns the display of dotted lines around margins and columns in Web layout or Print view on and off for a specified window
Vertical ruler	`Window.DisplayVerticalRuler`	Turns the display of the vertical ruler on the left side of the window in the Print view on and off for a specified window
Optional hyphens	`Window.View.ShowHyphens`	Turns the display of optional hyphens on and off for a specified window

Option	Property	Description
All	`Window.View.ShowAll`	Turns the display of nonprinting characters on and off for a specified window
Wrap to window	`Window.View.Display-VerticalScrollBar`	Determines whether the text in the specified window should be Word wrapped
Draft font	`Window.View.Draft`	Turns the display of draft font on and off for a specified window
Style area width	`Window.StyleAreaWidth`	Sets the width of the style area for a specified area in points

General Tab

The General tab contains options that enable you to modify miscellaneous Word options. Similar to the View tab, most of these options are check boxes and can be used by certain VBA property controls. Figure 23-2 displays the General tab of the Options dialog box.

Table 23-2 lists the components in the General tab along with their property control and description.

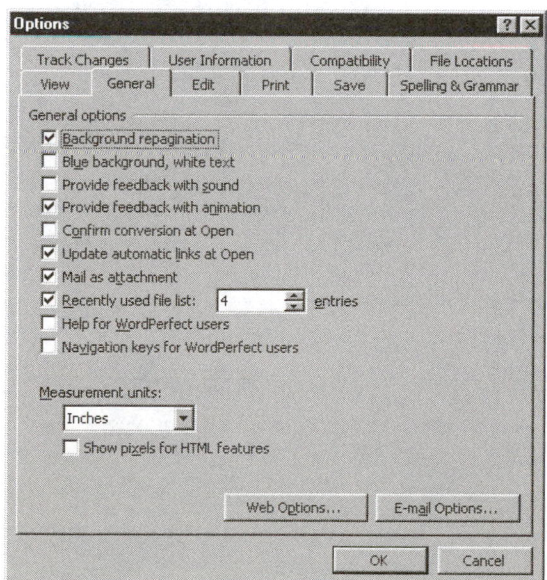

FIGURE 23-2 *The General tab of the Options dialog box*

Table 23-2 General Tab Controls

Option	Property	Description
Background repagination	`Options.Pagination`	Sets background repagination on or off
Blue background, white text	`Options.BlueScreen`	Sets the display of a blue screen with white text on or off
Provide feedback with sound	`Options.EnableSound`	Sets sound on or off while performing Word events
Provide feedback with animation	`Options.AnimateScreenMovements`	Sets mouse animations and other animated movements on or off
Confirm conversion at Open	`Options.ConfirmConversions`	Enables or disables you to choose a file converter from the available file converters
Update automatic links at Open	`Options.UpdateLinksAtOpen`	Sets the automatic updating of document links on or off
Mail as attachment	`Options.SentMailAttach`	Sends documents as attachments or text
Recently used file list	`Application.DisplayRecentFiles`	Enables or disables the display of recently opened files and uses RecentFiles.Maximum to control the number of recently opened files to be displayed
Help for WordPerfect users	`Options.WPHelp`	Sets WordPerfect help on or off
Navigation keys for WordPerfect users	`Options.DocNavKeys`	Sets WordPerfect navigation keys on or off
Measurement units	`Options.MeasurementUnit`	Specifies the measurement unit to be used. The Inches, Centimeters, Points, and Picas items are set after adding the words wd without any space before them.

Edit Tab

The third key tab in the Options dialog box is the Edit tab. This tab contains options that enable you to modify various keyboard- and mouse-based editing settings. Figure 23-3 displays the Edit tab of the Options dialog box.

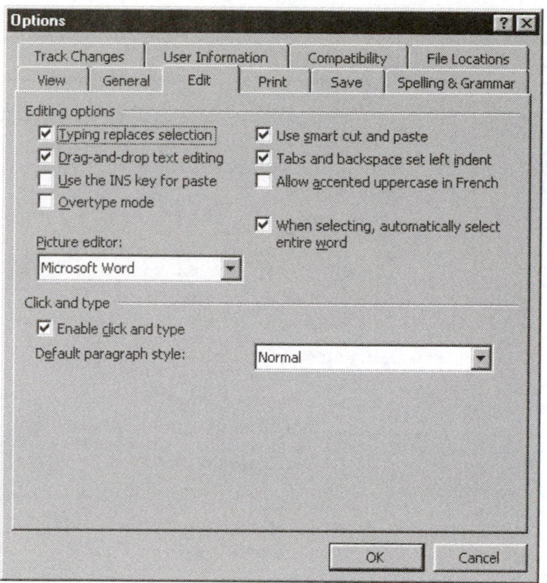

FIGURE 23-3 *The Edit tab of the Options dialog box*

Table 23-3 lists the components of the Edit tab along with their property control and description.

Table 23-3 Edit Tab Controls

Option	Property	Description
Typing replaces selection	`Options.ReplaceSelection`	Specifies whether a key press replaces selection
Drag-and-drop text editing	`Options.AllowDragAndDrop`	Specifies whether drag-and-drop editing is enabled
Use the INS key for paste	`Options.INSKeyForPaste`	Specifies whether the Insert key can be used to paste Clipboard contents
Overtype mode	`Options.Overtype`	Specifies whether overtype mode is on
User smart cut and paste	`Options.SmartCutAndPaste`	Specifies whether extra spaces are added or deleted while cutting or pasting text

continues

Table 23-3 continued

Option	Property	Description
Tabs and backspace left indent	`Options.TabIndetKey`	Specifies whether Tab is used for indenting text and Backspace for outdenting text
Allow accented in French	`Options.Allow-AccentedUppercase`	Specifies whether text formatted as French can use accented uppercase letters
When selecting, automatically select entire word	`Options.AutoWordSelection`	Specifies whether dragging the mouse can select entire word at one time
Picture editor	`Options.PictureEditor`	Specifies the editor to be used to edit pictures
Enable click and type	`Options.ClickAndTypeMouse`	Enables or disables the click and type feature of Word
Default paragraph style	`Document.ClickAnd-TypeParagraphStyle`	Specifies the default paragraph style for the click and type feature of Word

The following sections discuss the Word Application objects in detail.

Word Application Object

In addition to the properties and methods of the `Application` object in VBA, Word has a few unique properties and methods for the `Application` object.

Application Object Properties

Following are a few properties of the `Application` object that may be useful while creating VBA applications:

- `ActivePrinter`
- `Application.CapsLock`
- `Application.DefaultSaveFormat`

ActivePrinter

The `ActivePrinter` property enables you to set the name of the active or default printer. However, it is important to note that you can only specify the name of an existing printer.

The following command enables you to set the printer named `MyPrinterOne` on the local computer as the active printer:

```
ActivePrinter = "MyPrinterOne local on LPT1:"
```

Application.CapsLock

The `CapsLock` property of the `Application` object stores the status of the Caps Lock key on the keyboard. If Caps Lock is activated, the `Application.CapsLock` property stores the `Boolean` value `True`.

The following command enables you to switch Caps Lock on:

```
Application.CapsLock = True
```

Application.DefaultSaveFormat

The `DefaultSaveFormat` property of the `Application` object enables you to read or specify the default file format that is to be used while saving a Word document.

The following command enables you to set the default format in which Word documents should be saved to Word 6.0/95:

```
Application.DefaultSaveFormat = "MSWord6Exp"
```

Table 23-4 lists some file formats used by Word along with their file format name.

Table 23-4 Word File Formats

Format Name	Converter Class Name
Word document	<null strings>
Document Template	dot
Text Only	Text
Text Only with Line Breaks	CRText
MS-DOS Text	8Text
MS-DOS Text with Line Breaks	8CRText
Rich Text Format	Rtf
Unicode Text	Unicode

Application.DefaultTableSeparator

The `Application.DefaultTableSeparator` property enables you to set the default character used to separate text.

The following command enables you to set the Tab character as the default text separator:

```
Application.DefaultTableSeparator = vbTab
```

Application.MouseAvailable

The `Application.MouseAvailable` property enables you to check whether the computer has a mouse attached to it. This property returns the `Boolean` value `True` if a mouse is attached and `False` if the computer does not have a mouse.

Application.NormalTemplate

The `Application.NormalTemplate` property stores a Template object that represents the Normal Template in Word.

Application.NumLock

The `NumLock` property of the `Application` object enables you to check whether the Num Lock key is activated. This property returns the `Boolean` value `True` if the Num Lock key is activated. For example, the following code displays the status of the `NumLock` key:

```
Sub CheckNumLock()
If (Application.NumLock = True) Then
MsgBox ("Numlock on")
Else
MsgBox ("Numlock off")
End If
End Sub
```

Application.StartUpPath

The `Application.StartUpPath` property enables you to set the path of Word's startup folder.

Application.UserInitials

The `Application.UserInitials` property enables you to set the initials of the user using Word. The initials specified in this property are then used in comments created in Word.

Every object has properties and methods associated with it. The next section discusses the methods of the `Application` object.

Application Object Methods

The methods of the `Application` object are as follows:

- `ChangeFileOpenDirectory`
- `OnTime`
- `Move`
- `Resize`
- `Quit`

Application.ChangeFileOpenDirectory

This method of the `Application` object is used to set the folder in which Word documents will be opened from and saved by default.

The syntax for this method is as follows:

```
Application.ChangeFileOpenDirectory(Path)
```

In this syntax, `Path` represents the path of the folder in which all Word documents are opened from and saved by default.

For example, if you want to change the default file folder for Word documents to C:\Official, use the following command:

```
Application.ChangeFileOpenDirectory "C:\Official"
```

Application.OnTime

This method of the `Application` object is used to run a procedure at a specified time.

The syntax for this method is as follows:

```
Application.OnTime(When, Name, Tolerance)
```

In this syntax:

- `When` represents the time and date at which a procedure is required to be run. You can represent time by using the `TimeValue(Time)` method in which the `Time` parameter is represented by time.
- `Name` represents the name of the procedure that should be run when the time and date specified in the `When` parameter is reached.
- `Tolerance` represents a number of seconds to wait before running the procedure specified in the `Name` parameter if Word is not ready. If you do not specify this parameter, Word waits indefinitely until it is ready to run the specified procedure.

For example, if you want to run the `MakeBackup` procedure at 3:00 PM and want Word to wait for 15 seconds if it is not ready, you can use the following code:

```
Application.OnTime
    When:=TimeValue("3:00PM")
    Name:="MakeBackup"
    Tolerance:=15
```

Application.Move

This method of the `Application` object is used to move a Word application window according to the specified coordinates. However, this method works only if the application window is not maximized or minimized.

The syntax for this method is as follows:

```
Application.Move(Left, Right)
```

In this syntax:

- `Left` represents the horizontal screen position of the left edge of the application window. This value is represented in points.
- `Right` represents the vertical screen position of the top edge of the application window. This value is also represented in points.

For example, if you want to move the application window to the upper-left corner of the screen, you can use the following command:

```
Application.Move 0,0
```

Application.Resize

This method of the `Application` object is used to change the size of the application window.

The syntax for this method is as follows:

```
Application.Resize(Width, Height)
```

In this syntax:

- `Width` represents the horizontal size of the application window. This value is represented in points.
- `Height` represents the vertical size of the application window. This value is also represented in points.

For example, if you want to change the size of the application window to 400 points in width and 300 points in height, you can use the following command:

```
Application.Resize 400,300
```

Application.Quit

This method of the `Application` object is used to close Word. When this method is run, you are prompted to save the unsaved open documents.

The syntax for this method is as follows:

```
Application.Quit
```

Notice that the syntax for this method does not have any parameters.

For example, if you want to close Word, you can use the following command:

```
Application.Quit
```

Word Document Object

After the `Application` object, one of the most important objects in Word is the `Document` object. This object is below the `Application` object. You can use this object in VBA to create, open, and delete documents.

The following sections discuss working with Word `Document` objects using VBA.

Specifying a Document Object

Before you can use a Word document or its contents, you first need to specify the document to be used.

You can specify the Word document by using the `Documents` object. The `Documents` object is a collection of all open Word documents. You can specify the document to be used by specifying the index number of the document or by specifying the name of the document.

For example, if you need to work on the document that was opened first in Word, you can use the following command:

```
Documents(1)
```

Alternatively, if you want to specify the open document named `MyFile.doc`, you can use the following command:

```
Documents("MyFile.doc")
```

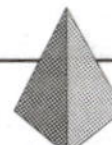

TIP

You can also use the `ActiveDocument` object and `ThisDocument` object to refer to the document currently with focus and the document on which VBA code is being executed, respectively.

Opening a Document Object

If the document that is to be used is not open, you can use the `Open` method of the `Documents` collection to open the document.

The basic syntax of the `Open` method is as follows:

```
Documents.Open(FileName)
```

In this syntax, `FileName` is used to represent the full name of the file that is to be opened. The full name should consist of the entire path of the file along with the name of the file.

The code for opening the file `MyFile.doc` in the Projects folder in the C drive of your computer is as follows:

```
Documents.Open "C:\Projects\MyFile.doc"
```

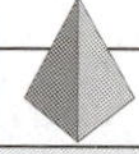

TIP

If the file that is to be opened is in the current drive and folder, you need not specify the path of the document.

Creating a New Document

You can also create a new Word document by using VBA. This can be done using the `Documents` object. The syntax for creating a new Word document is as follows:

```
Documents.Add(Template, NewTemplate, DocumentType, Visible)
```

In this syntax:

- `Template` is used to specify the template file that is to be used to create the new document. This file should be a file with the extension `dot` and should be specified with the full path. If a template is not specified, the new document is created based on the Normal template.
- `NewTemplate` is a `Boolean` constant and is used to accept the values `True` or `False`. If you specify the value `True`, the command creates a new template instead of a new document of the specified type.
- `DocumentType` represents the type of document that is to be created. This parameter uses one of the constants specified in Table 23-5.

Table 23-5 Constants Accepted by the DocumentType Parameter

Constant	Type of Document
`wdNewBlankDocument`	Creates a new blank Word document
`wdNewEmailMessage`	Creates a new e-mail message
`wdNewFrameset`	Creates a new Web page containing frames
`wdNewWebPage`	Creates a new Web page

The last parameter is `Visible`. This parameter accepts a `Boolean` value. This value determines whether the new document created by the command is displayed to the user. This is `True` by default.

RecentFiles Object

The `RecentFiles` object is another object that can be used to open Word documents. This object enables you to open the most recently opened files. The syntax for opening recently opened files is as follows:

```
RecentFiles.Item(Index).Open
```

In this syntax, `Index` represents a numeric value according to the order in which a document was opened. Therefore, the most recently opened document will have the value 1, the second most recently opened file will have the value 2, and so on. For example, the following code opens the third most recently opened file:

```
RecentFiles.Item(3).Open
```

The `RecentFiles` object also contains certain properties. Table 23-6 lists these properties along with their value stored.

Table 23-6 Properties of the RecentFiles Object

Property	Value Stored
`RecentFiles.Maximum`	The maximum number of documents stored as recently opened files.
`RecentFiles.Application`	The application with which the specified recent files are attached.
`RecentFiles.Count`	The number of documents stored as recently opened files.

Properties of the Document Object

The `Document` object contains properties that enable you to refer to a collection of other objects in the document. Some common properties are listed in Table 23-7.

Table 23-7 Document Object Properties

Property	Description
`Document.Bookmarks`	Contains all the bookmarks defined for the specified document as `Bookmark` objects
`Document.Characters`	Contains all the characters defined for the specified document as `Character` objects

Property	Description
`Document.ClickAndType-ParagraphStyle`	Returns or sets the paragraph style that is applied while inserting text
`Document.Endnotes`	Contains all the endnotes defined for the specified document as `Endnotes` collection
`Document.Envelope`	Contains the envelope option that is defined for the specified document as `Envelope` object
`Document.Footnotes`	Contains all the footnotes defined for the specified document as `Footnotes` collection
`Document.FullName`	Contains the full path and name of the specified document
`Document.GrammarChecked`	Contains the value `True` if the document is grammar-checked and `False` if the document contains grammatical errors
`Document.IsMasterDocument`	Contains the value `True` if the document is a master document and `False` otherwise
`Document.IsSubDocument`	Contains the value `True` if the document is a sub-document and `False` otherwise
`Document.Name`	Contains the file name of the document
`Document.Paragraphs`	Contains all the paragraphs in the specified document as `Paragraph` objects
`Document.Path`	Contains the complete path of the document
`Document.Sentences`	Contains all the sentences in the specified document as `Sentences` objects
`Document.ReadOnly`	Contains the value `True` if the document is read-only and `False` otherwise
`Document.Revisions`	Contains all the revisions in the specified document as `Revisions` objects
`Document.Saved`	Contains the value `True` if the document does not contain unsaved changes and `False` otherwise
`Document.SaveFormat`	Contains the format in which the document was saved

continues

Table 23-7 continued

Property	Description
Document.Sections	Contains all the sections in the specified document as Sections objects
Document.ShowRevisions	Contains the value True if the document should display revision marks and False otherwise
Document.SpellingChecked	Contains the value True if the document is spell-checked and False if the document contains spelling errors
Document.Styles	Contains all the styles defined in the specified document as Style objects
Document.Subdocuments	Contains all the subdocuments in the specified document as Subdocuments objects
Document.Tables	Contains all the tables in the specified document as Tables objects
Document.VBASigned	Contains the value True if the document is digitally signed and False otherwise
Document.Words	Contains all the words in the specified document as Words objects

Methods of the Document Object

The Document object contains methods that enable you to refer to a collection of other objects in the document. The following sections explain the methods of the Document object.

Document.AcceptAllRevisions

This method of the Document object is used to accept all the changes made in the Word document with the revision marks turned on. This method does not require any parameters and is used as is. Therefore, you only need to specify the document on which the task is to be performed instead of Document.

Document.Activate

This method of the `Document` object is used to activate the specified open Word document. This command does not require any parameters and is used as is. Therefore, you only need to specify the document on which the task is to be performed instead of `Document`.

For example, if you want to activate the Word document `Status.doc`, use the following command:

```
Documents("Status.doc").Activate
```

Document.CheckGrammar

This method of the `Document` object is used to check the grammar of the text in the specified document. This method too does not require any parameters and is used as is. Therefore, you only need to specify the document on which the task is to be performed instead of `Document`.

Document.Close

This method of the `Document` object is used to close the specified document.

The syntax for this method is as follows:

```
Document.Close(SaveChanges, OriginalFormat, RouteDocument)
```

In this syntax:

- `Document` represents the document that is to be closed.
- `SaveChanges` represents the action to be taken if the document contains unsaved changes. To save the unsaved changes, `wdSaveChanges` is required. However, if you do not want to save the changes, `wdDoNotSave Changes` is specified. Further, if you want to ensure that the option for saving changes is with the user of the application, you can specify `wdPromptToSave`.
- `OriginalFormat` represents the format that is to be used to save the document. To save the document in its existing format, `wdOriginalFormat` is specified. To save the document as a Word document, `wdWordDocument` is specified. However, if you want to ask the user to specify the format in which the document is to be saved, `wdPromptUser` is specified.
- `RouteDocument` accepts the values `True` or `False`. If the value `True` is specified here, Word routes the document to the next recipient.

For example, if you want to close the currently open document after saving the changes made in the document and want to prompt the user to specify the format of the document, use the following command:

```
ActiveDocument.Close(wdSaveChanges, wdPromptUser, False)
```

Document.CopyStylesFromTemplate

This method of the `Document` object is used to copy the styles for the specified template to the document specified by the `Document` parameter.

The syntax for this method is as follows:

```
Document.CopyStylesFromTemplate(Template)
```

In this syntax:

- `Document` represents the document in which styles are to be copied.
- `Template` represents the path and file name of the template file from which document styles are to be copied.

For example, if you want copy all the styles from the `ProjectOne.dot` template in the `C:\Projects\Templates` folder to the active document, use the following command:

```
ActiveDocument.CopyStylesFromTemplate "C:\Projects\Templates\ProjectOne.dot"
```

Document.GoTo

This method of the `Document` object is used to go to a specified position in a document.

The syntax for this method is as follows:

```
Document.GoTo(What, Which, Count, Name)
```

In this syntax:

- `Document` represents the document that is to be closed.
- `What` represents the type of object that you want to reach. This parameter accepts 17 different constants. The most common ones are `wdGoToBookmark`, `wdGoToComment`, `wdGotToEndnote`, `wdGoToFootnote`, `wdGoToGraphic`, `wdGoToLine`, `wdGotToObject`, `wdGoToPage`, `wdGoToSection`, and `wdGoToTable`.

- `Which` represents the way in which Word navigates to the specified object. Table 23-8 displays the list of constants for this parameter with their functions.

Table 23-8 Navigation Constants

Constant	Function
wdGoToAbsolute	Goes to the absolute position of the item
wdGoToFirst	Goes to the first instance of the item
wdGoToLast	Goes to the last instance of the item
wdGoToNext	Goes to the next instance of the item
wdGoToPrevious	Goes to the previous position of the item
wdGoToRelative	Goes to the relative position of the item

After specifying the appropriate constant in the `Which` parameter, you specify the value for `RouteDocument`. This parameter accepts positive numeric values that represent the number of the item. For example, if you want to locate the third instance of the specified object in the document, you provide the value 3.

The last parameter in the displayed syntax is `Name`. This parameter is used to supply the name of the searched object. For example, if you want to search for a `Bookmark` or `Field` object, you specify the name of the bookmark or field in this parameter.

If you want to go to the first bookmark in the active document, use the following command:

```
ActiveDocument.GoTo _
What:=wdGoToBookmark, _
Which:=wdGoToAbsolute, _
Count:=1
```

Notice that the `Name` parameter is not specified. This is because this parameter is optional and is not required in this instance.

Document.PrintOut

This method of the `Document` object is used to print the contents of the specified document.

The syntax for this method is as follows:

```
Document.PrintOut(Background, Append, Range, OutPutFileName, From, To, Item, Copies,
   Pages, PageType, PrintToFile, Collate)
```

In this syntax:

- `Document` represents the document in which styles are to be copied.
- `Background` specifies whether the procedure continues to run while the document is being printed. This parameter contains either the constant `True` or the constant `False`.
- `Append` specifies whether the output of the specified document is to be appended to the document specified in the `OutPutFileName` parameter. This parameter also contains either the constant `True` or the constant `False`.
- `Range` specifies the range of the text in the specified document to be printed. The `Range` parameter accepts the constants in Table 23-9.

Table 23-9 Range Constants

Constant	Function
`wdPrintAllDocument`	Specifies that the complete document is to be printed
`wdPrintCurrentPage`	Specifies that only the current page is to be printed
`wdPrintFromTo`	Specifies that only the pages starting from the page number specified in the `From` parameter to the `To` parameter are to be printed
`wdPrintRangeOfPages`	Specifies that only the range of pages specified in the `Pages` parameter are to be printed
`wdPrintPrintSelection`	Specifies that only the selected text is to be printed

- `OutputFileName` specifies the name of the file to which the contents of the document are to be printed. However, when this parameter is used, the value of the `PrintToFile` parameter needs to be set to `True`.

- `From` specifies a positive integer that represents the starting page number of the range of pages to be printed. This parameter is used only if the `wdPrintFromTo` constant is specified in the `Range` parameter.
- `Item` specifies the item that is to be printed. This parameter is used to specify a constant from `wdPrintAutoTextEntries`, `wdPrintComments`, `wdPrintDocumentContent`, `wdPrintKeyAssignments`, `wdPrintPrintProperties`, or `wdPrintStyles`.
- `To` specifies a positive integer that represents the ending page number of the range of pages to be printed. This parameter is used only if the `wdPrintFromTo` constant is specified in the `Range` parameter.
- `Copies` specifies a positive integer that represents the number of copies of the specified document that are to be printed.
- `Pages` specifies a positive integer that represents the range of pages that are to be printed. This parameter is used only if the `wdPrintRangeOfPages` constant is specified in the `Range` parameter.
- `PageType` specifies the pages that are to be printed and contains the `wdPrintAllPages`, `wdPrintEvenPagesOnly`, or `wdPrintOddPagesOnly` constants.
- `PrintToFile` specifies either the constant `True` or the constant `False`. This parameter is used only when you want to print the specified items in the document to a file instead of a printer.
- `Collate` specifies either the constant `True` or the constant `False` to specify whether you want to print the entire document first and then print another copy. This parameter is used only if the value in the `Copies` parameter is greater than one.

Document.PrintPreview

This method of the `Document` object is used to display the specified document in the Print Preview window. This method does not require any parameters and is used as is. Therefore, you only need to specify the document on which the task is to be performed instead of `Document`.

Document.Redo

This method of the Document object is used to redo the last action or actions that were undone. The syntax for this method is as follows:

```
Document.Redo(Times)
```

In this syntax, the parameter Times is used to specify the number of actions that are to be redone. This is specified as a positive integer.

Document.RejectAllRevisions

This method of the Document object is used to reject all the changes made to the specified document that were made as revision marks. This method does not require any parameters and is used as is. Therefore, you only need to specify the document on which the task is to be performed instead of Document.

Document.Repaginate

This method of the Document object is used to number the pages of the document again. This method does not require any parameters and is used as is. Therefore, you only need to specify the document on which the task is to be performed instead of Document.

Document.Save

This method of the Document object is used to save the specified document. This method does not require any parameters and is used as is. Therefore, you only need to specify the document on which the task is to be performed instead of Document. However, if you have created a new document, you need to use the Document.SaveAs method.

Document.SaveAs

This method of the Document object is used to save the contents of the specified open Word document in another file.

The syntax for this method is as follows:

```
Document.SaveAs(FileName, FileFormat)
```

In this syntax:

- `FileName` is used to specify the full name of the document to which you want to save the contents of the specified document. The full name should also contain the complete path of the new document.
- `FileFormat` is used to specify the format in which the new document is to be saved. You can use the predefined Word file format constants for this parameter.

For example, if you want to save the contents of the active Word document to `Status.doc`, use the following command:

```
ActiveDocument.SaveAs "C:\Projects\Satus.doc", wdWordDocument
```

Document.Select

This method of the `Document` object is used to select all the text in the specified document. This method does not require any parameters and is used as is. Therefore, you only need to specify the document on which the task is to be performed instead of `Document`.

Document.Undo

This method of the `Document` object is used to undo the last action or actions that were performed. The syntax for this method is as follows:

```
Document.Undo(Times)
```

In this syntax, the parameter `Times` is used to specify the number of actions that are to be undone. This is specified as a positive integer.

Text Representation Objects

In addition to representing documents as `Document` objects, Word also represents text in these documents in various objects. The most important of these objects are as follows:

- `Range` object
- `Section` object
- `Characters` object

- Words object
- Sentences object
- Paragraph object

The Range Object

In a Word document, text is represented using the Range object. This object can contain single characters, words, sentences, paragraphs, or even the entire document.

This object can be returned either by using the Range method of the Document object or by using the Range property.

The Range method enables you to specify the starting and ending points for a range. The syntax of this method is as follows:

```
Document.Range(Start,End)
```

In this syntax, Start depicts the starting character position, and End depicts the ending character position.

However, in contrast to the Range method, the Range property is an object that is present for each object containing a collection of characters. This object has certain properties of its own that determine the features of the characters in a document. These properties are listed in Table 23-10.

Table 23-10 Range Object Properties

Property	Description
Range.Bold	Makes the text bold and is specified by constants True, False, and undefined (if only part of the text is bold)
Range.Case	Changes the case of the text and is specified by constants wdLowerCase, wdTitleSentence, wdTitleWord, wdToggleCase, and wdUpperCase
Range.Characters	Contains all the characters in the text
Range.End	Specifies the position of the last character in the text
Range.Font	Specifies the font of the text
Range.Italic	Makes the text italicized and is specified by constants True, False, and undefined (if only part of the text is italic)

Property	Description
`Range.Paragraphs`	Contains all the paragraphs in the text
`Range.Revisions`	Contains all the changes made in revision marks in the text
`Range.Sentences`	Contains all the sentences in the text
`Range.Start`	Specifies the position of the first character in the text
`Range.Text`	Specifies the text in the range
`Range.Words`	Contains all the words in the text

In addition to properties, the `Range` object also contains certain methods. Table 23-11 lists these methods along with their description.

Table 23-11 Range Object Methods

Method	Description
`Range.CheckGrammar`	Checks the grammar in a specified page of a document
`Range.CheckSpelling`	Checks the spelling in a specified page of a document
`Range.Collapse`	Unselects the currently selected text and positions the cursor
`Range.ConvertToTable`	Converts the selected text into a table
`Range.Copy`	Copies the range to the Clipboard
`Range.Cut`	Cuts the selected range from the text and places it in the Clipboard
`Range.Delete`	Deletes the specified text
`Range.InsertAfter`	Inserts the contents of the Clipboard after the specified range
`Range.InsertBefore`	Inserts the contents of the Clipboard before the specified range
`Range.InsertParagraph`	Inserts a paragraph by replacing the specified text
`Range.InsertParagraphAfter`	Inserts a paragraph after the specified text
`Range.InsertParagraphBefore`	Inserts a paragraph before the specified text
`Range.Paste`	Pastes the contents of the Clipboard at the existing cursor position
`Range.Select`	Selects the specified text

The Selection Object

Another object that represents text in Word is the Selection object. This object refers either to the selected text or to the position of the cursor. The selection object has various properties. Table 23-12 lists the unique properties of this object.

Table 23-12 Properties of the Selection Object

Property	Description
ExtendMode	Returns the value True if the selection mode of Word is activated
Information(Type)	Returns information about the Selection object, such as whether Word is in the overtype mode
IPAtEndOfLine	Returns the value True if the cursor is positioned at the end of a sentence
ISEndOfRowMark	Returns the value True if the cursor is positioned at the end of a row in a table
Type	Returns the type of selection, such as wdNoSelection, wdSelectionColumn, wdSelectionIP, wdSelectionNormal, and wdSelectionRow

In addition to properties, the Selection object also contains certain methods. Table 23-13 lists the Selection object methods along with their description.

Table 23-13 Selection Object Methods

Method	Description
Collapse	Removes the selection in a document
EndKey	Extends the selection in a document
EndOf	Extends the selection in a document and returns the number of characters that were moved
EscapeKey	Cancels the extend mode
Expand	Expands the specified selection
Extend	Activates the extend mode in Word and extends the current selection

Method	Description
HomeKey	Extends the selection in a document and returns the number of characters that were moved
InRange	Checks whether the specified range is in the current selection
Move	Collapses the current selection and moves the insertion point by a specified number of units
MoveDown	Moves the insertion point down by a specified number of units
MoveEnd	Moves the end point of a selection by a specified number of units
MoveLeft	Moves the insertion point to the left by a specified number of units
MoveRight	Moves the insertion point to the right by a specified number of units
MoveStart	Moves the start point of a selection by a specified number of units
MoveUp	Moves the insertion point up by a specified number of units
SelectCurrentAlignment	Extends the current selection until it reaches text that is formatted with a different alignment
SelectCurrentColor	Extends the current selection until it reaches text that is formatted with a different color
SelectCurrentFont	Extends the current selection until it reaches text that is formatted with a different font
SelectCurrentIndent	Extends the current selection until it reaches text that is formatted with a different indent
SelectCurrentSpacing	Extends the current selection until it reaches text that is formatted with a different spacing
SelectCurrentTabs	Extends the current selection until it reaches text that is formatted with different Tab stops
StartOf	Extends or moves the insertion point to the start of a specified selection by a specified number of units
TypeBackspace	Performs the function of the Backspace key
TypeParagraph	Performs the function of the Enter key

The Characters Object

The Characters object also represents text in Word. This object represents a collection of all the characters in the specified document.

You can refer to the characters in a document by specifying the index number of the character.

For example, to refer to the first character that is in the font size 20 in the active document, you use the following command:

```
ActiveDocument.Characters(1).Font.Size = 20
```

In addition, if you want to count the number of characters in the active document and store them in the TotalCharacters variable, you can use the following command:

```
TotalCharacters = ActiveDocument.Characters.Count
```

The Words Object

Similar to the Characters object, the Words object also represents text. However, the Words object represents the collection of words in a document instead of characters.

Similar to the Characters object, the Words object is also referred to by its index number.

For example, to refer to the first character that is italicized in the active document, you use the following command:

```
ActiveDocument.Words(1).Font.Italic = True
```

In addition, if you want to count the number of words in the active document and store them in the TotalWords variable, you can use the following command:

```
TotalWords = ActiveDocument.Words.Count
```

The Sentences Object

Another collection object representing text is the Sentences object. This object contains a collection of all the sentences in a document and is also referred by an index number.

For example, to refer to the first sentence in the active document, you use the following command:

```
ActiveDocument.Sentences(1)
```

In addition, if you want to count the number of sentences in the active document and store them in the `TotalSentences` variable, you can use the following command:

```
TotalSentences = ActiveDocument.Sentences.Count
```

The Paragraph Object

Another object representing text is the `Paragraph` object. This object represents all the paragraphs that are present in a document.

The `Sentences` object has various properties. Table 23-14 lists the unique properties of this object.

Table 23-14 Properties of the Sentences Object

Property	Description
`Paragraph.KeepTogether`	Specifies whether a paragraph should be printed together in the same page after repagination
`Paragraph.KeepWithNext`	Specifies whether a paragraph should be printed together in the same page with the following paragraph after repagination
`Paragraph.LeftIndent`	Specifies the left indent of the specified paragraph
`Paragraph.LineSpacing`	Specifies the line spacing of the specified paragraph
`Paragraph.RightIndent`	Specifies the right indent of the specified paragraph
`Paragraph.SpaceAfter`	Specifies the spacing in points after the specified paragraph
`Paragraph.SpaceBefore`	Specifies the spacing in points before the specified paragraph
`Paragraph.Style`	Specifies the style used for the specified paragraph

In addition to properties, the `Paragraph` object also contains certain methods. Table 23-15 lists these methods along with their functions.

Table 23-15 Paragraph Object Methods

Method	Function
`Paragraph.Indent`	Indents a specified paragraph to the next Tab stop
`Paragraph.Next`	Moves from a specified paragraph to the next one in a document
`Paragraph.Outdent`	Outdents a specified paragraph to the next Tab stop
`Paragraph.Previous`	Moves from a specified paragraph to the previous one in a document
`Paragraph.Space1`	Sets single spacing for the specified paragraph
`Paragraph.Space15`	Sets 1.5 line spacing for the specified paragraph
`Paragraph.Space2`	Sets double spacing for the specified paragraph

Summary

In this chapter, you learned about the VBA Word object model. You learned the various Word objects, their properties, and methods that are used to enable an application to interact with Word. You will use these Word objects to code the Word Checker tool in the next chapter.

Chapter 24

Coding the Application

In this chapter, you will learn to code the Word Checker tool. You will also learn about the logic of the Word Checker tool and the various methods of the application.

Understanding the Logic of the Word Checker Tool

As discussed in Chapter 22, "Project Case Study: Writers and Editors Inc.," the Word Checker tool consists of two screens, the `Splash` screen and the `Main` screen. The `Main` screen is the Word Checker screen where the user specifies the path of the documents. Using this screen, a user can specify the following options:

- Path of the document on which the tool is to be run
- Path of the standard control file against which the document is to be checked
- Path of the output report file where the final output needs to be stored

The user can browse through a path to specify the correct path by using the `Browse` button of the tool. The `Browse` button opens a dialog box where you can specify the paths to the relevant files.

When the tool runs, it reads from the standard control file and then opens the document file to be checked, which is read line-by-line by the tool. After reading the document, an output report is generated. The errors in the document file are listed in a tabular format. The report specifies the location of an error in the document file and offers a suggestion for the change to be implemented. In addition to this, the tool also highlights the incorrect words as present in the standard control file.

Figure 24-1 illustrates the various functions that the application uses along with a brief description of each function.

The `OpenScriptAndStartProcessing()` function also calls the `ActivateWindow()` function to activate the Output file window. The `Active Window()` function is then called again in the `LogErr()` function to activate the Output File window. It also activates the document file to start processing the error words in the document file. The `Trimmer()` function is also called in the application to trim strings for special characters.

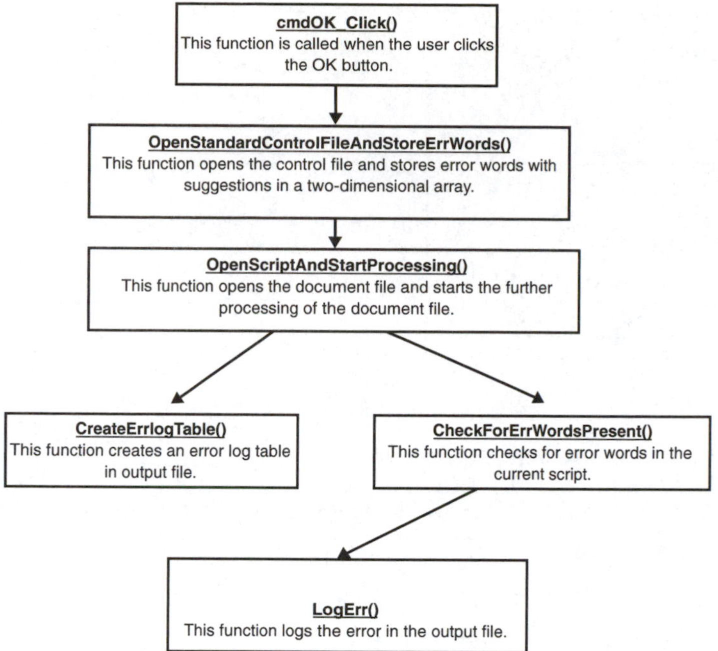

FIGURE 24-1 *The flowchart for the Word Checker tool, as decided by the development team*

The following sections discuss each of the functions used in the Word Checker tool in detail.

The cmdOK_Click() Function

The `cmdOK_Click()` function is called when the user clicks on the `OK` button. It is the main function that is called when the user specifies the path of the document file, the path of the standard control file, and the path of the output report on the Word Checker `Main` screen. Figure 24-2 displays the Word Checker `Main` screen.

The tool begins processing using the `cmdOK_Click()` function. This function declares seven variables:

- `IsDriveExist`. This stores the value returned after checking for drive existence.
- `Checkdrive`. This stores the value of the drive letter in string format.

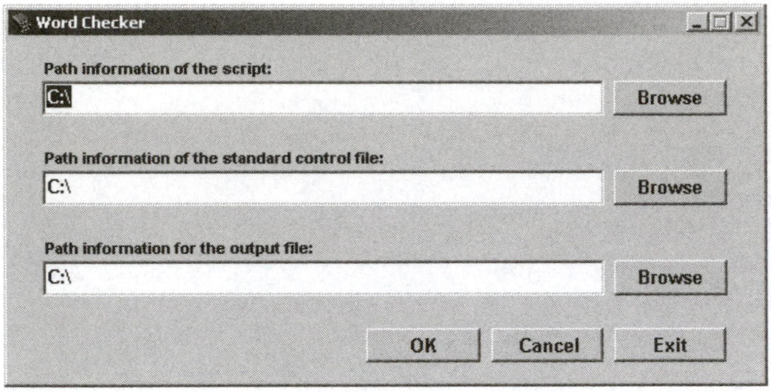

FIGURE 24-2 Main *screen of the Word Checker tool*

- `LastPos`. This stores the position value of the document.
- `res`. This stores the temporary value of the document.
- `OutputPath`. This stores the output text as entered by the user.
- `ControlFilePath`. This stores the location of the standard control file as entered by the user.
- `ScriptPath`. This stores the path of the document file as entered by the user.

The preceding variables hold the information entered by the user, such as the document file path, the output file path, and the control file path. If the information entered by the user is incorrect, an error message is displayed to the user.

The `cmdOK_Click()` function also checks for the format of the files as specified by the user. If the format specified by the user is incorrect, an error message is displayed.

In addition to this, the function also checks for the valid drive letter and write permission on the drive.

Listing 24-1 contains the code for the `cmdOK_Click()` function.

Listing 24-1 The cmdOK_Click() Function

```
    'This function is invoked when the OK button is clicked by the user
Private Sub cmdOK_Click(ByVal eventSender As System.Object, ByVal eventArgs As
  System.EventArgs) Handles cmdOk.Click
```

```
Dim IsUnconventionalErrorFound As Boolean
Dim IsDriveExist As Boolean
Dim CheckDrive As String
Dim LastPos As Integer
Dim res As Object
Dim OutputPath As String
Dim ControlFilePath As String
Dim ScriptPath As String

    Code starts from here to validate the path information entered for the
       script, control and
    output file
    If Trim(txtScriptFilePath.Text) = Trim(txtOutputPath.Text) Then
     MsgBox("The path information for the script file and the output file is the
        same.
    Please   check!!!",
    MsgBoxStyle.OKOnly + MsgBoxStyle.Exclamation, "Word Checker")
    txtOutputPath.Focus()
    GoTo OutOfHere
    End If
    PunctuationErr = ""
    Dim HasWritePermission As Boolean
    HasWritePermission = True
    ScriptPath = LTrim(RTrim(txtScriptFilePath.Text))
    Code to validate the Script file path information
    If Len(ScriptPath) = 0 Then
    MsgBox("Please enter path information for script file", MsgBoxStyle.OKOnly +
    MsgBoxStyle.Exclamation, "Word Checker")
    txtScriptFilePath.Focus()
    GoTo OutOfHere
    End If
    ControlFilePath = LTrim(RTrim(txtControlFilePath.Text))

    Code to validate the Control file path information
    If Len(ControlFilePath) = 0 Then
    MsgBox("Please enter path information for standard control file",
       MsgBoxStyle.OKOnly + MsgBoxStyle.Exclamation, "Word Checker")
    txtControlFilePath.Focus()
```

```
GoTo OutOfHere
End If
OutputPath = LTrim(RTrim(txtOutputPath.Text))

Code to validate the Output file path information
If Len(OutputPath) = 0 Then
MsgBox("Please enter path information for output file", MsgBoxStyle.OKOnly +
MsgBoxStyle.Exclamation, "Word Checker")
txtOutputPath.Focus()
GoTo OutOfHere
End If
If Mid(ScriptPath, 2, 2) <> ":\" Then
MsgBox("Invalid path information for script file.
If the file is on the network then make sure   that the
path is mapped", MsgBoxStyle.OKOnly + MsgBoxStyle.Exclamation,
   "Word Checker")
txtScriptFilePath.Focus()
GoTo OutOfHere
End If
If Mid(ControlFilePath, 2, 2) <> ":\" Then
MsgBox("Invalid path information for standard control file.
If the file is on the network then make sure
that the path is mapped", MsgBoxStyle.OKOnly + MsgBoxStyle.Exclamation,
"Word Checker")
txtControlFilePath.Focus()
GoTo OutOfHere
End If
If Mid(OutputPath, 2, 2) <> ":\" Then
MsgBox("Invalid path information for output file.
If the file is on the network then make sure that the
path is mapped", MsgBoxStyle.OKOnly + MsgBoxStyle.Exclamation,
   "Word Checker")
txtOutputPath.Focus()
GoTo OutOfHere
End If
Dim testdir1 As String
testdir1 = Dir(ScriptPath, FileAttribute.Normal)
```

```
If (testdir1 = "") Then
MsgBox("Path information of script file " + ScriptPath + " does not exist.",
MsgBoxStyle.OKOnly +
MsgBoxStyle.Exclamation, "Word Checker")
txtScriptFilePath.Focus()
GoTo OutOfHere
Else
If UCase(Microsoft.VisualBasic.Right(ScriptPath, 4)) <> UCase(".doc") Then
MsgBox("Invalid file format selected in the input path information of script
   file." & Chr(13) & Chr(13)
&
"File selected is not a .rtf or .doc File.", MsgBoxStyle.OKOnly +
   MsgBoxStyle.Exclamation,
"Word Checker")
txtScriptFilePath.Focus()
GoTo OutOfHere
End If
End If
testdir1 = Dir(ControlFilePath, FileAttribute.Normal)
If (testdir1 = "") Then
MsgBox("Path information of standard control file " + ControlFilePath + "
   does not exist.",
MsgBoxStyle.OKOnly + MsgBoxStyle.Exclamation, "Word Checker")
txtControlFilePath.Focus()
GoTo OutOfHere
ElseIf UCase(Microsoft.VisualBasic.Right(ControlFilePath, 4)) <>
   UCase(".doc") Then
MsgBox("Invalid file format selected in the input path information
   of standard control file.
" & Chr(13) &
Chr(13) & "File selected is not a .doc File.", MsgBoxStyle.OKOnly +
MsgBoxStyle.Exclamation, "Word
Checker")
txtControlFilePath.Focus()
GoTo OutOfHere
End If
If UCase(Microsoft.VisualBasic.Right(OutputPath, 4)) <> UCase(".doc") Then
MsgBox("Invalid file format selected in the path information for the output
   file." & Chr(13) &
```

```
Chr(13) & "File selected is not a .doc File.", MsgBoxStyle.OKOnly +
MsgBoxStyle.Exclamation, "Word Checker")
txtOutputPath.Focus()
GoTo OutOfHere
ElseIf UCase(Microsoft.VisualBasic.Right(OutputPath, 5)) = UCase("\.doc") Or
UCase(Microsoft.VisualBasic.Right(OutputPath, 5)) = UCase("/.doc") Or
UCase(Microsoft.VisualBasic.Right(OutputPath, 5)) = UCase(":.doc") Or
UCase(Microsoft.VisualBasic.Right(OutputPath, 5)) = UCase("*.doc") Or
UCase(Microsoft.VisualBasic.Right(OutputPath, 5)) = UCase("?.doc") Or
UCase(Microsoft.VisualBasic.Right(OutputPath, 5)) = UCase("""".doc") Or
UCase(Microsoft.VisualBasic.Right(OutputPath, 5)) = UCase(">.doc") Or
UCase(Microsoft.VisualBasic.Right(OutputPath, 5)) = UCase("<.doc") Or
UCase(Microsoft.VisualBasic.Right(OutputPath, 5)) = UCase("¦.doc") Then
MsgBox("Invalid file name selected in the output path information for the
   output file.",
MsgBoxStyle.OKOnly + MsgBoxStyle.Exclamation, "Word Checker")
txtOutputPath.Focus()
GoTo OutOfHere
Else
End If
LastPos = InStrRev(OutputPath, "\")
CheckDrive = ""
If LastPos > 3 Then
CheckDrive = Microsoft.VisualBasic.Left(OutputPath, LastPos - 1)
Else
CheckDrive = Microsoft.VisualBasic.Left(OutputPath, LastPos)
End If
Dim drv As Object

'Code to validate the drive letter information entered for the output file path
drv = CreateObject("Scripting.FileSystemObject")
IsDriveExist = drv.DriveExists(Microsoft.VisualBasic.Left(OutputPath, 3))
If IsDriveExist = False Then
MsgBox("Drive " & Microsoft.VisualBasic.Left(OutputPath, 3) & "
specified in the output path information does not exist.
If the path is on the network, then make sure that it is mapped.",
MsgBoxStyle.OKOnly + MsgBoxStyle.Exclamation, "Word Checker")
```

```
txtOutputPath.Focus()
GoTo OutOfHere
End If
HasWritePermission = False
On Error GoTo OutOfHere
If Microsoft.VisualBasic.Right(CheckDrive, 1) <> "\" Then

'Code to check for write permission for the path information entered for
   output file
MkDir(CheckDrive + "\CheckWritePermission")
RmDir(CheckDrive + "\CheckWritePermission")
Else
MkDir(CheckDrive + "CheckWritePermission")
RmDir(CheckDrive + "CheckWritePermission")
End If
HasWritePermission = True
If Trim(txtScriptFilePath.Text) = Trim(txtControlFilePath.Text) Then
MsgBox("The path information for the script file and the control file is the same.
Please Check!!!", MsgBoxStyle.OKOnly + MsgBoxStyle.Exclamation, "Word Checker")
txtControlFilePath.Focus()
GoTo OutOfHere
ElseIf Trim(txtScriptFilePath.Text) = Trim(txtOutputPath.Text) Then
MsgBox("The path information for the script file and the output file is the same.
Please Check!!!", MsgBoxStyle.OKOnly + MsgBoxStyle.Exclamation, "Word Checker")
txtOutputPath.Focus()
GoTo OutOfHere
ElseIf Trim(txtControlFilePath.Text) = Trim(txtOutputPath.Text) Then
MsgBox("The path information for the control file and the output file is the same.
Please Check!!!", MsgBoxStyle.OKOnly + MsgBoxStyle.Exclamation, "Word Checker")
txtOutputPath.Focus()
GoTo OutOfHere
End If
```

```
'Code ends here to validate the path information entered for the script,
control and output file
Word1 = New Word.Application()
Word1.Application.Visible = True
Word1.Activate()
IsUnconventionalErrorFound = False
OpenStandardControlFileAndStoreErrWords(ControlFilePath, ScriptPath, OutputPath)
'Function to open control file & store error words
Call cmdExit_Click(cmdExit, New System.EventArgs())
OutOfHere:
If HasWritePermission = False Then
MsgBox("Invalid output path information.
Make sure that you have write permission on the output path.",
MsgBoxStyle.OKOnly + MsgBoxStyle.Exclamation, "Word Checker")
txtOutputPath.Focus()
End If
End Sub
```

The `cmdOK_Click()` function calls the `OpenStandardControlFileAndStoreErrWords()` function, which is discussed in the following section.

The OpenStandardControlFileAndStoreErrWords() Function

The `OpenStandardControlFileAndStoreErrWords()` function opens the control file and stores error words along with suggestions in a two-dimensional array.

The `OpenStandardControlFileAndStoreErrWords()` function opens the standard control file by using the `FileOpen` statement, which, in turn, opens the specified document. The error words along with the suggestions are stored in a two-dimensional array called `ErrorWordsAndSuggestions`.

This function accepts three parameters:

- `ControlFilePath`. This is the path information related to the control file.
- `ScriptPath`. This is the path information of the document file.
- `OutputPath`. This is the path of the output file.

The `Trimmer()` function is used to trim the contents of a string for any special characters that are present in an application.

Listing 24-2 contains the code for the `OpenStandardControlFileAndStoreErrWords()` function.

Listing 24-2 The OpenStandardControlFileAndStoreErrWords() Function

```
'This subroutine opens the control file and stores the error words
Sub OpenStandardControlFileAndStoreErrWords(ByRef ControlFilePath As Object,
ByRef ScriptPath
As Object, ByRef OutputPath As Object)
Dim IsUnconventionalErrorFound As Boolean
Dim res As Object
Dim LastRowOfInputFile As Integer
CounterErrorWordsAndSuggestions = 0
Word1.WordBasic.FileOpen(Name:=ControlFilePath, ConfirmConversions:=0,
   ReadOnly:=0,
AddToMru:=0, PasswordDoc:="", PasswordDot:="", Revert:=0,
   WritePasswordDoc:="",
WritePasswordDot:="")
LastRowOfInputFile = 0
Word1.WordBasic.EndOfDocument()
If Word1.WordBasic.CmpBookmarks("\Sel", "\StartOfDoc") = 0 Then
Word1.WordBasic.MsgBox("Standard control file '" + ControlFilePath +
   "' has been altered and is blank.", "Word Checker")
GoTo EnoughStoringFromControlFile
End If
ReadString = Word1.WordBasic.Selection()
res = Trimmer(ReadString)
While Len(Trim(ReadString)) <= 1
Word1.WordBasic.CharLeft(1)
ReadString = Word1.WordBasic.Selection()
res = Trimmer(ReadString)
If Len(ReadString) > 1 Then
If Word1.WordBasic.SelInfo(12) <> -1 Then
IsUnconventionalErrorFound = True
```

```
Word1.WordBasic.MsgBox("An entry is found below the table in '" +
   ControlFilePath +
"'.", "Word Checker")
GoTo EnoughStoringFromControlFile
End If
LastRowOfInputFile = Word1.WordBasic.SelInfo(13)
GoTo LastRowStored
End If
If LastRowOfInputFile > 1150 Then
Word1.WordBasic.MsgBox("Standard control file '" + ControlFilePath +
"' contains more than 1150 rows/error words.", "Word Checker")
GoTo EnoughStoringFromControlFile
End If
If Word1.WordBasic.CmpBookmarks("\Sel", "\StartOfDoc") = 0 Then
  Word1.WordBasic.MsgBox("Standard control file '" + ControlFilePath +
"' has been altered and it does not contain any text.", "Word Checker")
GoTo EnoughStoringFromControlFile
End If
End While
LastRowStored:
Var(0) = Chr(45)
Var(1) = Chr(150)
Var(2) = Chr(151)
Var(3) = Chr(173)
Var(4) = Chr(40)
Var(5) = Chr(123)
Var(6) = Chr(91)
Var(7) = Chr(41)
Var(8) = Chr(125)
Var(9) = Chr(93)
Var(10) = " "
Var(11) = Chr(13)
Word1.WordBasic.StartOfDocument()
While Word1.WordBasic.SelInfo(12) <> -1
Word1.WordBasic.CharRight(1)
If Word1.WordBasic.CmpBookmarks("\Sel", "\EndOfDoc") = 0 Then
IsUnconventionalErrorFound = True
Word1.WordBasic.MsgBox("The file '" + ControlFilePath +
```

```
"' does not contain any table.", "Word Checker")
GoTo EnoughStoringFromControlFile
End If
End While
Word1.WordBasic.NextCell()
Word1.WordBasic.PrevCell()
While Word1.WordBasic.SelInfo(13) <= LastRowOfInputFile
If Word1.WordBasic.SelInfo(16) <> 1 Then
Word1.WordBasic.MsgBox("The first entry in the file '" + ControlFilePath +
"' is not in the first column.", "Word Checker")
GoTo EnoughStoringFromControlFile
Else
ReadString = Word1.WordBasic.Selection()
res = Trimmer(ReadString)
If Len(ReadString) > 0 Then
ErrorWordsAndSuggestions(CounterErrorWordsAndSuggestions, 0) = ReadString
Word1.WordBasic.NextCell()
If Word1.WordBasic.SelInfo(16) <> 2 Then
Word1.WordBasic.MsgBox("The second entry in the file
'" + ControlFilePath + "' is not in the second column.", "Word Checker")
GoTo EnoughStoringFromControlFile
Else
ReadString = Word1.WordBasic.Selection()
res = Trimmer(ReadString)
If Len(ReadString) > 0 Then
ErrorWordsAndSuggestions(CounterErrorWordsAndSuggestions, 1) = ReadString
End If
If Word1.WordBasic.SelInfo(13) <> LastRowOfInputFile Then
Word1.WordBasic.NextCell()
Else
GoTo OutOfStoring
End If
End If
CounterErrorWordsAndSuggestions = CounterErrorWordsAndSuggestions + 1
Else
If Word1.WordBasic.SelInfo(13) <> LastRowOfInputFile Then
Word1.WordBasic.NextCell()
Word1.WordBasic.NextCell()
```

```
Else
GoTo OutOfStoring
End If
End If
End If
End While
OutOfStoring:
OpenScriptAndStartProcessing(ScriptPath, OutputPath)
'Function to open the script file and start it's processing
EnoughStoringFromControlFile:
End Sub
```

The `OpenStandardControlFileAndStoreErrWords()` function calls the `OpenScriptAndStartProcessing()` `function`, which is discussed in the following section.

The OpenScriptAndStartProcessing() Function

The `OpenScriptAndProcessing()` function reads the standard control file and stores the error words and suggestions in an output report.

The `OpenScriptAndStartProcessing()` function reads the document file line by line and processes each selected line for the presence of error words, if any. The `OpenScriptAndStartProcessing()` function accepts two parameters: `ScriptPath` and `OutputPath`.

Internally, the function calls two more functions, the `CreateErrorLogTable()` function, which creates a table in the output file, and the `CheckForErrorWordsPresent()` function, which checks the selected line for incorrect words. Valid lines are then passed through the `CheckForErrWordspresent()` function, which accepts the following three parameters:

- `ReadString`. This is the current selected line in the document file.
- `ScriptWindow`. This is the name of the document file.
- `ErrFileWindow`. This is the name of the output report.

The document file is checked for the presence of error words. If error words are encountered, they are logged in the output report file. The `HighlightControlWordsNonTabular` procedure, which highlights the error words found in the document file, is called.

Listing 24-3 lists the code for the `OpenScriptAndProcessing()` function.

Listing 24-3 The OpenScriptAndStartProcessing() Function

```
Sub OpenScriptAndStartProcessing(ByRef ScriptPath As Object,
ByRef OutputPath As Object)
Dim i As Integer
Dim DoNotCheck As Boolean
Dim res As Object
Dim IsBlank As Boolean
Dim ScriptWindow As String
Dim Flagstr As Object
Dim ErrFileWindow As String
NumberOfErrors = 0
PartialFound = False
Word1.WordBasic.FileNewDefault()
ErrFileWindow = Word1.WordBasic.WindowName()
CreateErrlogTable((Flagstr))
Word1.WordBasic.Fileopen (Name:=ScriptPath,
ConfirmConversions:=0, ReadOnly:=0, AddToMru:=0, PasswordDoc:="", PasswordDot:="",
Revert:=0, WritePasswordDoc:="", WritePasswordDot:="")
Word1.WordBasic.ViewNormal()
ScriptWindow = Word1.WordBasic.WindowName()
Word1.WordBasic.StartOfDocument()
Word1.WordBasic.ParaDown(1, 1)
If Word1.WordBasic.CmpBookmarks("\Sel", "\StartOfDoc") = 0 Then
Word1.WordBasic.MsgBox("Script file '" + ScriptPath + "' is blank.", "Word
   Checker")
GoTo EnoughOpenScriptAndStartProcessing
End If
IsBlank = True
While Word1.WordBasic.CmpBookmarks("\Sel", "\EndOfDoc")
Word1.WordBasic.CharRight(1)
If Word1.WordBasic.SelInfo(12) = -1 Then
Word1.WordBasic.MsgBox("Script file '" + ScriptPath + "' is in a tabular
   format." + Chr(13)
+ Chr(13) + "Please run the tool again selecting the correct options.",
   "Word Checker")
GoTo EnoughOpenScriptAndStartProcessing
End If
```

```
Word1.WordBasic.ParaDown(1, 1)
ReadString = Word1.WordBasic.Selection()
res = Trimmer(ReadString)
If Len(ReadString) > 0 Then
IsBlank = False
DoNotCheck = False
CheckForErrWordsPresent(ReadString, ScriptWindow, ErrFileWindow)
'Function to check for the error words in the current selection of the
'script file
End If
End While
If ErrorWordsFoundCtr > 0 Then
'Loop to go to the start of document and start highlighting the error words
   in the script file
Word1.WordBasic.StartOfDocument()
For i = 0 To ErrorWordsFoundCtr - 1
Word1.WordBasic.EditFind(Find:=ErrorWordsFound(i), WholeWord:=1)
Word1.WordBasic.HighlightColor(3)
Word1.WordBasic.CharRight(1)
Next
Word1.WordBasic.Filesave()
End If
If IsBlank = True Then
Word1.WordBasic.MsgBox("Script file '" + ScriptPath + "' is blank.",
   "Word Checker")
GoTo EnoughOpenScriptAndStartProcessing
End If
'Function called to activate the output file
ActivateWindow((ErrFileWindow))
If NumberOfErrors = 0 Then
Word1.WordBasic.NextCell()
Word1.WordBasic.ParaDown(3, 1)
Word1.WordBasic.TableMergeCells()
Word1.WordBasic.CharLeft(1)
Word1.WordBasic.Insert("No Errors.")
Else
Word1.WordBasic.EndOfDocument()
Word1.WordBasic.InsertPara()
```

```
'To log the total number of error words as found in the script file
Word1.WordBasic.Insert("Number of error words found is " &
   Str(NumberOfErrors)
'To log the total number of error words as found in the script file
If NumberOfErrors >= 1000 Then
Word1.WordBasic.Insert
("The tool is unable to highlight all the error words in blue as the number
   of error words
are too many.")
End If
End If
Word1.WordBasic.FileSaveAs(Name:=OutputPath, Format:=0, LockAnnot:=0,
   Password:="",
AddToMru:=1, WritePassword:="", RecommendReadOnly:=0, EmbedFonts:=0,
NativePictureFormat:=0, FormsData:=0, SaveAsAOCELetter:=0)
Word1.WordBasic.FileClose(1)
Word1.WordBasic.Fileopen(Name:=OutputPath, ConfirmConversions:=0,
   ReadOnly:=0,
AddToMru:=0, PasswordDoc:="", PasswordDot:="", Revert:=0,
   WritePasswordDoc:="",
WritePasswordDot:="")
EnoughOpenScriptAndStartProcessing:
End Sub
```

The `OpenScriptAndStartProcessing()` function calls the `LogError()` function, which is discussed in the following section.

The LogErr() Function

The `LogErr()` function logs the error in the output file.

The `LogErr() function` is called by the `CheckForErrWordsPresent()` function when error words are found in the document file. The `LogErr()` function logs an error in the output report. The function accepts five parameters, based on which function is carried out. The parameters are as follows:

- `ScriptWindow`. This is the name of the document file.
- `ErrFileWindow`. This is the name of the output document.
- `ChkCtr`. This positions the error word element in the output report.

- Page Number. This specifies the page number in the document file where an error is found.
- Line Number. This is the line number in the document file where the error is found.

The error count in the document is calculated by the NumberOfErrors variable, which is incremented every time an error is encountered in the document. The error count is then written in the document by using the Insert method, which inserts text at any specified insertion point.

The ActiveWindow function, which accepts a window name as a parameter, activates the specified window. The complete output report is then saved using the FileSaveAs method.

Listing 24-4 contains the code for the LogErr() function.

Listing 24-4 The LogErr() Function

```
Sub CreateErrlogTable(ByRef Flagstr As Object)
Word1.WordBasic.TableInsertTable(ConvertFrom:="", NumColumns:="3",
NumRows:="2", InitialColWidth:="Auto", Format:="0", Apply:="167")
Word1.WordBasic.FormatBordersAndShading(ApplyTo:=3, Shadow:=0, TopBorder:=2,
LeftBorder:=2, BottomBorder:=2, RightBorder:=2, HorizBorder:=1,
   VertBorder:=1,
TopColor:=0, LeftColor:=0, BottomColor:=0, RightColor:=0, HorizColor:=0,
   VertColor:=0,
FromText:="0 pt", Shading:=0, Foreground:=0, Background:=0, TAB:="0",
   FineShading:=-1)
Word1.WordBasic.ParaDown(6, 1)
Word1.WordBasic.CenterPara()
Word1.WordBasic.CharLeft(1)
Word1.WordBasic.ParaDown(4, 1)
Word1.WordBasic.Bold()
Word1.WordBasic.CharLeft(1)
Word1.WordBasic.Insert("Incorrect Words")
Word1.WordBasic.TableColumnWidth(ColumnWidth:="1.5" & Chr(34),
SpaceBetweenCols:="0.15" & Chr(34), RulerStyle:="0")
Word1.WordBasic.NextCell()
Word1.WordBasic.Insert("Pg# Ln#.")
```

```
Word1.WordBasic.TableColumnWidth(ColumnWidth:="1.2" & Chr(34),
SpaceBetweenCols:="0.15" & Chr(34), RulerStyle:="0")
Word1.WordBasic.NextCell()
Word1.WordBasic.Insert("Suggestion.")
Word1.WordBasic.TableColumnWidth(ColumnWidth:="3.3" & Chr(34),
SpaceBetweenCols:="0.15" & Chr(34), RulerStyle:="0")
Word1.WordBasic.LineDown(1)
Word1.WordBasic.ParaDown(1, 1)
Word1.WordBasic.LeftPara()
Word1.WordBasic.LineUp(1)
Word1.WordBasic.NextCell()
End Sub
```

Basic Functions Used in the Application

In addition to the main functions, some basic word functions also help in the application of the `Word Checker` tool. The additional functions with the applications are listed in Table 24-1 along with their functions.

Table 24-1 Additional Functions

Function Name	Application
`Activate()`	Used to activate a specified window along with the window name
`FileOpen()`	Used to open a specified document
`EndOfDocument()`	Used to move the insertion point to the end of a selected document
`CmpBookmarks()`	Used to compare the contents of two bookmarks
`Selection()`	Used to select the unformatted text that is returned
`CharLeft()`	Used to move the insertion point to the left by the number of characters specified
`SellInfo()`	Used to select the type of information returned in terms of predefined values, such as, 1, 2, and so on, which perform specific functions
`StartOfDocument()`	Used to move the insertion point to the beginning of a document

continues

Table 24-1 continued

Function Name	Application
`CharRight()`	Used to move the insertion point to the right by the number of characters specified
`NextCell()`	Used to select the contents in the next cell of a table
`PrevCell()`	Used to select the contents in the previous cell of a table
`FileNewDefault()`	Used to create a new document depending on the template used
`ParaDown()`	Used to select the contents in the previous cell of a table
`EditFind()`	Used to find the instance of the next block of specified text
`HighlightColor()`	Used to set the color selected for text
`InsertPara()`	Used to insert a paragraph at the marked insertion point
`CenterPara()`	Used to center selected paragraphs
`Bold()`	Used to add or remove the format of bold characters for the current selection
`TableColumnWidth()`	Used to set the space and width of columns for selected cells
`LineDown()`	Used to move the insertion point down by the specified number of lines
`LeftPara()`	Used to left align a selected paragraph
`LineUp()`	Used to move the insertion point up by the specified number of lines
`NextCell()`	Used to select the contents of the next cell in a table
`CountWindows()`	Used to return the number of the document opened
`WindowList()`	Used to activate a window that is listed on the Window menu

Complete Code for the Word Checker Tool

The `Splash` screen is the first screen you will see when the Word Checker tool is executed. The screen mainly specifies the name of the tool and its version number along with the copyright text of the tool. Listing 24-5 contains the code for the `Splash` screen.

Listing 24-5 Code for the Splash Screen

```
Dim FirstEntry As Boolean
Private Sub frmSplash_KeyPress(ByVal eventSender As System.Object,
ByVal eventArgs As System.Windows.Forms.KeyPressEventArgs) Handles
  MyBase.KeyPress
Call DoTasks()
End Sub
Private Sub Image1_Click(ByVal eventSender As System.Object,
ByVal eventArgs As System.EventArgs) Handles Image1.Click
Call DoTasks()
End Sub
Private Sub lblProductName_Click(ByVal eventSender As System.Object,
ByVal eventArgs As System.EventArgs) Handles lblProductName.Click
Call DoTasks()
End Sub
Private Sub lblWarning_Click(ByVal eventSender As System.Object,
ByVal eventArgs As System.EventArgs) Handles lblWarning.Click
Call DoTasks()
End Sub
Function DoTasks()
If FirstEntry = False Then
Dim MainForm As New frmMainScreen()
Me.Hide()
MainForm.Show()
FirstEntry = True
End If
End Function
Private Sub Timer1_Tick(ByVal sender As Object,
ByVal e As System.EventArgs) Handles Timer1.Tick
Call DoTasks()
End Sub
```

The `Main` screen is instantly shown after the `Splash` screen. You can specify the path of the document file for which the check is to be run, the path of the standard control file, and the path for the output report. Listing 24-6 contains the code for the `Main` screen.

Listing 24-6 Code for the Main Screen

```
Dim Word1 As New Word.Application
Dim ErrorWordsAndSuggestions(1150, 1) As Object
'Array variable to store the error words and suggestions
Dim ErrorWordsFound(1000) As String
Dim ErrorWordsFoundCtr As Short
Dim ReadString As String
Dim CounterErrorWordsAndSuggestions As Short
Dim NumberOfErrors As Short
Dim Var(11) As String
Dim PunctuationErr As String
Dim LoggedWords(20) As String
Dim LoggedWordsctr As Short
Dim PartialFound As Boolean
Private Sub cmdBrowse1_Click(ByVal eventSender As System.Object,
ByVal eventArgs As System.EventArgs) Handles cmdBrowseScript.Click
OpenFileDialog1.InitialDirectory = Application.ExecutablePath
'This function is invoked when the Browse button for selecting the Script
'file is clicked
OpenFileDialog1.Title = "Select the Script File"
OpenFileDialog1.Filter = "MS-Word Documents¦*.doc"
OpenFileDialog1.FilterIndex = 1
If OpenFileDialog1.ShowDialog() <> DialogResult.Cancel Then
txtScriptFilePath.Text = OpenFileDialog1.FileName
Else
txtScriptFilePath.Text = ""
End If
End Sub
Private Sub cmdBrowse2_Click(ByVal eventSender As System.Object,
ByVal eventArgs As System.EventArgs) Handles cmdBrowseControlFile.Click
OpenFileDialog1.InitialDirectory = Application.ExecutablePath
'This function is invoked when the Browse button for selecting the Control
'file is clicked
OpenFileDialog1.Title = "Select the Control File"
OpenFileDialog1.Filter = "MS-Word Documents¦*.doc"
OpenFileDialog1.FilterIndex = 1
If OpenFileDialog1.ShowDialog() <> DialogResult.Cancel Then
```

```
txtControlFilePath.Text = OpenFileDialog1.FileName
Else
txtControlFilePath.Text = ""
End If
End Sub
Private Sub cmdBrowse3_Click(ByVal eventSender As System.Object,
ByVal eventArgs As System.EventArgs) Handles cmdBrowseOutput.Click
SaveFileDialog1.Title = "Specify Output File"
'This function is invoked when the Browse button for selecting the Output
'file is clicked
SaveFileDialog1.Filter = "MS-Word Documents¦*.doc"
SaveFileDialog1.FilterIndex = 1
SaveFileDialog1.OverwritePrompt = True
If SaveFileDialog1.ShowDialog() <> DialogResult.Cancel Then
txtOutputPath.Text = SaveFileDialog1.FileName
Else
txtOutputPath.Text = ""
End If
End Sub
Private Sub cmdCancel_Click(ByVal eventSender As System.Object,
ByVal eventArgs As System.EventArgs) Handles cmdCancel.Click
txtControlFilePath.Text = "C:\"
'This function is invoked when the Cancel button is clicked
txtScriptFilePath.Text = "C:\"
txtOutputPath.Text = "C:\"
End Sub
Private Sub cmdExit_Click(ByVal eventSender As System.Object,
ByVal eventArgs As System.EventArgs) Handles cmdExit.Click
End
End Sub
Private Sub cmdOK_Click(ByVal eventSender As System.Object,
ByVal eventArgs As System.EventArgs) Handles cmdOk.Click
Dim IsUnconventionalErrorFound As Boolean
'This function is invoked when the OK button is clicked by the user
Dim IsDriveExist As Boolean
Dim CheckDrive As String
Dim LastPos As Integer
Dim res As Object
```

```
Dim OutputPath As String
Dim ControlFilePath As String
Dim ScriptPath As String

' Code starts from here to validate the path information entered for the script,
control and output file
If Trim(txtScriptFilePath.Text) = Trim(txtOutputPath.Text) Then
MsgBox("The path information for the script file and the output file is the
   same.
Please check!!!", MsgBoxStyle.OKOnly + MsgBoxStyle.Exclamation,
   "Word Checker")
txtOutputPath.Focus()
GoTo OutOfHere
End If
PunctuationErr = ""
Dim HasWritePermission As Boolean
HasWritePermission = True
ScriptPath = LTrim(RTrim(txtScriptFilePath.Text))
'Code to validate the Script file path information
If Len(ScriptPath) = 0 Then
MsgBox("Please enter path information for script file",
MsgBoxStyle.OKOnly + MsgBoxStyle.Exclamation, "Word Checker")
txtScriptFilePath.Focus()
GoTo OutOfHere
End If
ControlFilePath = LTrim(RTrim(txtControlFilePath.Text))
'Code to validate the Control file path information
If Len(ControlFilePath) = 0 Then
MsgBox("Please enter path information for standard control file",
MsgBoxStyle.OKOnly + MsgBoxStyle.Exclamation, "Word Checker")
txtControlFilePath.Focus()
GoTo OutOfHere
End If
  OutputPath = LTrim(RTrim(txtOutputPath.Text))

'Code to validate the Output file path information
If Len(OutputPath) = 0 Then
```

```
MsgBox("Please enter path information for output file",
MsgBoxStyle.OKOnly + MsgBoxStyle.Exclamation,
"Word Checker")
VtxtOutputPath.Focus()
GoTo OutOfHere
End If
If Mid(ScriptPath, 2, 2) <> ":\" Then
MsgBox("Invalid path information for script file.
If the file is on the network then make sure that the path is mapped",
 MsgBoxStyle.OKOnly + MsgBoxStyle.Exclamation, "Word Checker")
txtScriptFilePath.Focus()
GoTo OutOfHere
End If
If Mid(ControlFilePath, 2, 2) <> ":\" Then
MsgBox("Invalid path information for standard control file.
If the file is on the network then make sure that the path is mapped",
MsgBoxStyle.OKOnly + MsgBoxStyle.Exclamation, "Word Checker")
txtControlFilePath.Focus()
GoTo OutOfHere
End If
If Mid(OutputPath, 2, 2) <> ":\" Then
MsgBox("Invalid path information for output file.
If the file is on the network then make sure that the path is mapped",
MsgBoxStyle.OKOnly + MsgBoxStyle.Exclamation, "Word Checker")
txtOutputPath.Focus()
GoTo OutOfHere
End If
Dim testdir1 As String
testdir1 = Dir(ScriptPath, FileAttribute.Normal)
If (testdir1 = "") Then
MsgBox("Path information of script file " + ScriptPath + " does not exist.",
MsgBoxStyle.OKOnly + MsgBoxStyle.Exclamation, "Word Checker")
txtScriptFilePath.Focus()
GoTo OutOfHere
Else
If UCase(Microsoft.VisualBasic.Right(ScriptPath, 4)) <> UCase(".doc") Then
MsgBox("Invalid file format selected in the input path information of script
   file.
```

```
" & Chr(13) & Chr(13) & "File selected is not a .rtf or .doc File.",
MsgBoxStyle.OKOnly + MsgBoxStyle.Exclamation, "Word Checker")
txtScriptFilePath.Focus()
GoTo OutOfHere
End If
End If
testdir1 = Dir(ControlFilePath, FileAttribute.Normal)
If (testdir1 = "") Then
MsgBox("Path information of standard control file " + ControlFilePath + "
   does not exist.",
MsgBoxStyle.OKOnly + MsgBoxStyle.Exclamation, "Word Checker")
txtControlFilePath.Focus()
GoTo OutOfHere
ElseIf UCase(Microsoft.VisualBasic.Right(ControlFilePath, 4)) <>
   UCase(".doc") Then
MsgBox("Invalid file format selected in the input path information of
   standard control file.
" & Chr(13) & Chr(13) & "File selected is not a .doc File.",
MsgBoxStyle.OKOnly + MsgBoxStyle.Exclamation, "Word Checker")
txtControlFilePath.Focus()
GoTo OutOfHere
End If
If UCase(Microsoft.VisualBasic.Right(OutputPath, 4)) <> UCase(".doc") Then
MsgBox("Invalid file format selected in the path information for the output
   file.
" & Chr(13) & Chr(13) & "File selected is not a .doc File.",
MsgBoxStyle.OKOnly + MsgBoxStyle.Exclamation, "Word Checker")
txtOutputPath.Focus()
GoTo OutOfHere
ElseIf UCase(Microsoft.VisualBasic.Right(OutputPath, 5)) = UCase("\.doc") Or
UCase(Microsoft.VisualBasic.Right(OutputPath, 5)) = UCase("/.doc") Or
UCase(Microsoft.VisualBasic.Right(OutputPath, 5)) = UCase(":.doc") Or
UCase(Microsoft.VisualBasic.Right(OutputPath, 5)) = UCase("*.doc") Or
UCase(Microsoft.VisualBasic.Right(OutputPath, 5)) = UCase("?.doc") Or
UCase(Microsoft.VisualBasic.Right(OutputPath, 5)) = UCase(""".doc") Or
UCase(Microsoft.VisualBasic.Right(OutputPath, 5)) = UCase(">.doc") Or
UCase(Microsoft.VisualBasic.Right(OutputPath, 5)) = UCase("<.doc") Or
UCase(Microsoft.VisualBasic.Right(OutputPath, 5)) = UCase("¦.doc") Then
MsgBox("Invalid file name selected in the output path information for the
```

```
  output file.",
MsgBoxStyle.OKOnly + MsgBoxStyle.Exclamation, "Word Checker")
txtOutputPath.Focus()
 GoTo OutOfHere
 Else
 End If

 LastPos = InStrRev(OutputPath, "\")
 CheckDrive = ""
 If LastPos > 3 Then
 CheckDrive = Microsoft.VisualBasic.Left(OutputPath, LastPos - 1)
 Else
 CheckDrive = Microsoft.VisualBasic.Left(OutputPath, LastPos)
  End If

  Dim drv As Object
' Code to validate the drive letter information entered for the output file
' path
 drv = CreateObject("Scripting.FileSystemObject")
  IsDriveExist = drv.DriveExists(Microsoft.VisualBasic.Left(OutputPath, 3))

  If IsDriveExist = False Then
  MsgBox("Drive " & Microsoft.VisualBasic.Left(OutputPath, 3) &
" specified in the output path information does not exist.
If the path is on the network, then make sure that it is mapped.",
MsgBoxStyle.OKOnly + MsgBoxStyle.Exclamation, "Word Checker")
  txtOutputPath.Focus()
 GoTo OutOfHere
 End If

 HasWritePermission = False

 On Error GoTo OutOfHere

 If Microsoft.VisualBasic.Right(CheckDrive, 1) <> "\" Then
' Code to check for write permission for the path information entered for
' output file
 MkDir(CheckDrive + "\CheckWritePermission")
 RmDir(CheckDrive + "\CheckWritePermission")
```

```
Else
MkDir(CheckDrive + "CheckWritePermission")
RmDir(CheckDrive + "CheckWritePermission")
End If
HasWritePermission = True

 If Trim(txtScriptFilePath.Text) = Trim(txtControlFilePath.Text) Then
 MsgBox("The path information for the script file and the control file is
    the same.
 Please Check!!!", MsgBoxStyle.OKOnly + MsgBoxStyle.Exclamation, "Word
    Checker")
 txtControlFilePath.Focus()
 GoTo OutOfHere
 ElseIf Trim(txtScriptFilePath.Text) = Trim(txtOutputPath.Text) Then
 MsgBox("The path information for the script file and the output file is
    the same.
 Please Check!!!", MsgBoxStyle.OKOnly + MsgBoxStyle.Exclamation, "Word
    Checker")
 txtOutputPath.Focus()
 GoTo OutOfHere
 ElseIf Trim(txtControlFilePath.Text) = Trim(txtOutputPath.Text) Then
 MsgBox("The path information for the control file and the output file is
    the same.
 Please Check!!!", MsgBoxStyle.OKOnly + MsgBoxStyle.Exclamation, "Word
    Checker")
txtOutputPath.Focus()
GoTo OutOfHere
End If

' Code ends here to validate the path information entered for the script, control
' and output file
Word1 = New Word.Application()
Word1.Application.Visible = True
Word1.Activate()

IsUnconventionalErrorFound = False
OpenStandardControlFileAndStoreErrWords(ControlFilePath, ScriptPath,
   OutputPath)
 'Function to open control file & store error words
```

```
Call cmdExit_Click(cmdExit, New System.EventArgs())
OutOfHere:
If HasWritePermission = False Then
MsgBox("Invalid output path information.
Make sure that you have write permission on the output path.",
MsgBoxStyle.OKOnly + MsgBoxStyle.Exclamation, "Word Checker")
txtOutputPath.Focus()
End If
End Sub

Sub OpenStandardControlFileAndStoreErrWords(ByRef ControlFilePath As Object
 ByRef ScriptPath As Object, ByRef OutputPath As Object)
Dim IsUnconventionalErrorFound As Boolean
'This subroutine opens the control file and stores the error words
Dim res As Object
Dim LastRowOfInputFile As Integer
CounterErrorWordsAndSuggestions = 0

 Word1.WordBasic.FileOpen(Name:=ControlFilePath, ConfirmConversions:=0,
    ReadOnly:=0,
 AddToMru:=0, PasswordDoc:="", PasswordDot:="", Revert:=0,
    WritePasswordDoc:="",
 WritePasswordDot:="")
LastRowOfInputFile = 0
Word1.WordBasic.EndOfDocument()

If Word1.WordBasic.CmpBookmarks("\Sel", "\StartOfDoc") = 0 Then
Word1.WordBasic.MsgBox("Standard control file '
" + ControlFilePath + "' has been altered and is blank.", "Word Checker")
GoTo EnoughStoringFromControlFile
End If

ReadString = Word1.WordBasic.Selection()
res = Trimmer(ReadString)

While Len(Trim(ReadString)) <= 1
Word1.WordBasic.CharLeft(1)
ReadString = Word1.WordBasic.Selection()
res = Trimmer(ReadString)
```

```
If Len(ReadString) > 1 Then
If Word1.WordBasic.SelInfo(12) <> -1 Then
IsUnconventionalErrorFound = True
Word1.WordBasic.MsgBox("An entry is found below the table in
'" + ControlFilePath + "'.", "Word Checker")
GoTo EnoughStoringFromControlFile
End If
LastRowOfInputFile = Word1.WordBasic.SelInfo(13)
GoTo LastRowStored
 End If

 If LastRowOfInputFile > 1150 Then
 Word1.WordBasic.MsgBox("Standard control file
'" + ControlFilePath + "' contains more than 1150 rows/error words.", "Word
   Checker")
 GoTo EnoughStoringFromControlFile
  End If

 If Word1.WordBasic.CmpBookmarks("\Sel", "\StartOfDoc") = 0 Then
 Word1.WordBasic.MsgBox("Standard control file
'" + ControlFilePath + "' has been altered and it does not contain any text.",
   "Word Checker")
 GoTo EnoughStoringFromControlFile
  End If
  End While
LastRowStored:

   Var(0) = Chr(45)
    Var(1) = Chr(150)
    Var(2) = Chr(151)
    Var(3) = Chr(173)
    Var(4) = Chr(40)
    Var(5) = Chr(123)
    Var(6) = Chr(91)
    Var(7) = Chr(41)
    Var(8) = Chr(125)
    Var(9) = Chr(93)
    Var(10) = " "
```

```
 Var(11) = Chr(13)

Word1.WordBasic.StartOfDocument()
While Word1.WordBasic.SelInfo(12) <> -1
Word1.WordBasic.CharRight(1)
If Word1.WordBasic.CmpBookmarks("\Sel", "\EndOfDoc") = 0 Then
IsUnconventionalErrorFound = True
Word1.WordBasic.MsgBox("The file
'" + ControlFilePath + "' does not contain any table.", "Word Checker")
GoTo EnoughStoringFromControlFile
End If
End While

Word1.WordBasic.NextCell()
Word1.WordBasic.PrevCell()
While Word1.WordBasic.SelInfo(13) <= LastRowOfInputFile
If Word1.WordBasic.SelInfo(16) <> 1 Then
Word1.WordBasic.MsgBox("The first entry in the file
'" + ControlFilePath + "' is not in the first column.", "Word Checker")
GoTo EnoughStoringFromControlFile
 Else
ReadString = Word1.WordBasic.Selection()
res = Trimmer(ReadString)
If Len(ReadString) > 0 Then
ErrorWordsAndSuggestions(CounterErrorWordsAndSuggestions, 0) = ReadString
Word1.WordBasic.NextCell()
If Word1.WordBasic.SelInfo(16) <> 2 Then
Word1.WordBasic.MsgBox("The second entry in the file
'" + ControlFilePath + "' is not in the second column.", "Word Checker")
GoTo EnoughStoringFromControlFile
 Else
 ReadString = Word1.WordBasic.Selection()
 res = Trimmer(ReadString)
 If Len(ReadString) > 0 Then
 ErrorWordsAndSuggestions(CounterErrorWordsAndSuggestions, 1) = ReadString
 End If
 If Word1.WordBasic.SelInfo(13) <> LastRowOfInputFile Then
 Word1.WordBasic.NextCell()
  Else
```

```
                GoTo OutOfStoring
                End If
                End If
            CounterErrorWordsAndSuggestions = CounterErrorWordsAndSuggestions + 1
            Else
            If Word1.WordBasic.SelInfo(13) <> LastRowOfInputFile Then
            Word1.WordBasic.NextCell()
            Word1.WordBasic.NextCell()
            Else
            GoTo OutOfStoring
            End If
            End If
            End If
            End While
OutOfStoring:
        OpenScriptAndStartProcessing(ScriptPath, OutputPath)
     'Function to open the script file and start its processing
EnoughStoringFromControlFile:
        End Sub

       Function Trimmer(ByRef RString As Object) As Object
       ReadString = RString
         While (Microsoft.VisualBasic.Right(ReadString, 1) = Chr(7) Or
Microsoft.VisualBasic.Right(ReadString, 1) = Chr(11) Or
Microsoft.VisualBasic.Right(ReadString, 1) = Chr(13) Or
Microsoft.VisualBasic.Right(ReadString, 1) = Chr(9) Or
Microsoft.VisualBasic.Right(ReadString, 1) = Chr(32) Or
Microsoft.VisualBasic.Right(ReadString, 1) = Chr(160) Or
Microsoft.VisualBasic.Right(ReadString, 1) = Chr(10) Or
Microsoft.VisualBasic.Right(ReadString, 1) = Chr(12) Or
Microsoft.VisualBasic.Right(ReadString, 1) = (Chr(13) & Chr(10)))
         ReadString = Microsoft.VisualBasic.Left(ReadString, Len(ReadString) - 1)
         End While
         While (Microsoft.VisualBasic.Left(ReadString, 1) = Chr(7) Or
Microsoft.VisualBasic.Left(ReadString, 1) = Chr(11) Or
Microsoft.VisualBasic.Left(ReadString, 1) = Chr(13) Or
Microsoft.VisualBasic.Left(ReadString, 1) = Chr(9) Or
Microsoft.VisualBasic.Left(ReadString, 1) = Chr(32) Or
```

```
Microsoft.VisualBasic.Left(ReadString, 1) = Chr(160) Or
Microsoft.VisualBasic.Left(ReadString, 1) = Chr(10) Or
Microsoft.VisualBasic.Left(ReadString, 1) = (Chr(13) & Chr(10)) Or
Microsoft.VisualBasic.Left(ReadString, 1) = Chr(12))
        ReadString = Microsoft.VisualBasic.Right(ReadString, Len(ReadString) - 1)
        End While
        End Function
        Sub OpenScriptAndStartProcessing(ByRef ScriptPath As Object,
        ByRef OutputPath As Object)
        Dim i As Integer
        Dim DoNotCheck As Boolean
        Dim res As Object
        Dim IsBlank As Boolean
        Dim ScriptWindow As String
        Dim Flagstr As Object
        Dim ErrFileWindow As String

        NumberOfErrors = 0
        PartialFound = False
        Word1.WordBasic.FileNewDefault()
        ErrFileWindow = Word1.WordBasic.WindowName()
        CreateErrlogTable((Flagstr))
'Function to create the error log table in the output file

        Word1.WordBasic.Fileopen(Name:=ScriptPath, ConfirmConversions:=0,
           ReadOnly:=0, AddToMru:=0, PasswordDoc:="", PasswordDot:="", Revert:=0,
           WritePasswordDoc:="", WritePasswordDot:="")
        Word1.WordBasic.ViewNormal()
        ScriptWindow = Word1.WordBasic.WindowName()

        Word1.WordBasic.StartOfDocument()
        Word1.WordBasic.ParaDown(1, 1)

        If Word1.WordBasic.CmpBookmarks("\Sel", "\StartOfDoc") = 0 Then
        Word1.WordBasic.MsgBox("Script file '" + ScriptPath + "' is blank.", "Word
           Checker")
        GoTo EnoughOpenScriptAndStartProcessing
        End If
```

```
IsBlank = True

While Word1.WordBasic.CmpBookmarks("\Sel", "\EndOfDoc")
Word1.WordBasic.CharRight(1)
If Word1.WordBasic.SelInfo(12) = -1 Then
Word1.WordBasic.MsgBox("Script file '" + ScriptPath + "' is in a tabular
   format." + Chr(13) +
Chr(13) + "Please run the tool again selecting the correct options.", "Word
   Checker")
GoTo EnoughOpenScriptAndStartProcessing
End If

Word1.WordBasic.ParaDown(1, 1)
ReadString = Word1.WordBasic.Selection()
res = Trimmer(ReadString)
If Len(ReadString) > 0 Then
IsBlank = False
DoNotCheck = False

'Function to check for the error words in the current selection of the script file

CheckForErrWordsPresent(ReadString, ScriptWindow, ErrFileWindow)
   End If
End While

If ErrorWordsFoundCtr > 0 Then
'Loop to go to the start of document and start highlighting the error words
'in the script file
Word1.WordBasic.StartOfDocument()
For i = 0 To ErrorWordsFoundCtr - 1
Word1.WordBasic.EditFind(Find:=ErrorWordsFound(i), WholeWord:=1)
Word1.WordBasic.HighlightColor(3)
Word1.WordBasic.CharRight(1)
Next
Word1.WordBasic.Filesave()
End If
```

```
        If IsBlank = True Then
        Word1.WordBasic.MsgBox("Script file '" + ScriptPath + "' is blank.", "Word
           Checker")
        GoTo EnoughOpenScriptAndStartProcessing
        End If

         ActivateWindow((ErrFileWindow))
'Function called to activate the output file
         If NumberOfErrors = 0 Then
         Word1.WordBasic.NextCell()
         Word1.WordBasic.ParaDown(3, 1)
         Word1.WordBasic.TableMergeCells()
         Word1.WordBasic.CharLeft(1)
         Word1.WordBasic.Insert("No Errors.")
         Else
         Word1.WordBasic.EndOfDocument()
         Word1.WordBasic.InsertPara()
         Word1.WordBasic.Insert("Number of error words found is " &
Str(NumberOfErrors))
           'To log the total number of error words as found in the script file

         If NumberOfErrors >= 1000 Then
         Word1.WordBasic.Insert("The tool is unable to highlight all the error words
            in blue as the number of error words are too many.")
          End If

          End If

          Word1.WordBasic.FileSaveAs(Name:=OutputPath, Format:=0, LockAnnot:=0,
             Password:="", AddToMru:=1, WritePassword:="", RecommendReadOnly:=0,
             EmbedFonts:=0, NativePictureFormat:=0, FormsData:=0,
             SaveAsAOCELetter:=0)
          Word1.WordBasic.FileClose(1)
          Word1.WordBasic.Fileopen(Name:=OutputPath, ConfirmConversions:=0,
             ReadOnly:=0, AddToMru:=0, PasswordDoc:="", PasswordDot:="", Revert:=0,
             WritePasswordDoc:="", WritePasswordDot:="")

EnoughOpenScriptAndStartProcessing:
```

```
End Sub
 Sub CheckForErrWordsPresent(ByRef ReadString As Object,
ByRef ScriptWindow As Object, ByRef ErrFileWindow As Object)
 Dim RightSide As Integer
 Dim LeftSide As Integer
 Dim ChkOfRightPlus As String
 Dim CtrRight As Integer
 Dim ChkOfRight As String
 Dim VarCtr As Integer
 Dim ChkOfLeft As String
 Dim LineNo As Integer
 Dim PageNo As Integer
 Dim ErrorWordFound As Integer
 Dim ChkCtr As Integer
 Dim LeftChkErrReported As Integer
 Dim RightChkErrReported As Integer
 Dim RightPlusErrReported As Integer
 Dim RightPlusChecked As Integer
 Dim IsRightAnyOfTheVar As Integer

 IsRightAnyOfTheVar = 0
 RightPlusChecked = 0
 RightPlusErrReported = 0
 RightChkErrReported = 0
 LeftChkErrReported = 0
 For ChkCtr = 0 To CounterErrorWordsAndSuggestions
     ErrorWordFound = 0
     If UCase(ErrorWordsAndSuggestions(ChkCtr, 0)) = "(S)" Then
         ErrorWordFound = InStr(UCase(ReadString),
UCase(ErrorWordsAndSuggestions(ChkCtr, 0)))
If ErrorWordFound <> 0 Then
PageNo = Word1.WordBasic.SelInfo(1)
LineNo = Word1.WordBasic.SelInfo(10)
LogErr(ScriptWindow, ErrFileWindow, ChkCtr, PageNo, LineNo)
'Function to log the error in the output file
If LoggedWordsctr < 20 Then
LoggedWords(LoggedWordsctr) = ErrorWordsAndSuggestions(ChkCtr, 0)
LoggedWordsctr = LoggedWordsctr + 1
```

```
End If

End If
Else
If LeftChkErrReported = 0 Then
ErrorWordFound = 0
ChkOfLeft = UCase(Microsoft.VisualBasic.Left(ReadString,
  Len(ErrorWordsAndSuggestions(ChkCtr, 0))))
If UCase(ChkOfLeft) = UCase(ErrorWordsAndSuggestions(ChkCtr, 0)) Then
For VarCtr = 0 To 11
If Mid(ReadString, Len(ChkOfLeft) + 1, 1) = Var(VarCtr) Then
ErrorWordFound = 1
Exit For
End If
Next
End If
If ErrorWordFound <> 0 Then
LeftChkErrReported = 1
PageNo = Word1.WordBasic.SelInfo(1)
LineNo = Word1.WordBasic.SelInfo(10)

'Function to log the error in the output file
LogErr(ScriptWindow, ErrFileWindow, ChkCtr, PageNo, LineNo)
   If LoggedWordsctr < 20 Then
LoggedWords(LoggedWordsctr) = ErrorWordsAndSuggestions(ChkCtr, 0)
LoggedWordsctr = LoggedWordsctr + 1
End If

End If
End If

If RightChkErrReported = 0 Then
  ErrorWordFound = 0
 ChkOfRight = UCase(Microsoft.VisualBasic.Right(ReadString,
   Len(ErrorWordsAndSuggestions(ChkCtr, 0))))
If UCase(ChkOfRight) = UCase(ErrorWordsAndSuggestions(ChkCtr, 0)) Then
For VarCtr = 0 To 11
If Mid(ReadString, Len(ReadString) - Len(ChkOfRight), 1) = Var(VarCtr)
```

```
Then
             ErrorWordFound = 1
             Exit For
             End If
             Next
             End If

            If ErrorWordFound <> 0 Then
            RightChkErrReported = 1
            PageNo = Word1.WordBasic.SelInfo(1)
            LineNo = Word1.WordBasic.SelInfo(10)
            LogErr(ScriptWindow, ErrFileWindow, ChkCtr, PageNo, LineNo)
        'Function to log the error in the output file
            If LoggedWordsctr < 20 Then
            LoggedWords(LoggedWordsctr) = ErrorWordsAndSuggestions(ChkCtr, 0)
            LoggedWordsctr = LoggedWordsctr + 1
            End If

            End If
            End If

            If RightPlusChecked = 0 Then
           For CtrRight = 0 To 11
           If Microsoft.VisualBasic.Right(ReadString, 1) = Var(CtrRight) Then
           IsRightAnyOfTheVar = 1
           Exit For
           End If
          Next
          RightPlusChecked = 1
          End If

          If RightPlusErrReported = 0 Then
          ErrorWordFound = 0
          If IsRightAnyOfTheVar = 0 Then
             ChkOfRightPlus = UCase(Microsoft.VisualBasic.Right(ReadString,
                 Len(ErrorWordsAndSuggestions(ChkCtr, 0)) + 1))
             If UCase(Microsoft.VisualBasic.Left(ChkOfRightPlus,
                 Len(ErrorWordsAndSuggestions(ChkCtr, 0)))) =
```

```
   UCase(ErrorWordsAndSuggestions(ChkCtr, 0)) Then
For VarCtr = 0 To 11
If Mid(ReadString, Len(ReadString) - Len(ChkOfRightPlus), 1) = Var(VarCtr)
   Then
ErrorWordFound = 1
Exit For
End If
Next
End If

If ErrorWordFound <> 0 Then
RightPlusErrReported = 1
PageNo = Word1.WordBasic.SelInfo(1)
LineNo = Word1.WordBasic.SelInfo(10)
LogErr(ScriptWindow, ErrFileWindow, ChkCtr, PageNo, LineNo)
   'Function to log the error in the output file
If LoggedWordsctr < 20 Then
LoggedWords(LoggedWordsctr) = ErrorWordsAndSuggestions(ChkCtr, 0)
LoggedWordsctr = LoggedWordsctr + 1
End If

End If
End If
End If

For LeftSide = 0 To 11
For RightSide = 0 To 11
ErrorWordFound = InStr(UCase(ReadString), Var(LeftSide) &
   UCase(ErrorWordsAndSuggestions(ChkCtr, 0)) & Var(RightSide))
If ErrorWordFound <> 0 Then
PageNo = Word1.WordBasic.SelInfo(1)
LineNo = Word1.WordBasic.SelInfo(10)
LogErr(ScriptWindow, ErrFileWindow, ChkCtr, PageNo, LineNo)
   'Function to log the error in the output file
If LoggedWordsctr < 20 Then
LoggedWords(LoggedWordsctr) = ErrorWordsAndSuggestions(ChkCtr, 0)
LoggedWordsctr = LoggedWordsctr + 1
End If
```

```
        End If
        Next
        Next
        End If
        Next

EOFCheckForErrWordsPresent:
        End Sub

        Sub LogErr(ByRef ScriptWindow As Object, ByRef ErrFileWindow As Object,
           ByRef ChkCtr As Object, ByRef PageNo As Object, ByRef LineNo As Object)
        ActivateWindow((ErrFileWindow))     'To activate the output file window

        NumberOfErrors = NumberOfErrors + 1
        Word1.WordBasic.Insert(ErrorWordsAndSuggestions(ChkCtr, 0))
        If ErrorWordsFoundCtr < 1000 Then
        ErrorWordsFound(ErrorWordsFoundCtr) = ErrorWordsAndSuggestions(ChkCtr, 0)
        ErrorWordsFoundCtr = ErrorWordsFoundCtr + 1
        End If

        Word1.WordBasic.NextCell()
        Word1.WordBasic.Insert("Pg " & Str(PageNo) & " Ln " & Str(LineNo))
        Word1.WordBasic.NextCell()
        Word1.WordBasic.Insert(ErrorWordsAndSuggestions(ChkCtr, 1))
        Word1.WordBasic.NextCell()

        ActivateWindow((ScriptWindow))      'To activate the script file window
        End Sub

        Sub CreateErrlogTable(ByRef Flagstr As Object)
        Word1.WordBasic.TableInsertTable(ConvertFrom:="", NumColumns:="3",
           NumRows:="2", InitialColWidth:="Auto", Format:="0", Apply:="167")
        Word1.WordBasic.FormatBordersAndShading(ApplyTo:=3, Shadow:=0,
           TopBorder:=2, LeftBorder:=2, BottomBorder:=2, RightBorder:=2,
           HorizBorder:=1, VertBorder:=1, TopColor:=0, LeftColor:=0, BottomColor:=0,
           RightColor:=0, HorizColor:=0, VertColor:=0, FromText:="0 pt", Shading:=0,
           Foreground:=0, Background:=0, TAB:="0", FineShading:=-1)
        Word1.WordBasic.ParaDown(6, 1)
```

```
Word1.WordBasic.CenterPara()
Word1.WordBasic.CharLeft(1)
Word1.WordBasic.ParaDown(4, 1)
Word1.WordBasic.Bold()
Word1.WordBasic.CharLeft(1)
Word1.WordBasic.Insert("Incorrect Words")
Word1.WordBasic.TableColumnWidth(ColumnWidth:="1.5" & Chr(34),
   SpaceBetweenCols:="0.15" & Chr(34), RulerStyle:="0")
Word1.WordBasic.NextCell()
Word1.WordBasic.Insert("Pg# Ln#.")
Word1.WordBasic.TableColumnWidth(ColumnWidth:="1.2" & Chr(34),
   SpaceBetweenCols:="0.15" & Chr(34), RulerStyle:="0")
Word1.WordBasic.NextCell()
Word1.WordBasic.Insert("Suggestion.")
Word1.WordBasic.TableColumnWidth(ColumnWidth:="3.3" & Chr(34),
   SpaceBetweenCols:="0.15" & Chr(34), RulerStyle:="0")
Word1.WordBasic.LineDown(1)
Word1.WordBasic.ParaDown(1, 1)
Word1.WordBasic.LeftPara()
Word1.WordBasic.LineUp(1)
Word1.WordBasic.NextCell()
End Sub
'For this subroutine to work, the window should already be open.
' This will just bring it to the front.
Private Sub ActivateWindow(ByRef WindowToOpen As Object)
Dim numwin As Integer
Dim i As Integer

Dim leave_Renamed As Integer
Dim winname As String
numwin = Word1.WordBasic.CountWindows()
If numwin <> 0 Then
i = 1
While i <= numwin And leave_Renamed <> 1
winname = Word1.WordBasic.WindowName(i)
If InStr(winname, WindowToOpen) Then leave_Renamed = 1
If leave_Renamed <> 1 Then i = i + 1
End While
```

```
End If
If InStr(winname, WindowToOpen) Then
Word1.WordBasic.WindowList(i)
Else
Word1.WordBasic.MsgBox("There is no window containing ", WindowToOpen)
End If
End Sub
```

Summary

In this chapter, you coded the application of the Word Checker tool. You also looked at the various methods and functions used in the application. In the next chapter, you will learn to execute the application of the Work Checker tool.

Chapter 25

Executing the Word Checker Tool

In this chapter, you will learn how to execute the Word Checker tool that you have developed. You will also learn the steps to distribute the application as an executable file.

Running the Application

To run the application, you need to install the Word Checker tool on your computer. To install this tool, you need to copy all the required files to the computer and run the setup.exe file, which will automatically install the tool on the default C drive. When the setup is complete, you can click on the shortcut to run the tool.

You need to click on Start and then choose the Word Checker tool from the Programs menu. The Word Checker tool is then executed. The `Splash` screen is the first screen to be displayed, and it disappears after some time. Figure 25-1 displays the `Splash` screen of the Word Checker tool.

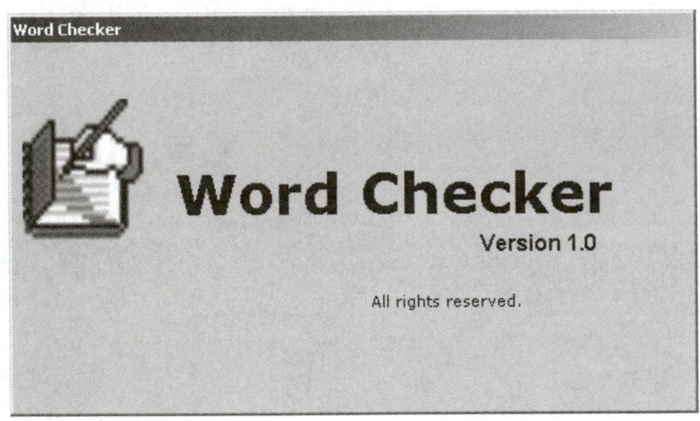

FIGURE 25-1 *The* `Splash` *screen of the Word Checker tool*

Next, the `Main` screen of the tool is displayed. In this screen the path of the script, the path of the standard control file, and the path for the output report have to be specified. The `Main` screen of the Word Checker tool is shown in Figure 25-2.

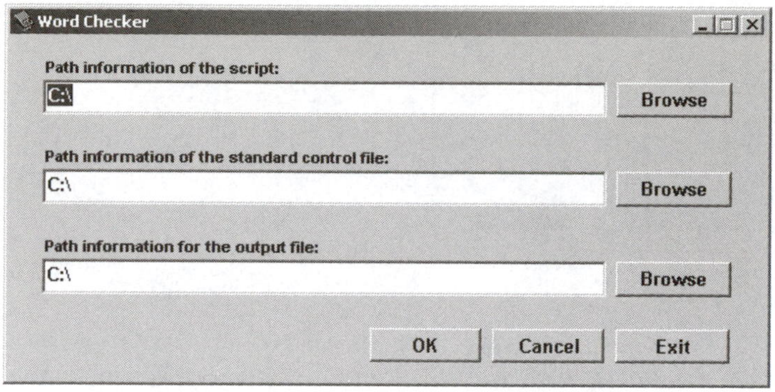

FIGURE 25-2 *The* `Main` *screen of the Word Checker tool*

Information related to all the paths for the document is specified using the `Browse` button, and then the tool is run. Figure 25-3 displays the complete screen.

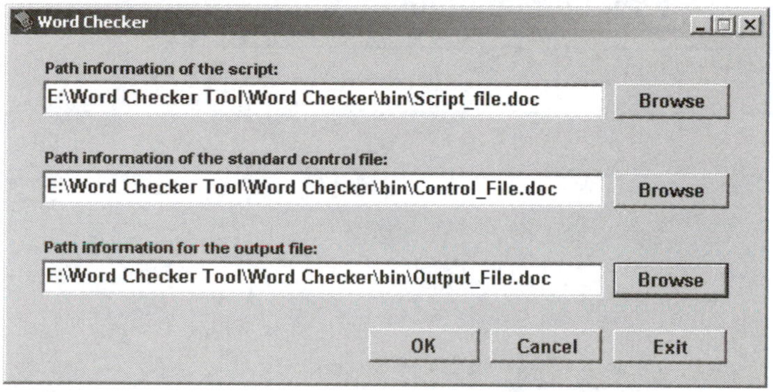

FIGURE 25-3 *The* `Main` *screen of the Word Checker Tool with the paths specified for the document file, control file, and the output file*

When the `OK` button is clicked, the tool checks the path specified for the output report. The Specify Output File message box is displayed if the selected output file already exists at the location specified in the output path. Clicking on `Yes` will replace the output file in the specified directory path. Figure 25-4 displays the message.

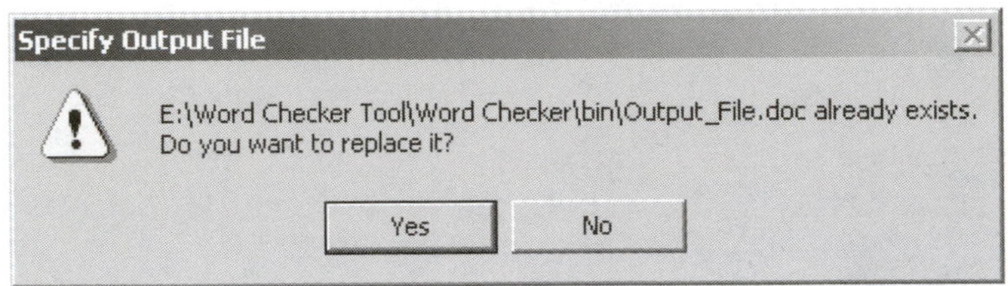

FIGURE 25-4 *The Specify Output File message box*

When the execution of the application starts, the Word Checker tool is run on the specified document. The output report is displayed in Figure 25-5.

Incorrect Words	Pg#Ln#	Suggestion
amongst	Pg 1 Ln 3	Use among instead of amongst.
Imbed	Pg 1 Ln 14	Use embed instead of imbed
Lock	Pg 1 Ln 25	Use write-protect, not lock, to refer to the action of protecting disks from being overwritten.
wastage	Pg 1 Ln 40	Use waste instead of wastage.

Number of error words found is 4

FIGURE 25-5 *The Output Report format of the Word Checker tool*

Distributing the Application

You can distribute the executable file to run the application. The application needs to be converted into an .exe file before it is executed.

To distribute the Word Checker application as an .exe file, perform the following steps to first build and compile the application setup program:

1. Specify the path of the Word Checker tool setup program. Figure 25-6 displays the path of the Word Checker tool.
2. Include the various files required by the Word Checker tool. Figure 25-7 displays the files required by the Word Checker tool.
3. Select the process of building the Word Checker tool. Figure 25-8 displays the process of building the Word Checker tool setup program. Select the Build Solution option from the Build menu.

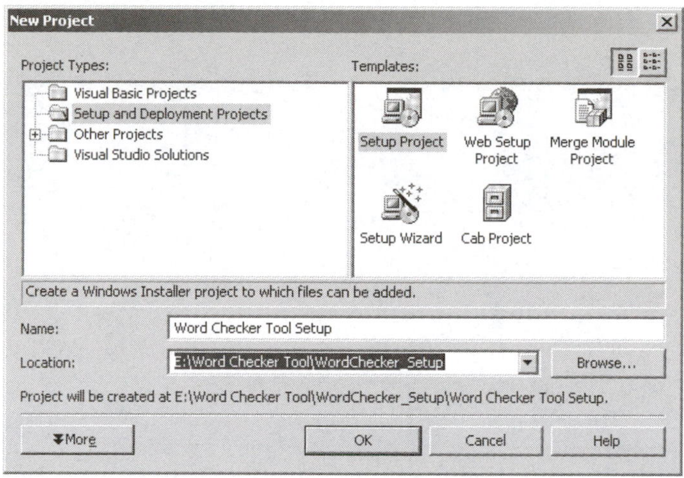

FIGURE 25-6 *The New Project dialog box that prompts for the path of the Word Checker tool to be specified*

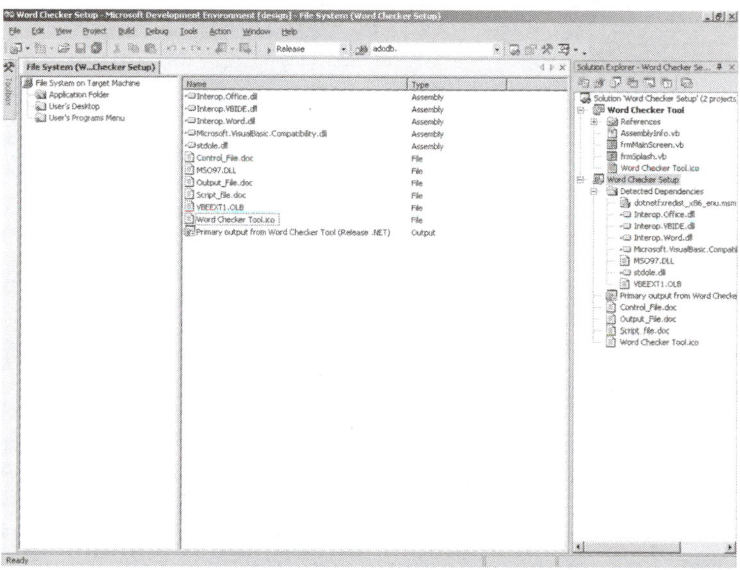

FIGURE 25-7 *All the files required by the Word Checker tool application*

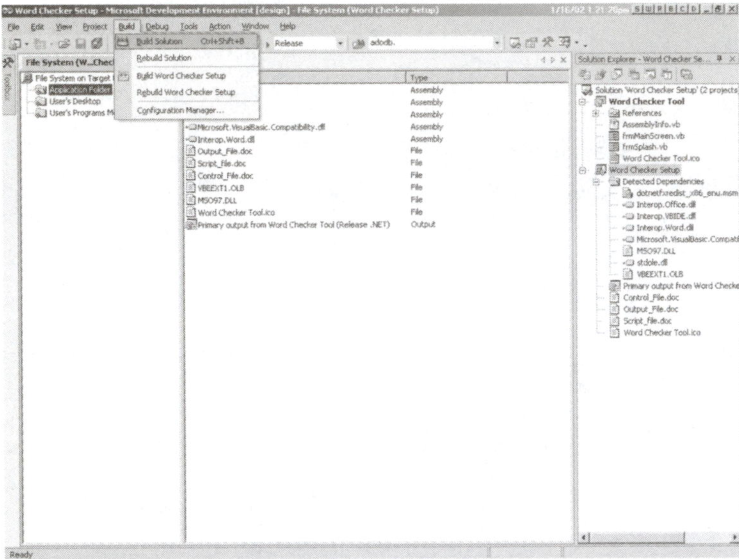

FIGURE 25-8 *The Build Solution option is used to build the Word Checker tool.*

The following setup files are included by the Word Checker tool application:

- Control_File.doc
- Output_File.doc
- Word Checker Tool.exe
- Word Checker Tool.ico
- Script_File.doc

After the setup is complete, the tool can be run directly by selecting the Word Checker tool icon on the Programs menu.

Summary

In this chapter, you learned to execute and run the Word Checker tool by using the .exe file. You also learned about the procedure for converting the application into an .exe file and then distributing the application to run automatically on the document file.

PART VI

Professional Project 4

Project 4

Creating the Easy Selling Application

Project 4 Overview

The Easy Selling application can be used by salespeople to record the details of their clients. This application can be effectively used by salespeople to create proposals, presentations, and reports.

The application has the following functionalities:

- The application stores all client-specific details in a database.
- The application helps generate a proposal in Word for the client.
- The application generates an Excel report.
- The application generates a presentation in PowerPoint for management review with the client.

The Easy Selling application has been built using Visual Basic .NET. You will learn to work with Excel and PowerPoint objects in this application. In addition, the following concepts have been used to code this application:

- Working with Windows Forms in .NET
- Working with controls in .NET and creating and changing properties
- Working with the List view control and its methods
- Working with MDI Forms in .NET
- Details of how to create parent and child forms
- Concept of shared members, properties, and methods
- Working with data types and defining variables and type conversions
- Creating functions and procedures
- Error trapping
- Working with AxBrowser control to show HTML help files
- Data Access through OleDB by using `OleDbConnection`, `OleDbCommand`, and `OleDbDataReader`

- Data Access through ADO Method using `ADODB.Connection` and `ADODB.Recordset`
- Basic concepts of SQL, such as how to read data, update data, delete data, and add data through Structured Query Language
- Methods used to create a Word Application instance and create and manipulate the Word document
- Methods used to create an Excel Application instance and create and manipulate the Excel spreadsheet
- Methods used to create a PowerPoint Application instance and create and manipulate the PowerPoint presentation

Chapter 26

Project Case Study: Perfect Stationery Inc.

Perfect Stationery Inc. is a well-known company that sells stationery to corporate clients. The company is a $200M company with its headquarters in Washington state and operates from six offices in the United States. The company buys high-quality stationery supplies such as computer paper, copy paper, gel ink pens, highlighters, Scotch tape, and Glue Stic from manufacturers and sells them to different organizations.

The company has an experienced staff of salespeople who have the responsibility of meeting prospective clients and getting orders for the company. The salespeople meet these clients and identify details such as the company's profile, need, problems encountered, and other competition-related details. The salesperson records these details, and, based on the input from the client, a proposal is created. If the proposal is accepted, a contract is signed between Perfect Stationery Inc. and the client.

As part of this activity, the salesperson is sometimes required to convince the client to buy by giving him a comparison with the competitor's product. The senior management also gives presentations to corporate clients based on their needs and the products that Perfect Stationery Inc. offers.

The salespeople are responsible for all of the following tasks:

- Meeting the customer
- Identifying details
- Preparing a proposal for the client in Word
- Preparing an Excel sheet to give a comparison of the products with the competitor
- Preparing a PowerPoint presentation for the client

All these tasks are handled individually and take a lot of time and effort.

The company has decided to automate the above-mentioned tasks by creating an application that can be used by the salesperson. The application will perform the following tasks:

- Store all client-specific details in a database.
- Generate a proposal in Word based on the client and product details.
- Generate an Excel sheet for the comparative analysis with the competitor.
- Generate a presentation in PowerPoint for the senior management.

The company appointed a five-member team to the project. The team named the project "Easy Selling." The team decided on the following phases of the DLC:

1. Requirements analysis
2. Design
3. Coding
4. Testing
5. Executing and distributing the application

The various phases of the DLC are discussed in the next section.

Requirements Analysis

Requirements analysis is the first phase of the DLC. In this phase, the requirements for the application are gathered. The requirements of the Easy Selling application as identified by the development team are as follows:

- The application will consist of user input screens to store details related to the following:
  - Client-specific details
  - Product-specific details
  - Salesperson-related details
  - Client problem- or issue-related details
  - Solutions offered by Perfect Stationery Inc. in response to the client's issues
  - Type of output to be generated, such as a proposal, Excel sheet, or a presentation
- The application will make use of a database to store the details of multiple clients.
- The application will allow the salesperson to add, modify, and delete client details using forms.
- When adding, modifying, or deleting data in forms, validations will ensure that correct data is entered in the database.
- The application will be able to automate the process of generating a proposal in Word, an Excel sheet, or a presentation in PowerPoint depending upon the user's choice.

Design

This is the second phase of the DLC and is used to create a broad-level design for the application based on the requirements of the project, as identified in the requirements analysis phase. The team needs to design the database and the screens for the application. The following section discusses the database design for the application.

Designing the Database

The team identified that they need to create eight tables for the database. These eight tables will store the following details:

- Client expectation details
- Client contact details
- Solutions that can be offered to the client
- Product- and competitor-related details
- Database usage-related details
- Sales representative details
- Standard expectations of the client from Perfect Stationery Inc.
- Standard solutions that Perfect Stationery Inc. can offer to its clients

The next section discusses the user input screens for the application.

Designing the User-Input Screens

The team decided to have the following user-input screens for the application.

The Main Screen

This is the first screen displayed to the user when the user runs the application. A sketch of the screen is depicted in Figure 26-1.

The `Main` screen has five buttons at the left of the window: `Customers`, `Issues`, `Solutions`, `Outputs`, and `Exit`. Clicking each button displays the corresponding user-input screen to the user.

The screen also has three tabs associated with it. The three tabs are `Customers`, `About You`, and `Help`. Figure 26-1 displays the `Main` screen with its Customers tab

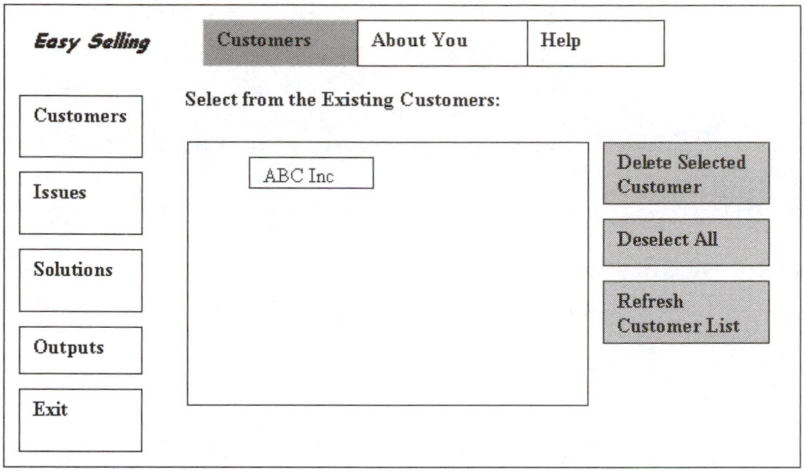

FIGURE 26-1 *The* `Main` *screen of the Easy Selling application with the* `Customers` *tab clicked*

clicked. The `Customers` page of the `Main` screen gives a listing of the existing customers. Buttons will also be provided for deleting existing customers, deselecting all the customers, and refreshing the customer list.

When the user clicks on the `About You` tab, the `About You` page is displayed. The next section discusses the `About You` page.

The About You Page of the Main Screen

The `About You` page is displayed when the user clicks on the `About You` tab of the `Main` screen. A sketch of the `About You` page is displayed in Figure 26-2.

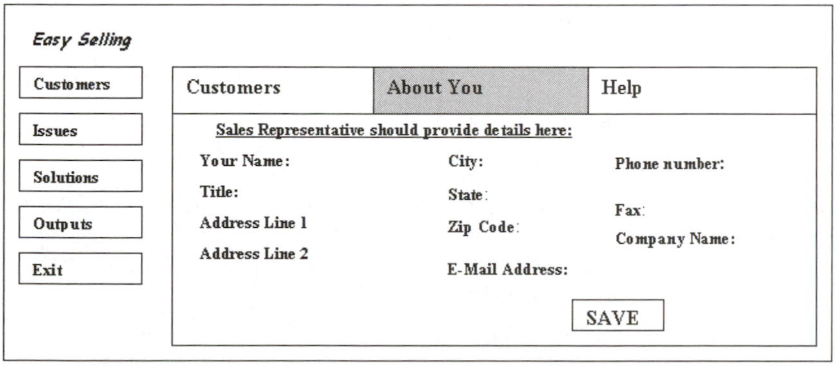

FIGURE 26-2 *The* `About You` *page of the* `Main` *screen*

The About You page is used to enter the details of the salesperson such as the name, address, title, city, state, zip code, phone number, fax, and the company name.

Clicking on the Help tab of the Main screen displays the Help page. The Help page is discussed next.

The Help Page of the Main Screen

The Help page is displayed when the user clicks on the Help tab on the Main screen. A sketch of the Help page is displayed in Figure 26-3.

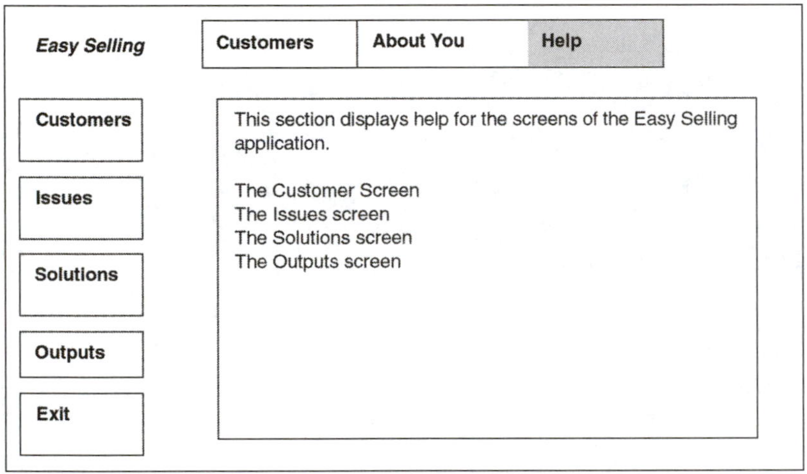

FIGURE 26-3 *The* Help *page of the* Main *screen displays help for the application.*

The Help page is used to display help for the screens used in the Easy Selling application.

The Customers Screen

This screen is displayed to the user when the user clicks on the Customers button, which is displayed at the left of the Main screen. A sketch of this screen is displayed in Figure 26-4.

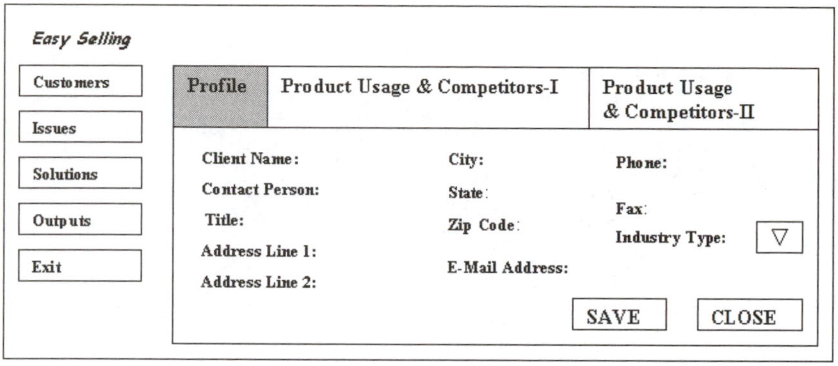

FIGURE 26-4 *The* `Profile` *page of the* `Customers` *screen*

Just as the `Main` screen, the `Customers` screen also has a set of tabs associated with it. The tabs for the `Customers` screen are `Profile`, `Product Usage & Competitors-I`, and `Product Usage & Competitors-II`. Figure 26-4 displays the `Customers` screen with its `Profile` tab clicked.

The `Profile` page is used by the salesperson to enter customer details such as the client name, contact person's name, title, address, city, state, zip code, e-mail address, phone, fax, and industry type.

The product- and competition-specific details are stored in the `Product Usage & Competitors-I` page. The next section discusses the design of this page.

The Product Usage & Competitors-I Page of the Customers Screen

This page is displayed when the user clicks on the `Product Usage & Competitors-I` tab on the `Customers` screen. A sketch of this page is displayed in Figure 26-5.

This page is used to store the product- and competition-specific details of the customer. The page contains a category for all the products of Perfect Stationery Inc. and stores the customer details for each product such as the order frequency, annual order value, and the current provider for the product.

The `Product Usage & Competitors-II` tab displays the `Product Usage & Competitors-II` page of the `Customers` screen. The design of this page is discussed in the following section.

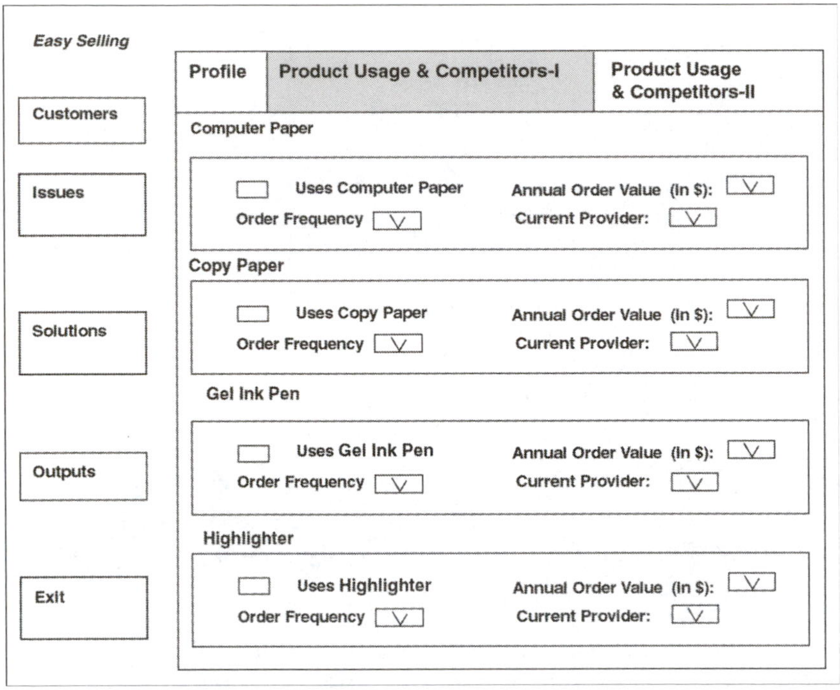

FIGURE 26-5 *The* `Product Usage & Competitors-I` *page of the* `Customers` *screen*

The Product Usage & Competitors-II Page of the Customers Screen

This screen also stores the product- and competition-specific details for the customer. A sketch of this page is displayed in Figure 26-6.

This page is displayed when the user clicks on the `Product Usage & Competitors-II` tab of the `Customers` screen. This page is used to store the product- and competition-specific details for the customer. This page also contains a note on the past experience of the client with the company's products.

The next section discusses the design of the `Issues` screen.

The Issues Screen

The `Issues` screen is displayed when the user clicks on the `Issues` button. A sketch of the `Issues` screen is displayed in Figure 26-7.

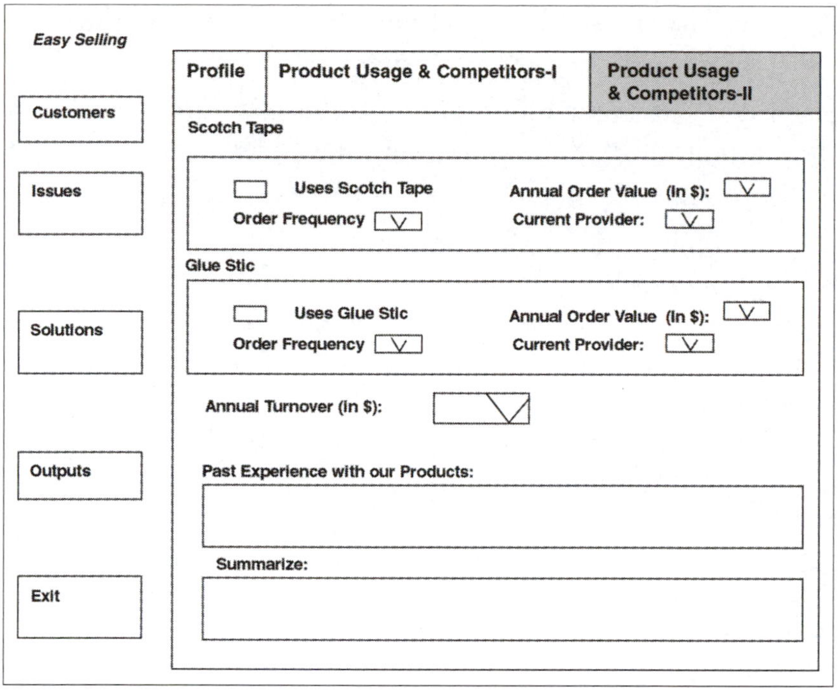

Easy Selling

Profile	Product Usage & Competitors-I	Product Usage & Competitors-II

Customers

Issues

Solutions

Outputs

Exit

Scotch Tape

Uses Scotch Tape — Annual Order Value (In $):

Order Frequency — Current Provider:

Glue Stic

Uses Glue Stic — Annual Order Value (In $):

Order Frequency — Current Provider:

Annual Turnover (In $):

Past Experience with our Products:

Summarize:

FIGURE 26-6 *The* `Product Usage & Competitors-II` *page of the* `Customers` *screen*

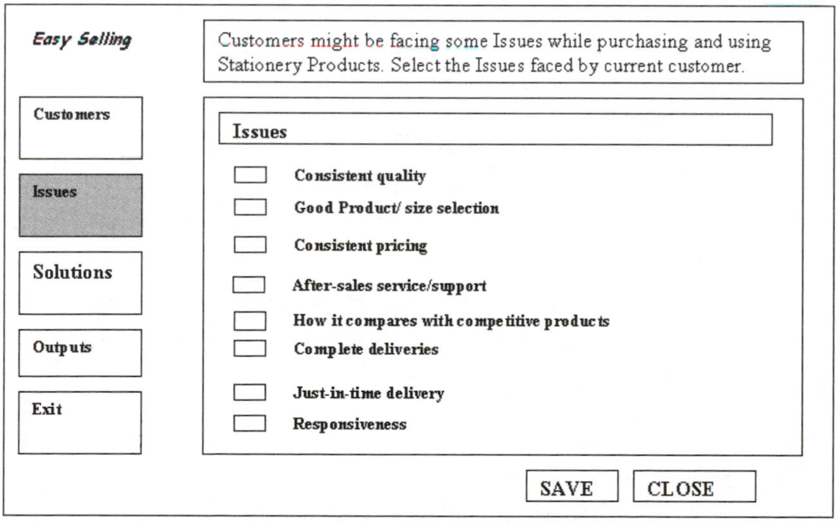

Easy Selling

Customers might be facing some Issues while purchasing and using Stationery Products. Select the Issues faced by current customer.

Customers

Issues

Solutions

Outputs

Exit

Issues

- Consistent quality
- Good Product/ size selection
- Consistent pricing
- After-sales service/support
- How it compares with competitive products
- Complete deliveries
- Just-in-time delivery
- Responsiveness

SAVE | CLOSE

FIGURE 26-7 *The* `Issues` *screen*

The salesperson uses the `Issues` screen to identify the various issues of the customer. The user can select from a list of available issues.

The application also provides a list of solutions offered by the company in response to the issues faced by the customer. The `Solutions` screen is discussed next.

The Solutions Screen

This screen is used by the salesperson to offer solutions for customer issues. The salesperson can choose from a list of solutions available. A sketch of the `Solutions` screen is displayed in Figure 26-8.

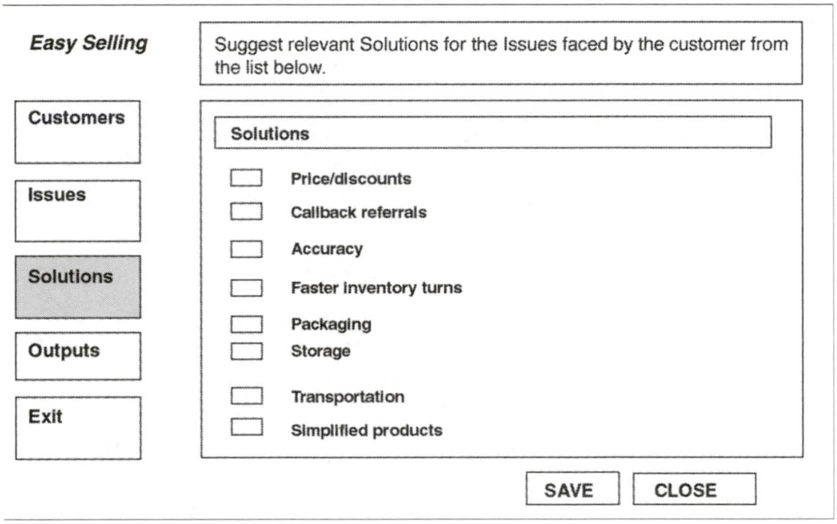

FIGURE 26-8 *The* `Solutions` *screen*

Output needs to be generated based on the details captured by the salesperson. The `Outputs` screen is used to specify the type of output to be generated: a Word proposal, an Excel sheet, or a PowerPoint presentation.

The Outputs Screen

The `Outputs` screen is displayed when the user clicks on the `Outputs` button. A sketch of the `Outputs` screen is displayed in Figure 26-9.

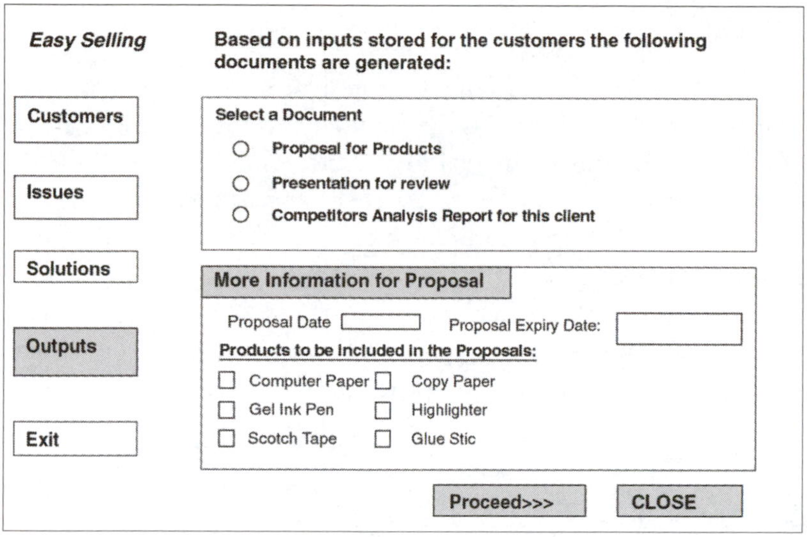

Easy Selling

Based on inputs stored for the customers the following documents are generated:

Customers
Issues
Solutions
Outputs
Exit

Select a Document

- Proposal for Products
- Presentation for review
- Competitors Analysis Report for this client

More Information for Proposal

Proposal Date Proposal Expiry Date:

Products to be Included in the Proposals:

- Computer Paper
- Copy Paper
- Gel Ink Pen
- Highlighter
- Scotch Tape
- Glue Stic

Proceed>>> CLOSE

FIGURE 26-9 *The* `Outputs` *screen*

The `Outputs` screen will be used to specify the output of the application to be generated. The output can be a proposal document, a PowerPoint presentation, or an Excel sheet.

The next section discusses the Coding phase of the application.

Coding

Coding is the third phase of the DLC for the Easy Selling application. The input for this phase is the design document, and the design is translated into code in this phase. During this phase, the development team divided the responsibilities of coding the application among the team members. Some team members were assigned the task of creating the interface and the database, and the others were assigned the task of coding the application. The database design of the application is discussed in Chapter 27, "Creating the Database."

Testing

In this phase, the application is tested. The development team decided on a *test plan outline* that consisted of details such as the requirements for the project, items to be tested, test deliverables, environmental needs, and so on. A *test specification document* was then prepared to help the testers check the application. The test specification document lists the procedures for testing the application. The testing team prepared a *test analysis report* after they tested the application. The report was submitted to the development team who then made changes to the code based upon the feedback in the report. A separate QA team was formed to ensure that the final application conformed to the defined levels of quality.

Executing and Distributing the Application

This is the final phase in the DLC of the Easy Selling application. After the tool has been successfully tested, it needs to be distributed so that all employees in the organization have access to the application. However, it is important to obtain a QA team's approval before the project is distributed. The development team of the tool has the responsibility of providing constant support to all the employees using the application in terms of installation and debugging any errors.

Summary

In this chapter, you looked at the DLC of the Easy Selling application. The phases of the DLC of the Easy Selling application were also discussed. In the next chapter, you will look at the database creation for the application.

Chapter 27

Creating the Database

In this chapter, you will create the database for the use in the Easy Selling application. You will also learn about the datatypes and fields of each table in the database.

Easy Selling Application Database

You need to create the following tables for the Easy Selling database:

- `tblClientExpectations`
- `tblClients`
- `tblClientSolutions`
- `tblInstalldecide`
- `tblProductUsageAndCompAnalysis`
- `tblSalesRep`
- `tblStandardExpectations`
- `tblStandardSolutions`

The following sections discuss each table of this database in detail.

The tblClientExpectations Table

The `tblClientExpectations` table stores the data related to client expectations. Data is inserted into this table, and the sales representatives can check for any selected data that applies to a particular client. Table 27-1 shows the structure of the `tblClientExpectations` table.

Table 27-1 tblClientExpectations

Field Name	Type	Size (in characters)	Description
`Client_ID`	Long integer	4	This field stores the ID of the client.
`Selected`	Yes/No	1	This field indicates whether the expectation mentioned in this current record is selected or NOT.
`Expectation`	Text	50	This field stores one of the client expectations.

The tblClients Table

The `tblClients` table stores the client contact details. Table 27-2 shows the structure of the `tblClients` table.

Table 27-2 tblClients

Field Name	Type	Size (in characters)	Description
`Clients_ID`	Long Integer	4	This field stores the ID of the client.
`Client_Name`	Text	50	This field stores the name of the client.
`Contact_Person`	Text	50	This field stores the name of the contact person for a particular client.
`Title`	Text	20	This field stores the title or designation that the contact person holds.
`Address_Line1`	Text	30	This field stores the first line of address of the contact person.
`Address_Line2`	Text	30	This field stores the second line of address of the contact person.
`City`	Text	25	This field stores the city of the address.
`State`	Text	20	This field stores the state name of the address.
`ZipCode`	Text	6	This field stores the zip code of the address.
`Remarks`	Text	100	This field stores any comments that the salesperson might have related to the contact person of the client.
`CellPhone-Number`	Text	20	This field stores the cell phone number of the contact person.
`PhoneNumber`	Text	15	This field stores the phone number of the contact person.
`Fax`	Text	15	This field stores the fax number of the contact person.
`EmailAddress`	Text	30	This field stores the e-mail address of the contact person.

The tblClientSolutions Table

The `tblClientSolutions` table stores the data related to solutions that are suggested for a particular client. Data is inserted into this table from the `tblStandardSolutions` table. The sales representatives can select the appropriate information that applies to a particular client. Table 27-3 shows the structure of the `tblClientSolutions` table.

Table 27-3 tblClientsSolutions

Field Name	Type	Size (in characters)	Description
`Client_ID`	Long Integer	4	This field stores the ID of the client.
`Selected`	Yes/No	1	This field indicates whether the solution mentioned in this current record is selected or NOT.
`Solution`	Text	50	This field stores one of the solutions for client expectations.

The tblInstalldecide Table

The `tblInstalldecide` table stores the database indicator showing whether the application is being run for the first time. It prompts the sales representatives to fill in more information, if required. Table 27-4 shows the structure of the `tblInstalldecide` table.

Table 27-4 tblInstalldecide

Field Name	Type	Size (in characters)	Description
`First_time`	Text	1	This parameter is set to N initially but is set to Y once the application is used. This helps the application in the initial steps.

The tblProductUsageAndCompAnalysis Table

The `tblProductUsageAndCompAnalysis` table stores the data related to all other products and competitors of a particular product. Table 27-5 shows the structure of the `tblProductUsageAndCompAnalysis` table.

Table 27-5 tblProductUsageAndCompAnalysis

Field Name	Type	Size (in characters)	Description
`Client_ID`	Long Integer	4	This field stores the ID of the client.
`Type_Of_Industry`	Text	15	This field stores the type of the industry.
`Is_Computer-Paper_Used`	Yes/No	1	This field stores whether the client is using Computer Paper. All the `Is` type of fields represent the same information for respective products.
`ComPaper-OrdFreq`	Text	15	This field stores the frequency at which the client is ordering Computer Paper. All the `OrdFreq` type of fields represent the same information for respective products.
`ComPaper-OrdValue`	Number	18	This field stores the annual order value in dollars for Computer Paper. All the `OrdValue` type of fields represent the same information for respective products.
`ComPaper-CurrProvider`	Text	30	This field stores the name of the current provider of Computer Paper for the client. All the `CurrProvider` type of fields represent the same information for respective products.
`Is_Copy-Paper_Used`	Yes/No	1	This field stores whether the client uses Copy Paper.
`CopyPaper-OrdFreq`	Text	15	This field stores the frequency at which the client orders Copy Paper.
`CopyPaper-OrdValue`	Currency	8	This field stores the annual order value in dollars for Copy Paper.

continues

Table 27-5 continued

Field Name	Type	Size (in characters)	Description
`CopyPaper-CurrProvider`	Text	30	This field stores the name of the current provider of Copy Paper for the client.
`Is_GelInk-Pen_Used`	Yes/No	1	This field stores whether the client uses Gel Ink Pens.
`GelInkPen-OrdFreq`	Text	15	This field stores the frequency at which the client orders Gel Ink Pens.
`GelInkPen-OrdValue`	Currency	8	This field stores the annual order value in dollars for Gel Ink Pens.
`GelInkPenCurr-Provider`	Text	30	This field stores the name of the current provider of Gel Ink Pens for the client.
`Is_High-Lighter_Used`	Yes/No	1	This field stores whether the client uses Highlighters.
`HighLighter-OrdFreq`	Text	15	This field stores the frequency at which the client orders Highlighters.
`HighLighter-OrdValue`	Currency	8	This field stores the annual order value in dollars for Highlighters.
`HighLighter-CurrProvider`	Text	30	This field stores the name of the current provider of Highlighters for the client.
`Is_Scotch-Tape_Used`	Yes/No	1	This field stores whether the client uses Scotch Tape.
`ScotchTape-OrdFreq`	Text	15	This field stores the frequency at which the client orders Scotch Tape.
`ScotchTape-OrdValue`	Currency	8	This field stores the annual order value in dollars for Scotch Tape.
`ScotchTape-CurrProvider`	Text	30	This field stores the name of the current provider of Scotch Tape for the client.
`Is_Glue-Stics_Used`	Yes/No	1	This field stores whether the client uses Glue Stic.
`GlueSticsOrdFreq`	Text	15	This field stores the frequency at which the client orders Glue Stic.

Field Name	Type	Size (in characters)	Description
GlueStics-OrdValue	Currency	8	This field stores the annual order value in dollars for Glue Stic.
GlueStics-CurrProvider	Text	30	This field stores the name of the current provider of Glue Stic for the client.
General_Comments	Text	100	This field provides some extra information that client might provide, for example, information on some products they are using or planning to use.
UsedOur-ProductsBefore	Text	100	This field is used to store information on past experiences of the client with Perfect Stationery, if any.
AnnualTurnOver	Currency	8	This field stores the annual turnover figure of the client.

The tblSalesRep Table

The `tblSalesRep` table stores the data related to sales representatives who use the application. Table 27-6 shows the structure of the `tblSalesRep` table.

Table 27-6 tblSalesRep

Field Name	Type	Size (in characters)	Description
SalesRep_id	Long Integer	4	This field stores the ID of the sales representative.
SalesRep_Name	Text	30	This field stores the name of the sales representative using the application.
SalesRep_Title	Text	20	This field stores the title or designation that the sales representative holds.
Address_Line1	Text	30	This field stores the first line of address of the sales representative.
Address_Line2	Text	30	This field stores the second line of address of the sales representative.

continues

Table 27-6 continued

Field Name	Type	Size (in characters)	Description
`City`	Text	25	This field stores the city name that is a part of address.
`State`	Text	20	This field stores the state name that is a part of address.
`ZipCode`	Text	6	This field stores the zip code that is a part of address.
`PhoneNumber`	Text	20	This field stores the phone number of the sales personnel.
`CellPhoneNumber`	Text	20	This field stores the cell phone number of the sales representative.
`Fax`	Text	15	This field stores the fax number of the sales representative.
`EmailAddress`	Text	30	This field stores the email address of the sales representative.
`CompanyName`	Text	30	This field stores the name of the company; in this case it will be Perfect Stationery or the complete name.

The tblStandardExpectations Table

The `tblStandardExpectations` table stores the data related to all standard expectations that the client has from the products and services offered by Perfect Stationery Inc. The company defines these expectations and adds to it, if required. Table 27-7 shows the structure of the `tblStandardExpectations` table.

Table 27-7 tblStandardExpectations

Field Name	Type	Size (in characters)	Description
`Expectations`	Text	50	This field stores he standard client expectations maintained in the database.

The tblStandardSolutions Table

The `tblStandardSolutions` table stores the data related to all standard solutions that Perfect Stationery Inc. could offer to the client, based on their expectations. The company predefines these expectations; records can be added, if required. Table 27-8 shows the structure of the `tblStandardSolutions` table.

Table 27-8 tblStandardSolutions

Field Name	Type	Size (in characters)	Description
`Solutions`	Text	50	This field stores one of the standard solutions of client expectations maintained in the database.

Summary

In this chapter, you learned about the database used in the Easy Selling application. You also learned about the data types, fields, and descriptions of each table in the database.

Chapter 28

Designing the Forms of the Application

In the previous chapter, you created the database for the Easy Selling application. In this chapter, you will create the user-input forms of the application in VB.NET.

Creating the Forms

You need to create the following forms for the Easy Selling application:

- The `MainMDI` form
- The `StartApplication` form
- The `ClientInfo` form
- The `ClientIssues` form
- The `ClientSolutions` form
- The `ClientDocuments` form

Each of these forms is discussed in the following sections.

The MainMDI Form

All the forms of the application have a set of buttons at the left of each window. These buttons are `Customers`, `Issues`, `Solutions`, `Outputs`, and `Exit`. Therefore, a main form that contains these five buttons is created. At the time of execution, every form is integrated with this main form and is then displayed to the user. Create the main form in VB.NET as displayed in Figure 28-1.

The form displayed in Figure 28-1 is named as the `MainMDI` form. This form consists of six `PictureBox` controls. The six controls are `PictureBox1` for the `EasySelling` button, `PictureBox2` for the `Customers` button, `PictureBox3` for the `Issues` button, `PictureBox4` for the `Solutions` button, `PictureBox5` for the `Outputs` button, and `PictureBox6 for` the `Exit` button. This form is integrated with all the other forms of the application at run-time to display the buttons on each form. You will attach functionality to these buttons while coding the application.

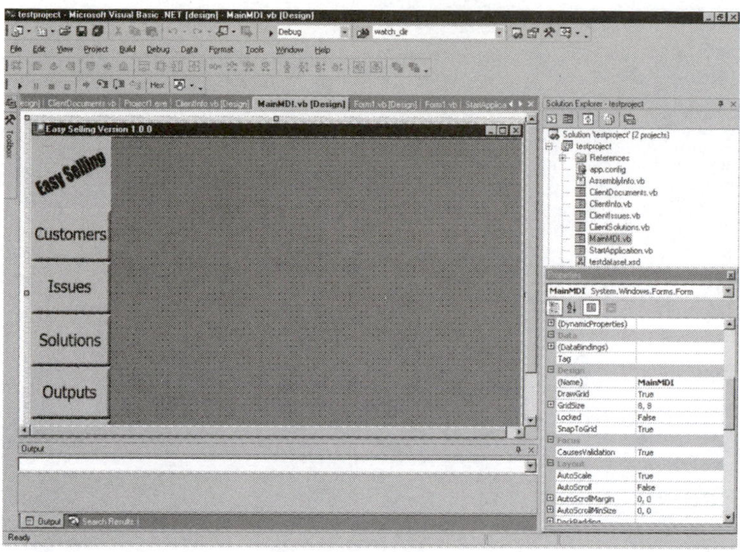

FIGURE 28-1 *The* `MainMDI` *form of the Easy Selling application*

The StartApplication Form

The `StartApplication` form is used to display the `Main` screen, which is the start screen of the application, to the user. The form is integrated with the `MainMDI` form at run-time and then displayed to the user. This form consists of three tabs: `Customers`, `About You`, and `Help`. The `Customers` page of the `StartApplication` form is displayed in Figure 28-2.

This page consists of five controls: a `Label` control, a `ListBox` control, and three `CommandButton` controls. The `Label` control is used to display static text at the top of the `ListBox` control. The `ListBox` control is used to display a list of existing customers to the user. The list of customers is picked from the database when the form is loaded and will be displayed to the user.

The page consists of three buttons at the right of the screen. The `Delete Selected Customer` button is used to delete an existing customer. The user will need to select a customer from the list and then click on this button. The corresponding record for the customer will then be removed from the database. The `Deselect All` button is used to deselect all the selected customers. The `Refresh Customer List` button is used to refresh the customer name list. Once a new customer is added, the user will be able to view the name of the newly added customer in the list by clicking on this button.

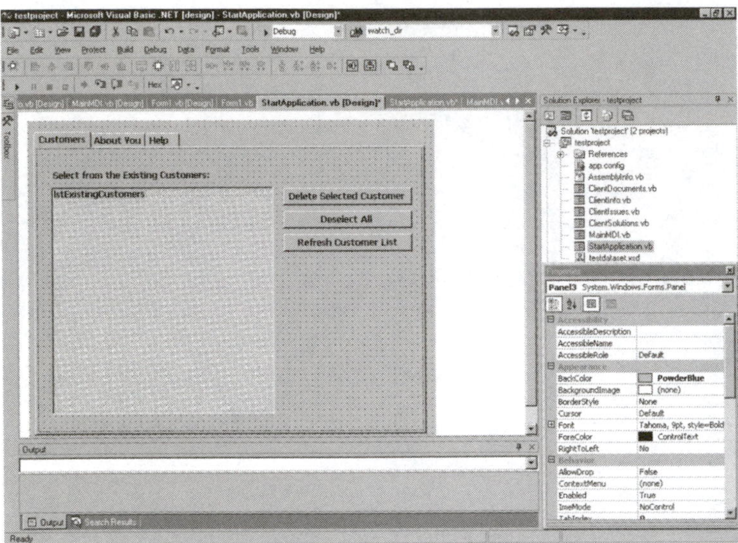

FIGURE 28-2 *The* `Customers` *page of the* `StartApplication` *form*

NOTE

The functionality will be added to the buttons while coding the application, which you will learn in the next few chapters of the project.

Next, you create the `About You` page of the `StartApplication` form.

The About You Page of the StartApplication Form

This page is displayed when the user clicks on the `About You` tab. The page is displayed in Figure 28-3.

This page is used to capture the details of the salesperson using this application. These details are required to generate the output documents.

The page consists of `Label` controls, `TextBox` controls, and a `CommandButton` control. Next you create the `Help` page.

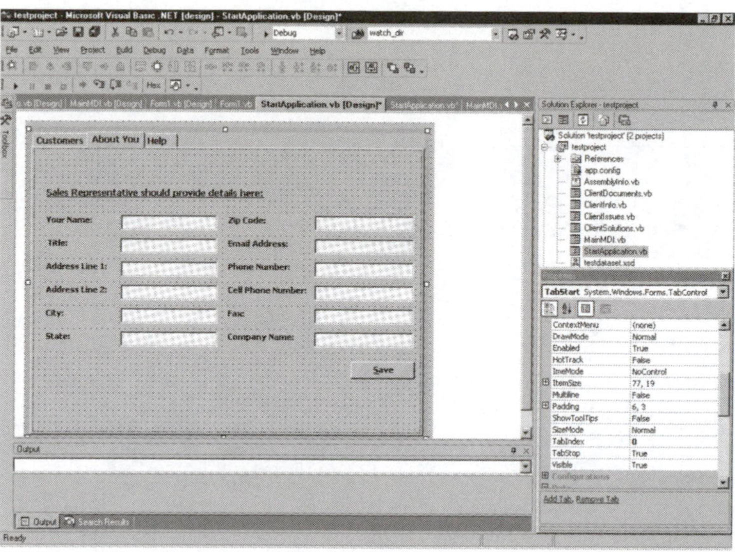

FIGURE 28-3 *The* `About You` *page of the* `StartApplication` *form*

The Help Page of the StartApplication Form

This page is displayed when the user clicks on the `Help` tab on the `StartApplication` form. The page is displayed in Figure 28-4.

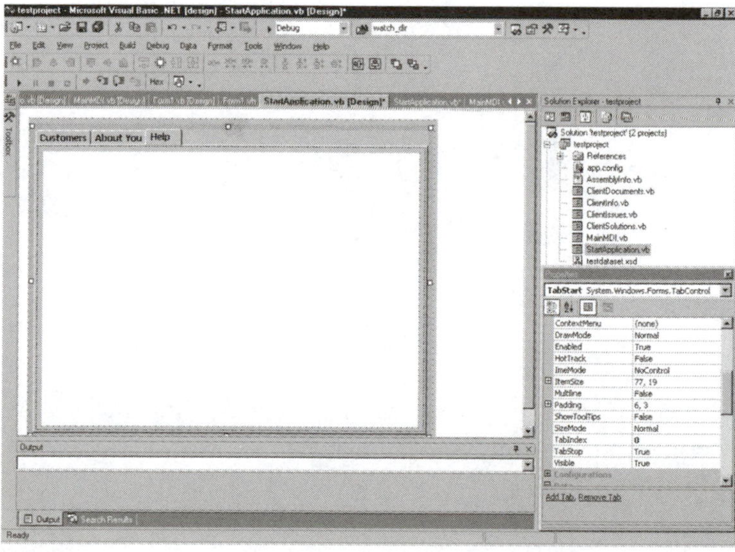

FIGURE 28-4 *The* `Help` *page of the* `StartApplication` *form*

The `Help` page is used to display an HTML file in the Web browser. The file gets picked up at run-time.

NOTE

The HTML file will be created later while coding the application.

You have created the `StartApplication` form of the application in this section. In the next section, you create the `ClientInfo` form.

The ClientInfo Form

The salesperson uses this form to capture the client and product details. As stated earlier, this form will also be integrated with the `MainMDI` form at the time of execution. This form consists of three tabs: `Profile`, `Product Usage and Competitors - I`, and `Product Usage and Competitors - II`. The `Profile` page of the `ClientInfo` form is displayed in Figure 28-5.

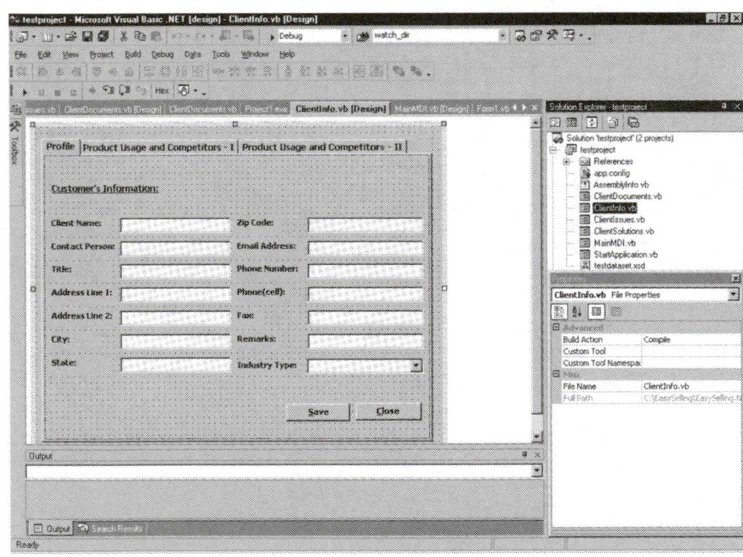

FIGURE 28-5 *The* `Profile` *page of the* `ClientInfo` *form*

This page consists of `Label` controls, `TextBox` controls, and `CommandButton` controls and is used to capture client details.

The `Product Usage and Competitors - I` page is discussed next.

The Product Usage and Competitors – I Page of the ClientInfo Form

This page is displayed when the user clicks on the `Product Usage and Competitors - I` tab. It would be used to capture product- and competitor-related information from the client. The page is displayed in Figure 28-6.

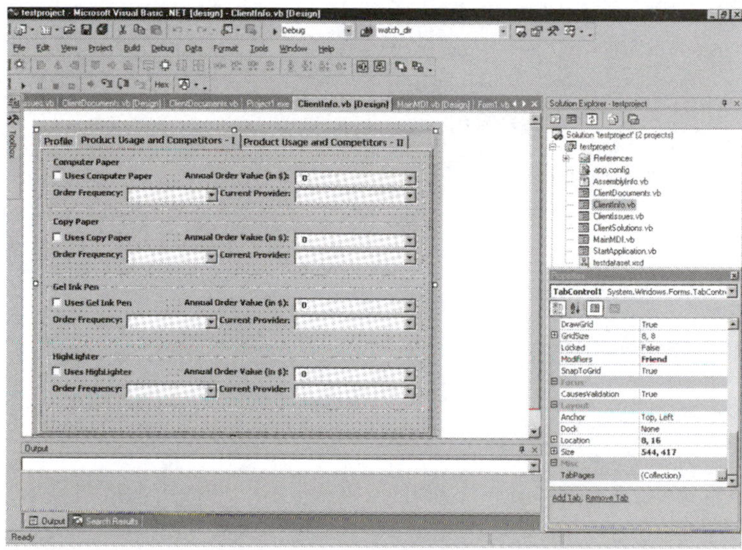

FIGURE 28-6 *The* `Product Usage and Competitors - I` *page of the* `ClientInfo` *form*

The page consists of the various product options that Perfect Stationery Inc. offers to its clients. The salesperson captures the order frequency, the annual order value, and the name of the current provider of the client for each product by using this form. The information entered in the page is then stored in the database. The page consists of the following controls: `Label`, `ComboBox`, `CheckBox`, and `Frame`. The salesperson can select a value from the available options in the combo box. There is another page related to product and competition details, which is discussed next.

The Product Usage and Competitors – II Page of the ClientInfo Form

This page is a continuation of the `Product Usage and Competitors - I` page. It is displayed when the user clicks on the `Product Usage and Competitors - II` tab. The page is displayed in Figure 28-7.

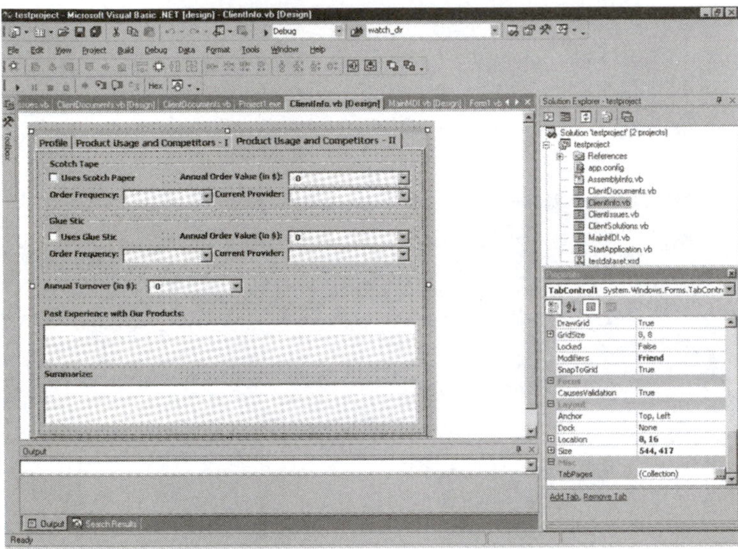

FIGURE 28-7 *The* `Product Usage and Competitors – II` *page of the* `ClientInfo` *form*

This page is also used for entering product- and competitor-related details. The user selects the values from the options available in the combo box. The salesperson also records any other feedback from the client based on the past experience with the company and prepares a summary. This page consists of various controls such as `Label`, `CheckBox`, `ComboBox`, and `Frame`.

The next section discusses the `ClientIssues` form.

The ClientIssues Form

This form is displayed when the user clicks on the `Issues` button of the `MainMDI` form. The `ClientIssues` form is used to display a list of issues that a customer might have, and the salesperson is able to choose from the available options based on the conversation with the client. The `ClientIssues` form is displayed in Figure 28-8.

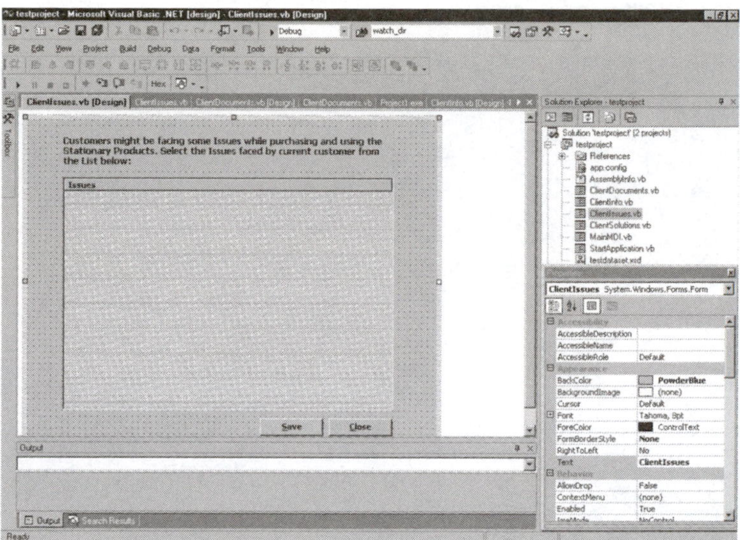

FIGURE 28-8 *The* `ClientIssues` *form*

As with all forms, this form is also integrated with the `MainMDI` form at run-time. The form displays check boxes with a list of issues against them. You will add the check boxes and the issues while coding the application. The salesperson can then select from these issues depending upon the client. Once the salesperson has chosen the issues, they are stored in the database.

Based on the issues, the salesperson suggests solutions, which are captured using the `ClientSolutions` form, to the client. The `ClientSolutions` form is created next.

The ClientSolutions Form

This form is displayed when the user clicks on the `Solutions` button of the `MainMDI` form. The `ClientSolutions` form is displayed in Figure 28-9.

This form is used to display a list of solutions to the client based on their issues. The list of solutions to be displayed is picked up from the database.

The form displays check boxes with a list of solutions against them. The user can choose from the available options.

The form is integrated with the `MainMDI` form at run-time.

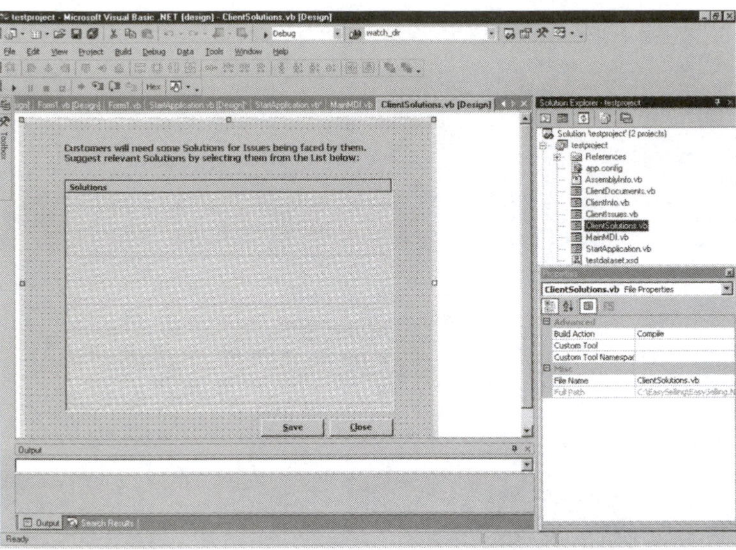

FIGURE 28-9 *The* `ClientSolutions` *form*

The ClientDocuments Form

This form is displayed when the user clicks on the `Outputs` button of the `MainMDI` form. The form is displayed in Figure 28-10.

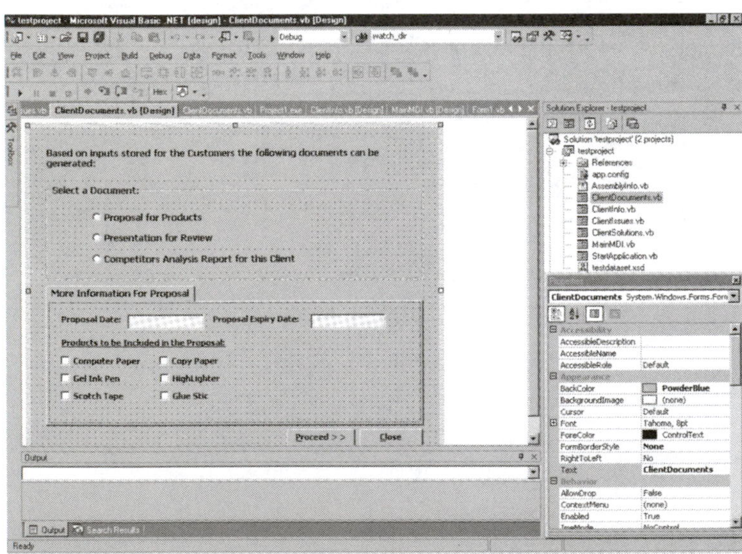

FIGURE 28-10 *The* `ClientDocuments` *form*

This screen is used to specify the type of output to be generated. The type of output could be a Word proposal, an Excel sheet, or a PowerPoint presentation. If the user opts for a Word proposal, additional information such as the products to be included in the proposal is captured using this form.

Summary

In this chapter, you created the user forms of the Easy Selling application. You also looked at the controls and functionality of each form. In the next chapter, you will learn about VBA Excel and PowerPoint objects. You will use the knowledge of Excel and PowerPoint objects while coding the application.

Chapter 29

Working with Excel Objects

In this chapter, you will learn about working with the key objects of the Excel object model. You will also learn to work with the properties, methods, and events of the Application, Workbook, Worksheet, and Range objects.

The VBA Objects for Excel

The discussion begins with the objects that VBA provides for accessing and manipulating workbooks and worksheets in Excel. There are four objects that you can use:

- The Application object
- The Workbook object
- The Worksheet object
- The Range object

The following sections discuss each of these objects in detail.

Using the Application Object of Excel

An Application object is common to all the programs. It acts as a container for all the program objects, because it refers to the application as a whole. The Application object provides many properties and methods that are accessible to all the programs. The functions, properties, and methods of the Application object are discussed next.

Functions of the Application Object

VBA provides various Excel-specific worksheet-related functions. These functions can be accessed through a property of the Application object called WorksheetFunctions. Some of these functions are as follows:

- Average()
- Ceiling()
- IsError()
- Replace()
- Sum()

- `Max()`
- `Min()`
- `Radian()`
- `Round()`
- `Count()`
- `Rate()`
- `Sum()`
- `Replace()`

Each of these functions works in the same manner as they work in a worksheet. For example, consider the following statement.

```
Totalsales=Application.WorksheetFunctions.Sum(Range("Sales"))
```

This statement uses the `Sum()` function of the `WorksheetFunctions` property. It calculates the sum of the values in the `Sales` range and stores the result in a variable called `TotalSales`.

Properties of the Application Object

The `Application` object has dozens of properties that affect the Excel environment in one way or another. Some of these properties are discussed next.

Application.CalculationVersion

This property returns a number of the form `ECCCC`. Here, `E` is the Excel version number. The Excel version number is 9 for Excel 2000 and 0 for all prior versions. `CCCC` is the version number of the Excel calculation engine. `CCCC` has the value 0000 for the versions prior to 2000.

Application.Caller

This property is used to identify the caller of the current procedure. It is normally used to identify the cell that invoked the function. The statement to identify the address of the caller cell is as follows:

```
Application.Caller.Address
```

Application.CanPlaySounds

This property can be used to identify whether the system can play sounds. You cannot modify this property. The property returns `True` if the system can play sounds.

Application.CanRecordSounds

This property can be used to identify whether the system can record sounds. You cannot modify this property. The property returns `True` if the system can record sounds.

Application.CutCopyMode

This property can be used to set the `Cut` or `Copy` mode of Excel. While working with Excel worksheets, you might have noticed that when you copy and paste a range of cells, the moving borders remain visible even after you have pasted the cells. In addition, the message `"Select destination and press Enter or select Paste"` is displayed on the status bar. You can hide the moving border and the message on the status bar by using the following statement:

```
Application.CutCopyMode=False
```

Application.EnableEvents

This property enables you to turn the events on or off. You can turn off the events by using the following statement:

```
Application.EnableEvents = False
```

Application.MemoryFree

This property returns the available memory, in bytes, that Excel can use. The following is an example of this property:

```
FrMemory= Application.MemoryFree
```

Application.OperatingSystem

This property is used to identify the name and version of the operating system. This is useful in situations where you want to perform some OS-specific tasks.

Methods of the Application Object

The `Application` object provides many methods that you can use to perform actions in an Excel environment. Some of the common methods are discussed next.

The Calculate Method

This method calculates all those formulas whose cell precedents have changed. You do not need to specify the `Application` object before the `Calculate` method declaration. The following is an example that uses the `Calculate` method:

```
Sub Calc1()
    Range("E9").Select
    ActiveCell.FormulaR1C1 = "=SUM(R[-6]C:R[-4]C)"
    Calculate
End Sub
```

The Application.CalculateFull Method

This method recalculates every formula in all the open workbooks. The recalculation is performed irrespective of whether the cell precedents have changed or not. The following is an example of the `Application.CalculateFull` method:

```
Sub Calc1()
    Range("E9").Select
    ActiveCell.FormulaR1C1 = "=SUM(R[-6]C:R[-4]C)"
    Application.CalculateFull
End Sub
```

The Application.DoubleClick Method

This method opens the current cell for editing if in-cell editing is activated. Otherwise, the comment of the cell, if any, is opened for editing. This method simulates a double-click in a cell within a worksheet. The following is an example of the `Application.DoubleClick` method:

```
Sub Calc1()
    Range("E10").Select
    Application.DoubleClick
End Sub
```

The Evaluate Method

This method converts an Excel object into a string. The syntax for using this method is as follows:

```
Evaluate(<name>)
```

In this code, `<name>` is a cell address, a range, or a defined name.

The Application.Quit Method

This method closes the open workbooks. If there is any unsaved data, Excel prompts you to save the data. You can suppress the message displayed by Excel by setting the `DisplayAlerts` property to `False`.

The Application.SaveWorkspace Method

This method saves the current workspace. The syntax to use the method is as follows:

```
Application.SaveWorkspace(<Filename>)
```

In this syntax, `<Filename>` is the name of the file in which the workspace will be saved.

The Application.Volatile Method

This method, if inserted in a user-defined function, prompts Excel to recalculate the function every time the worksheet is calculated. If you do not declare this method inside a user-defined function, Excel recalculates the function only when the input cells, which are passed as arguments to the function, change.

The Application.Wait Method

This method is used to pause a macro for a specified time duration. The syntax to use this method is as follows:

```
Application.Wait (<Time>)
```

In this syntax, `<time>` is the duration for which you want to pause the macro. Here is an example that stops a macro for a minute:

```
Application.Wait Now + TimeValue("00:01:00")
```

Event-Related Methods

The `Application` object contains some methods to handle events such as the press of a key on the keyboard. Some of these methods are

- `OnKey`
- `OnTime`
- `OnRepeat`
- `OnUndo`

The OnKey Method

The `OnKey` method of the `Application` object enables you to specify the procedures to be executed on the press of a specific key or a combination of keys. The syntax of the `OnKey` method is as follows:

```
Application.OnKey(<keys>, <procedure>)
```

Here, `<keys>` is the key or key combination that will invoke the procedure, `<procedure>`. The values that you can specify for the `<keys>` parameter are listed in Table 29-1.

Table 29-1 The <Keys> Parameter Values

Key	String to Be Used
Backspace	"{BACKSPACE}" or "{BS}"
Break	"{BREAK}"
Caps Lock	"{CAPSLOCK}"
Delete	"{DELETE}" or "{DEL}"
Down arrow	"{DOWN}"
End	"{END}"
Enter (keypad)	"{ENTER}"
Enter	"~"
Esc	"{ESCAPE}" or "{ESC}"
Help	"{HELP}"
Home	"{HOME}"
Insert	"{INSERT}"

continues

Table 29-1 continued

Key	String to Be Used
Left arrow	"{LEFT}"
Num lock	"{NUMLOCK}"
Page down	"{PGDN}"
Page up	"{PGUP}"
Right arrow	"{RIGHT}"
Scroll lock	"{SCROLLLOCK}"
Tab	"{TAB}"
Up arrow	"{UP}"
F1 – F12 Keys	"{F1}" – "{F12}"
You can also combine keys with the `Alt`, `Ctrl`, and `Shift` keys. The symbols that you use for these keys are:	
Alt	%
Ctrl	^
Shift	+

The OnTime Method

The `OnTime` method is used to run a specified procedure at a particular time. The syntax for the method is as follows:

```
Application.OnTime(<time>, <procedure>, <end_time>, <true/false>)
```

Following is an explanation of the arguments of the `OnTime` method:

- The `<time>` argument represents the date and time when the `<procedure>` would run.
- The `<procedure>` argument is the name of the procedure that will be executed at the specified time, `<time>`.
- If Excel is not in the ready mode, `<end_time>` is the date and time when VBA tries to run the procedure. If the `<end_time>` argument is omitted, VBA keeps trying to run the procedure until Excel is ready.

- The <true/false> value identifies whether the procedure will run at the specified <time>. If <true/false> is omitted or if it is True, the procedure runs at the specified time, <time>. If <true/false> is False, the previous OnTime setting is canceled.

Following is as example of the OnTime method:

```
Application.OnTime(TimeValue("12:00PM"),"RunAt12")
```

In this example, the RunAt12 procedure will be executed at 12:00 PM.

The OnRepeat Method

The OnRepeat method is used to specify the procedure that should run when the user selects the Repeat command from the Edit menu. The method also customizes the name of the Repeat menu item in the Edit menu. The syntax of the method is as follows:

```
Application.OnRepeat(<menu_text>, <procedure>)
```

In this syntax, <menu_text> is the newly defined name of the Repeat menu item. The <procedure> argument specifies the procedure that runs when Repeat is selected from the Edit menu.

The OnUndo Method

The OnUndo method is used to specify the procedure that should run when the user selects the Undo command from the Edit menu. The method also customizes the name of the Undo menu item in the Edit menu. The syntax of the OnUndo method is as follows:

```
Application.OnUndo(<menu_text>, <procedure>)
```

In this syntax, <menu_text> is the newly defined name of the Undo menu item. The <procedure> argument specifies the procedure that runs when Undo is selected from the Edit menu.

Using the Workbook Object

VBA enables you to `create`, `open`, `save`, `close`, and `delete` workbooks. You can perform all these activities by using the `Workbook` object. The `Workbook` object appears below the `Application` object in the objects hierarchy in VBA.

Declaring a Workbook Object

You need to specify the workbook upon which you want to perform some action. For example, to open a workbook, you need to declare a `Workbook` object in VBA that contains a reference to the workbook. There are three ways in which you can declare a `Workbook` object:

- Using the `Workbooks` object
- Using the `ActiveWorkbook` object
- Using the `ThisWorkbook` object

Using the Workbooks Object

The `Workbooks` object represents all the workbooks that are currently open. You can specify a particular workbook either by using the index number of the workbook or by using the name of the workbook. For example, consider the following `Workbooks` objects:

```
Workbooks(4)
Workbooks("MyWorkBook.xls")
```

Using the ActiveWorkbook Object

The `ActiveWorkbook` object represents the currently active workbook. For example, the following statement will close the currently active workbook:

```
ActiveWorkbook.Close
```

Using the ThisWorkbook Object

The `ThisWorkbook` object represents the workbook in which the VBA procedure is being executed. This object is used when a procedure deals with several workbooks at a time. Consider the following statement:

ThisWorkbook.close

This statement will close the workbook that contains the procedure in which the statement is written.

Opening a Workbook

To open a workbook, you need to use the `Open` method of the `Workbooks` collection. The syntax of the `Open` method is as follows:

```
Workbooks.Open(<filename>, [<update_links>], [<readOnly>], [<format>], [<password>],
[<writeResPassword>], [<IgnoreReadOnlyRecommended>], [<Origin>], [<Delimiter>],
[<Editable>], [<Notify>], [<converter>], [<AddToMru>])
```

Notice that in this syntax, all the other parameters except `<filename>` are optional. For example, the following statement will open a workbook:

```
Workbooks.Open("MyWorkbook.xls")
```

Creating a New Workbook

To create a new workbook, use the `Add` method of the `Workbooks` collection. The syntax to use the `Add` method is as follows:

```
Workbooks.Add([<templates>])
```

Here, `<templates>` is an optional argument used to specify the template of the workbook. The value of `<templates>` determines the format of the workbook that will be created. `<templates>` can take one of the following constant values:

- `xlWBATWorksheet`. This constant creates a workbook with a single worksheet.
- `xlWBATChart`. This constant creates a workbook with a single chart sheet.
- `xlWBATExcel4MacroSheet`. This constant creates a worksheet with a single Excel 4 macro sheet.
- `xlWBATExcel4IntMacroSheet`. This constant creates a workbook with a single Excel 4 international macro sheet.

You can also specify an Excel file name as `<templates>`. In such a situation, the file will be used as a template for the new files.

Workbook Object Properties

There are various properties associated with the `Workbook` object. Some of these properties are as follows:

- `Workbook.CalculationVersion`. This property returns a number of the form, `ECCCC`. Here, `E` is the Excel version number. The Excel version number is 9 for Excel 2000 and 0 for all prior versions. `CCCC` is the version number of the Excel calculation engine. CCCC has the value 0000 for the versions prior to 2000.
- `Workbook.FullName`. This property returns the complete path of the workbook. The path will include the file name along with the drive and folder names.
- `Workbook.Name`. This property returns the file name of the workbook.
- `Workbook.Path`. This property returns the path of the workbook file.
- `Workbook.Saved`. This property determines if there are any unsaved changes in the workbook. If there are no unsaved changes, `False` is returned.

Workbook Object Methods

You can use the `Workbook` objects to perform various activities such as saving and closing a workbook. Some of the `Workbook` object methods are as follows:

- `Workbook.Activate`. This method activates the specified workbook. For example, the following statement activates `MyWorkbook.xls`:

  ```
  Workbooks("MyWorkbook.xls").Activate
  ```
- `Workbook.AddToFavorites`. This method adds a shortcut for the specified workbook to the `Favorites` folder.
- `Workbook.close`. This method closes the specified workbook. The syntax of this method is:

  ```
  Workbook.close(<save_changes>, <filename>, <routeworkbook>)
  ```

  The `<save_changes>` argument is used to specify whether Excel should save any unsaved changes in the workbook. The `<save_changes>` argument can take the `True`, `False`, or `Omitted` value. The `<filename>` argument contains the name of the file in which the workbook will be saved. The `<routeworkbook>` argument routes the workbook. The value that can be assigned to `<routeworkbook>` is `True`, `False`, or `Omitted`.

- `Workbook.PrintOut`. This method prints the specified workbook. The syntax of the `Printout` method is:

  ```
  Workbook.PrintOut(From, To, Copies, Preview, ActivePrinter,
  PrintToFile, Collate, PrToFileName)
  ```

  The preceding statement prints `<Copies>` number of copies from the page `<From>` to the page `<To>` of the current workbook. The printer is `<ActivePrinter>`. The value, `True`, for `<Preview>` will force Excel to display a preview before printing. If `<PrintToFile>` is `True`, the workbook is printed to a file and the user will be prompted for a file name. If `<Collate>` is `True` and `<Copies>` is greater than 1, Excel collates the copies. `<PrToFileName>` is the file to which the workbook will be printed, given that the `<PrintToFile>` value is `True`.
- `Workbook.PrintPreview`. This method displays the specified workbook in the `Print Preview` window.
- `Workbook.Protect`. This method protects the specified workbook. The syntax of the `Protect` method is as follows:

  ```
  Workbook.Protect(<password>, <structure>, <windows>)
  ```

  In this syntax, `<password>` is the text that a user needs to know to access the content of the workbook. If `<structure>` is `True`, the workbook's structure is protected. If `<windows>` is `True`, the workbook's window is protected.
- `Workbook.Save`. This method saves the specified workbook.
- `Workbook.SaveAs`. This method saves the specified workbook to a different file, if the workbook is already saved in a file. The syntax of the `Workbook.SaveAs` method is as follows:

  ```
  Workbook.SaveAs(<filename>)
  ```

  The `Workbook.SaveAs` method accepts more arguments but all the other options except `<filename>` are optional. The `<filename>` option contains the full path of the file including the drive and the folder.

Workbook Object Events

The following list describes some of the events handled by the `Workbook` object:

- `Activate`. This event is fired when a workbook is activated. A workbook is activated in any of the following ways: when the user selects the workbook from the Window menu, when the workbook's `Activate` method is executed, when a user opens a workbook, or when the VBA code runs the `Workbook.Open` method. The event-handler code is written in the `Workbook_Activate` procedure. This procedure is provided by VBA, and you can access it from the procedure list of the workbook.

- `BeforeClose`. This event is fired when the user closes a workbook by selecting the Close command from the File menu or when the close method of the workbook is executed. The event-handler code is written in the `Workbook_BeforeClose` procedure. The code in the procedure is run before the workbook is closed and before the user is prompted to save changes.
- `BeforePrint`. This event is fired when the user selects the Print command from the File menu or the `PrintOut` method of the workbook is executed by VBA. The event-handler code is written in the `Workbook_BeforePrint` procedure. The code inside this procedure is executed before the workbook is printed and the Print dialog box appears.
- `BeforeSave`. This event is fired when the user selects either the Save or Save As command from the File menu. It is also fired when the `Save` and `SaveAs` methods of the workbook are called. The event-handler code is written in the `Workbook_BeforeSave` procedure.
- `Deactivate`. This event is fired when a workbook loses focus. However, it is not fired when the user switches to a different application. The code for handling the event is written in the `Workbook_Deactivate` procedure. Excel opens the other workbook before executing the event-handling code.
- `NewSheet`. This event is fired when the user creates a new sheet in a workbook either by selecting the Insert menu or by executing the `Add` method of the worksheet object. The event-handler code is written in the `Workbook_NewSheet` procedure. The code in the procedure is executed after the new sheet is inserted.
- `Open`. This event is fired when the user selects the Open command from the File menu or when the `Open` method of the workbook is executed. The event handler code is defined in the `Workbook_Open` procedure.

The Worksheet Object

The `Worksheet` object provides several properties, methods, and events. You can use these to perform activities such as adding, deleting, and copying worksheets.

Declaring the Worksheets Object

You need to specify the worksheet upon which you want to perform an action. For example, to perform a calculation on a range of cells in a particular worksheet, you need to provide a reference of the worksheet to Excel. You can specify a worksheet by using the `Worksheets` object. The `Worksheets` object is a collection of worksheets in a particular workbook. A particular worksheet can be referenced either by indicating the index number or the worksheet name. For example:

```
Workbooks (1)
Worksheets ("MySheet")
```

Creating a New Worksheet

You can use the `Add` method of the `Worksheets` object to insert a new sheet in the workbook. The syntax for the `Add` method is as follows:

```
Worksheets.Add(<before>, <after>, <count>, <type>)
```

If `<before>` is specified, the new worksheet is inserted before the `<before>` sheet. Similarly, if `<after>` is specified, the new worksheet is inserted after the `<after>` sheet. You cannot specify both `<before>` and `<after>` at the same time. The `<count>` argument is the number of worksheets to be inserted. The `<type>` argument represents the type of worksheets, which can be `xlWorksheet`, `xlExcel4MacroSheet`, or `xlExcel4IntMacroSheet`.

Properties of the Worksheet Object

The properties of the `Worksheet` object are listed in Table 29-2.

Table 29-2 Properties of the Worksheet Object

Property	Description
`Worksheet.Name`	This property is used to obtain or set the name of a worksheet. The statement to set the name of the second worksheet to `MyData` is `Worksheets(2).Name="MyData"`.
`Worksheet.ProtectContents`	This property returns `True` if the specified worksheet is protected.
`Worksheet.Protect-DrawingObjects`	This property returns `True` if the drawing objects on the specified worksheet are protected.

continues

Table 29-2 continued

Property	Description
`Worksheet.ProtectionMode`	This property returns `True` if the user-interface-only protection is activated for the specified worksheet.
`Worksheet.ProtectScenarios`	This property returns `True` if the scenarios in the specified worksheet are protected.
`Worksheet.StandardHeight`	This property returns the standard height of the rows in the specified worksheet.
`Worksheet.StandardWidth`	This property returns the standard width of the columns in the specified worksheet.
`Worksheet.UsedRange`	This property returns a range object representing the used range in the specified worksheet.
`Worksheet.Visible`	This property is used to specify the visibility setting of the worksheet. For example, to hide a worksheet, you would use the statement, `Worksheets ("Sales").Visible = False`.

Methods of the Worksheet Object

The methods of the `Worksheet` object are discussed in the following sections.

Worksheet.Activate

This method makes the specified worksheet active. For example, consider the following statement:

```
Workbooks ("AnnualSales.xls").Worksheets("August").Activate
```

This statement, when executed, will make the `August` worksheet of the `AnnualSales.xls` workbook active.

Worksheet.CheckSpelling

This method displays the Spelling dialog box to check the spelling in the specified worksheet. The syntax of the method is as follows:

```
Worksheet.CheckSpelling(<customDirectory>, <ignoreUpperCase>, <alwaysSuggest>, <language>)
```

In this syntax, `<customDirectory>` is the file name of a custom dictionary that Excel will look up in case the word is not found in the main dictionary. If `<ignoreUpperCase>` is set to `True`, the words in all uppercase are ignored. Setting `<alwaysSuggest>` to `True` enables Excel to display a list of suggested words for the misspelled words found. The `<language>` argument specifies the language of the dictionary.

Worksheet.Copy

This method copies the specified worksheet. The syntax of the `Worksheet.Copy` method is as follows:

```
Worksheet.Copy(<Before>, <After>)
```

The worksheet will be copied before the `<before>` worksheet. Otherwise, the worksheet will be copied after the `<after>` worksheet. You cannot specify both the `<before>` and `<after>` arguments together.

Worksheet.Delete

This method deletes the specified worksheet. For example, to delete the `August` worksheet, execute the following statement:

```
Worksheets("August").Delete
```

To delete the active worksheet, execute the following statement:

```
ActiveSheet.Delete
```

Worksheets.FillAcrossSheets

This method fills or formats data in a range in the specified worksheets. The syntax of the `Worksheets.FillAcrossSheets` method is as follows:

```
Worksheets.FillAcrossSheets(<range>, <type>)
```

Here, `<range>` is the range in which you need to fill data or formatting, and `<type>` is an optional argument that specifies what will be filled in the `<range>`.

Worksheet.Move

This method moves the specified worksheet. The syntax to use this method is as follows:

```
Worksheet.Move (<before>, <after>)
```

The worksheet will be moved before the `<before>` worksheet or after the `<after>` worksheet. You cannot specify both `<before>` and `<after>` at the same time. If you omit both the arguments, a new workbook is created to which the worksheet will be moved.

Worksheet.Protect

This method sets the protection for the specified worksheet. The following is the syntax to use this method:

```
Worksheet.Protect(<password>, <drawingObjects>, <contents>, <scenarios>,
<userInterfaceOnly>)
```

Here, `<password>` is the text that a user would need to supply to use the worksheet. If `<drawingObjects>`, `<contents>`, `<scenarios>`, and `<userInterfaceOnly>` are set to `True`, Excel protects the worksheet's drawing objects, cell contents, scenarios, and user interfaces, respectively.

Worksheet.SetBackgroundPicture

This method sets the background of the specified worksheet. The syntax to use this method is as follows:

```
Worksheet.SetBackgroundPicture (<image>)
```

Here, `<image>` is the name of the image that you need to set as the background. For example:

```
Worksheets(1).SetBackgroundPicture "C:\ bronze_coin.jpg"
```

This statement sets the background of the first worksheet of the workbook.

Worksheet.Unprotect

This method removes protection from the worksheet. The syntax to use the method is as follows:

```
Worksheet.Unprotect (<password>)
```

Here, `<password>` is the password that you have specified for the worksheet. This password is removed once the preceding statement is executed.

The Worksheet Object Events

The following sections discuss some of the events handled by the `Worksheet` object.

Activate

This event is fired when the worksheet gains focus. User activity such as clicking on the worksheet tab fires this event. This event is not fired when the user switches from one workbook to another or from one application to another. The code to handle this event is written in the `Worksheet_Activate` procedure.

Calculate

This event is fired when the worksheet is recalculated. If no user-defined function has been declared as volatile, the `Calculate` event is fired in the following situations:

- When the cursor re-enters a cell containing a formula
- When the value of any input cell for the formula changes
- When the VBA code executes the `Calculate` method

If a function has been declared as volatile, the `Calculate` event is fired not only in the preceding situations but also in the following situations:

- When the user presses the F9 button or clicks the Calc Now or the Calc Sheet button in the Calculation tab of the Options dialog box
- When the value of a cell that is used indirectly in a calculation changes

The event-handler code for the `Calculate` event is written in the `Worksheet_Calculate` procedure.

Change

This event is fired when the user changes the value of any cell in the worksheet or when the code changes the value property of a cell. The event-handler code of the `Change` event is written in the `Worksheet_Change` procedure.

Deactivate

This event is fired when a worksheet loses focus. A worksheet loses focus due to activities such as a user clicking on the tab of another worksheet or the VBA code calling the `Activate` method of another worksheet. The code for handling the event is written in the `Workbook_Deactivate` procedure. Excel switches to the other worksheet before running the event handler.

Using the Range Object

While working with an Excel spreadsheet, you use cells and ranges to store data, manipulate data, and perform other activities. You can edit the values in these cells and ranges directly. However, while using VBA, you need a mechanism to refer to the cells in the worksheets.

VBA enables you to access and refer to the cells in a worksheet by using the `Range` object. A `Range` object can be a single cell, a row, a column, or a selection of cells.

Using the Range Method

The `Range` method is used to identify a cell or a range. The syntax of the `Range` method is as follows:

```
Worksheet.Range(<name>)
Worksheet.Range(<upper_left_cell>, <lower_right_cell>)
```

In the first syntax, the `<name>` argument is the range reference or the name entered as text. In the second syntax, the `<upper_left_cell>` and `<lower_right_cell>` arguments are the upper-left corner cell and the lower-right corner cell, respectively, of a range of cells. The `<upper_left_cell>` and `<lower_right_cell>` values can be a cell address, a `Range` object, or an entire column or row.

Using the Cells Method

The `Cells` method returns a single cell as a `Range` object. The syntax of the method is as follows:

```
Object.Cells(<rowIndex>, <colIndex>)
```

Here, `<rowIndex>` is the row number of the cell. If the `Object` is a worksheet, the `<rowIndex>` value of 1 refers to row 1 in the worksheet. If the `Object` is a range, the value of 1 for `<rowIndex>` refers to the first row of the range.

In the preceding syntax, `<colIndex>` is the column of the cell. The column can be specified either by using a text or a number. If the `Object` is a worksheet, the `<colIndex>` argument having the value A or 1 refers to column A of the sheet. If the `Object` is a range, the value of A or 1 refers to the first column of the range.

Using the Rows Method

The `Rows` method is used to refer to a row of either a worksheet or a range. The syntax of the `Rows` method is as follows:

```
Object.Rows(<rowIndex>)
```

If the `Object` is a worksheet, the value of 1 for the `<rowIndex>` argument refers to the first row in the worksheet. On the other hand, if the `Object` is a range, the value of 1 for `<rowIndex>` refers to the first row of the range. If the `<rowIndex>` argument is omitted, VBA returns a collection of all the rows in the `Object`.

Using the Columns Method

The `Columns` method is used to refer to a column of either a worksheet or a range. The syntax of the `Columns` method is as follows:

```
Object.Columns(<col_Index>)
```

If the `Object` is a worksheet, the value of 1 or A for the `<col_Index>` argument refers to column A in the worksheet. On the other hand, if the `Object` is a range, the value of 1 or A for `<col_Index>` refers to the first column of the range. If the `<col_Index>` argument is omitted, VBA returns a collection of all the columns in the `Object`.

Using the Offset Method

While working with a range or a collection of cells, you might not know the address of the range. Therefore, to refer to the cell in the second row and fourth column of the range, you need to identify the address of the active cell and then calculate the address of the other cell. Using the `Offset` method of VBA provides you an easy alternative. The Offset method returns a Range object that is offset from a specified range by a certain number of arrows and columns. The syntax of the Offset method is as follows:

```
Range.Offset(<rowOffset>, <colOffset>)
```

Here, the <rowOffset> and <colOffset> arguments represent the row and column offsets, respectively. If any of these offsets is omitted, VBA assumes 0 as the offset.

Consider the following example.

```
Range("A1:C5").Offset(1,1).Font.Bold = True
```

This statement will make the range, B2:D6, bold.

Using the Cut Method

The Cut method cuts the specified range to the clipboard or to a new destination. The syntax of the Cut method is as follows:

```
Range.Cut(<destination>)
```

In this syntax, <destination> is the cell or range where the cut range will be pasted. For example:

```
Range("A1:B3").Cut Destination:=Range("C10")
```

This statement will cut a range from cells A1 to B3 and paste it to the cell C10. The range in which the cells will be pasted is C10:D12.

Using the Copy Method

The Copy method copies the specified range to the clipboard or to a new destination. The syntax of the Copy method is as follows:

```
Range.Copy(<destination>)
```

Here, <destination> is the cell or range where the copied range will be pasted. For example, consider the following statement:

```
Range("A1:B3").Copy Destination:=Range("C10")
```

This statement will copy a range from A1 to B3 and paste it to the cell C10. The range in which the cells will be pasted is C10:D12.

Using the Clear Method

The `Clear` method clears the specified range. The content, formatting, and comments, if any, are removed. You can individually remove the content, formatting, and comments from a range. To remove the content, you need to use the `Range.ClearContents` method. To remove the comments, you can use the `Range.ClearComments` method. To remove the formats, you should use the `Range.ClearFormats` method.

Using the DataSeries Method

The `DataSeries` method creates a data series in a range. The syntax of the `DataSeries` method is as follows:

```
Range.DataSeries(<row_col>, <type>, <date>, <step>, <stop>, <trend>)
```

Following is an explanation of the arguments of the method:

- <row_col>. This argument enables you to specify whether you need to enter the data in rows or columns. To enter the data in rows, use `xlRows`, or to enter the data in columns, use `xlColumns`.
- <type>. This argument specifies the series type. This argument can take values such as `xlLinear`, `xlGrowth`, `xlChronological`, and `xlAutoFill`.
- <date>. If you are using the `xlChronological` value for the <type> argument, you need to specify the date series. The <date> argument can take values such as `xlDay`, `xlWeekday`, `xlMonth`, and `xlYear`.
- <step>. This argument sets the step value for the series.
- <stop>. This argument specifies the stop value for the series.
- <trend>. This argument determines whether to create a growth series or a standard series. When <trend> is `False`, a standard series is created. If <trend> is `True`, a linear or growth trend series is created.

Using the Fill Methods

There are various fill methods for the `Range` object. Some of these methods are as follows:

- `Range.FillDown`. This method fills the range downward based on the contents and formatting of the top row.

- Range.FillLeft. This method fills the range leftward based on the contents and formatting of the rightmost column.
- Range.FillRight. This method fills the range rightward based on the contents and formatting of the leftmost column.
- Range.FillUp. This method fills the range upward based on the contents and formatting of the bottom row.

Using the Insert Method

The Insert method is used to insert cells in the specified range. The syntax to use the Insert method is as follows:

```
Range.Object.Insert(<direction>)
```

Here, <direction> is the direction in which the existing cells will shift after the insertion process. The <direction> argument can have either the value xlShift-ToRight or xlShiftDown.

Using the Resize Method

The Resize method resizes a range. The syntax for this method is as follows:

```
Range.Resize(<rowsize>, <colsize>)
```

Here, <rowsize> and <colsize> specify the number of rows and columns in the new range.

The Range Object Properties

Following are some of the Range object properties:

- Range.Address. This property returns the address of the specified Range.
- Range.Column. This property returns the number of the first column in the Range.
- Range.Count. This property returns the number of cells in the Range.
- Range.CurrentRegion. This property returns a Range object representing the region in which the specified Range resides. A range's region is the region surrounding the range that is bound by at least one empty row above and below and one empty column on the left and right.

- `Range.Formula`. This property returns a formula for the specified `Range`. It can also be used to set a formula for the specified `Range`.
- `Range.FormulaArray`. This property returns an array formula for the specified `Range`. It can also be used to set an array formula for the specified `Range`.
- `Range.NumberFormat`. This property returns the numeric format for the specified `Range`. It can also be used to set the numeric format for the specified `Range`.
- `Range.Row`. This property returns the number of the first row in the specified `Range`.
- `Range.Value`. This property is used to obtain or set the value in the specified `Range`.

Writing a Simple VBA Application for Excel

In this section, you create a simple VBA application. This application creates an Excel worksheet and generates a report by importing data from a database. It uses a table, `Emp_Master`, created in MS Access. This table contains the details of employees, and the sample data is given in Table 29-3.

Table 29-3 The Emp_Master Table

Emp_ID	Emp_Name	Emp_DOJ	Emp_Salary
E000001	Mark Smith	1/12/2001	$3,500.00
E000002	Jim Wilkins	2/12/2001	$4,000.00

Following is the code that is used to import data from this table and generate a report in Excel:

```
Imports System.Data.OleDb
Public Class Form1
    Inherits System.Windows.Forms.Form
' THIS IS A WINDOWS GENERATED CODE
#Region " Windows Form Designer generated code "
```

```
Public Sub New()
    MyBase.New()

    'This call is required by the Windows Form Designer.
    InitializeComponent()

    'Add any initialization after the InitializeComponent() call

End Sub

'Form overrides dispose to clean up the component list.
Protected Overloads Overrides Sub Dispose(ByVal disposing As Boolean)
    If disposing Then
        If Not (components Is Nothing) Then
            components.Dispose()
        End If
    End If
    MyBase.Dispose(disposing)
End Sub
Friend WithEvents Button1 As System.Windows.Forms.Button
Friend WithEvents Label1 As System.Windows.Forms.Label

'Required by the Windows Form Designer
Private components As System.ComponentModel.IContainer

'NOTE: The following procedure is required by the Windows Form Designer
'It can be modified using the Windows Form Designer.
'Do not modify it using the code editor.
<System.Diagnostics.DebuggerStepThrough()> Private Sub InitializeComponent()
    Me.Button1 = New System.Windows.Forms.Button()
    Me.Label1 = New System.Windows.Forms.Label()
    Me.SuspendLayout()
    '
    'Button1
    '
    Me.Button1.Font = New System.Drawing.Font("Microsoft Sans Serif", 8.25!,
       System.Drawing.FontStyle.Bold, System.Drawing.GraphicsUnit.Point,
       CType(0, Byte))
    Me.Button1.Location = New System.Drawing.Point(72, 88)
```

```
        Me.Button1.Name = "Button1"
        Me.Button1.Size = New System.Drawing.Size(144, 24)
        Me.Button1.TabIndex = 0
        Me.Button1.Text = "Show Employee Data"
        '
        'Label1
        '
        Me.Label1.Font = New System.Drawing.Font("Microsoft Sans Serif", 8.25!,
           (System.Drawing.FontStyle.Bold Or System.Drawing.FontStyle.Underline),
           System.Drawing.GraphicsUnit.Point, CType(0, Byte))
        Me.Label1.Location = New System.Drawing.Point(56, 32)
        Me.Label1.Name = "Label1"
        Me.Label1.Size = New System.Drawing.Size(216, 24)
        Me.Label1.TabIndex = 1
        Me.Label1.Text = "Click to View Employee Data"
        Me.Label1.TextAlign = System.Drawing.ContentAlignment.MiddleCenter
        '
        'Form1
        '
        Me.AutoScaleBaseSize = New System.Drawing.Size(5, 13)
        Me.ClientSize = New System.Drawing.Size(292, 273)
        Me.Controls.AddRange(New System.Windows.Forms.Control() {Me.Label1,
           Me.Button1})
        Me.Name = "Form1"
        Me.Text = "Form1"
        Me.ResumeLayout(False)

    End Sub

#End Region
' THE ABOVE CODE IS WINDOWS GENERATED
Private Sub Button1_Click(ByVal sender As System.Object, ByVal e As
   System.EventArgs) Handles Button1.Click
' Specify a connection with the Employee.mdb database
        Dim ourConn As String = "Provider=Microsoft.Jet.OLEDB.4.0;
           Data Source=D:\VBA_Excel\Employee.mdb;Persist Security Info=False"
        Dim clientConnection As OleDbConnection = New OleDbConnection(ourConn)
        Dim strSqlStatement As String
```

```
        Dim xlApp As Excel.Application
        Dim clientCommand As OleDbCommand
        Dim clientDataReader As OleDbDataReader
        Dim xlBook As Excel.Workbook
        Dim xlSheet As Excel.Worksheet
        Dim varIndustryType As String
        Dim varTotalValue As Decimal
        Dim varEmpID, varEmpName As String
        Dim varEmpDOJ As New DateTime()
        Dim varEmpSalary, varTotSal As Double

        Dim i As Integer
        i = 3
        varTotSal = 0


        Try
            'create a new workbook and add a worksheet to it
' Create an Excel workbook and add a worksheet to it
            xlApp = CType(CreateObject("Excel.Application"), Excel.Application)
            xlBook = CType(xlApp.Workbooks.Add, Excel.Workbook)
            xlSheet = CType(xlBook.Worksheets(1), Excel.Worksheet)

            ' Place some text in the second row of the sheet.
' Display the text "Employee Data" in the specified text
            xlSheet.Cells(1, 1) = "Employee Data"
            'execute the SQL statement to query for data In Emp_Master table
' Declare the SQL statement and execute the statement
            clientConnection.Open()
            strSqlStatement = "SELECT * FROM Emp_Master"
            clientCommand = New OleDbCommand(strSqlStatement, clientConnection)
            clientDataReader = clientCommand.ExecuteReader()
            xlSheet.Cells(2, 1) = "Emp ID"
            xlSheet.Cells(2, 2) = "Employee Name"
            xlSheet.Cells(2, 3) = "DOJ"
            xlSheet.Cells(2, 4) = "Salary"
            'Display data in the Excel worksheet
```

```
' Read the records returned by the SQL statement and display the results in the
' worksheet
            While clientDataReader.Read

                varEmpID = clientDataReader.Item(0)
                varEmpName = clientDataReader.Item(1)
                varEmpDOJ = clientDataReader.Item(2)
                varEmpSalary = clientDataReader.Item(3)
                varTotSal = varTotSal + varEmpSalary
                xlSheet.Cells(i, 1) = varEmpID
                xlSheet.Cells(i, 2) = varEmpName
                xlSheet.Cells(i, 3) = varEmpDOJ
                xlSheet.Cells(i, 4) = varEmpSalary

                i = i + 1

            End While
            i = i + 2
            xlSheet.Cells(i, 2) = "Total Salary Paid to Employees: "
            xlSheet.Cells(i, 4) = varTotSal
            clientDataReader.Close()
            clientConnection.Close()

            xlSheet.Application.Visible = True
            xlSheet = Nothing
            xlBook = Nothing
            xlApp = Nothing
        Catch
            MsgBox(Err.Description)
        End Try

    End Sub
End Class
```

The output of the preceding code is displayed in Figure 29-1.

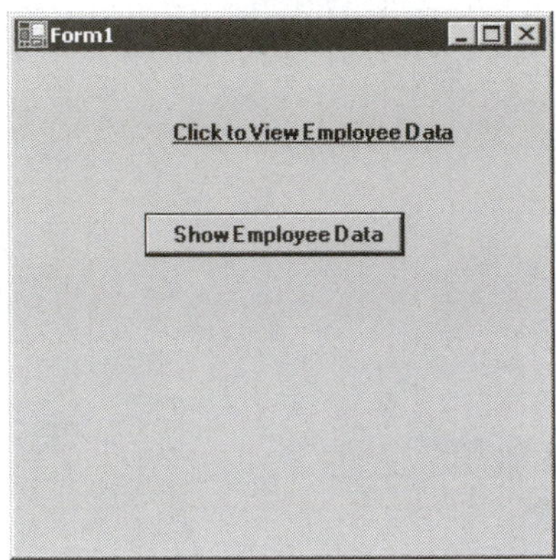

FIGURE 29-1 *The output of the code*

When you click on the "`Show Employee Data`" button in the form displayed in Figure 29-1, the Excel worksheet that is generated is displayed, as shown in Figure 29-2.

Microsoft Excel - Book1

	A	B	C	D	E	F
1	Employee Data					
2	Emp ID	Employee Name	DOJ	Salary		
3	E000001	Mark Smith	1/12/2001	3500		
4	E000002	Jim Wilkins	2/12/2001	4000		
5						
6						
7		Total Salary Paid to Employees:		7500		
8						
9						
10						
11						

FIGURE 29-2 *The generated Excel worksheet*

Summary

In this chapter, you learned to use the key objects of the Excel object model. You also learned to use the properties, methods, and events of the `Application`, `Workbook`, `Worksheet`, and `Range` objects, which are used to represent and manipulate workbooks and worksheets in Excel. Finally, you learned to create a simple application that uses these objects to create an Excel worksheet.

Chapter 30

Working with PowerPoint Objects

In this chapter, you will learn to use the key objects of the PowerPoint object model. You will learn to work with the properties and methods of the `Application`, `Presentation`, `Slides`, and `Shapes` objects that VBA provides for PowerPoint.

The VBA Objects for PowerPoint

The discussion begins with the objects provided by VBA for accessing and manipulating PowerPoint presentations. There are four such objects that you can use:

- The `Application` object
- The `Presentation` object
- The `Slide` object
- The `Shapes` object

The following sections discuss each of these objects in detail.

Using the Application Object of PowerPoint

You already know that the `Application` object is common to all the programs. It acts as a container for all the program objects since it refers to the application as a whole. You have seen the properties and methods of the `Application` object in the previous chapters on Word and Excel. Here some PowerPoint-specific properties of the `Application` object:

- `ActivePresentation`. This property returns a `Presentation` object that represents the currently active presentation.
- `ActivePrinter`. This property returns the name of the active printer. You can also use this property to change the active printer to another printer.
- `Presentations`. This property returns a collection of all the open presentations.
- `SlideShowWindows`. This property returns a collection of all the open slide show windows.

The next object is the `Presentation` object. It represents a PowerPoint presentation.

Using the Presentation Object

You need to specify the presentation on which you want to perform an action. That is, to work with a presentation, you need to tell PowerPoint which presentation to use.

Declaring a PowerPoint Object

There are three ways in which you can specify a `Presentation` object. These are as follows:

- Using the `Presentations` object
- Using the `ActivePresentation` object
- Using the `Presentation` property

The Presentations Object

The `Presentations` object is a collection of all the presentations that are open. You can refer to a particular presentation in the collection by using either the index number of the presentation or its name. The index numbers start from 1. Therefore, the first presentation in a collection will have the index number 1. The following statements refer to a specific presentation:

```
Presentations(1)
Presentations("FirstPresentation.ppt")
```

The ActivePresentation Object

The `ActivePresentation` object refers to the currently active presentation. You can use this object to identify and work with the presentation that has focus at a particular time.

The Presentation Property

PowerPoint slide shows have a `Presentation` property that returns the name of the presentation. For example, the following statement returns the name of the first slide show and stores it in a variable:

```
VarFirstSlide = SlideShowWindows(1).Presentation
```

The Presentation Object Properties

The properties of the `Presentation` object are as follows:

- `Presentation.FullName`. This property returns the full path, including the drive and the folder name, of the presentation.
- `Presentation.HandoutMaster`. This property returns the `Master` object. This `Master` object represents the handout master for the presentation.
- `Presentation.HasTitleMaster`. This property is used to determine if the specified presentation has a title master. If a title master is found, this property returns `True`.
- `Presentation.Name`. This property returns the name of the presentation.
- `Presentation.Path`. This property returns the path of the presentation file.
- `Presentation.Saved`. This property is used to determine if there is any unsaved change in the presentation.
- `Presentation.SlideMaster`. This property returns the slide master for the presentation.
- `Presentation.Slides`. This property returns a `Slides` object. This `Slides` object contains information about the slide objects present in the presentation.
- `Presentation.SlideShowSettings`. This property is used to obtain information about the settings of the slide shows in a presentation.
- `Presentation.TemplateName`. This property is used to determine the design template used in the presentation.
- `Presentation.TitleMaster`. This property is used to determine the title master for the presentation.
- `Presentation.VBASigned`. This property returns `True` if the presentation is signed digitally.

The Presentation Object Methods

The `Presentation` object provides various methods for tasks such as closing, saving, and printing presentations. Some of the commonly used methods are as follows:

- `Presentation.AddTitleMaster`. This method is used to add a title master to a presentation. A presentation can have only one title master. An error is generated if you try to assign a title master to a presentation that already has one. Therefore, before adding a title master by using this method, you should check whether the specified presentation already has a title master. You can do this by using the `HasProperty` method.

- `Presentation.AddToFavorites`. This method adds the presentation to the favorites list.
- `Presentation.ApplyTemplate`. This method is used to apply a template to a presentation. The syntax of this method is as follows:

  ```
  Presentation.ApplyTemplate(<filename>)
  ```

  Here, `<filename>` is the name of the template file. The template file has the extension `.POT`.
- `Presentation.Close`. This method is used to close presentations. Users are prompted to save the presentation if there are unsaved changes in it.
- `Presentation.NewWindow`. This method opens a presentation in a new window.
- `Presentation.PrintOut`. This method prints a presentation. The syntax of the `PrintOut` method is as follows:

  ```
  Presentation.PrintOut(<from>, <to>, <printtofile>, <copies>,
     <collate>)
  ```

  Here, `<from>` and `<to>` are the starting and ending page, respectively. The file will be printed to `<printtofile>`, if specified. The printer will print `<copies>` number of copies. If the `<collate>` option is `True` and `<copies>` is more than one, VBA collates the copies.
- `Presentation.Save`. This method enables you to save a presentation.
- `Presentation.SaveAs`. This method is used to save a presentation to a new file if the file that contains the presentation has been saved at least once. However, if the file containing the presentation is new, the `SaveAs` method is used to save the file. The syntax of the `Presentation.SaveAs` method is as follows:

  ```
  Presentation.SaveAs (<filename>, <fileformat>, <embedTrueTypeFonts>)
  ```

  Here, `<filename>` is the full name, including the complete path description along with the drive and folder name of the presentation file. The `<fileformat>` argument specifies the format that will be used for the file. The `<fileformat>` argument can have the `ppSaveAs` constant values such as ppSaveAsPresentation and ppSaveAsHTML. The <embedTrueType-Fonts> argument is used to specify whether or not PowerPoint embeds the TrueType fonts in a new file.

Using the Slide Objects

A PowerPoint presentation consists of a number of slides. VBA provides the Slide objects that you can use to manipulate slides. The Slide object represents a slide of the PowerPoint presentation. You can use the various properties and methods provided by Slide object to perform activities such as setting a slide's layout, specifying the transition effects, and copying and deleting slides from the presentation.

Declaring a Slides Object

To work with a slide, you need to access it. You can use the Slides object to obtain a reference to a particular slide. The Slides object enables you to access a slide either by specifying an index number or the slide name. The index numbers of the slides in the Slides object start from 1. For example, if the name of the first slide of the active presentation is FirstSlide, you can use following statements to refer to the slide:

```
ActivePresentation.Slides(1)
ActivePresentation.Slides("FirstSlide")
```

You can also find a slide by its slide ID number. Each slide in a presentation is assigned a unique ID number. The Slides.FindBySlideID method enables you to find a slide by its ID. The syntax of the Slides.FindBySlideID is as follows:

```
Presentation.Slides.FindBySlideID(<slide_ID>)
```

Here, <slide_ID> is the slide ID. You can use the Range method to refer to multiple slides. The syntax of the Range method is as follows:

```
Presentation.Slides.Range(<index>)
```

Here, <index> is an array that specifies the slides. An example of the Range method is as follows:

```
ActivePresentation.Slides.Range(Array("SlideA", "SlideB", "SlideC"))
```

The preceding example uses slide names. In addition to slide names, you can also use the index numbers or the slide ID. The preceding example also uses the `Array` method to declare an array.

To refer to every slide in a presentation, you can use the following statement:

```
ActivePresentation.Slides.Range
```

The Slide Object Properties

VBA enables you to customize slides. Using the properties of the `Slide` object, you can customize a slide's properties such as its layout, background, color scheme, and name. Following are some of the frequently used `Slide` object properties:

- `Slide.Background`. This property returns a slide's background. You can also use it to set the background of a slide. This property can be used with the slide master to set the background of all the slides in a presentation.
- `Slide.DisplayMasterShapes`. This property is used to identify whether a slide in the presentation displays a shape declared in the slide master. For example, if a slide master contains an image and the `DisplayMasterShapes` property is set to `False` for a particular slide, that slide will not display the image. However, you can display the slide master image in a slide by setting the `DisplayMasterShapes` property to `True`.
- `Slide.FollowMasterBackground`. This property is used to identify whether a particular slide uses the same background as that of the slide master. The `True` value returned by the `FollowMasterBackground` property indicates that the slide uses the same background as the slide master. You can assign the slide the same background as that of the slide master by setting the `FollowMasterBackground` property to `True`.
- `Slide.Layout`. This property is used to identify the layout of a particular slide. It returns a constant representing the layout. You can also assign a layout to the slide using this property.
- `Slide.Master`. This property returns the slide master of the slide.
- `Slide.Name`. This property enables you to obtain or modify the name of a particular slide.
- `Slide.Shapes`. This property returns a `Shapes` collection. The `Shapes` collection contains a list of all the `Shape` objects that are contained in a slide.

- `Slide.SlideID`. This property is used to obtain the slide ID of a particular slide.
- `Slide.SlideIndex`. This property is used to obtain the index number of a particular slide in a presentation.
- `Slide.SlideShowTransition`. This property returns an object that represents the transition special effect that has been applied to the slide.

The Slide Object Methods

VBA provides the `Slide` object methods that enable you to perform activities such as copying, deleting, and exporting slides. These methods are discussed in the following list:

- `Slide.Copy`. This method copies a slide to the clipboard.
- `Slide.Paste`. This method enables you to paste a slide, which has been copied to the clipboard, into another presentation. The syntax of the `Paste` method is as follows:

  ```
  Presentation.Slides.Paste(<index>)
  ```

  Here, the slide will be pasted before the slide having the index number `<index>`. The following are examples of the `Copy` and `Paste` methods:

  ```
  Presentations(1).Slides(1).Copy
  Presentations(2).Slides.Paste (1)
  ```

  In the preceding example, the first slide in the first presentation is copied and pasted in the second presentation. The copied slide is pasted before the first slide of the second presentation.
- `Slide.Cut`. This method cuts a slide and places it on the clipboard. This slide can be pasted in any other presentation by using the `Slide.Paste` method.
- `Slide.Delete`. This method, when used, will delete a specified slide.
- `Slide.Duplicate`. This method creates a copy of a specified slide and places the copy immediately next to the specified slide.
- `Slide.Export`. This method is capable of exporting a slide to a file in a graphic format. The syntax of this method is as follows:

  ```
  Slide.Export (<filename>, <format>, <scaleWidth>, <scaleHeight>)
  ```

Here, `<filename>` is the name of the file to which the slide will be exported. The file will be exported in the `<format>` format. While being exported, the slide will be scaled horizontally and vertically to the factors, `<scaleWidth>` and `<scaleHeight>`, respectively.

- `Slide.Select`. This method selects the specified slide.

  In addition to the preceding methods, VBA provides methods for adding slides to a presentation. Two such methods are

- The `Add` method
- The `InsertFromFile` method

The following sections look at how to add slides to a presentation by using these methods.

Adding New Slides to a Presentation

VBA enables you to add slides to a presentation. You can use the `Add` method of the `Slides` object to do so. The syntax of the `Add` method is as follows:

```
Presentation.Slides.Add(<index>, <layout>)
```

Here, `<index>` is the index number of the slide in the `Slides` object. To refer to the first slide in the presentation, use the value 1 for `<index>`. You can refer to the last slide in a presentation by assigning the value `Slides.Count + 1`.

The `<layout>` parameter specifies the layout of the new slide. Some of the layout constants that you can assign are `ppLayoutText`, `ppLayoutChart`, and `ppLayoutBlank`.

```
ActivePresentation.Slides.Add(1, ppLayoutText)
```

This statement will insert a text-only slide as the first slide in the presentation.

Adding Slides from Other Files

At times, you might need to add slides from an existing presentation to another presentation. VBA enables you to do this by providing the `InsertFromFile` method. The syntax of the `InsertFromFile` method is as follows:

```
Presentation.Slides. InsertFromFile(<filename>, <index>, <begin_slide>, <end_slide>)
```

The following list provides an explanation of the arguments of the InsertFromFile method:

- <filename>. This argument represents the file name, including the complete path information such as the drive and the folder name, from where the slides need to be imported.
- <index>. The <index> argument specifies the index number from where the slides will be imported into the current presentation. For example, if <index> is 2, the slides will be inserted from the second position onward.
- <begin_slide>. The <begin_slide> argument specifies the index number of the slide starting from which the subsequent slides from <filename> will be copied.
- <end_slide>. The <end_slide> argument is the index number of the slide where the slides need to be copied from <filename>. The slides from index number <begin_slide> till <end_slide> will be copied from <filename>.

Using the Shape Objects

A slide in PowerPoint consists of many ingredients such as titles, texts, pictures, images, tables, and so on. VBA considers each of these as a Shape object. Therefore, in order to know VBA for PowerPoint in detail, you should know about the Shape objects.

Specifying a Shape Object

You can refer to a shape by using the Shapes object. A Shapes object is a collection of the available Shape objects in a particular slide. To select a particular shape, you can use either the index number of the Shape object in the Shapes object or the name of the Shape object. For example, if there is a Shape object named Text1 in a slide and it is also the first Shape in the Shapes object, the statements to refer to the Text1 shape object is as follows:

```
ActivePresentation.Shapes("Text1")
ActivePresentation.Shapes(1)
```

Similar to the slides, if you need to work with multiple shapes, you can use the Range object. The syntax for using the Range object is given here:

```
Slide.Shapes.Range(<array>)
```

Next you will learn the methods that VBA provides for adding shapes to a slide.

Adding Shapes to a Slide

The `Slides` object has many methods that enable you to insert shapes into a slide. These methods are explained in the following sections.

Slides.Shapes.AddCallout

This method adds a callout to the specified slide. The syntax of this method is as follows:

```
Slide.Shapes.AddCallout(<type>, <left>, <top>, <width>, <height>)
```

Here, `<type>` specifies the type of the callout. This argument can take any one of the constants defined by VBA. Some such constants are as follow:

- `msoCalloutOn`. This defines a single-segment callout that can be oriented either horizontally or vertically.
- `msoCalloutTwo`. This defines a single-segment callout that can be oriented in any direction.
- `msoCalloutThree`. This defines a double-segment callout.
- `msoCalloutFour`. This defines a triple-segment callout.

The `<left>` argument in the syntax is the distance between the left edges of the shape and the slide window. The `<top>` argument is the distance between the top edges of the shape and the slide window. The `<width>` and `<height>` arguments are respectively the width and height of the shape in points.

Slide.Shapes.AddComment

This method adds a comment to the specified shape. The syntax of this method is as follows:

```
Slide.Shapes.AddComment(<left>, <top>, <width>, <height>)
```

The `<left>` argument in the syntax is the distance between the left edges of the shape and the slide window. The `<top>` argument is the distance between the top edges of the shape and the slide window. `<width>` and `<height>` are respectively the width and height of the shape in points.

Slide.Shapes.AddConnector

This method adds a connector to the specified slide. The syntax of the method is as follows:

```
Slide.Shapes.AddConnector (<type>, <beginX>, <beginY>, <endX>, <endY>)
```

Here, `<type>` is a constant that specifies the connector type. The `<type>` argument can take one of the following values:

- `msoConnectorCurve`
- `msoConnectorElbow`
- `msoConnectorStraight`

Slide.Shapes.AddCurve

This method adds a curve to the specified slide. The syntax to use this method is as follows:

```
Slide.Shapes.AddCurve(<ArrayOfPoints>)
```

Here, `<ArrayOfPoints>` is an array of coordinates and vertices of the curves and polylines in a slide.

Slide.Shapes.AddLabel

This method adds a label to the specified slide. The syntax to use the `AddLabel` method is as follows:

```
Slide.Shapes.AddLabel(<orientation>, <left>, <top>, <width>, <height>)
```

Here, the `<orientation>` argument specifies the orientation of text in a label or a text box. This argument can take one of the following two constants:

- `msoTextOrientationHorizontal`
- `msoTextOrientationVerticalFarEast`

Slide.Shapes.AddLine

This method is used to add a straight line to a slide. The syntax of the `Slide.Shapes.AddLine` method is as follows:

```
Slide.Shapes.AddLine(<beginX>, <beginY>, <endX>, <endY>)
```

The following is an explanation of each argument:

- `<beginX>`. This is the distance between the shape's starting point and the left edge of the slide window.
- `<beginY>`. This is the distance between the shape's starting point and the top edge of the slide window.
- `<endX>`. This is the distance between the shape's ending point and the left edge of the slide window.
- `<endY>`. This is the distance between the shape's ending point and the top edge of the slide window.

Slide.Shapes.AddMediaObject

This method adds a multimedia file to a specified slide. The syntax of this method is as follows:

```
Slide.Shapes.AddMediaObject (<filename>, <left>, <top>, <width>, <height>)
```

Here, `<filename>` is the path of the file from where the shape needs to be imported. The `<left>` argument represents the distance in points between the left edge of the shape and the left edge of the slide window. The `<top>` argument represents the distance in points between the top edge of the shape and the top edge of the slide window.

In the syntax, the `<width>` and `<height>` arguments are used to specify the width and height of the shape.

Slide.Shapes.AddOLEObject

This method adds an OLE object to a specified slide. The syntax to use this method is as follows:

```
Slide.Shapes.AddOLEObject(<left>, <top>, <height>, <className>, <fileName>,
   <DisplayAsIcon>, <IconFileName>, <IconIndex>, <IconLabel>, <Link>)
```

The following is an explanation of each argument:

- `<left>`. This argument represents the distance in points between the left edge of the shape and the left edge of the slide window.
- `<top>`. This argument represents the distance in points between the top edge of the shape and the top edge of the slide window.

- `<height>`. This argument represents the height of the shape.
- `<className>`. This argument specifies the class name for the OLE object.
- `<filename>`. This argument represents the file to be used to create the OLE object.
- `<DisplayAsIcon>`. This argument, if set to `True`, displays the object as an icon.
- `<IconLabel>`. If `<DisplayAsIcon>` is `True`, this argument represents the label that will be displayed below the icon.
- `<Link>`. This argument sets up a link to `<filename>`. If `<filename>` is specified, setting this argument to `True` will set up a link between the shape and the original file.

Slide.Shapes.AddPicture

This method adds a graphic to a specified slide. The syntax to use this method is as follows:

```
Slide.Shapes.AddPicture (<filename>, <linktofile>, <saveWithDocument>, <left>,
   <top>, <width>, <height>)
```

The following is an explanation of each argument:

- `<filename>`. This argument represents the name of the file that contains the graphic.
- `<linktofile>`. This argument, if set to `True`, sets up a link of the shape to the file. If `<linktofile>` is `False`, an independent copy of the graphic is stored on the slide.
- `<saveWithDocument>`. This argument determines whether the graphic will be saved along with the presentation.
- `<left>`. This argument represents the distance in points between the left edge of the shape and the left edge of the slide window.
- `<top>`. This argument represents the distance in points between the top edge of the shape and the top edge of the slide window.
- `<height>`. This argument represents the height of the shape.
- `<width>`. This argument represents the width of the shape.

Slide.Shapes.AddPolyline

This method is used to add a polyline or a polygon to a slide. The syntax is as follows:

```
Slide.Shapes.AddPolyline(<arrayOfPoints>)
```

Here, `<arrayOfPoints>` is an array of coordinate pairs that specify the vertices for the shape.

Slide.Shapes.AddShape

This method adds an `AutoShape` to the specified slide. The syntax is as follows:

```
Slide.Shapes.AddShape (<type>, <left>, <top>, <width>, <height>)
```

The following is an explanation of each argument:

- `<type>`. This argument is a constant and specifies the `AutoShape` that you need to add.
- `<left>`. This argument represents the distance in points between the left edge of the shape and the left edge of the slide window.
- `<top>`. This argument represents the distance in points between the top edge of the shape and the top edge of the slide window.
- `<height>`. This argument represents the height of the shape.
- `<width>`. This argument represents the width of the shape.

Slide.Shapes.AddTable

This method adds a table to a specified slide. The syntax is as follows:

```
Slide.Shapes.AddTable(<numrows>, <numcols>, <left>, <top>, <width>, <height>)
```

The following is an explanation of each argument:

- `<numrows>`. This argument specifies the number of rows in the table.
- `<numcols>`. This argument specifies the number of columns in the table.
- `<left>`. This argument represents the distance in points between the left edge of the shape and the left edge of the slide window.
- `<top>`. This argument represents the distance in points between the top edge of the shape and the top edge of the slide window.

- `<height>`. This argument represents the height of the shape.
- `<width>`. This argument represents the width of the shape.

Slide.Shapes.AddTextbox

The method adds a text box to the slide. The syntax of the method is as follows:

```
Slide.Shapes.AddTextbox (<left>, <top>, <width>, <height>)
```

The following is an explanation of each argument:

- `<left>`. This argument represents the distance in points between the left edge of the shape and the left edge of the slide window.
- `<top>`. This argument represents the distance in points between the top edge of the shape and the top edge of the slide window.
- `<height>`. This argument represents the height of the shape.
- `<width>`. This argument represents the width of the shape.

Slide.Shapes.AddTextEffect

This method is used to add WordArt effects to the specified slide. The syntax of the `Slide.Shapes.AddTextEffect` method is as follows:

```
Slide.Shapes.AddTextEffect(<presetTextEffect>, <text>, <fontname>, <fontsize>,
   <fontbold>, <fontitalic>, <left>, <top>)
```

The following is an explanation of each argument:

- `<presetTextEffect>`. This argument has a constant value that specifies the WordArt to use.
- `<text>`. This argument contains the text to be displayed.
- `<fontname>`. This argument specifies the font that needs to be applied to <text>.
- `<fontsize>`. This argument specifies the font size.
- `<fontbold>`. This argument, if set to `True`, will make the text bold.
- `<fontitalic>`. This argument, if set to `True`, will italicize the text.
- `<left>`. This argument represents the distance in points between the left edge of the shape and the left edge of the slide window.
- `<top>`. This argument represents the distance in points between the top edge of the shape and the top edge of the slide window.

Slide.Shapes.AddTitle

This method adds a title to a slide. This method throws an error if you try to assign a title to a slide that already has a title.

Shape Object Properties

The properties of the `Shape` object control characteristics such as the dimensions and positions of a shape, whether a shadow is displayed, and so on. The following sections look at some of the properties.

Shape.AnimationSettings

This property is used to obtain the `AnimationSettings` object for the specified shape. The `AnimationSettings` object represents the various settings that are applied to the shape. In addition, the `AnimationSettings` object contains various settings that can be used to apply effects to the shape. Some of the constants that play a role in the animation settings are as follows:

- `AdvanceMode`. This constant determines how the animation will proceed. The animation can proceed either on the click of a mouse or after a specified period of time. For automatic advancement, you need to use the `ppAdvanceOnTime` constant whereas for advancement on a mouse click, you need to use the `ppAdvanceOnClick` constant.
- `AfterEffect`. This constant determines how the shape appears after the animation is complete.
- `Animate`. This constant controls the animation of the shape by turning it on or off.
- `AnimateTextInReverse`. This Boolean constant, if `True`, enables PowerPoint to display the text animation in reverse order.
- `EntryEffect`. This constant argument determines the initial special animation effect that is applied to the shape.
- `TextUnitEffect`. This constant determines how PowerPoint animates the text, by paragraph, word, or letter.

Shape.AutoShapeType

This property returns the shape type for the specified shape. It is also used to set the shape type.

Shape.Fill

This property returns a `FillFormat` object that represents the fill formatting for a specified shape. The methods of the `FillFormat` object that you can use to control the fill formatting of a shape are as follows:

- `Background`. This sets the fill to match the slide's background.
- `OneColorGradient`. This sets the fill to one-color gradient.
- `Patterned`. This sets the fill to a pattern.
- `PresetGradient`. This sets the fill to one of PowerPoint's preset gradients.
- `PresetTextured`. This sets the fill to one of PowerPoint's preset textures.
- `Solid`. This sets the fill to a solid color.
- `TwoColorGradient`. This sets the fill to a two-color gradient.
- `UserPicture`. This sets the fill to a graphic file that you specify.

Shape.HasTable

This method returns a Boolean value that determines whether the specified shape is a table.

Shape.Height

This property is used to obtain, in points, the height of a specified shape. You can also modify the height by using this property.

Shape.Table

This property returns a `Table` object for a specified shape. You can use the `HashTable` property to determine whether the shape has a table.

Shape.TextFrame

This property is used to obtain a `TextFrame` area for a specified object. `TextFrame` is an area within a shape that can contain text. The `TextRange` object represents the frame's text as a whole. The actual text is represented by the `Text` property of the `TextRange` object. Therefore, to refer to a shape's text, you need to use the following statement:

```
Shape.TextFrame.TextRange.Text
```

Shape Object Methods

The `Shape` object has various methods that enable you to perform activities such as copying, deleting, and flipping slides. The useful methods of the `Shape` object are as follows:

- `Shape.Apply`. This method applies a particular formatting to the specified shape.
- `Shape.Copy`. This method copies the specified shape to the clipboard.
- `Shape.Cut`. This method cuts the specified shape and places it on the clipboard.
- `Shape.Delete`. This method deletes the specified shape.
- `Shape.Duplicate`. This method makes a copy of the specified shape in the same slide. The new shape is added to the `Shapes` object immediately after the specified shape.
- `Shape.Flip`. This method flips the specified shape along with its horizontal or vertical axis.
- `Shape.IncrementLeft`. This method moves the specified shape horizontally.
- `Shape.IncrementRotation`. This method rotates the specified shape along with its z-axis.
- `Shape.IncrementTop`. This method moves the specified shape vertically.
- `Shape.PickUp`. This method copies the formatting of a specified shape.
- `Shape.Select`. This method selects the specified shape.

Operating a Slide Show

In this section, you will learn how VBA enables you to add transition effects and settings to slide shows. You will also learn to run the slide shows by using VBA statements.

Slide Show Transitions

Every `Slide` object has a property called `SlideShowTransition`, which determines the slide transition settings in a slide show. The `SlideShowTransition` property is actually a `SlideShowTransitions` object. You can modify the transition effects by using the `SlideShowTransitions` object's properties. Some of these properties are as follows:

- `Slide.SlideShowTransition.AdvanceOnClick`. This property determines whether the slide will advance on the click of a mouse. If this property is set to `True`, the slide will advance on a mouse click.
- `Slide.SlideShowTransition.AdvanceOnTime`. This property determines whether the specified slide will advance after a particular period of time.
- `Slide.SlideShowTransition.AdvanceTime`. This property is used to specify the time in seconds after which the specified slide will advance. For this property to function properly, the `SlideShowTransition.AdvanceOnTime` property should be set to true.
- `Slide.SlideShowTransition.EntryEffect`. This is a constant that determines the effects used in the transition for the specified slide.
- `Slide.SlideShowTransition.Hidden`. This property is used to determine whether the specified slide is hidden during the slide show.
- `Slide.SlideShowTransition.Speed`. This property is used to specify the speed for the specified slide. This property can take constant values such as `ppTransitionSpeedSlow`, `ppTransitionSpeedMedium`, and `ppTransitionSpeedMixed`.

Slide Show Settings

The `SlideShowSettings` property of the `Presentation` object enables you to control the settings for the slide show. Some of the most frequently used settings are as follows:

- `Presentation.SlideShowSettings.AdvanceMode`. This property enables you to specify how the slides will advance for the specified presentation.
- `Presentation.SlideShowSettings.EndingSlide`. This property enables you to specify the index number that is to be displayed in the presentation.
- `Presentation.SlideShowSettings.LoopUntilStopped`. This property, if set to `True`, will cause the PowerPoint slide show to play continuously.
- `Presentation.SlideShowSettings.PointerColor`. This property can be used to set the color of the mouse pointer during the slide show for the specified presentation.

- `Presentation.SlideShowSettings.ShowType`. This property enables you to specify whether the slide show will run full screen or in a window.
- `Presentation.SlideShowSettings.ShowWithAnimation`. This property is used to specify the animation settings applied to each slide's shapes.
- `Presentation.SlideShowSettings.StartingSlide`. This property is used to specify the name of the first slide that will be displayed during the slide show.

Running the Slide Show

To run a slide show using VBA, you can use the `SlideShowSettings` property. The syntax to run a slide show is as follows:

```
Presentation.SlideShowSettings.Run
```

You have now learned about the VBA objects for PowerPoint. The next section shows you an example that uses these objects.

Writing a Simple VBA Application for PowerPoint

In this section, you create a simple VBA application. This application creates a PowerPoint presentation. The application picks the data from a database and displays the data in the slides of the presentation. It uses a table `EmpMaster` created in MS Access to store data. This table contains details of employees and sample data is given in the Table 30-1.

Table 30-1 EmpMaster Table

EmpID	EmpName	EmpAddress
E00001	Mark Smith	New York
E00002	Jim Wilkins	Washington

The code for the application is as follows:

```
Imports System.Data.OleDb
Public Class Form1
    Inherits System.Windows.Forms.Form
' THIS IS A WINDOWS GENERATED CODE
#Region " Windows Form Designer generated code "

    Public Sub New()
        MyBase.New()

        'This call is required by the Windows Form Designer.
        InitializeComponent()

        'Add any initialization after the InitializeComponent() call

    End Sub

    'Form overrides dispose to clean up the component list.
    Protected Overloads Overrides Sub Dispose(ByVal disposing As Boolean)
        If disposing Then
            If Not (components Is Nothing) Then
                components.Dispose()
            End If
        End If
        MyBase.Dispose(disposing)
    End Sub
    Friend WithEvents Button1 As System.Windows.Forms.Button
    Friend WithEvents Label1 As System.Windows.Forms.Label

    'Required by the Windows Form Designer
    Private components As System.ComponentModel.IContainer

    'NOTE: The following procedure is required by the Windows Form Designer
    'It can be modified using the Windows Form Designer.
    'Do not modify it using the code editor.
    <System.Diagnostics.DebuggerStepThrough()> Private Sub InitializeComponent()
        Me.Button1 = New System.Windows.Forms.Button()
```

```
        Me.Label1 = New System.Windows.Forms.Label()
        Me.SuspendLayout()
        '
        'Button1
        '
        Me.Button1.Font = New System.Drawing.Font("Microsoft Sans Serif", 8.25!,
           System.Drawing.FontStyle.Bold, System.Drawing.GraphicsUnit.Point,
           CType(0, Byte))
        Me.Button1.Location = New System.Drawing.Point(64, 96)
        Me.Button1.Name = "Button1"
        Me.Button1.Size = New System.Drawing.Size(160, 32)
        Me.Button1.TabIndex = 0
        Me.Button1.Text = "Click to view Presentation"
        '
        'Label1
        '
        Me.Label1.Font = New System.Drawing.Font("Microsoft Sans Serif", 8.25!,
           System.Drawing.FontStyle.Bold, System.Drawing.GraphicsUnit.Point,
           CType(0, Byte))
        Me.Label1.Location = New System.Drawing.Point(24, 40)
        Me.Label1.Name = "Label1"
        Me.Label1.Size = New System.Drawing.Size(248, 23)
        Me.Label1.TabIndex = 1
        Me.Label1.Text = "Click the Button to View Presentation"
        Me.Label1.TextAlign = System.Drawing.ContentAlignment.MiddleCenter
        '
        'Form1
        '
        Me.AutoScaleBaseSize = New System.Drawing.Size(5, 13)
        Me.ClientSize = New System.Drawing.Size(292, 273)
        Me.Controls.AddRange(New System.Windows.Forms.Control() {Me.Label1,
           Me.Button1})
        Me.Name = "Form1"
        Me.Text = "Form1"
        Me.ResumeLayout(False)

    End Sub

#End Region
```

```
' THE ABOVE IS  WINDOWS GENERATED
' Setup the connection to a specified database.
    Private ourConn As String = "Provider=Microsoft.Jet.OLEDB.4.0;
       Data Source=E:\EmpMaster.mdb;Persist Security Info=False"
    Private clientConnection As OleDbConnection = New OleDbConnection(ourConn)
    Private clientCommand As OleDbCommand
    Private clientDataReader As OleDbDataReader

    Private Sub Button1_Click(ByVal sender As System.Object, ByVal e As
       System.EventArgs) Handles Button1.Click
        Dim strSqlStatement As String
        Dim ppApp As PowerPoint.Application
        Dim ppOne As PowerPoint.Presentation
        Dim ppTwo As PowerPoint.Presentation
        Dim ppslide As PowerPoint.Slide
        Dim ppShape As PowerPoint.Shape
        Dim varLength As Long
        Dim EmpCode As String
        Dim EmpName As String
        Dim EmpAddress As String
        Dim Count As Integer
        Count = 0

        Try
' Create a PowerPoint Application
            ppApp = CType(CreateObject("PowerPoint.Application"),
               PowerPoint.Application)
            ppApp.Visible = True
            ppApp.Presentations.Add()
' Get a reference to the active presentation
            ppOne = ppApp.ActivePresentation
' Apply a template to the presentation and add a slide from the mentioned file
            ppOne.ApplyTemplate("E:\EmpTemplate.pot")
            varLength = ppOne.Slides.InsertFromFile("E:\EmpTemplate.ppt", 0, 1, 1)

' Open the connection with the database, execute the SQL query, and obtain the result
            clientConnection.Open()
```

```
            strSqlStatement = "SELECT * FROM EmpDetail"
            clientCommand = New OleDbCommand(strSqlStatement, clientConnection)
            clientDataReader = clientCommand.ExecuteReader()

' Loop while there's any data in the recordset
            While clientDataReader.Read

' Store the values from the rows in variables
                EmpCode = clientDataReader.Item(0)
                EmpName = clientDataReader.Item(1)
                EmpAddress = clientDataReader.Item(2)


                For Each ppslide In ppOne.Slides
                    For Each ppShape In ppslide.Shapes
                        If ppShape.HasTextFrame = True Then

' Find and replace the tags with the data
                            ppShape.TextFrame.TextRange.Replace("<<Employee
                               Code>>", EmpCode)
                            ppShape.TextFrame.TextRange.Replace("<<Employee
                               Name>>", EmpName)
                            ppShape.TextFrame.TextRange.Replace("<<Employee
                               Address>>", EmpAddress)
                        End If
                    Next
                Next
                Count = Count + 1
                ppOne.Slides.InsertFromFile("E:\EmpTemplate.ppt", Count)
            End While
            clientDataReader.Close()
            clientConnection.Close()
            ppShape = Nothing
            ppslide = Nothing
            ppOne = Nothing
            ppApp = Nothing
        Catch
            MsgBox(Err.Description)
```

```
        End Try

    End Sub

    Private Sub Label1_Click(ByVal sender As System.Object, ByVal e As
       System.EventArgs) Handles Label1.Click

    End Sub
End Class
```

The output of the preceding code is displayed in the Figure 30-1.

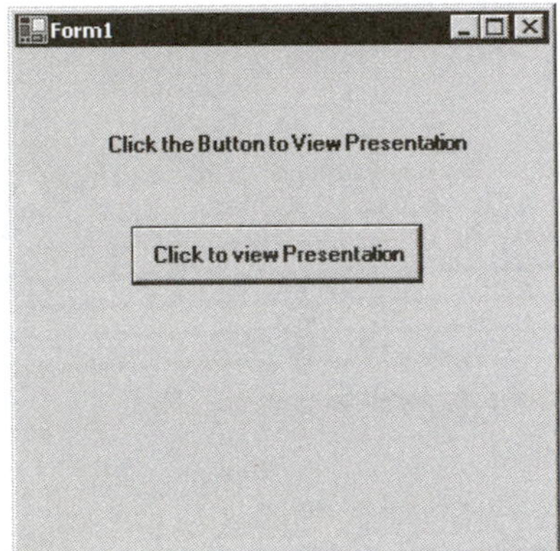

FIGURE 30-1 *The output of the code*

When you click on the "Click to view Presentation" button in the form displayed in Figure 30-1, the PowerPoint presentation that is generated is displayed, as shown in Figure 30-2.

Notice in the code that the new slides are imported from the `EmpTemplate.ppt` presentation, as shown in Figure 30-3.

Notice in Figure 30-3 that the slide contains some text in tags such as `<<Employee Code>>`, `<<Employee Name>>`, and `<<Employee Address>>`. These tags are replaced with the data from the database as displayed in the Figure 30-2.

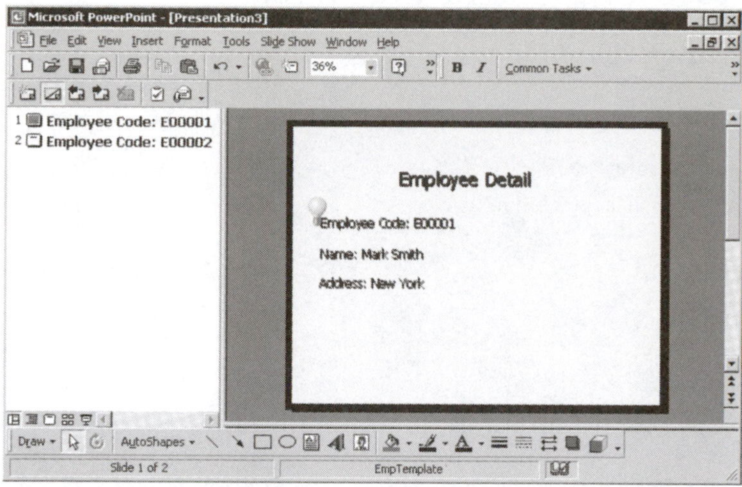

FIGURE 30-2 *The generated PowerPoint presentation*

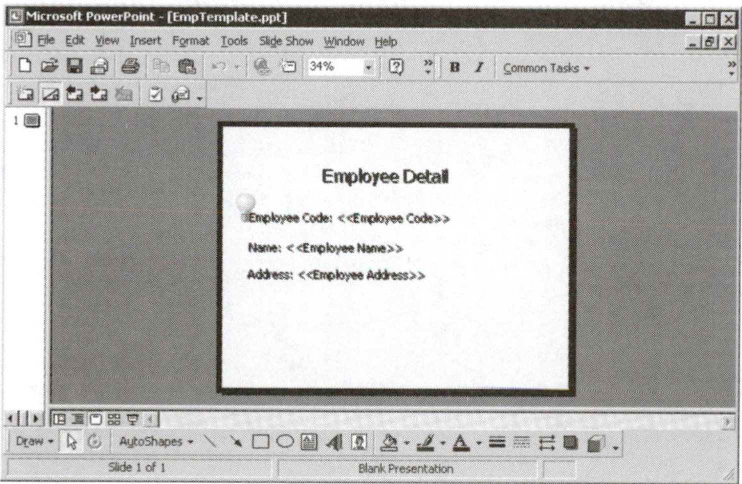

FIGURE 30-3 *The presentation from where slides are imported*

Summary

In this chapter, you learned to use the key objects of the PowerPoint object model. You also learned to use properties and methods of `Application`, `Presentation`, `Slide`, and `Shapes` objects. You can use these objects to represent and modify presentations. Finally, you learned to create a simple application that uses these objects to create a PowerPoint presentation. You will code the Easy Selling Application in the coming chapters.

Chapter 31

Coding the Main Screen of the Easy Selling Application

Chapter 28, "Designing the Forms of the Application," discussed the different screens of the Easy Selling application. In this chapter, you will learn the code for the `Main` screen and add functionality to the Easy Selling application.

Working of the Main Screen of the Easy Selling Application

This section discusses the procedures and functions used in the `Main` screen of the Easy Selling application. The `Main` screen is shown in Figure 31-1.

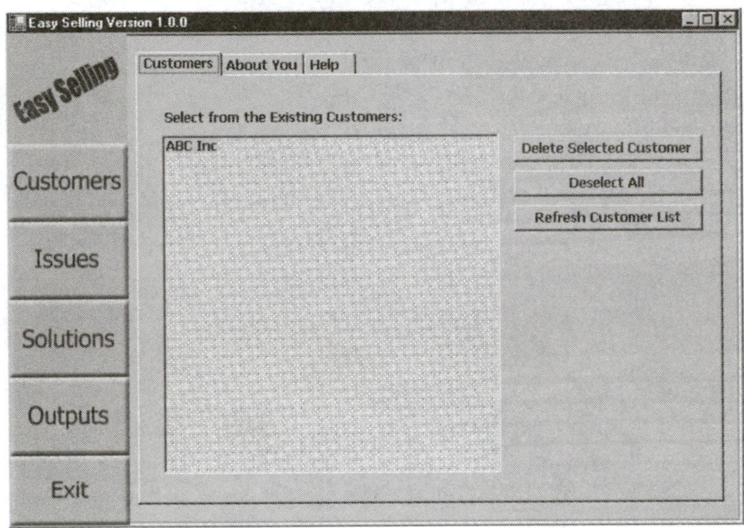

FIGURE 31-1 *The* `Main` *screen of the Easy Selling application*

The `Main` screen is a combination of the `MainMDI` form and the `StartApplication` form. The framework of the Easy Selling application is based on the concept of MDI parent-child forms. When an instance of an MDI parent form is initiated, on the form load event, the MDI parent form and the `StartApplication` forms are initiated. The `MainMDI` form is the parent form of the Easy Selling application. It comprises the left navigation bar. The `StartApplication` form comprises the tabs at the top of the screen and the command buttons on the right side of the screen.

Figure 31-2 depicts the procedures and functions used in the two forms of the `Main` screen of the Easy Selling application.

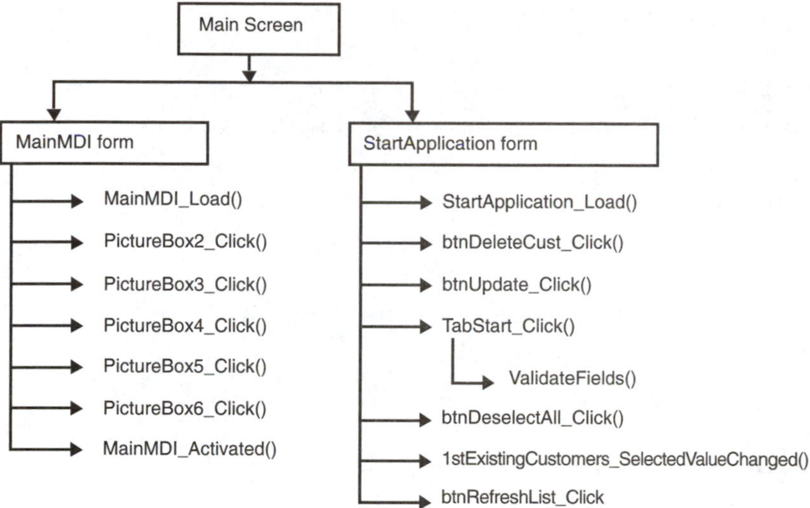

FIGURE 31-2 *The procedures and functions used in the* `MainMDI` *form and the* `StartApplication` *form*

Listing 31-1 contains the code of the `MainMDI` form of the Easy Selling application.

Listing 31-1 Code for the MainMDI Form

```
Public Class MainMDI
     Inherits System.Windows.Forms.Form
Private varCompanyName As New StartApplication.ShareClass()
Private Sub MainMDI_Load(ByVal sender As System.Object, ByVal e As
   System.EventArgs) Handles MyBase.Load
         Dim NewMDIChild As New StartApplication()
         NewMDIChild.MdiParent = Me
         NewMDIChild.Show()
         NewMDIChild.Left = 110
         NewMDIChild.Top = 0
End Sub
Private Sub PictureBox2_Click(ByVal sender As System.Object, ByVal e As
   System.EventArgs) Handles PictureBox2.Click
         Dim NewMDIChild As New ClientInfo()
```

```
            NewMDIChild.MdiParent = Me
            NewMDIChild.Show()
            NewMDIChild.Left = 110
            NewMDIChild.Top = 0
    PictureBox2.Image =
       System.Drawing.Image.FromFile("c:\easyselling\Customers_sel.jpg")
    PictureBox3.Image = System.Drawing.Image.FromFile("c:\easyselling\Issues_def.jpg")
    PictureBox4.Image =
       System.Drawing.Image.FromFile("c:\easyselling\solutions_def.jpg")
    PictureBox5.Image = System.Drawing.Image.FromFile("c:\easyselling\outputs_def.jpg")
    End Sub
    Private Sub PictureBox6_Click(ByVal sender As System.Object, ByVal e As
       System.EventArgs) Handles PictureBox6.Click
            End
    End Sub
    Private Sub PictureBox3_Click(ByVal sender As System.Object, ByVal e As
       System.EventArgs) Handles PictureBox3.Click
            If (Trim(varCompanyName.SharedValue) = "" Or varCompanyName.SharedClientID
               = 0) Then
                MsgBox("Select a Customer from the List", MsgBoxStyle.Information, "No
                   Customer Selected")
            Else
                Dim NewMDIChild As New ClientIssues()
                NewMDIChild.MdiParent = Me
                NewMDIChild.Show()
                NewMDIChild.Left = 110
                NewMDIChild.Top = 0
                PictureBox3.Image =
                   System.Drawing.Image.FromFile("c:\easyselling\Issues_sel.jpg")
                PictureBox2.Image =
                   System.Drawing.Image.FromFile("c:\easyselling\customers_def.jpg")
                PictureBox4.Image =
                   System.Drawing.Image.FromFile("c:\easyselling\solutions_def.jpg")
                PictureBox5.Image =
                   System.Drawing.Image.FromFile("c:\easyselling\outputs_def.jpg")
            End If
        End Sub
    Private Sub PictureBox4_Click(ByVal sender As System.Object, ByVal e As
```

```
    System.EventArgs) Handles PictureBox4.Click
        If (Trim(varCompanyName.SharedValue) = "" Or
                varCompanyName.SharedClientID = 0) Then
MsgBox("Select a Customer from the List", MsgBoxStyle.Information, "No
    Customer Selected")
        Else
                Dim NewMDIChild As New ClientSolutions()
        NewMDIChild.MdiParent = Me
        NewMDIChild.Show()
        NewMDIChild.Left = 110
        NewMDIChild.Top = 0
        PictureBox4.Image =
          System.Drawing.Image.FromFile("c:\easyselling\solutions_sel.jpg")
        PictureBox2.Image =
          System.Drawing.Image.FromFile("c:\easyselling\customers_def.jpg")
        PictureBox3.Image =
          System.Drawing.Image.FromFile("c:\easyselling\Issues_def.jpg")
        PictureBox5.Image =
          System.Drawing.Image.FromFile("c:\easyselling\outputs_def.jpg")
        End If
    End Sub
Private Sub PictureBox5_Click(ByVal sender As System.Object, ByVal e As
    System.EventArgs) Handles PictureBox5.Click
        If (Trim(varCompanyName.SharedValue) = "" Or
            varCompanyName.SharedClientID = 0) Then
            MsgBox("Select a Customer from the List", MsgBoxStyle.Information, "No
               Customer Selected")
      Else
          Dim NewMDIChild As New ClientDocuments()
          NewMDIChild.MdiParent = Me
          NewMDIChild.Show()
          NewMDIChild.Left = 110
          NewMDIChild.Top = 0
          PictureBox5.Image =
             System.Drawing.Image.FromFile("c:\easyselling\outputs_sel.jpg")
          PictureBox2.Image =
             System.Drawing.Image.FromFile("c:\easyselling\customers_def.jpg")
          PictureBox3.Image =
```

```
                System.Drawing.Image.FromFile("c:\easyselling\Issues_def.jpg")
              PictureBox4.Image =
                System.Drawing.Image.FromFile("c:\easyselling\solutions_def.jpg")
          End If
      End Sub
Private Sub MainMDI_Activated(ByVal sender As Object, ByVal e As System.EventArgs)
   Handles MyBase.Activated
PictureBox2.Image =
   System.Drawing.Image.FromFile("c:\easyselling\customers_def.jpg")
PictureBox3.Image = System.Drawing.Image.FromFile("c:\easyselling\Issues_def.jpg")
PictureBox4.Image =
   System.Drawing.Image.FromFile("c:\easyselling\solutions_def.jpg")
PictureBox5.Image = System.Drawing.Image.FromFile("c:\easyselling\outputs_def.jpg")
End Sub
End Class
```

I will now discuss each procedure declared in form1 of the `Main` screen of the `Easy Selling` application.

The MainMDI_Load Procedure

The `MainMDI_Load` procedure is executed when the Easy Selling application is started. This procedure shows the `MainMDI` form and then positions the `StartApplication` form at the appropriate position. The code for the `MainMDI_Load` procedure is as follows:

```
Private Sub MainMDI_Load(ByVal sender As System.Object, ByVal e As
   System.EventArgs) Handles MyBase.Load
        Dim NewMDIChild As New StartApplication()
'sets the Parent Form of the Child window
        NewMDIChild.MdiParent = Me
'displays the new form
        NewMDIChild.Show()
'positions the displayed form
        NewMDIChild.Left = 110
        NewMDIChild.Top = 0
End Sub
```

The PictureBox2_Click Procedure

The PictureBox2_Click procedure is executed when the sales representative clicks the Customers button. It displays the form associated with the Customers button. This procedure also sets the images of the Issues, Solutions, Outputs, and Exit buttons. The code for the PictureBox2_Click procedure is as follows:

```
Private Sub PictureBox2_Click(ByVal sender As System.Object, ByVal e As
   System.EventArgs) Handles PictureBox2.Click
         Dim NewMDIChild As New ClientInfo()
'sets the Parent Form of the Child window
         NewMDIChild.MdiParent = Me
'displays the new form
         NewMDIChild.Show()
'positions the displayed form
         NewMDIChild.Left = 110
         NewMDIChild.Top = 0
'sets the proper images in picture boxes according to the state that they should be in
PictureBox2.Image = System.Drawing.Image.FromFile("c:\easyselling\Customers_sel.jpg")
PictureBox3.Image = System.Drawing.Image.FromFile("c:\easyselling\Issues_def.jpg")
PictureBox4.Image = System.Drawing.Image.FromFile("c:\easyselling\solutions_def.jpg")
PictureBox5.Image = System.Drawing.Image.FromFile("c:\easyselling\outputs_def.jpg")
End Sub
```

The PictureBox3_Click Procedure

The PictureBox3_Click procedure is executed when the sales representative clicks the Issues button. It displays the form associated with the Issues button. This procedure displays an error message if no customer is selected in the Main screen. In addition, it also sets the images of the Customers, Solutions, Outputs, and Exit buttons. The code for the PictureBox3_Click procedure is as follows:

```
Private Sub PictureBox3_Click(ByVal sender As System.Object, ByVal e As
   System.EventArgs) Handles PictureBox3.Click
'checks if a customer is selected or not
         If (Trim(varCompanyName.SharedValue) = "" Or varCompanyName.SharedClientID
            = 0) Then
             MsgBox("Select a Customer from the List", MsgBoxStyle.Information, "No
                Customer Selected")
```

```
        Else
            Dim NewMDIChild As New ClientIssues()
'sets the Parent Form of the Child window
            NewMDIChild.MdiParent = Me
'displays the new form
            NewMDIChild.Show()
'positions the displayed form
            NewMDIChild.Left = 110
            NewMDIChild.Top = 0
'sets the proper images in picture boxes according to the state that they should be in
            PictureBox3.Image =
               System.Drawing.Image.FromFile("c:\easyselling\Issues_sel.jpg")
            PictureBox2.Image =
               System.Drawing.Image.FromFile("c:\easyselling\customers_def.jpg")
            PictureBox4.Image =
               System.Drawing.Image.FromFile("c:\easyselling\solutions_def.jpg")
            PictureBox5.Image =
               System.Drawing.Image.FromFile("c:\easyselling\outputs_def.jpg")
        End If
    End Sub
```

The PictureBox4_Click Procedure

The `PictureBox4_Click` procedure is executed when the sales representative clicks the `Solutions` button. This procedure is similar to the `PictureBox5_Click` procedure. It displays the form associated with the `Solutions` button. The `PictureBox4_Click` procedure also displays a message if no customer is selected in the `Main` screen. In addition, it also sets the images of the `Customers`, `Solutions`, `Outputs`, and `Exit` buttons. The code for the `PictureBox4_Click` procedure is as follows:

```
Private Sub PictureBox4_Click(ByVal sender As System.Object, ByVal e As
   System.EventArgs) Handles PictureBox4.Click
'checks if a customer is selected or not
If (Trim(varCompanyName.SharedValue) = "" Or
    varCompanyName.SharedClientID = 0) Then
MsgBox("Select a Customer from the List", MsgBoxStyle.Information, "No Customer
   Selected")
```

```
        Else
            Dim NewMDIChild As New ClientSolutions()
'sets the Parent Form of the Child window
            NewMDIChild.MdiParent = Me
'displays the new form
            NewMDIChild.Show()
'positions the displayed form
            NewMDIChild.Left = 110
            NewMDIChild.Top = 0
'sets the proper images in picture boxes according to the state that they should be in
PictureBox4.Image =
   System.Drawing.Image.FromFile("c:\easyselling\solutions_sel.jpg")
PictureBox2.Image =
   System.Drawing.Image.FromFile("c:\easyselling\customers_def.jpg")
PictureBox3.Image = System.Drawing.Image.FromFile("c:\easyselling\Issues_def.jpg")
PictureBox5.Image = System.Drawing.Image.FromFile("c:\easyselling\outputs_def.jpg")
        End If
End Sub
```

The PictureBox5_Click Procedure

The `PictureBox5_Click` procedure is executed when the sales representative clicks the `Outputs` button. This procedure is similar to the procedures that get triggered when the `Issues` and `Solutions` buttons are clicked. The `PictureBox5_Click` procedure displays the form associated with the `Outputs` button. The `PictureBox5_Click` procedure also displays a message if no customer is selected in the `Main` screen. In addition, it also sets the images of the `Customers`, `Solutions`, `Outputs`, and `Exit` buttons. The code for the `PictureBox5_Click` procedure is as follows:

```
Private Sub PictureBox5_Click(ByVal sender As System.Object, ByVal e As
   System.EventArgs) Handles PictureBox5.Click
'checks if a customer is selected or not
        If (Trim(varCompanyName.SharedValue) = "" Or
             varCompanyName.SharedClientID = 0) Then
MsgBox("Select a Customer from the List", MsgBoxStyle.Information, "No Customer
   Selected")
        Else
```

```
            Dim NewMDIChild As New ClientDocuments()
'sets the Parent Form of the Child window.
            NewMDIChild.MdiParent = Me
'displays the new form
            NewMDIChild.Show()
'positions the displayed form
            NewMDIChild.Left = 110
            NewMDIChild.Top = 0
'sets the proper images in picture boxes according to the state that they should be in
            PictureBox5.Image =
               System.Drawing.Image.FromFile("c:\easyselling\outputs_sel.jpg")
            PictureBox2.Image =
               System.Drawing.Image.FromFile("c:\easyselling\customers_def.jpg")
            PictureBox3.Image =
               System.Drawing.Image.FromFile("c:\easyselling\Issues_def.jpg")
            PictureBox4.Image =
               System.Drawing.Image.FromFile("c:\easyselling\solutions_def.jpg")
        End If
End Sub
```

The PictureBox6_Click Procedure

The `PictureBox6_Click` procedure is executed when the sales representative clicks the `Exit` button. The Easy Selling application is closed after this procedure is triggered. The code for the `PictureBox6_Click` procedure is as follows:

```
Private Sub PictureBox6_Click(ByVal sender As System.Object, ByVal e As
   System.EventArgs) Handles PictureBox6.Click
        End
End Sub
```

The MainMDI_Activated Procedure

The `MainMDI_Activated` procedure is executed when the `Main` screen gets the focus. The code is as follows:

```
Private Sub MainMDI_Activated(ByVal sender As Object, ByVal e As System.EventArgs)
   Handles MyBase.Activated
PictureBox2.Image =
   System.Drawing.Image.FromFile("c:\easyselling\customers_def.jpg")
```

```
PictureBox3.Image = System.Drawing.Image.FromFile("c:\easyselling\Issues_def.jpg")
PictureBox4.Image =
   System.Drawing.Image.FromFile("c:\easyselling\solutions_def.jpg")
PictureBox5.Image = System.Drawing.Image.FromFile("c:\easyselling\outputs_def.jpg")
End Sub
End Class
```

Listing 31-2 contains the code for the second form of the Main screen, the `StartApplication` form.

Listing 31-2 Code for the StartApplication Form of the Main Screen

```
Imports System.Data.OleDb
Public Class StartApplication
     Inherits System.Windows.Forms.Form
     Public Class ShareClass
          Public Shared SharedValue As String
          Public Shared SharedClientID As Long
     End Class

Private ourConn As String = "Provider=Microsoft.Jet.OLEDB.4.0;
   Data Source=C:\EasySelling\EasySelling.mdb;Persist Security Info=False"
Private clientConnection As OleDbConnection = New OleDbConnection(ourConn)
     Private clientCommand As OleDbCommand
     Private clientDataReader As OleDbDataReader
     Private strSqlStatement As String
     Friend WithEvents editName As System.Windows.Forms.TextBox
     Friend WithEvents btnDeselectAll As System.Windows.Forms.Button
     Friend WithEvents btnRefreshList As System.Windows.Forms.Button
     Private checkFirstTime As String

Private Sub StartApplication_Load(ByVal sender As System.Object, ByVal e As
   System.EventArgs) Handles MyBase.Load
          Try
               clientConnection.Open()
               strSqlStatement = "SELECT Client_Name FROM tblClients"
               clientCommand = New OleDbCommand(strSqlStatement, clientConnection)
               clientDataReader = clientCommand.ExecuteReader()
               While clientDataReader.Read
```

```
            lstExistingCustomers.Items.Add(clientDataReader.Item(0))
        End While
        clientDataReader.Close()
        strSqlStatement = "SELECT * FROM tblSalesRep"
        clientCommand = New OleDbCommand(strSqlStatement, clientConnection)
        clientDataReader = clientCommand.ExecuteReader()
        While clientDataReader.Read
editName.Text = IIf(IsDBNull(clientDataReader.Item(1)), "",
clientDataReader.Item(1))
ditTitle.Text = IIf(IsDBNull(clientDataReader.Item(2)), "",
clientDataReader.Item(2))
ditAddress_Line1.Text = IIf(IsDBNull(clientDataReader.Item(3)), "",
clientDataReader.Item(3))
ditAddress_Line2.Text = IIf(IsDBNull(clientDataReader.Item(4)), "",
clientDataReader.Item(4))
editCity.Text = IIf(IsDBNull(clientDataReader.Item(5)), "",
clientDataReader.Item(5))
editState.Text = IIf(IsDBNull(clientDataReader.Item(6)), "",
clientDataReader.Item(6))
editZipCode.Text =  IIf(IsDBNull(clientDataReader.Item(7)), "",
clientDataReader.Item(7))
editPhoneNumber.Text = IIf(IsDBNull(clientDataReader.Item(8)), "",
clientDataReader.Item(8))
editCellPhoneNumber.Text = IIf(IsDBNull(clientDataReader.Item(9)), "",
clientDataReader.Item(9))
editFax.Text = IIf(IsDBNull(clientDataReader.Item(10)), "",
clientDataReader.Item(10))
editEmailAddress.Text = IIf(IsDBNull(clientDataReader.Item(11)), "",
clientDataReader.Item(11))
editCompany.Text = IIf(IsDBNull(clientDataReader.Item(12)), "",
clientDataReader.Item(12))
       End While
          clientDataReader.Close()
          clientConnection.Close()
          AxWebBrowser1.Navigate2("c:\easyselling\help.html")
          AxWebBrowser1.BackColor = System.Drawing.Color.PowderBlue
Catch
     MsgBox(Err.Description)
```

```
        End Try
    End Sub
Private Sub btnDeleteCust_Click(ByVal sender As System.Object, ByVal e As
  System.EventArgs) Handles btnDeleteCust.Click
        Try
            Dim varReply As Integer
                If ShareClass.SharedValue = "" Then
          MsgBox("Select a Customer Name from the List.", MsgBoxStyle.Exclamation,
            "No Customer Selected")
                Else
          varReply = MsgBox("Do you Really want to Delete this Record?",
            MsgBoxStyle.YesNo,  "Confirmation")
                    If varReply = 6 Then
          strSqlStatement = "DELETE FROM tblClients WHERE Client_Name = '" &
          lstExistingCustomers.SelectedItem & "'"
                      clientConnection.Open()
          clientCommand = New OleDbCommand(strSqlStatement, clientConnection)
                      clientCommand.ExecuteNonQuery()
          strSqlStatement = "DELETE FROM tblClientExpectations WHERE Client_ID = " &
          ShareClass.SharedClientID
          clientCommand = New OleDbCommand(strSqlStatement, clientConnection)
                      clientCommand.ExecuteNonQuery()
            strSqlStatement = "DELETE FROM tblClientSolutions WHERE
              Client_ID = " & ShareClass.SharedClientID
           clientCommand = New OleDbCommand(strSqlStatement, clientConnection)
                      clientCommand.ExecuteNonQuery()
           strSqlStatement = "DELETE FROM tblProductUsageAndCompAnalysis WHERE
             Client_ID =     " &
           ShareClass.SharedClientID
       clientCommand = New OleDbCommand(strSqlStatement, clientConnection)
                      clientCommand.ExecuteNonQuery()
                      clientConnection.Close()
                      clientConnection = Nothing
                      clientConnection = New OleDbConnection(ourConn)
                      clientConnection.Open()
                      lstExistingCustomers.Items.Clear()
                      strSqlStatement = "SELECT Client_Name FROM tblClients"
            clientCommand = New OleDbCommand(strSqlStatement, clientConnection)
```

```
                clientDataReader = clientCommand.ExecuteReader()
            While clientDataReader.Read
             lstExistingCustomers.Items.Add(clientDataReader.Item(0))
                    End While
                            ShareClass.SharedValue = ""
                            clientConnection.Close()
        End If
    End If
    Catch
        MsgBox(Err.Description)
    End Try
End Sub
Private Sub btnUpdate_Click(ByVal sender As System.Object, ByVal e As
   System.EventArgs) Handles btnUpdate.Click
        Dim adoConn As New ADODB.Connection()
        Dim rsSalesRep As New ADODB.Recordset()
        Try
       adoConn.Open("Provider=Microsoft.Jet.OLEDB.4.0;Data
       Source=C:\EasySelling\EasySelling.mdb;Persist Security Info=False")
        Catch
       MsgBox("Could not open database", MsgBoxStyle.Critical,
         "Problem with Database Open")
              End
        End Try
       rsSalesRep.Open("select * from tblSalesRep", adoConn,
          ADODB.CursorTypeEnum.adOpenDynamic, ADODB.LockTypeEnum.adLockOptimistic)
        If checkFirstTime = "N" Then
          If ValidateFields() = True Then
               rsSalesRep.Fields("SalesRep_Name").Value = Trim(editName.Text)
               rsSalesRep.Fields("SalesRep_Title").Value = editTitle.Text
        rsSalesRep.Fields("Address_Line1").Value = editAddress_Line1.Text
        rsSalesRep.Fields("Address_Line2").Value = editAddress_Line2.Text
                rsSalesRep.Fields("city").Value = editCity.Text
               rsSalesRep.Fields("state").Value = editState.Text
               rsSalesRep.Fields("zipcode").Value = editZipCode.Text
        rsSalesRep.Fields("PhoneNumber").Value = Trim(editPhoneNumber.Text)
               rsSalesRep.Fields("CellPhoneNumber").Value = editCellPhoneNumber.Text
               rsSalesRep.Fields("Fax").Value = editFax.Text
```

```
            rsSalesRep.Fields("EmailAddress").Value = Trim(editEmailAddress.Text)
            rsSalesRep.Fields("CompanyName").Value = Trim(editCompany.Text)
            rsSalesRep.Update()
            MsgBox("Record Saved Successfully.", MsgBoxStyle.Information,
               "Record Saved")
     End If
    Else
       If ValidateFields() = True Then
             rsSalesRep.AddNew()
    rsSalesRep.Fields("SalesRep_Name").Value =
    Trim(editName.Text)
             rsSalesRep.Fields("SalesRep_Title").Value =
            editTitle.Text
            rsSalesRep.Fields("Address_Line1").Value =
            editAddress_Line1.Text
            rsSalesRep.Fields("Address_Line2").Value =
            editAddress_Line2.Text
            rsSalesRep.Fields("city").Value = editCity.Text
            rsSalesRep.Fields("state").Value = editState.Text
            rsSalesRep.Fields("zipcode").Value = editZipCode.Text
            rsSalesRep.Fields("PhoneNumber").Value =
            Trim(editPhoneNumber.Text)
            rsSalesRep.Fields("CellPhoneNumber").Value =
            editCellPhoneNumber.Text
            rsSalesRep.Fields("Fax").Value = editFax.Text
            rsSalesRep.Fields("EmailAddress").Value =
           Trim(editEmailAddress.Text)
           rsSalesRep.Fields("CompanyName").Value =
           Trim(editCompany.Text)
           rsSalesRep.Update()
           MsgBox("Record Saved Successfully.",
           MsgBoxStyle.Information, "Record Saved")
           strSqlStatement = "UPDATE tblInstallDecide SET
           First_time = 'N'"
           clientConnection.Open()
           clientCommand = New OleDbCommand(strSqlStatement,
           clientConnection)
           clientCommand.ExecuteNonQuery()
```

```
                clientConnection.Close()
            End If
        End If
            rsSalesRep.Close()
            adoConn.Close()
    End Sub
Private Sub TabStart_Click(ByVal sender As Object, ByVal e As System.EventArgs)
Handles TabStart.Click
        If TabStart.SelectedIndex = 1 Then
            clientConnection.Open()
            strSqlStatement = "SELECT First_Time FROM tblInstalldecide"
            clientCommand = New OleDbCommand(strSqlStatement, clientConnection)
            clientDataReader = clientCommand.ExecuteReader()
            While clientDataReader.Read
                checkFirstTime = clientDataReader.Item(0)
            End While
           If checkFirstTime = "Y" Then
     MsgBox("The Sales Representative's details are required to generate
        documents.Please fill in your details.", MsgBoxStyle.Information,
        "Welcome to EasySelling")
           End If
                 clientDataReader.Close()
                clientConnection.Close()
        End If
    End Sub
    Private Function ValidateFields() As Boolean
        If Trim(editName.Text) = "" Then
           MsgBox("Sales Representative's Name cannot be empty.",
           MsgBoxStyle.Critical, "Information Missing")
           editName.Focus()
           Return False
            Exit Function
        End If
        If Trim(editPhoneNumber.Text) = "" Then
           MsgBox("Phone Number for Sales Representative cannot be
           empty.", MsgBoxStyle.Critical, "Information Missing")
           editPhoneNumber.Focus()
           Return False
```

```
            Exit Function
        End If
        If Trim(editEmailAddress.Text) = "" Then
            MsgBox("Email Address for Sales Representative cannot be
               empty.", MsgBoxStyle.Critical, "Information Missing")
            editEmailAddress.Focus()
            Return False
             Exit Function
        End If
        If Trim(editCompany.Text) = "" Then
            MsgBox("Parent Company for Sales Representative cannot be
               empty.", MsgBoxStyle.Critical, "Information Missing")
            editCompany.Focus()
            Return False
             Exit Function
        End If
        Return True
    End Function
Private Sub btnDeselectAll_Click(ByVal sender As System.Object, ByVal e As
   System.EventArgs) Handles btnDeselectAll.Click
        lstExistingCustomers.ClearSelected()
End Sub
Private Sub lstExistingCustomers_SelectedValueChanged(ByVal sender As Object,
   ByVal e As System.EventArgs) Handles lstExistingCustomers.SelectedValueChanged
        ShareClass.SharedValue = lstExistingCustomers.SelectedItem
        clientConnection.Open()
        strSqlStatement = "SELECT Client_ID FROM tblClients WHERE
        Client_Name = '" & lstExistingCustomers.SelectedItem & "'"
        clientCommand = New OleDbCommand(strSqlStatement,
        clientConnection)
        clientDataReader = clientCommand.ExecuteReader()
        While clientDataReader.Read
            ShareClass.SharedClientID = clientDataReader.Item(0)
        End While
        clientDataReader.Close()
        clientConnection.Close()
    End Sub
    Private Sub btnRefreshList_Click(ByVal sender As System.Object,
```

```
        ByVal e As System.EventArgs) Handles btnRefreshList.Click
         lstExistingCustomers.Items.Clear()
         clientConnection.Open()
         strSqlStatement = "SELECT Client_Name FROM tblClients"
         clientCommand = New OleDbCommand(strSqlStatement,
         clientConnection)
         clientDataReader = clientCommand.ExecuteReader()
         While clientDataReader.Read
             lstExistingCustomers.Items.Add(clientDataReader.Item(0))
         End While
         clientDataReader.Close()
         clientConnection.Close()
    End Sub
End Class
```

The following sections discuss the procedures and functions of the second form on the `Main` screen.

The StartApplication_Load Procedure

The `StartApplication_Load` procedure is triggered when the Easy Selling application is started. The procedure creates a connection with the `EasySelling.mdb` database that stores the details about each client and the respective sales representative. Once the connection with the database is established, the list of customers from the `tblClients` table is displayed in the `Select from the Existing Customers:` list box on the `Main` screen. The data from the `tblSalesRep` table is displayed in the `About You` tab on the `Main` screen showing the details of the sales representative. The `StartApplication_Load` procedure also loads the help file in the `Help` tab on the `Main` screen.

This procedure uses the `try..catch..finally` structure. This structure is used to trap errors. If any error occurs while running this procedure, the statements written within `catch` are executed. If you want a particular statement or set of statements to be executed irrespective of whether an error is trapped or not, you can place them in the `finally` part of the structure. The code for the `StartApplication_Load` procedure is as follows:

```
Private Sub StartApplication_Load(ByVal sender As System.Object, ByVal e As
   System.EventArgs) Handles MyBase.Load
         Try
'loads the list of customers in the Select from the Existing Customers: list box
```

```
            clientConnection.Open()
            strSqlStatement = "SELECT Client_Name FROM tblClients"
            clientCommand = New OleDbCommand(strSqlStatement, clientConnection)
            clientDataReader = clientCommand.ExecuteReader()
            While clientDataReader.Read
                lstExistingCustomers.Items.Add(clientDataReader.Item(0))
            End While
            clientDataReader.Close()
'loads data in the About You tab on the Main screen
            strSqlStatement = "SELECT * FROM tblSalesRep"
           clientCommand = New OleDbCommand(strSqlStatement, clientConnection)
           clientDataReader = clientCommand.ExecuteReader()
           While clientDataReader.Read
             editName.Text = IIf(IsDBNull(clientDataReader.Item(1)), "",
                clientDataReader.Item(1)
             editTitle.Text = IIf(IsDBNull(clientDataReader.Item(2)), "",
                clientDataReader.Item(2))
             editAddress_Line1.Text = IIf(IsDBNull(clientDataReader.Item(3)), "",
                clientDataReader.Item(3))
             editAddress_Line2.Text = IIf(IsDBNull(clientDataReader.Item(4)), "",
                clientDataReader.Item(4))
             editCity.Text = IIf(IsDBNull(clientDataReader.Item(5)), "",
                clientDataReader.Item(5))
             editState.Text = IIf(IsDBNull(clientDataReader.Item(6)), "",
                clientDataReader.Item(6))
             editZipCode.Text =  IIf(IsDBNull(clientDataReader.Item(7)), "",
                clientDataReader.Item(7))
             editPhoneNumber.Text = IIf(IsDBNull(clientDataReader.Item(8)), "",
                clientDataReader.Item(8))
             editCellPhoneNumber.Text = IIf(IsDBNull(clientDataReader.Item(9)), "",
                clientDataReader.Item(9))
             editFax.Text = IIf(IsDBNull(clientDataReader.Item(10)), "",
                clientDataReader.Item(10))
             editEmailAddress.Text = IIf(IsDBNull(clientDataReader.Item(11)), "",
                clientDataReader.Item(11))
             editCompany.Text = IIf(IsDBNull(clientDataReader.Item(12)), "",
                clientDataReader.Item(12))
         End While
```

```
                clientDataReader.Close()
                clientConnection.Close()
'loads the help html file in the Help tab on the Main Screen
                AxWebBrowser1.Navigate2("c:\easyselling\help.html")
                AxWebBrowser1.BackColor = System.Drawing.Color.PowderBlue
        Catch
            MsgBox(Err.Description)
        End Try
    End Sub
```

The btnDeleteCust_Click Procedure

The `btnDeleteCust_Click` procedure is triggered when the `Delete Selected Customer` button is clicked. This procedure deletes the selected customer records from the database. If a customer name is not selected, a message is displayed indicating that it is mandatory to select a customer name in the `Main` screen before clicking the `Delete Selected Customer` button. The code for the `btnDeleteCust_Click` procedure is as follows:

```
Private Sub btnDeleteCust_Click(ByVal sender As System.Object, ByVal e As
    System.EventArgs) Handles btnDeleteCust.Click
        Try
            Dim varReply As Integer
                If ShareClass.SharedValue = "" Then
              MsgBox("Select a Customer Name from the List.",
                 MsgBoxStyle.Exclamation, "No Customer Selected")
                Else
              varReply = MsgBox("Do you Really want to Delete this Record?",
                 MsgBoxStyle.YesNo, "Confirmation")
                If varReply = 6 Then
'deletes record from tblClients
              strSqlStatement = "DELETE FROM tblClients WHERE Client_Name = '" &
              lstExistingCustomers.SelectedItem & "'"
                 clientConnection.Open()
              clientCommand = New OleDbCommand(strSqlStatement, clientConnection)
                 clientCommand.ExecuteNonQuery()
'deletes record from tblClientExpections
              strSqlStatement = "DELETE FROM tblClientExpectations WHERE Client_ID = "
```

```
                & ShareClass.SharedClientID
                clientCommand = New OleDbCommand(strSqlStatement, clientConnection)
                   clientCommand.ExecuteNonQuery()

'deletes record from tblClientSolutions
                strSqlStatement = "DELETE FROM tblClientSolutions WHERE Client_ID = " &
                ShareClass.SharedClientID
                clientCommand = New OleDbCommand(strSqlStatement, clientConnection)
                   clientCommand.ExecuteNonQuery()
'deletes record from tblClientSolutions
                strSqlStatement = "DELETE FROM tblProductUsageAndCompAnalysis WHERE
                  Client_ID = " & ShareClass.SharedClientID
                clientCommand = New OleDbCommand(strSqlStatement, clientConnection)
                   clientCommand.ExecuteNonQuery()
                                 clientConnection.Close()
                                 clientConnection = Nothing
                                 clientConnection = New OleDbConnection(ourConn)
                                 clientConnection.Open()
                                 lstExistingCustomers.Items.Clear()
                                strSqlStatement = "SELECT Client_Name FROM tblClients"
                clientCommand = New OleDbCommand(strSqlStatement, clientConnection)
                   clientDataReader = clientCommand.ExecuteReader()
                        While clientDataReader.Read

lstExistingCustomers.Items.Add(clientDataReader.Item(0))
                     End While
                ShareClass.SharedValue = ""
                   clientConnection.Close()
           End If
        End If
      Catch
            MsgBox(Err.Description)
        End Try
    End Sub
```

The btnUpdate_Click Procedure

The btnUpdate_Click procedure is triggered when the sales representative saves the changes made in any screen. This procedure is also triggered when the sales representative clicks the Proceed button on the Outputs screen. This procedure establishes a connection with the database. If the connection is not established, the application displays an error message indicating that the database could not be opened. If the application is being used for the first time, the details of the sales representative are filled in on the About You tab on the Main screen. Subsequently, the tblInstallDecide table is updated with the details of the sales representative. The code for the btnUpdate_Click procedure is as follows:

```
Private Sub btnUpdate_Click(ByVal sender As System.Object, ByVal e As
   System.EventArgs) Handles btnUpdate.Click
         Dim adoConn As New ADODB.Connection()
         Dim rsSalesRep As New ADODB.Recordset()
         Try
        adoConn.Open("Provider=Microsoft.Jet.OLEDB.4.0;Data
           Source=C:\EasySelling\EasySelling.mdb;Persist Security Info=False")
         Catch
        MsgBox("Could not open database", MsgBoxStyle.Critical,
           "Problem with Database Open")
                 End
         End Try
        rsSalesRep.Open("select * from tblSalesRep", adoConn,
        ADODB.CursorTypeEnum.adOpenDynamic, ADODB.LockTypeEnum.adLockOptimistic)
'checks if the application is being run the first time, if 'N' then edit or addnew
                    If checkFirstTime = "N" Then
                                 If ValidateFields() = True Then
                             rsSalesRep.Fields("SalesRep_Name").Value =
                           Trim(editName.Text)
        rsSalesRep.Fields("SalesRep_Title").Value = editTitle.Text
        rsSalesRep.Fields("Address_Line1").Value =
           editAddress_Line1.Text
        rsSalesRep.Fields("Address_Line2").Value =
           editAddress_Line2.Text
        rsSalesRep.Fields("city").Value = editCity.Text
        rsSalesRep.Fields("state").Value = editState.Text
```

```
        rsSalesRep.Fields("zipcode").Value =
           editZipCode.Text
        rsSalesRep.Fields("PhoneNumber").Value
           = Trim(editPhoneNumber.Text)
        rsSalesRep.Fields("CellPhoneNumber").Value =
           editCellPhoneNumber.Text
        rsSalesRep.Fields("Fax").Value =
           editFax.Text
        rsSalesRep.Fields("EmailAddress").Value =
           Trim(editEmailAddress.Text)
        rsSalesRep.Fields("CompanyName").Value =
           Trim(editCompany.Text)
        rsSalesRep.Update()
           MsgBox("Record Saved Successfully.", MsgBoxStyle.Information,
           "Record  Saved")
                    End If
         Else
'if the data for sales rep is not entered as yet then add a new record
              If ValidateFields() = True Then
                 rsSalesRep.AddNew()
                 rsSalesRep.Fields("SalesRep_Name").Value =
                 Trim(editName.Text)
                 rsSalesRep.Fields("SalesRep_Title").Value =
                 editTitle.Text
                 rsSalesRep.Fields("Address_Line1").Value =
                 editAddress_Line1.Text
                 rsSalesRep.Fields("Address_Line2").Value =
                 editAddress_Line2.Text
                 rsSalesRep.Fields("city").Value = editCity.Text
                 rsSalesRep.Fields("state").Value = editState.Text
                 rsSalesRep.Fields("zipcode").Value = editZipCode.Text
                 rsSalesRep.Fields("PhoneNumber").Value =
                 Trim(editPhoneNumber.Text)
                 rsSalesRep.Fields("CellPhoneNumber").Value =
                 editCellPhoneNumber.Text
                 rsSalesRep.Fields("Fax").Value = editFax.Text
```

```
                    rsSalesRep.Fields("EmailAddress").Value =
                    Trim(editEmailAddress.Text)
                    rsSalesRep.Fields("CompanyName").Value =
                    Trim(editCompany.Text)
                    rsSalesRep.Update()
                    MsgBox("Record Saved Successfully.",
                    MsgBoxStyle.Information, "Record Saved")
'sets the flag for tblInstalldecide as 'N' to indicate that sales rep record
 'has been added
                    strSqlStatement = "UPDATE tblInstallDecide SET
                    First_time = 'N'"
                    clientConnection.Open()
                    clientCommand = New OleDbCommand(strSqlStatement,
                    clientConnection)
                    clientCommand.ExecuteNonQuery()
                    clientConnection.Close()
                 End If
               End If
                rsSalesRep.Close()
                adoConn.Close()
          End Sub
```

The TabStart_Click Procedure

The `TabStart_Click` procedure is triggered when the sales representative clicks on the `About You` tab on the `Main` screen. If the application is being used for the first time, a message is displayed indicating that the details of the sales representative need to be filled out before entering the details of any customer. This procedure also contains a `ValidateFields` function. There are a few mandatory fields in the `About You` page, such as name, phone number, e-mail, address, and company name of the sales representative. If any one of these fields is empty, the document is not saved in the database, and an error message is displayed. The code for the `TabStart Click` procedure is as follows:

```
Private Sub TabStart_Click(ByVal sender As Object, ByVal e As System.EventArgs)
   Handles TabStart.Click
         If TabStart.SelectedIndex = 1 Then
 'checks if running for the first time and give a message
              clientConnection.Open()
```

```
            strSqlStatement = "SELECT First_Time FROM tblInstalldecide"
            clientCommand = New OleDbCommand(strSqlStatement, clientConnection)
            clientDataReader = clientCommand.ExecuteReader()
            While clientDataReader.Read
                checkFirstTime = clientDataReader.Item(0)
            End While
            If checkFirstTime = "Y" Then
MsgBox("The Sales Representative's details are required to generate
   documents.Please fill in your details.", MsgBoxStyle.Information,
   "Welcome to EasySelling")
            End If
                 clientDataReader.Close()
                 clientConnection.Close()

        End If
    End Sub

    Private Function ValidateFields() As Boolean
'the name, phone number, emailaddress and company name are required fields
        If Trim(editName.Text) = "" Then
                          MsgBox("Sales Representative's Name cannot be empty.",
                          MsgBoxStyle.Critical, "Information Missing")
              editName.Focus()
           Return False
            Exit Function
        End If
        If Trim(editPhoneNumber.Text) = "" Then
            MsgBox("Phone Number for Sales Representative cannot be
            empty.", MsgBoxStyle.Critical, "Information Missing")
            editPhoneNumber.Focus()
            Return False
            Exit Function
        End If
        If Trim(editEmailAddress.Text) = "" Then
           MsgBox("Email Address for Sales Representative cannot be
           empty.", MsgBoxStyle.Critical, "Information Missing")
           editEmailAddress.Focus()
```

```
            Return False
             Exit Function
        End If
        If Trim(editCompany.Text) = "" Then
            MsgBox("Parent Company for Sales Representative cannot be
            empty.", MsgBoxStyle.Critical, "Information Missing")
            editCompany.Focus()
            Return False
             Exit Function
        End If
        Return True
    End Function
```

The btnDeselectAll_Click Procedure

The `btnDeselectAll_Click` procedure is triggered when the sales representative clicks the `Deselect All` button on the `Main` screen. This procedure deletes all the customer records from the database. The code for the `btnDeselectAll_Click` procedure is as follows:

```
Private Sub btnDeselectAll_Click(ByVal sender As System.Object, ByVal e As
System.EventArgs) Handles btnDeselectAll.Click
'clears the list box
        lstExistingCustomers.ClearSelected()
    End Sub
```

The lstExistingCustomers_SelectedValueChanged Procedure

The `lstExistingCustomers_SelectedValueChanged` procedure is triggered when a customer name is selected in the `Select from the Existing Customers:` list box on the `Main` screen. This procedure sets the selected customer as the current customer. The code for the `lstExistingCustomers_SelectedValueChanged` procedure is as follows:

```
Private Sub lstExistingCustomers_SelectedValueChanged(ByVal sender As Object, ByVal e
   As System.EventArgs) Handles lstExistingCustomers.SelectedValueChanged
  'sets the selected customer as the current customer
        ShareClass.SharedValue = lstExistingCustomers.SelectedItem
        clientConnection.Open()
```

```
        strSqlStatement = "SELECT Client_ID FROM tblClients WHERE
        Client_Name = '" & lstExistingCustomers.SelectedItem & "'"
        clientCommand = New OleDbCommand(strSqlStatement,
        clientConnection)
        clientDataReader = clientCommand.ExecuteReader()
        While clientDataReader.Read
            ShareClass.SharedClientID = clientDataReader.Item(0)
        End While
        clientDataReader.Close()
        clientConnection.Close()
    End Sub
```

The btnRefreshList_Click Procedure

The `btnRefreshList_Click` procedure is triggered when the sales representative clicks the `Refresh Customer List` button on the `Main` screen. This procedure is used to list the client names stored in the `tblClients` table. The procedure refreshes the list of customers from the database. The code for the `btnRefreshList_Click` procedure is as follows:

```
Private Sub btnRefreshList_Click(ByVal sender As System.Object,
   ByVal e As System.EventArgs) Handles btnRefreshList.Click
'refreshes the list of customer from the database to reflect the latest entries
        lstExistingCustomers.Items.Clear()
        clientConnection.Open()
        strSqlStatement = "SELECT Client_Name FROM tblClients"
        clientCommand = New OleDbCommand(strSqlStatement,
        clientConnection)
        clientDataReader = clientCommand.ExecuteReader()
        While clientDataReader.Read
            lstExistingCustomers.Items.Add(clientDataReader.Item(0))
        End While
        clientDataReader.Close()
        clientConnection.Close()
    End Sub
End Class
```

Summary

In this chapter, you coded the `Main` screen of the Easy Selling application. You learned the main procedures and functions used in the forms. In the next chapter, you will learn to code the `Customers` screen of the Easy Selling application.

Chapter 32

Coding the Customers Screen of the Easy Selling Application

Chapter 31, "Coding the Main Screen of the Easy Selling Application," discussed the working of the `Main` screen. This chapter discusses the code of the `Customers` screen of the Easy Selling application.

Working of the Customers Screen of the Easy Selling Application

This section discusses the procedures and functions used in the `Customers` screen of the Easy Selling application. This screen comprises three tabs: `Profile`, `Product Usage and Competitors - I`, and `Product Usage and Competitors - II`.

Figures 32-1, 32-2, and 32-3 show the three tabs and their respective pages used in the `Customers` screen of the Easy Selling application.

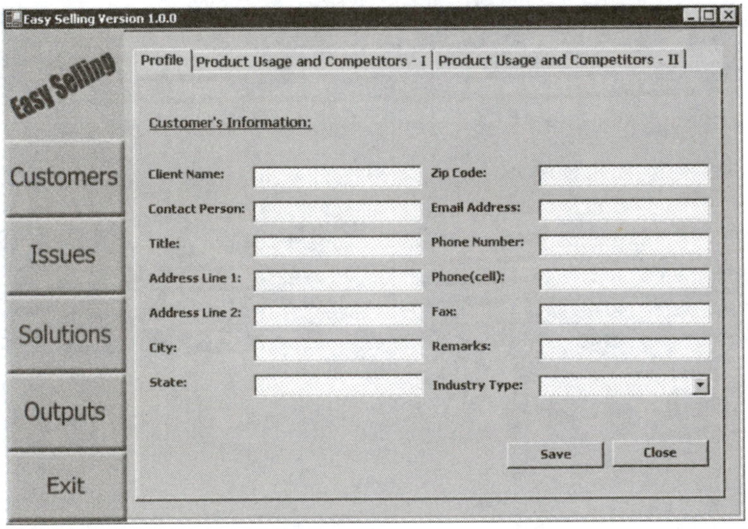

FIGURE 32-1 *The* `Profile` *tab of the* `Customers` *screen*

The `Customers` screen is a combination of the `MainMDI` form and the `ClientInfo` form. The `ClientInfo` form is initiated when the sales representative clicks on the `Customers` button in the navigation bar. Figure 32-4 depicts the procedures and functions used in the `Customers` screen of the Easy Selling application.

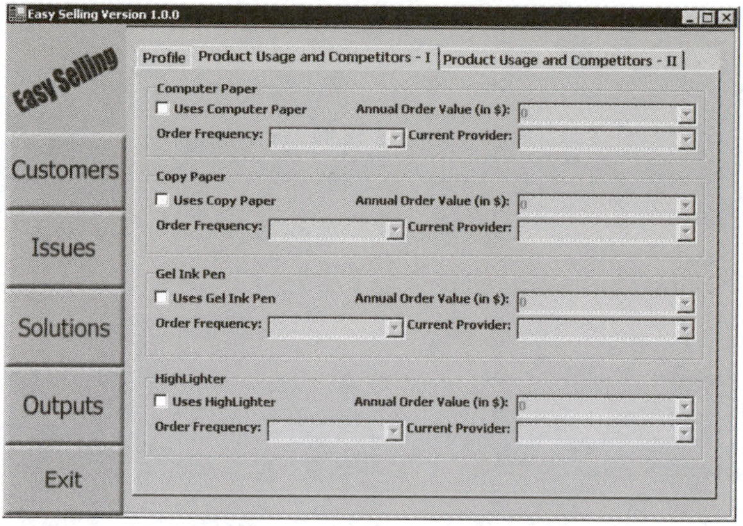

FIGURE 32-2 *The* `Product Usage and Competitors - I` *tab of the* `Customers` *screen*

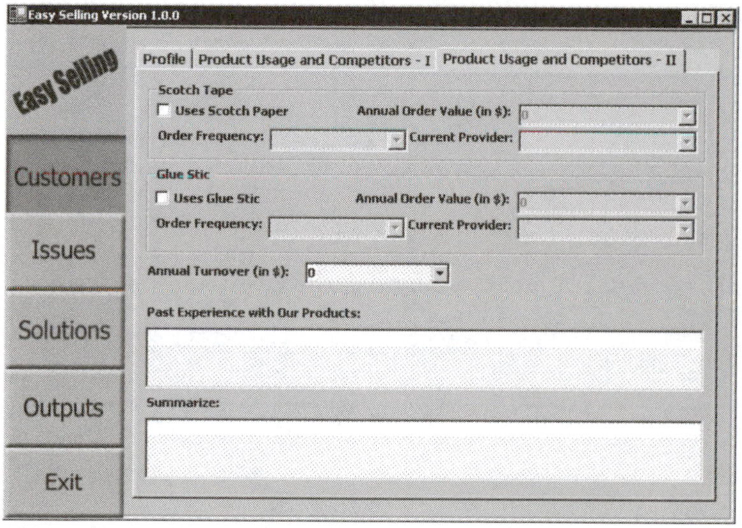

FIGURE 32-3 *The* `Product Usage and Competitors - II` *tab of the* `Customers` *screen*

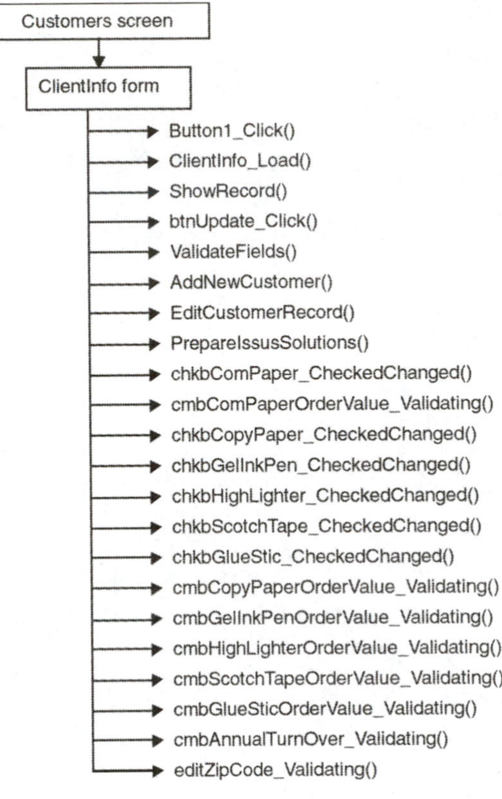

FIGURE 32-4 *The procedures and functions used in the* `ClientInfo` *form*

Listing 32-1 shows the code of the `ClientInfo` form of the Easy Selling application.

Listing 32-1 Code for the ClientInfo Form

```
Imports System.Data.OleDb
Public Class ClientInfo
    Inherits System.Windows.Forms.Form
    Private ourConn As String = "Provider=Microsoft.Jet.OLEDB.4.0;
       Data Source=C:\EasySelling\EasySelling.mdb;Persist Security Info=False"
    Private clientConnection As OleDbConnection = New OleDbConnection(ourConn)
    Private clientCommand As OleDbCommand
    Private clientDataReader As OleDbDataReader
    Friend WithEvents chkbComPaper As System.Windows.Forms.CheckBox
    Friend WithEvents cmbComPaperOrderValue As System.Windows.Forms.ComboBox
```

```
    Friend WithEvents cmbComPaperOrdFreq As System.Windows.Forms.ComboBox
    Friend WithEvents cmbComPaperCurrPro As System.Windows.Forms.ComboBox
    Friend WithEvents cmbCopyPaperOrderValue As System.Windows.Forms.ComboBox
    Friend WithEvents cmbCopyPaperOrdFreq As System.Windows.Forms.ComboBox
    Friend WithEvents chkbCopyPaper As System.Windows.Forms.CheckBox
    Friend WithEvents cmbCopyPaperCurrPro As System.Windows.Forms.ComboBox
    Friend WithEvents cmbGelInkPenOrderValue As System.Windows.Forms.ComboBox
    Friend WithEvents chkbGelInkPen As System.Windows.Forms.CheckBox
    Friend WithEvents cmbGelInkPenOrdFreq As System.Windows.Forms.ComboBox
    Friend WithEvents cmbGelInkPenCurrPro As System.Windows.Forms.ComboBox
    Friend WithEvents chkbHighLighter As System.Windows.Forms.CheckBox
    Friend WithEvents cmbHighLighterCurrPro As System.Windows.Forms.ComboBox
    Friend WithEvents cmbHighLighterOrderValue As System.Windows.Forms.ComboBox
    Friend WithEvents cmbHighLighterOrdFreq As System.Windows.Forms.ComboBox
    Friend WithEvents cmbScotchTapeOrderValue As System.Windows.Forms.ComboBox
    Friend WithEvents chkbScotchTape As System.Windows.Forms.CheckBox
    Friend WithEvents cmbScotchTapeOrdFreq As System.Windows.Forms.ComboBox
    Friend WithEvents cmbScotchTapeCurrPro As System.Windows.Forms.ComboBox
    Friend WithEvents cmbGlueSticOrderValue As System.Windows.Forms.ComboBox
    Friend WithEvents chkbGlueStic As System.Windows.Forms.CheckBox
    Friend WithEvents cmbGlueSticCurrPro As System.Windows.Forms.ComboBox
    Friend WithEvents cmbGlueSticOrdFreq As System.Windows.Forms.ComboBox
    Friend WithEvents cmbAnnualTurnOver As System.Windows.Forms.ComboBox
    Friend WithEvents txtGeneralComments As System.Windows.Forms.TextBox
    Friend WithEvents txtPastExp As System.Windows.Forms.TextBox
    Private strSqlStatement As String
    Private varCompanyName As New StartApplication.ShareClass()
    Private clientID As Long
    Private adoConn As New ADODB.Connection()
    Private rsSalesRep As New ADODB.Recordset()

Private Sub Button1_Click(ByVal sender As System.Object, ByVal e As
   System.EventArgs) Handles Button1.Click
        Dim NewMDIParent As New MainMDI()
        NewMDIParent.Show()
        NewMDIParent.Hide()
        Me.Close()
    End Sub
```

```
Private Sub ClientInfo_Load(ByVal sender As System.Object, ByVal e As
   System.EventArgs) Handles MyBase.Load
        If (Trim(varCompanyName.SharedValue) = "" Or varCompanyName.SharedClientID
           = 0) Then
        Else
            Call ShowRecord(varCompanyName.SharedValue)
            editClientName.Enabled = False
        End If
    End Sub
    Private Sub ShowRecord(ByVal strCustName As String)
        Try
            clientConnection.Open()
            strSqlStatement = "SELECT * FROM tblClients WHERE Client_Name = '" &
               strCustName & "'"
            clientCommand = New OleDbCommand(strSqlStatement, clientConnection)
            clientDataReader = clientCommand.ExecuteReader()
            While clientDataReader.Read
                editClientName.Text = IIf(IsDBNull(clientDataReader.Item(1)), "",
                   clientDataReader.Item(1))
                editContactPerson.Text = IIf(IsDBNull(clientDataReader.Item(2)), "",
                clientDataReader.Item(2))
                editTitle.Text = IIf(IsDBNull(clientDataReader.Item(3)), "",
                   clientDataReader.Item(3))
                editAddressLine1.Text = IIf(IsDBNull(clientDataReader.Item(4)), "",
                clientDataReader.Item(4))
                editAddressLine2.Text = IIf(IsDBNull(clientDataReader.Item(5)), "",
                clientDataReader.Item(5))
                editCity.Text = IIf(IsDBNull(clientDataReader.Item(6)), "",
                   clientDataReader.Item(6))
                editState.Text = IIf(IsDBNull(clientDataReader.Item(7)), "",
                   clientDataReader.Item(7))
                editZipCode.Text = IIf(IsDBNull(clientDataReader.Item(8)), "",
                   clientDataReader.Item(8))
                editRemarks.Text = IIf(IsDBNull(clientDataReader.Item(9)), "",
                   clientDataReader.Item(9))
```

```
        editCellPhoneNumber.Text =
            IIf(IsDBNull(clientDataReader.Item(10)), "",
        clientDataReader.Item(10))
        editPhoneNumber.Text = IIf(IsDBNull(clientDataReader.Item(11)), "",
        clientDataReader.Item(11))
        editFax.Text = IIf(IsDBNull(clientDataReader.Item(12)), "",
            clientDataReader.Item(12))
        editEmailAddress.Text = IIf(IsDBNull(clientDataReader.Item(13)), "",
        clientDataReader.Item(13))
End While
clientDataReader.Close()
strSqlStatement = "SELECT Client_ID FROM tblClients WHERE Client_Name
    = '" & strCustName
& "'"
clientCommand = New OleDbCommand(strSqlStatement, clientConnection)
clientDataReader = clientCommand.ExecuteReader()
While clientDataReader.Read
        clientID = clientDataReader.Item(0)
End While
clientDataReader.Close()
strSqlStatement = "SELECT * FROM tblProductUsageAndCompAnalysis WHERE
    Client_ID = " &
clientID
clientCommand = New OleDbCommand(strSqlStatement, clientConnection)
clientDataReader = clientCommand.ExecuteReader()
While clientDataReader.Read
        cmbIndustryType.Text = IIf(IsDBNull(clientDataReader.Item(1)), "",
        clientDataReader.Item(1))
        chkbComPaper.Checked = IIf(IsDBNull(clientDataReader.Item(2)), "",
        clientDataReader.Item(2))
        cmbComPaperOrdFreq.Text = IIf(IsDBNull(clientDataReader.Item(3)), "",
        clientDataReader.Item(3))
        cmbComPaperOrderValue.Text = IIf(IsDBNull(clientDataReader.Item(4)), "",
        clientDataReader.Item(4))
        cmbComPaperCurrPro.Text = IIf(IsDBNull(clientDataReader.Item(5)), "",
        clientDataReader.Item(5))
        chkbCopyPaper.Checked = IIf(IsDBNull(clientDataReader.Item(6)), "",
        clientDataReader.Item(6))
```

```
cmbCopyPaperOrdFreq.Text = IIf(IsDBNull(clientDataReader.Item(7)), "",
clientDataReader.Item(7))
cmbCopyPaperOrderValue.Text =
   IIf(IsDBNull(clientDataReader.Item(8)), "",
clientDataReader.Item(8))
cmbCopyPaperCurrPro.Text = IIf(IsDBNull(clientDataReader.Item(9)), "",
clientDataReader.Item(9))
chkbGelInkPen.Checked = IIf(IsDBNull(clientDataReader.Item(10)), "",
clientDataReader.Item(10))
cmbGelInkPenOrdFreq.Text =
   IIf(IsDBNull(clientDataReader.Item(11)), "",
clientDataReader.Item(11))
cmbGelInkPenOrderValue.Text =
   IIf(IsDBNull(clientDataReader.Item(12)), "",
clientDataReader.Item(12))
cmbGelInkPenCurrPro.Text =
   IIf(IsDBNull(clientDataReader.Item(13)), "",
clientDataReader.Item(13))
chkbHighLighter.Checked = IIf(IsDBNull(clientDataReader.Item(14)), "",
clientDataReader.Item(14))
cmbHighLighterOrdFreq.Text =
   IIf(IsDBNull(clientDataReader.Item(15)), "",
clientDataReader.Item(15))
cmbHighLighterOrderValue.Text =
   IIf(IsDBNull(clientDataReader.Item(16)), "",
clientDataReader.Item(16))
cmbHighLighterCurrPro.Text =
   IIf(IsDBNull(clientDataReader.Item(17)), "",
clientDataReader.Item(17))
chkbScotchTape.Checked = IIf(IsDBNull(clientDataReader.Item(18)), "",
clientDataReader.Item(18))
cmbScotchTapeOrdFreq.Text =
   IIf(IsDBNull(clientDataReader.Item(19)), "",
clientDataReader.Item(19))
cmbScotchTapeOrderValue.Text =
   IIf(IsDBNull(clientDataReader.Item(20)), "",
clientDataReader.Item(20))
cmbScotchTapeCurrPro.Text =
```

```
IIf(IsDBNull(clientDataReader.Item(21)), "",
                        clientDataReader.Item(21))
                        chkbGlueStic.Checked = IIf(IsDBNull(clientDataReader.Item(22)), "",
                        clientDataReader.Item(22))
                        cmbGlueSticOrdFreq.Text = IIf(IsDBNull(clientDataReader.Item(23)), "",
                        clientDataReader.Item(23))
                        cmbGlueSticOrderValue.Text =
                           IIf(IsDBNull(clientDataReader.Item(24)), "",
                        clientDataReader.Item(24))
                        cmbGlueSticCurrPro.Text = IIf(IsDBNull(clientDataReader.Item(25)), "",
                        clientDataReader.Item(25))
                        txtGeneralComments.Text = IIf(IsDBNull(clientDataReader.Item(26)), "",
                        clientDataReader.Item(26))
                        txtPastExp.Text = IIf(IsDBNull(clientDataReader.Item(27)), "",
                           clientDataReader.Item(27))
                        cmbAnnualTurnOver.Text = IIf(IsDBNull(clientDataReader.Item(28)), "",
                        clientDataReader.Item(28))
                  End While
                  clientDataReader.Close()
                  clientConnection.Close()
            Catch
                  MsgBox(Err.Description())
            End Try
      End Sub

Private Sub btnUpdate_Click(ByVal sender As System.Object, ByVal e As
   System.EventArgs) Handles btnUpdate.Click
            Try
                  adoConn.Open("Provider=Microsoft.Jet.OLEDB.4.0;Data
                  Source=C:\EasySelling\EasySelling.mdb;Persist Security Info=False")
            Catch
                  MsgBox("Could not open database", MsgBoxStyle.Critical, "Problem with
                     Database Open")
            End Try

            If (Trim(varCompanyName.SharedValue) = "" Or varCompanyName.SharedClientID
               = 0) Then
                  Call AddNewCustomer()
```

```
    Else
        Call EditCustomerRecord()
    End If
End Sub
Private Function ValidateFields() As Boolean
    Try

        If Trim(editClientName.Text) = "" Then
            MsgBox("Customer's Name cannot be empty.", MsgBoxStyle.Critical,
               "Information Missing")
            editClientName.Focus()
            adoConn.Close()
            Return False
            Exit Function
        End If
        If Trim(editContactPerson.Text) = "" Then
            MsgBox("Contact Name cannot be empty.", MsgBoxStyle.Critical,
               "Information Missing")
            editContactPerson.Focus()
            adoConn.Close()
            Return False
            Exit Function
        End If
        If Trim(editTitle.Text) = "" Then
            MsgBox("Title cannot be empty.", MsgBoxStyle.Critical,
               "Information Missing")
            editTitle.Focus()
            adoConn.Close()
            Return False
            Exit Function
        End If
        If Trim(editAddressLine1.Text) = "" Then
            MsgBox("Address Line 1 cannot be empty.", MsgBoxStyle.Critical,
               "Information Missing")
            editAddressLine1.Focus()
            adoConn.Close()
            Return False
            Exit Function
```

```
            End If
            If Trim(cmbIndustryType.Text) = "" Then
                MsgBox("Industry Type cannot be empty.", MsgBoxStyle.Critical,
                   "Information Missing")
                cmbIndustryType.Focus()
                adoConn.Close()
                Return False
                Exit Function
            End If
            Return True
        Catch
            MsgBox(Err.Description())
        End Try
    End Function

    Private Function CheckDuplicate() As Boolean
        Try
            Dim varRecordCount As Integer
            If Trim(editClientName.Text) <> "" Then
                varRecordCount = 0
                clientConnection.Open()
                strSqlStatement = "SELECT count(*) FROM tblClients WHERE
                   Client_Name = '" &
                editClientName.Text & "'"
                clientCommand = New OleDbCommand(strSqlStatement, clientConnection)
                clientDataReader = clientCommand.ExecuteReader()
                While clientDataReader.Read
                    varRecordCount = clientDataReader.Item(0)
                End While
                clientDataReader.Close()
                clientConnection.Close()
                If varRecordCount > 0 Then
                    MsgBox("Record for This Customer Already Exists.",
                       MsgBoxStyle.Critical, "Duplicate
                    Record")
                    editClientName.Focus()
                    adoConn.Close()
                    Return False
```

```
                Exit Function
            End If
        End If
        Return True
    Catch
        MsgBox(Err.Description())
    End Try
End Function

Private Sub AddNewCustomer()
    Try
        If ValidateFields() = True Then
            If CheckDuplicate() = True Then
                'add new record
                strSqlStatement = "SELECT * FROM tblClients"
                rsSalesRep.Open(strSqlStatement, adoConn,
                ADODB.CursorTypeEnum.adOpenDynamic,
                   ADODB.LockTypeEnum.adLockOptimistic)
                rsSalesRep.AddNew()
                rsSalesRep.Fields("Client_Name").Value =
                   Trim(editClientName.Text)
                rsSalesRep.Fields("Contact_Person").Value =
                   editContactPerson.Text
                rsSalesRep.Fields("Title").Value = editTitle.Text
                rsSalesRep.Fields("Address_Line1").Value =
                   editAddressLine1.Text
                rsSalesRep.Fields("Address_Line2").Value =
                   editAddressLine2.Text
                rsSalesRep.Fields("city").Value = editCity.Text
                rsSalesRep.Fields("state").Value = editState.Text
                rsSalesRep.Fields("zipcode").Value = editZipCode.Text
                rsSalesRep.Fields("Remarks").Value = Trim(editRemarks.Text)
                rsSalesRep.Fields("CellPhoneNumber").Value =
                   editCellPhoneNumber.Text
                rsSalesRep.Fields("PhoneNumber").Value =
                   Trim(editPhoneNumber.Text)
                rsSalesRep.Fields("Fax").Value = editFax.Text
                rsSalesRep.Fields("EmailAddress").Value =
```

```
    Trim(editEmailAddress.Text)
  rsSalesRep.Update()
  rsSalesRep.Close()
  adoConn.Close()
  clientConnection.Open()
  strSqlStatement = "SELECT Client_ID FROM tblClients WHERE
    Client_Name = '" &
  editClientName.Text & "'"
  clientCommand = New OleDbCommand(strSqlStatement,
    clientConnection)
  clientDataReader = clientCommand.ExecuteReader()
  While clientDataReader.Read
      clientID = clientDataReader.Item(0)
  End While
  clientDataReader.Close()
  clientConnection.Close()
  adoConn.Open("Provider=Microsoft.Jet.OLEDB.4.0;Data
  Source=C:\EasySelling\EasySelling.mdb;Persist Security
    Info=False")
  strSqlStatement = "SELECT * FROM
    tblProductUsageAndCompAnalysis WHERE Client_ID =
  " & clientID
  rsSalesRep.Open(strSqlStatement, adoConn,
ADODB.CursorTypeEnum.adOpenDynamic,
   ADODB.LockTypeEnum.adLockOptimistic)
  rsSalesRep.AddNew()
  rsSalesRep.Fields("Client_ID").Value =
    Convert.ToInt32(clientID)
  rsSalesRep.Fields("Type_Of_Industry").Value =
    cmbIndustryType.Text
  rsSalesRep.Fields("Is_ComputerPaper_Used").Value =
    chkbComPaper.Checked
  rsSalesRep.Fields("ComPaperOrdFreq").Value =
    cmbComPaperOrdFreq.Text
  rsSalesRep.Fields("ComPaperOrdValue").Value =
  IIf(IsDBNull(cmbComPaperOrderValue.Text), 0,
Convert.ToDecimal(cmbComPaperOrderValue.Text))
```

```
rsSalesRep.Fields("ComPaperCurrProvider").Value =
   cmbComPaperCurrPro.Text
rsSalesRep.Fields("Is_CopyPaper_Used").Value =
   chkbCopyPaper.Checked
rsSalesRep.Fields("CopyPaperOrdFreq").Value =
   cmbCopyPaperOrdFreq.Text
rsSalesRep.Fields("CopyPaperOrdValue").Value =
IIf(IsDBNull(cmbCopyPaperOrderValue.Text), 0,
Convert.ToDecimal(cmbCopyPaperOrderValue.Text))
rsSalesRep.Fields("CopyPaperCurrProvider").Value =
   cmbCopyPaperCurrPro.Text
rsSalesRep.Fields("Is_GelInkPen_Used").Value =
   chkbGelInkPen.Checked
rsSalesRep.Fields("GelInkPenOrdFreq").Value =
   cmbGelInkPenOrdFreq.Text
rsSalesRep.Fields("GelInkPenOrdValue").Value =
IIf(IsDBNull(cmbGelInkPenOrderValue.Text), 0,
Convert.ToDecimal(cmbGelInkPenOrderValue.Text))
rsSalesRep.Fields("GelInkPenCurrProvider").Value =
   cmbGelInkPenCurrPro.Text
rsSalesRep.Fields("Is_HighLighter_Used").Value =
   chkbHighLighter.Checked
rsSalesRep.Fields("HighLighterOrdFreq").Value =
   cmbHighLighterOrdFreq.Text
rsSalesRep.Fields("HighLighterOrdValue").Value =
IIf(IsDBNull(cmbHighLighterOrderValue.Text), 0,
Convert.ToDecimal(cmbHighLighterOrderValue.Text))
rsSalesRep.Fields("HighLighterCurrProvider").Value =
   cmbHighLighterCurrPro.Text
rsSalesRep.Fields("Is_ScotchTape_Used").Value =
   chkbScotchTape.Checked
rsSalesRep.Fields("ScotchTapeOrdFreq").Value =
   cmbScotchTapeOrdFreq.Text
rsSalesRep.Fields("ScotchTapeOrdValue").Value =
IIf(IsDBNull(cmbScotchTapeOrderValue.Text), 0,
Convert.ToDecimal(cmbScotchTapeOrderValue.Text))
rsSalesRep.Fields("ScotchTapeCurrProvider").Value =
   cmbScotchTapeCurrPro.Text
```

```
                rsSalesRep.Fields("Is_GlueStics_Used").Value =
                   chkbGlueStic.Checked
                rsSalesRep.Fields("GlueSticsOrdFreq").Value =
                   cmbGlueSticOrdFreq.Text
                rsSalesRep.Fields("GlueSticsOrdValue").Value =
                IIf(IsDBNull(cmbGlueSticOrderValue.Text), 0,
               Convert.ToDecimal(cmbGlueSticOrderValue.Text))
                rsSalesRep.Fields("GlueSticsCurrProvider").Value =
                   cmbGlueSticCurrPro.Text
                rsSalesRep.Fields("General_Comments").Value =
                   txtGeneralComments.Text
                rsSalesRep.Fields("UsedOurProductsBefore").Value =
                   txtPastExp.Text
                rsSalesRep.Fields("AnnualTurnOver").Value =
                   cmbAnnualTurnOver.Text
                rsSalesRep.Update()
                rsSalesRep.Close()
                adoConn.Close()
                Call PrepareIssuesSolutions()
                MsgBox("New Customer Record Saved Successfully.",
                   MsgBoxStyle.Information, "New
                Record Saved")
                varCompanyName.SharedValue = Trim(editClientName.Text)
                varCompanyName.SharedClientID = 0
            End If
        End If
    Catch
        MsgBox(Err.Description())
    End Try
End Sub
Private Sub EditCustomerRecord()
    Try
        If ValidateFields() = True Then
            strSqlStatement = "SELECT * FROM tblClients WHERE Client_ID=" &
               clientID
            rsSalesRep.Open(strSqlStatement, adoConn,
               ADODB.CursorTypeEnum.adOpenDynamic,
            ADODB.LockTypeEnum.adLockOptimistic)
```

```
rsSalesRep.Fields("Client_Name").Value = Trim(editClientName.Text)
rsSalesRep.Fields("Contact_Person").Value = editContactPerson.Text
rsSalesRep.Fields("Title").Value = editTitle.Text
rsSalesRep.Fields("Address_Line1").Value = editAddressLine1.Text
rsSalesRep.Fields("Address_Line2").Value = editAddressLine2.Text
rsSalesRep.Fields("city").Value = editCity.Text
rsSalesRep.Fields("state").Value = editState.Text
rsSalesRep.Fields("zipcode").Value = editZipCode.Text
rsSalesRep.Fields("Remarks").Value = Trim(editRemarks.Text)
rsSalesRep.Fields("CellPhoneNumber").Value =
   editCellPhoneNumber.Text
rsSalesRep.Fields("PhoneNumber").Value =
   Trim(editPhoneNumber.Text)
rsSalesRep.Fields("Fax").Value = editFax.Text
rsSalesRep.Fields("EmailAddress").Value =
   Trim(editEmailAddress.Text)
rsSalesRep.Update()
rsSalesRep.Close()
'edit data in tblProductUsageAndCompAnalysis table
strSqlStatement = "SELECT * FROM tblProductUsageAndCompAnalysis
   WHERE Client_ID = "
& clientID
rsSalesRep.Open(strSqlStatement, adoConn,
   ADODB.CursorTypeEnum.adOpenDynamic,
ADODB.LockTypeEnum.adLockOptimistic)
rsSalesRep.Fields("Type_Of_Industry").Value = cmbIndustryType.Text
rsSalesRep.Fields("Is_ComputerPaper_Used").Value =
   chkbComPaper.Checked
rsSalesRep.Fields("ComPaperOrdFreq").Value =
   cmbComPaperOrdFreq.Text
rsSalesRep.Fields("ComPaperOrdValue").Value =
IIf(IsDBNull(cmbComPaperOrderValue.Text), 0,
Convert.ToDecimal(cmbComPaperOrderValue.Text))
rsSalesRep.Fields("ComPaperCurrProvider").Value =
   cmbComPaperCurrPro.Text
```

```
 rsSalesRep.Fields("Is_CopyPaper_Used").Value =
    chkbCopyPaper.Checked
 rsSalesRep.Fields("CopyPaperOrdFreq").Value =
    cmbCopyPaperOrdFreq.Text
 rsSalesRep.Fields("CopyPaperOrdValue").Value =
 IIf(IsDBNull(cmbCopyPaperOrderValue.Text), 0,
Convert.ToDecimal(cmbCopyPaperOrderValue.Text))
 rsSalesRep.Fields("CopyPaperCurrProvider").Value =
    cmbCopyPaperCurrPro.Text
 rsSalesRep.Fields("Is_GelInkPen_Used").Value =
    chkbGelInkPen.Checked
 rsSalesRep.Fields("GelInkPenOrdFreq").Value =
    cmbGelInkPenOrdFreq.Text
 rsSalesRep.Fields("GelInkPenOrdValue").Value =
 IIf(IsDBNull(cmbGelInkPenOrderValue.Text), 0,
Convert.ToDecimal(cmbGelInkPenOrderValue.Text))
 rsSalesRep.Fields("GelInkPenCurrProvider").Value =
    cmbGelInkPenCurrPro.Text
 rsSalesRep.Fields("Is_HighLighter_Used").Value =
    chkbHighLighter.Checked
 rsSalesRep.Fields("HighLighterOrdFreq").Value =
    cmbHighLighterOrdFreq.Text
 rsSalesRep.Fields("HighLighterOrdValue").Value =
 IIf(IsDBNull(cmbHighLighterOrderValue.Text), 0,
Convert.ToDecimal(cmbHighLighterOrderValue.Text))
 rsSalesRep.Fields("HighLighterCurrProvider").Value =
    cmbHighLighterCurrPro.Text

 rsSalesRep.Fields("Is_ScotchTape_Used").Value =
    chkbScotchTape.Checked
 rsSalesRep.Fields("ScotchTapeOrdFreq").Value =
    cmbScotchTapeOrdFreq.Text
 rsSalesRep.Fields("ScotchTapeOrdValue").Value =
 IIf(IsDBNull(cmbScotchTapeOrderValue.Text), 0,
Convert.ToDecimal(cmbScotchTapeOrderValue.Text))
```

```
                rsSalesRep.Fields("ScotchTapeCurrProvider").Value =
                   cmbScotchTapeCurrPro.Text
                rsSalesRep.Fields("Is_GlueStics_Used").Value =
                   chkbGlueStic.Checked
                rsSalesRep.Fields("GlueSticsOrdFreq").Value =
                   cmbGlueSticOrdFreq.Text
                rsSalesRep.Fields("GlueSticsOrdValue").Value =
                   IIf(IsDBNull(cmbGlueSticOrderValue.Text),
                0, Convert.ToDecimal(cmbGlueSticOrderValue.Text))
                rsSalesRep.Fields("GlueSticsCurrProvider").Value =
                   cmbGlueSticCurrPro.Text
                rsSalesRep.Fields("General_Comments").Value =
                   txtGeneralComments.Text
                rsSalesRep.Fields("UsedOurProductsBefore").Value = txtPastExp.Text
                rsSalesRep.Fields("AnnualTurnOver").Value = cmbAnnualTurnOver.Text
                rsSalesRep.Update()
                rsSalesRep.Close()
                adoConn.Close()
                MsgBox("Record Saved Successfully.", MsgBoxStyle.Information,
                   "Record Saved")
            End If
        Catch
            MsgBox(Err.Description())
        End Try
    End Sub
    Private Sub PrepareIssuesSolutions()
        Dim varfalse As Boolean
        varfalse = False
        Try
            strSqlStatement = "INSERT INTO tblClientExpectations SELECT " &
               clientID & " AS Client_ID," &
            varfalse & " AS selected,Expectations AS Expectation FROM
               tblStandardExpectations"
            clientConnection.Open()
            clientCommand = New OleDbCommand(strSqlStatement, clientConnection)
            clientCommand.ExecuteNonQuery()
```

```
            clientConnection.Close()
        Catch
            MsgBox(Err.Description())
        End Try
        Try
            strSqlStatement = "INSERT INTO tblClientSolutions SELECT " & clientID
               & " AS Client_ID," &
            varfalse & " AS selected,Solutions AS Solution FROM
               tblStandardSolutions"
            clientConnection.Open()
            clientCommand = New OleDbCommand(strSqlStatement, clientConnection)
            clientCommand.ExecuteNonQuery()
            clientConnection.Close()
        Catch
            MsgBox(Err.Description())
        End Try
    End Sub
Private Sub chkbComPaper_CheckedChanged(ByVal sender As System.Object, ByVal e As
   System.EventArgs) Handles chkbComPaper.CheckedChanged
        'if the check box is selected then enable the remaining fields for this
           product
        'else disable the remaining fields and set default values
        If chkbComPaper.Checked = True Then
            cmbComPaperOrderValue.Enabled = True
            cmbComPaperOrdFreq.Enabled = True
            cmbComPaperCurrPro.Enabled = True
        Else
            cmbComPaperOrderValue.Text = 0
            cmbComPaperOrdFreq.Text = ""
            cmbComPaperCurrPro.Text = ""
            cmbComPaperOrderValue.Enabled = False
            cmbComPaperOrdFreq.Enabled = False
            cmbComPaperCurrPro.Enabled = False
        End If
    End Sub
```

```
Private Sub cmbComPaperOrderValue_Validating(ByVal sender As Object, ByVal e As
   System.ComponentModel.CancelEventArgs) Handles cmbComPaperOrderValue.Validating
        'check if the value entered is numeric or not
        If Not IsNumeric(cmbComPaperOrderValue.Text) Then
            MsgBox("Enter a Numeric Value", MsgBoxStyle.Critical, "Incorrect
               DataType")
            cmbComPaperOrderValue.Focus()
        End If
    End Sub

Private Sub chkbCopyPaper_CheckedChanged(ByVal sender As System.Object, ByVal e As
   System.EventArgs) Handles chkbCopyPaper.CheckedChanged
        'if the check box is selected then enable the remaining fields for this
           product
        'else disable the remaining fields and set default values
        If chkbCopyPaper.Checked = True Then
            cmbCopyPaperOrderValue.Enabled = True
            cmbCopyPaperOrdFreq.Enabled = True
            cmbCopyPaperCurrPro.Enabled = True
        Else
            cmbCopyPaperOrderValue.Text = 0
            cmbCopyPaperOrdFreq.Text = ""
            cmbCopyPaperCurrPro.Text = ""
            cmbCopyPaperOrderValue.Enabled = False
            cmbCopyPaperOrdFreq.Enabled = False
            cmbCopyPaperCurrPro.Enabled = False
        End If
    End Sub

Private Sub chkbGelInkPen_CheckedChanged(ByVal sender As System.Object, ByVal e As
   System.EventArgs) Handles chkbGelInkPen.CheckedChanged
        'if the check box is selected then enable the remaining fields for this
           product
        'else disable the remaining fields and set default values
        If chkbGelInkPen.Checked = True Then
            cmbGelInkPenOrderValue.Enabled = True
```

```
            cmbGelInkPenOrdFreq.Enabled = True
            cmbGelInkPenCurrPro.Enabled = True
        Else
            cmbGelInkPenOrderValue.Text = 0
            cmbGelInkPenOrdFreq.Text = ""
            cmbGelInkPenCurrPro.Text = ""
            cmbGelInkPenOrderValue.Enabled = False
            cmbGelInkPenOrdFreq.Enabled = False
            cmbGelInkPenCurrPro.Enabled = False
        End If
    End Sub

Private Sub chkbHighLighter_CheckedChanged(ByVal sender As System.Object, ByVal e
   As System.EventArgs) Handles chkbHighLighter.CheckedChanged
        'if the check box is selected then enable the remaining fields for this
           product
        'else disable the remaining fields and set default values
        If chkbHighLighter.Checked = True Then
            cmbHighLighterOrderValue.Enabled = True
            cmbHighLighterOrdFreq.Enabled = True
            cmbHighLighterCurrPro.Enabled = True
        Else
            cmbHighLighterOrderValue.Text = 0
            cmbHighLighterOrdFreq.Text = ""
            cmbHighLighterCurrPro.Text = ""
            cmbHighLighterOrderValue.Enabled = False
            cmbHighLighterOrdFreq.Enabled = False
            cmbHighLighterCurrPro.Enabled = False
        End If
    End Sub

Private Sub chkbScotchTape_CheckedChanged(ByVal sender As System.Object, ByVal e As
   System.EventArgs) Handles chkbScotchTape.CheckedChanged
        'if the check box is selected then enable the remaining fields for this
           product
```

```
        'else disable the remaining fields and set default values
        If chkbScotchTape.Checked = True Then
            cmbScotchTapeOrderValue.Enabled = True
            cmbScotchTapeOrdFreq.Enabled = True
            cmbScotchTapeCurrPro.Enabled = True
        Else
            cmbScotchTapeOrderValue.Text = 0
            cmbScotchTapeOrdFreq.Text = ""
            cmbScotchTapeCurrPro.Text = ""
            cmbScotchTapeOrderValue.Enabled = False
            cmbScotchTapeOrdFreq.Enabled = False
            cmbScotchTapeCurrPro.Enabled = False
        End If
    End Sub

Private Sub chkbGlueStic_CheckedChanged(ByVal sender As System.Object, ByVal e As
   System.EventArgs) Handles chkbGlueStic.CheckedChanged
        'if the check box is selected then enable the remaining fields for this
           product
        'else disable the remaining fields and set default values
        If chkbGlueStic.Checked = True Then
            cmbGlueSticOrderValue.Enabled = True
            cmbGlueSticOrdFreq.Enabled = True
            cmbGlueSticCurrPro.Enabled = True
        Else
            cmbGlueSticOrderValue.Text = 0
            cmbGlueSticOrdFreq.Text = ""
            cmbGlueSticCurrPro.Text = ""
            cmbGlueSticOrderValue.Enabled = False
            cmbGlueSticOrdFreq.Enabled = False
            cmbGlueSticCurrPro.Enabled = False
        End If
    End Sub

Private Sub cmbCopyPaperOrderValue_Validating(ByVal sender As Object, ByVal e As
   System.ComponentModel.CancelEventArgs) Handles cmbCopyPaperOrderValue.Validating
```

```
        'check if the value entered is numeric or not
        If Not IsNumeric(cmbCopyPaperOrderValue.Text) Then
            MsgBox("Enter a Numeric Value", MsgBoxStyle.Critical, "Incorrect
              DataType")
            e.Cancel = True
        End If
    End Sub

Private Sub cmbGelInkPenOrderValue_Validating(ByVal sender As Object, ByVal e As
   System.ComponentModel.CancelEventArgs) Handles cmbGelInkPenOrderValue.Validating
        'check if the value entered is numeric or not
        If Not IsNumeric(cmbGelInkPenOrderValue.Text) Then
            MsgBox("Enter a Numeric Value", MsgBoxStyle.Critical, "Incorrect
              DataType")
            e.Cancel = True
        End If
    End Sub

Private Sub cmbHighLighterOrderValue_Validating(ByVal sender As Object, ByVal e As
   System.ComponentModel.CancelEventArgs) Handles
   cmbHighLighterOrderValue.Validating
        'check if the value entered is numeric or not
        If Not IsNumeric(cmbHighLighterOrderValue.Text) Then
            MsgBox("Enter a Numeric Value", MsgBoxStyle.Critical, "Incorrect
              DataType")
            e.Cancel = True
        End If
    End Sub

Private Sub cmbScotchTapeOrderValue_Validating(ByVal sender As Object, ByVal e As
   System.ComponentModel.CancelEventArgs) Handles cmbScotchTapeOrderValue.Validating
        'check if the value entered is numeric or not
        If Not IsNumeric(cmbScotchTapeOrderValue.Text) Then
            MsgBox("Enter a Numeric Value", MsgBoxStyle.Critical, "Incorrect
              DataType")
            e.Cancel = True
        End If
    End Sub
```

```
Private Sub cmbGlueSticOrderValue_Validating(ByVal sender As Object, ByVal e As
   System.ComponentModel.CancelEventArgs) Handles cmbGlueSticOrderValue.Validating
        'check if the value entered is numeric or not
        If Not IsNumeric(cmbGlueSticOrderValue.Text) Then
            MsgBox("Enter a Numeric Value", MsgBoxStyle.Critical, "Incorrect
               DataType")
            e.Cancel = True
        End If
    End Sub

Private Sub cmbAnnualTurnOver_Validating(ByVal sender As Object, ByVal e As
   System.ComponentModel.CancelEventArgs) Handles cmbAnnualTurnOver.Validating
        'check if the value entered is numeric or not
        If Not IsNumeric(cmbAnnualTurnOver.Text) Then
            MsgBox("Enter a Numeric Value", MsgBoxStyle.Critical, "Incorrect
               DataType")
            e.Cancel = True
        End If
    End Sub


Private Sub editZipCode_Validating(ByVal sender As Object, ByVal e As
   System.ComponentModel.CancelEventArgs) Handles editZipCode.Validating
        'validate the zip code field
        If Len(editZipCode.Text) > 6 Then
            MsgBox("Enter only 6 digits", MsgBoxStyle.Critical, "Incorrect
               DataType")
            e.Cancel = True
        End If
        If Not IsNumeric(editZipCode.Text) Then
            MsgBox("Enter Numeric Values Only.", MsgBoxStyle.Critical, "Incorrect
               DataType")
            e.Cancel = True
        End If
    End Sub
End Class
```

The following sections discuss the procedures used in the ClientInfo form.

The Button1_Click Procedure

The Button1_Click procedure is executed when the sales representative clicks on the Close button on the Profile page of the Customers screen. This procedure hides the Customers screen and shows the Main screen. The code for the Button1_Click procedure is as follows:

```
Private Sub Button1_Click(ByVal sender As System.Object, ByVal e As
   System.EventArgs) Handles Button1.Click
         Dim NewMDIParent As New MainMDI()
         'shows the main mdi form again to activate it
         NewMDIParent.Show()
         NewMDIParent.Hide()
         Me.Close()
    End Sub
```

The ClientInfo_Load Procedure

The ClientInfo_Load procedure is executed when the sales representative clicks on the Customers button. It displays the form associated with the Customers button. This procedure checks whether the ClientInfo form is loaded with a client or without a client. If a client is selected in the Main screen, the ClientInfo_Load procedure is called in the ShowRecord procedure. The ShowRecord procedure is used to display details of the selected client on the Customers screen. The details in the Profile tab are extracted from the tblClients table. The details on the Product Usage and Competitors - I screen are extracted from the tblProductUsageAndCompAnalysis table. The code for the ClientInfo_Load procedure is as follows:

```
Private Sub ClientInfo_Load(ByVal sender As System.Object, ByVal e As
   System.EventArgs) Handles MyBase.Load
If (Trim(varCompanyName.SharedValue) = "" Or varCompanyName.SharedClientID = 0)
Then
         Else
             Call ShowRecord(varCompanyName.SharedValue)
             editClientName.Enabled = False
         End If
End Sub
```

```
Private Sub ShowRecord(ByVal strCustName As String)
    Try
        clientConnection.Open()
        strSqlStatement = "SELECT * FROM tblClients WHERE Client_Name = '" &
          strCustName & "'"
        clientCommand = New OleDbCommand(strSqlStatement, clientConnection)
        clientDataReader = clientCommand.ExecuteReader()
        While clientDataReader.Read
            editClientName.Text = IIf(IsDBNull(clientDataReader.Item(1)), "",
              clientDataReader.Item(1))
            editContactPerson.Text = IIf(IsDBNull(clientDataReader.Item(2)),
              "",
            clientDataReader.Item(2))
            editTitle.Text = IIf(IsDBNull(clientDataReader.Item(3)), "",
              clientDataReader.Item(3))
            editAddressLine1.Text = IIf(IsDBNull(clientDataReader.Item(4)),
              "",
            clientDataReader.Item(4))
            editAddressLine2.Text = IIf(IsDBNull(clientDataReader.Item(5)),
              "",
            clientDataReader.Item(5))
            editCity.Text = IIf(IsDBNull(clientDataReader.Item(6)), "",
              clientDataReader.Item(6))
            editState.Text = IIf(IsDBNull(clientDataReader.Item(7)), "",
              clientDataReader.Item(7))
            editZipCode.Text = IIf(IsDBNull(clientDataReader.Item(8)), "",
              clientDataReader.Item(8))
            editRemarks.Text = IIf(IsDBNull(clientDataReader.Item(9)), "",
              clientDataReader.Item(9))
            editCellPhoneNumber.Text =
              IIf(IsDBNull(clientDataReader.Item(10)), "",
            clientDataReader.Item(10))
            editPhoneNumber.Text = IIf(IsDBNull(clientDataReader.Item(11)),
              "",
            clientDataReader.Item(11))
            editFax.Text = IIf(IsDBNull(clientDataReader.Item(12)), "",
              clientDataReader.Item(12))
            editEmailAddress.Text = IIf(IsDBNull(clientDataReader.Item(13)),
              "",
```

```
    clientDataReader.Item(13))
End While
clientDataReader.Close()
strSqlStatement = "SELECT Client_ID FROM tblClients WHERE Client_Name
   = '" & strCustName
& "'"
clientCommand = New OleDbCommand(strSqlStatement, clientConnection)
clientDataReader = clientCommand.ExecuteReader()
While clientDataReader.Read
    clientID = clientDataReader.Item(0)
End While
strSqlStatement = "SELECT * FROM tblProductUsageAndCompAnalysis WHERE
   Client_ID = " &
clientID
clientCommand = New OleDbCommand(strSqlStatement, clientConnection)
clientDataReader = clientCommand.ExecuteReader()
While clientDataReader.Read
    cmbIndustryType.Text = IIf(IsDBNull(clientDataReader.Item(1)), "",
    clientDataReader.Item(1))
    chkbComPaper.Checked = IIf(IsDBNull(clientDataReader.Item(2)), "",
    clientDataReader.Item(2))
    cmbComPaperOrdFreq.Text = IIf(IsDBNull(clientDataReader.Item(3)),
       "",
    clientDataReader.Item(3))
    cmbComPaperOrderValue.Text =
       IIf(IsDBNull(clientDataReader.Item(4)), "",
    clientDataReader.Item(4))
    cmbComPaperCurrPro.Text = IIf(IsDBNull(clientDataReader.Item(5)),
       "",
    clientDataReader.Item(5))
    chkbCopyPaper.Checked = IIf(IsDBNull(clientDataReader.Item(6)),
       "",
    clientDataReader.Item(6))
    cmbCopyPaperOrdFreq.Text = IIf(IsDBNull(clientDataReader.Item(7)),
       "",
    clientDataReader.Item(7))
    cmbCopyPaperOrderValue.Text =
       IIf(IsDBNull(clientDataReader.Item(8)), "",
```

```
clientDataReader.Item(8))
cmbCopyPaperCurrPro.Text = IIf(IsDBNull(clientDataReader.Item(9)),
   "",
clientDataReader.Item(9))
chkbGelInkPen.Checked = IIf(IsDBNull(clientDataReader.Item(10)),
   "",
clientDataReader.Item(10))
cmbGelInkPenOrdFreq.Text =
   IIf(IsDBNull(clientDataReader.Item(11)), "",
clientDataReader.Item(11))
cmbGelInkPenOrderValue.Text =
   IIf(IsDBNull(clientDataReader.Item(12)), "",
clientDataReader.Item(12))
cmbGelInkPenCurrPro.Text =
   IIf(IsDBNull(clientDataReader.Item(13)), "",
clientDataReader.Item(13))
chkbHighLighter.Checked = IIf(IsDBNull(clientDataReader.Item(14)),
   "",
clientDataReader.Item(14))
cmbHighLighterOrdFreq.Text =
   IIf(IsDBNull(clientDataReader.Item(15)), "",
clientDataReader.Item(15))
cmbHighLighterOrderValue.Text =
   IIf(IsDBNull(clientDataReader.Item(16)), "",
clientDataReader.Item(16))
cmbHighLighterCurrPro.Text =
   IIf(IsDBNull(clientDataReader.Item(17)), "",
clientDataReader.Item(17))
chkbScotchTape.Checked = IIf(IsDBNull(clientDataReader.Item(18)),
   "",
clientDataReader.Item(18))
cmbScotchTapeOrdFreq.Text =
   IIf(IsDBNull(clientDataReader.Item(19)), "",
clientDataReader.Item(19))
cmbScotchTapeOrderValue.Text =
   IIf(IsDBNull(clientDataReader.Item(20)), "",
clientDataReader.Item(20))
cmbScotchTapeCurrPro.Text =
```

```
            IIf(IsDBNull(clientDataReader.Item(21)), "",
        clientDataReader.Item(21))
        chkbGlueStic.Checked = IIf(IsDBNull(clientDataReader.Item(22)),
            "",
        clientDataReader.Item(22))
        cmbGlueSticOrdFreq.Text = IIf(IsDBNull(clientDataReader.Item(23)),
            "",
        clientDataReader.Item(23))
        cmbGlueSticOrderValue.Text =
            IIf(IsDBNull(clientDataReader.Item(24)), "",
        clientDataReader.Item(24))
        cmbGlueSticCurrPro.Text = IIf(IsDBNull(clientDataReader.Item(25)),
            "",
        clientDataReader.Item(25))
        txtGeneralComments.Text = IIf(IsDBNull(clientDataReader.Item(26)),
            "",
        clientDataReader.Item(26))
        txtPastExp.Text = IIf(IsDBNull(clientDataReader.Item(27)), "",
            clientDataReader.Item(27))
        cmbAnnualTurnOver.Text = IIf(IsDBNull(clientDataReader.Item(28)),
            "",
        clientDataReader.Item(28))
    End While
    clientDataReader.Close()
    clientConnection.Close()
Catch
    MsgBox(Err.Description())
End Try
End Sub
```

The btnUpdate_Click Procedure

The `btnUpdate_Click` procedure is triggered when the sales representative clicks on the `Save` button. When this procedure is executed, a connection is established with the `EasySelling.mdb` database. After the connection with the database is established, the procedure checks whether a new record has to be added or the existing record has to be modified. When the sales representative adds a new record, the details are updated in the database. The code for the btnUpdate_Click procedure is as follows:

```
Private Sub btnUpdate_Click(ByVal sender As System.Object, ByVal e As
   System.EventArgs) Handles btnUpdate.Click
        Private Sub btnUpdate_Click(ByVal sender As System.Object, ByVal e As
           System.EventArgs) Handles btnUpdate.Click
        Try
            adoConn.Open("Provider=Microsoft.Jet.OLEDB.4.0;Data
            Source=C:\EasySelling\EasySelling.mdb;Persist Security Info=False")
        Catch
            MsgBox("Could not open database", MsgBoxStyle.Critical, "Problem with
               Database Open")
        End Try

        If (Trim(varCompanyName.SharedValue) = "" Or varCompanyName.SharedClientID
           = 0) Then
            Call AddNewCustomer()
        Else
            Call EditCustomerRecord()
        End If
    End Sub
```

The AddNewCustomer Procedure

The AddNewCustomer procedure is triggered when the sales representative adds a new customer. The fields in the Customers screen are filled in. The data in the Customers screen is then stored in the EasySelling.mdb database. When data is entered by the sales representative, certain validations need to be performed on the data. The procedures and functions used for validating are discussed later in the chapter. The code for the AddNewCustomer procedure is as follows:

```
Private Sub AddNewCustomer()
    Try
        If ValidateFields() = True Then
            If CheckDuplicate() = True Then
                'add new record
                strSqlStatement = "SELECT * FROM tblClients"
                rsSalesRep.Open(strSqlStatement, adoConn,
```

```
ADODB.CursorTypeEnum.adOpenDynamic,
   ADODB.LockTypeEnum.adLockOptimistic)
rsSalesRep.AddNew()
rsSalesRep.Fields("Client_Name").Value =
   Trim(editClientName.Text)
rsSalesRep.Fields("Contact_Person").Value =
   editContactPerson.Text
rsSalesRep.Fields("Title").Value = editTitle.Text
rsSalesRep.Fields("Address_Line1").Value =
   editAddressLine1.Text
rsSalesRep.Fields("Address_Line2").Value =
   editAddressLine2.Text
rsSalesRep.Fields("city").Value = editCity.Text
rsSalesRep.Fields("state").Value = editState.Text
rsSalesRep.Fields("zipcode").Value = editZipCode.Text
rsSalesRep.Fields("Remarks").Value = Trim(editRemarks.Text)
rsSalesRep.Fields("CellPhoneNumber").Value =
   editCellPhoneNumber.Text
rsSalesRep.Fields("PhoneNumber").Value =
   Trim(editPhoneNumber.Text)
rsSalesRep.Fields("Fax").Value = editFax.Text
rsSalesRep.Fields("EmailAddress").Value =
   Trim(editEmailAddress.Text)
rsSalesRep.Update()
rsSalesRep.Close()
adoConn.Close()

'get the new id that is generated
clientConnection.Open()
strSqlStatement = "SELECT Client_ID FROM tblClients WHERE
   Client_Name = '" &
editClientName.Text & "'"
clientCommand = New OleDbCommand(strSqlStatement,
   clientConnection)
clientDataReader = clientCommand.ExecuteReader()
While clientDataReader.Read
    clientID = clientDataReader.Item(0)
End While
```

```
clientDataReader.Close()
clientConnection.Close()

'add data to tblProductUsageAndCompAnalysis table
adoConn.Open("Provider=Microsoft.Jet.OLEDB.4.0;Data
Source=C:\EasySelling\EasySelling.mdb;Persist Security
   Info=False")
strSqlStatement = "SELECT * FROM
   tblProductUsageAndCompAnalysis WHERE Client_ID =
" & clientID
rsSalesRep.Open(strSqlStatement, adoConn,
ADODB.CursorTypeEnum.adOpenDynamic,
  ADODB.LockTypeEnum.adLockOptimistic)

rsSalesRep.AddNew()

rsSalesRep.Fields("Client_ID").Value =
   Convert.ToInt32(clientID)
rsSalesRep.Fields("Type_Of_Industry").Value =
   cmbIndustryType.Text

rsSalesRep.Fields("Is_ComputerPaper_Used").Value =
   chkbComPaper.Checked
rsSalesRep.Fields("ComPaperOrdFreq").Value =
   cmbComPaperOrdFreq.Text
rsSalesRep.Fields("ComPaperOrdValue").Value =
IIf(IsDBNull(cmbComPaperOrderValue.Text), 0,
Convert.ToDecimal(cmbComPaperOrderValue.Text))
rsSalesRep.Fields("ComPaperCurrProvider").Value =
   cmbComPaperCurrPro.Text

rsSalesRep.Fields("Is_CopyPaper_Used").Value =
   chkbCopyPaper.Checked
rsSalesRep.Fields("CopyPaperOrdFreq").Value =
   cmbCopyPaperOrdFreq.Text
rsSalesRep.Fields("CopyPaperOrdValue").Value =
IIf(IsDBNull(cmbCopyPaperOrderValue.Text), 0,
Convert.ToDecimal(cmbCopyPaperOrderValue.Text))
```

```
 rsSalesRep.Fields("CopyPaperCurrProvider").Value =
    cmbCopyPaperCurrPro.Text

 rsSalesRep.Fields("Is_GelInkPen_Used").Value =
    chkbGelInkPen.Checked
 rsSalesRep.Fields("GelInkPenOrdFreq").Value =
    cmbGelInkPenOrdFreq.Text
 rsSalesRep.Fields("GelInkPenOrdValue").Value =
 IIf(IsDBNull(cmbGelInkPenOrderValue.Text), 0,
Convert.ToDecimal(cmbGelInkPenOrderValue.Text))
 rsSalesRep.Fields("GelInkPenCurrProvider").Value =
    cmbGelInkPenCurrPro.Text

 rsSalesRep.Fields("Is_HighLighter_Used").Value =
    chkbHighLighter.Checked
 rsSalesRep.Fields("HighLighterOrdFreq").Value =
    cmbHighLighterOrdFreq.Text
 rsSalesRep.Fields("HighLighterOrdValue").Value =
 IIf(IsDBNull(cmbHighLighterOrderValue.Text), 0,
Convert.ToDecimal(cmbHighLighterOrderValue.Text))
 rsSalesRep.Fields("HighLighterCurrProvider").Value =
    cmbHighLighterCurrPro.Text

 rsSalesRep.Fields("Is_ScotchTape_Used").Value =
    chkbScotchTape.Checked
 rsSalesRep.Fields("ScotchTapeOrdFreq").Value =
    cmbScotchTapeOrdFreq.Text
 rsSalesRep.Fields("ScotchTapeOrdValue").Value =
 IIf(IsDBNull(cmbScotchTapeOrderValue.Text), 0,
Convert.ToDecimal(cmbScotchTapeOrderValue.Text))
 rsSalesRep.Fields("ScotchTapeCurrProvider").Value =
    cmbScotchTapeCurrPro.Text

 rsSalesRep.Fields("Is_GlueStics_Used").Value =
    chkbGlueStic.Checked
 rsSalesRep.Fields("GlueSticsOrdFreq").Value =
    cmbGlueSticOrdFreq.Text
 rsSalesRep.Fields("GlueSticsOrdValue").Value =
```

```
                    IIf(IsDBNull(cmbGlueSticOrderValue.Text), 0,
                   Convert.ToDecimal(cmbGlueSticOrderValue.Text))
                    rsSalesRep.Fields("GlueSticsCurrProvider").Value =
                       cmbGlueSticCurrPro.Text

                    rsSalesRep.Fields("General_Comments").Value =
                       txtGeneralComments.Text
                    rsSalesRep.Fields("UsedOurProductsBefore").Value =
                       txtPastExp.Text
                    rsSalesRep.Fields("AnnualTurnOver").Value =
                       cmbAnnualTurnOver.Text

                    rsSalesRep.Update()
                    rsSalesRep.Close()
                    adoConn.Close()
                    Call PrepareIssuesSolutions()
                    MsgBox("New Customer Record Saved Successfully.",
                       MsgBoxStyle.Information, "New
                    Record Saved")
                    varCompanyName.SharedValue = Trim(editClientName.Text)
                    varCompanyName.SharedClientID = 0
                End If
            End If
        Catch
            MsgBox(Err.Description())
        End Try
    End Sub
```

The EditCustomerRecord Procedure

The `EditCustomerRecord` procedure is triggered when the sales representative edits a record. The data that is edited in the `Customers` screen is updated in the `EasySelling.mdb` database. When a sales representative enters data or edits existing records, a few validations are performed on the data. The code for the `EditCustomerRecord` procedure is as follows:

```
Private Sub EditCustomerRecord()
    Try
        If ValidateFields() = True Then
```

```
strSqlStatement = "SELECT * FROM tblClients WHERE Client_ID=" &
   clientID
rsSalesRep.Open(strSqlStatement, adoConn,
   ADODB.CursorTypeEnum.adOpenDynamic,
ADODB.LockTypeEnum.adLockOptimistic)

rsSalesRep.Fields("Client_Name").Value = Trim(editClientName.Text)
rsSalesRep.Fields("Contact_Person").Value = editContactPerson.Text
rsSalesRep.Fields("Title").Value = editTitle.Text
rsSalesRep.Fields("Address_Line1").Value = editAddressLine1.Text
rsSalesRep.Fields("Address_Line2").Value = editAddressLine2.Text
rsSalesRep.Fields("city").Value = editCity.Text
rsSalesRep.Fields("state").Value = editState.Text
rsSalesRep.Fields("zipcode").Value = editZipCode.Text
rsSalesRep.Fields("Remarks").Value = Trim(editRemarks.Text)
rsSalesRep.Fields("CellPhoneNumber").Value =
   editCellPhoneNumber.Text
rsSalesRep.Fields("PhoneNumber").Value =
   Trim(editPhoneNumber.Text)
rsSalesRep.Fields("Fax").Value = editFax.Text
rsSalesRep.Fields("EmailAddress").Value =
   Trim(editEmailAddress.Text)
rsSalesRep.Update()
rsSalesRep.Close()
'edit data in tblProductUsageAndCompAnalysis table
strSqlStatement = "SELECT * FROM tblProductUsageAndCompAnalysis
   WHERE Client_ID = "
& clientID
rsSalesRep.Open(strSqlStatement, adoConn,
   ADODB.CursorTypeEnum.adOpenDynamic,
ADODB.LockTypeEnum.adLockOptimistic)
rsSalesRep.Fields("Type_Of_Industry").Value = cmbIndustryType.Text
rsSalesRep.Fields("Is_ComputerPaper_Used").Value =
   chkbComPaper.Checked
rsSalesRep.Fields("ComPaperOrdFreq").Value =
   cmbComPaperOrdFreq.Text
rsSalesRep.Fields("ComPaperOrdValue").Value =
IIf(IsDBNull(cmbComPaperOrderValue.Text), 0,
```

```
Convert.ToDecimal(cmbComPaperOrderValue.Text))
 rsSalesRep.Fields("ComPaperCurrProvider").Value =
    cmbComPaperCurrPro.Text
 rsSalesRep.Fields("Is_CopyPaper_Used").Value =
    chkbCopyPaper.Checked
 rsSalesRep.Fields("CopyPaperOrdFreq").Value =
    cmbCopyPaperOrdFreq.Text
 rsSalesRep.Fields("CopyPaperOrdValue").Value =
 IIf(IsDBNull(cmbCopyPaperOrderValue.Text), 0,
Convert.ToDecimal(cmbCopyPaperOrderValue.Text))
 rsSalesRep.Fields("CopyPaperCurrProvider").Value =
    cmbCopyPaperCurrPro.Text
 rsSalesRep.Fields("Is_GelInkPen_Used").Value =
    chkbGelInkPen.Checked
 rsSalesRep.Fields("GelInkPenOrdFreq").Value =
    cmbGelInkPenOrdFreq.Text
 rsSalesRep.Fields("GelInkPenOrdValue").Value =
 IIf(IsDBNull(cmbGelInkPenOrderValue.Text), 0,
Convert.ToDecimal(cmbGelInkPenOrderValue.Text))
 rsSalesRep.Fields("GelInkPenCurrProvider").Value =
    cmbGelInkPenCurrPro.Text
 rsSalesRep.Fields("Is_HighLighter_Used").Value =
    chkbHighLighter.Checked
 rsSalesRep.Fields("HighLighterOrdFreq").Value =
    cmbHighLighterOrdFreq.Text
 rsSalesRep.Fields("HighLighterOrdValue").Value =
 IIf(IsDBNull(cmbHighLighterOrderValue.Text), 0,
Convert.ToDecimal(cmbHighLighterOrderValue.Text))
 rsSalesRep.Fields("HighLighterCurrProvider").Value =
    cmbHighLighterCurrPro.Text

 rsSalesRep.Fields("Is_ScotchTape_Used").Value =
    chkbScotchTape.Checked
 rsSalesRep.Fields("ScotchTapeOrdFreq").Value =
    cmbScotchTapeOrdFreq.Text
 rsSalesRep.Fields("ScotchTapeOrdValue").Value =
 IIf(IsDBNull(cmbScotchTapeOrderValue.Text), 0,
Convert.ToDecimal(cmbScotchTapeOrderValue.Text))
```

```
                rsSalesRep.Fields("ScotchTapeCurrProvider").Value =
                  cmbScotchTapeCurrPro.Text
                rsSalesRep.Fields("Is_GlueStics_Used").Value =
                  chkbGlueStic.Checked
                rsSalesRep.Fields("GlueSticsOrdFreq").Value =
                  cmbGlueSticOrdFreq.Text
                rsSalesRep.Fields("GlueSticsOrdValue").Value =
                  IIf(IsDBNull(cmbGlueSticOrderValue.Text),
                0, Convert.ToDecimal(cmbGlueSticOrderValue.Text))
                rsSalesRep.Fields("GlueSticsCurrProvider").Value =
                  cmbGlueSticCurrPro.Text
                rsSalesRep.Fields("General_Comments").Value =
                  txtGeneralComments.Text
                rsSalesRep.Fields("UsedOurProductsBefore").Value = txtPastExp.Text
                rsSalesRep.Fields("AnnualTurnOver").Value = cmbAnnualTurnOver.Text
                rsSalesRep.Update()
                rsSalesRep.Close()
                adoConn.Close()
                MsgBox("Record Saved Successfully.", MsgBoxStyle.Information,
                  "Record Saved")
            End If
        Catch
            MsgBox(Err.Description())
        End Try
    End Sub
```

The procedures and functions used for validating data entry in the `ClientInfo` form are listed in Table 32-1 along with their descriptions.

Table 32-1 Validation Checks used in the Customers Screen

Procedure/Function Name	Description
`ValidateFields()`	This function is used to validate the data before saving the record in the `tblclients` table. The validations are performed when the sales representative enters data in the `Profile` tab of the `Customers` screen. This function checks whether Client Name, Contact Person, Title, Address Line 1, and Industry Type fields are filled in. The record will not be saved unless these fields are filled in.

continues

Table 32-1 continued

Procedure/Function Name	Description
`CheckDuplicate()`	This function is used to check for duplicate records. The validation is done on the basis of the client name.
`chkbComPaper_Checked-Changed()`	This procedure is used to enable or disable fields under the `Computer Paper` group box depending on whether the `Uses Computer Paper` check box is selected. If the `Uses Computer Paper` check box is selected, the remaining fields in the group box are enabled. If the `Uses Computer Paper` check box is deselected, the remaining fields are disabled.
`chkbCopyPaper_Checked-Changed()`	This procedure is used to enable or disable fields under the `Copy Paper` group box depending on whether the `Copy Paper` check box is selected. If the `Copy Paper` check box is selected, the remaining fields in the group box are enabled. If the `Copy Paper` check box is deselected, the remaining fields are disabled.
`chkbGelInkPen_Checked-Changed()`	This procedure is used to enable or disable fields under the `Gel Ink Pen` group box depending on whether the `Gel Ink Pen` check box is selected. If the `Gel Ink Pen` check box is selected, the remaining fields in the group box are enabled. If the `Gel Ink Pen` check box is deselected, the remaining fields are disabled
`chkbHighLighter_Checked-Changed()`	This procedure is used to enable or disable fields under the `HighLighter` group box depending on whether the `HighLighter` check box is selected. If the `HighLighter` check box is selected, the remaining fields in the group box are enabled. If the `HighLighter` check box is deselected, the remaining fields are disabled.
`chkbScotchTape_Checked-Changed()`	This procedure is used to enable or disable fields under the `Scotch Tape` group box depending on whether the `Scotch Tape` check box is selected. If the `Scotch Tape` check box is selected, the remaining fields in the group box are enabled. If the `Scotch Tape` check box is deselected, the remaining fields are disabled.

Procedure/Function Name	Description
chkbGlueStic_Checked-Changed()	This procedure is used to enable or disable fields under the Glue Stic group box depending on whether the Glue Stic check box is selected. If the Glue Stic check box is selected, the remaining fields in the group box are enabled. If the Glue Stic check box is deselected, the remaining fields are disabled.
cmbComPaperOrderValue_Validating()	This procedure is used to check whether the data entered in the Annual Order Value (in $) combo box in the Computer Paper group box is numeric.
cmbCopyPaperOrderValue_Validating()	This procedure is used to check whether the data entered in the Annual Order Value (in $) combo box in the Copy Paper group box is numeric.
cmbGelInkPenOrderValue_Validating()	This procedure is used to check whether the data entered in the Annual Order Value (in $) combo box in the Gel Ink Pen group box is numeric.
cmbHighLighterOrderValue_Validating()	This procedure is used to check whether the data entered in the Annual Order Value (in $) combo box in the HighLighter group box is numeric.
cmbScotchTapeOrderValue_Validating()	This procedure is used to check whether the data entered in the Annual Order Value (in $) combo box in the Scotch Tape group box is numeric.
cmbGlueSticOrderValue_Validating()	This procedure is used to check whether the data entered in the Annual Order Value (in $) combo box in the Glue Stic group box is numeric.
cmbAnnualTurnOver_Validating()	This procedure is used to check whether the data entered in the Annual Order Value (in $) combo box on the Product Usage and Competitors-II. tab is numeric.
editZipCode_Validating()	This procedure is used to check whether the data entered in the Zip Code: text box on the Profile tab is of six characters and numeric.

The PrepareIssuesSolutions Procedure

The PrepareIssuesSolutions procedure is triggered when a new record is created. This procedure inserts data in the tblClientExpectations and tblClientSolutions tables from tblStandardExpectations and tblStandardSolutions tables. The tblStandardExpectations and tblStandardSolutions tables contain a list of standard issues and solutions, respectively. The code for the PrepareIssuesSolutions procedure is as follows:

```
Private Sub PrepareIssuesSolutions()
        Dim varfalse As Boolean
        varfalse = False
        Try
            strSqlStatement = "INSERT INTO tblClientExpectations SELECT
            " & clientID & " AS Client_ID," & varfalse & " AS
            selected,Expectations AS Expectation FROM
            tblStandardExpectations"
            clientConnection.Open()
            clientCommand = New OleDbCommand(strSqlStatement,
            clientConnection)
            clientCommand.ExecuteNonQuery()
            clientConnection.Close()
        Catch
            MsgBox(Err.Description())
        End Try
        Try
            strSqlStatement = "INSERT INTO tblClientSolutions SELECT " &
            clientID & " AS Client_ID," & varfalse & " AS
            selected,Solutions AS Solution FROM tblStandardSolutions"
            clientConnection.Open()
            clientCommand = New OleDbCommand(strSqlStatement,
            clientConnection)
            clientCommand.ExecuteNonQuery()
            clientConnection.Close()
        Catch
            MsgBox(Err.Description())
        End Try
    End Sub
```

Summary

In this chapter, you coded the `Customers` screen of the Easy Selling application. You also learned all the procedures and functions used in the form. In the next chapter, you will learn to code the `Issues` screen of the Easy Selling application.

Chapter 33

Coding the Issues Screen of the Easy Selling Application

Chapter 32, "Coding the Customers Screen of the Easy Selling Application," discussed the working of the `Customers` screen. This chapter discusses the code of the `Issues` screen of the Easy Selling application.

Working of the Issues Screen of the Easy Selling Application

This section discusses the procedures and functions used in the `Issues` screen of the Easy Selling application.

Figure 33-1 shows the `Issues` screen of the Easy Selling application.

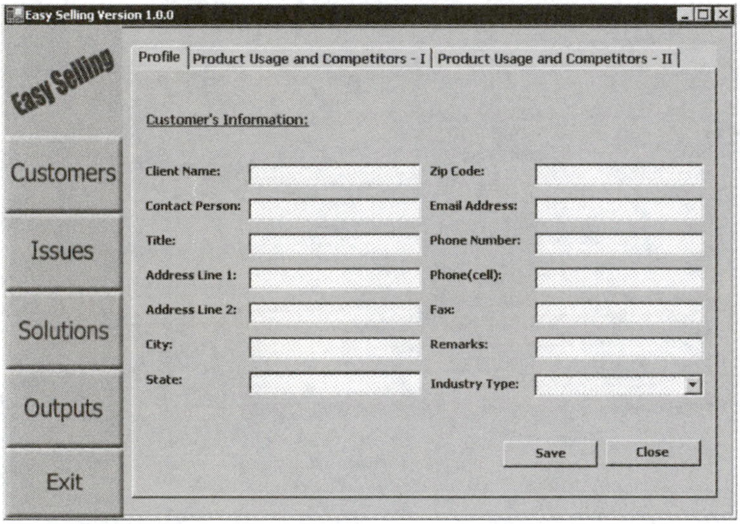

FIGURE 33-1 *The* `Issues` *screen of the Easy Selling application*

The `Issues` screen is a combination of the `MainMDI` form and the `ClientIssues` form. The `ClientIssues` form is initiated when the sales representative clicks on the `Issues` button in the navigation bar.

Figure 33-2 depicts the procedures and functions used in the `Issues` screen of the Easy Selling application.

Listing 33-1 contains the code of the `ClientIssues` form of the Easy Selling application.

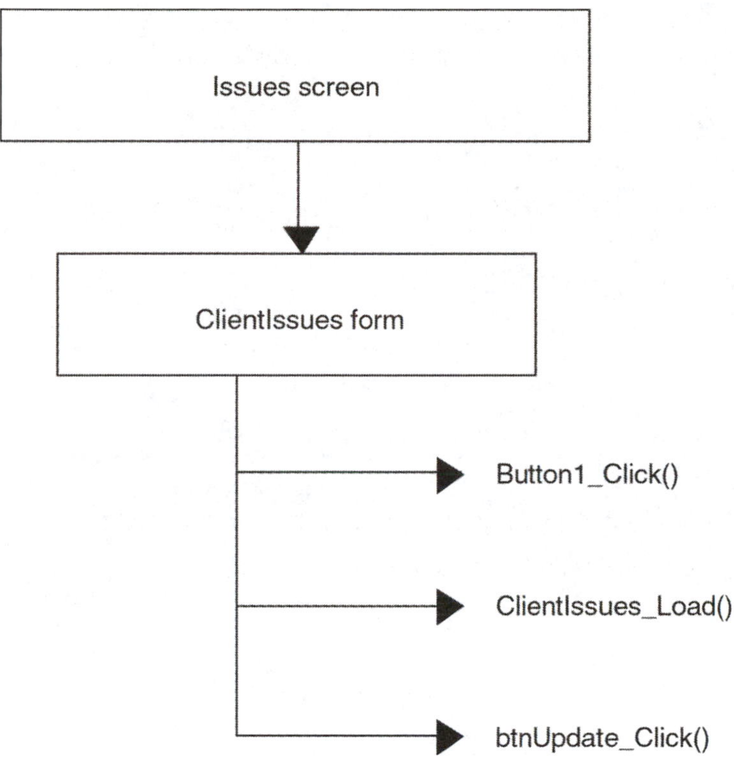

FIGURE 33-2 *The procedures and functions used in the* `ClientIssues` *form*

Listing 33-1 Code for the ClientIssues Form

```
Imports System.Data.OleDb
Public Class ClientIssues
    Inherits System.Windows.Forms.Form

    Private varCompanyName As New StartApplication.ShareClass()
    Private ourConn As String = "Provider=Microsoft.Jet.OLEDB.4.0;Data
    Source=C:\EasySelling\EasySelling.mdb;Persist Security Info=False"
    Private clientConnection As OleDbConnection = New
    OleDbConnection(ourConn)
    Private clientCommand As OleDbCommand
    Private clientDataReader As OleDbDataReader
    Friend WithEvents lstvIssues As System.Windows.Forms.ListView
    Private strSqlStatement As String
```

```
    Private varClientID As Long
    Declare Sub Sleep Lib "kernel32" (ByVal dwmilliseconds As Long)

Private Sub Button1_Click(ByVal sender As System.Object, ByVal e As
   System.EventArgs) Handles Button1.Click
        Dim NewMDIParent As New MainMDI()
        NewMDIParent.Show()
        NewMDIParent.Hide()
        Me.Close()
End Sub

Private Sub ClientIssues_Load(ByVal sender As System.Object, ByVal e As
   System.EventArgs) Handles MyBase.Load

        Dim issueCount As Integer
        issueCount = 0
        Try
            clientConnection.Open()
'on the basis of the customer name selected In the main screen the the code selects
'the clientid from tblClients table
            strSqlStatement = "SELECT Client_ID FROM tblClients WHERE
            Client_Name = '" & varCompanyName.SharedValue & "'"
            clientCommand = New OleDbCommand(strSqlStatement,
            clientConnection)
            clientDataReader = clientCommand.ExecuteReader()
            While clientDataReader.Read
                varClientID = clientDataReader.Item(0)
            End While
            clientDataReader.Close()
            strSqlStatement = "SELECT Expectation,selected FROM
            tblClientExpectations WHERE Client_ID = " & varClientID
            clientCommand = New OleDbCommand(strSqlStatement,
            clientConnection)
            clientDataReader = clientCommand.ExecuteReader()
            While clientDataReader.Read
                lstvIssues.Items().Add(clientDataReader.Item(0),
                issueCount)
                If clientDataReader.Item(1) = True Then
```

```
                lstvIssues.Items(issueCount).Checked = True
            End If
            issueCount = issueCount + 1
        End While
        clientDataReader.Close()
        clientConnection.Close()
    Catch
        MsgBox(Err.Description())
    End Try

End Sub

Private Sub btnUpdate_Click(ByVal sender As System.Object, ByVal e As
  System.EventArgs) Handles btnUpdate.Click
    Dim varCollection As
    System.Windows.Forms.ListView.CheckedListViewItemCollection
    Dim varitem As ListViewItem
    Try
        varCollection = lstvIssues.CheckedItems()
        clientConnection.Open()
        For Each varitem In varCollection
            strSqlStatement = "UPDATE tblClientExpectations SET
            Selected = True WHERE Client_ID=" & varClientID & " AND
            Expectation = '" & varitem.Text & "'"
            clientCommand = New OleDbCommand(strSqlStatement,
            clientConnection)
            clientCommand.ExecuteNonQuery()
        Next
        clientConnection.Close()
        MsgBox("Record Saved Successfully.",
        MsgBoxStyle.Information, "Record Saved")
    Catch
        MsgBox(Err.Description())
    End Try
End Sub
End Class
```

The Button1_Click Procedure

The `Button1_Click` procedure is triggered when the sales representative clicks on the `Close` button on the `Issues` screen. This procedure closes the `Issues` screen and displays the `Main` screen. The code for the `Button1_Click` procedure is as follows:

```
Private Sub Button1_Click(ByVal sender As System.Object, ByVal e As
   System.EventArgs) Handles Button1.Click
        Dim NewMDIParent As New MainMDI()
        NewMDIParent.Show()
        NewMDIParent.Hide()
        Me.Close()
End Sub
```

The ClientIssues_Load Procedure

The `ClientIssues_Load` procedure is triggered when the sales representative clicks on the `Issues` button. It displays the `ClientIssues` form. The form displays a list of issues that the customers might be facing. The `ClientIssues_Load` procedure establishes a connection with the `Easyselling.mdb` file and enables the sales representative to select issues faced by the customer and store them in the `tblClientExpectations` table. The data displayed on the `Issues` screen depends on the customer name selected in the `Main` screen. The issues are extracted from the `tblClientExpectations` table on the basis of the `clientid`. In case of a new customer, the issues appear unchecked. The code for the `ClientIssues_Load` procedure is as follows:

```
Private Sub ClientIssues_Load(ByVal sender As System.Object, ByVal e As
   System.EventArgs) Handles MyBase.Load
        Dim issueCount As Integer
        issueCount = 0
        Try
            clientConnection.Open()
            strSqlStatement = "SELECT Client_ID FROM tblClients WHERE
            Client_Name = '" & varCompanyName.SharedValue & "'"
            clientCommand = New OleDbCommand(strSqlStatement,
            clientConnection)
            clientDataReader = clientCommand.ExecuteReader()
            While clientDataReader.Read
                varClientID = clientDataReader.Item(0)
```

```
            End While
            clientDataReader.Close()
            strSqlStatement = "SELECT Expectation,selected FROM
            tblClientExpectations WHERE Client_ID = " & varClientID
            clientCommand = New OleDbCommand(strSqlStatement,
            clientConnection)
            clientDataReader = clientCommand.ExecuteReader()
            While clientDataReader.Read
                lstvIssues.Items().Add(clientDataReader.Item(0),
                issueCount)
                If clientDataReader.Item(1) = True Then
                    lstvIssues.Items(issueCount).Checked = True
                End If
                issueCount = issueCount + 1
            End While
            clientDataReader.Close()
            clientConnection.Close()
        Catch
            MsgBox(Err.Description())
        End Try
    End Sub
```

The btnUpdate_Click Procedure

The `btnUpdate_Click` procedure is triggered when the sales representative clicks on the `Save` button. It saves the issues selected by the sales representative in the `tblClientExpectations` table. After saving the issues faced by the customer, this procedure displays a message indicating that the record in the database has been saved successfully. The code for the `btnUpdate_Click` procedure is as follows:

```
Private Sub btnUpdate_Click(ByVal sender As System.Object, ByVal e As
   System.EventArgs) Handles btnUpdate.Click
        Dim varCollection As
        System.Windows.Forms.ListView.CheckedListViewItemCollection
        Dim varitem As ListViewItem
        Try
            varCollection = lstvIssues.CheckedItems()
            clientConnection.Open()
            For Each varitem In varCollection
```

```
                strSqlStatement = "UPDATE tblClientExpectations SET
                Selected = True WHERE Client_ID=" & varClientID & " AND
                Expectation = '" & varitem.Text & "'"
                clientCommand = New OleDbCommand(strSqlStatement,
                clientConnection)
                clientCommand.ExecuteNonQuery()
            Next
            clientConnection.Close()
            MsgBox("Record Saved Successfully.",
            MsgBoxStyle.Information, "Record Saved")
        Catch
            MsgBox(Err.Description())
        End Try
    End Sub
End Class
```

Summary

In this chapter, you coded the `Issues` screen of the Easy Selling application. You also learned all the main procedures and functions used in the form. In the next chapter, you will learn to code the `Solutions` screen of the Easy Selling application.

Chapter 34

Coding the Solutions Screen of the Easy Selling Application

Chapter 33, "Coding the Issues Screen of the Easy Selling Application," discussed the working of the `Issues` screen. This chapter discusses the code of the `Solutions` screen of the Easy Selling application.

Working of the Solutions Screen of the Easy Selling Application

This section discusses the procedures and functions used in the `Solutions` screen of the Easy Selling application. The `Solutions` screen is shown in Figure 34-1.

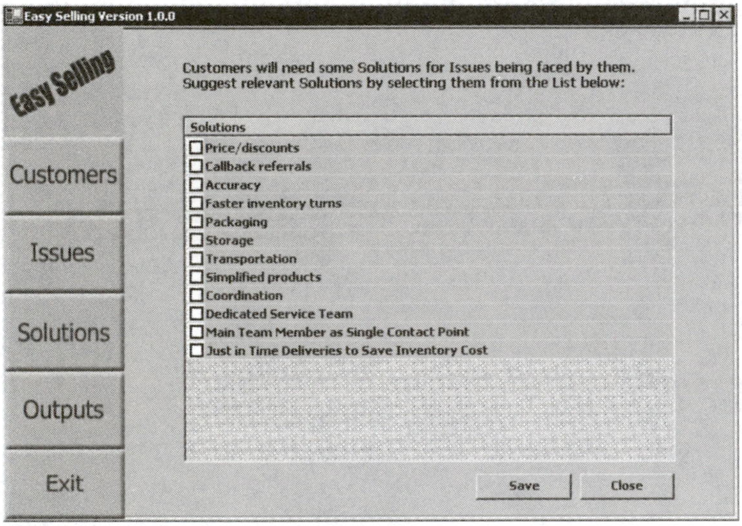

Easy Selling Version 1.0.0

Easy Selling

Customers

Issues

Solutions

Outputs

Exit

Customers will need some Solutions for Issues being faced by them.
Suggest relevant Solutions by selecting them from the List below:

Solutions

- [ ] Price/discounts
- [ ] Callback referrals
- [ ] Accuracy
- [ ] Faster inventory turns
- [ ] Packaging
- [ ] Storage
- [ ] Transportation
- [ ] Simplified products
- [ ] Coordination
- [ ] Dedicated Service Team
- [ ] Main Team Member as Single Contact Point
- [ ] Just in Time Deliveries to Save Inventory Cost

Save Close

FIGURE 34-1 *The* `Solutions` *screen of the Easy Selling application*

The `Solutions` screen is a combination of the `MainMDI` form and the `ClientSolutions` form. The `ClientSolutions` form is initiated when the sales representative clicks on the `Solutions` button in the navigation bar.

Figure 34-2 depicts the procedures and functions used in the `Solutions` screen of the Easy Selling application.

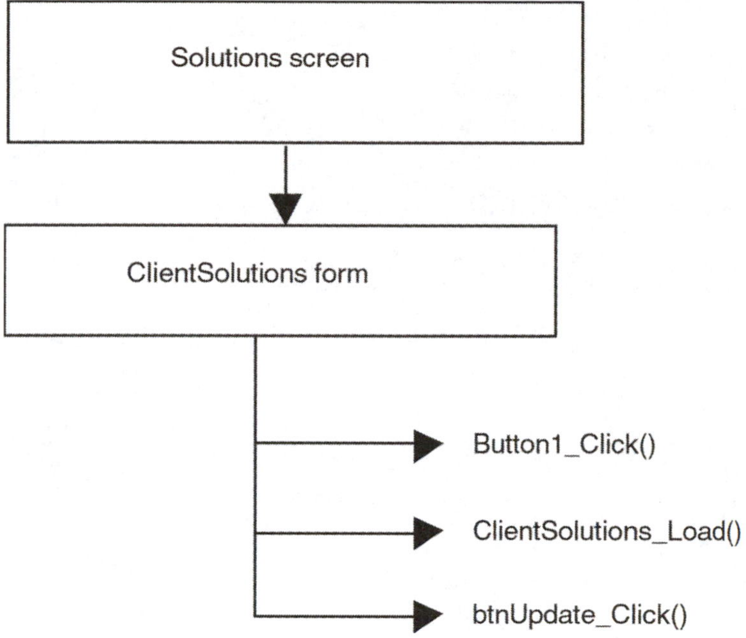

FIGURE 34-2 *The procedures and functions used in the* `ClientSolutions` *form*

Listing 34-1 shows the code of the `ClientSolutions` form of the Easy Selling application.

Listing 34-1 Code for the ClientSolutions Form

```
Imports System.Data.OleDb
Public Class ClientSolutions
    Inherits System.Windows.Forms.Form
    Private varCompanyName As New StartApplication.ShareClass()
    Private ourConn As String = "Provider=Microsoft.Jet.OLEDB.4.0;Data
    Source=C:\EasySelling\EasySelling.mdb;Persist Security Info=False"
    Private clientConnection As OleDbConnection = New
    OleDbConnection(ourConn)
    Private clientCommand As OleDbCommand
    Private clientDataReader As OleDbDataReader
    Private strSqlStatement As String
    Private varClientID As Long
```

```
Private Sub Button1_Click(ByVal sender As System.Object, ByVal e As
   System.EventArgs) Handles Button1.Click
         Dim NewMDIParent As New MainMDI()
         NewMDIParent.Show()
         NewMDIParent.Hide()

         Me.Close()
End Sub

Private Sub ClientSolutions_Load(ByVal sender As System.Object, ByVal e As
   System.EventArgs) Handles MyBase.Load
         Dim issueCount As Integer
         issueCount = 0
         Try
              clientConnection.Open()

              strSqlStatement = "SELECT Client_ID FROM tblClients WHERE
              Client_Name = '" & varCompanyName.SharedValue & "'"
              clientCommand = New OleDbCommand(strSqlStatement,
              clientConnection)
              clientDataReader = clientCommand.ExecuteReader()
              While clientDataReader.Read
                   varClientID = clientDataReader.Item(0)
              End While
              clientDataReader.Close()

              strSqlStatement = "SELECT solution,selected FROM
              tblClientSolutions WHERE Client_ID = " & varClientID
              clientCommand = New OleDbCommand(strSqlStatement,
              clientConnection)
              clientDataReader = clientCommand.ExecuteReader()
              While clientDataReader.Read
                   lstvSolutions.Items().Add(clientDataReader.Item(0),
                   issueCount)
                   If clientDataReader.Item(1) = True Then
                        lstvSolutions.Items(issueCount).Checked = True
                   End If
```

```
                issueCount = issueCount + 1
            End While
            clientDataReader.Close()
            clientConnection.Close()
        Catch
            MsgBox(Err.Description())
        End Try
    End Sub

Private Sub btnUpdate_Click(ByVal sender As System.Object, ByVal e As
   System.EventArgs) Handles btnUpdate.Click
        Dim varCollection As
        System.Windows.Forms.ListView.CheckedListViewItemCollection
        Dim varitem As ListViewItem
        Try
            varCollection = lstvSolutions.CheckedItems()
            clientConnection.Open()
            For Each varitem In varCollection
                strSqlStatement = "UPDATE tblClientSolutions SET
                Selected = True WHERE Client_ID=" & varClientID & " AND
                solution = '" & varitem.Text & "'"
                clientCommand = New OleDbCommand(strSqlStatement,
                clientConnection)
                clientCommand.ExecuteNonQuery()
            Next
            clientConnection.Close()
            MsgBox("Record Saved Successfully.",
            MsgBoxStyle.Information, "Record Saved")
        Catch
            MsgBox(Err.Description())
        End Try
    End Sub
End Class
```

The following sections discuss the procedures used in the `ClientSolutions` form.

The Button1_Click Procedure

The Button1_Click procedure is triggered when the sales representative clicks the Close button on the Solutions screen. This procedure closes the Solutions screen and displays the Main screen. The code for the Button1_Click procedure is as follows:

```
Private Sub Button1_Click(ByVal sender As System.Object, ByVal e As
   System.EventArgs) Handles Button1.Click
        Dim NewMDIParent As New MainMDI()
        NewMDIParent.Show()
        NewMDIParent.Hide()

        Me.Close()
End Sub
```

The ClientSolutions_Load Procedure

The ClientSolutions_Load procedure is triggered when the sales representative clicks the Solutions button. It displays the ClientSolutions form. The Solutions screen displays the solutions that could be used to avoid the existing issues faced by the customer. The ClientSolutions_Load procedure establishes a connection with the Easyselling.mdb file and enables the sales representative to select solutions faced by the customer and store them in the tblClientSolutions table. The data displayed on the Solutions screen depends on the customer name selected in the Main screen. The solutions are extracted from the tblClientSolutions table on the basis of the clientid of the selected customer. If the selected customer is a new customer then all the solutions are displayed as unchecked. The code for the ClientSolutions_Load procedure is as follows:

```
Private Sub ClientSolutions_Load(ByVal sender As System.Object, ByVal e As
   System.EventArgs) Handles MyBase.Load
        Dim issueCount As Integer
        issueCount = 0
        Try
            clientConnection.Open()
            strSqlStatement = "SELECT Client_ID FROM tblClients WHERE
            Client_Name = '" & varCompanyName.SharedValue & "'"
            clientCommand = New OleDbCommand(strSqlStatement,
            clientConnection)
```

```
            clientDataReader = clientCommand.ExecuteReader()
            While clientDataReader.Read
                varClientID = clientDataReader.Item(0)
            End While
            clientDataReader.Close()

            strSqlStatement = "SELECT solution,selected FROM
            tblClientSolutions WHERE Client_ID = " & varClientID
            clientCommand = New OleDbCommand(strSqlStatement,
            clientConnection)
            clientDataReader = clientCommand.ExecuteReader()
            While clientDataReader.Read
                lstvSolutions.Items().Add(clientDataReader.Item(0),
                issueCount)
                If clientDataReader.Item(1) = True Then
                    lstvSolutions.Items(issueCount).Checked = True
                End If
                issueCount = issueCount + 1
            End While
            clientDataReader.Close()
            clientConnection.Close()
        Catch
            MsgBox(Err.Description())
        End Try
    End Sub
```

The btnUpdate_Click Procedure

The `btnUpdate_Click` procedure is triggered when the sales representative clicks the `Save` button. It saves the solutions selected by the sales representative in the `tblClientSolutions` table. After saving the solutions given by the customer, this procedure displays a message indicating that the record in the database has been saved successfully. The code for the `btnUpdate_Click` procedure is as follows:

```
Private Sub btnUpdate_Click(ByVal sender As System.Object, ByVal e As
   System.EventArgs) Handles btnUpdate.Click
        Dim varCollection As
        System.Windows.Forms.ListView.CheckedListViewItemCollection
        Dim varitem As ListViewItem
```

```
        Try
            varCollection = lstvSolutions.CheckedItems()
            clientConnection.Open()
            For Each varitem In varCollection
                strSqlStatement = "UPDATE tblClientSolutions SET
                Selected = True WHERE Client_ID=" & varClientID & " AND
                solution = '" & varitem.Text & "'"
                clientCommand = New OleDbCommand(strSqlStatement,
                clientConnection)
                clientCommand.ExecuteNonQuery()
            Next
            clientConnection.Close()
            MsgBox("Record Saved Successfully.",
            MsgBoxStyle.Information, "Record Saved")

        Catch
            MsgBox(Err.Description())
        End Try
    End Sub
End Class
```

Summary

In this chapter, you coded the `Solutions` screen of the Easy Selling application. You also learned all the main procedures and functions used in the form. In the next chapter, you will learn to code the `Outputs` screen of the Easy Selling application.

Chapter 35

Coding the Outputs Screen of the Easy Selling Application

Chapter 34, "Coding the Solutions Screen of the Easy Selling Application," discussed the working of the `Solutions` screen. This chapter discusses the code of the `Outputs` screen of the Easy Selling application.

Working of the Outputs Screen of the Easy Selling Application

This section discusses the procedures and functions used in the `Outputs` screen of the Easy Selling application.

Figure 35-1 shows the `Outputs` screen of the Easy Selling application.

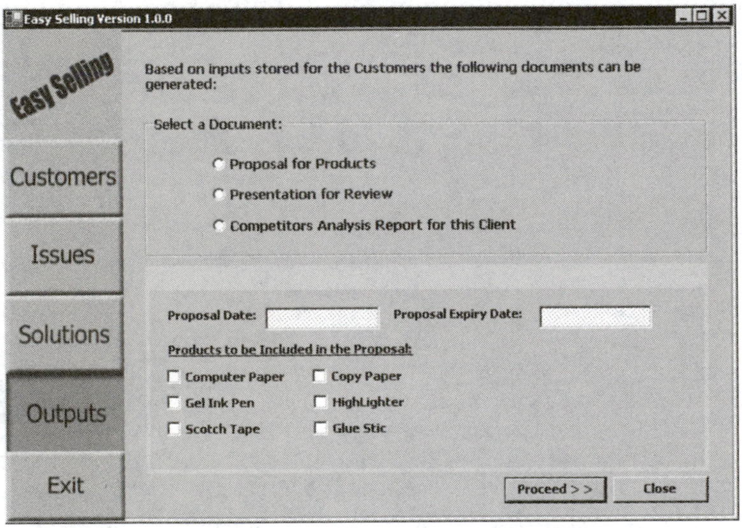

FIGURE 35-1 *The* `Outputs` *screen of the Easy Selling application*

The `Outputs` screen is a combination of the `MainMDI` form and the `ClientDocuments` form. The `ClientDocuments` form is initiated when the sales representative clicks on the `Outputs` button in the navigation bar.

Figure 35-2 depicts the procedures and functions used in the `Outputs` screen of the Easy Selling application.

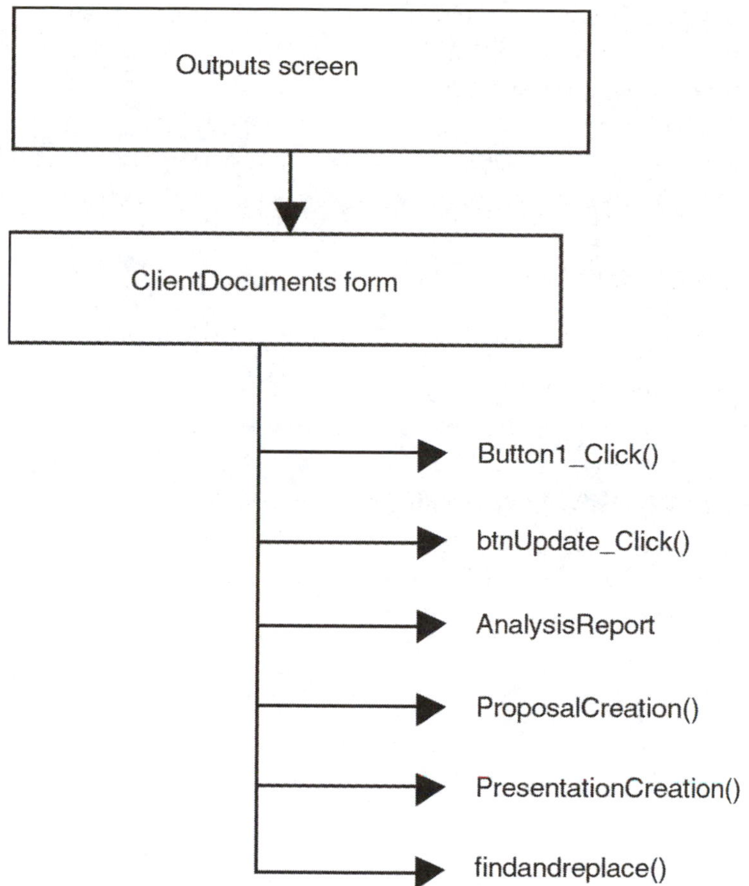

FIGURE 35-2 *The procedures and functions used in the* `ClientDocuments` *form*

Listing 35-1 contains the code of the `ClientDocuments` form of the Easy Selling application.

Listing 35-1 Code for the ClientDocuments Form

```
Imports System.Data.OleDb
Public Class ClientDocuments
    Inherits System.Windows.Forms.Form
    Private varCompanyName As New StartApplication.ShareClass()
    Private ourConn As String = "Provider=Microsoft.Jet.OLEDB.4.0;Data
    Source=C:\EasySelling\EasySelling.mdb;Persist Security Info=False"
```

```
    Private clientConnection As OleDbConnection = New OleDbConnection(ourConn)
    Private clientCommand As OleDbCommand
    Private clientDataReader As OleDbDataReader
    Friend WithEvents grpDocumentOption As System.Windows.Forms.GroupBox
    Friend WithEvents radbAnalysis As System.Windows.Forms.RadioButton
    Friend WithEvents radbPresentation As System.Windows.Forms.RadioButton
    Friend WithEvents radbProposal As System.Windows.Forms.RadioButton
    Private strSqlStatement As String
    Friend WithEvents chkbGlueStic As System.Windows.Forms.CheckBox
    Friend WithEvents chkbScotchTape As System.Windows.Forms.CheckBox
    Friend WithEvents chkbHighlighter As System.Windows.Forms.CheckBox
    Friend WithEvents chkbGelInkPen As System.Windows.Forms.CheckBox
    Friend WithEvents chkbCompPaper As System.Windows.Forms.CheckBox
    Friend WithEvents chkbCopyPaper As System.Windows.Forms.CheckBox
    Friend WithEvents ExpiryDate As System.Windows.Forms.TextBox
    Friend WithEvents ProposalDate As System.Windows.Forms.TextBox
    Private docApp As Word.Application

Private Sub Button1_Click(ByVal sender As System.Object, ByVal e As
  System.EventArgs) Handles Button1.Click
        Dim NewMDIParent As New MainMDI()
        NewMDIParent.Show()
        NewMDIParent.Hide()
        Me.Close()
    End Sub

Private Sub btnUpdate_Click(ByVal sender As System.Object, ByVal e As
  System.EventArgs) Handles btnUpdate.Click
        If radbAnalysis.Checked = True Then
            Call AnalysisReport()
        End If
        If radbProposal.Checked = True Then
            Call ProposalCreation()
        End If
        If radbPresentation.Checked = True Then
            Call PresentationCreation()
        End If
    End Sub
```

```
Private Sub AnalysisReport()
    Dim xlApp As Excel.Application
    Dim xlBook As Excel.Workbook
    Dim xlSheet As Excel.Worksheet
    Dim varIndustryType As String
    Dim varTotalValue As Decimal

    Try
        xlApp = CType(CreateObject("Excel.Application"), Excel.Application)
        xlBook = CType(xlApp.Workbooks.Add, Excel.Workbook)
        xlSheet = CType(xlBook.Worksheets(1), Excel.Worksheet)
        xlSheet.Cells(1, 1) = "This is Competitor Analysis Report for
           Customer: " &
        varCompanyName.SharedValue & "  Customer ID: " &
           varCompanyName.SharedClientID
        clientConnection.Open()
        strSqlStatement = "SELECT * FROM tblProductUsageAndCompAnalysis WHERE
           Client_ID = " &
        varCompanyName.SharedClientID
        clientCommand = New OleDbCommand(strSqlStatement, clientConnection)
        clientDataReader = clientCommand.ExecuteReader()
        While clientDataReader.Read
            varIndustryType = clientDataReader.Item(1)
            xlSheet.Cells(2, 1) = "Customer's Industry Type is: " &
               varIndustryType
            xlSheet.Cells(4, 1) = "Products"
            xlSheet.Cells(4, 2) = "Order Value(in Dollars)"
            xlSheet.Cells(4, 3) = "Current Provider"
            xlSheet.Cells(4, 4) = "% of Total Order Value"
            xlSheet.Cells(6, 1) = "Computer Paper"
            xlSheet.Cells(6, 2) = IIf(IsDBNull(clientDataReader.Item(4)), 0,
               clientDataReader.Item(4))
            xlSheet.Cells(6, 3) = IIf(IsDBNull(clientDataReader.Item(5)),
               "NA", clientDataReader.Item(5))
            xlSheet.Cells(7, 1) = "Copy Paper"
            xlSheet.Cells(7, 2) = IIf(IsDBNull(clientDataReader.Item(8)), 0,
               clientDataReader.Item(8))
            xlSheet.Cells(7, 3) = IIf(IsDBNull(clientDataReader.Item(9)),
```

```
        "NA", clientDataReader.Item(9))
    xlSheet.Cells(8, 1) = "Gel Ink Pen"
    xlSheet.Cells(8, 2) = IIf(IsDBNull(clientDataReader.Item(12)), 0,
        clientDataReader.Item(12))
    xlSheet.Cells(8, 3) = IIf(IsDBNull(clientDataReader.Item(13)), "NA",
    clientDataReader.Item(13))
    xlSheet.Cells(9, 1) = "Highlighter"
    xlSheet.Cells(9, 2) = IIf(IsDBNull(clientDataReader.Item(16)), 0,
        clientDataReader.Item(16))
    xlSheet.Cells(9, 3) = IIf(IsDBNull(clientDataReader.Item(17)), "NA",
    clientDataReader.Item(17))
    xlSheet.Cells(10, 1) = "Scotch Tape"
    xlSheet.Cells(10, 2) = IIf(IsDBNull(clientDataReader.Item(20)), 0,
    clientDataReader.Item(20))
    xlSheet.Cells(10, 3) = IIf(IsDBNull(clientDataReader.Item(21)), 0,
    clientDataReader.Item(21))
    xlSheet.Cells(11, 1) = "Glue Stic"
    xlSheet.Cells(11, 2) = IIf(IsDBNull(clientDataReader.Item(24)), 0,
    clientDataReader.Item(24))
    xlSheet.Cells(11, 3) = IIf(IsDBNull(clientDataReader.Item(25)), "NA",
    clientDataReader.Item(25))
End While
clientDataReader.Close()
clientConnection.Close()
xlSheet.Cells(13, 1) = "Total Order Value is: "
xlSheet.Range("A1:D13").Select()
xlApp.Selection.Font.Bold = True
xlSheet.Columns("A:A").ColumnWidth = 20
xlSheet.Columns("B:B").ColumnWidth = 25
xlSheet.Columns("C:C").ColumnWidth = 25
xlSheet.Range("B6:B13").Select()
xlSheet.Range("B13").Activate()
xlApp.ActiveCell.FormulaR1C1 = "=SUM(R[-7]C:R[-1]C)"
xlSheet.Range("B13").Select()
xlApp.Selection.Font.Bold = True
```

```
            xlSheet.Range("D6").Select()
            xlApp.ActiveCell.FormulaR1C1 = "=(RC[-2]/R[7]C[-2])*100"
            xlSheet.Range("D7").Select()
            xlApp.ActiveCell.FormulaR1C1 = "=(RC[-2]/R[6]C[-2])*100"
            xlSheet.Range("D8").Select()
            xlApp.ActiveCell.FormulaR1C1 = "=(RC[-2]/R[5]C[-2])*100"
            xlSheet.Range("D9").Select()
            xlApp.ActiveCell.FormulaR1C1 = "=(RC[-2]/R[4]C[-2])*100"
            xlSheet.Range("D10").Select()
            xlApp.ActiveCell.FormulaR1C1 = "=(RC[-2]/R[3]C[-2])*100"
            xlSheet.Range("D11").Select()
            xlApp.ActiveCell.FormulaR1C1 = "=(RC[-2]/R[2]C[-2])*100"
            xlSheet.Range("D6:D11").Select()
            xlApp.Selection.NumberFormat = "0.00"
            xlSheet.Range("D6:D13").Select()
            xlSheet.Range("D13").Activate()
            xlApp.ActiveCell.FormulaR1C1 = "=SUM(R[-7]C:R[-1]C)"
            xlSheet.Range("B6:B13").Select()
            With xlApp.Selection
                .HorizontalAlignment = -4108
            End With
            xlSheet.Range("H1:H1").Select()
            xlSheet.Application.Visible = True
            xlSheet = Nothing
            xlBook = Nothing
            xlApp = Nothing
        Catch
            MsgBox(Err.Description)
        End Try
    End Sub
    Private Sub ProposalCreation()
        Dim tempDoc As Word.Document
        Dim mainDoc As Word.Document
        Dim newDocName As String
        Dim varProducts As String
        Dim varIssues As String
        Dim varSolutions As String
        Try
```

```
docApp = CType(CreateObject("Word.Application"), Word.Application)
docApp.Visible = True
docApp.Application.Documents.Open("c:\easyselling\ProposalTemplate.doc")
tempDoc = CType(docApp.ActiveDocument, Word.Document)
docApp.Selection.WholeStory()
docApp.Selection.Copy()
mainDoc = CType(docApp.Documents.Add, Word.Document)
docApp.Selection.Paste()
docApp.Selection.HomeKey(unit:=6)
clientConnection.Open()
strSqlStatement = "SELECT * FROM tblClients WHERE Client_ID = " &
varCompanyName.SharedClientID
clientCommand = New OleDbCommand(strSqlStatement, clientConnection)
clientDataReader = clientCommand.ExecuteReader()
While clientDataReader.Read
    Call findandreplace("<<CLIENT BUSINESS NAME>>",
       IIf(IsDBNull(clientDataReader.Item(1)),
    "NA", clientDataReader.Item(1)))
    Call findandreplace("<<ADDRESS LINE>>",
       IIf(IsDBNull(clientDataReader.Item(4)), "NA",
    clientDataReader.Item(4)) + Chr(13) +
       IIf(IsDBNull(clientDataReader.Item(5)), "NA",
    clientDataReader.Item(5)))
    Call findandreplace("<<CITY>>",
       IIf(IsDBNull(clientDataReader.Item(6)), "NA",
    clientDataReader.Item(6)) + Chr(13) +
       IIf(IsDBNull(clientDataReader.Item(7)), "NA",
    clientDataReader.Item(7)) + Chr(13) +
       IIf(IsDBNull(clientDataReader.Item(8)), "NA",
    clientDataReader.Item(8)))
End While
clientDataReader.Close()
clientConnection.Close()
clientConnection.Open()
strSqlStatement = "SELECT * FROM tblSalesRep"
clientCommand = New OleDbCommand(strSqlStatement, clientConnection)
clientDataReader = clientCommand.ExecuteReader()
```

```
While clientDataReader.Read
     Call findandreplace("<<SALESREP>>",
        IIf(IsDBNull(clientDataReader.Item(1)), "NA",
     clientDataReader.Item(1)))
     Call findandreplace("<<OUR ADDRESS LINE>>",
        IIf(IsDBNull(clientDataReader.Item(3)),
     "NA", clientDataReader.Item(3)) + Chr(13) +
        IIf(IsDBNull(clientDataReader.Item(4)), "NA",
     clientDataReader.Item(4)))
     Call findandreplace("<<OURCITY>>",
        IIf(IsDBNull(clientDataReader.Item(5)), "NA",
     clientDataReader.Item(5)) + Chr(13) +
        IIf(IsDBNull(clientDataReader.Item(6)), "NA",
     clientDataReader.Item(6)) + Chr(13) +
        IIf(IsDBNull(clientDataReader.Item(7)), "NA",
     clientDataReader.Item(7)))
End While
clientDataReader.Close()
clientConnection.Close()
clientConnection.Open()
strSqlStatement = "SELECT Expectation FROM tblClientExpectations WHERE
   selected = True
AND Client_ID = " & varCompanyName.SharedClientID
clientCommand = New OleDbCommand(strSqlStatement, clientConnection)
clientDataReader = clientCommand.ExecuteReader()
varIssues = "The Following Issues were discussed:" + Chr(13) + Chr(13)

While clientDataReader.Read
     varIssues = varIssues + clientDataReader.Item(0) + Chr(13) + Chr(13)
End While
clientDataReader.Close()
clientConnection.Close()
Call findandreplace("<<ISSUESMENTIONED>>", varIssues)
clientConnection.Open()
strSqlStatement = "SELECT solution FROM tblClientSolutions WHERE
   selected = True AND
Client_ID = " & varCompanyName.SharedClientID
```

```
        clientCommand = New OleDbCommand(strSqlStatement, clientConnection)
        clientDataReader = clientCommand.ExecuteReader()
        varSolutions = "The Following Solutions are Suggested:" + Chr(13) + Chr(13)
        While clientDataReader.Read
        varSolutions = varSolutions + clientDataReader.Item(0) + Chr(13) + Chr(13)
        End While
        clientDataReader.Close()
        clientConnection.Close()
        Call findandreplace("<<SUGGESTEDSOLUTIONS>>", varSolutions)
        varProducts = "This Proposal is offered for following product(s):" + Chr(13)
        If chkbCompPaper.Checked = True Then
            varProducts = varProducts + Chr(13) + "Computer Paper"
        End If
        If chkbCopyPaper.Checked = True Then
            varProducts = varProducts + Chr(13) + "Copy Paper"
        End If
        If chkbGelInkPen.Checked = True Then
            varProducts = varProducts + Chr(13) + "Gel Ink Pen"
        End If
        If chkbHighlighter.Checked = True Then
            varProducts = varProducts + Chr(13) + "HighLighter"
        End If
        If chkbScotchTape.Checked = True Then
            varProducts = varProducts + Chr(13) + "Scotch Tape"
        End If
        If chkbGlueStic.Checked = True Then
            varProducts = varProducts + Chr(13) + "Glue Stic"
        End If
        Call findandreplace("<<PRODUCTS>>", varProducts)
        Call findandreplace("<<PDATE>>", ProposalDate.Text)
        Call findandreplace("<<EDATE>>", ExpiryDate.Text)
        tempDoc = Nothing
        mainDoc = Nothing
        docApp = Nothing
    Catch
```

```
        MsgBox(Err.Description)
    End Try
End Sub

Public Sub PresentationCreation()
    Dim ppApp As PowerPoint.Application
    Dim ppOne As PowerPoint.Presentation
    Dim ppTwo As PowerPoint.Presentation
    Dim ppslide As PowerPoint.Slide
    Dim ppShape As PowerPoint.Shape
    Dim varLength As Long
    Dim varSalesRepInfo As String
    Dim varSalesRepName As String
    Dim varIssues As String
    Dim IssuesCount As Integer
    Dim SolutionsCount As Integer
    Dim VarSlideNumber As Integer
    Dim varSolutions As String
    Try
        ppApp = CType(CreateObject("PowerPoint.Application"),
           PowerPoint.Application)
        ppApp.Visible = True
        ppApp.Presentations.Add()
        ppOne = ppApp.ActivePresentation
        ppOne.ApplyTemplate("c:\easyselling\presentation.ppt")
        varLength = ppOne.Slides.InsertFromFile("c:\easyselling\presentation.ppt",
           0, 1, 6)
        clientConnection.Open()
        strSqlStatement = "SELECT * FROM tblSalesRep"
        clientCommand = New OleDbCommand(strSqlStatement, clientConnection)
        clientDataReader = clientCommand.ExecuteReader()
        While clientDataReader.Read
            varSalesRepName = IIf(IsDBNull(clientDataReader.Item(1)), "NA",
            clientDataReader.Item(1))
            varSalesRepInfo = IIf(IsDBNull(clientDataReader.Item(1)), "NA",
               clientDataReader.Item(1))
            + Chr(13)
            varSalesRepInfo = varSalesRepInfo +
```

```
            IIf(IsDBNull(clientDataReader.Item(2)), "NA",
        clientDataReader.Item(2)) + Chr(13)
        varSalesRepInfo = varSalesRepInfo +
            IIf(IsDBNull(clientDataReader.Item(11)), "NA",
        clientDataReader.Item(11)) + Chr(13)

    End While
    clientDataReader.Close()
    clientConnection.Close()
    clientConnection.Open()
    strSqlStatement = "SELECT Expectation FROM tblClientExpectations
       WHERE selected = True
    AND Client_ID = " & varCompanyName.SharedClientID
    clientCommand = New OleDbCommand(strSqlStatement, clientConnection)
    clientDataReader = clientCommand.ExecuteReader()
    While clientDataReader.Read
        varIssues = varIssues + clientDataReader.Item(0) + Chr(13)
    End While
    clientDataReader.Close()
    clientConnection.Close()
    clientConnection.Open()
    strSqlStatement = "SELECT solution FROM tblClientSolutions
       WHERE selected = True AND
    Client_ID = " & varCompanyName.SharedClientID
    clientCommand = New OleDbCommand(strSqlStatement, clientConnection)
    clientDataReader = clientCommand.ExecuteReader()
    While clientDataReader.Read
        varSolutions = varSolutions + clientDataReader.Item(0) + Chr(13)
    End While
    clientDataReader.Close()
    clientConnection.Close()
    For Each ppslide In ppOne.Slides
        For Each ppShape In ppslide.Shapes
            If ppShape.HasTextFrame = True Then
                ppShape.TextFrame.TextRange.Replace("<<Customer Company>>",
                varCompanyName.SharedValue)
                ppShape.TextFrame.TextRange.Replace("<<SalesRep>>",
                   varSalesRepInfo)
```

```
                    ppShape.TextFrame.TextRange.Replace("<<SalesRepName>>",
                       varSalesRepName)
                    ppShape.TextFrame.TextRange.Replace("<<IssuesItems>>",
                       varIssues)
                    ppShape.TextFrame.TextRange.Replace("<<SolutionItems>>",
                       varSolutions)

                End If
            Next
        Next

        ppShape = Nothing
        ppslide = Nothing
        ppOne = Nothing
        ppApp = Nothing
    Catch
        MsgBox(Err.Description)
    End Try
End Sub
Public Sub findandreplace(ByVal findtext As String, ByVal replacementText As
   String)
    Dim flag As Integer
    Dim var As Boolean
    docApp.Selection.Find.ClearFormatting()
    docApp.Selection.Find.Replacement.ClearFormatting()
    With docApp.Selection.Find
        .Text = findtext
        .Replacement.Text = replacementText
        .Forward = True
        .Wrap = 1
        .Format = False
        .MatchCase = False
        .MatchWholeWord = False
        .MatchWildcards = False
        .MatchSoundsLike = False
        .MatchAllWordForms = False
    End With
```

```
            flag = 1
            Do While flag = 1
                var = docApp.Selection.Find.Execute
                If var = True Then
                    With docApp.Selection
                        If .Find.Forward = True Then
                            .Collapse(Direction:=1)
                        Else
                            .Collapse(Direction:=0)
                        End If
                        .Find.Execute(Replace:=1)
                        If .Find.Forward = True Then
                            .Collapse(Direction:=0)
                        Else
                            .Collapse(Direction:=1)
                        End If

                    End With
                Else
                    flag = 0
                End If
            Loop
        End Sub
End Class
```

The Button1_Click Procedure

The `Button1_Click` procedure is triggered when the sales representative clicks on the `Close` button. This procedure closes the `Outputs` screen and displays the `Main` screen. The code for the `Button1_Click` procedure is as follows:

```
Private Sub Button1_Click(ByVal sender As System.Object, ByVal e As
   System.EventArgs) Handles Button1.Click
         Dim NewMDIParent As New MainMDI()
         NewMDIParent.Show()
         NewMDIParent.Hide()
         Me.Close()
    End Sub
```

The btnUpdate_Click Procedure

The `btnUpdate_Click` procedure is triggered when the sales representative clicks on the `Proceed` button. It displays the document created. The document is either a Word document, an Excel workbook, or a PowerPoint presentation depending upon the radio button selected in the `Select a Document` group box. The code for the `btnUpdate_Click` procedure is as follows:

```
Private Sub btnUpdate_Click(ByVal sender As System.Object, ByVal e As
   System.EventArgs) Handles btnUpdate.Click
        If radbAnalysis.Checked = True Then
            Call AnalysisReport()
        End If
        If radbProposal.Checked = True Then
            Call ProposalCreation()
        End If
        If radbPresentation.Checked = True Then
            Call PresentationCreation()
        End If
    End Sub
```

The AnalysisReport Procedure

The `AnalysisReport` procedure is triggered when the sales representative selects the `Competitors Analysis Report for this Client` radio button in the `Select a Document` group box. This procedure is used to create an Excel workbook. The `AnalysisReport` procedure automates the process of creating the analysis report by extracting data from the `tblProductUsageAndCompAnalysis` table such as customer name, customer id, industry type, and the details of each product usage. In addition to adding data to the Excel worksheet, the procedure does calculations on the data. The `AnalysisReport` procedure calculates the total order amount for the client. It also calculates the percentage of order value that the product holds. The code for the `AnalysisReport` procedure is as follows:

```
Private Sub AnalysisReport()
        Dim xlApp As Excel.Application
        Dim xlBook As Excel.Workbook
        Dim xlSheet As Excel.Worksheet
        Dim varIndustryType As String
        Dim varTotalValue As Decimal
```

```
        Try
            xlApp = CType(CreateObject("Excel.Application"), Excel.Application)
            xlBook = CType(xlApp.Workbooks.Add, Excel.Workbook)
            xlSheet = CType(xlBook.Worksheets(1), Excel.Worksheet)
'places text in the second row of the sheet
            xlSheet.Cells(1, 1) = "This is Competitor Analysis Report for
               Customer: " &
            varCompanyName.SharedValue & "  Customer ID: " &
               varCompanyName.SharedClientID
            clientConnection.Open()
            strSqlStatement = "SELECT * FROM tblProductUsageAndCompAnalysis
               WHERE Client_ID = " &
            varCompanyName.SharedClientID
            clientCommand = New OleDbCommand(strSqlStatement, clientConnection)
            clientDataReader = clientCommand.ExecuteReader()
            While clientDataReader.Read
                varIndustryType = clientDataReader.Item(1)
                xlSheet.Cells(2, 1) = "Customer's Industry Type is: " &
                   varIndustryType
                xlSheet.Cells(4, 1) = "Products"
                xlSheet.Cells(4, 2) = "Order Value(in Dollars)"
                xlSheet.Cells(4, 3) = "Current Provider"
                xlSheet.Cells(4, 4) = "% of Total Order Value"
                xlSheet.Cells(6, 1) = "Computer Paper"
                xlSheet.Cells(6, 2) = IIf(IsDBNull(clientDataReader.Item(4)), 0,
                   clientDataReader.Item(4))
                xlSheet.Cells(6, 3) = IIf(IsDBNull(clientDataReader.Item(5)),
                   "NA", clientDataReader.Item(5))
                xlSheet.Cells(7, 1) = "Copy Paper"
                xlSheet.Cells(7, 2) = IIf(IsDBNull(clientDataReader.Item(8)), 0,
                   clientDataReader.Item(8))
                xlSheet.Cells(7, 3) = IIf(IsDBNull(clientDataReader.Item(9)),
                   "NA", clientDataReader.Item(9))
                xlSheet.Cells(8, 1) = "Gel Ink Pen"
                xlSheet.Cells(8, 2) = IIf(IsDBNull(clientDataReader.Item(12)), 0,
                   clientDataReader.Item(12))
                xlSheet.Cells(8, 3) = IIf(IsDBNull(clientDataReader.Item(13)), "NA",
```

```
            clientDataReader.Item(13))
            xlSheet.Cells(9, 1) = "Highlighter"
            xlSheet.Cells(9, 2) = IIf(IsDBNull(clientDataReader.Item(16)), 0,
               clientDataReader.Item(16))
            xlSheet.Cells(9, 3) = IIf(IsDBNull(clientDataReader.Item(17)), "NA",
            clientDataReader.Item(17))
            xlSheet.Cells(10, 1) = "Scotch Tape"
            xlSheet.Cells(10, 2) = IIf(IsDBNull(clientDataReader.Item(20)), 0,
            clientDataReader.Item(20))
            xlSheet.Cells(10, 3) = IIf(IsDBNull(clientDataReader.Item(21)), 0,
            clientDataReader.Item(21))
            xlSheet.Cells(11, 1) = "Glue Stic"
            xlSheet.Cells(11, 2) = IIf(IsDBNull(clientDataReader.Item(24)), 0,
            clientDataReader.Item(24))
            xlSheet.Cells(11, 3) = IIf(IsDBNull(clientDataReader.Item(25)), "NA",
            clientDataReader.Item(25))
        End While
        clientDataReader.Close()
        clientConnection.Close()
        xlSheet.Cells(13, 1) = "Total Order Value is: "
        xlSheet.Range("A1:D13").Select()
        xlApp.Selection.Font.Bold = True
        xlSheet.Columns("A:A").ColumnWidth = 20
        xlSheet.Columns("B:B").ColumnWidth = 25
        xlSheet.Columns("C:C").ColumnWidth = 25
        xlSheet.Range("B6:B13").Select()
        xlSheet.Range("B13").Activate()
        xlApp.ActiveCell.FormulaR1C1 = "=SUM(R[-7]C:R[-1]C)"
        xlSheet.Range("B13").Select()
        xlApp.Selection.Font.Bold = True
        xlSheet.Range("D6").Select()
'calculates the percentage
        xlApp.ActiveCell.FormulaR1C1 = "=(RC[-2]/R[7]C[-2])*100"
        xlSheet.Range("D7").Select()
        xlApp.ActiveCell.FormulaR1C1 = "=(RC[-2]/R[6]C[-2])*100"
        xlSheet.Range("D8").Select()
```

```
                xlApp.ActiveCell.FormulaR1C1 = "=(RC[-2]/R[5]C[-2])*100"
                xlSheet.Range("D9").Select()
                xlApp.ActiveCell.FormulaR1C1 = "=(RC[-2]/R[4]C[-2])*100"
                xlSheet.Range("D10").Select()
                xlApp.ActiveCell.FormulaR1C1 = "=(RC[-2]/R[3]C[-2])*100"
                xlSheet.Range("D11").Select()
                xlApp.ActiveCell.FormulaR1C1 = "=(RC[-2]/R[2]C[-2])*100"
                xlSheet.Range("D6:D11").Select()
                xlApp.Selection.NumberFormat = "0.00"
                xlSheet.Range("D6:D13").Select()
                xlSheet.Range("D13").Activate()
                xlApp.ActiveCell.FormulaR1C1 = "=SUM(R[-7]C:R[-1]C)"
                xlSheet.Range("B6:B13").Select()
                With xlApp.Selection
                    .HorizontalAlignment = -4108
                End With
                xlSheet.Range("H1:H1").Select()
' shows the sheet
                xlSheet.Application.Visible = True
                xlSheet = Nothing
                xlBook = Nothing
                xlApp = Nothing
            Catch
                MsgBox(Err.Description)
            End Try
        End Sub
```

The ProposalCreation Procedure

The `ProposalCreation` procedure is triggered when the sales representative selects the `Proposal for Products` radio button in the `Select a Document` group box. This procedure is used to create a Word document. The `ProposalCreation` procedure automates the process of creating the proposal. A default template `ProposalTemplate.doc` is used to create the final proposal. This procedure extracts data from the `tblClients`, `tblSalesRep`, `tblClientExpectations`, and `tblClientSolutions` tables. The `ProposalCreation` procedure uses the `findandreplace` procedure to find and replace customer-specific details such as customer name, customer's address, details of the sales representative attending the customer, expectation of the customer, and solutions that can be provided to avoid existing issues. The code for the `ProposalCreation` procedure is as follows:

```
Private Sub ProposalCreation()
        Dim tempDoc As Word.Document
        Dim mainDoc As Word.Document
        Dim newDocName As String
        Dim varProducts As String
        Dim varIssues As String
        Dim varSolutions As String
        Try
            docApp = CType(CreateObject("Word.Application"), Word.Application)
            docApp.Visible = True
            docApp.Application.Documents.Open("c:\easyselling\ProposalTemplate.doc")
            tempDoc = CType(docApp.ActiveDocument, Word.Document)
            docApp.Selection.WholeStory()
            docApp.Selection.Copy()
            mainDoc = CType(docApp.Documents.Add, Word.Document)
            docApp.Selection.Paste()
            docApp.Selection.HomeKey(unit:=6)
'start replacing customer data values.
            clientConnection.Open()
            strSqlStatement = "SELECT * FROM tblClients WHERE Client_ID = " &
            varCompanyName.SharedClientID
            clientCommand = New OleDbCommand(strSqlStatement, clientConnection)
            clientDataReader = clientCommand.ExecuteReader()
            While clientDataReader.Read
                Call findandreplace("<<CLIENT BUSINESS NAME>>",
                   IIf(IsDBNull(clientDataReader.Item(1)),
                "NA", clientDataReader.Item(1)))
                Call findandreplace("<<ADDRESS LINE>>",
                   IIf(IsDBNull(clientDataReader.Item(4)), "NA",
                clientDataReader.Item(4)) + Chr(13) +
                   IIf(IsDBNull(clientDataReader.Item(5)), "NA",
                clientDataReader.Item(5)))
                Call findandreplace("<<CITY>>",
                   IIf(IsDBNull(clientDataReader.Item(6)), "NA",
```

```
            clientDataReader.Item(6)) + Chr(13) +
               IIf(IsDBNull(clientDataReader.Item(7)), "NA",
            clientDataReader.Item(7)) + Chr(13) +
               IIf(IsDBNull(clientDataReader.Item(8)), "NA",
            clientDataReader.Item(8)))
        End While
        clientDataReader.Close()
        clientConnection.Close()
'start replacing sales rep data
        clientConnection.Open()
        strSqlStatement = "SELECT * FROM tblSalesRep"
        clientCommand = New OleDbCommand(strSqlStatement, clientConnection)
        clientDataReader = clientCommand.ExecuteReader()
        While clientDataReader.Read
            Call findandreplace("<<SALESREP>>",
               IIf(IsDBNull(clientDataReader.Item(1)), "NA",
            clientDataReader.Item(1)))
            Call findandreplace("<<OUR ADDRESS LINE>>",
               IIf(IsDBNull(clientDataReader.Item(3)),
            "NA", clientDataReader.Item(3)) + Chr(13) +
               IIf(IsDBNull(clientDataReader.Item(4)), "NA",
            clientDataReader.Item(4)))
            Call findandreplace("<<OURCITY>>",
               IIf(IsDBNull(clientDataReader.Item(5)), "NA",
            clientDataReader.Item(5)) + Chr(13) +
               IIf(IsDBNull(clientDataReader.Item(6)), "NA",
            clientDataReader.Item(6)) + Chr(13) +
               IIf(IsDBNull(clientDataReader.Item(7)), "NA",
            clientDataReader.Item(7)))
        End While
        clientDataReader.Close()
        clientConnection.Close()
'collects the issues for this customer and replace in Proposal
        clientConnection.Open()
        strSqlStatement = "SELECT Expectation FROM tblClientExpectations
           WHERE selected = True
        AND Client_ID = " & varCompanyName.SharedClientID
        clientCommand = New OleDbCommand(strSqlStatement, clientConnection)
```

```
            clientDataReader = clientCommand.ExecuteReader()
            varIssues = "The Following Issues were discussed:" + Chr(13) + Chr(13)
            While clientDataReader.Read
                varIssues = varIssues + clientDataReader.Item(0) + Chr(13) + Chr(13)
            End While
            clientDataReader.Close()
            clientConnection.Close()
            Call findandreplace("<<ISSUESMENTIONED>>", varIssues)
'collects the solutions for this customer and replace in Proposal
            clientConnection.Open()
            strSqlStatement = "SELECT solution FROM tblClientSolutions
               WHERE selected = True AND
            Client_ID = " & varCompanyName.SharedClientID
            clientCommand = New OleDbCommand(strSqlStatement, clientConnection)
            clientDataReader = clientCommand.ExecuteReader()
            varSolutions = "The Following Solutions are Suggested:" + Chr(13) + Chr(13)
            While clientDataReader.Read
            varSolutions = varSolutions + clientDataReader.Item(0) + Chr(13) + Chr(13)
            End While
            clientDataReader.Close()
            clientConnection.Close()
            Call findandreplace("<<SUGGESTEDSOLUTIONS>>", varSolutions)
            varProducts = "This Proposal is offered for following product(s):" + Chr(13)
            If chkbCompPaper.Checked = True Then
                varProducts = varProducts + Chr(13) + "Computer Paper"
            End If
            If chkbCopyPaper.Checked = True Then
                varProducts = varProducts + Chr(13) + "Copy Paper"
            End If
            If chkbGelInkPen.Checked = True Then
                varProducts = varProducts + Chr(13) + "Gel Ink Pen"
            End If
            If chkbHighlighter.Checked = True Then
                varProducts = varProducts + Chr(13) + "HighLighter"
```

```
            End If
            If chkbScotchTape.Checked = True Then
                varProducts = varProducts + Chr(13) + "Scotch Tape"
            End If
            If chkbGlueStic.Checked = True Then
                varProducts = varProducts + Chr(13) + "Glue Stic"
            End If
            Call findandreplace("<<PRODUCTS>>", varProducts)
            Call findandreplace("<<PDATE>>", ProposalDate.Text)
            Call findandreplace("<<EDATE>>", ExpiryDate.Text)
            tempDoc = Nothing
            mainDoc = Nothing
            docApp = Nothing
        Catch
            MsgBox(Err.Description)
        End Try
    End Sub
```

The PresentationCreation Procedure

The PresentationCreation procedure is triggered when the sales representative selects the Presentation for Review radio button in the Select a Document group box. This procedure is used to create a PowerPoint presentation. The PresentationCreation procedure automates the process of creating the presentation. A default template presentation.ppt is used to create the final presentation. This procedure extracts data from tblSalesRep, tblClientExpectations, and tblClientSolutions tables. The ProposalCreation procedure uses the findandreplace procedure to find and replace customer-specific details such as customer name, customer's address, details of the sales representative attending the customer, expectation of the customer, and solutions that can be provided to avoid existing issues. The code for the PresentationCreation procedure is as follows:

```
Public Sub PresentationCreation()
        Dim ppApp As PowerPoint.Application
        Dim ppOne As PowerPoint.Presentation
        Dim ppTwo As PowerPoint.Presentation
        Dim ppslide As PowerPoint.Slide
        Dim ppShape As PowerPoint.Shape
        Dim varLength As Long
```

```
        Dim varSalesRepInfo As String
        Dim varSalesRepName As String
        Dim varIssues As String
        Dim IssuesCount As Integer
        Dim SolutionsCount As Integer
        Dim VarSlideNumber As Integer
        Dim varSolutions As String

        Try
            ppApp = CType(CreateObject("PowerPoint.Application"),
               PowerPoint.Application)
            ppApp.Visible = True
            ppApp.Presentations.Add()
            ppOne = ppApp.ActivePresentation
            ppOne.ApplyTemplate("c:\easyselling\presentation.ppt")
            varLength = ppOne.Slides.InsertFromFile("c:\easyselling\presentation.ppt",
               0, 1, 6)
'gets sales rep data
            clientConnection.Open()
            strSqlStatement = "SELECT * FROM tblSalesRep"
            clientCommand = New OleDbCommand(strSqlStatement, clientConnection)
            clientDataReader = clientCommand.ExecuteReader()
            While clientDataReader.Read
                varSalesRepName = IIf(IsDBNull(clientDataReader.Item(1)), "NA",
                clientDataReader.Item(1))
                varSalesRepInfo = IIf(IsDBNull(clientDataReader.Item(1)), "NA",
                   clientDataReader.Item(1))
                + Chr(13)
                varSalesRepInfo = varSalesRepInfo +
                   IIf(IsDBNull(clientDataReader.Item(2)), "NA",
                clientDataReader.Item(2)) + Chr(13)
                varSalesRepInfo = varSalesRepInfo +
                   IIf(IsDBNull(clientDataReader.Item(11)), "NA",
                clientDataReader.Item(11)) + Chr(13)

            End While
            clientDataReader.Close()
            clientConnection.Close()
```

```
'gets issues
            clientConnection.Open()
            strSqlStatement = "SELECT Expectation FROM tblClientExpectations
               WHERE selected = True
            AND Client_ID = " & varCompanyName.SharedClientID
            clientCommand = New OleDbCommand(strSqlStatement, clientConnection)
            clientDataReader = clientCommand.ExecuteReader()
            While clientDataReader.Read
                varIssues = varIssues + clientDataReader.Item(0) + Chr(13)
            End While
            clientDataReader.Close()
            clientConnection.Close()
'gets solutions
            clientConnection.Open()
            strSqlStatement = "SELECT solution FROM tblClientSolutions WHERE
               selected = True AND
            Client_ID = " & varCompanyName.SharedClientID
            clientCommand = New OleDbCommand(strSqlStatement, clientConnection)
            clientDataReader = clientCommand.ExecuteReader()
            While clientDataReader.Read
                varSolutions = varSolutions + clientDataReader.Item(0) + Chr(13)
            End While
            clientDataReader.Close()
            clientConnection.Close()
'replaces data
            For Each ppslide In ppOne.Slides
                For Each ppShape In ppslide.Shapes
                    If ppShape.HasTextFrame = True Then
                        ppShape.TextFrame.TextRange.Replace("<<Customer Company>>",
                        varCompanyName.SharedValue)
                        ppShape.TextFrame.TextRange.Replace("<<SalesRep>>",
                           varSalesRepInfo)
                        ppShape.TextFrame.TextRange.Replace("<<SalesRepName>>",
                           varSalesRepName)
                        ppShape.TextFrame.TextRange.Replace("<<IssuesItems>>",
                           varIssues)
                        ppShape.TextFrame.TextRange.Replace("<<SolutionItems>>",
                           varSolutions)
```

```
                End If
            Next
        Next
        ppShape = Nothing
        ppslide = Nothing
        ppOne = Nothing
        ppApp = Nothing
    Catch
        MsgBox(Err.Description)
    End Try
End Sub
```

The findandreplace Procedure

The `findandreplace` procedure finds and replaces customer-specific details in the templates used for creating customer-specific proposals and presentations. The procedure works on the concept of selecting the default text in the document and then replacing the selected text with the specific text extracted from the database. The code for the `findandreplace` procedure is as follows:

```
Public Sub findandreplace(ByVal findtext As String,
   ByVal replacementText As String)
    Dim flag As Integer
    Dim var As Boolean
    docApp.Selection.Find.ClearFormatting()
    docApp.Selection.Find.Replacement.ClearFormatting()
    With docApp.Selection.Find
        .Text = findtext
        .Replacement.Text = replacementText
        .Forward = True
        .Wrap = 1
        .Format = False
        .MatchCase = False
        .MatchWholeWord = False
        .MatchWildcards = False
        .MatchSoundsLike = False
        .MatchAllWordForms = False
```

```
            End With
            flag = 1
            Do While flag = 1
                var = docApp.Selection.Find.Execute
                If var = True Then
                    With docApp.Selection
                        If .Find.Forward = True Then
                            .Collapse(Direction:=1)
                        Else
                            .Collapse(Direction:=0)
                        End If
                        .Find.Execute(Replace:=1)
                        If .Find.Forward = True Then
                            .Collapse(Direction:=0)
                        Else
                            .Collapse(Direction:=1)
                        End If

                    End With
                Else
                    flag = 0
                End If
            Loop
        End Sub
End Class
```

Summary

In this chapter, you coded the `Outputs` screen of the Easy Selling application. You also learned all the main procedures and functions used in the form. In the next chapter, you will learn to execute the application.

Chapter 36

Executing the Easy Selling Application

In this chapter, you will learn to execute the Easy Selling application. You will also learn the steps to distribute the application as an executable file.

Running the Application

To run the application, you need to execute the following steps:

1. Create a folder named `EasyTemp`.
2. Extract the files from the `EasySelling.zip` folder to the `EasyTemp` folder.

   You will see a folder named `EasySelling`. Within this folder, you will see the `EasySelling.NET` folder.
3. Move the `EasySelling` folder to C:\. You have the `C:\EasySelling\EasySelling.NET` structure ready.
4. Run the .exe from the bin folder within the `EasySelling.NET` folder. The application will start.

NOTE

The prerequisite for running this application is the installation of VB.NET and Office 2000 products on the computer.

When the application starts, the first screen to be displayed is the `Main` screen. The `Main` screen is discussed in the following section.

The Main Screen

Figure 36-1 displays the `Customers` page of the `Main` screen of the Easy Selling application.

At the left of the `Main` screen are the buttons for the various screen options. These screens are discussed throughout this chapter.

The `Main` screen consists of three tabs:

- The `Customers` tab
- The `About You` tab
- The `Help` tab

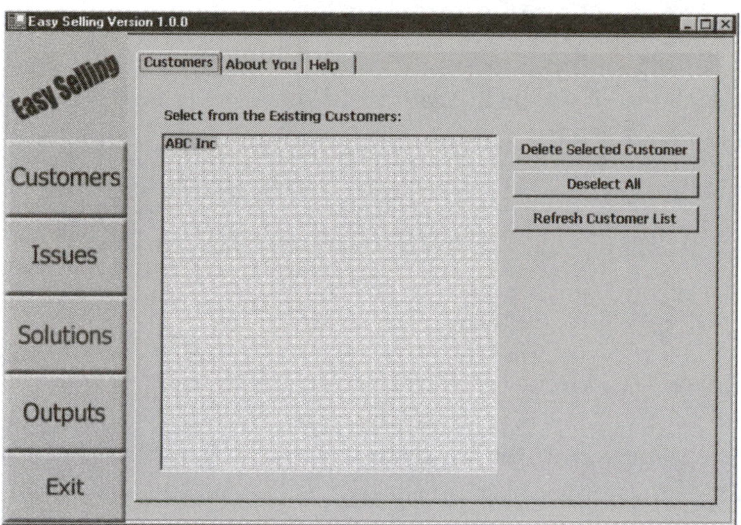

FIGURE 36-1 *The* `Customers` *page of the* `Main` *Screen of the Easy Selling application*

The `Customers` page is discussed in the following section.

The Customers Page of the Main Screen

This page consists of five controls: a label, a list box, and three command buttons. This list is filled with customer names when the form loads. The names of customers are picked from the database. You can select the name of an existing customer from this list.

NOTE

The list box is displayed empty if there are no records for existing customers in the database.

The three command buttons on the `Customers` page are as follows:

- `Delete Selected Customer`
- `Deselect All`
- `Refresh Customer List`

You can use the `Delete Selected Customer` button to delete the record of an existing customer from the database. Before deleting, you need to select a customer name from the list box. If you do not select a customer, an error message is displayed as shown in Figure 36-2.

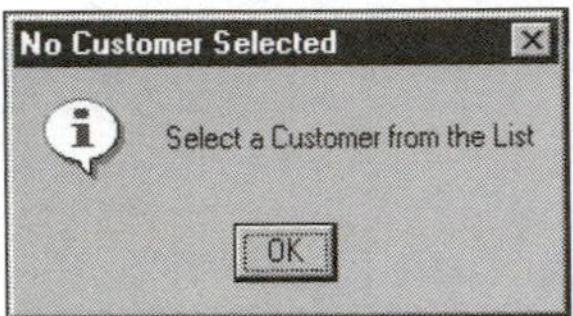

FIGURE 36-2 *The* `No Customer Selected` *error message*

After you select the customer from the list and click on the `Delete Selected Customer` button, a confirmation message is displayed as shown in Figure 36-3.

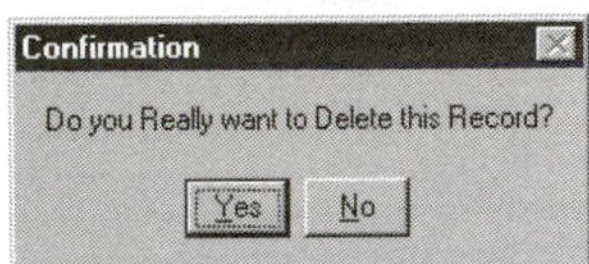

FIGURE 36-3 *A confirmation message for deleting a record*

If you click on the `Yes` button, the record is deleted from the database. If you click on the `No` button, the record is not deleted. After you delete the customer, you can refresh the customer list by clicking on the `Refresh Customer List` button.

You can click on the `Deselect All` button on the form to deselect all the customer names in the list. You can also use this button if you want to add a new customer because to add a new customer, none of the existing customers should be selected. After adding a new customer, you again need to click on the `Refresh Customer List` button to view the newly added customer.

The About You Page of the Main Screen

You can use this page to capture information related to the sales representative who would be using this application. Figure 36-4 displays the `About You` page of the `Main` screen.

Some of the fields on the `About You` page are mandatory and must be filled in before saving the record. The application also checks for correct data being entered by the user. It validates that the user has left none of the mandatory fields

FIGURE 36-4 *The* `About You` *page of the* `Main` *screen*

empty. For example, if the user leaves the `Your Name` field empty, the message box shown in Figure 36-5 is displayed.

If you leave the `Phone Number` field empty, the message box shown in Figure 36-6 is displayed.

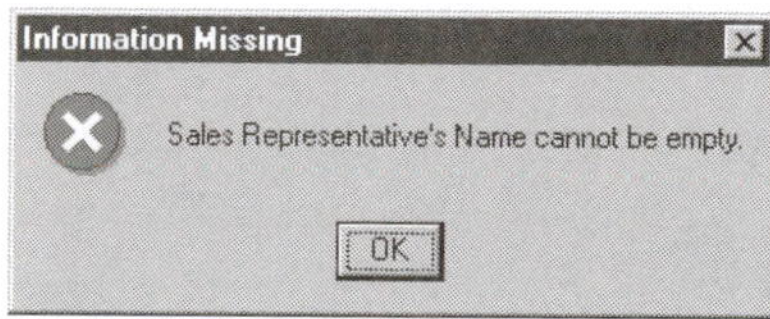

FIGURE 36-5 *This message box is displayed when the user does not enter the name.*

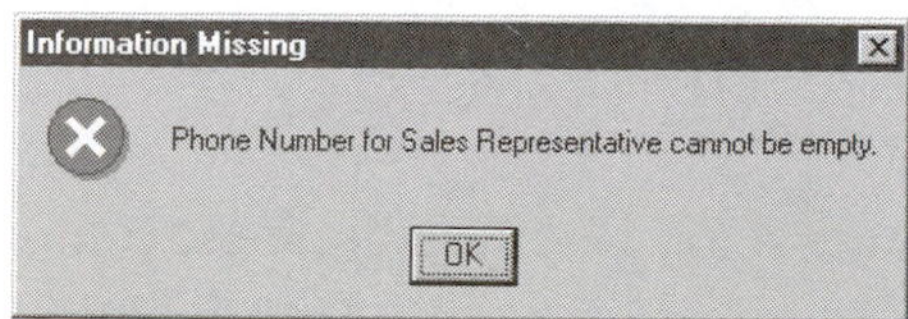

FIGURE 36-6 *This message box is displayed when the user does not enter the phone number.*

If you leave the `Email Address` field blank, the message box shown in Figure 36-7 is displayed.

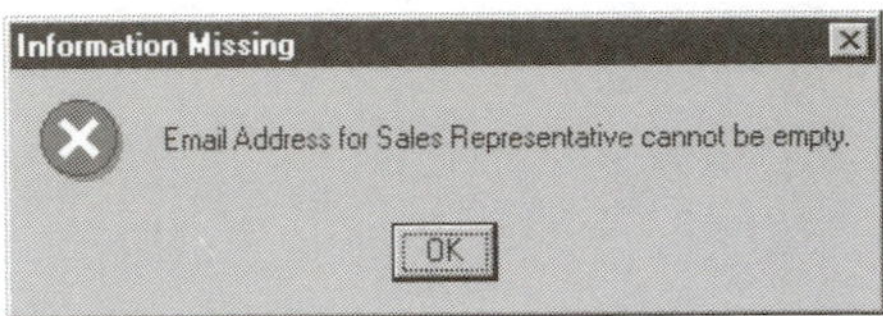

FIGURE 36-7 *This message box is displayed when the user does not enter the e-mail address.*

If the user leaves the `Company Name` field blank, the message box shown in Figure 36-8 is displayed.

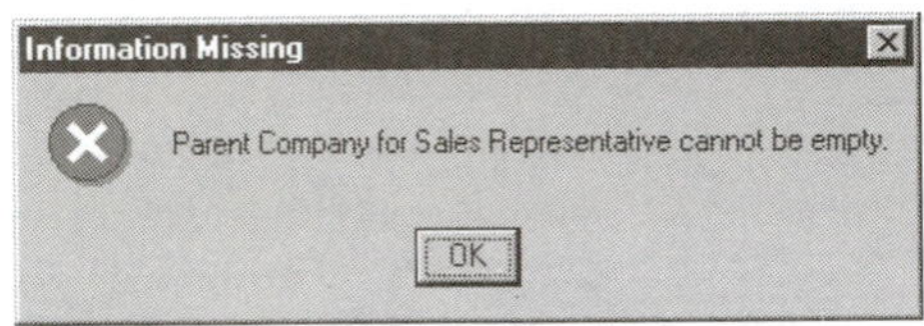

FIGURE 36-8 *This message box is displayed when the user does not enter the company name.*

After you enter all the details and click on the `Save` button, the record is saved and a message as shown in Figure 36-9 is displayed.

FIGURE 36-9 *This message box is displayed when the record is successfully saved.*

The Help Page of the Main Screen

The `Help` page displays help on using the application. The page consists of an HTML file that is being displayed in the Web browser. The `Help` page of the `Main` screen is displayed in Figure 36-10.

You can use the buttons of the `MainMDI` form to move to different screens in this application. You can click on the `Customers` button to navigate to the `Customers` screen.

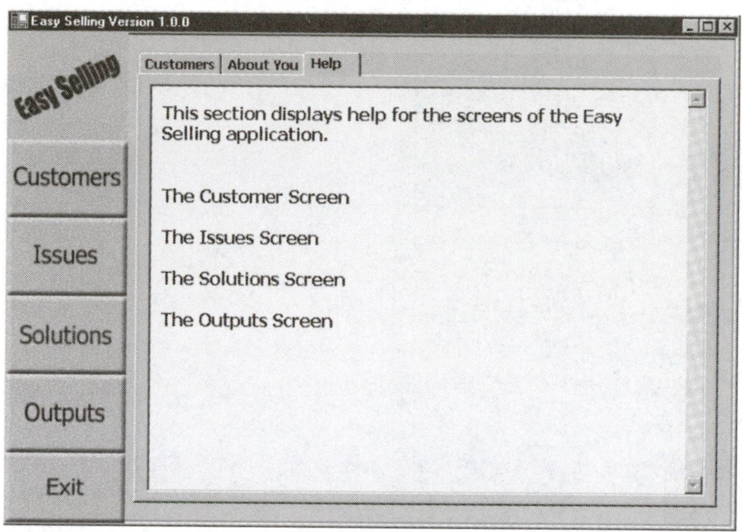

FIGURE 36-10 *The* `Help` *page of the* `Main` *screen*

The Customers Screen

The `Customers` screen is used to capture customer, product, and competition-related information. The `Customer` screen consists of three tabs:

- The `Profile` tab
- The `Product Usage and Competitor - I` tab
- The `Product Usage and Competitor - II` tab

You can click on each of these tabs to display the corresponding page. The following sections discuss each of these tabs.

The Profile Page of the Customers Screen

The `Profile` page is used to capture the customer details such as customer name, address, city, state, ZIP code, e-mail address, phone number, fax number, client contact name, and industry type. Validations ensure that no incorrect data is entered by the salesperson. The salesperson can save the record after entering the customer's details by clicking on the `Save` button on the form. The `Profile` page is displayed in Figure 36-11.

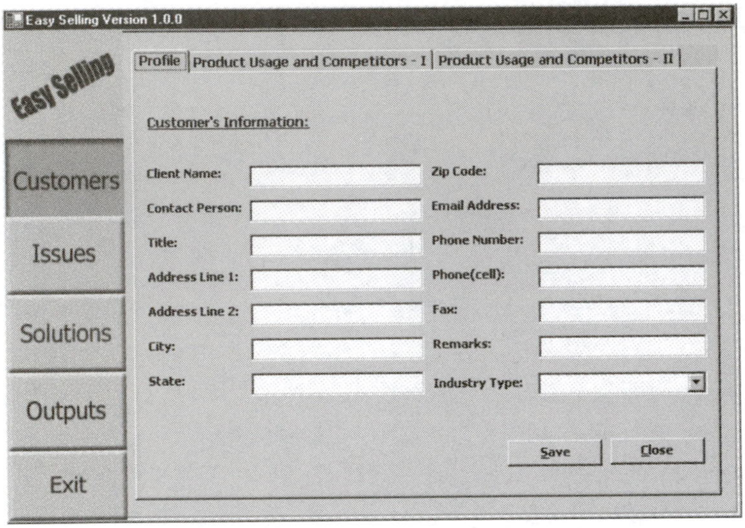

FIGURE 36-11 *The* `Profile` *page of the* `Customers` *screen*

The field `Client Name` is a mandatory field on this page. If the user does not enter the client name, a message box as shown in Figure 36-12 is displayed.

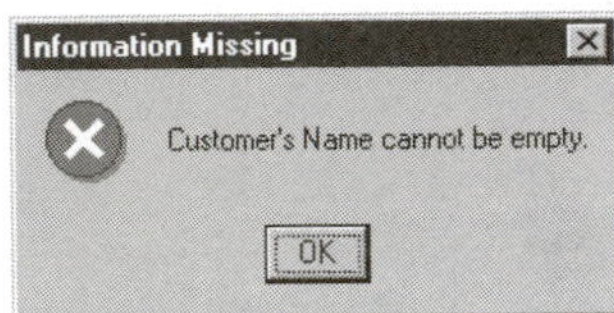

FIGURE 36-12 *This message box is displayed when the user does not enter the customer's name.*

After a new customer is added, you need to click on the `Save` button to add the record to the database. A confirmation message is then displayed to the sales person as shown in Figure 36-13.

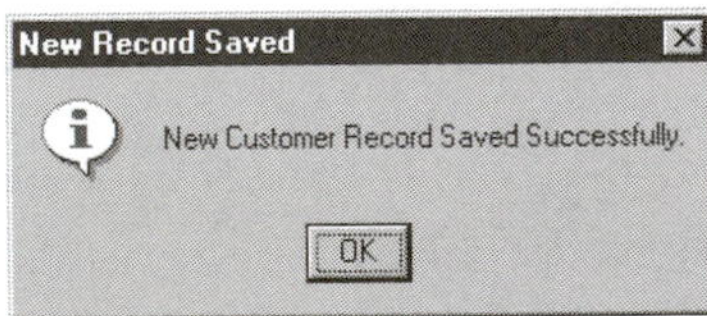

FIGURE 36-13 *This message box is displayed when a new customer record is added successfully.*

The `Save` button also saves the information recorded in the second and the third page of the form.

The Product Usage and Competitors – I Page of the Customers Screen

This page is used to capture the product- and competition-related details. The page is displayed in Figure 36-14.

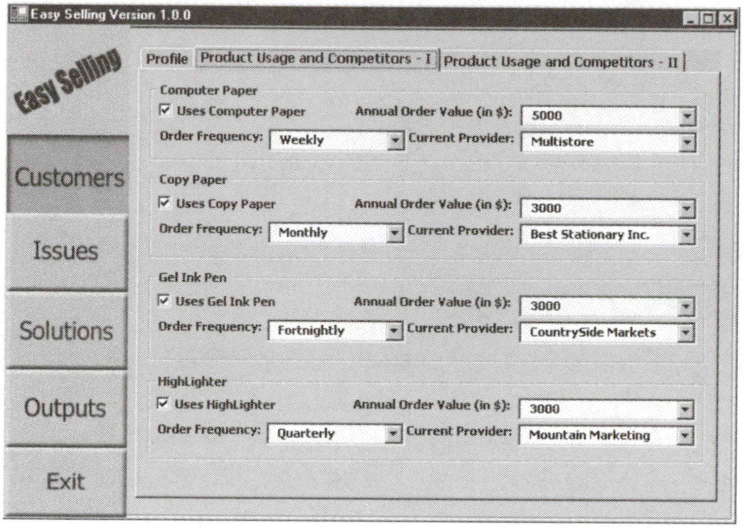

FIGURE 36-14 *The* `Product Usage and Competitors - I` *page of the* `Customers` *screen*

The salesperson can use this screen to capture information related to the product's usage in the company. It also helps capture the competitor's details. The salesperson can click on the check boxes provided on the form, based on the discussion with the client on the product's usage and its competitor's. For example, if the customer uses Computer Paper the salesperson can click on the `Computer Paper` check box. This activates the other three fields in the group, namely `Annual Order Value`, `Order Frequency`, and `Current Provider`. These are drop-down fields. However, the salesperson can also enter values in these list boxes. The list boxes check for correct data being entered.

The Product Usage and Competitors – II Page of the Customers Screen

The `Product Usage and Competitors - II` page is a continuation of the `Product Usage and Competitors - I` page. This page is displayed in Figure 36-15.

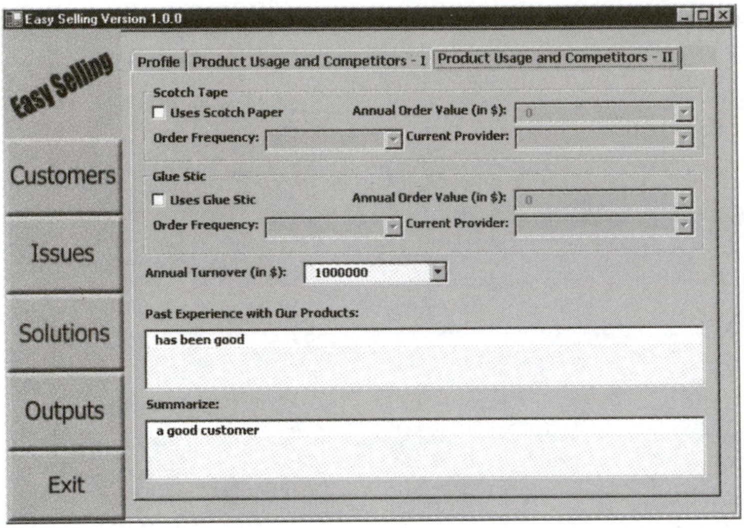

FIGURE 36-15 *The* `Product Usage and Competitors - II` *page of the* `Customers` *screen*

This page displays two more products and some extra fields such as `Annual Turnover (in $)`, `Past experience with our products`, and `Summarize` fields. These fields can be used by the salesperson to capture details such as the customer's annual turnover in dollars, a summary of product usage and competitor analysis, and any other comments.

You can click on the `Issues` button to navigate to the `Issues` screen.

The Issues Screen

The `Issues` screen is used to record the issues faced by the customer. The `Issues` screen is displayed in Figure 36-16.

The salesperson can move to this screen by selecting a customer and clicking on the `Issues` button. If the salesperson tries to select this option without selecting a customer, the message shown in Figure 36-17 is displayed.

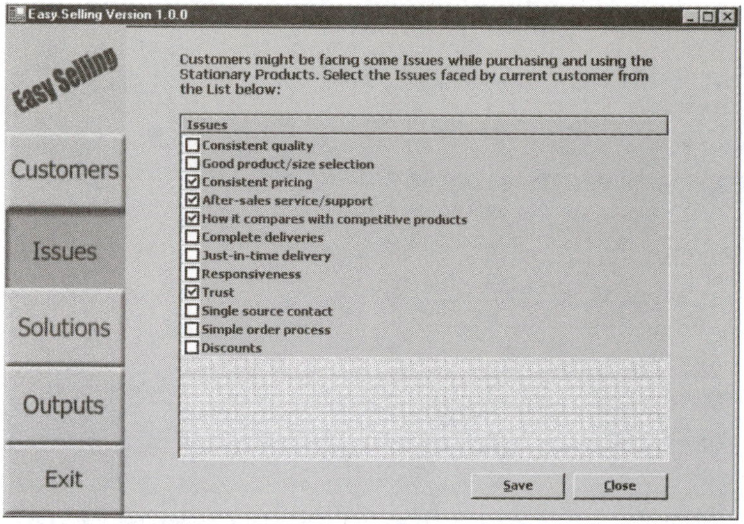

FIGURE 36-16 *The* `Issues` *screen*

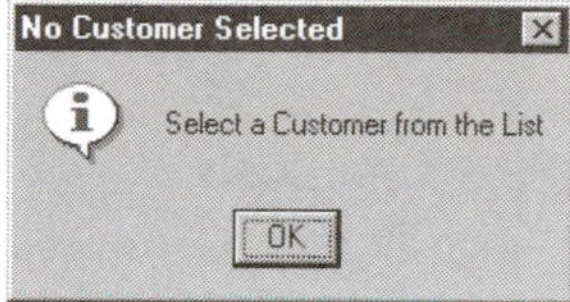

FIGURE 36-17 *This message box is displayed when the user clicks on the* `Issues` *button without selecting the customer.*

The issues listed on the `Issues` screen are standardized. The salesperson can select these issues based on the discussion with the customer. After selecting the issues, the salesperson can save the data in the database by clicking on the `Save` button. The information selected by the salesperson is used by the application to generate the output documents. The application displays a message "Record Saved Successfully" after the record is saved in the database as shown in Figure 36-18.

You can click on the `Solutions` button to navigate to the `Solutions` screen.

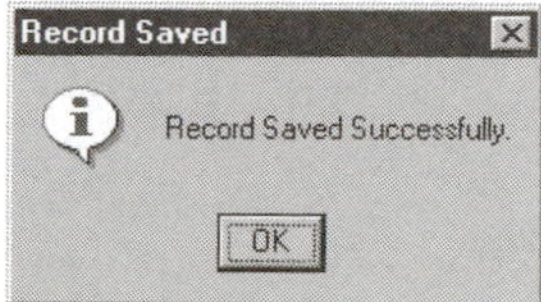

FIGURE 36-18 *This message box is displayed when the record for the* `Issues` *screen is saved successfully.*

The Solutions Screen

The salesperson can use the `Solutions` screen to offer solutions to the customer for the issues faced by them. The `Solutions` screen is displayed in Figure 36-19.

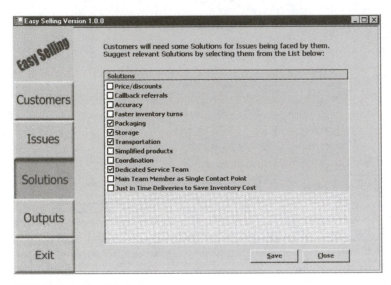

FIGURE 36-19 *The* `Solutions` *screen*

To navigate to this screen, the salesperson needs to select a customer first. If the salesperson clicks on the `Solutions` button without highlighting the customer name from the list, a message box appears as shown in Figure 36-20.

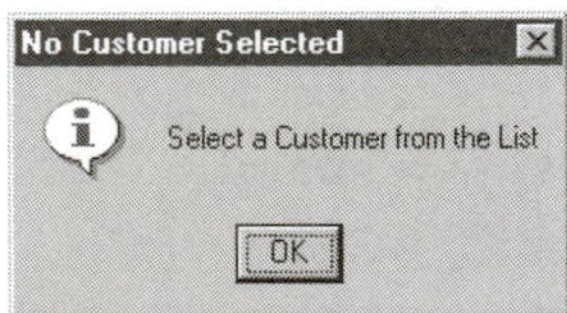

FIGURE 36-20 *This message box is displayed when the user clicks on the* `Solutions` *button without selecting a customer name.*

The solutions displayed on this screen are standardized. The salespeople can select the solutions on this screen and click on the `Save` button to save the data in the database. A message as shown in Figure 36-21 is displayed when the record is saved successfully.

FIGURE 36-21 *This message box is displayed when the solutions record is successfully added to the database.*

The information selected by the salesperson is used to create output documents by the application.

The Outputs Screen

The `Outputs` screen is used to generate the output documents: Word proposal, PowerPoint presentation, and the Excel report based on the data entered. Figure 36-22 displays the `Outputs` screen.

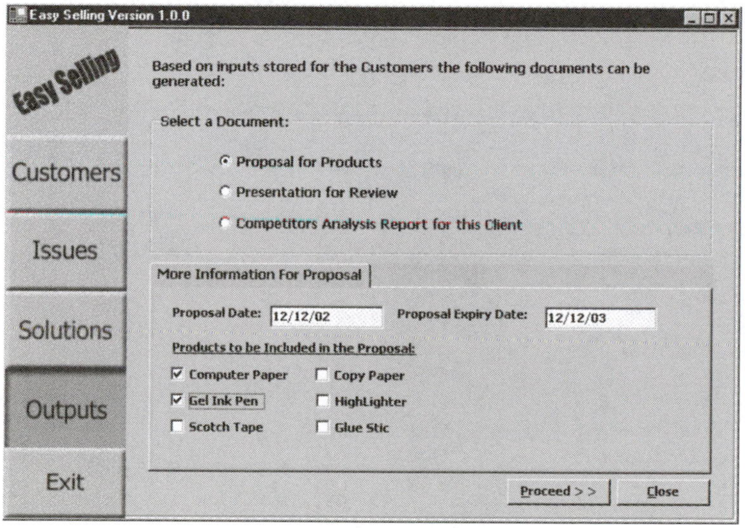

FIGURE 36-22 *The* `Outputs` *screen*

The `Outputs` screen has two sections. The first section is used to select the document that needs to be generated, that is, a proposal, a presentation, or a competitor analysis report. The second section is used to capture information related to the proposal document.

The Proposal for Products Option

When the salesperson selects the `Proposal for Products` option, the salesperson needs to provide the proposal date in the `Proposal Date` text box. This is the date on which the proposal is made. The salesperson also needs to specify the validity period of the generated proposal by specifying a date in the `Expiry Date` text box. The salesperson can specify the products to be included in the proposal by selecting the check boxes provided. The second tab in this section displays details of the salesperson. This information can be modified. Note that the information modified here is not saved in the database. The information is used in the generated document only.

NOTE

The output documents that are generated are kept open for the user to work with them. For example, when a proposal document is generated, the template document remains open along with the new document. The documents need to be closed by the user explicitly.

A sample of the Proposal document is shown in Figure 36-23.

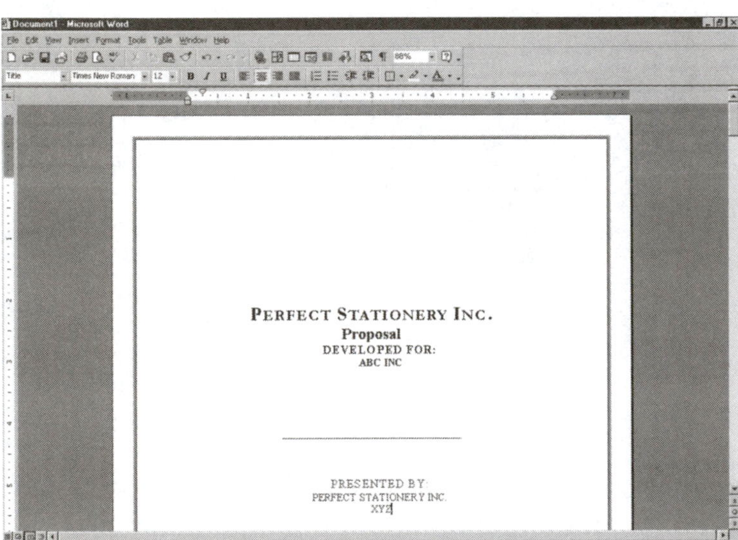

FIGURE 36-23 *A sample Proposal document generated*

The Presentation for Review Option

The salesperson can select this option to create a PowerPoint presentation. The salesperson can specify the products he wants to include by selecting the products listed. The second section of this screen displays a second tab, which shows the details of the salesperson. The salesperson can modify information here. However, the information is not saved in the database. The information is used in the generated document.

A sample of the PowerPoint presentation is shown in Figure 36-24.

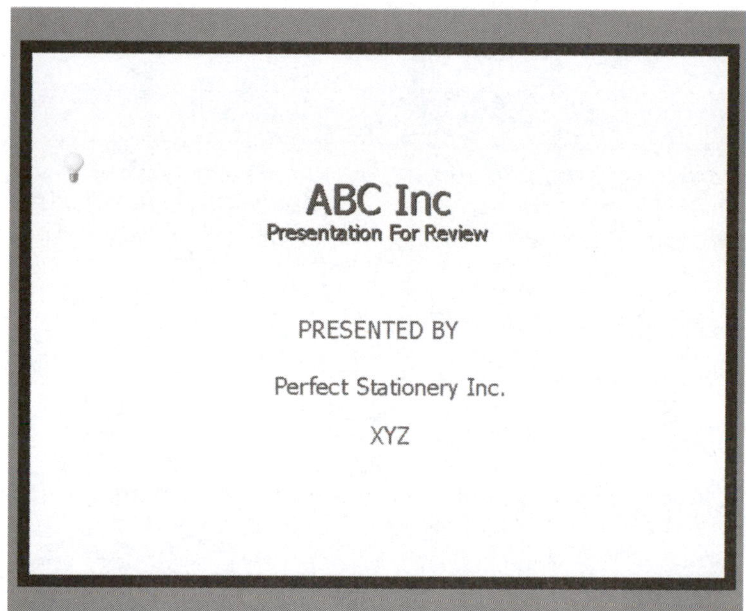

FIGURE 36-24 *A sample PowerPoint presentation*

The Competitor Analysis Report Option

The competitor analysis report is generated in Excel. This report is used by the salesperson to generate an analysis report for the selected customer. This report is not affected by any parameters on the screen. The format for this report is standard. The report gives information about who is holding what share in this customer's purchase capacity.

To generate the output documents, the salesperson needs to select a document and click on the `Proceed` button on the form. The documents are templates, which are filled with relevant data. Before generating the documents, the application checks for all relevant information.

A sample of the competitor's analysis report is shown in Figure 36-25.

This is Competitor Analysis Report for Customer: ABC Inc Customer ID: 1

Customer's Industry Type is:

Products	Order Value(in Dollars)	Current Provider	% of Total Order Value
Computer Paper	5000	Multistore	35.71
Copy Paper	3000	Best Stationary Inc.	21.43
Gel Ink Pen	3000	CountrySide Markets	21.43
Highlighter	3000	Mountain Marketing	21.43
Scotch Tape	0		0.00
Glue Stic	0		0.00
Total Order Value is:	14000		100.00

FIGURE 36-25 *A sample analysis report*

The Exit Button

The salesperson can close the application by clicking on the `Exit` button in the application.

Distributing the Application

You can distribute the Easy Selling application as an .exe file. The steps to create a setup for the Easy Selling application are the standard steps that you followed for distributing the Skill Search application in Chapter 21, "Executing the Skill Search Application."

Summary

In this chapter, you learned to execute the Easy Selling application. You also learned about the different screens of this application. Finally, you learned to distribute the application.

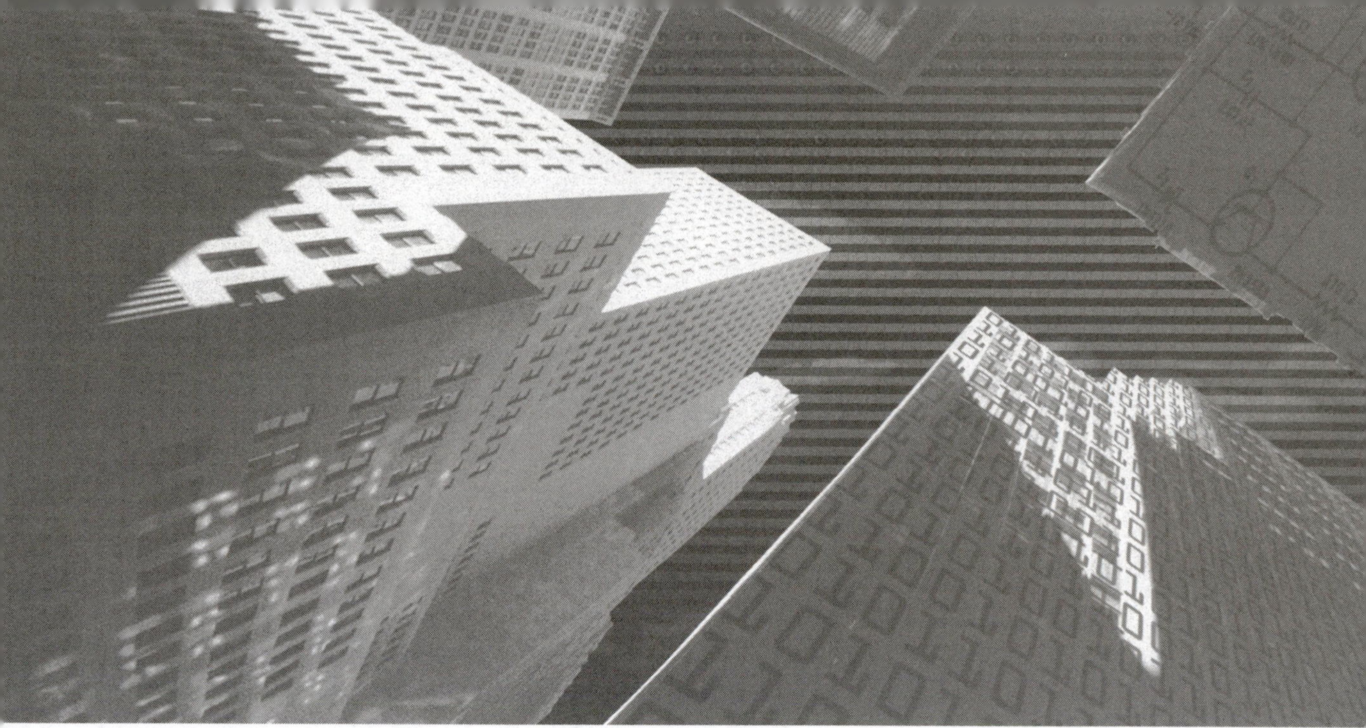

PART VII

Beyond the Lab

Chapter 37

XML and .NET

Over the years, the Internet has seen explosive growth. The drawbacks of HTML (*HyperText Markup Language*) as a Web application development language were apparent and led to the development of XML (*eXtensible Markup Language*). By using XML, you can create Web applications. Moreover, XML can be used with other technologies. This chapter provides an introduction to XML. You will also learn how XML documents are created and read using the .NET Framework. VB.NET is used for illustrating the concepts.

An Introduction to XML

Because XML was designed as a markup language, it is fast becoming the primary markup language for representing data. Some inherent features of XML make it a valid language for Web-based applications

Following are some key features of XML that make it a unique markup language:

- XML is used for structuring data.
- XML is platform-independent.
- XML supports internationalization.
- XML supports localization.
- XML is Unicode-compliant.

The following section discusses the differences between XML and HTML.

Differences Between XML and HTML

Similar to HTML, XML makes use of tags and attributes. In HTML, all the tags and attributes are defined and cannot be changed. For example, the <B> tag means that the text following the <B> tag should appear as bold. XML allows you as a developer to name each tag and define its meaning. In addition, it permits you to name each attribute and define its meaning. Consider the following HTML code snippet. Assume that you are developing an application that displays the quantity of motherboards.

```
<B>Product Name: Network Cards</B>
<B>Quantity: 100</B>
<B>Product Name: Motherboards</B>
<B>Quantity: 10</B>
```

Because the tags used in the preceding code do not define the meaning of the content, it is difficult to produce an application for the specified purpose.

The tags in the following code snippet describe the text that they define:

```
<Product>Network Cards</Product>
    <Quantity>100</Quantity>
<Product>Motherboards</Product>
    <Quantity>10</Quantity>
```

Therefore, it is easier to use XML code to develop an application that displays the quantity of motherboards.

Unlike HTML, the XML specification is strict on the formatting of an XML document. In HTML, a missing closing tag is acceptable. The HTML script does not stop running. The XML specifications do not allow an application to execute an XML document that has missing tags or attributes. The following code is for an XML document with a missing closing tag. An application will not be able to read the data in this document.

```
<Product>Network Cards<Product>
    <Quantity>100</Quantity>
<Product>Motherboards</Product>
    <Quantity>10</Quantity>
```

In addition, XML is case sensitive. If there are two tags, `<Product>` and `<product>`, XML does not treat them as the same. XML recognizes them as two different tags with different meanings.

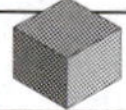

NOTE

You can develop applications using XML, and XML is absolutely free of cost. Therefore, when you select a technology, XML is always worth considering.

You have seen the key features of XML that make it a valid markup language for developing a Web application. The following section looks at how to create an XML document.

Creating a Basic XML Document

An XML document consists of tags and attributes. Consider the XML document shown in Listing 37-1.

Listing 37-1 Sample XML Code

```
<?xml version="1.0"?>
<Inventory>
<Product>Network Cards</Product>
    <Quantity>100</Quantity>
<Product>Motherboards</Product>
    <Quantity>10</Quantity>
</Inventory>
```

The first line of code is the XML declaration. This line identifies the document as an XML document. This document has three elements: `Product`, `Quantity`, and `Inventory`. An element has a start tag and an end tag. For example, the `Product` element has the start tag, `<Product>`, and the end tag, `</Product>`. Elements can be further classified by using attributes.

An attribute consists of a name and value pair that is used to define an additional property of an element. It is located inside the start tags and after the element name. All attribute values must be enclosed within quotes. Attributes are used to further classify an element. Following is an example of the code:

```
<?xml version="1.0"?>
<Inventory>
<Product id="001">Network Cards</Product>
    <Quantity>100</Quantity>
<Product id="002">Motherboards</Product>
    <Quantity>10</Quantity>
</Inventory>
```

In this code, `id` is an attribute of the `Product` element.

You can insert comments in an XML document to enhance the readability of the code. A comment is enclosed within the following characters, <!- - and - - >. It is a piece of code that is not executed. Comments are written in plain and simple English. The following code illustrates a comment inserted in an XML document:

```
<?xml version="1.0"?>
<!--This is a comment-->
<Inventory>
<Product id="001">Network Cards</Product>
    <Quantity>100</Quantity>
<Product id="002">Motherboards</Product>
    <Quantity>10</Quantity>
</Inventory>
```

You have learned how to create a basic and well-formed XML document. The next section discusses Document Type Definition (DTD).

Document Type Definition (DTD)

Consider a scenario. You and a friend are designing an XML-based application that requires the creation of 50 XML documents. You share the work among yourselves. To avoid confusion at a later stage, you create an XML vocabulary of all the elements and attributes to be used in the application. You also define the sequencing of the elements. By creating an XML vocabulary, you have created a DTD. A DTD essentially specifies a formal structure and the permissible values of XML documents. It is not mandatory to create a DTD, however it is a good practice to create one.

You use the following syntax to declare the elements in a DTD:

```
<!ELEMENT elementname (content-type or content-model)>
```

In this syntax:

- `elementname` represents the name of the element.
- `content-type` or `content-model` represents the content of an element. The content of an element can be either textual data or other elements.

Consider the following DTD code. This DTD is specific for the XML code given in Listing 37-1.

```
<!ELEMENT Inventory (Product,Quantity)>
<!ELEMENT Product (#PCData)>
<!ELEMENT Quantity (#PCData)>
```

In this code, `PCData` specifies that the type of data enclosed by this element is of the character string type. Suppose you type this code and save the document as

`Inventory.DTD`. You can include this DTD in the XML document as given in the following code:

```
<?xml version="1.0"?>
<!DOCTYPE Inventory SYSTEM "Inventory.DTD">
<Inventory>
<Product>Network Cards</Product>
    <Quantity>100</Quantity>
<Product>Motherboards</Product>
    <Quantity>10</Quantity>
</Inventory>
```

Notice the second line of the preceding code. This is the syntax used to include the DTD in the XML document. On including this DTD, you cannot introduce any new elements in the XML document. The only way to introduce new elements in the XML document is to declare them first in `Inventory.DTD`. If this is not done, an error is reported.

There are some drawbacks for a DTD. One drawback is that you can define two elements with the same name across multiple DTDs. Such a scenario can cause ambiguity and a name collision. This drawback is solved with XML Namespaces.

XML Namespaces

Namespaces are a collection of names that are used in XML documents as element types and attribute names. Consider an XML document that uses two DTDs, `Inventory.DTD` and `Order.DTD`. If these DTDs have some common element names, there will be a name collision. To avoid this, you can create namespaces. You can declare a namespace for every element that you are going to use.

There are three parts to a namespace declaration: a reserved keyword, a namespace prefix, and a URI. A URI can be the name of a DTD on your server. An example is given below:

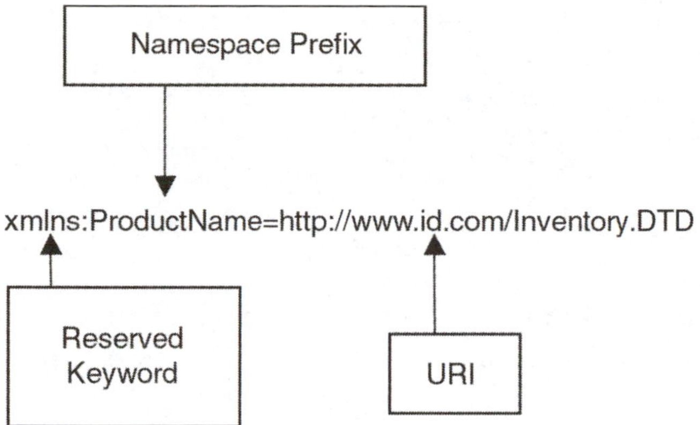

To refer to the `Product` element in the `Inventory.DTD` file, you would use the prefix, `ProductName`, to make it clear. For example:

```
<ProductName:Product />
```

Here is some food for thought. From all that you have learned so far, can you create your own data type? If your answer is NO, you are on the right track. A Schema is required for such a task. The following section discusses XML Schemas.

XML Schemas

You can think of an XML Schema as a way of constraining the choice of tags a user can use in an XML document. A DTD is a type of schema. Some of the advantages of an XML Schema over a DTD are that an XML Schema permits you to do the following:

- Create your own data type
- Restrict the type of data stored in the XML document
- Have greater control over the data assigned to elements

You looked at how the DTD for the XML document displayed in Listing 37-1 was developed. The following code illustrates a schema defining the XML document displayed in Listing 37-1.

```
<Schema …>
    <element name="Inventory">
        <type>
```

```
            <element name="Product" type="string"
                minOccurs="0" maxOccurs="1" />
            <element name="Quantity" type="integer"
                minOccurs="0" maxOccurs="1" />
        </type>
    </element>
</Schema>
```

In this code, each element name has three other attributes that can be declared. These variables help in constraining the user as per the requirements. The attribute type declares the data type. The attribute, `minOccurs`, specifies the minimum number of instances in which this element can occur in the XML document. The `maxOccurs` attribute defines the maximum number of instances in which this element can occur in the XML document. For example, consider the following line of code:

```
<element name="Quantity" type="integer"
minOccurs="0" maxOccurs="1" />
```

In this case, the name of the element is `Quantity`. The type of data this element can contain is integer. This element can never occur in the XML document or can occur only once.

NOTE

Microsoft has developed a language called XML Schema Definition (XSD) for defining the schema of an XML document. You can use the XSD language to define the structure and data types for XML documents.

So far, you have learned how XML can be used to structure data. You still have not looked at how you can access an XML document from your programs. The XML Document Object Model (DOM), discussed in the following section, is one of the ways of accessing an XML document.

XML Document Object Model (DOM)

Web browsers have used a DOM in one form or another. Unfortunately, each browser has implemented the DOM in its own manner. The W3C produced specifications to standardize the DOM, so that there is a standardized way of accessing and manipulating the document structure over the Web. You access the objects in the DOM to read, search, modify, and delete from a document. The DOM defines a standard method for document navigation and manipulation of the content of HTML and XML documents. This section discusses the XML DOM with respect to the .NET Framework.

There are two specifications on the DOM: Level 1 and Level 2. DOM (Core) Level 1 contains the specification for interfaces that allow access to XML documents. Figure 37-1 illustrates the objects that make up the DOM. DOM Level 2 is a superset of the DOM Level 1 model. In addition to all the objects that are found in DOM Level 1, DOM Level 2 includes the following:

- Support for namespaces
- An object model for style sheets
- Definitions of the methods of filtering an XML document
- An event model
- Ranges

All the XML documents generated using a DOM model guarantee that the document will be well formed.

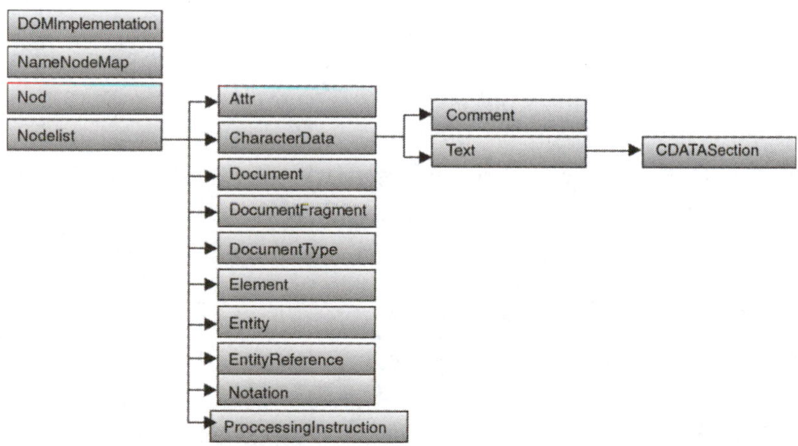

FIGURE 37-1 *XML DOM class hierarchy*

Web applications create and read XML documents. The .NET Framework is the backbone of creating such Web applications. The next section discusses the use of XML in the .NET Framework.

NOTE

Chapter 15, "Overview of the .NET Framework," gave you a basic understanding of the .NET Framework.

The .NET Framework Class Library

The .NET Framework includes classes, interfaces, and value types. The .NET Framework types are common language specification (CLS) compliant. Therefore, you can use any programming language that conforms to the CLS to achieve inter-language operability. You use the .NET Framework types to built .NET applications, components, and controls.

The .NET Framework provides a set of interfaces and abstract and non-abstract classes. You can use the non-abstract classes as they are, or you can derive your own classes from them. You can use an interface by creating a class that implements that interface. The following section discusses the System namespace.

The System Namespace

The System namespace is the root namespace in the .NET Framework. This namespace has classes that represent the base data types. These base data types include `Object`, `Byte`, `Char`, and so on. The System namespace also contains second-level namespaces. You use the second-level namespace, `System.XML`, to process XML documents.

The .NET Framework XML Classes

The .NET Framework XML classes are also referred to as .NET XML APIs. These classes are built on key industry standards, such as DOM Level 2 and XML Schemas. In addition to the classic DOM, the .NET Framework XML classes utilize a stream-based API that offers a pull model interface.

The .NET Framework XML classes are included in the `System.XML` namespace. Figure 37-3, later in the chapter, displays the classes in the `System.XML` namespace architecture. Before using the .NET Framework XML classes, you must import the `System.XML` namespace into your code. You use the `import` directive to do this.

For example:

```
import System.Xml
```

You have learned how to import the System.XML namespace. Next, you will learn how to read and create an XML document. You can do this by using the two abstract classes: XmlReader and XmlWriter.

Abstract Base Classes

XmlReader provides a fast, forward-only, read-only cursor for processing an XML document stream. XmlWriter provides an interface for producing XML document streams that conform to W3C's XML 1.0 + Namespaces Recommendations. So what does all this jargon mean? Well, in a nutshell, when you develop applications for processing XML documents, use XmlReader. For applications that produce XML documents, use XmlWriter. Neither class requires an in-memory cache. This is why they are such viable alternatives to the classic DOM approach. The DOM approach is discussed later in this chapter.

Because XmlReader and XmlWriter are abstract base classes, they define the functionality that all derived classes must support. XmlReader has three implementations: XmlTextReader, XmlNodeReader, and XslReader. Similarly, XmlWriter has one implementation, XmlTextWriter. By using XmlTextReader and XmlTextWriter, you can read from and write to a text-based stream. In addition, you can use XmlNodeReader to work with in-memory DOM trees. You can also build your own XML readers and XML writers. Figure 37-2 illustrates the DOM trees in XmlReader and XmlWriter.

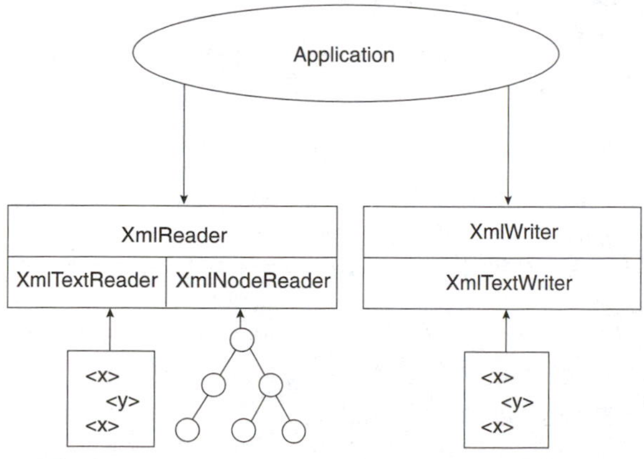

FIGURE 37-2 *DOM trees*

The following sections discuss the XmlReader and XmlWriter classes in more detail.

The XmlReader Class

The basic method of streaming through an XML document is provided by the Read method. The Read method goes through the document stream one node at a time in the document order. The document order is defined as the depth of the first traversal in the document's logical structure.

Reading an XML Document Using XmlReader

You can use the XmlReader class to read an XML document. Before reading the XML document, the position (node) of the reader cursor should be known. This is because the reader reads from this node. You call the Read method to advance the cursor to the next node. When reading more than one node, the Read method is usually performed inside a while loop.

You can position the reader at any element or attribute of an XML document. You can use the MoveToAttribute and MoveToElement methods to do this.

You can use two methods to read the attribute and element values: ReadInnerXml and ReadOuterXml.

The ReadInnerXml Method

The ReadInnerXml method returns values depending on the node type. When you call the ReadInnerXml method on an element node, the text stored in that node is returned. For example, consider the following XML code:

```
<Quantity>
    10
</Quantity>
```

If you call the ReadInnerXml method on this node, then the value, 10, is returned.

However, if this method is called on an attribute node, the value returned will be the value of the first attribute. For example:

```
<Quantity attr="val1" attr val2>
    10
</Quantity>
```

In this case, val1 will be returned. All other XmlNode types return string.empty.

The ReadOuterXml Method

The ReadOuterXml method is different from the ReadInnerXml method because in the former method, the start tag, the end tag, and the content of an element are all returned. When you call on an attribute node, both the attribute name and the attribute value are returned. For the previous code, the ReadOuterXml method would display attr="val1". Similar to the ReadInnerXml method, this method also returns a string.empty when called on any other XMLNode type.

So far, you have looked at methods that enable you to read content from an XML document in a sequential manner. These methods are not helpful when you want to read specific content in an XML document. The two methods that allow you to move through an XML document are MoveToContent and Skip.

The MoveToContent Method

The MoveToContent method skips all the nodes except the CDATA, Text, Element, EndElement, EntityReference, and EndEntity nodes. Consider the following XML code:

```
<?xml version="1.0">
<!—This is an illustration—>
<Quantity>10</Quantity>
```

You can use the MoveToContent method to move to the Quantity element. You can use the following code snippet to accomplish this:

```
If readr.MoveToContent() = XmlNodeType.Element And readr.Name = "Quantity" then
    readr.ReadString()
End If
```

The Skip Method

When you call the Skip method, the reader is moved to the next element. For example, consider the following code:

```
<Product name="Motherboards">
<x />
1000
<y />
</Product>
<Manufacturer>…
</Manufacturer>
```

The reader is positioned at the `Product` element. If you call the `Skip` method, the reader will be moved to the `Manufacturer` element.

`XmlTextReader`, which is discussed in the following section, is an implementation of the `XmlReader` class.

The XmlTextReader Class

The `XMLTextReader` class is derived from the abstract `XMLReader` class. This class supports validation against DTDs and XSD Schemas. By default, `XMLTextReader` auto-detects DTDs and schemas to process entities and attribute values. You use `Validation.Handler` to turn on the validation. `Validation.Handler` is an event-handler that is used when a reader encounters validation errors.

You have just seen how to use the classes that permit you to read an XML document. Earlier you learned that for applications to produce XML documents they need to use `XmlWriter`, as discussed next.

The XMLWriter Class

`XmlWriter` is an abstract class that is used to produce document streams. The `XmlWriter` class has methods and properties that permit you to do the following:

- Specify whether to support namespaces
- Write well-formed XML
- Encode binary bytes as base64 and as binhex
- Manage the output with the `WriteState` property
- Write multiple documents to one output stream
- Flush or close the output
- Report `xml:lang`, the current namespace prefix, or the `xml:space` scope
- Write name tokens, valid names, and qualified names

`XmlTextWriter`, discussed next, is an implementation of `XmlWriter`.

The XmlTextWriter Class

`XmlTextWriter` is a class derived from `XmlWriter`. You can use this class for writing character streams. The output stream types supported are as follows:

- file URI
- Stream
- TextWriter

The XmlTextWriter class is a highly configurable class. This class permits you to specify namespace support, indentation options, and even lexical representation for typed values. There are four methods in this class:

- WriteAttributeString. You use this method to write the text content of the attribute.
- WriteString. You use this method to write special characters, replacing them with appropriate characters, such as & < > and numeric character entities.
- WriteBase64. You use this method to encode the base64 bytes, which can then be read using ReadBinary on XmlReader.
- Close. You use this method to check if it is an invalid XML document. If it is invalid, an exception, InvalidOperationException, is thrown.

XmlTextWriter uses these methods to produce a well-formed XML document. In addition, XMLTextWriter ensures that the XML elements are written in the correct order. Next you will learn how XMLWriter can be used to generate XML streams.

Generating XML Streams Using XmlWriter

XMLWriter can be used to create an XML document. Consider the following code snippet:

```
<Product name="Motherboard">
    <Quantity>10</Quantity>
</Product>
```

Now, we will look at a VB.NET code snippet that generates the preceding XML code:

```
Shared Sub WriteQuote(writers As XmlWriter, attr As String, Quantity As Integer)
    writers.WriteStartElement("Product")
    writers.WriteAttributeString("attr", attr)
    writers.WriteElementString("Quantity", XmlConvert.ToString(Quantity))
    writers.WritersEndElement()
End Sub
```

```
Public Shared Sub Main()
    Dim writers As new XmlTextWriter(Console.Out)
    writers.Formatting = Formatting.Indented
    WriteQuote(writers, "Motherboards", 10)
    writers.close()
End Sub
```

The input to the `WriteQuote` method comes as the string, `Motherboards`, and the integer, 10. The `WriteStartElement` method is used to output the `Product` element. The `WriteAttributeString` method is used to display the `attr` attribute. The `WriteElementString` method is used to display the element, `Quantity`, and the value, 10. This value is converted to string by the `Xml.Convert` class.

The `XmlReader` class is used to read an XML document. When you use this class, the XML document is read in a forward-only mode. What if you need to go back and forth in a XML document? This class would not be suitable. This is one drawback in using the `XmlReader` class.

The `XMLWriter` class is used to generate an XML document. What if you need to modify an existing XML document? In such a case, you cannot use the `XmlWriter` class. Such drawbacks can be handled by the .NET DOM implementation, which is discussed in the following section.

The .NET DOM Implementation

`System.Xml.XmlDocument` is the .NET DOM implementation. It supports all of DOM Level 1 and all of DOM Level 2 Core. You can extend DOM interaction with your applications in several ways because DOM loading is built on top of `XmlReader`, and DOM serialization is built on `XmlWriter`. Figure 37-3 displays the .NET DOM class hierarchy. Table 37-1 displays the class names and their description.

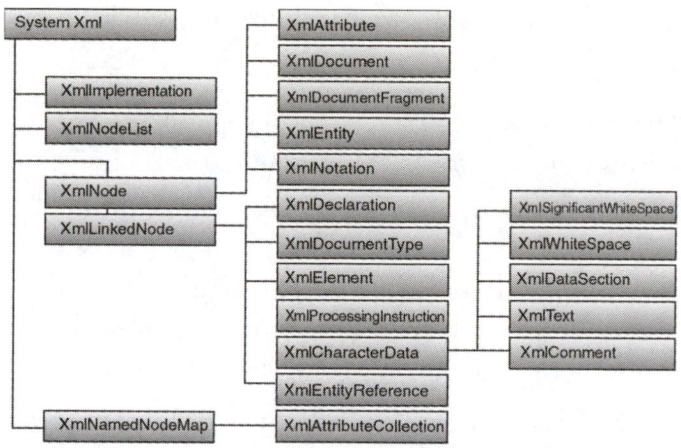

FIGURE 37-3 *The .NET DOM class hierarchy*

Table 37-1 Class Names and Their Description

DOM Node Type	Description
`XmlCharacterData`	This object represents the higher-level objects, such as `Text`, `CDATASection`, and `Comment` objects.
`XmlDeclaration`	This object represents the `<?xml version="1.0"` ...>.
`XmlDocumentType`	This object is equivalent to the `<!DOCTYPE`...> node. It contains information about the DTD or schema for the XML document.
`XmlElement`	This object represents the elements in a document.
`XmlEntityReference`	This object represents the non-expanded entity text.
`XmlProcessingInstruction`	This object represents a processing-instruction node.
`XmlAttribute`	This object represents the attribute of an element.
`XmlDocument`	This object is the container of all the nodes in the tree. It is also known as the root object for an XML document.
`XmlDocumentFragment`	This object is a temporary place where one or more nodes are stored without any tree structure. It is useful for tree insert operations
`XmlEntity`	This object represents the `<!ENTITY` ...> element found in an internal or external DTD of an XML document.
`XmlNotation`	This object represents a `<!NOTATION` ...> found in an internal or external DTD of an XML document.

There are some higher-level objects in this DOM class hierarchy, as follows:

- `XmlComment`. This represents a comment.
- `XmlText`. This represents the text of an element and an attribute.
- `XmlCDATASection`. This represents the `CDATA` section.
- `XmlWhitespace`. This represents the whitespace in the content of an element.
- `XmlSignificantWhitespace`. This represents a whitespace in the mixed content of an element. When a whitespace appears in an element-only content model for readability purposes, it is considered insignificant.

The `XmlDocument` class models the document information item. You use the overloaded `Load` methods for building a DOM tree from an input stream. The `XmlDocument` class permits you to do the following:

- Retrieve entire nodes. In addition, you can retrieve the information the node contains, such as the text in an element node.
- Access and modify nodes. Attribute nodes, element nodes, and entity reference nodes can be modified and accessed.

If you do not require these capabilities, the `XmlReader` and `XmlWriter` classes can be used. The next section discusses the conceptual representation of an XML document when using the DOM.

Node Tree Diagram

The DOM implements an XML document in-memory. This means that the conceptual representation of an XML document is in the form of a tree. Consider the following XML code snippet:

```
<Product>
    <Name>Motherboard</Name>
</Product>
```

This code snippet is represented as the tree diagram shown in Figure 37-4 with the assigned node type properties.

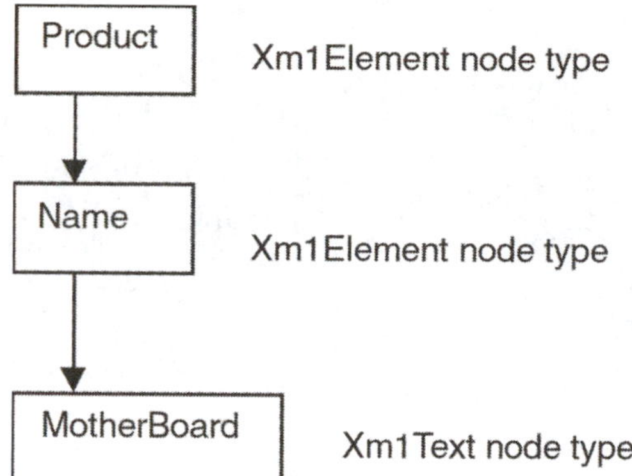

FIGURE 37-4 *Node tree diagram*

The node tree representation provides a visual representation of the types of nodes that are available. Because each type of node has its own methods and properties, it is vital for you to know the type of node. By doing so, you can determine the types of actions that can be carried out. For example, you could perform a `Read` operation on a node. Therefore, mapping the DOM object model to the XML document is a vital task.

You have learned about the classes used in the .NET DOM implementation and the conceptual representation of an XML document. Next, you will learn how an XML document is created using the `XMLDocument` class.

Creating an XML Document

You can create an XML document by using the `XMLDocument` class. The following VB.NET code snippet demonstrates how to create an XML document:

```
Dim DocXml As New XmlDocument ()
```

After you have created a document, you can load it by using data from a stream, a URL, or `XmlReader`. This is done using the `Load` method.

Reading an XML Document in the DOM

Reading an XML document in the DOM requires you to load the document in the memory. This procedure is called loading. A document can be loaded from a string or from a reader.

Loading From a String

You can load an XML document into the memory from a stream, a URL, a text reader, or `XmlReader`. The `Load` method is used to read data to the memory. This method has several overloaded methods to support data loading from different formats. The `LoadXML` method enables loading from a string. The following code snippet enables you to load a document:

```
Dim DocXml As New XmlDocument ()
DocXml.LoadXml(("<Product>" & _
"<Name>Motherboard</Name>" & _
"</Product>"))
```

You can save the output document to a file by calling the `Save` method. For example:

```
docXml.Save("Product.xml")
```

Loading From a Reader

When you load a document using `XMLReader`, certain considerations have to be kept in mind:

- **Consideration 1.** If the reader is in its initial state, the `Load` method uses all the contents of the reader to build the DOM.
- **Consideration 2.** If the reader is already positioned somewhere in the XML document, then the `Load` method reads the current node and all its siblings. This is done up to the closing of the current depth. When loading XML documents that are not well formed, the `Load` method throws an exception.
- **Consideration 3.** If the reader is positioned on a whitespace or attribute node, the reader will continue to read the document until it reaches a node that can be used for a root node.

The `Load` method does not check for validity against a DTD or XML Schema.

Validating an XML Document

To validate an XML document while it is loading, you need to pass `XmlValidatingReader` to the `Load` method. You need to set the `ValidationType` property to `Auto`, `DTD`, `Schema`, or `XDR`. You also need to provide the event-handler, `ValidationEventHandler`. After this is done, the `Load` method notifies you of validation errors. Unless you code to stop the load process, the loading will continue even with errors.

Now that you know how to load an XML document in the DOM, the next section shows you how to insert nodes into an existing XML document.

Inserting Nodes

To create new nodes in an existing XML document, you need to use the `Create` method in the `XmlDocument` class. This method is used for creating all types of nodes. The following list contains some of the important methods to create nodes:

- `CreateComment`
- `CreateCDataSection`
- `CreateDocumentFragment`
- `CreateDocumentType`
- `CreateElement`
- `CreateProcessingInstruction`
- `CreateTextNode`
- `CreateXmlDeclaration`
- `CreateWhitespace`
- `CreateSignificantWhitespace`

After the nodes are created, you can use one of the methods listed in Table 37-2 to insert them into an XML document.

Table 37-2 Insert Methods

Method	Action
`InsertBefore`	The new node is inserted immediately before the reference node.
`InsertAfter`	The new node is inserted immediately after the reference node.
`AppendChild`	The new node is inserted at the end of the list of child nodes for a given node.
`Append`	An attribute (`XmlAttribute`) is appended to the end of the list of attributes for a given element.

Next, you will learn how to edit an existing XML document.

Editing an Existing XML Document

An XML document can be edited in many ways. Table 37-3 shows the methods that you can use to edit an XML document.

Table 37-3 Edit Methods

Method	Edit Action
`XmlNode.Value`	To change the value of nodes
`XmlNode.InnerXml Property`	To replace an existing set of nodes with new nodes
`XmlNode.ReplaceChild`	To replace an existing set of child nodes with new nodes
`XmlCharacter.AppendData`	To append characters to an existing node that inherits from the `XmlCharacter` class
`XmlCharacter.InsertData`	To insert characters into an existing node that inherits from the `XmlCharacter` class
`XmlCharacter.ReplaceData`	To replace characters in an existing node that inherits from the `XmlCharacter` class
`DeleteData`	To delete the contents of nodes that inherit from the `XmlCharacterData` class
`SetAttribute`	To modify the value of an attribute

A simple way to change the value of a node is by using the following code:

```
node.Value = "new Value";
```

You can use this method to modify the contents for the following node types:

- `Attribute`
- `CDataSection`
- `Comment`
- `ProcessingInstruction`
- `Text`
- `XmlDeclaration`

- `Whitespace`
- `SignificantWhitespace`

You cannot set the value on any other node type. An exception, `InvalidOperationException`, will be thrown if you try to set the value of any other node type.

Summary

This chapter gave you an overview of XML. You learned that XML is a markup language used to structure data. This language allows you to describe the content of a document. You also learned to apply standard rules for XML documents by using DTDs and XML Schemas. In addition, an introduction to the DOM was covered.

In this chapter, you were also introduced to the .NET Framework XML classes. You also learned to create, read, and edit an XML document using the .NET Framework. Finally, you learned about the .NET DOM implementation.

PART VIII

Appendices

Appendix A

VBA Tips and Tricks

Working with VBA Code

When you develop applications using VBA, there are certain programming strategies and optimization techniques that you can apply to your VBA code. These strategies and techniques affect the way your application works and control both the performance and the speed of the application. You may choose to follow some or all of the strategies and techniques when writing VBA code.

However, before you apply the programming strategies and optimization techniques, you need to consider a few factors that affect an application's performance. These are as follows:

- Hardware and memory configuration of the computer
- Design of the backend database
- Design of the forms
- Design of the application, as single-user versus multiple-user
- VBA code

The discussion starts with general optimization strategies and then specific programming techniques that you can apply to your VBA code.

Optimization Strategies

When writing VBA code, you can perform the same task in different ways. Because of the flexibility of the Visual Basic language, you may need to optimize the performance of an application such that the application works faster and utilizes a minimum of memory.

Some of the optimization strategies that you can apply to your VBA code are discussed in the following sections. You must note that to increase an application's performance, you may need to trade-off with other factors, such as usability and maintainability of an application.

Use Macro Recorder

The easiest manner to learn VBA programming is to use Macro Recorder. Although you cannot use Macro Recorder to record all tasks, you can use it to learn the code generated for specific tasks. For example, you might use Macro Recorder to figure out the code required to modify the formatting of specific text or use it to find the name of a property or method used to perform a task. You can then look for specific information about the property or the method using online help.

However, when using Macro Recorder, you may consider removing any unnecessary recorded expressions. Consider the following example. Here, Macro Recorder has been used to record the code for selecting a range of cells and modifying the font property to bold. Because Macro Recorder cannot distinguish between the options that have been changed, it explicitly sets all options. The following code is generated when you select a range of cells in Excel and apply the font style as bold using the Font dialog box:

```
Option Explicit


Sub Macro1()
'
' Macro1 Macro
' Macro recorded 1/29/2002 by TG
''
    Range("A1:B1").Select
    With Selection.Font
        .Name = "Arial"
        .FontStyle = "Bold"
        .Size = 10
        .Strikethrough = False
        .Superscript = False
        .Subscript = False
        .OutlineFont = False
        .Shadow = False
        .Underline = xlUnderlineStyleNone
        .ColorIndex = xlAutomatic
    End With
End Sub
```

You can perform the same task using a single line of code as follows:

```
    Range("A1:B1").Font.FontStyle = "Bold"
```

Therefore, when using Macro Recorder, you must experiment by recording the same task using various methods to generate optimized code.

Use Option Explicit

When writing code using the Visual Basic Editor, it is recommended that you keep Option Explicit *on*. You can either add the previous statement to your code or make it a permanent feature by selecting the Require Variable Declaration option in the Options dialog box from the Tools menu.

When you use the Option Explicit option, you need to declare all variables used in the code. Although this might add more development effort, it saves time while debugging the code. For example, if you do not use the Option Explicit option, you may spell a variable name incorrectly. The code will compile without any errors, but the application may not give the desired results. Therefore, it is always recommend that you declare all variables explicitly.

Minimize OLE References

In addition to using Macro Recorder and declaring all variables explicitly, you can optimize code by minimizing OLE references used in VBA code. The more methods and properties called in a VBA statement, the more time it takes to execute the statement. Consider two VBA statements, statement A and statement B.

Statement A is as follows:

```
Workbooks(1).Sheets(1).Range("A1").Value = 10
```

Statement B is as follows:

```
ActiveWindow.Left = 200
```

When you execute these statements, statement B will be executed faster than statement A.

In addition to minimizing OLE references, you can specify a variable for an object reference that you need to use repeatedly. This will ensure that the variable is called instead of the object reference being made multiple times.

Avoid Object Activation

When you use Macro Recorder, the code generated invariably activates or selects an object before applying any methods or properties. This is, however, not required in all instances. Therefore, when writing VBA code you need not activate or select each object before performing any task on that object.

Minimize Usage of the Variant Variable

While coding in VBA, you may use the `Variant` variable for convenience. If you do not specify any variable type, VBA automatically defines all variables as `Variant`. However, `Variant` type variables require more processing time than a variable that you store using an explicit data type, such as `Integer` or `Long`.

Note that you should use explicit data types only when working with VBA. If you are working with data stored in tables within your codes or working with the Jet database, it is recommended that you use `Variant` data types. This is because the Jet database integrates and works with Access using `Variant` data types. Therefore, if you specify explicit data types, VBA code needs to convert data types, and this may lead to slower performance of the application.

The following section discusses some of the specific programming techniques that you can apply to your VBA code to ensure faster execution of code.

Programming Techniques

In addition to applying general code optimization strategies, you can use various programming techniques. These techniques can help you read, maintain, and debug code easier and also contribute significantly toward the performance of the application.

Use the With Statement

To minimize the usage of object references, you can use a `With` statement. You can use a `With` statement to perform a series of tasks on a specified object without repeating the object reference. Consider the following example. Here, a `With` statement is used to specify the font properties of selected text:

```
With Selection.Font
         .Name = "Comic Sans MS"
         .Size = 12
         .Bold = True
         .Italic = True
End With
```

You can also nest `With` statements. For example, in the following code, `With` statements are nested to increase the code efficiency:

```
With Workbooks("Book1").Worksheets("Sheet1").Cells(1, 1)
        .Formula = "=SQRT(20)"
        With .Font
            .Name = " Comic Sans MS "
            .Bold = True
            .Size = 10
        End With
    End With
```

Use the For Each...Next Loop

You can also use the `For Each...Next` loop to ensure faster execution of code. When you use the `For Each...Next` loop, a set of statements is executed for each object stored in a collection or an array. By using the `For Each...Next` loop, the code becomes more manageable such that you can read, debug, and maintain the code easily as it becomes shorter.

Consider the following example. Here, `myform` is an `Object`, and `Forms` is a collection. Using the `For Each...Next` loop, for each `myform` in the `Forms` collection, the name of `myform` is displayed:

```
Dim myform As Form
For Each myform In Forms
Print myform.name
Next myform
```

Use Len() to Check for Empty Strings

Although there are multiple methods to check for empty strings, it is preferable to use the `Len()` function. To test for zero-length strings, you might choose to compare the string with “” or compare the length of the string to 0. However, these methods take more time to execute than using the `Len()` function.

When you apply the `Len()` function to a string and the function returns a zero value, it automatically indicates that the string is empty or a zero-length string.

You can use the `Len()` function to check for empty strings. Note that since a nonzero value is considered as `True` within an `If` statement, you do not need to compare the string to “” or 0. This reduces the processing time, and therefore, the application is executed faster.

Use Asc() to Check for ANSI Value

In VBA, you can use the `Chr$()` function to convert a number to a character and determine the ANSI value, but it is better to use the `Asc()` function to convert the string character to a number and then determine its ANSI value. If you need to perform a limited number of such checks it may not make much difference to the efficiency of the code. However, if you need to perform such checks within multiple loops, it may save processing time and help the code execute faster.

Appendix B

Working with the Access Object Model

Access Object Model

The Access object model contains a collection of objects where each object has unique properties, methods, and events. In addition the collection of objects, the Access object model consists of *Data Access Objects*. These Data Access Objects are a different collection of objects, which are not dependent on Access. You can use these objects to work with databases, tables, and queries in Access.

The Application Object

Just like the object models available for other Microsoft products, such as Word and Excel, the `Application` object is the root object for Access. However, the Access object model is much different from other object models. First, in Access you use VBA to work with databases and not documents or worksheets. Second, you need to work with tables, forms, and reports programmatically, which is a little more difficult than simply referring to a document name or cell number in a worksheet.

Besides the `Application` object, the Access object model consists of the following main objects:

- Forms
- Reports
- Control

The discussion starts with some of the main properties and methods of the `Application` object and then moves on to the other main objects available in the Access object model.

Application Object Properties

Some of the main properties of the `Application` object and their brief description are listed in Table B-1.

Table B-1 *Application* Object Properties

Property	Description
`Application.CurrentObjectName`	Returns the name of the object on which the VBA code is being currently executed
`Application.CurrentObjectType`	Returns the object type of the object on which the VBA code is being currently executed
`Application.CodeContextObject`	Returns the object in which the VBA code is currently being executed
`Application.IsCompiled`	Returns `True` if the current VBA Access project has been compiled and `False` if the project has not been compiled
`Application.UserControl`	Returns `True` if the current VBA Access application is started by a user and `False` if the application is started using OLE Automation
`Application.Visible`	Returns whether the application window is minimized (`False`) or maximized (`True`)

Application Object Methods

Some of the important methods of the `Application` object and their brief description are listed in Table B-2.

Table B-2 *Application* Object Methods

Method	Description
`Application.CurrentDB`	Returns the Database object that represents the current database open in Access
`Application.CodeDB`	Returns the Database object that represents the database in which the code is currently being executed
`Application.NewCurrentDatabase`	Creates a new database in Access
`Application.CloseCurrentDatabase`	Closes the current database open in Access
`Application.OpenCurrentDatabase`	Opens the specified database
`Application.Quit`	Exits the Access application

The *Form* Object

Forms is a collection that contains all the open Form objects in the database currently active in Access. A Form object is any open form in the active database. To refer to a specific form, you need to use the following syntax:

```
Forms!FormName
```

Here, FormName is the name of the form that you need to access. However, if the name of the form includes spaces, you need to enclose FormName within parentheses as follows:

```
Forms![Form Name]
```

Form Object Properties

Although the Form object has many properties, this discussion is limited to a few important properties. These properties guide the look and feel of forms, such as the height and the width of form. Some of the important properties of the Form object and their brief description are listed in Table B-3.

Table B-3 *Form* Object Properties

Properties	Description
Form.Caption	Specifies or returns the caption that appears in the title bar of the specified form
Form.Name	Specifies or returns the name of the specified form
Form.OrderBy	Specifies the order to sort records contained in the specified form
Form.ActiveControl	Shifts the control to the specified form
Form.CurrentView	Specifies how the specified form is displayed
Form.Filter	Filters the records in the specified form
Form.NewRecord	Returns True if the current record contained in the specified form is a new record
Form.RecordSource	Specifies the record source for the specified form
Form.Visible	Sets the form property to False to hide the specified form

The OpenForm Method

When you open a form, you automatically add the form to the `Forms` collection. You can open a form by using the `OpenForm` method of `DoCmd` object.

The syntax for the `OpenForm` method is as follows:

```
DoCmd.OpenForm FormName, View, FilterName, WhereCondition, DataMode, WindowMode,
   OpenArgs
```

Here, `FormName` is the name of the form that you need to open and work with. You can use View to specify how the form is launched. For example, you can specify constants such as `acNormal` to open the form in the default form view or `acDesign` to open the form in the design view.

`FilterName` is the name of the query from the currently active database. You can use `WhereCondition` to provide a valid SQL statement that specifies the records to be displayed. In the syntax, `DataMode` refers to the mode in which the form is opened for data entry. For example, to open the form in the Edit mode, you can specify the `acEdit` constant for `DataMode`. Similarly, to open the form in the read-only mode, you can specify the `acReadOnly` constant.

You can also specify the window mode in which you need to open the form using the `WindowMode` option in the syntax. For `WindowMode`, you can specify constants such as `acNormal` to open the form in the normal default view. You can also choose to open the form as an icon by using the `acIcon` constant.

Finally, you can specify one or more arguments using string expressions. These `OpenArgs` can control the way in which the form opens.

The CreateForm Method

To create a new form, you can use the `CreateForm` method. The syntax of the `CreateForm` method is as follows:

```
CreateForm (Database, FormTemplate)
```

Here, `Database` refers to the database that contains the form on the basis of which you need to create the new form. By default, the current Access database is used. The `FormTemplate` option refers to the name of the form in the database that you need to use as a base for the new form. By default, the form template specified in the Form Template box of the Forms/Reports tab in the Options dialog box is used.

The Close Method

To close an open form, you can use the `DoCmd` object's `Close` method. The syntax of the `Close` method is as follows:

```
DoCmd.Close ObjectType, ObjectName, Save
```

Here, `ObjectType` refers to the type of object that you need to close. For example, you can specify the `actable` constant to close a table, `acForm` to close a form, and `acReport` to close a report. By default, the active project is closed if no arguments are supplied.

`ObjectName` specifies the name of the form that you need to close. You can also specify constants to determine how a form is saved in case any design modifications have been made to the form. For example, you can specify the `acPrompt` constant to specify that the user should be prompted to save the changes before closing the form.

Other Form Object Methods

In addition to creating a new form and opening and closing existing forms, you can also use other methods to work with forms. Some of the other `Form` object methods and their brief description are given in Table B-4.

Table B-4 *Form* Object Methods

Methods	Description
`Form.Undo`	Ignores all modifications made to the current record in the specified form
`Form.SetFocus`	Shifts the current focus to the specified form
`Form.Refresh`	Updates the records in the specified form as per the latest modifications
`Form.Recalc`	Recalculates all the calculated controls in the specified form
`Form.Requery`	Reruns the query on which the records in the specified form are based

The *Report* Object

Apart from working with the `Application` and `Form` objects, you can work with the Access `Report` object. A `Report` object specifies an open report in the current Access database. You can use the `Reports` collection to refer to a specific report as follows:

```
Reports!ReportName
```

Here, `ReportName` is the name of the report that you need to access. Just like forms, you need to enclose the report name in parentheses in case there are spaces within the report name. Consider the following example. Here, `Analysis 2002` refers to the name of the report:

```
Reports![Analysis 2002]
```

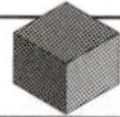

NOTE

You can also refer to a report using the reports index. `Index` is the report's index within the `Reports` collection. For instance, the first report contained in the collection is given index 0, the second has index 1, and so on. The syntax used to access reports using the index is `Reports(Index)`.

The OpenReport Method

You can open a report using the `OpenReport` method of the `DoCmd` object. The syntax of the `OpenReport` method is as follows:

```
DoCmd.OpenReport ReportName, View, FilterName, WhereCondition
```

In this syntax, `ReportName` is the name of the report that you need to open in the current database. The `View` option in the syntax specifies the manner in which the report is opened. For example, you can specify constants such as `acViewNormal`, `acViewDesign`, and `acViewPreview` to open the report in the normal report view, design view, and print preview, respectively.

You can also specify additional arguments using the `WhereCondition` option. You can use a valid SQL clause to specify the records to be displayed based on a category.

Consider the following example. Here, a report named `Analysis 2000` is opened in the design view. Only the records where the category name is `January` are to be displayed:

```
DoCmd.OpenReport: = "Analysis 2000", View:= acViewDesign, WhereCondition: =
   "CategoryName Like January"
```

The CreateReport Method

To create a new report, you can use the `CreateReport` method of the `Application` object. The syntax of the `CreateReport` method is as follows:

```
CreateReport (Database, ReportTemplate)
```

In this syntax, the `Database` option refers to the database that contains the report that acts as a template for the new report that you need to create. By default, Access uses the current database. You can also specify the template that you need to use to create the new report by using the `ReportTemplate` option. You need to specify the name of the report in the database that you want to use as a base for the new report. By default, the report template specified in the Report Template box of the Forms/Reports tab in the Options dialog box is used.

The Close Method

To close an existing open report, you can use the `Close` method of the `DoCmd` object. The syntax for the `Close` method is as follows:

```
DoCmd.Close ObjectType, ObjectName, Save
```

Here, `ObjectType` refers to the type of object that you need to close. For example, you can specify constants such as `acReport` to close the active report. By default, if no arguments are specified, the current project is closed.

In the syntax, you can also specify the name of the report that you need to close by using the `ObjectName` option. In addition, you can specify the save options for the report in case any design modifications have been made to the report. For example, you can use constants such as `acPrompt`, `acSaveYes`, and `acSaveNo` to prompt the user to save changes, save the changes automatically, and ignore the changes, respectively.

The *Control* Object

In the Access object model, a `Control` object refers to a control, such as a command button or a text box. This control can exist on a form or a report. You can refer to a control using the following syntax:

```
Object!ControlName
```

Here, Object refers to the Form or the Report object that contains the control, and the ControlName option is used to specify the name of the control. Consider the following example. In this example, a variable is defined as a Control object on the Analysis form:

```
Dim MyCtrl as Control
Set MyCtrl = Forms!Analysis! [Customer ID]
```

In addition to using the Control object, you can also use the Controls object to refer to all the controls contained on the specified form. You can use the Controls object to specify a similar property for all the controls at one time.

Appendix C

Upgrading Applications to VB.NET

You will agree that upgrading your existing VB 6.0 applications to the corresponding VB.NET applications is one of the biggest advantages in VB.NET. However, you might have a number of issues and concerns about upgrading applications in VB.NET, such as what the code will look like after it has been upgraded to VB.NET. There are a number of features that are supported by VB 6.0 that are not supported by VB.NET. These features are not upgraded by the Visual Basic Upgrade Wizard and need to be done manually. Therefore, you should have a good understanding of VB.NET before upgrading your applications to VB.NET.

The Upgrading Methodology

The methodology that Visual Basic Upgrade Wizard uses to upgrade applications is simple. It converts all the components of VB 6.0 to their corresponding counterparts in VB.NET. To list them all, the wizard converts the project in VB 6.0 to the corresponding project type in VB.NET, the forms in VB 6.0 to the corresponding Windows forms in VB.NET, the intrinsic controls in VB 6.0 to the equivalent controls in VB.NET, and so on.

However, the wizard either does not upgrade or only partially upgrades the following features:

- ActiveX EXE projects
- OLE Container Control
- Dynamic Data Exchange (DDE)
- Drag and drop
- Web classes
- Graphics controls
- User controls
- Visual Basic add-ins
- Games
- `Variant` data type
- Windows APIs
- ActiveX DHTML Page applications

The lack of support for the above-mentioned features in VB.NET means that certain types of Visual Basic applications are not suited for a VB.NET upgrade. However, you can still communicate with your Visual Basic application from VB.NET. For example, you might want to leave your ActiveX DLL as is rather than upgrading it. In that case, you can create a VB.NET application that interacts with the existing ActiveX DLL. This proves to be a time saver, because you can create the VB.NET applications more quickly if you use the existing ActiveX components. This ability of VB.NET to interact with the existing ActiveX components is known as *COM interop*.

Upgrading Projects

You must be familiar with the term *project* by now. A project can be considered as a repository of files, such as resource files and source files, that are required to create an output file such as an EXE or a DLL. A project consists of components such as project types, attributes, and filenames. The following sections discuss how these components are upgraded.

Upgrading Project Types

Projects created in VB 6.0 are upgraded to the equivalent project types in VB.NET. The equivalent project types in VB.NET for projects in VB 6.0 are listed in Table C-1.

Table C-1 Project Types in VB 6.0 and VB.NET

VB 6.0	VB.NET
Standard EXE	Windows application
ActiveX DLL	Class Library
ActiveX EXE	No equivalent project type exists for ActiveX EXE. The user is given a choice to either upgrade to Windows application or to Class Library project.
WebClass-based project	XML Web forms

Upgrading Project Attributes

Each VB project consists of a number of attributes such as name, version information, help settings, and so on. The behavior of all these attributes while upgrading is discussed in the following list:

- When upgraded, the project name of a VB 6.0 application becomes the *Assembly Name* and the *Root Namespace* for the VB.NET application. Assembly Name is the name that is used by other applications to load the EXE or the DLL that contains your project, and Root Namespace name is the name that is used by other applications to refer to your .NET application or library. The Root Namespace name is roughly equivalent to the VB 6.0 project name.
- Because VB 6.0 and VB.NET compilers generate different types of instructions, the compiler options for both are entirely different. Therefore, the Upgrade Wizard does not upgrade any of the compiler options to VB.NET.
- The project filename in VB 6.0 is `.vbp`, and the equivalent for the same in VB.NET is the `.vbproj` file. For example, if the name of your project file in VB 6.0 is `TestProject.vbp`, the same will be changed to `TestProject.vbproj` in VB.NET after upgrading.
- The individual filenames in a VB 6.0 project remains the same after upgrade in VB.NET. The extension to all the upgraded files in VB.NET is changed to `.vb`.

Forms and Other Controls

The Upgrade Wizard upgrades forms and other controls to their equivalent in VB.NET. Controls such as `CommandButton`, `TextBox`, `CheckBox`, and so on are converted to the Windows Forms package equivalent in VB.NET. You may find some of the controls with a red label inserted on the form after the upgrade process. The red label indicates that the Upgrade Wizard could not upgrade a control. The appearance and layout of your form is preserved after the upgrade process. Table C-2 lists the equivalent control class for VB 6.0 controls in VB.NET.

Table C-2 Control Classes in VB 6.0 and VB.NET

VB 6.0	VB.NET
`VB.CheckBox`	`System.Windows.Forms.CheckBox`
`VB.ComboBox`	`System.Windows.Forms.ComboBox`
`VB.CommandButton`	`System.windows.Forms.Button`
`VB.Image`	`System.Windows.Forms.Picture`
`VB.Frame`	`System.Windows.Forms.GroupBox` or `System.Windows.Forms.Panel`
`VB.Label`	`System.Windows.Forms.Label`
`VB.ListBox`	`System.Windows.Forms.ListBox`
`VB.OptionButton`	`System.Windows.Forms.OptionButton`
`VB.PictureBox`	`System.Windows.Forms.PictureBox` or `System.Windows.Forms.Panel`
`VB.TextBox`	`System.Windows.Forms.TextBox`
`VB.Timer`	`System.Windows.Forms.Timer`

Unlike VB 6.0, which stores the design-time properties of a form or a control inside the .frm file, VB.NET stores them as part of the code in a special hidden section called the Windows Form Designer Generated Code. The design-time properties for a Windows Form are stored in the `InitializeComponent()` subroutine inside this hidden section. The Upgrade Wizard uses the VB 6.0 design-time settings to generate code in the `InitializeComponent()`.

Control Arrays

A control array is used to group controls that share the same events and initial property settings. Therefore, you can apply the same behavior to these controls. You need to write code to create a control array in VB.NET. You declare an array by using code and then add controls to this array. You can then write additional code to attach events to each member of the control array. However, this is a time-consuming effort if you are writing code for a number of control arrays. To provide a solution, VB.NET offers the *compatibility library*.

A compatibility library is a feature provided by VB.NET to help you work with upgraded applications. This library supports a range of features such as ADO data binding and support for control arrays. The Upgrade Wizard automatically adds a reference to the compatibility library.

The compatibility library includes an array class for each type of control. For example, the array class for the `Button` control is the `ButtonArray` class. The control array class includes methods and events for all the underlying controls in the application.

The Upgrade Wizard upgrades the VB 6.0 control arrays to their corresponding control array classes in VB.NET.

ActiveX Controls and ActiveX References

The ActiveX controls and references remain as is in VB.NET after the upgrade process. However, because the VB 6.0 and VB.NET ActiveX control hosting environments are different, there might be a few changes. VB.NET interacts with ActiveX components through the COM interop layer, as discussed earlier. An important point to note here is that an ActiveX control or reference is not always upgraded to use the same component. At times, an ActiveX control or reference might be upgraded to use a native .NET component.

VB 6.0 also allows you to place the ActiveX ADO Data Control, however, you cannot integrate the same with the Windows form controls in VB.NET.

Code Changes

VB.NET uses the same keywords, statements, and expressions as in VB 6.0. Therefore, the Upgrade Wizard will upgrade most of your code as is without any major changes to it. This section covers the code changes in VB.NET.

Basic Code Conversions

Some of the basic Visual Basic language statements such as `If…Then`, `For…Next`, `Select…Case`, `Do…Loop`, and so on are upgraded to VB.NET without any change to them. However, some statements such as `IsEmpty`, `IsNothing`, and `IsObject` are not supported by VB.NET because these statements operate on the `Variant` data type, which is not supported by VB.NET.

Another difference between VB 6.0 and VB.NET is in data type conversions. VB.NET does not support direct assignments to incompatible data types. For example, you cannot directly assign a string value to an `Integer` data type. You need to explicitly convert the data type to store incompatible values.

TIP

If you need to convert types in your VB.NET code, you can use the methods in the `System.Convert` class.

The basic math functions in VB 6.0 such as `Abs`, `Cos`, and `Sqrt` are upgraded to .NET equivalents. For example, consider the following code:

```
Dim MyInt as Integer
MyInt = Abs (-1)
```

This code snippet when upgraded to VB.NET transforms to the following:

```
Dim MyInt as Integer
MyInt = System.Math.Abs (-1)
```

You must be aware that the `Option Explicit` statement is used in VB 6.0 to declare all variables explicitly. However, if you are not using this statement in VB 6.0, the Upgrade Wizard includes this statement in all forms and modules and takes care of declaring all variables.

In addition to all the code-related changes that have been discussed, the storage size for various data types have also been changed in VB.NET. For example, an `Integer` data type in VB 6.0 takes 16 bits, and in VB.NET it takes 32 bits. However, you do not need to bother about this change because the Upgrade Wizard automatically declares all the numeric types to use the VB.NET equivalent based on the size. The various changes in data types with their corresponding upgrades to VB.NET are listed in Table C-3.

Table C-3 Upgrades to Data Types

VB 6.0	VB.NET
Integer	Short
Long	Integer
Currency	Decimal
Variant	Object

Parameters in VB 6.0 are passed by reference as the default calling convention. However, in VB.NET, all parameters must be specified by the `ByVal` or the `ByRef` keyword. Because the default in VB 6.0 is `ByRef`, the Upgrade Wizard automatically qualifies all the unqualified parameters with the `ByRef` keyword. For example, consider the following code snippet in VB 6.0:

```
Sub Calculate (MyInt As Integer)
    MyInt = 10
End Sub
```

This code snippet when upgraded to VB.NET is as follows:

```
Sub Calculate (ByRef MyInt As Integer)
    MyInt = 10
End Sub
```

The functions and statements that cannot be upgraded to their equivalent in VB.NET are listed in the report that the wizard generates at the end of the upgrade process. A sample Upgrade Wizard report is displayed in Figure C-1.

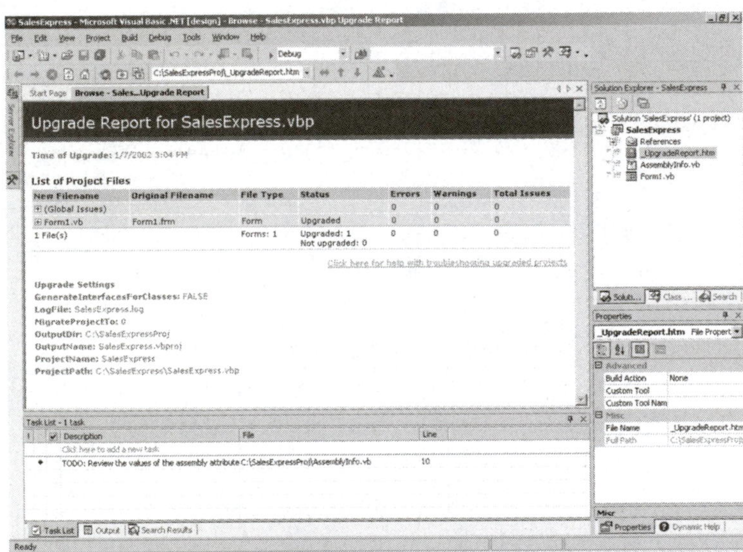

FIGURE C-1 *A sample upgrade report*

It is a good idea to know about VB.NET before upgrading your applications. This helps you get a clear understanding of how the upgrade process handles each piece of your code.

Appendix D

VBA Constants

Word VBA Constants

Table D-1 lists some of the important Word constants and their values.

Table D-1 Word VBA Constants

Constant	Value
WdMailSystem	
wdNoMailSystem	0
wdMAPI	1
wdPowerTalk	2
wdMAPIandPowerTalk	3
WdTemplateType	
wdNormalTemplate	0
wdGlobalTemplate	1
wdAttachedTemplate	2
WdContinue	
wdContinueDisabled	0
wdResetList	1
wdContinueList	2
WdIndexSortBy	
wdIndexSortByStroke	0
wdIndexSortBySyllable	1
WdJustificationMode	
wdJustificationModeExpand	0
wdJustificationModeCompress	1
wdJustificationModeCompressKana	2

Constant	Value
WdFarEastLineBreakLevel	
wdFarEastLineBreakLevelNormal	0
wdFarEastLineBreakLevelStrict	1
wdFarEastLineBreakLevelCustom	2
WdCaptionPosition	
wdCaptionPositionAbove	0
wdCaptionPositionBelow	1
WdCountry	
WdUS	1
wdCanada	2
wdLatinAmerica	3
wdNetherlands	31
wdFrance	33
wdSpain	34
wdItaly	39
wdUK	44
wdDenmark	45
wdSweden	46
wdNorway	47
wdGermany	49
wdPeru	51
wdMexico	52
wdArgentina	54
wdBrazil	55
wdChile	56

Table D-1 continued

Constant	Value
wdVenezuela	58
wdJapan	81
wdTaiwan	886
wdChina	86
wdKorea	82
wdFinland	358
wdIceland	354
WdHeadingSeparator	
wdHeadingSeparatorNone	0
wdHeadingSeparatorBlankLine	1
wdHeadingSeparatorLetter	2
wdHeadingSeparatorLetterLow	3
wdHeadingSeparatorLetterFull	4
WdSeparatorType	
wdSeparatorHyphen	0
wdSeparatorPeriod	1
wdSeparatorColon	2
wdSeparatorEmDash	3
wdSeparatorEnDash	4
WdPageNumberAlignment	
wdAlignPageNumberLeft	0
wdAlignPageNumberCenter	1
wdAlignPageNumberRight	2

Constant	Value
wdAlignPageNumberInside	3
wdAlignPageNumberOutside	4
WdBorderType	
wdBorderTop	-1
wdBorderLeft	-2
wdBorderBottom	-3
wdBorderRight	-4
wdBorderHorizontal	-5
wdBorderVertical	-6
WdAnimation	
wdAnimationNone	0
wdAnimationLasVegasLights	1
wdAnimationBlinkingBackground	2
wdAnimationSparkleText	3
wdAnimationMarchingBlackAnts	4
wdAnimationMarchingRedAnts	5
wdAnimationShimmer	6
WdCharacterCase	
wdNextCase	-1
wdLowerCase	0
wdUpperCase	1
wdTitleWord	2
wdTitleSentence	4
wdToggleCase	5

Table D-1 continued

Constant	Value
WdSummaryMode	
wdSummaryModeHighlight	0
wdSummaryModeHideAllButSummary	1
wdSummaryModeInsert	2
wdSummaryModeCreateNew	3
WdSummaryLength	
wd10Sentences	-2
wd20Sentences	-3
wd100Words	-4
wd500Words	-5
wd10Percent	-6
wd25Percent	-7
wd50Percent	-8
wd75Percent	-9
WdStyleType	
wdStyleTypeParagraph	1
wdStyleTypeCharacter	2
WdUnits	
wdCharacter	1
wdWord	2
wdSentence	3
wdParagraph	4
wdLine	5

Constant	Value
wdStory	6
wdScreen	7
wdSection	8
wdColumn	9
wdRow	10
wdWindow	11
wdCell	12
wdCharacterFormatting	13
wdParagraphFormatting	14
wdTable	15
wdItem	16
WdGoToItem	
wdGoToBookmark	-1
wdGoToSection	0
wdGoToPage	1
wdGoToTable	2
wdGoToLine	3
wdGoToFootnote	4
wdGoToEndnote	5
wdGoToComment	6
WdGoToDirection	
wdGoToFirst	1
wdGoToLast	-1
wdGoToNext	2
wdGoToRelative	2

Table D-1 continued

Constant	Value
`wdGoToPrevious`	3
`wdGoToAbsolute`	1
`WdCollapseDirection`	
`wdCollapseStart`	1
`wdCollapseEnd`	0
`WdRowHeightRule`	
`wdRowHeightAuto`	0
`wdRowHeightAtLeast`	1
`wdRowHeightExactly`	2
`WdFrameSizeRule`	
`wdFrameAuto`	0
`wdFrameAtLeast`	1
`wdFrameExact`	2
`WdInsertCells`	
`wdInsertCellsShiftRight`	0
`wdInsertCellsShiftDown`	1
`wdInsertCellsEntireRow`	2
`wdInsertCellsEntireColumn`	3
`WdDeleteCells`	
`wdDeleteCellsShiftLeft`	0
`wdDeleteCellsShiftUp`	1

Constant	Value
wdDeleteCellsEntireRow	2
wdDeleteCellsEntireColumn	3
WdCursorType	
wdCursorWait	0
wdCursorIBeam	1
wdCursorNormal	2
wdCursorNorthwestArrow	3
WdParagraphAlignment	
wdAlignParagraphLeft	0
wdAlignParagraphCenter	1
wdAlignParagraphRight	2
wdAlignParagraphJustify	3
WdParagraphAlignmentHID	
wdAlignParagraphDistribute	4
WdListLevelAlignment	
wdListLevelAlignLeft	0
wdListLevelAlignCenter	1
wdListLevelAlignRight	2
WdRowAlignment	
wdAlignRowLeft	0
wdAlignRowCenter	1
wdAlignRowRight	2

Table D-1 continued

Constant	Value
WdTabAlignment	
wdAlignTabLeft	0
wdAlignTabCenter	1
wdAlignTabRight	2
wdAlignTabDecimal	3
wdAlignTabBar	4
wdAlignTabList	6
WdVerticalAlignment	
wdAlignVerticalTop	0
wdAlignVerticalCenter	1
wdAlignVerticalJustify	2
wdAlignVerticalBottom	3
WdCellVerticalAlignment	
wdCellAlignVerticalTop	0
wdCellAlignVerticalCenter	1
wdCellAlignVerticalBottom	3
WdTrailingCharacter	
wdTrailingTab	0
wdTrailingSpace	1
wdTrailingNone	2
WdListGalleryType	
wdBulletGallery	1

Constant	Value
wdNumberGallery	2
wdOutlineNumberGallery	3
WdListNumberStyle	
wdListNumberStyleArabic	0
wdListNumberStyleUppercaseRoman	1
wdListNumberStyleLowercaseRoman	2
wdListNumberStyleUppercaseLetter	3
wdListNumberStyleLowercaseLetter	4
wdListNumberStyleOrdinal	5
wdListNumberStyleCardinalText	6
wdListNumberStyleOrdinalText	7
wdListNumberStyleArabicLZ	22
wdListNumberStyleBullet	23
wdListNumberStyleLegal	253
wdListNumberStyleLegalLZ	254
wdListNumberStyleNone	255
WdStatistic	
wdStatisticWords	0
wdStatisticLines	1
wdStatisticPages	2
wdStatisticCharacters	3
wdStatisticParagraphs	4
wdStatisticCharactersWithSpaces	5
WdBuiltInProperty	

Table D-1 continued

Constant	Value
wdPropertyTitle	1
wdPropertySubject	2
wdPropertyAuthor	3
wdPropertyKeywords	4
wdPropertyComments	5
wdPropertyTemplate	6
wdPropertyLastAuthor	7
wdPropertyRevision	8
wdPropertyAppName	9
wdPropertyTimeLastPrinted	10
wdPropertyTimeCreated	11
wdPropertyTimeLastSaved	12
wdPropertyVBATotalEdit	13
wdPropertyPages	14
wdPropertyWords	15
wdPropertyCharacters	16
wdPropertySecurity	17
wdPropertyCategory	18
wdPropertyFormat	19
WdLineSpacing	
wdLineSpaceSingle	0
wdLineSpace1pt5	1
wdLineSpaceDouble	2
wdLineSpaceAtLeast	3
wdLineSpaceExactly	4
wdLineSpaceMultiple	5

Constant	Value
WdNumberType	
wdNumberParagraph	1
wdNumberListNum	2
wdNumberAllNumbers	3
WdListType	
wdListNoNumbering	0
wdListListNumOnly	1
wdListBullet	2
wdListSimpleNumbering	3
wdListOutlineNumbering	4
wdListMixedNumbering	5
WdStoryType	
wdMainTextStory	1
wdFootnotesStory	2
wdEndnotesStory	3
wdCommentsStory	4
wdTextFrameStory	5
wdEvenPagesHeaderStory	6
wdPrimaryHeaderStory	7
wdEvenPagesFooterStory	8
wdPrimaryFooterStory	9
wdFirstPageHeaderStory	10
wdFirstPageFooterStory	11

Table D-1 continued

Constant	Value
WdSaveFormat	
wdFormatDocument	0
wdFormatTemplate	1
wdFormatText	2
wdFormatTextLineBreaks	3
wdFormatDOSText	4
wdFormatDOSTextLineBreaks	5
wdFormatRTF	6
wdFormatUnicodeText	7
WdOpenFormat	
wdOpenFormatAuto	0
wdOpenFormatDocument	1
wdOpenFormatTemplate	2
wdOpenFormatRTF	3
wdOpenFormatText	4
wdOpenFormatUnicodeText	5
WdHeaderFooterIndex	
wdHeaderFooterPrimary	1
wdHeaderFooterFirstPage	2
wdHeaderFooterEvenPages	3
WdTocFormat	
wdTOCTemplate	0
wdTOCClassic	1

Constant	Value
wdTOCDistinctive	2
wdTOCFancy	3
wdTOCModern	4
wdTOCFormal	5
wdTOCSimple	6
WdLineStyle	
wdLineStyleNone	0
wdLineStyleSingle	1
wdLineStyleDot	2
wdLineStyleDashSmallGap	3
wdLineStyleDashLargeGap	4
wdLineStyleDashDot	5
wdLineStyleDashDotDot	6
wdLineStyleDouble	7
wdLineStyleTriple	8
wdLineStyleThinThickSmallGap	9
wdLineStyleThickThinSmallGap	10
wdLineStyleThinThickThinSmallGap	11
wdLineStyleThinThickMedGap	12
wdLineStyleThickThinMedGap	13
wdLineStyleThinThickThinMedGap	14
WdLineWidth	
wdLineWidth025pt	2
wdLineWidth050pt	4
wdLineWidth075pt	6

Table D-1 continued

Constant	Value
wdLineWidth100pt	8
wdLineWidth150pt	12
wdLineWidth225pt	18
wdLineWidth300pt	24
wdLineWidth450pt	36
wdLineWidth600pt	48
WdBreakType	
wdSectionBreakNextPage	2
wdSectionBreakContinuous	3
wdSectionBreakEvenPage	4
wdSectionBreakOddPage	5
wdLineBreak	6
wdPageBreak	7
wdColumnBreak	8
WdTabLeader	
wdTabLeaderSpaces	0
wdTabLeaderDots	1
wdTabLeaderDashes	2
wdTabLeaderLines	3
WdTabLeaderHID	
wdTabLeaderHeavy	4
wdTabLeaderMiddleDot	5

Constant	Value
WdMeasurementUnits	
wdInches	0
wdCentimeters	1
wdPoints	3
wdPicas	4
WdMeasurementUnitsHID	
wdMillimeters	2
WdDropPosition	
wdDropNone	0
wdDropNormal	1
wdDropMargin	2
WdNumberingRule	
wdRestartContinuous	0
wdRestartSection	1
wdRestartPage	2
WdTableFieldSeparator	
wdSeparateByParagraphs	0
wdSeparateByTabs	1
wdSeparateByCommas	2
wdSeparateByDefaultListSeparator	3
WdSortFieldType	
wdSortFieldAlphanumeric	0

Table D-1 continued

Constant	Value
wdSortFieldNumeric	1
wdSortFieldDate	2
wdSortOrder	
wdSortOrderAscending	0
wdSortOrderDescending	1
WdTableFormat	
wdTableFormatNone	0
wdTableFormatSimple1	1
wdTableFormatSimple2	2
wdTableFormatSimple3	3
wdTableFormatClassic1	4
wdTableFormatClassic2	5
wdTableFormatClassic3	6
wdTableFormatClassic4	7
wdTableFormatColorful1	8
wdTableFormatColorful2	9
wdTableFormatColorful3	10
wdTableFormatColumns1	11
wdTableFormatColumns2	12
wdTableFormatColumns3	13
wdTableFormatColumns4	14
wdTableFormatColumns5	15
wdTableFormatGrid1	16
wdTableFormatGrid2	17
wdTableFormatGrid3	18

Constant	Value
wdTableFormatGrid4	19
wdTableFormatGrid5	20
wdTableFormatGrid6	21
wdTableFormatGrid7	22
wdTableFormatGrid8	23
wdTableFormatList1	24
wdTableFormatList2	25
WdTableFormatApply	
wdTableFormatApplyBorders	1
wdTableFormatApplyShading	2
wdTableFormatApplyFont	4
wdTableFormatApplyColor	8
wdTableFormatApplyAutoFit	16
wdTableFormatApplyHeadingRows	32
wdTableFormatApplyLastRow	64
wdTableFormatApplyFirstColumn	128
wdTableFormatApplyLastColumn	256
WdLanguageID	
wdLanguageNone	0
wdNoProofing	1024
wdDanish	1030
wdGerman	1031
wdSwissGerman	2055
wdEnglishAUS	3081
wdEnglishUK	2057

Table D-1 continued

Constant	Value
wdEnglishUS	1033
wdEnglishCanadian	4105
wdEnglishNewZealand	5129
wdEnglishSouthAfrica	7177
WdFieldType	
wdFieldEmpty	-1
wdFieldRef	3
wdFieldIndexEntry	4
wdFieldFootnoteRef	5
wdFieldSet	6
wdFieldIf	7
wdFieldIndex	8
wdFieldTOCEntry	9
wdFieldStyleRef	10
wdFieldRefDoc	11
wdFieldSequence	12
wdFieldTOC	13
wdFieldInfo	14
wdFieldTitle	15
wdFieldSubject	16
wdFieldAuthor	17
wdFieldKeyWord	18
wdFieldComments	19
wdFieldLastSavedBy	20
wdFieldCreateDate	21
wdFieldSaveDate	22

Constant	Value
WdTextFormFieldType	
wdRegularText	0
wdNumberText	1
wdDateText	2
wdCurrentDateText	3
wdCurrentTimeText	4
wdCalculationText	5
WdMailMergeMainDocType	
wdNotAMergeDocument	-1
wdFormLetters	0
wdMailingLabels	1
wdEnvelopes	2
wdCatalog	3
WdMailMergeDestination	
wdSendToNewDocument	0
wdSendToPrinter	1
wdSendToEmail	2
wdSendToFax	3
WdMailMergeActiveRecord	
wdNoActiveRecord	-1
wdNextRecord	-2
wdPreviousRecord	-3
wdFirstRecord	-4
wdLastRecord	-5

Table D-1 continued

Constant	Value
WdMailMergeDefaultRecord	
wdDefaultFirstRecord	1
wdDefaultLastRecord	-16
WdMailMergeDataSource	
wdNoMergeInfo	-1
wdMergeInfoFromWord	0
wdMergeInfoFromAccessDDE	1
wdMergeInfoFromExcelDDE	2
wdMergeInfoFromMSQueryDDE	3
wdMergeInfoFromODBC	4
WdWindowState	
wdWindowStateNormal	0
wdWindowStateMaximize	1
wdWindowStateMinimize	2
WdWindowType	
wdWindowDocument	0
wdWindowTemplate	1
WdViewType	
wdNormalView	1
wdOutlineView	2
wdPageView	3
wdPrintPreview	4

Constant	Value
wdMasterView	5
wdOnlineView	6
WdPageFit	
wdPageFitNone	0
wdPageFitFullPage	1
wdPageFitBestFit	2
WdPaperTray	
wdPrinterDefaultBin	0
wdPrinterUpperBin	1
wdPrinterOnlyBin	1
wdPrinterLowerBin	2
wdPrinterMiddleBin	3
wdPrinterManualFeed	4
wdPrinterEnvelopeFeed	5
wdPrinterManualEnvelopeFeed	6
wdPrinterAutomaticSheetFeed	7
WdOrientation	
wdOrientPortrait	0
wdOrientLandscape	1
WdSelectionType	
wdNoSelection	0
wdSelectionIP	1
wdSelectionNormal	2

Table D-1 continued

Constant	Value
wdSelectionFrame	3
wdSelectionColumn	4
wdSelectionRow	5
wdSelectionBlock	6
wdSelectionInlineShape	7
wdSelectionShape	8
WdSaveOptions	
wdDoNotSaveChanges	0
wdSaveChanges	-1
wdPromptToSaveChanges	-2
WdDocumentKind	
wdDocumentNotSpecified	0
wdDocumentLetter	1
wdDocumentEmail	2
WdDocumentType	
wdTypeDocument	0
wdTypeTemplate	1
WdPaperSize	
wdPaper10x14	0
wdPaper11x17	1
wdPaperLetter	2
wdPaperLetterSmall	3

Constant	Value
wdPaperLegal	4
wdPaperExecutive	5
wdPaperA3	6
wdPaperA4	7
wdPaperA4Small	8
wdPaperA5	9
wdPaperB4	10
wdPaperB5	11
wdPaperEnvelope9	24
wdPaperEnvelope10	25
wdPaperEnvelope11	26
WdProtectionType	
wdNoProtection	-1
wdAllowOnlyRevisions	0
wdAllowOnlyComments	1
wdAllowOnlyFormFields	2
WdEditionType	
wdPublisher	0
wdSubscriber	1
WdEditionOption	
wdCancelPublisher	0
wdSendPublisher	1
wdSelectPublisher	2
wdAutomaticUpdate	3

Table D-1 continued

Constant	Value
wdManualUpdate	4
wdChangeAttributes	5
wdUpdateSubscriber	6
wdOpenSource	7
WdOLEType	
wdOLELink	0
wdOLEEmbed	1
wdOLEControl	2
WdMovementType	
wdMove	0
wdExtend	1
WdPrintOutItem	
wdPrintDocumentContent	0
wdPrintProperties	1
wdPrintComments	2
wdPrintStyles	3
wdPrintAutoTextEntries	4
wdPrintKeyAssignments	5
wdPrintEnvelope	6
WdPrintOutPages	
wdPrintAllPages	0
wdPrintOddPagesOnly	1
wdPrintEvenPagesOnly	2

Constant	Value
WdPrintOutRange	
wdPrintAllDocument	0
wdPrintSelection	1
wdPrintCurrentPage	2
wdPrintFromTo	3
wdPrintRangeOfPages	4
WdSpellingErrorType	
wdSpellingCorrect	0
wdSpellingNotInDictionary	1
wdSpellingCapitalization	2
WdProofreadingErrorType	
wdSpellingError	0
wdGrammaticalError	1
WdTextOrientation	
wdTextOrientationHorizontal	0
wdTextOrientationUpward	2
wdTextOrientationDownward	3
WdReplace	
wdReplaceNone	0
wdReplaceOne	1
wdReplaceAll	2

Excel VBA Constants

Table D-2 lists some of the important Excel constants and their values.

Table D-2 Excel VBA Constants

Constant	Value
`xl24HourClock`	33
`xl3DArea`	-4098
`xl3DAreaStacked`	78
`xl3DAreaStacked100`	79
`xl3DBar`	-4099
`xl3DBarClustered`	60
`xl3DBarStacked`	61
`xl3DBarStacked100`	62
`xl3DColumn`	-4100
`xl3DColumnClustered`	54
`xl3DColumnStacked`	55
`xl3DEffects1`	13
`xl3DPie`	-4102
`xl3DPieExploded`	70
`xlAbsolute`	1
`xlAbsRowRelColumn`	2
`xlAccounting1`	4
`xlAccounting2`	5
`xlAccounting3`	6
`xlAccounting4`	17
`xlAll`	-4104
`xlAllAtOnce`	2
`xlAllChanges`	2

Constant	Value
xlArea	1
xlAreaStacked	76
xlAreaStacked100	77
xlArrangeStyleCascade	7
xlArrangeStyleHorizontal	-4128
xlArrangeStyleTiled	1
xlArrangeStyleVertical	-4166
xlAscending	1
xlAutoClose	2
xlAutoFill	4
xlAutomatic	-4105
xlAutomaticScale	-4105
xlAutomaticUpdate	4
xlAutoOpen	1
xlAverage	-4106
xlAxis	21
xlAxisTitle	17
xlBackgroundAutomatic	-4105
xlBackgroundOpaque	3
xlBackgroundTransparent	2
xlBar	2
xlBarClustered	57
xlBarStacked	58
xlBox	0
xlBubble	15
xlButton	15
xlButtonControl	0

Table D-2 continued

Constant	Value
xlByColumns	2
xlByRows	1
xlCalculationAutomatic	-4105
xlCalculationManual	-4135
xlCalculationSemiautomatic	2
xlCancel	1
xlCellTypeConstants	2
xlCellTypeFormulas	-4123
xlCellTypeVisible	12
xlCellValue	1
xlCenter	-4108
xlChangeAttributes	6
xlChart	-4109
xlChartArea	2
xlChartAsWindow	5
xlChartInPlace	4
xlChartTitle	4
xlCircle	8
xlClassic1	1
xlClassic2	2
xlClassic3	3
xlClipboard	3
xlClipboardFormatBIFF	8
xlClipboardFormatBinary	15
xlClipboardFormatBitmap	9
xlClipboardFormatEmbeddedObject	21
xlClipboardFormatEmbedSource	22

Constant	Value
xlClipboardFormatLink	11
xlClipboardFormatLinkSource	23
xlClipboardFormatLinkSourceDesc	32
xlClipboardFormatObjectDesc	31
xlClosed	3
xlCodePage	2
xlColor1	7
xlColor2	8
xlColor3	9
xlColorIndexAutomatic	-4105
xlColorIndexNone	-4142
xlColumn	3
xlColumnClustered	51
xlColumnField	2
xlColumnHeader	-4110
xlColumnItem	5
xlColumnLabels	2
xlColumns	2
xlColumnSeparator	14
xlColumnStacked	52
xlColumnStacked100	53
xlColumnThenRow	2
xlCombination	-4111
xlCommand	2
xlCommandUnderlinesAutomatic	-4105
xlCommandUnderlinesOff	-4146
xlCommandUnderlinesOn	1

Table D-2 continued

Constant	Value
xlComplete	4
xlConeBarClustered	102
xlConeBarStacked	103
xlConeBarStacked100	104
xlConstant	1
xlConstants	2
xlContents	2
xlContext	-5002
xlContinuous	1
xlCopy	1
xlCount	-4112
xlCountNums	-4113
xlCountryCode	1
xlCountrySetting	2
xlCross	4
xlCSVMac	22
xlCSVMSDOS	24
xlCSVWindows	23
xlCurrencyBefore	37
xlCurrencyCode	25
xlCurrencyDigits	27
xlCurrencyLeadingZeros	40
xlCurrencyMinusSign	38
xlCurrencyNegative	28
xlCurrencySpaceBefore	36
xlCurrencyTrailingZeros	39

Constant	Value
xlCustom	-4114
xlCut	2
xlCylinder	3
xlCylinderBarClustered	95
xlCylinderBarStacked	96
xlCylinderBarStacked100	97
xlDash	-4115
xlDashDot	4
xlDashDotDot	5
xlDataAndLabel	0
xlDatabase	1
xlDataField	4
xlDataHeader	3
xlDataItem	7
xlDataLabel	0
xlDataLabelsShowLabel	4
xlDataLabelsShowLabelAndPercent	5
xlDataLabelsShowNone	-4142
xlDataLabelsShowPercent	3
xlDataLabelsShowValue	2
xlDataOnly	2
xlDataTable	7
xlDate	2
xlDateOrder	32
xlDateSeparator	17
xlDay	1
xlDayCode	21

Table D-2 continued

Constant	Value
xlDayLeadingZero	42
xlDefault	-4143
xlDefaultAutoFormat	-1
xlDescending	2
xlDesktop	9
xlDiagonalDown	5
xlDiagonalUp	6
xlDialogActivate	103
xlDialogActiveCellFont	476
xlDialogAddChartAutoformat	390
xlDialogAlignment	43
xlDialogApplyNames	133
xlDialogApplyStyle	212
xlDialogAppMove	170
xlDialogAppSize	171
xlDialogArrangeAll	12
xlDialogAssignToObject	213
xlDialogAssignToTool	293
xlDialogAttachText	80
xlDialogAutoCorrect	485
xlDialogAxes	78
xlDialogBorder	45
xlDialogCalculation	32
xlDialogCellProtection	46
xlDialogChartAddData	392
xlDialogChartLocation	527

Constant	Value
xlDialogChartOptionsDataLabels	505
xlDialogChartSourceData	541
xlDialogChartTrend	350
xlDialogChartType	526
xlDialogChartWizard	288
xlDialogCheckboxProperties	435
xlDialogClear	52
xlDialogCopyChart	147
xlDialogCopyPicture	108
xlDialogCreateNames	62
xlDialogCreatePublisher	217
xlDialogCustomizeToolbar	276
xlDialogCustomViews	493
xlDialogDataDelete	36
xlDialogDataLabel	379
xlDialogDataSeries	40
xlDialogDataValidation	525
xlDialogDefineName	61
xlDialogDefineStyle	229
xlDialogDeleteFormat	111
xlDialogDeleteName	110
xlDialogDemote	203
xlDialogDisplay	27
xlDialogEditboxProperties	438
xlDialogEditColor	223
xlDialogEditDelete	54
xlDialogEditionOptions	251

Table D-2 continued

Constant	Value
xlDialogEditSeries	228
xlDialogErrorbarX	463
xlDialogErrorbarY	464
xlDialogExtract	35
xlDialogFileDelete	6
xlDialogFileSharing	481
xlDialogFilter	447
xlDialogFilterAdvanced	370
xlDialogFindFile	475
xlDialogFont	26
xlDialogFontProperties	381
xlDialogFormatAuto	269
xlDialogFormatChart	465
xlDialogFormatCharttype	423
xlDialogFormatFont	150
xlDialogFormatMain	225
xlDialogFormatMove	128
xlDialogFormatNumber	42
xlDialogFormatSize	129
xlDialogFormatText	89
xlDialogFormulaReplace	130
xlDialogGoalSeek	198
xlDialogGridlines	76
xlDialogInsert	55
xlDialogInsertHyperlink	596
xlDialogInsertNameLabel	496

Constant	Value
xlDialogInsertObject	259
xlDialogInsertPicture	342
xlDialogInsertTitle	380
xlDialogLabelProperties	436
xlDialogMainChart	85
xlDialogMainChartType	185
xlDialogMove	262
xlDialogNew	119
xlDialogObjectProperties	207
xlDialogOpen	1
xlDialogOpenLinks	2
xlDialogOpenMail	188
xlDialogOptionsChart	325
xlDialogOptionsEdit	319
xlDialogOptionsGeneral	356
xlDialogOptionsView	320
xlDialogOutline	142
xlDialogPageSetup	7
xlDialogPasteSpecial	53
xlDialogPatterns	84
xlDialogPivotCalculatedField	570
xlDialogPivotCalculatedItem	572
xlDialogPivotFieldGroup	433
xlDialogPivotFieldProperties	313
xlDialogPivotFieldUngroup	434
xlDialogPivotTableOptions	567
xlDialogPivotTableWizard	312

Table D-2 continued

Constant	Value
xlDialogPlacement	300
xlDialogPrint	8
xlDialogPrinterSetup	9
xlDialogPrintPreview	222
xlDialogProperties	474
xlDialogRowHeight	127
xlDialogRun	17
xlDialogSaveAs	5
xlDialogSaveCopyAs	456
xlDialogSaveNewObject	208
xlDialogSaveWorkbook	145
xlDialogSaveWorkspace	285
xlDialogScale	87
xlDialogSelectSpecial	132
xlDialogSendMail	189
xlDialogSheet	-4116
xlDialogShowDetail	204
xlDialogShowToolbar	220
xlDialogSize	261
xlDialogSort	39
xlDialogSortSpecial	192
xlDialogSplit	137
xlDialogStandardFont	190
xlDialogStandardWidth	472
xlDialogStyle	44
xlDialogSubscribeTo	218

Constant	Value
xlDialogSubtotalCreate	398
xlDialogSummaryInfo	474
xlDialogTable	41
xlDialogTabOrder	394
xlDialogTextToColumns	422
xlDialogUnhide	94
xlDialogUpdateLink	201
xlDialogVbaInsertFile	328
xlDialogVbaMakeAddin	478
xlDialogVbaProcedureDefinition	330
xlDialogView3d	197
xlDialogWindowMove	14
xlDialogWindowSize	13
xlDialogWorkbookAdd	281
xlDialogWorkbookCopy	283
xlDialogWorkbookInsert	354
xlDialogWorkbookMove	282
xlDialogWorkbookName	386
xlDialogWorkbookNew	302
xlDialogWorkbookOptions	284
xlDialogWorkbookProtect	417
xlDialogWorkbookUnhide	384
xlDialogWorkgroup	199
xlDialogWorkspace	95
xlDialogZoom	256
xlDiamond	2
xlDIF	9

Table D-2 continued

Constant	Value
xlDifferenceFrom	2
xlDirect	1
xlDisabled	0
xlDisplayShapes	-4104
xlDistributed	-4117
xlDivide	5
xlDoNotSaveChanges	2
xlDot	-4118
xlDouble	-4119
xlDoubleAccounting	5
xlDoubleClosed	5
xlDoubleOpen	4
xlDoubleQuote	1
xlDoughnut	-4120
xlDoughnutExploded	80
xlDown	-4121
xlDownBars	20
xlDownThenOver	1
xlDownward	-4170
xlDrawingObject	14
xlDropDown	2
xlDropLines	26
xlDRW	4
xlDXF	5
xlEdgeBottom	9
xlEdgeLeft	7

Constant	Value
xlEdgeRight	10
xlEdgeTop	8
xlEditBox	3
xlEditionDate	2
xlEnd	2
xlEndSides	3
xlEntireChart	20
xlEPS	8
xlEqual	3
xlErrDiv0	2007
xlErrNA	2042
xlErrName	2029
xlErrNull	2000
xlErrNum	2036
xlErrorBars	9
xlErrorBarTypeCustom	-4114
xlErrorBarTypeFixedValue	1
xlErrorBarTypePercent	2
xlErrorHandler	2
xlErrors	16
xlErrRef	2023
xlErrValue	2015
xlExcel2	16
xlExcel2FarEast	27
xlExcel3	29
xlExcel4	33
xlExcel4IntlMacroSheet	4

Table D-2 continued

Constant	Value
xlExcel4MacroSheet	3
xlExcel4Workbook	35
xlExcel5	39
xlExcel7	39
xlExcel9795	43
xlExcelLinks	1
xlExcelMenus	1
xlExclusive	3
xlExponential	5
xlExpression	2
xlExtended	3
xlExternal	2
xlFill	5
xlFillCopy	1
xlFillDays	5
xlFillDefault	0
xlFillFormats	3
xlFillMonths	7
xlFillSeries	2
xlFillValues	4
xlFillWeekdays	6
xlFillWithAll	-4104
xlFillWithContents	2
xlFillWithFormats	-4122
xlFillYears	8
xlFilterCopy	2

Constant	Value
xlFilterInPlace	1
xlFirst	0
xlFitToPage	2
xlFixedValue	1
xlFixedWidth	2
xlFloating	5
xlFloor	23
xlFormats	-4122
xlFormula	5
xlFormulas	-4123
xlFreeFloating	3
xlFront	4
xlFrontEnd	6
xlFrontSides	5
xlFullPage	3
xlFunction	1
xlGeneral	1
xlGeneralFormatName	26
xlGray16	17
xlGray25	-4124
xlGray50	-4125
xlGray75	-4126
xlGray8	18
xlGreater	5
xlGreaterEqual	7
xlGregorian	2
xlGrid	15

Table D-2 continued

Constant	Value
xlGridline	22
xlGroupBox	4
xlGrowth	2
xlGrowthTrend	10
xlGuess	0
xlHairline	1
xlHAlignCenter	-4108
xlHAlignCenterAcrossSelection	7
xlHAlignDistributed	-4117
xlHAlignFill	5
xlHAlignGeneral	1
xlHAlignJustify	-4130
xlHAlignLeft	-4131
xlHAlignRight	-4152
xlHGL	6
xlHidden	0
xlHide	3
xlHigh	-4127
xlHorizontal	-4128
xlHourCode	22
xlIBeam	3
xlIcons	1
xlIMEModeAlpha	8
xlIMEModeAlphaFull	7
xlIMEModeDisable	3
xlIMEModeNoControl	0

Constant	Value
xlIMEModeOff	2
xlIMEModeOn	1
xlImmediatePane	12
xlIndex	9
xlInfo	-4129
xlInsertDeleteCells	1
xlInsertEntireRows	2
xlInside	2
xlInsideHorizontal	12
xlInsideVertical	11
xlInteger	2
xlInterpolated	3
xlInterrupt	1
xlIntlMacro	25
xlJustify	-4130
xlLabel	5
xlLabelOnly	1
xlLabelPositionAbove	0
xlLabelPositionBelow	1
xlLabelPositionBestFit	5
xlLabelPositionCenter	-4108
xlLabelPositionCustom	7
xlLabelPositionInsideBase	4
xlLabelPositionInsideEnd	3
xlLabelPositionLeft	-4131
xlLabelPositionRight	-4152
xlLandscape	2

Table D-2 continued

Constant	Value
xlLast	1
xlLastCell	11
xlLatin	-5001
xlLeaderLines	29
xlLeft	-4131
xlLeftBrace	12
xlLeftBracket	10
xlLeftToRight	2
xlLegend	24
xlLegendEntry	12
xlLegendKey	13
xlLegendPositionBottom	-4107
xlLegendPositionCorner	2
xlLegendPositionLeft	-4131
xlLegendPositionRight	-4152
xlLegendPositionTop	-4160
xlLess	6
xlLessEqual	8
xlLightDown	13
xlLightHorizontal	11
xlLightUp	14
xlLightVertical	12
xlLine	4
xlLinear	-4132
xlLinearTrend	9
xlLineMarkers	65

Constant	Value
xlLineMarkersStacked	66
xlLineMarkersStacked100	67
xlLineStacked	63
xlLineStacked100	64
xlLineStyleNone	-4142
xlList1	10
xlList2	11
xlList3	12
xlListBox	6
xlListSeparator	5
xlLocalFormat1	15
xlLocationAsNewSheet	1
xlLocationAsObject	2
xlLocationAutomatic	3
xlLogarithmic	-4133
xlLogical	4
xlLogicalCursor	1
xlLong	3
xlLotusHelp	2
xlLow	-4134
xlLowerCaseColumnLetter	9
xlLowerCaseRowLetter	8
xlLTR	-5003
xlMacintosh	1
xlMacrosheetCell	7
xlMajorGridlines	15
xlManual	-4135

Table D-2 continued

Constant	Value
xlManualUpdate	5
xlMAPI	1
xlMax	-4136
xlMaximized	-4137
xlMaximum	2
xlMDY	44
xlMedium	-4138
xlMin	-4139
xlMinimized	-4140
xlMinimum	4
xlMinorGridlines	16
xlMinusValues	3
xlMinuteCode	23
xlMixed	2
xlMixedLabels	3
xlModule	-4141
xlMonth	3
xlMonthCode	20
xlMonthLeadingZero	41
xlMonthNameChars	30
xlMonths	1
xlMove	2
xlMoveAndSize	1
xlMultiply	4
xlNarrow	1
xlNext	1

Constant	Value
xlNextToAxis	4
xlNo	2
xlNoButton	0
xlNoButtonChanges	1
xlNoCap	2
xlNoChange	1
xlNoChanges	4
xlNoConversion	3
xlNoDocuments	3
xlNoIndicator	0
xlNormal	-4143
xlNormalView	1
xlNoSelection	-4142
xlNotBetween	2
xlNotEqual	4
xlNothing	28
xlNotXLM	3
xlNumber	-4145
xlOff	-4146
xlOLEControl	2
xlOLEEmbed	1
xlOLELink	0
xlOLELinks	2
xlOn	1
xlOpen	2
xlOpenSource	3
xlOptionButton	7

Table D-2 continued

Constant	Value
xlOr	2
xlOrigin	3
xlOtherSessionChanges	3
xlOutside	3
xlOverThenDown	2
xlOverwriteCells	0
xlPageBreakAutomatic	-4105
xlPageBreakFull	1
xlPageHeader	2
xlPaper10x14	16
xlPaper11x17	17
xlPaperA3	8
xlPaperA4	9
xlPaperA4Small	10
xlPaperA5	11
xlPaperB4	12
xlPaperB5	13
xlPaperCsheet	24
xlPaperDsheet	25
xlPaperEnvelope10	20
xlPaperEnvelope11	21
xlPaperEnvelope12	22
xlPaperEnvelope14	23
xlPaperEnvelope9	19
xlPart	2
xlPartial	3

Constant	Value
xlPasteAll	-4104
xlPasteComments	-4144
xlPasteFormats	-4122
xlPasteFormulas	-4123
xlPasteValues	-4163
xlPatternAutomatic	-4105
xlPatternChecker	9
xlPatternCrissCross	16
xlPatternDown	-4121
xlPatternGray16	17
xlPatternGray25	-4124
xlPatternGrid	15
xlPatternHorizontal	-4128
xlPatternLightHorizontal	11
xlPatternLightUp	14
xlPatternNone	-4142
xlPatternSemiGray75	10
xlPatternSolid	1
xlPatternUp	-4162
xlPatternVertical	-4166
xlPCT	13
xlPCX	10
xlPercent	2
xlPercentDifferenceFrom	4
xlPercentOf	3
xlPercentOfColumn	7
xlPercentOfRow	6

Table D-2 continued

Constant	Value
xlPercentOfTotal	8
xlPicture	-4147
xlPie	5
xlPivotTable	-4148
xlPlaceholders	2
xlPlotArea	19
xlPortrait	1
xlPrevious	2
xlPrimaryButton	1
xlPrinter	2
xlProduct	-4149
xlPrompt	0
xlPublisher	1
xlPublishers	5
xlRadar	-4151
xlRadarAxisLabels	27
xlRadarFilled	82
xlRadarMarkers	81
xlRange	2
xlRangeAutoFormat3DEffects1	13
xlRangeAutoFormat3DEffects2	14
xlRangeAutoFormatAccounting1	4
xlRangeAutoFormatAccounting2	5
xlRangeAutoFormatClassic1	1
xlRangeAutoFormatColor1	7
xlReadOnly	3

Constant	Value
xlReadWrite	2
xlReference	4
xlRelative	4
xlRight	-4152
xlRightBrace	13
xlRightBracket	11
xlRowField	1
xlRowHeader	-4153
xlRowItem	4
xlRowLabels	1
xlRows	1
xlRowSeparator	15
xlSaveChanges	1
xlScreen	1
xlScrollBar	8
xlSecondary	2
xlSemiautomatic	2
xlSemiGray75	10
xlSheetHidden	0
xlSheetVisible	-1
xlShiftDown	-4121
xlShiftToLeft	-4159
xlShiftToRight	-4161
xlShiftUp	-4162
xlShort	1
xlShowLabel	4
xlShowLabelAndPercent	5

Table D-2 continued

Constant	Value
xlShowPercent	3
xlShowValue	2
xlSides	1
xlSolid	1
xlSortColumns	1
xlSortLabels	2
xlSortRows	2
xlSortValues	1
xlStrict	2
xlStroke	2
xlSubscriber	2
xlSubtract	3
xlSum	-4157
xlSurface	83
xlSurfaceTopView	85
xlTabPositionFirst	0
xlTabPositionLast	1
xlTemplate	17
xlText	-4158
xlTextBox	16
xlTextValues	2
xlTimeScale	3
xlTimeSeparator	18
xlTitleBar	8
xlToLeft	-4159
xlToolbar	1

Constant	Value
xlTransparent	2
xlTrendline	8
xlUnlockedCells	1
xlValidateInputOnly	0
xlValidateList	3
xlValidateTime	5
xlVAlignBottom	-4107
xlVAlignCenter	-4108
xlVAlignDistributed	-4117
xlVAlignJustify	-4130
xlVAlignTop	-4160
xlVertical	-4166
xlVeryHidden	2
xlVisible	12
xlVisualCursor	2
xlWhole	1
xlWide	3
xlWorkbook	1
xlWorksheet	-4167
xlWorksheet4	1
xlWorksheetCell	3

Access VBA Constants

Table D-3 lists some of the important Access constants and their values.

Table D-3 Access VBA Constants

Constant	Value
acCmdAboutMicrosoftAccess	35
acCmdAddWatch	201
acCmdAdvancedFilterSort	99
acCmdAlignBottom	46
acCmdAlignLeft	43
acCmdAlignRight	44
acCmdAlignToGrid	47
acCmdAlignTop	45
acCmdAlignToShortest	153
acCmdAlignToTallest	154
acCmdAnalyzePerformance	283
acCmdAnalyzeTable	284
acCmdAnswerWizard	235
acCmdApplyDefault	55
acCmdApplyFilterSort	93
acCmdAppMaximize	10
acCmdAppMinimize	11
acCmdAppMove	12
acCmdAppRestore	9
acCmdAppSize	13
acCmdArrangeIconsAuto	218
acCmdArrangeIconsByCreated	216
acCmdArrangeIconsByModified	217

Constant	Value
acCmdArrangeIconsByName	214
acCmdArrangeIconsByType	215
acCmdAutoCorrect	261
acCmdAutoDial	192
acCmdAutoFormat	270
acCmdCallStack	172
acCmdChangeToCheckBox	231
acCmdChangeToComboBox	230
acCmdChangeToImage	234
acCmdChangeToLabel	228
acCmdChangeToListBox	229
acCmdChangeToOptionButton	233
acCmdChangeToTextBox	227
acCmdChangeToToggleButton	232
acCmdClearAll	146
acCmdClearAllBreakpoints	132
acCmdClearGrid	71
acCmdClearHyperlink	343
acCmdClearItemDefaults	237
acCmdClose	58
acCmdCloseWindow	186
acCmdColumnWidth	117
acCmdCompactDatabase	4
acCmdCompileAllModules	125
acCmdCompileAndSaveAllModules	126
acCmdCompileLoadedModules	290
acCmdCompleteWord	306

Table D-3 continued

Constant	Value
acCmdConnection	383
acCmdControlWizardsToggle	197
acCmdConvertDatabase	171
acCmdConvertMacrosToVisualBasic	279
acCmdCopy	190
acCmdCopyHyperlink	328
acCmdCreateMenuFromMacro	334
acCmdCreateRelationship	150
acCmdCreateReplica	263
acCmdCreateShortcut	219
acCmdCreateShortcutMenuFromMacro	336
acCmdCreateToolbarFromMacro	335
acCmdCut	189
acCmdDataAccessPageBrowse	344
acCmdDataAccessPageDesignView	385
acCmdDatabaseProperties	256
acCmdDataEntry	78
acCmdDatasheetView	282
acCmdDateAndTime	226
acCmdDebugWindow	123
acCmdDelete	337
acCmdDeletePage	332
acCmdDeleteQueryColumn	81
acCmdDeleteRecord	223
acCmdDeleteRows	188
acCmdDeleteTab	255

Constant	Value
acCmdDeleteTableColumn	271
acCmdDeleteWatch	267
acCmdDemote	388
acCmdDesignView	183
acCmdDiagramAddRelatedTables	373
acCmdDiagramAutosizeSelectedTables	378
acCmdDiagramDeleteRelationship	382
acCmdDiagramLayoutDiagram	380
acCmdDiagramLayoutSelection	379
acCmdDiagramModifyUserDefinedView	375
acCmdDiagramNewLabel	372
acCmdDiagramNewTable	381
acCmdDiagramRecalculatePageBreaks	377
acCmdDiagramShowRelationshipLabels	374
acCmdDiagramViewPageBreaks	376
acCmdDocMaximize	15
acCmdDocMinimize	60
acCmdDocMove	16
acCmdDocRestore	14
acCmdDocSize	17
acCmdDocumenter	285
acCmdDuplicate	34
acCmdEditHyperlink	325
acCmdEditingAllowed	70
acCmdEditRelationship	151
acCmdEditTriggers	384
acCmdEditWatch	202

Table D-3 continued

Constant	Value
acCmdEncryptDecryptDatabase	5
acCmdEnd	198
acCmdExit	3
acCmdFavoritesAddTo	299
acCmdFavoritesOpen	298
acCmdFieldList	42
acCmdFilterByForm	207
acCmdFilterBySelection	208
acCmdFilterExcludingSelection	277
acCmdFind	30
acCmdFindNext	341
acCmdFindNextWordUnderCursor	313
acCmdFindPrevious	120
acCmdFindPrevWordUnderCursor	312
acCmdFitToWindow	245
acCmdFont	19
acCmdFormatCells	77
acCmdFormHdrFtr	36
acCmdFormView	281
acCmdFreezeColumn	105
acCmdGoBack	294
acCmdGoContinue	127
acCmdGoForward	295
acCmdGroupByTable	387
acCmdGroupControls	484
acCmdHideColumns	79

Constant	Value
acCmdHidePane	365
acCmdHideTable	147
acCmdHorizontalSpacingDecrease	158
acCmdHorizontalSpacingIncrease	159
acCmdHorizontalSpacingMakeEqual	157
acCmdHyperlinkDisplayText	329
acCmdImport	257
acCmdIndent	205
acCmdIndexes	152
acCmdInsertActiveXControl	258
acCmdInsertChart	293
acCmdInsertFile	39
acCmdInsertFileIntoModule	118
acCmdInsertHyperlink	259
acCmdInsertLookupColumn	273
acCmdInsertLookupField	291
acCmdInsertMovieFromFile	469
acCmdInsertObject	33
acCmdInsertPage	331
acCmdInsertPicture	222
acCmdPivotTable	470
acCmdInsertProcedure	262
acCmdInsertQueryColumn	82
acCmdInsertRows	187
acCmdInsertSpreadsheet	471
acCmdInsertSubdatasheet	499
acCmdInsertTableColumn	272

Table D-3 continued

Constant	Value
acCmdInsertUnboundSection	472
acCmdInvokeBuilder	178
acCmdJoinProperties	72
acCmdLastPosition	339
acCmdLayoutPreview	141
acCmdLineUpIcons	213
acCmdLinkTableManager	519
acCmdLinkTables	102
acCmdListConstants	303
acCmdLoadFromQuery	95
acCmdMacroConditions	87
acCmdMacroNames	86
acCmdMakeMDEFile	7

Index

B

C

D

E

G

H

I

J

K

L

M

N

O

P

Q

R

S

T

U

V

W

X

Z